名著英汉对照双语版

格列佛游记

Gulliver's Travels

[英]乔纳森·斯威夫特（Jonathan Swift）著

纪飞 译

清华大学出版社

北 京

内 容 简 介

　　《格列佛游记》是世界上最伟大的童话、讽刺小说之一。故事讲述主人公格列佛在四个完全不同的国度——小人国、大人国、飞岛国和慧骃国的冒险经历和非凡奇遇。格列佛遇海难，来到小人国，这里的人身高仅六英寸，君臣贪婪、国家战祸连绵，作者以巨人的角度，俯视人类的荒唐和渺小。格列佛误闯大人国，这里的人身高如塔，国威显赫，作者以小矮人的角度，仰视人类的粗俗和无情。格列佛遇海盗，造访飞岛国，这里的城市和乡村颓败、荒芜，作者以平常的心态，平视人类的疯狂和邪恶本性。格列佛游访慧骃国，这里的统治者高度理性，人形动物邪恶、低劣，作者以理性动物的角度，审视人类的本质。该书问世近300年，已被译成几十种文字，还多次被改编成电影。在中国，它是最具影响力的外国文学作品之一，被列入语文新课程标准推荐阅读书目。无论是作为语言学习的课本，还是作为通俗的文学读本，本书对当代中国的青少年读者都将产生积极的影响。

图书在版编目（CIP）数据

　　格列佛游记：名著英汉对照双语版 /（英）乔纳森·斯威夫特（Jonathan Swift）著；纪飞译 . —北京：清华大学出版社，2024.1

　　ISBN 978-7-302-64506-1

　　Ⅰ . ①格…　Ⅱ . ①乔…②纪…　Ⅲ . ①英语－汉语－对照读物　Ⅳ . ① H319.4

　　中国国家版本馆 CIP 数据核字 (2023) 第 163001 号

责任编辑：陈　莉
封面设计：刘　晶
版式设计：方加青
责任校对：成凤进
责任印制：杨　艳

出版发行：清华大学出版社
　　　　网　　　址：https://www.tup.com.cn，https://www.wqxuetang.com
　　　　地　　　址：北京清华大学学研大厦 A 座　　　　邮　　编：100084
　　　　社 总 机：010-83470000　　　　　　　　　　邮　　购：010-62786544
　　　　投稿与读者服务：010-62776969，c-service@tup.tsinghua.edu.cn
　　　　质 量 反 馈：010-62772015，zhiliang@tup.tsinghua.edu.cn
印 装 者：河北鹏润印刷有限公司
经　　销：全国新华书店
开　　本：170mm×260mm　　　印　　张：18.5　　　字　　数：472 千字
版　　次：2024 年 1 月第 1 版　　　印　　次：2024 年 1 月第 1 次印刷
定　　价：69.80 元

产品编号：100067-01

前　言

　　乔纳森·斯威夫特 (Jonathan Swift，1667—1745)，英国启蒙运动中激进民主派的创始人，18 世纪英国最杰出的政论家和讽刺文学大师之一。

　　1667 年 11 月 30 日，乔纳森·斯威夫特出生在爱尔兰都柏林的一个贫苦家庭。他出生前七个月的时候父亲去世，由叔父抚养长大。1686 年，他获得都柏林三一学院学士学位；1692 年，获得牛津大学硕士学位；1701 年，获都柏林三一学院博士学位。在大学期间，虽然主修的是哲学和神学，但他却对文学和历史产生了浓厚的兴趣。在此期间，斯威夫特曾任穆尔庄园主人威廉·邓波尔爵士的私人秘书、英国国教会教士及乡村牧师等。1710—1714 年，为托利党主编《考察报》。1714 年，托利党失势后，他回到爱尔兰，在都柏林圣帕特里克大教堂任副主教，同时着手研究爱尔兰现状，积极支持并投入争取爱尔兰独立自由的斗争。1745 年 10 月 19 日，斯威夫特去世，葬于圣帕特里克大教堂。

　　斯威夫特一生发表了大量的政论、讽刺诗和散文等，抨击地主、豪绅和英国殖民主义政策，受到民众的热烈欢迎。而他的讽刺小说影响更为深广，其代表作《格列佛游记》是一部杰出的游记体长篇小说，是世界文学史上最伟大的讽刺小说之一。1726 年，《格列佛游记》一经出版，便震惊了当时的英国社会，成为当时最畅销、最受关注的作品之一。小说以格列佛船长的口吻叙述了周游小人国、大人国、飞岛国和慧骃国的经历，作者以神奇的想象、夸张的语言、寓言的笔法对英国政体进行了批判，尤其对统治阶级的腐败、无能、毒辣、荒淫、贪婪、自大等做了痛快淋漓的鞭挞。该书问世近 300 年，已被译成几十种文字，是世界各国人民最喜爱的经典文学作品之一。

　　在中国，《格列佛游记》同样是最受广大青少年读者欢迎的经典小说之一，自 20 世纪初引入中国以来，各种版本总计不下百种。作为世界文学宝库中的经典之作，它影响了一代又一代中国人的美丽童年、少年直至成年。基于以上原因，我们决定翻译本书，并采用英汉双语的形式出版。我们相信，该经典著作的引进对加强当代中国读者，特别对青少年读者的人文修养是非常有帮助的。

　　本书配有英文音频，读者可在每章章标题处获取音频二维码，扫码听书。

纪 飞

2023 年 3 月

目　录

The Publisher to the Reader / 1

　　给读者的话 / 163

A Letter from Captain Gulliver to his Cousin Sympson / 2

　　格列佛船长致其表兄辛普森的一封信 / 164

Part I　A Voyage to Lilliput / 5

　　第一卷　利立浦特游记 / 166

Part II　A Voyage to Brobdingnag / 41

　　第二卷　布罗丁格奈格游记 / 194

Part III　A Voyage to Laputa, Balnibarbi, Luggnagg, Glubbdubdrib, and Japan / 80

　　第三卷　拉普塔、巴尔尼巴比、鲁格奈格、格鲁布杜德利卜、日本游记 / 226

Part IV　A Voyage to the Country of the Houyhnhnms / 116

　　第四卷　慧骃国游记 / 254

The Publisher to the Reader

The author of these Travels, Mr. Lemuel Gulliver, is my ancient and intimate friend; there is likewise some relation between us on the mother's side. About three years ago, Mr. Gulliver growing weary of the concourse of curious people coming to him at his house in Redriff, made a small purchase of land, with a convenient house, near Newark, in Nottinghamshire, his native country; where he now lives retired, yet in good esteem among his neighbours.

Although Mr. Gulliver was born in Nottinghamshire, where his father dwelt, yet I have heard him say his family came from Oxfordshire; to confirm which, I have observed in the churchyard at Banbury in that county, several tombs and monuments of the Gullivers.

Before he quitted Redriff, he left the custody of the following papers in my hands, with the liberty to dispose of them as I should think fit. I have carefully perused them three times. The style is very plain and simple; and the only fault I find is, that the author, after the manner of travellers, is a little too circumstantial. There is an air of truth apparent through the whole; and indeed the author was so distinguished for his veracity, that it became a sort of proverb among his neighbours at Redriff, when any one affirmed a thing, to say, it was as true as if Mr. Gulliver had spoken it.

By the advice of several worthy persons, to whom, with the author's permission, I communicated these papers, I now venture to send them into the world, hoping they may be, at least for some time, a better entertainment to our young noblemen, than the common scribbles of politics and party.

This volume would have been at least twice as large, if I had not made bold to strike out innumerable passages relating to the winds and tides, as well as to the variations and bearings in the several voyages, together with the minute descriptions of the management of the ship in storms, in the style of sailors; likewise the account of longitudes and latitudes; wherein I have reason to apprehend, that Mr. Gulliver may be a little dissatisfied. But I was resolved to fit the work as much as possible to the general capacity of readers. However, if my own ignorance in sea affairs shall have led me to commit some mistakes, I alone am answerable for them. And if any traveller hath a curiosity to see the whole work at large, as it came from the hands of the author, I will be ready to gratify him.

As for any further particulars relating to the author, the reader will receive satisfaction from the first pages of the book.

Richard Sympson

A Letter from Captain Gulliver to his Cousin Sympson

I hope you will be ready to own publicly, whenever you shall be called to it, that by your great and frequent urgency you prevailed on me to publish a very loose and incorrect account of my travels, with directions to hire some young gentleman of either university to put them in order, and correct the style, as my cousin Dampier did, by my advice, in his book called, *A Voyage round the world*. But I do not remember I gave you power to consent that anything should be omitted, and much less that anything should be inserted; therefore, as to the latter, I do here renounce everything of that kind; particularly a paragraph about her Majesty Queen Anne, of most pious and glorious memory; although I did reverence and esteem her more than any of human species. But you, or your interpolator, ought to have considered, that it was not my inclination, so was it not decent to praise any animal of our composition before my master *Houyhnhnm*: And besides, the fact was altogether false; for to my knowledge, being in England during some part of her Majesty's reign, she did govern by a chief minister; nay even by two successively, the first whereof was the lord of Godolphin, and the second the lord of Oxford; so that you have made me say the thing that was not. Likewise in the account of the academy of projectors, and several passages of my discourse to my master *Houyhnhnm*, you have either omitted some material circumstances, or minced or changed them in such a manner, that I do hardly know my own work. When I formerly hinted to you something of this in a letter, you were pleased to answer that you were afraid of giving offence; that people in power were very watchful over the press, and apt not only to interpret, but to punish everything which looked like an innuendo (as I think you call it). But, pray how could that which I spoke so many years ago, and at about five thousand leagues distance, in another reign, be applied to any of the *Yahoos*, who now are said to govern the herd; especially at a time when I little thought, or feared, the unhappiness of living under them? Have not I the most reason to complain, when I see these very *Yahoos* carried by *Houyhnhnms* in a vehicle, as if they were brutes, and those the rational creatures? And indeed to avoid so monstrous and detestable a sight was one principal motive of my retirement hither.

Thus much I thought proper to tell you in relation to yourself, and to the trust I reposed in you.

I do in the next place, complain of my own great want of judgment, in being prevailed upon by the entreaties and false reasoning of you and some others, very much against my own opinion, to suffer my travels to be published. Pray bring to your mind how often I desired you to consider, when you insisted on the motive of public good, that the *Yahoos* were a species of animals utterly incapable of amendment by precept or example: and so it has proved; for, instead of seeing a full stop put to all abuses and corruptions, at least in this little island, as I had reason to expect; behold, after above six months warning, I cannot learn that my book has produced one single effect according to my intentions. I desired you would let me know, by a letter, when party and faction were extinguished; judges learned and upright; pleaders honest and modest, with some tincture of common sense, and Smithfield blazing with pyramids of law books; the young nobility's education entirely changed; the physicians banished; the female *Yahoos* abounding in virtue, honor, truth, and good sense; courts and levees of great ministers thoroughly weeded and swept; wit, merit, and learning rewarded; all disgracers of the press in prose and verse condemned to eat nothing but their own cotton, and quench their thirst with their own ink. These, and a thousand other reformations, I firmly counted upon by your encouragement; as indeed they were plainly deducible from the precepts delivered in my book. And it must be owned, that seven months were a sufficient time to correct every vice and folly to which *Yahoos* are subject, if their natures had been capable of the least disposition to virtue or wisdom. Yet, so far have you been from answering my expectation in any of your letters; that on the contrary you are loading our carrier every week with libels, and keys, and reflections, and memoirs, and second parts; wherein I see myself accused of reflecting upon great state folk; of degrading human nature (for so they have still the confidence to style it), and of abusing the female sex. I find likewise that the writers of those bundles are not agreed among themselves; for some of them will not allow me to be the author of my own travels; and others make me author of books to which I am wholly a stranger.

I find likewise that your printer has been so careless as to confound the times, and mistake the dates, of my several voyages and returns; neither assigning the true year, nor the true month, nor day of the month; and I hear the original manuscript is all destroyed since the publication of my book; neither have I any copy left; however, I have sent you some corrections, which you may insert, if ever there should be a second edition: and yet I cannot stand to them; but shall leave that matter to my judicious and candid readers to adjust it as they please.

I hear some of our sea *Yahoos* find fault with my sea-language, as not proper in many parts, nor now in use. I cannot help it. In my first voyages, while I was young, I was instructed by the oldest mariners, and learned to speak as they did. But I have since found that the sea *Yahoos* are apt, like the land ones, to become new-fangled in their words, which the latter change every year; insomuch, as I remember upon each return to my own country their old dialect was so altered, that I could hardly understand the new. And I observe, when any *Yahoo* comes from London out of curiosity to visit me at my house, we neither of us are able to deliver our conceptions in a manner intelligible to the other.

If the censure of the *Yahoos* could any way affect me, I should have great reason to complain, that some of them are so bold as to think my book of travels a mere fiction out of mine own brain, and have gone so far as to drop hints, that the *Houyhnhnms* and *Yahoos* have no more existence than the inhabitants of Utopia.

Indeed I must confess, that as to the people of Lilliput, Brobdingrag (for so the word should have been spelt, and not erroneously Brobdingnag), and Laputa, I have never yet heard of any *Yahoo* so presumptuous as to dispute their being, or the facts I have related concerning them; because the truth immediately strikes every reader with conviction. And is there less probability in my account of the *Houyhnhnms* or *Yahoos*, when it is manifest as to the latter, there are so many thousands even in this country, who only differ from their brother brutes in *Houyhnhnmland*, because they use a sort of jabber, and do not go naked? I wrote for their amendment, and not their approbation. The united praise of the whole race would be of less consequence to me, than the neighing of those two degenerate *Houyhnhnms* I keep in my stable; because from these, degenerate as they are, I still improve in some virtues without any mixture of vice.

Do these miserable animals presume to think, that I am so degenerated as to defend my veracity? *Yahoo* as I am, it is well known through all *Houyhnhnmland*, that, by the instructions and example of my illustrious master, I was able in the compass of two years (although I confess with the utmost difficulty) to remove that infernal habit of lying, shuffling, deceiving, and equivocating, so deeply rooted in the very souls of all my species; especially the Europeans.

I have other complaints to make upon this vexatious occasion; but I forbear troubling myself or you any further. I must freely confess, that since my last return, some corruptions of my *Yahoo* nature have revived in me by conversing with a few of your species, and particularly those of my own family, by an unavoidable necessity; else I should never have attempted so absurd a project as that of reforming the *Yahoo* race in this kingdom; But I have now done with all such visionary schemes for ever.

April 2, 1727

Part I
A Voyage to Lilliput

∼⌢∼ **Chapter I** ∼⌢∼

The author gives some account of himself and family. His first inducements to travel. He is shipwrecked, and swims for his life. Gets safe on shore in the country of Lilliput; is made a prisoner, and carried up the country.

My father had a small estate in Nottinghamshire; I was the third of five sons. He sent me to Emanuel College in Cambridge at fourteen years old, where I resided three years, and applied myself close to my studies; but the charge of maintaining me, although I had a very scanty allowance, being too great for a narrow fortune, I was bound apprentice to Mr. James Bates, an eminent surgeon in London, with whom I continued four years. My father now and then sending me small sums of money, I laid them out in learning navigation, and other parts of the mathematics, useful to those who intend to travel, as I always believed it would be, sometime or other, my fortune to do. When I left Mr. Bates, I went down to my father; where, by the assistance of him and my uncle John, and some other relations, I got forty pounds, and a promise of thirty pounds a year to maintain me at Leyden; there I studied physic two years and seven months, knowing it would be useful in long voyages.

Soon after my return from Leyden, I was recommended by my good master, Mr. Bates, to be surgeon to the Swallow, Captain Abraham Pannel, commander; with whom I continued three years and a half, making a voyage or two into the Levant, and some other parts. When I came back I resolved to settle in London; to which Mr. Bates, my master, encouraged me, and by him I was recommended to several patients. I took part of a small house in the Old Jewry; and being advised to alter my condition, I married Mrs. Mary Burton, second daughter to Mr. Edmund Burton, hosier, in Newgate-street, with whom I received four hundred pounds for a portion.

But my good master Bates dying in two years after, and I having few friends, my business began to fail; for my conscience would not suffer me to imitate the bad practice of too many among my brethren. Having therefore consulted with my wife, and some of my acquaintance, I determined to go again to sea. I was surgeon successively in two ships, and made several voyages, for six years, to the East and West Indies, by which I got some addition to my fortune. My hours of leisure I spent in reading the best authors, ancient and modern, being always provided with a good number of books; and when I was ashore, in observing the manners and dispositions of the people, as well as learning their language; wherein I had a great facility, by the strength of my memory.

The last of these voyages not proving very fortunate, I grew weary of the sea, and intended to stay at home with my wife and family. I removed from the Old Jewry to Fetter Lane, and from thence to Wapping, hoping to get business among the sailors; but it would not turn to account. After three years expectation that things would mend, I accepted an advantageous offer from Captain William Prichard, master of the Antelope, who was making a voyage to the South Sea. We set sail from Bristol, May 4, 1699, and our voyage was at first very prosperous.

It would not be proper, for some reasons, to trouble the reader with the particulars of our adventures in those seas; let it suffice to inform him, that in our passage from thence to the East Indies, we were driven by a violent storm to the north-west of Van Diemen's Land. By an observation, we found ourselves in the latitude of 30 degrees 2 minutes south. Twelve of our crew were dead by immoderate labor and ill food; the rest were in a very weak condition. On the 5th of November, which was the beginning of summer in those parts, the weather being very hazy, the seamen spied a rock within half a cable's length of the ship; but the wind was so strong, that we were driven directly upon it, and immediately split. Six of the crew, of whom I was one, having let down the boat into the sea, made a shift to get clear of the ship and the rock. We rowed, by my computation, about three leagues, till we were able to work no longer, being already spent with labor while we were in the ship. We therefore trusted ourselves to the mercy of the waves, and in about half an hour the boat was overset by a sudden flurry from the north. What became of my companions in the boat, as well as of those who escaped on the rock, or were left in the vessel, I cannot tell; but conclude they were all lost. For my own part, I swam as fortune directed me, and was pushed forward by wind and tide. I often let my legs drop, and could feel no bottom; but when I was almost gone, and able to struggle no longer, I found myself within my depth; and by this time the storm was much abated. The declivity was so small, that I walked near a mile before I got to the shore, which I conjectured was about eight o'clock in the evening. I then advanced forward near half a mile, but could not discover any sign of houses or inhabitants; at least I was in so weak a condition, that I did not observe them. I was extremely tired, and with that, and the heat of the weather, and about half a pint of brandy that I drank as I left the ship, I found myself much inclined to sleep. I lay down on the grass, which was very short and soft, where I slept sounder than ever I remembered to have done in my life, and, as I reckoned, about nine hours; for when I awaked, it was just day-light. I attempted to rise, but was not able to stir: for, as I happened to lie on my back, I found my arms and legs were strongly fastened on each side to the ground; and my hair, which was long and thick, tied down in the same manner. I likewise felt several slender ligatures across my body, from my arm-pits to my thighs. I could only look upwards; the sun began to grow hot, and the light offended my eyes. I heard a confused noise about me; but in the posture I lay, could see nothing except the sky. In a little time I felt something alive moving on my left leg, which advancing gently forward over my breast, came almost up to my chin; when, bending my eyes downwards as much as I could, I perceived it to be a human creature not six inches high, with a bow and arrow in his hands, and a quiver at his back. In the meantime, I felt at least forty more of the same kind (as I conjectured) following the first. I was in the utmost astonishment, and roared so loud, that they all ran back in a fright; and some of them, as I was afterwards told, were hurt with the falls they got by leaping from my sides upon the ground. However, they soon returned, and one of them, who ventured so far as to get a full sight of my face, lifting up his hands and eyes by way of admiration, cried out in a shrill but distinct voice, *Hekinah degul*; the others repeated the same words several times, but then I knew not what they meant. I lay all this while, as the reader may believe, in great uneasiness. At length, struggling to get loose, I had the fortune to break the strings, and wrench out the pegs that fastened my left arm to the ground; for, by lifting it up to my face, I discovered the methods they had taken to bind me, and at the same time with a violent pull, which gave me excessive pain, I a little loosened the strings that tied down my hair on the left side, so that I was just able to turn my head about two inches. But the creatures ran off a second time, before I could seize them; whereupon there was a great shout in a very shrill accent, and after it ceased I heard one of them cry aloud *Tolgo phonac*; when in an instant I felt above a hundred arrows discharged on my left hand, which pricked me like so many needles; and besides, they shot another flight into the air, as we do bombs in Europe, whereof many, I suppose, fell on my body, (though I felt them not), and some on my face, which I immediately covered with my left hand. When this shower of arrows was over, I fell a groaning with grief and pain; and then striving again to get loose, they discharged another volley larger than the first, and some of them attempted with spears to stick me in the sides; but by good luck I had on a buff jerkin, which they could not pierce. I thought it the most prudent method to lie still, and my design was to continue so till night, when my left hand being already loose, I could easily free myself; and as for the inhabitants, I had reason to believe I might be a match for the greatest army they could bring against me, if they were all of the same size with him that I saw. But fortune disposed otherwise of me. When the people observed I was quiet, they discharged no more arrows; but, by the noise I heard, I knew their numbers increased; and about four yards from me, over against my right ear, I heard a knocking for above an hour, like that of people at work; when turning my head that way, as well as the pegs and strings would permit me, I saw a stage erected about a foot and a half from the ground, capable of holding four of the inhabitants, with two or three ladders to mount it: from whence one of them, who seemed to be a person of quality, made me a long speech, whereof I understood not one syllable. But I should have mentioned, that before the principal person began his oration, he cried out three times, *Langro dehul san* (these words and the former were afterwards repeated and explained to me); whereupon, immediately, about fifty of the inhabitants came and cut the strings that fastened the left side of my head, which gave me the liberty of turning it to the right, and of observing the person and gesture of him that was to speak. He appeared to be of a middle age, and taller than any of the other three who attended him, whereof one was a page that held up his train, and seemed to be somewhat longer than my middle finger; the other two stood one on each side to support him. He acted every part of an orator, and I could observe many periods of threatening, and others of promises, pity, and kindness. I answered in a few words, but in the most submissive manner, lifting up my left hand, and both my eyes to the sun, as calling him for a witness; and being almost famished with hunger, having not eaten a morsel for some hours before I left the ship, I found the demands of nature so strong upon me, that I could not forbear showing my impatience (perhaps against the strict rules of decency) by putting my finger frequently to my mouth, to signify that I wanted food. The *hurgo* (for so they call a great lord, as I afterwards learnt) understood me very well. He descended from the stage, and commanded that several ladders should be applied to my sides, on which above a hundred of the inhabitants mounted and walked towards my mouth, laden with baskets full of meat, which had been provided and sent thither by the king's orders, upon the first intelligence he received of me. I observed there was the flesh of several animals, but could not distinguish them by the taste. There were shoulders, legs, and loins, shaped like those of mutton, and very well dressed, but smaller than the wings of a lark. I ate them by two or three at a mouthful, and took three loaves at a time, about the bigness of musket bullets. They supplied me as fast as they could, showing a thousand marks of wonder and astonishment at my bulk and appetite. I then made another sign, that I wanted drink. They found by my eating that a small quantity would not suffice me; and being a most ingenious people, they slung up, with great dexterity, one of their largest hogsheads, then rolled it towards my hand, and beat out the top; I drank it off at a draught, which I might well do, for it did not hold half a pint, and tasted like a small wine of Burgundy, but much more delicious. They brought me a second hogshead, which I drank in the same manner, and made signs for more; but they had none to give me. When I had performed these wonders, they shouted for joy, and danced upon my breast, repeating several times as they did at first, *Hekinah degul*. They made me a sign that I should throw down the two hogsheads, but first warning the people below to stand out of the way, crying aloud, *Borach mevolah*; and when they saw the vessels in the air, there was a universal shout of *Hekinah degul*. I confess I was often tempted, while they were passing backwards and forwards on my body, to seize forty or fifty of the first that came in my reach, and dash them against the ground. But the remembrance of what I had felt, which probably might not be the worst they could do, and the promise of honor I made them — for so I interpreted my submissive behaviour — soon drove out these imaginations. Besides, I now considered myself as bound by the laws of hospitality, to a people who had treated me with so much expense and magnificence. However, in my thoughts I could not sufficiently wonder at the intrepidity of these diminutive mortals, who durst venture to mount and walk upon my body, while one of my hands was at liberty, without trembling at the very sight of so prodigious a creature as I must appear to them. After some time, when they observed that I made no more demands for meat, there appeared before me a person of high rank from his imperial Majesty. His excellency, having mounted on the small of my right leg, advanced forwards up to my face, with about a dozen of his retinue; and producing his credentials under the signet royal, which he applied close to my eyes, spoke about ten minutes without any signs of anger, but with a kind of determinate resolution, often pointing forwards, which, as I afterwards found, was towards the capital city, about half a mile distant; whither it was agreed by his Majesty in council that I must be conveyed. I answered in few words, but to no purpose, and made a sign with my hand that was loose, putting it to the other (but over his excellency's head for fear of hurting him or his train) and then to my own head and body, to signify that I desired my liberty. It appeared that he understood me well enough, for he shook his head by way of disapprobation, and held his hand in a posture to show that I must be carried as a prisoner. However, he made other signs to let me understand that I should have meat and drink enough, and very good treatment. Whereupon I once more thought of attempting to break my bonds; but again, when I felt the smart of their arrows upon my face and hands, which were all in blisters, and many of the darts still sticking in them, and observing likewise that the number of my enemies increased, I gave tokens to let them know that they might do with me what they pleased. Upon this, the *hurgo* and his train withdrew, with much civility and cheerful countenances. Soon after I heard a general shout, with frequent repetitions of the words *Peplom selan*; and I felt great numbers of people on my left side relaxing the cords to such a degree, that I was able to turn upon my right, and to ease myself with making water; which I very plentifully did, to the great astonishment of the people; who, conjecturing by my motion what I was going to do, immediately opened to the right and left on that side, to avoid the torrent, which fell with such noise and violence from me. But before this, they had daubed my face and both my hands with a sort of ointment, very pleasant to the smell, which, in a few minutes, removed all the smart of their arrows. These circumstances, added to the refreshment I had received by their victuals and drink, which were very nourishing, disposed me to sleep. I slept about eight hours, as I was afterwards assured; and it was no wonder, for the physicians, by the emperor's order, had mingled a sleepy potion in the hogsheads of wine.

It seems, that upon the first moment I was discovered sleeping on the ground, after my landing, the emperor had early notice of it by an express; and determined in council, that I should be tied in the manner I have related, (which was done in the night while I slept;) that plenty of meat and drink should be sent to me, and a machine prepared to carry me to the capital city.

This resolution perhaps may appear very bold and dangerous, and I am confident would not be imitated by any prince in Europe on the like occasion. However, in my opinion, it was extremely prudent, as well as generous: for, supposing these people had endeavored to kill me with their spears and arrows, while I was asleep, I should certainly have awaked with the first sense of smart, which might so far have roused my rage and strength, as to have enabled me to break the strings wherewith I was tied; after which, as they were not able to make resistance, so they could expect no mercy.

These people are most excellent mathematicians, and arrived to a great perfection in mechanics, by the countenance and encouragement of the emperor, who is a renowned patron of learning. This prince has several machines fixed on wheels, for the carriage of trees and other great weights. He often builds his largest men of war, whereof some are nine feet long, in the woods where the timber grows, and has them carried on these engines three or four hundred yards to the sea. Five hundred carpenters and engineers were immediately set at work to prepare the greatest engine they had. It was a frame of wood raised three inches from the ground, about seven feet long, and four wide, moving upon twenty-two wheels. The shout I heard was upon the arrival of this engine, which, it seems, set out in four hours after my landing. It was brought parallel to me, as I lay. But the principal difficulty was to raise and place me in this vehicle. Eighty poles, each of one foot high, were erected for this purpose, and very strong cords, of the bigness of packthread, were fastened by hooks to many bandages, which the workmen had girt round my neck, my hands, my body, and my legs. Nine hundred of the strongest men were employed to draw up these cords, by many pulleys fastened on the poles; and thus, in less than three hours, I was raised and slung into the engine, and there tied fast. All this I was told; for, while the operation was performing, I lay in a profound sleep, by the force of that soporiferous medicine infused into my liquor. Fifteen hundred of the emperor's largest horses, each about four inches and a half high, were employed to draw me towards the metropolis, which, as I said, was half a mile distant.

About four hours after we began our journey, I awaked by a very ridiculous accident; for the carriage being stopped a while, to adjust something that was out of order, two or three of the young natives had the curiosity to see how I looked when I was asleep; they climbed up into the engine, and advancing very softly to my face, one of them, an officer in the guards, put the sharp end of his half-pike a good way up into my left nostril, which tickled my nose like a straw, and made me sneeze violently; whereupon they stole off unperceived, and it was three weeks before I knew the cause of my waking so suddenly. We made a long march the remaining part of the day, and, rested at night with five hundred guards on each side of me, half with torches, and half with bows and arrows, ready to shoot me if I should offer to stir. The next morning at sunrise we continued our march, and arrived within two hundred yards of the city gates about noon. The emperor, and all his court, came out to meet us; but his great officers would by no means suffer his Majesty to endanger his person by mounting on my body.

At the place where the carriage stopped there stood an ancient temple, esteemed to be the largest in the whole kingdom; which, having been polluted some years before by an unnatural murder, was, according to the zeal of those people, looked upon as profane, and therefore had been applied to common use, and all the ornaments and furniture carried away. In this edifice it was determined I should lodge. The great gate fronting to the north was about four feet high, and almost two feet wide, through which I could easily creep. On each side of the gate was a small window, not above six inches from the ground; into that on the left side, the king's smith conveyed fourscore and eleven chains, like those that hang to a lady's watch in Europe, and almost as large, which were locked to my left leg with six-and-thirty padlocks. Over against this temple, on the other side of the great highway, at twenty feet distance, there was a turret at least five feet high. Here the emperor ascended, with many principal lords of his court, to have an opportunity of viewing me, as I was told, for I could not see them. It was reckoned that above a hundred thousand inhabitants came out of the town upon the same errand; and, in spite of my guards, I believe there could not be fewer than ten thousand at several times, who mounted my body by the help of ladders. But a proclamation was soon issued, to forbid it upon pain of death. When the workmen found it was impossible for me to break loose, they cut all the strings that bound me; whereupon I rose up, with as melancholy a disposition as ever I had in my life. But the noise and astonishment of the people, at seeing me rise and walk, are not to be expressed. The chains that held my left leg were about two yards long, and gave me not only the liberty of walking backwards and forwards in a semicircle, but, being fixed within four inches of the gate, allowed me to creep in, and lie at my full length in the temple.

ᘯᕳ **Chapter II** ᘯᕳ

The emperor of Lilliput, attended by several of the nobility, comes to see the author in his confinement. The emperor's person and habit described. Learned men appointed to teach the author their language. He gains favor by his mild disposition. His pockets are searched, and his sword and pistols taken from him.

When I found myself on my feet, I looked about me, and must confess I never beheld a more entertaining prospect. The country around appeared like a continued garden, and the enclosed fields, which were generally forty feet square, resembled so many beds of flowers. These fields were intermingled with woods of half a stang, and the tallest trees, as I could judge, appeared to be seven feet high. I viewed the town on my left hand, which looked like the painted scene of a city in a theatre.

I had been for some hours extremely pressed by the necessities of nature; which was no wonder, it being almost two days since I had last disburdened myself. I was under great difficulties between urgency and shame. The best expedient I could think of, was to creep into my house, which I accordingly did; and shutting the gate after me, I went as far as the length of my chain would suffer, and discharged my body of that uneasy load. But this was the only time I was ever guilty of so uncleanly an action; for which I cannot but hope the candid reader will give some allowance, after he has maturely and impartially considered my case, and the distress I was in. From this time my constant practice was, as soon as I rose, to perform that business in open air, at the full extent of my chain; and due care was taken every morning before company came, that the offensive matter should be carried off in wheel-barrows, by two servants appointed for that purpose. I would not have dwelt so long upon a circumstance that, perhaps, at first sight, may appear not very momentous, if I had not thought it necessary to justify my character, in point of cleanliness, to the world; which, I am told, some of my maligners have been pleased, upon this and other occasions, to call in question.

When this adventure was at an end, I came back out of my house, having occasion for fresh air. The emperor was already descended from the tower, and advancing on horseback towards me, which had like to have cost him dear; for the beast, though very well trained, yet wholly unused to such a sight, which appeared as if a mountain moved before him, reared up on its hinder feet; but that prince, who is an excellent horseman, kept his seat, till his attendants ran in, and held the bridle, while his Majesty had time to dismount. When he alighted, he surveyed me round with great admiration; but kept beyond the length of my chain. He ordered his cooks and butlers, who were already prepared, to give me victuals and drink, which they pushed forward in a sort of vehicles upon wheels, till I could reach them. I took these vehicles and soon emptied them all; twenty of them were filled with meat, and ten with liquor; each of the former afforded me two or three good mouthfuls; and I emptied the liquor of ten vessels, which was contained in earthen vials, into one vehicle, drinking it off at a draught; and so I did with the rest. The empress, and young princes of the blood of both sexes, attended by many ladies, sat at some distance in their chairs; but upon the accident that happened to the emperor's horse, they alighted, and came near his person, which I am now going to describe. He is taller by almost the breadth of my nail, than any of his court; which alone is enough to strike an awe into the beholders. His features are strong and masculine, with an Austrian lip and arched nose, his complexion olive, his countenance erect, his body and limbs well proportioned, all his motions graceful, and his deportment majestic. He was then past his prime, being twenty-eight years and three quarters old, of which he had reigned about seven in great felicity, and generally victorious. For the better convenience of beholding him, I lay on my side, so that my face was parallel to his, and he stood but three yards off: however, I have had him since many times in my hand, and therefore cannot be deceived in the description. His dress was very plain and simple, and the fashion of it between the Asiatic and the European; but he had on his head a light helmet of gold, adorned with jewels, and a plume on the crest. He held his sword drawn in his hand to defend himself, if I should happen to break loose; it was almost three inches long; the hilt and scabbard were gold enriched with diamonds. His voice was shrill, but very clear and articulate; and I could distinctly hear it when I stood up. The ladies and courtiers were all most magnificently clad; so that the spot they stood upon seemed to resemble a petticoat spread upon the ground, embroidered with figures of gold and silver. His imperial Majesty spoke often to me, and I returned answers, but neither of us could understand a syllable. There were several of his priests and lawyers present (as I conjectured by their habits), who were commanded to address themselves to me; and I spoke to them in as many languages as I had the least smattering of, which were High and Low Dutch, Latin, French, Spanish, Italian, and Lingua Franca, but all to no purpose. After about two hours the court retired, and I was left with a strong guard, to prevent the impertinence, and probably the malice of the rabble, who were very impatient to crowd about me as near as they durst; and some of them had the impudence to shoot their arrows at me, as I sat on the ground by the door of my house, whereof one very narrowly missed my left eye. But the colonel ordered six of the ringleaders to be seized, and thought no punishment so proper as to deliver them bound into my hands; which some of his soldiers accordingly did, pushing them forward with the butt-ends of their pikes into my reach. I took them all in my right hand, put five of them into my coat-pocket; and as to the sixth, I made a countenance as if I would eat him alive. The poor man squalled terribly, and the colonel and his officers were in much pain, especially when they saw me take out my penknife, but I soon put them out of fear; for, looking mildly, and immediately cutting the strings he was bound with, I set him gently on the ground, and away he ran. I treated the rest in the same manner, taking them one by one out of my pocket; and I observed both the soldiers and people were highly delighted at this mark of my clemency, which was represented very much to my advantage at court.

Towards night I got with some difficulty into my house, where I lay on the ground, and continued to do so about a fortnight; during which time, the emperor gave orders to have a bed prepared for me. Six hundred beds of the common measure were brought in carriages, and worked up in my house; a hundred and fifty of their beds, sewn together, made up the breadth and length; and these were four double, which, however, kept me but very indifferently from the hardness of the floor, that was of smooth stone. By the same computation, they provided me with sheets, blankets, and coverlets, tolerable enough for one who had been so long inured to hardships.

As the news of my arrival spread through the kingdom, it brought prodigious numbers of rich, idle, and curious people to see me; so that the villages were almost emptied; and great neglect of tillage and household affairs must have ensued, if his imperial Majesty had not provided, by several proclamations and orders of state, against this inconveniency. He directed that those who had already beheld me should return home, and not presume to come within fifty yards of my house, without license from the court; whereby the secretaries of state got considerable fees.

In the meantime the emperor held frequent councils, to debate what course should be taken with me; and I was afterwards assured by a particular friend, a person of great quality, who was as much in the secret as any, that the court was under many difficulties concerning me. They apprehended my breaking loose; that my diet would be very expensive, and might cause a famine. Sometimes they determined to starve me; or at least to shoot me in the face and hands with poisoned arrows, which would soon dispatch me; but again they considered, that the stench of so large a carcass might produce a plague in the metropolis, and probably spread through the whole kingdom. In the midst of these consultations, several officers of the army went to the door of the great council-chamber, and two of them being admitted, gave an account of my behaviour to the six criminals above-mentioned; which made so favorable an impression in the breast of his Majesty and the whole board, in my behalf, that an imperial commission was issued out, obliging all the villages, nine hundred yards round the city, to deliver in every morning six beeves, forty sheep, and other victuals for my sustenance; together with a proportionable quantity of bread, and wine, and other liquors; for the due payment of which his Majesty gave assignments upon his treasury, for this prince lives chiefly upon his own demesnes; seldom, except upon great occasions, raising any subsidies upon his subjects, who are bound to attend him in his wars at their own expense. An establishment was also made of six hundred persons to be my domestics, who had board-wages allowed for their maintenance, and tents built for them very conveniently on each side of my door. It was likewise ordered, that three hundred tailors should make me a suit of clothes, after the fashion of the country; that six of his Majesty's greatest scholars should be employed to instruct me in their language; and lastly, that the emperor's horses, and those of the nobility and troops of guards, should be frequently exercised in my sight, to accustom themselves to me. All these orders were duly put in execution; and in about three weeks I made a great progress in learning their language; during which time the emperor frequently honoured me with his visits, and was pleased to assist my masters in teaching me. We began already to converse together in some sort; and the first words I learnt, were to express my desire "that he would please give me my liberty;" which I every day repeated on my knees. His answer, as I could comprehend it, was, that this must be a work of time, not to be thought on without the advice of his council, and that first I must *lumos kelmin pesso desmar lon emposo*; that is, swear a peace with him and his kingdom. However, that I should be used with all kindness. And he advised me to acquire, by my patience and discreet behaviour, the good opinion of himself and his subjects. He desired I would not take it ill, if he gave orders to certain proper officers to search me; for probably I might carry about me several weapons, which must needs be dangerous things, if they answered the bulk of so prodigious a person. I said, His Majesty should be satisfied; for I was ready to strip myself, and turn up my pockets before him. This I delivered part in words, and part in signs. He replied, "that, by the laws of the kingdom, I must be searched by two of his officers; that he knew this could not be done without my consent and assistance; and he had so good an opinion of my generosity and justice, as to trust their persons in my hands; that whatever they took from me, should be returned when I left the country, or paid for at the rate which I would set upon them." I took up the two officers in my hands, put them first into my coat-pockets, and then into every other pocket about me, except my two fobs, and another secret pocket, which I had no mind should be searched, wherein I had some little necessaries that were of no consequence to any but myself. In one of my fobs there was a silver watch, and in the other a small quantity of gold in a purse. These gentlemen, having pen, ink, and paper, about them, made an exact inventory of everything they saw; and when they had done, desired I would set them down, that they might deliver it to the emperor. This inventory I afterwards translated into English, and is, word for word, as follows:

Imprimis, In the right coat-pocket of the Great Man Mountain (for so I interpret the words *quinbus flestrin*) after the strictest search, we found only one great piece of coarse-cloth, large enough to be a foot-cloth for your Majesty's chief room of state. In the left pocket we saw a huge silver chest, with a cover of the same metal, which we, the searchers, were not able to lift. We desired it should be opened, and one of us stepping into it, found himself up to the mid leg in a sort of dust, some part whereof flying up to our faces set us both a sneezing for several times together. In his right waistcoat-pocket we found a prodigious bundle of white thin substances, folded one over another, about the bigness of three men, tied with a strong cable, and marked with black figures; which we humbly conceive to be writings, every letter almost half as large as the palm of our hands. In the left there was a sort of engine, from the back of which were extended twenty long poles, resembling the pallisades before your Majesty's court; wherewith we conjecture the Man-Mountain combs his head; for we did not always trouble him with questions, because we found it a great difficulty to make him understand us. In the large pocket, on the right side of his middle cover (so I translate the word *ranfulo*, by which they meant my breeches), we saw a hollow pillar of iron, about the length of a man, fastened to a strong piece of timber larger than the pillar; and upon one side of the pillar, were huge pieces of iron sticking out, cut into strange figures, which we know not what to make of. In the left pocket, another engine of the same kind. In the smaller pocket on the right side, were several round flat pieces of white and red metal, of different bulk; some of the white, which seemed to be silver, were so large and heavy, that my comrade and I could hardly lift them. In the left pocket were two black pillars irregularly shaped; we could not, without difficulty, reach the top of them, as we stood at the bottom of his pocket. One of them was covered, and seemed all of a piece; but at the upper end of the other there appeared a white round substance, about twice the bigness of our heads. Within each of these was enclosed a prodigious plate of steel; which, by our orders, we obliged him to show us, because we apprehended they might be dangerous engines. He took them out of their cases, and told us, that in his own country his practice was to shave his beard with one of these, and cut his meat with the other. There were two pockets which we could not enter: these he called his fobs; they were two large slits cut into the top of his middle cover, but squeezed close by the pressure of his belly. Out of the right fob hung a great silver chain, with a wonderful kind of engine at the bottom. We directed him to draw out whatever was at the end of that chain; which appeared to be a globe, half silver, and half of some transparent metal; for, on the transparent side, we saw certain strange figures circularly drawn, and thought we could touch them, till we found our fingers stopped by the lucid substance. He put this engine into our ears, which made an incessant noise, like that of a water-mill. and we conjecture it is either some unknown animal, or the god that he worships; but we are more inclined to the latter opinion, because he assured us (if we understood him right, for he expressed himself very imperfectly) that he seldom did anything without consulting it. He called it his oracle, and said, it pointed out the time for every action of his life. From the left fob he took out a net almost large enough for a fisherman, but contrived to open and shut like a purse, and served him for the same use: we found therein several massy pieces of yellow metal, which, if they be real gold, must be of immense value.

Having thus, in obedience to your Majesty's commands, diligently searched all his pockets, we observed a girdle about his waist made of the hide of some prodigious animal, from which, on the left side, hung a sword of the length of five men; and on the right, a bag or pouch divided into two cells, each cell capable of holding three of your Majesty's subjects. In one of these cells were several globes, or balls, of a most ponderous metal, about the bigness of our heads, and requiring a strong hand to lift them; the other cell contained a heap of certain black grains, but of no great bulk or weight, for we could hold above fifty of them in the palms of our hands.

This is an exact inventory of what we found about the body of the Man-Mountain, who used us with great civility, and due respect to your Majesty's commission. Signed and sealed on the fourth day of the eighty-ninth moon of your Majesty's auspicious reign.

Clefrin Frelock, Marsi Frelock.

When this inventory was read over to the emperor, he directed me, although in very gentle terms, to deliver up the several particulars. He first called for my scimitar, which I took out, scabbard and all. In the meantime he ordered three thousand of his choicest troops (who then attended him) to surround me at a distance, with their bows and arrows just ready to discharge; but I did not observe it, for mine eyes were wholly fixed upon his Majesty. He then desired me to draw my Scymiter, which, although it had got some rust by the sea water, was, in most parts, exceeding bright. I did so, and immediately all the troops gave a shout between terror and surprise; for the sun shone clear, and the reflection dazzled their eyes, as I waved the scimitar to and fro in my hand. His Majesty, who is a most magnanimous prince, was less daunted than I could expect; he ordered me to return it into the scabbard, and cast it on the ground as gently as I could, about six feet from the end of my chain. The next thing he demanded was one of the hollow iron pillars; by which he meant my pocket pistols. I drew it out, and at his desire, as well as I could, expressed to him the use of it; and charging it only with powder, which, by the closeness of my pouch, happened to escape wetting in the sea (an inconvenience against which all prudent mariners take special care to provide,) I first cautioned the emperor not to be afraid, and then I let it off in the air. The astonishment here was much greater than at the sight of my scimitar. Hundreds fell down as if they had been struck dead; and even the emperor, although he stood his ground, could not recover himself for some time. I delivered up both my pistols in the same manner as I had done my scimitar, and then my pouch of powder and bullets; begging him that the former might be kept from fire, for it would kindle with the smallest spark, and blow up his imperial palace into the air. I likewise delivered up my watch, which the emperor was very curious to see, and commanded two of his tallest yeomen of the guards to bear it on a pole upon their shoulders, as dray-men in England do a barrel of ale. He was amazed at the continual noise it made, and the motion of the minute-hand, which he could easily discern, for their sight is much more acute than ours; he asked the opinions of his learned men about it, which were various and remote, as the reader may well imagine without my repeating; although indeed I could not very perfectly understand them. I then gave up my silver and copper money, my purse, with nine large pieces of gold, and some smaller ones; my knife and razor, my comb and silver snuff-box, my handkerchief and journal-book. My scimitar, pistols, and pouch, were conveyed in carriages to his Majesty's stores; but the rest of my goods were returned me.

I had as I before observed, one private pocket, which escaped their search, wherein there was a pair of spectacles (which I sometimes use for the weakness of mine eyes,) a pocket perspective, and some other little conveniences; which, being of no consequence to the emperor, I did not think myself bound in honor to discover, and I apprehended they might be lost or spoiled if I ventured them out of my possession.

Chapter III

The author diverts the emperor, and his nobility of both sexes, in a very uncommon manner. The diversions of the court of Lilliput described. The author has his liberty granted him upon certain conditions.

My gentleness and good behaviour had gained so far on the emperor and his court, and indeed upon the army and people in general, that I began to conceive hopes of getting my liberty in a short time. I took all possible methods to cultivate this favorable disposition. The natives came, by degrees, to be less apprehensive of any danger from me. I would sometimes lie down, and let five or six of them dance on my hand; and at last the boys and girls would venture to come and play at hide-and-seek in my hair. I had now made a good progress in understanding and speaking the language. The emperor had a mind one day to entertain me with several of the country shows, wherein they exceed all nations I have known, both for dexterity and magnificence. I was diverted with none so much as that of the rope-dancers, performed upon a slender white thread, extended about two feet, and twelve inches from the ground. Upon which I shall desire liberty, with the reader's patience, to enlarge a little.

This diversion is only practiced by those persons who are candidates for great employments, and high favor at court. They are trained in this art from their youth, and are not always of noble birth, or liberal education. When a great office is vacant, either by death or disgrace (which often happens,) five or six of those candidates petition the emperor to entertain his Majesty and the court with a dance on the rope; and whoever jumps the highest, without falling, succeeds in the office. Very often the chief ministers themselves are commanded to show their skill, and to convince the emperor that they have not lost their faculty. Flimnap, the treasurer, is allowed to cut a caper on the straight rope, at least an inch higher than any other lord in the whole empire. I have seen him do the summerset several times together, upon a trencher fixed on a rope which is no thicker than a common packthread in England. My friend Reldresal, principal secretary for private affairs, is, in my opinion, if I am not partial, the second after the treasurer; the rest of the great officers are much upon a par.

These diversions are often attended with fatal accidents, whereof great numbers are on record. I myself have seen two or three candidates break a limb. But the danger is much greater, when the ministers themselves are commanded to show their dexterity; for, by contending to excel themselves and their fellows, they strain so far that there is hardly one of them who has not received a fall, and some of them two or three. I was assured that, a year or two before my arrival, Flimnap would infallibly have broken his neck, if one of the king's cushions, that accidentally lay on the ground, had not weakened the force of his fall.

There is likewise another diversion, which is only shown before the emperor and empress, and first minister, upon particular occasions. The emperor lays on the table three fine silken threads of six inches long; one is blue, the other red, and the third green. These threads are proposed as prizes for those persons whom the emperor has a mind to distinguish by a peculiar mark of his favor. The ceremony is performed in his Majesty's great chamber of state, where the candidates are to undergo a trial of dexterity very different from the former, and such as I have not observed the least resemblance of in any other country of the new or old world. The emperor holds a stick in his hands, both ends parallel to the horizon, while the candidates advancing, one by one, sometimes leap over the stick, sometimes creep under it, backward and forward, several times, according as the stick is advanced or depressed. Sometimes the emperor holds one end of the stick, and his first minister the other; sometimes the minister has it entirely to himself. Whoever performs his part with most agility, and holds out the longest in leaping and creeping, is rewarded with the blue-coloured silk; the red is given to the next, and the green to the third, which they all wear girt twice round about the middle; and you see few great persons about this court who are not adorned with one of these girdles.

The horses of the army, and those of the royal stables, having been daily led before me, were no longer shy, but would come up to my very feet without starting. The riders would leap them over my hand, as I held it on the ground; and one of the emperor's huntsmen, upon a large courser, took my foot, shoe and all; which was indeed a prodigious leap. I had the good fortune to divert the emperor one day after a very extraordinary manner. I desired he would order several sticks of two feet high, and the thickness of an ordinary cane, to be brought me; whereupon his Majesty commanded the master of his woods to give directions accordingly; and the next morning six woodmen arrived with as many carriages, drawn by eight horses to each. I took nine of these sticks, and fixing them firmly in the ground in a quadrangular figure, two feet and a half square, I took four other sticks, and tied them parallel at each corner, about two feet from the ground; then I fastened my handkerchief to the nine sticks that stood erect; and extended it on all sides, till it was tight as the top of a drum; and the four parallel sticks, rising about five inches higher than the handkerchief, served as ledges on each side. When

I had finished my work, I desired the emperor to let a troop of his best horses twenty-four in number, come and exercise upon this plain. His Majesty approved of the proposal, and I took them up, one by one, in my hands, ready mounted and armed, with the proper officers to exercise them. As soon as they got into order they divided into two parties, performed mock skirmishes, discharged blunt arrows, drew their swords, fled and pursued, attacked and retired, and in short discovered the best military discipline I ever beheld. The parallel sticks secured them and their horses from falling over the stage; and the emperor was so much delighted, that he ordered this entertainment to be repeated several days, and once was pleased to be lifted up and give the word of command; and with great difficulty persuaded even the empress herself to let me hold her in her close chair within two yards of the stage, when she was able to take a full view of the whole performance. It was my good fortune, that no ill accident happened in these entertainments; only once a fiery horse, that belonged to one of the captains, pawing with his hoof, struck a hole in my handkerchief, and his foot slipping, he overthrew his rider and himself; but I immediately relieved them both, and covering the hole with one hand, I set down the troop with the other, in the same manner as I took them up. The horse that fell was strained in the left shoulder, but the rider got no hurt; and I repaired my handkerchief as well as I could; however, I would not trust to the strength of it any more, in such dangerous enterprises.

About two or three days before I was set at liberty, as I was entertaining the court with this kind of feat, there arrived an express to inform his Majesty, that some of his subjects, riding near the place where I was first taken up, had seen a great black substance lying on the around, very oddly shaped, extending its edges round, as wide as his Majesty's bedchamber, and rising up in the middle as high as a man; that it was no living creature, as they at first apprehended, for it lay on the grass without motion; and some of them had walked round it several times; that, by mounting upon each other's shoulders, they had got to the top, which was flat and even, and, stamping upon it, they found that it was hollow within; that they humbly conceived it might be something belonging to the Man-Mountain; and if his Majesty pleased, they would undertake to bring it with only five horses. I presently knew what they meant, and was glad at heart to receive this intelligence. It seems, upon my first reaching the shore after our shipwreck, I was in such confusion, that before I came to the place where I went to sleep, my hat, which I had fastened with a string to my head while I was rowing, and had stuck on all the time I was swimming, fell off after I came to land; the string, as I conjecture, breaking by some accident, which I never observed, but thought my hat had been lost at sea. I entreated his Imperial Majesty to give orders it might be brought to me as soon as possible, describing to him the use and the nature of it; and the next day the waggoners arrived with it, but not in a very good condition; they had bored two holes in the brim, within an inch and half of the edge, and fastened two hooks in the holes; these hooks were tied by a long cord to the harness, and thus my hat was dragged along for above half an English mile; but, the ground in that country being extremely smooth and level, it received less damage than I expected.

Two days after this adventure, the emperor, having ordered that part of his army which quarters in and about his metropolis, to be in readiness, took a fancy of diverting himself in a very singular manner. He desired I would stand like a Colossus, with my legs as far asunder as I conveniently could. He then commanded his general (who was an old experienced leader, and a great patron of mine) to draw up the troops in close order, and march them under me; the foot by twenty-four abreast, and the horse by sixteen, with drums beating, colours flying, and pikes advanced. This body consisted of three thousand foot, and a thousand horse. His Majesty gave orders, upon pain of death, that every soldier in his march should observe the strictest decency with regard to my person; which however could not prevent some of the younger officers from turning up their eyes as they passed under me. And, to confess the truth, my breeches were at that time in so ill a condition, that they afforded some opportunities for laughter and admiration.

I had sent so many memorials and petitions for my liberty, that his Majesty at length mentioned the matter, first in the cabinet, and then in a full council; where it was opposed by none, except Skyresh Bolgolam, who was pleased, without any provocation, to be my mortal enemy. But it was carried against him by the whole board, and confirmed by the emperor. That minister was galbet, or admiral of the realm, very much in his master's confidence, and a person well versed in affairs, but of a morose and sour complexion. However, he was at length persuaded to comply; but prevailed that the articles and conditions upon which I should be set free, and to which I must swear, should be drawn up by himself. These articles were brought to me by Skyresh Bolgolam in person attended by two under-secretaries, and several persons of distinction. After they were read, I was demanded to swear to the performance of them; first in the manner of my own country, and afterwards in the method prescribed by their laws; which was, to hold my right foot in my left hand, and to place the middle finger of my right hand on the crown of my head, and my thumb on the tip of my right ear. But because the reader may be curious to have some idea of the style and manner of expression peculiar to that people, as well as to know the article upon which I recovered my liberty, I have made a translation of the whole instrument, word for word, as near as I was able, which I here offer to the public.

Golbasto Momarem Evlame Gurdilo Shefin Mully Ully Gue, most mighty Emperor of Lilliput, delight and terror of the universe, whose dominions extend five thousand blustrugs (about twelve miles in circumference) to the extremities of the globe; monarch of all monarchs, taller than the sons of men; whose feet press down to the centre, and whose head strikes against the sun; at whose nod the princes of the earth shake their knees; pleasant as the spring, comfortable as the summer, fruitful as autumn, dreadful as winter. His most sublime Majesty proposes to the Man-Mountain, lately arrived at our celestial dominions, the following articles, which, by a solemn oath, he shall be obliged to perform:

1st, The Man-Mountain shall not depart from our dominions, without our license under our great seal.

2nd, He shall not presume to come into our metropolis, without our express order; at which time, the inhabitants shall have two hours warning to keep within doors.

3rd, The said Man-Mountain shall confine his walks to our principal high roads, and not offer to walk, or lie down, in a meadow or field of corn.

4th, As he walks the said roads, he shall take the utmost care not to trample upon the bodies of any of our loving subjects, their horses, or carriages, nor take any of our subjects into his hands without their own consent.

5th, If an express requires extraordinary dispatch, the Man-Mountain shall be obliged to carry, in his pocket, the messenger and horse a six days journey, once in every moon, and return the said messenger back (if so required) safe to our imperial presence.

6th, He shall be our ally against our enemies in the island of Blefuscu, and do his utmost to destroy their fleet, which is now preparing to invade us.

7th, That the said Man-Mountain shall, at his times of leisure, be aiding and assisting to our workmen, in helping to raise certain great stones, towards covering the wall of the principal park, and other our royal buildings.

8th, that the said Man-Mountain shall, in two moons' time, deliver in an exact survey of the circumference of our dominions, by a computation of his own paces round the coast.

Lastly, that, upon his solemn oath to observe all the above articles, the said Man-Mountain shall have a daily allowance of meat and drink sufficient for the support of 1724 of our subjects, with free access to our royal person, and other marks of our favor. Given at our palace at Belfaborac, the twelfth day of the ninety-first moon of our reign.

I swore and subscribed to these articles with great cheerfulness and content, although some of them were not so honourable as I could have wished; which proceeded wholly from the malice of Skyresh Bolgolam, the high-admiral: whereupon my chains were immediately unlocked, and I was at full liberty. The emperor himself, in person, did me the honor to be by at the whole ceremony. I made my acknowledgements by prostrating myself at his Majesty's feet; but he commanded me to rise; and after many gracious expressions, which, to avoid the censure of vanity, I shall not repeat, he added, that he hoped I should prove a useful servant, and well deserve all the favours he had already conferred upon me, or might do for the future.

The reader may please to observe, that, in the last article of the recovery of my liberty, the emperor stipulates to allow me a quantity of meat and drink sufficient for the support of 1724 Lilliputians. Sometime after, asking a friend at court how they came to fix on that determinate number, he told me that his Majesty's mathematicians, having taken the height of my body by the help of a quadrant, and finding it to exceed theirs in the proportion of twelve to one, they concluded from the similarity of their bodies, that mine must contain at least 1724 of theirs, and consequently would require as much food as was necessary to support that number of Lilliputians. By which the reader may conceive an idea of the ingenuity of that people, as well as the prudent and exact economy of so great a prince.

⌒～ **Chapter IV** ～⌒

Mildendo, the metropolis of Lilliput, described, together with the emperor's palace. A conversation between the author and a principal secretary, concerning the affairs of that empire. The author's offers to serve the emperor in his wars.

The first request I made, after I had obtained my liberty, was, that I might have license to see Mildendo, the metropolis; which the emperor easily granted me, but with a special charge to do no hurt either to the inhabitants or their houses. The people had notice, by proclamation, of my design to visit the town. The wall which encompassed it is two feet and a half high, and at least eleven inches broad, so that a coach and horses may be driven very safely round it; and it is flanked with strong towers at ten feet distance. I stepped over the great western gate, and passed very gently, and sidling, through the two principal streets, only in my short waistcoat, for fear of damaging the roofs and eaves of the houses with the skirts of my coat. I walked with the utmost circumspection, to avoid treading on any stragglers who might remain in the streets, although the orders were very strict, that all people should keep in their houses, at their own peril. The garret windows and tops of houses were so crowded with spectators, that I thought in all my travels I had not seen a more populous place. The city is an exact square, each side of the wall being five hundred feet long. The two great streets, which run across and divide it into four quarters, are five feet wide. The lanes and alleys, which I could not enter, but only view them as I passed, are from twelve to eighteen inches. The town is capable of holding five hundred thousand souls; The houses are from three to five stories; the shops and markets well provided.

The emperor's palace is in the centre of the city where the two great streets meet. It is enclosed by a wall of two feet high, and twenty feet distance from the buildings. I had his Majesty's permission to step over this wall; and, the space being so wide between that and the palace, I could easily view it on every side. The outward court is a square of forty feet, and includes two other courts; in the inmost are the royal apartments, which I was very desirous to see, but found it extremely difficult; for the great gates, from one square into another, were but eighteen inches high, and seven inches wide. Now the buildings of the outer court were at least five feet high, and it was impossible for me to stride over them without infinite damage to the pile, though the walls were strongly built of hewn stone, and four inches thick. At the same time the emperor had a great desire that I should see the magnificence of his palace; but this I was not able to do till three days after, which I spent in cutting down with my knife some of the largest trees in the royal park, about a hundred yards distant from the city. Of these trees I made two stools, each about three feet high, and strong enough to bear my weight. The people having received notice a second time, I went again through the city to the palace with my two stools in my hands. When I came to the side of the outer court, I stood upon one stool, and took the other in my hand; this I lifted over the roof, and gently set it down on the space between the first and second court, which was eight feet wide. I then stepped over the building very conveniently from one stool to the other, and drew up the first after me with a hooked stick. By this contrivance I got into the inmost court; and, lying down upon my side, I applied my face to the windows of the middle stories, which were left open on purpose, and discovered the most splendid apartments that can be imagined. There I saw the empress and the young princes, in their several lodgings, with their chief attendants about them. Her imperial Majesty was pleased to smile very graciously upon me, and gave me out of the window her hand to kiss.

But I shall not anticipate the reader with further descriptions of this kind, because I reserve them for a greater work, which is now almost ready for the press; containing a general description of this empire, from its first erection, through a long series of princes; with a particular account of their wars and politics, laws, learning, and religion; their plants and animals; their peculiar manners and customs, with other matters very curious and useful; my chief design at present being only to relate such events and transactions as happened to the public or to myself during a residence of about nine months in that empire.

One morning, about a fortnight after I had obtained my liberty, Reldresal, principal secretary (as they style him) for private affairs, came to my house attended only by one servant. He ordered his coach to wait at a distance, and desired I would give him an hour's audience; which I readily consented to, on account of his quality and personal merits, as well as of the many good offices he had done me during my solicitations at court. I offered to lie down that he might the more conveniently reach my ear, but he chose rather to let me hold him in my hand during our conversation. He began with compliments on my liberty; said, he might pretend to some merit in it; but, however, added, that if it had not been for the present situation of things at court, perhaps I might not have obtained it so soon. For, said he, "as flourishing a condition as we may appear to be in to foreigners, we labor under two mighty evils; a violent faction at home, and the danger of an invasion, by a most potent enemy, from abroad. As to the first, you are to understand, that for about seventy moons past there have been two struggling parties in this empire, under the names of Tramecksan and Slamecksan, from the high and low heels of their shoes, by which they distinguish themselves. It is alleged, indeed, that the high heels are most agreeable to our ancient constitution; but, however this be, his Majesty has determined to make use only of low heels in the administration of the government, and all offices in the gift of the crown, as you cannot but observe; and particularly that his Majesty's imperial heels are lower at least by a drurr than any of his court (drurr is a measure about the fourteenth part of an inch). The animosities between these two parties run so high, that they will neither eat, nor drink, nor talk with each other. We compute the Tramecksan, or high heels, to exceed us in number; but the power is wholly on our side. We apprehend his imperial highness, the heir to the crown, to have some tendency towards the high heels; at least we can plainly discover that one of his heels is higher than the other, which gives him a hobble in his gait. Now, in the midst of these intestine disquiets, we are threatened with an invasion from the island of Blefuscu, which is the other great empire of the universe, almost as large and powerful as this of his Majesty. For as to what we have heard you affirm, that there are other kingdoms and states in the world inhabited by human creatures as large as yourself, our philosophers are in much doubt, and would rather conjecture that you dropped from the moon, or one of the stars; because it is certain, that a hundred mortals of your bulk would in a short time destroy all the fruits and cattle of his Majesty's dominions; besides, our histories of six thousand moons make no mention of any other regions than the two great empires of Lilliput and Blefuscu. Which two mighty powers have, as I was going to tell you, been engaged in a most obstinate war for six-and-thirty moons past. It began upon the following occasion. It is allowed on all hands, that the primitive way of breaking eggs, before we eat them, was upon the larger end; but his present Majesty's grandfather, while he was a boy, going to eat an egg, and breaking it according to the ancient practice, happened to cut one of his fingers. Whereupon the emperor his father published an edict, commanding all his subjects, upon great penalties, to break the smaller end of their eggs. The people so highly resented this law, that our histories tell us, there have been six rebellions raised on that account; wherein one emperor lost his life, and another his crown. These civil commotions were constantly fomented by the monarchs of Blefuscu; and when they were quelled, the exiles always fled for refuge to that empire. It is computed that eleven thousand persons have at several times suffered death, rather than submit to break their eggs at the smaller end. Many hundred large volumes have been published upon this controversy; but the books of the Big-endians have been long forbidden, and the whole party rendered incapable by law of holding employments. During the course of these troubles, the emperors of Blefusca did frequently expostulate by their ambassadors, accusing us of making a schism in religion, by offending against a fundamental doctrine of our great prophet Lustrog, in the fifty-fourth chapter of the Blundecral. This, however, is thought to be a mere strain upon the text; for the words are these, that all true believers break their eggs at the convenient end. And which is the convenient end, seems, in my humble opinion to be left to every man's conscience, or at least in the power of the chief magistrate to determine. Now, the Big-endian exiles have found so much credit in the emperor of Blefuscu's court, and so much private assistance and encouragement from their party here at home, that a bloody war has been carried on between the two empires for six-and-thirty moons, with various success; during which time we have lost forty capital ships, and a much a greater number of smaller vessels, together with thirty thousand of our best seamen and soldiers; and the damage received by the enemy is reckoned to be somewhat greater than ours. However, they have now equipped a numerous fleet, and are just preparing to make a descent upon us; and his Imperial Majesty, placing great confidence in your velour and strength, has commanded me to lay this account of his affairs before you."

I desired the secretary to present my humble duty to the emperor; and to let him know, that I thought it would not become me, who was a foreigner, to interfere with parties; but I was ready, with the hazard of my life, to defend his person and state against all invaders.

⌒ **Chapter V** ⌒

The author, by an extraordinary stratagem, prevents an invasion. A high title of honor is conferred upon him. Ambassadors arrive from the emperor of Blefuscu, and sue for peace. The empress's apartment on fire by an accident; the author instrumental in saving the rest of the palace.

The empire of Blefuscu is an island situated to the north-east of Lilliput, from which it is parted only by a channel of eight hundred yards wide. I had not yet seen it, and upon this notice of an intended invasion, I avoided appearing on that side of the coast, for fear of being discovered, by some of the enemy's ships, who had received no intelligence of me; all intercourse between the two empires having been strictly forbidden during the war, upon pain of death, and an embargo laid by our emperor upon all vessels whatsoever. I communicated to his Majesty a project I had formed of seizing the enemy's whole fleet; which, as our scouts assured us, lay at anchor in the harbor, ready to sail with the first fair wind. I consulted the most experienced seamen upon the depth of the channel, which they had often plumbed; who told me, that in the middle, at high-water, it was seventy glumgluffs deep, which is about six feet of European measure; and the rest of it fifty glumgluffs at most. I walked towards the north-east coast, over against Blefuscu, where, lying down behind a hillock, I took out my small perspective glass, and viewed the enemy's fleet at anchor, consisting of about fifty men of war, and a great number of transports: I then came back to my house, and gave orders (for which I had a warrant) for a great quantity of the strongest cable and bars of iron. The cable was about as thick as packthread and the bars of the length and size of a knitting-needle. I trebled the cable to make it stronger, and for the same reason I twisted three of the iron bars together, bending the extremities into a hook. Having thus fixed fifty hooks to as many cables, I went back to the north-east coast, and putting off my coat, shoes, and stockings, walked into the sea, in my leathern jerkin, about half an hour before high water. I waded with what haste I could, and swam in the middle about thirty yards, till I felt ground. I arrived at the fleet in less than half an hour. The enemy was so frightened when they saw me, that they leaped out of their ships, and swam to shore, where there could not be fewer than thirty thousand souls. I then took my tackling, and, fastening a hook to the hole at the prow of each, I tied all the cords together at the end. While I was thus employed, the enemy discharged several thousand arrows, many of which stuck in my hands and face, and, beside the excessive smart, gave me much disturbance in my work. My greatest apprehension was for mine eyes, which I should have infallibly lost, if I had not suddenly thought of an expedient. I kept, among other little necessaries, a pair of spectacles in a private pocket, which, as I observed before, had escaped the emperor's searchers. These I took out and fastened as strongly as I could upon my nose, and thus armed, went on boldly with my work, in spite of the enemy's arrows, many of which struck against the glasses of my spectacles, but without any other effect, further than a little to discompose them. I had now fastened all the hooks, and, taking the knot in my hand, began to pull; but not a ship would stir, for they were all too fast held by their anchors, so that the boldest part of my enterprise remained. I therefore let go the cord, and leaving the hooks fixed to the ships, I resolutely cut with my knife the cables that fastened the anchors, receiving about two hundred shots in my face and hands; then I took up the knotted end of the cables, to which my hooks were tied, and with great ease drew fifty of the enemy's largest men of war after me.

The Blefuscudians, who had not the least imagination of what I intended, were at first confounded with astonishment. They had seen me cut the cables, and thought my design was only to let the ships run adrift or fall foul on each other; but when they perceived the whole fleet moving in order, and saw me pulling at the end, they set up such a scream of grief and despair as it is almost impossible to describe or conceive. When I had got out of danger, I stopped awhile to pick out the arrows that stuck in my hands and face; and rubbed on some of the same ointment that was given me at my first arrival, as I have formerly mentioned. I then took off my spectacles, and waiting about an hour, till the tide was a little fallen, I waded through the middle with my cargo, and arrived safe at the royal port of Lilliput.

The emperor and his whole court stood on the shore, expecting the issue of this great adventure. They saw the ships move forward in a large half-moon, but could not discern me, who was up to my breast in water. When I advanced to the middle of the channel, they were yet more in pain, because I was under water to my neck. The emperor concluded me to be drowned, and that the enemy's fleet was approaching in a hostile manner. But he was soon eased of his fears; for the channel growing shallower every step I made, I came in a short time within hearing, and holding up the end of the cable, by which the fleet was fastened, I cried in a loud voice, "Long live the most puissant king of Lilliput!" This great prince received me at my landing with all possible encomiums, and created me a nardac upon the spot, which is the highest title of honor among them.

His Majesty desired I would take some other opportunity of bringing all the rest of his enemy's ships into his ports. And so unmeasurable is the ambition of princes, that he seemed to think of nothing less than reducing the whole empire of Blefuscu into a province, and governing it, by a viceroy; of destroying the Big-endian exiles, and compelling that people to break the smaller end of their eggs, by which he would remain the sole monarch of the whole world. But I endeavored to divert him from this design, by many arguments drawn from the topics of policy as well as justice; and I plainly protested, that I would never be an instrument of bringing a free and brave people into slavery. And, when the matter was debated in council, the wisest part of the ministry were of my opinion.

This open bold declaration of mine was so opposite to the schemes and politics of his Imperial Majesty, that he could never forgive me. He mentioned it in a very artful manner at council, where I was told that some of the wisest appeared, at least by their silence, to be of my opinion; but others, who were my secret enemies, could not forbear some expressions which, by a side-wind, reflected on me. And from this time began an intrigue between his Majesty and a junto of ministers, maliciously bent against me, which broke out in less than two months, and had like to have ended in my utter destruction. Of so little weight are the greatest services to princes, when put into the balance with a refusal to gratify their passions.

About three weeks after this exploit, there arrived a solemn embassy from Blefuscu, with humble offers of a peace, which was soon concluded, upon conditions very advantageous to our emperor, wherewith I shall not trouble the reader. There were six ambassadors, with a train of about five hundred persons, and their entry was very magnificent, suitable to the grandeur of their master, and the importance of their business. When their treaty was finished, wherein I did them several good offices by the credit I now had, or at least appeared to have, at court, their excellencies, who were privately told how much I had been their friend, made me a visit in form. They began with many compliments upon my velour and generosity, invited me to that kingdom in the emperor their master's name, and desired me to show them some proofs of my prodigious strength, of which they had heard so many wonders; wherein I readily obliged them, but shall not trouble the reader with the particulars.

When I had for some time entertained their excellencies, to their infinite satisfaction and surprise, I desired they would do me the honor to present my most humble respects to the emperor their master, the renown of whose virtues had so justly filled the whole world with admiration, and whose royal person I resolved to attend, before I returned to my own country. Accordingly, the next time I had the honor to see our emperor, I desired his general license to wait on the Blefuscudian monarch, which he was pleased to grant me, as I could perceive, in a very cold manner; but could not guess the reason, till I had a whisper from a certain person, that Flimnap and Bolgolam had represented my intercourse with those ambassadors as a mark of disaffection; from which I am sure my heart was wholly free. And this was the first time I began to conceive some imperfect idea of courts and ministers.

It is to be observed, that these ambassadors spoke to me, by an interpreter, the languages of both empires differing as much from each other as any two in Europe, and each nation priding itself upon the antiquity, beauty, and energy of their own tongue, with an avowed contempt for that of their neighbour; yet our emperor, standing upon the advantage he had got by the seizure of their fleet, obliged them to deliver their credentials, and make their speech, in the Lilliputian tongue. And it must be confessed, that from the great intercourse of trade and commerce between both realms, from the continual reception of exiles which is mutual among them, and from the custom, in each empire, to send their young nobility and richer gentry to the other, in order to polish themselves by seeing the world, and understanding men and manners; there are few persons of distinction, or merchants, or seamen, who dwell in the maritime parts, but what can hold conversation in both tongues; as I found some weeks after, when I went to pay my respects to the emperor of Blefuscu, which, in the midst of great misfortunes, through the malice of my enemies, proved a very happy adventure to me, as I shall relate in its proper place.

The reader may remember, that when I signed those articles upon which I recovered my liberty, there were some which I disliked, upon account of their being too servile; neither could anything but an extreme necessity have forced me to submit. But being now a nardac of the highest rank in that empire, such offices were looked upon as below my dignity, and the emperor (to do him justice), never once mentioned them to me. However, it was not long before I had an opportunity of doing his Majesty, at least as I then thought, a most signal service. I was alarmed at midnight with the cries of many hundred people at my door; by which, being suddenly awaked, I was in some kind of terror. I heard the word Burglum repeated incessantly; several of the emperor's court, making their way through the crowd, entreated me to come immediately to the palace, where her imperial Majesty's apartment was on fire, by the carelessness of a maid of honor, who fell asleep while she was reading a romance. I got up in an instant; and orders being given to clear the way before me, and it being likewise a moonshine night, I made a shift to get to the palace without trampling on any of the people. I found they had already applied ladders to the walls of the apartment, and were well provided with buckets, but the water was at some distance. These buckets were about the size of large thimbles, and the poor people supplied me with them as fast as they could; but the flame was so violent that they did little good. I might easily have stifled it with my coat, which I unfortunately left behind me for haste, and came away only in my leathern jerkin. The case seemed wholly desperate and deplorable; and this magnificent palace would have infallibly been burnt down to the ground, if, by a presence of mind unusual to me, I had not suddenly thought of an expedient. I had, the evening before, drunk plentifully of a most delicious wine called *glimigrim*, (the Blefuscudians call it *flunec*, but ours is esteemed the better sort) which is very diuretic. By the luckiest chance in the world, I had not discharged myself of any part of it. The heat I had contracted by coming very near the flames, and by labouring to quench them, made the wine begin to operate by urine; which I voided in such a quantity, and applied so well to the proper places, that in three minutes the fire was wholly extinguished, and the rest of that noble pile, which had cost so many ages in erecting, preserved from destruction.

It was now day-light, and I returned to my house without waiting to congratulate with the emperor; because, although I had done a very eminent piece of service, yet I could not tell how his Majesty might resent the manner by which I had performed it; for, by the fundamental laws of the realm, it is capital in any person, of what quality soever, to make water within the precincts of the palace. But I was a little comforted by a message from his Majesty, that he would give orders to the grand justifier for passing my pardon in form; which, however, I could not obtain; and I was privately assured, that the empress, conceiving the greatest abhorrence of what I had done, removed to the most distant side of the court, firmly resolved that those buildings should never be repaired for her use; and, in the presence of her chief confidents could not forbear vowing revenge.

⌒ **Chapter VI** ⌒

Of the inhabitants of Lilliput; their learning, laws, and customs; the manner of educating their children. The author's way of living in that country. His vindication of a great lady.

Although I intend to leave the description of this empire to a particular treatise, yet, in the meantime, I am content to gratify the curious reader with some general ideas. As the common size of the natives is somewhat under six inches high, so there is an exact proportion in all other animals, as well as plants and trees; for instance, the tallest horses and oxen are between four and five inches in height, the sheep an inch and half, more or less; their geese about the bigness of a sparrow, and so the several gradations downwards till you come to the smallest, which to my sight, were almost invisible; but nature has adapted the eyes of the Lilliputians to all objects proper for their view; they see with great exactness, but at no great distance. And, to show the sharpness of their sight towards objects that are near, I have been much pleased with observing a cook pulling a lark, which was not so large as a common fly; and a young girl threading an invisible needle with invisible silk. Their tallest trees are about seven feet high; I mean some of those in the great royal park, the tops whereof I could but just reach with my fist clenched. The other vegetables are in the same proportion; but this I leave to the reader's imagination.

I shall say but little at present of their learning, which, for many ages, has flourished in all its branches among them; but their manner of writing is very peculiar, being neither from the left to the right, like the Europeans, nor from the right to the left, like the Arabians, nor from up to down, like the Chinese, but aslant, from one corner of the paper to the other, like ladies in England.

They bury their dead with their heads directly downward, because they hold an opinion, that in eleven thousand moons they are all to rise again; in which period the earth (which they conceive to be flat) will turn upside down, and by this means they shall, at their resurrection, be found ready standing on their feet. The learned among them confess the absurdity of this doctrine; but the practice still continues, in compliance to the vulgar.

There are some laws and customs in this empire very peculiar; and if they were not so directly contrary to those of my own dear country, I should be tempted to say a little in their justification. It is only to be wished they were as well executed. The first I shall mention, relates to informers. All crimes against the state, are punished here with the utmost severity; but, if the person accused makes his innocence plainly to appear upon his trial, the accuser is immediately put to an ignominious death; and out of his goods or lands the innocent person is quadruply recompensed for the loss of his time, for the danger he underwent, for the hardship of his imprisonment, and for all the charges he has been at in making his defence; or, if that fund be deficient, it is largely supplied by the crown. The emperor also confers on him some public mark of his favor, and proclamation is made of his innocence through the whole city.

They look upon fraud as a greater crime than theft, and therefore seldom fail to punish it with death; for they allege, that care and vigilance, with a very common understanding, may preserve a man's goods from thieves, but honesty has no defence against superior cunning; and, since it is necessary that there should be a perpetual intercourse of buying and selling, and dealing upon credit, where fraud is permitted and connived at, or has no law to punish it, the honest dealer is always undone, and the knave gets the advantage. I remember, when I was once interceding with the emperor for a criminal who had wronged his master of a great sum of money, which he had received by order and ran away with; and happening to tell his Majesty, by way of extenuation, that it was only a breach of trust, the emperor thought it monstrous in me to offer as a defence the greatest aggravation of the crime; and truly I had little to say in return, farther than the common answer, that different nations had different customs; for, I confess, I was heartily ashamed.

Although we usually call reward and punishment the two hinges upon which all government turns, yet I could never observe this maxim to be put in practice by any nation except that of Lilliput. Whoever can there bring sufficient proof, that he has strictly observed the laws of his country for seventy-three moons, has a claim to certain privileges, according to his quality or condition of life, with a proportionable sum of money out of a fund appropriated for that use; he likewise acquires the title of snilpall, or legal, which is added to his name, but does not descend to his posterity. And these people thought it a prodigious defect of policy among us, when I told them that our laws were enforced only by penalties, without any mention of reward. It is upon this account that the image of Justice, in their courts of judicature, is formed with six eyes, two before, as many behind, and on each side one, to signify circumspection; with a bag of gold open in her right hand, and a sword sheathed in her left, to show she is more disposed to reward than to punish.

In choosing persons for all employments, they have more regard to good morals than to great abilities; for, since government is necessary to mankind, they believe, that the common size of human understanding is fitted to some station or other; and that Providence never intended to make the management of public affairs a mystery to be comprehended only by a few persons of sublime genius, of which there seldom are three born in an age; but they suppose truth, justice, temperance, and the like, to be in every man's power; the practice of which virtues, assisted by experience and a good intention, would qualify any man for the service of his country, except where a course of study is required. But they thought the want of moral virtues was so far from being supplied by superior endowments of the mind, that employments could never be put into such dangerous hands as those of persons so qualified; and, at least, that the mistakes committed by ignorance, in a virtuous disposition, would never be of such fatal consequence to the public weal, as the practices of a man, whose inclinations led him to be corrupt, and who had great abilities to manage, to multiply, and defend his corruptions.

In like manner, the disbelief of a Divine Providence renders a man incapable of holding any public station; for, since kings avow themselves to be the deputies of Providence, the Lilliputians think nothing can be more absurd than for a prince to employ such men as disown the authority under which he acts.

In relating these and the following laws, I would only be understood to mean the original institutions, and not the most scandalous corruptions, into which these people are fallen by the degenerate nature of man. For, as to that infamous practice of acquiring great employments by dancing on the ropes, or badges of favor and distinction by leaping over sticks and creeping under them, the reader is to observe, that they were first introduced by the grandfather of the emperor now reigning, and grew to the present height by the gradual increase of party and faction.

Ingratitude is among them a capital crime, as we read it to have been in some other countries; for they reason thus; that whoever makes ill returns to his benefactor, must needs be a common enemy to the rest of mankind, from whom he has received no obligation, and therefore such a man is not fit to live.

Their notions relating to the duties of parents and children differ extremely from ours. For, since the conjunction of male and female is founded upon the great law of nature, in order to propagate and continue the species, the Lilliputians will needs have it, that men and women are joined together, like other animals, by the motives of concupiscence; and that their tenderness towards their young proceeds from the like natural principle; for which reason they will never allow that a child is under any obligation to his father for begetting him, or to his mother for bringing him into the world; which, considering the miseries of human life, was neither a benefit in itself, nor intended so by his parents, whose thoughts, in their love encounters, were otherwise employed. Upon these, and the like reasonings, their opinion is, that parents are the last of all others to be trusted with the education of their own children; and therefore they have in every town public nurseries, where all parents, except cottagers and labourers, are obliged to send their infants of both sexes to be reared and educated, when they come to the age of twenty moons, at which time they are supposed to have some rudiments of docility. These schools are of several kinds, suited to different qualities, and both sexes. They have certain professors well skilled in preparing children for such a condition of life as befits the rank of their parents, and their own capacities, as well as inclinations. I shall first say something of the male nurseries, and then of the female.

The nurseries for males of noble or eminent birth, are provided with grave and learned professors, and their several deputies. The clothes and food of the children are plain and simple. They are bred up in the principles of honor, justice, courage, modesty, clemency, religion, and love of their country; they are always employed in some business, except in the times of eating and sleeping, which are very short, and two hours for diversions consisting of bodily exercises. They are dressed by men till four years of age, and then are obliged to dress themselves, although their quality be ever so great; and the women attendant, who are aged proportionably to ours at fifty, perform only the most menial offices. They are never suffered to converse with servants, but go together in smaller or greater numbers to take their diversions, and always in the presence of a professor, or one of his deputies; whereby they avoid those early bad impressions of folly and vice, to which our children are subject. Their parents are suffered to see them only twice a year; the visit is to last but an hour; they are allowed to kiss the child at meeting and parting; but a professor, who always stands by on those occasions, will not suffer them to whisper, or use any fondling expressions, or bring any presents of toys, sweetmeats, and the like.

The pension from each family for the education and entertainment of a child, upon failure of due payment, is levied by the emperor's officers.

The nurseries for children of ordinary gentlemen, merchants, traders, and handicrafts, are managed proportionably after the same manner; only those designed for trades are put out apprentices at eleven years old, whereas those of persons of quality continue in their exercises till fifteen, which answers to twenty-one with us; but the confinement is gradually lessened for the last three years.

In the female nurseries, the young girls of quality are educated much like the males, only they are dressed by orderly servants of their own sex; but always in the presence of a professor or deputy, till they come to dress themselves, which is at five years old. And if it be found that these nurses ever presume to entertain the girls with frightful or foolish stories, or the common follies practised by chambermaids among us, they are publicly whipped thrice about the city, imprisoned for a year, and banished for life to the most desolate part of the country. Thus the young ladies are as much ashamed of being cowards and fools as the men, and despise all personal ornaments, beyond decency and cleanliness; neither did I perceive any difference in their education made by their difference of sex, only that the exercises of the females were not altogether so robust; and that some rules were given them relating to domestic life, and a smaller compass of learning was enjoined them: for their maxim is, that among peoples of quality, a wife should be always a reasonable and agreeable companion, because she cannot always be young. When the girls are twelve years old, which among them is the marriageable age, their parents or guardians take them home, with great expressions of gratitude to the professors, and seldom without tears of the young lady and her companions.

In the nurseries of females of the meaner sort, the children are instructed in all kinds of works proper for their sex, and their several degrees: those intended for apprentices are dismissed at seven years old, the rest are kept to eleven.

The meaner families who have children at these nurseries, are obliged, besides their annual pension, which is as low as possible, to return to the steward of the nursery a small monthly share of their gettings, to be a portion for the child; and therefore all parents are limited in their expenses by the law. For the Lilliputians think nothing can be more unjust, than for people, in subservience to their own appetites, to bring children into the world, and leave the burthen of supporting them on the public. As to persons of quality, they give security to appropriate a certain sum for each child, suitable to their condition; and these funds are always managed with good husbandry and the most exact justice.

The cottagers and labourers keep their children at home, their business being only to till and cultivate the earth, and therefore their education is of little consequence to the public: but the old and diseased among them, are supported by hospitals; for begging is a trade unknown in this empire.

And here it may, perhaps, divert the curious reader, to give some account of my domestics, and my manner of living in this country, during a residence of nine months, and thirteen days. Having a head mechanically turned, and being likewise forced by necessity, I had made for myself a table and chair convenient enough, out of the largest trees in the royal park. Two hundred seamstresses were employed to make me shirts, and linen for my bed and table, all of the strongest and coarsest kind they could get; which, however, they were forced to quilt together in several folds, for the thickest was some degrees finer than lawn. Their linen is usually three inches wide, and three feet make a piece. The seamstresses took my measure as I lay on the ground, one standing at my neck, and another at my mid-leg, with a strong cord extended, that each held by the end, while a third measured the length of the cord with a rule of an inch long. Then they measured my right thumb, and desired no more; for by a mathematical computation, that twice round the thumb is once round the wrist, and so on to the neck and the waist, and by the help of my old shirt, which I displayed on the ground before them for a pattern, they fitted me exactly. Three hundred tailors were employed in the same manner to make me clothes; but they had another contrivance for taking my measure. I kneeled down, and they raised a ladder from the ground to my neck; upon this ladder one of them mounted, and let fall a plumb-line from my collar to the floor, which just answered the length of my coat; but my waist and arms I measured myself. When my clothes were finished, which was done in my house (for the largest of theirs would not have been able to hold them), they looked like the patch-work made by the ladies in England, only that mine were all of a colour.

I had three hundred cooks to dress my victuals, in little convenient huts built about my house, where they and their families lived, and prepared me two dishes a-piece. I took up twenty waiters in my hand, and placed them on the table; a hundred more attended below on the ground, some with dishes of meat, and some with barrels of wine and other liquors slung on their shoulders; all which the waiters above drew up, as I wanted, in a very ingenious manner, by certain cords, as we draw the bucket up a well in Europe. A dish of their meat was a good mouthful, and a barrel of their liquor a reasonable draught. Their mutton yields to ours, but their beef is excellent. I have had a sirloin so large, that I have been forced to make three bites of it; but this is rare. My servants were astonished to see me eat it, bones and all, as in our country we do the leg of a lark. Their geese and turkeys I usually ate at a mouthful, and I confess they far exceed ours. Of their smaller fowl I could take up twenty or thirty at the end of my knife.

One day his Imperial Majesty, being informed of my way of living, desired that himself and his royal consort, with the young princes of the blood of both sexes, might have the happiness (as he was pleased to call it) of dining with me. They came accordingly, and I placed them in chairs of state, upon my table, just over against me, with their guards about them. Flimnap, the lord high treasurer, attended there likewise with his white staff; and I observed he often looked on me with a sour countenance, which I would not seem to regard, but ate more than usual, in honor to my dear country, as well as to fill the court with admiration. I have some private reasons to believe, that this visit from his Majesty gave Flimnap an opportunity of doing me ill offices to his master. That minister had always been my secret enemy, though he outwardly caressed me more than was usual to the moroseness of his nature. He represented to the emperor the low condition of his treasury; that he was forced to take up money at a great discount; that exchequer bills would not circulate under nine per cent. Below par; that I had cost his Majesty above a million and a half of sprugs (their greatest gold coin, about the bigness of a spangle) and, upon the whole, that it would be advisable in the emperor to take the first fair occasion of dismissing me.

I am here obliged to vindicate the reputation of an excellent lady, who was an innocent sufferer upon my account. The treasurer took a fancy to be jealous of his wife, from the malice of some evil tongues, who informed him that her grace had taken a violent affection for my person; and the court scandal ran for some time, that she once came privately to my lodging. This I solemnly declare to be a most infamous falsehood, without any grounds, further than that her Grace was pleased to treat me with all innocent marks of freedom and friendship. I own she came often to my house, but always publicly, nor ever without three more in the coach, who were usually her sister and young daughter, and some particular acquaintance; but this was common to many other ladies of the court. And I still appeal to my servants round, whether they at any time saw a coach at my door, without knowing what persons were in it. On those occasions, when a servant had given me notice, my custom was to go immediately to the door, and, after paying my respects, to take up the coach and two horses very carefully in my hands (for if there were six horses, the postilion always unharnessed four) and place them on a table, where I had fixed a movable rim quite round, of five inches high, to prevent accidents. And I have often had four coaches and horses at once on my table, full of company, while I sat in my chair, leaning my face towards them; and when I was engaged with one set, the coachmen would gently drive the others round my table. I have passed many an afternoon very agreeably in these conversations. But I defy the treasurer, or his two informers (I will name them, and let them make the best of it) Clustril and Drunlo, to prove that any person ever came to me incognito, except the secretary Reldresal, who was sent by express command of his Imperial Majesty, as I have before related. I should not have dwelt so long upon this particular, if it had not been a point wherein the reputation of a great lady is so nearly concerned, to say nothing of my own; though I then had the honor to be a nardac, which the treasurer himself is not; for all the world knows, that he is only a glumglum, a title inferior by one degree, as that of a marquis is to a duke in England; yet I allow him preceded me in right of his post. These false informations, which I afterwards came to the knowledge of by an accident not proper to mention, made the treasurer show his lady for some time an ill countenance, and me a worse; and although he was at last undeceived and reconciled to her, yet I lost all credit with him, and found my interest decline very fast with the emperor himself, who was, indeed, too much governed by that favourite.

〜 **Chapter VII** 〜

The author, being informed of a design to accuse him of high-treason, makes his escape to Blefuscu. His reception there.

Before I proceed to give an account of my leaving this kingdom, it may be proper to inform the reader of a private intrigue which had been for two months forming against me.

I had been hitherto, all my life, a stranger to courts, for which I was unqualified by the meanness of my condition. I had indeed heard and read enough of the dispositions of great princes and ministers, but never expected to have found such terrible effects of them, in so remote a country, governed, as I thought, by very different maxims from those in Europe.

When I was just preparing to pay my attendance on the emperor of Blefuscu, a considerable person at court (to whom I had been very serviceable, at a time when he lay under the highest displeasure of his Imperial Majesty) came to my house very privately at night, in a close chair, and, without sending his name, desired admittance. The chairmen were dismissed; I put the chair, with his lordship in it, into my coat-pocket; and, giving orders to a trusty servant, to say I was indisposed and gone to sleep, I fastened the door of my house, placed the chair on the table, according to my usual custom, and sat down by it. After the common salutations were over, observing his lordship's countenance full of concern, and inquiring into the reason, he desired I would hear him with patience, in a matter that highly concerned my honor and my life. His speech was to the following effect, for I took notes of it as soon as he left me:

"You are to know," said he, "that several committees of council have been lately called, in the most private manner, on your account; and it is but two days since his Majesty came to a full resolution."

"You are very sensible that Skyresh Bolgolam" (*galbet*, or high-admiral) "has been your mortal enemy, almost ever since your arrival. His original reasons I know not; but his hatred is increased since your great success against Blefuscu, by which his glory as admiral is much obscured. This lord, in conjunction with Flimnap the high-treasurer, whose enmity against you is notorious on account of his lady, Limtoc the general, Lalcon the chamberlain, and Balmuff the grand justiciary, have prepared articles of impeachment against you, for treason and other capital crimes."

This preface made me so impatient, being conscious of my own merits and innocence, that I was going to interrupt him; when he entreated me to be silent, and thus proceeded:

"Out of gratitude for the favours you have done me, I procured information of the whole proceedings, and a copy of the articles; wherein I venture my head for your service."

Articles of Impeachment against QUINBUS FLESTRIN, (the Man-Mountain.)

ARTICLE I.

Whereas, by a statute made in the reign of his imperial Majesty Calin Deffar Plune, it is enacted, that, whoever shall make water within the precincts of the royal palace, shall be liable to the pains and penalties of high-treason; notwithstanding, the said Quinbus Flestrin, in open breach of the said law, under colour of extinguishing the fire kindled in the apartment of his Majesty's most dear imperial consort, did maliciously, traitorously, and devilishly, by discharge of his urine, put out the said fire kindled in the said apartment, lying and being within the precincts of the said royal palace, against the statute in that case provided, etc. against the duty, etc.

ARTICLE II.

That the said Quinbus Flestrin, having brought the imperial fleet of Blefuscu into the royal port, and being afterwards commanded by his imperial Majesty to seize all the other ships of the said empire of Blefuscu, and reduce that empire to a province, to be governed by a viceroy from hence, and to destroy and put to death, not only all the Big-endian exiles, but likewise all the people of that empire who would not immediately forsake the Big-endian heresy, he, the said Flestrin, like a false traitor against his most auspicious, serene, imperial Majesty, did petition to be excused from the said service, upon presence of unwillingness to force the consciences, or destroy the liberties and lives of an innocent people.

ARTICLE III.

That, whereas certain ambassadors arrived from the Court of Blefuscu, to sue for peace in his Majesty's court, he, the said Flestrin, did, like a false traitor, aid, abet, comfort, and divert, the said ambassadors, although he knew them to be servants to a prince who was lately an open enemy to his imperial Majesty, and in an open war against his said Majesty.

ARTICLE IV.

That the said Quinbus Flestrin, contrary to the duty of a faithful subject, is now preparing to make a voyage to the court and empire of Blefuscu, for which he has received only verbal license from his Imperial Majesty; and, under colour of the said license, does falsely and traitorously intend to take the said voyage, and thereby to aid, comfort, and abet the emperor of Blefuscu, so lately an enemy, and in open war with his Imperial Majesty aforesaid.

"There are some other articles; but these are the most important, of which I have read you an abstract."

"In the several debates upon this impeachment, it must be confessed that his Majesty gave many marks of his great lenity; often urging the services you had done him, and endeavoring to extenuate your crimes. The treasurer and admiral insisted that you should be put to the most painful and ignominious death, by setting fire to your house at night, and the general was to attend with twenty thousand men, armed with poisoned arrows, to shoot you on the face and hands. Some of your servants were to have private orders to strew a poisonous juice on your shirts and sheets, which would soon make you tear your own flesh, and die in the utmost torture. The general came into the same opinion; so that for a long time there was a majority against you; but his Majesty resolving, if possible, to spare your life, at last brought off the chamberlain.

"Upon this incident, Reldresal, principal secretary for private affairs, who always approved himself your true friend, was commanded by the emperor to deliver his opinion, which he accordingly did; and therein justified the good thoughts you have of him. He allowed your crimes to be great, but that still there was room for mercy, the most commendable virtue in a prince, and for which his Majesty was so justly celebrated. He said, the friendship between you and him was so well known to the world, that perhaps the most honourable board might think him partial; however, in obedience to the command he had received, he would freely offer his sentiments. That if his Majesty, in consideration of your services, and pursuant to his own merciful disposition, would please to spare your life, and only give orders to put out both your eyes, he humbly conceived, that by this expedient justice might in some measure be satisfied, and all the world would applaud the lenity of the emperor, as well as the fair and generous proceedings of those who have the honour to be his counsellors. That the loss of your eyes would be no impediment to your bodily strength, by which you might still be useful to his Majesty; that blindness is an addition to courage, by concealing dangers from us; that the fear you had for your eyes, was the greatest difficulty in bringing over the enemy's fleet, and it would be sufficient for you to see by the eyes of the ministers, since the greatest princes do no more."

"This proposal was received with the utmost disapprobation by the whole board. Bolgolam, the admiral, could not preserve his temper, but, rising up in fury, said, he wondered how the secretary durst presume to give his opinion for preserving the life of a traitor; that the services you had performed were, by all true reasons of state, the great aggravation of your crimes; that you, who were able to extinguish the fire by discharge of urine in her Majesty's apartment (which he mentioned with horror), might, at another time, raise an inundation by the same means, to drown the whole palace; and the same strength which enabled you to bring over the enemy's fleet, might serve, upon the first discontent, to carry it back; that he had good reasons to think you were a Big-endian in your heart; and, as treason begins in the heart, before it appears in overt-acts, so he accused you as a traitor on that account, and therefore insisted you should be put to death."

"The treasurer was of the same opinion; he showed to what straits his Majesty's revenue was reduced, by the charge of maintaining you, which would soon grow insupportable; that the secretary's expedient of putting out your eyes, was so far from being a remedy against this evil, that it would probably increase it, as is manifest from the common practice of blinding some kind of fowls, after which they fed the faster, and grew sooner fat; that his sacred Majesty and the council, who are your judges, were, in their own consciences, fully convinced of your guilt, which was a sufficient argument to condemn you to death, without the formal proofs required by the strict letter of the law."

"But his Imperial Majesty, fully determined against capital punishment, was graciously pleased to say, that since the council thought the loss of your eyes too easy a censure, some other way may be inflicted hereafter. And your friend the secretary, humbly desiring to be heard again, in answer to what the treasurer had objected, concerning the great charge his Majesty was at in maintaining you, said, that his excellency, who had the sole disposal of the emperor's revenue, might easily provide against that evil, by gradually lessening your establishment; by which, for want of sufficient for you would grow weak and faint, and lose your appetite, and consequently, decay, and consume in a few months; neither would the stench of your carcass be then so dangerous, when it should become more than half diminished; and immediately upon your death five or six thousand of his Majesty's subjects might, in two or three days, cut your flesh from your bones, take it away by cart-loads, and bury it in distant parts, to prevent infection, leaving the skeleton as a monument of admiration to posterity."

"Thus, by the great friendship of the secretary, the whole affair was compromised. It was strictly enjoined, that the project of starving you by degrees should be kept a secret; but the sentence of putting out your eyes was entered on the books; none dissenting, except Bolgolam the admiral, who, being a creature of the empress, was perpetually instigated by her Majesty to insist upon your death, she having borne perpetual malice against you, on account of that infamous and illegal method you took to extinguish the fire in her apartment."

"In three days your friend the secretary will be directed to come to your house, and read before you the articles of impeachment; and then to signify the great lenity and favour of his Majesty and council, whereby you are only condemned to the loss of your eyes, which his Majesty does not question you will gratefully and humbly submit to; and twenty of his Majesty's surgeons will attend, in order to see the operation well performed, by discharging very sharp-pointed arrows into the balls of your eyes, as you lie on the ground."

"I leave to your prudence what measures you will take; and to avoid suspicion, I must immediately return in as private a manner as I came."

His lordship did so; and I remained alone, under many doubts and perplexities of mind.

It was a custom introduced by this prince and his ministry (very different, as I have been assured, from the practice of former times,) that after the court had decreed any cruel execution, either to gratify the monarch's resentment, or the malice of a favourite, the emperor always made a speech to his whole council, expressing his great lenity and tenderness, as qualities known and confessed by all the world. This speech was immediately published throughout the kingdom; nor did anything terrify the people so much as those encomiums on his Majesty's mercy; because it was observed, that the more these praises were enlarged and insisted on, the more inhuman was the punishment, and the sufferer more innocent. Yet, as to myself, I must confess, having never been designed for a courtier, either by my birth or education, I was so ill a judge of things, that I could not discover the lenity and favor of this sentence, but conceived it (perhaps erroneously) rather to be rigorous than gentle. I sometimes thought of standing my trial, for, although I could not deny the facts alleged in the several articles, yet I hoped they would admit of some extenuation. But having in my life perused many state-trials, which I ever observed to terminate as the judges thought fit to direct, I durst not rely on so dangerous a decision, in so critical a juncture, and against such powerful enemies. Once I was strongly bent upon resistance, for, while I had liberty the whole strength of that empire could hardly subdue me, and I might easily with stones pelt the metropolis to pieces; but I soon rejected that project with horror, by remembering the oath I had made to the emperor, the favours I received from him, and the high title of nardac he conferred upon me. Neither had I so soon learned the gratitude of courtiers, to persuade myself, that his Majesty's present seventies acquitted me of all past obligations.

At last, I fixed upon a resolution, for which it is probable I may incur some censure, and not unjustly; for I confess I owe the preserving of mine eyes, and consequently my liberty, to my own great rashness and want of experience; because, if I had then known the nature of princes and ministers, which I have since observed in many other courts, and their methods of treating criminals less obnoxious than myself, I should, with great alacrity and readiness, have submitted to so easy a punishment. But hurried on by the precipitancy of youth, and having his Imperial Majesty's license to pay my attendance upon the emperor of Blefuscu, I took this opportunity, before the three days were elapsed, to send a letter to my friend the secretary, signifying my resolution of setting out that morning for Blefuscu, pursuant to the leave I had got; and, without waiting for an answer, I went to that side of the island where our fleet lay. I seized a large man of war, tied a cable to the prow, and, lifting up the anchors, I stripped myself, put my clothes (together with my coverlet, which I carried under my arm) into the vessel, and, drawing it after me, between wading and swimming arrived at the royal port of Blefuscu, where the people had long expected me: they lent me two guides to direct me to the capital city, which is of the same name. I held them in my hands, till I came within two hundred yards of the gate, and desired them to signify my arrival to one of the secretaries, and let him know, I there waited his Majesty's command. I had an answer in about an hour, that his Majesty, attended by the royal family, and great officers of the court, was coming out to receive me. I advanced a hundred yards. The emperor and his train alighted from their horses, the empress and ladies from their coaches, and I did not perceive they were in any fright or concern. I lay on the ground to kiss his Majesty's and the empress's hands. I told his Majesty, that I was come according to my promise, and with the license of the emperor my master, to have the honor of seeing so mighty a monarch, and to offer him any service in my power, consistent with my duty to my own prince; not mentioning a word of my disgrace, because I had hitherto no regular information of it, and might suppose myself wholly ignorant of any such design; neither could I reasonably conceive that the emperor would discover the secret, while I was out of his power; wherein, however, it soon appeared I was deceived.

I shall not trouble the reader with the particular account of my reception at this court, which was suitable to the generosity of so great a prince; nor of the difficulties was I in for want of a house and bed, being forced to lie on the ground, wrapped up in my coverlet.

⌒⌒ **Chapter VIII** ⌒⌒

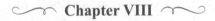

The author, by a lucky accident, finds means to leave Blefuscu; and, after some difficulties, returns safe to his native country.

Three days after my arrival, walking out of curiosity to the north-east coast of the island, I observed, about half a league off in the sea, somewhat that looked like a boat overturned. I pulled off my shoes and stockings, and, wailing two or three hundred yards, I found the object to approach nearer by force of the tide; and then plainly saw it to be a real boat, which I supposed might by some tempest have been driven from a ship. Whereupon, I returned immediately towards the city, and desired his Imperial Majesty to lend me twenty of the tallest vessels he had left, after the loss of his fleet, and three thousand seamen, under the command of his vice-admiral. This fleet sailed round, while I went back the shortest way to the coast, where I first discovered the boat. I found the tide had driven it still nearer. The seamen were all provided with cordage, which I had beforehand twisted to a sufficient strength. When the ships came up, I stripped myself, and waded till I came within a hundred yards off the boat, after which I was forced to swim till I got up to it. The seamen threw me the end of the cord, which I fastened to a hole in the fore-part of the boat, and the other end to a man of war; but I found all my labour to little purpose; for, being out of my depth, I was not able to work. In this necessity I was forced to swim behind, and push the boat forward, as often as I could, with one of my hands; and the tide favouring me, I advanced so far that I could just hold up my chin and feel the ground. I rested two or three minutes, and then gave the boat another shove, and so on, till the sea was no higher than my arm-pits; and now, the most laborious part being over, I took out my other cables, which were stowed in one of the ships, and fastened them first to the boat, and then to nine of the vessels which attended me; the wind being favourable, the seamen towed, and I shoved, until we arrived within forty yards of the shore; and, waiting till the tide was out, I got dry to the boat, and by the assistance of two thousand men, with ropes and engines, I made a shift to turn it on its bottom, and found it was but little damaged.

I shall not trouble the reader with the difficulties I was under, by the help of certain paddles, which cost me ten days making, to get my boat to the royal port of Blefuscu, where a mighty concourse of people appeared upon my arrival, full of wonder at the sight of so prodigious a vessel. I told the emperor that my good fortune had thrown this boat in my way, to carry me to some place whence I might return into my native country; and begged his Majesty's orders for getting materials to fit it up, together with his license to depart; which, after some kind expostulations, he was pleased to grant.

I did very much wonder, in all this time, not to have heard of any express relating to me from our emperor to the court of Blefuscu. But I was afterward given privately to understand, that his Imperial Majesty, never imagining I had the least notice of his designs, believed I was only gone to Blefuscu in performance of my promise, according to the license he had given me, which was well known at our court, and would return in a few days, when the ceremony was ended. But he was at last in pain at my long absence; and after consulting with the treasurer and the rest of that cabal, a person of quality was dispatched with the copy of the articles against me. This envoy had instructions to represent to the monarch of Blefuscu, the great lenity of his master, who was content to punish me no farther than with the loss of mine eyes; that I had fled from justice; and if I did not return in two hours, I should be deprived of my title of nardac, and declared a traitor. The envoy further added, that in order to maintain the peace and amity between both empires, his master expected that his brother of Blefuscu would give orders to have me sent back to Lilliput, bound hand and foot, to be punished as a traitor.

The emperor of Blefuscu, having taken three days to consult, returned an answer consisting of many civilities and excuses. He said, That as for sending me bound, his brother knew it was impossible; that, although I had deprived him of his fleet, yet he owed great obligations to me for many good offices I had done him in making the peace. That, however, both their majesties would soon be made easy; for I had found a prodigious vessel on the shore, able to carry me on the sea, which he had given orders to fit up, with my own assistance and direction; and he hoped, in a few weeks, both empires would be freed from so insupportable an encumbrance.

With this answer the envoy returned to Lilliput; and the monarch of Blefuscu related to me all that had passed; offering me at the same time (but under the strictest confidence) his gracious protection, if I would continue in his service; wherein, although I believed him sincere, yet I resolved never more to put any confidence in princes or ministers, where I could possibly avoid it; and therefore, with all due acknowledgments for his favourable intentions, I humbly begged to be excused. I told him, "that since fortune, whether good or evil, had thrown a vessel in my way, I was resolved to venture myself on the ocean, rather than be an occasion of difference between two such mighty monarchs." Neither did I find the emperor at all displeased; and I discovered, by a certain accident, that he was very glad of my resolution, and so were most of his ministers.

These considerations moved me to hasten my departure somewhat sooner than I intended;

to which the court, impatient to have me gone, very readily contributed. Five hundred workmen were employed to make two sails to my boat, according to my directions, by quilting thirteen folds of their strongest linen together. I was at the pains of making ropes and cables, by twisting ten, twenty, or thirty of the thickest and strongest of theirs. A great stone that I happened to find, after a long search, by the sea-shore, served me for an anchor. I had the tallow of three hundred cows, for greasing my boat, and other uses. I was at incredible pains in cutting down some of the largest timber-trees, for oars and masts, wherein I was, however, much assisted by his Majesty's ship-carpenters, who helped me in smoothing them, after I had done the rough work.

In about a month, when all was prepared, I sent to receive his Majesty's commands, and to take my leave. The emperor and royal family came out of the palace; I lay down on my face to kiss his hand, which he very graciously gave me; so did the empress and young princes of the blood. His Majesty presented me with fifty purses of two hundred sprugs a-piece, together with his picture at full length, which I put immediately into one of my gloves, to keep it from being hurt. The ceremonies at my departure were too many to trouble the reader with at this time.

I stored the boat with the carcases of a hundred oxen, and three hundred sheep, with bread and drink proportionable, and as much meat ready dressed as four hundred cooks could provide. I took with me six cows and two bulls alive, with as many ewes and rams, intending to carry them into my own country, and propagate the breed. And to feed them on board, I had a good bundle of hay, and a bag of corn. I would gladly have taken a dozen of the natives, but this was a thing the emperor would by no means permit; and, besides a diligent search into my pockets, his Majesty engaged my honour not to carry away any of his subjects, although with their own consent and desire.

Having thus prepared all things as well as I was able, I set sail on the twenty-fourth day of September 1701, at six in the morning; and when I had gone about four-leagues to the northward, the wind being at south-east, at six in the evening I descried a small island, about half a league to the north-west. I advanced forward, and cast anchor on the lee-side of the island, which seemed to be uninhabited. I then took some refreshment, and went to my rest. I slept well, and as I conjectured at least six hours, for I found the day broke in two hours after I awaked. It was a clear night. I ate my breakfast before the sun was up; and heaving anchor, the wind being favourable, I steered the same course that I had done the day before, wherein I was directed by my pocket compass. My intention was to reach, if possible, one of those islands. which I had reason to believe lay to the north-east of Van Diemen's Land. I discovered nothing all that day; but upon the next, about three in the afternoon, when I had by my computation made twenty-four leagues from Blefuscu, I descried a sail steering to the south-east; my course was due east. I hailed her, but could get no answer; yet I found I gained upon her, for the wind slackened. I made all the sail I could, and in half an hour she spied me, then hung out her ancient, and discharged a gun. It is not easy to express the joy I was in, upon the unexpected hope of once more seeing my beloved country, and the dear pledges I left in it. The ship slackened her sails, and I came up with her between five and six in the evening, September 26th; but my heart leaped within me to see her English colours. I put my cows and sheep into my coat-pockets, and got on board with all my little cargo of provisions. The vessel was an English merchantman, returning from Japan by the North and South seas; the captain, Mr. John

Biddel, of Deptford, a very civil man, and an excellent sailor.

We were now in the latitude of 30 degrees south; there were about fifty men in the ship; and here I met an old comrade of mine, one Peter Williams, who gave me a good character to the captain. This gentleman treated me with kindness, and desired I would let him know what place I came from last, and whither I was bound; which I did in a few words, but he thought I was raving, and that the dangers I underwent had disturbed my head; whereupon I took my black cattle and sheep out of my pocket, which, after great astonishment, clearly convinced him of my veracity. I then showed him the gold given me by the emperor of Blefuscu, together with his Majesty's picture at full length, and some other rarities of that country. I gave him two purses of two hundreds sprugs each, and promised, when we arrived in England, to make him a present of a cow and a sheep big with young.

I shall not trouble the reader with a particular account of this voyage, which was very prosperous for the most part. We arrived in the Downs on the 13th of April, 1702. I had only one misfortune, that the rats on board carried away one of my sheep; I found her bones in a hole, picked clean from the flesh. The rest of my cattle I got safe ashore, and set them a-grazing in a bowling-green at Greenwich, where the fineness of the grass made them feed very heartily, though I had always feared the contrary: neither could I possibly have preserved them in so long a voyage, if the captain had not allowed me some of his best biscuit, which, rubbed to powder, and mingled with water, was their constant food. The short time I continued in England, I made a considerable profit by showing my cattle to many persons of quality and others; and before I began my second voyage, I sold them for six hundred pounds. Since my last return I find the breed is considerably increased, especially the sheep, which I hope will prove much to the advantage of the woollen manufacture, by the fineness of the fleeces.

I stayed but two months with my wife and family, for my insatiable desire of seeing foreign countries, would suffer me to continue no longer. I left fifteen hundred pounds with my wife, and fixed her in a good house at Redriff. My remaining stock I carried with me, part in money and part in goods, in hopes to improve my fortunes. My eldest uncle John had left me an estate in land, near Epping, of about thirty pounds a year; and I had a long lease of the Black Bull in Fetter-Lane, which yielded me as much more; so that I was not in any danger of leaving my family upon the parish. My son Johnny, named so after his uncle, was at the grammar-school, and a cowardly child. My daughter Betty (who is now well married, and has children) was then at her needle-work. I took leave of my wife, and boy and girl, with tears on both sides, and went on board the Adventure, a merchant ship of three hundred tons, bound for Surat, Captain John Nicholas, of Liverpool, commander. But my account of this voyage must be referred to the Second Part of my Travels.

Part II
A Voyage to Brobdingnag

∽ **Chapter I** ∽

A great storm described; the long boat sent to fetch water; the author goes with it to discover the country. He is left on shore, is seized by one of the natives, and carried to a farmer's house. His reception, with several accidents that happened there. A description of the inhabitants.

Having been condemned, by nature and fortune, to active and restless life, in two months after my return, I again left my native country, and took shipping in the Downs, on the 20th day of June, 1702, in the Adventure, Captain John Nicholas, a Cornish man, commander, bound for Surat. We had a very prosperous gale, till we arrived at the Cape of Good Hope, where we landed for fresh water; but discovering a leak, we unshipped our goods and wintered there; for the captain falling sick of an ague, we could not leave the Cape till the end of March. We then set sail, and had a good voyage till we passed the Straits of Madagascar; but having got northward of that island, and to about five degrees south latitude, the winds, which in those seas are observed to blow a constant equal gale between the north and west, from the beginning of December to the beginning of May, on the 19th of April began to blow with much greater violence, and more westerly than usual, continuing so for twenty days together: during which time, we were driven a little to the east of the Molucca Islands, and about three degrees northward of the line, as our captain found by an observation he took the 2nd of May, at which time the wind ceased, and it was a perfect calm, whereat I was not a little rejoiced. But he, being a man well experienced in the navigation of those seas, bid us all prepare against a storm, which accordingly happened the day following: for the southern wind, called the southern monsoon, began to set in.

Finding it was likely to overblow, we took in our sprit-sail, and stood by to hand the fore-sail; but making foul weather, we looked the guns were all fast, and handed the mizen. The ship lay very broad off, so we thought it better spooning before the sea, than trying or hulling. We reefed the fore-sail and set him, and hauled aft the fore-sheet; the helm was hard a-weather. The ship wore bravely. We belayed the fore down-haul; but the sail was split, and we hauled down the yard, and got the sail into the ship, and unbound all the things clear of it. It was a very fierce storm; the sea broke strange and dangerous. We hauled off upon the laniard of the whip-staff, and helped the man at the helm. We would not get down our topmast, but let all stand, because she scudded before the sea very well, and we knew that the top-mast being aloft, the ship was the wholesomer, and made better way through the sea, seeing we had sea-room. When the storm was over, we set fore-sail and main-sail, and brought the ship to. Then we set the mizen, main-top-sail, and the fore-top-sail. Our course was east-north-east, the wind was at south-west. We got the starboard tacks aboard, we cast off our weather-braces and lifts; we set in the lee-braces, and hauled forward by the weather-bowlings, and hauled them tight, and belayed them, and hauled over the mizen tack to windward, and kept her full and by as near as she would lie.

During this storm, which was followed by a strong wind west-south-west, we were carried, by my computation, about five hundred leagues to the east, so that the oldest sailor on board could not tell in what part of the world we were. Our provisions held out well, our ship was staunch, and our crew all in good health; but we lay in the utmost distress for water. We thought it best to hold on the same course, rather than turn more northerly, which might have brought us to the north-west part of Great Tartary, and into the Frozen Sea.

On the 16th day of June, 1703, a boy on the top-mast discovered land. On the 17th, we came in full view of a great island or continent, (for we knew not whether) on the south side whereof was a small neck of land jutting out into the sea, and a creek too shallow to hold a ship of above one hundred tons. We cast anchor within a league of this creek, and our captain sent a dozen of his men well-armed in the long-boat, with vessels for water, if any could be found. I desired his leave to go with them, that I might see the country, and make what discoveries I could. When we came to land we saw no river or spring, nor any sign of inhabitants. Our men therefore wandered on the shore to find out some fresh water near the sea, and I walked alone about a mile on the other side, where I observed the country all barren and rocky. I now began to be weary, and seeing nothing to entertain my curiosity, I returned gently down towards the creek; and the sea being full in my view, I saw our men already got into the boat, and rowing for life to the ship. I was going to holla after them, although it had been to little purpose, when I observed a huge creature walking after them in the sea, as fast as he could: he waded not much deeper than his knees, and took prodigious strides; but our men had the start of him half a league, and, the sea thereabouts being full of sharp-pointed rocks, the monster was not able to overtake the boat. This I was afterwards told, for I durst not stay to see the issue of the adventure; but ran as fast as I could the way I first went, and then climbed up a steep hill, which gave me some prospect of the country. I found it fully cultivated; but that which first surprised me was the length of the grass, which, in those grounds that seemed to be kept for hay, was about twenty feet high.

I fell into a high road, for so I took it to be, though it served to the inhabitants only as a foot-path through a field of barley. Here I walked on for some time, but could see little on either side, it being now near harvest, and the corn rising at least forty feet. I was an hour walking to the end of this field, which was fenced in with a hedge of at least one hundred and twenty feet high, and the trees so lofty that I could make no computation of their altitude. There was a stile to pass from this field into the next. It had four steps, and a stone to cross over when you came to the uppermost. It was impossible for me to climb this stile, because every step was six-feet high, and the upper stone about twenty. I was endeavouring to find some gap in the hedge, when I discovered one of the inhabitants in the next field, advancing towards the stile, of the same size with him whom I saw in the sea pursuing our boat. He appeared as tall as an ordinary spire steeple, and took about ten yards at every stride, as near as I could guess. I was struck with the utmost fear and astonishment, and ran to hide myself in the corn, whence I saw him at the top of the stile looking back into the next field on the right hand, and heard him call in a voice many degrees louder than a speaking-trumpet; but the noise was so high in the air, that at first I certainly thought it was thunder. Whereupon seven monsters, like himself, came towards him with reaping-hooks in their hands, each hook about the largeness of six scythes. These people were not so well clad as the first, whose servants or labourers they seemed to be; for, upon some words he spoke, they went to reap the corn in the field where I lay. I kept from them at as great a distance as I could, but was forced to move with extreme difficulty, for the stalks of the corn were sometimes not above a foot distant, so that I could hardly squeeze my body betwixt them. However, I made a shift to go forward, till I came to a part of the field where the corn had been laid by the rain and wind. Here it was impossible for me to advance a step; for the stalks were so interwoven, that I could not creep through, and the beards of the fallen ears so strong and pointed, that they pierced through my clothes into my flesh. At the same time I heard the reapers not a hundred yards behind me. Being quite dispirited with toil, and wholly overcome by grief and despair, I lay down between two ridges, and heartily wished I might there end my days. I bemoaned my desolate widow and fatherless children. I lamented my own folly and willfulness, in attempting a second voyage, against the advice of all my friends and relations. In this terrible agitation of mind, I could not forbear thinking of Lilliput, whose inhabitants looked upon me as the greatest prodigy that ever appeared in the world; where I was able to draw an imperial fleet in my hand, and perform those other actions, which will be recorded for ever in the chronicles of that empire, while posterity shall hardly believe them, although attested by millions. I reflected what a mortification it must prove to me, to appear as inconsiderable in this nation, as one single Lilliputian would be among us. But this I conceived was to be the least of my misfortunes; for, as human creatures are observed to be more savage and cruel in proportion to their bulk, what could I expect but to be a morsel in the mouth of the first among these enormous barbarians that should happen to seize me? Undoubtedly philosophers are in the right, when they tell us that nothing is great or little otherwise than by comparison. It might have pleased fortune, to have let the Lilliputians find some nation, where the people were as diminutive with respect to them, as they were to me. And who knows but that even this prodigious race of mortals might be equally overmatched in some distant part of the world, whereof we have yet no discovery.

Scared and confounded as I was, I could not forbear going on with these reflections, when one of the reapers, approaching within ten yards of the ridge where I lay, made me apprehend that with the next step I should be squashed to death under his foot, or cut in two with his reaping-hook. And therefore, when he was again about to move, I screamed as loud as fear could make me. Whereupon the huge creature trod short, and, looking round about under him for some time, at last espied me as I lay on the ground. He considered awhile, with the caution of one who endeavours to lay hold on a small dangerous animal in such a manner that it shall not be able either to scratch or bite him, as I myself have sometimes done with a weasel in England. At length he ventured to take me behind, by the middle, between his fore-finger and thumb, and brought me within three yards of his eyes, that he might behold my shape more perfectly. I guessed his meaning, and my good fortune gave me so much presence of mind, that I resolved not to struggle in the least as he held me in the air above sixty feet from the ground, although he grievously pinched my sides, for fear I should slip through his fingers. All I ventured was to raise mine eyes towards the sun, and place my hands together in a supplicating posture, and to speak some words in a humble melancholy tone, suitable to the condition I then was in. For, I apprehended every moment that he would dash me against the ground, as we usually do any little hateful animal, which we have a mind to destroy. But my good star would have it, that he appeared pleased with my voice and gestures, and began to look upon me as a curiosity, much wondering to hear me pronounce articulate words, although he could not understand them. In the mean time I was not able to forbear groaning and shedding tears, and turning my head towards my sides; letting him know, as well as I could, how cruelly I was hurt by the pressure of his thumb and finger. He seemed to apprehend my meaning; for, lifting up the lappet of his coat, he put me gently into it, and immediately ran along with me to his master, who was a substantial farmer, and the same person I had first seen in the field.

The farmer having (as I suppose by their talk) received such an account of me as his servant could give him, took a piece of a small straw, about the size of a walking-staff, and therewith lifted up the lappets of my coat; which it seems he thought to be some kind of covering that nature had given me. He blew my hairs aside to take a better view of my face. He called his hinds about him, and asked them, as I afterwards learned, whether they had ever seen in the fields any little creature that resembled me. He then placed me softly on the ground upon all fours, but I got up immediately, and walked slowly backward and forward, to let those people see I had no intent to run away. They all sat down in a circle about me, the better to observe my motions. I pulled off my hat, and made a low bow towards the farmer. I fell on my knees, and lifted up my hands and eyes, and spoke several words as loud as I could; I took a purse of gold out of my pocket, and humbly presented it to him. He received it on the palm of his hand, then applied it close to his eye to see what it was, and afterwards turned it several times with the point of a pin (which he took out of his sleeve,) but could make nothing of it. Whereupon I made a sign that he should place his hand on the ground. I then took the purse, and, opening it, poured all the gold into his palm. There were six Spanish pieces of four pistols each, beside twenty or thirty smaller coins. I saw him wet the tip of his little finger upon his tongue, and take up one of my largest pieces, and then another; but he seemed to be wholly ignorant what they were. He made me a sign to put them again into my purse, and the purse again into my pocket, which, after offering it to him several times, I thought it best to do.

The farmer, by this time, was convinced I must be a rational creature. He spoke often to me; but the sound of his voice pierced my ears like that of a water-mill, yet his words were articulate enough. I answered as loud as I could in several languages, and he often laid his ear within two yards of me, but all in vain, for we were wholly unintelligible to each other. He then sent his servants to their work, and taking his handkerchief out of his pocket, he doubled and spread it on his left hand, which he placed flat on the ground with the palm upward, making me a sign to step into it, as I could easily do, for it was not above a foot in thickness. I thought it my part to obey, and, for fear of falling, laid myself at full length upon the handkerchief, with the remainder of which he lapped me up to the head for further security, and in this manner carried me home to his house. There he called his wife, and showed me to her; but she screamed and ran back, as women in England do at the sight of a toad or a spider. However, when she had a while seen my behaviour, and how well I observed the signs her husband made, she was soon reconciled, and by degrees grew extremely tender of me.

It was about twelve at noon, and a servant brought in dinner. It was only one substantial dish of meat (fit for the plain condition of a husbandman) in a dish of about four-and-twenty feet diameter. The company were, the farmer and his wife, three children, and an old grandmother. When they were sat down, the farmer placed me at some distance from him on the table, which was thirty feet high from the floor. I was in a terrible fright, and kept as far as I could from the edge, for fear of falling. The wife minced a bit of meat, then crumbled some bread on a trencher, and placed it before me. I made her a low bow, took out my knife and fork, and fell to eat, which gave them exceeding delight. The mistress sent her maid for a small dram cup, which held about two gallons, and filled it with drink; I took up the vessel with much difficulty in both hands, and in a most respectful manner drank to her ladyship's health, expressing the words as loud as I could in English, which made the company laugh so heartily, that I was almost deafened with the noise. This liquor tasted like a small cider, and was not unpleasant. Then the master made me a sign to come to his trencher side; but as I walked on the table, being in great surprise all the time, as the indulgent reader will easily conceive and excuse, I happened to stumble against a crust, and fell flat on my face, but received no hurt. I got up immediately, and observing the good people to be in much concern, I took my hat (which I held under my arm out of good manners) and waving it over my head, made three huzzas, to show I had got no mischief by the fall. But advancing forward towards my master (as I shall henceforth call him,) his youngest son, who sat next to him, an arch boy of about ten years old, took me up by the legs, and held me so high in the air, that I trembled every limb; but his father snatched me from him, and at the same time gave him such a box on the left ear, as would have felled an European troop of horse to the earth, ordering him to be taken from the table. But being afraid the boy might owe me a spite, and well remembering how mischievous all children among us naturally are to sparrows, rabbits, young kittens, and puppy dogs, I fell on my knees, and pointing to the boy, made my master to understand, as well as I could, that I desired his son might be pardoned. The father complied, and the lad took his seat again, whereupon I went to him, and kissed his hand, which my master took, and made him stroke me gently with it.

In the midst of dinner, my mistress's favourite cat leaped into her lap. I heard a noise behind me like that of a dozen stocking-weavers at work; and turning my head, I found it proceeded from the purring of that animal, who seemed to be three times larger than an ox, as I computed by the view of her head, and one of her paws, while her mistress was feeding and stroking her. The fierceness of this creature's countenance altogether discomposed me; though I stood at the farther end of the table, above fifty feet off; and although my mistress held her fast, for fear she might give a spring, and seize me in her talons. But it happened there was no danger, for the cat took not the least notice of me when my master placed me within three yards of her. And as I have been always told, and found true by experience in my travels, that flying or discovering fear before a fierce animal, is a certain way to make it pursue or attack you, so I resolved, in this dangerous juncture, to show no manner of concern. I walked with intrepidity five or six times before the very head of the cat, and came within half a yard of her; whereupon she drew herself back, as if she were more afraid of me: I had less apprehension concerning the dogs, whereof three or four came into the room, as it is usual in farmers' houses; one of which was a mastiff, equal in bulk to four elephants, and another a greyhound, somewhat taller than the mastiff, but not so large.

When dinner was almost done, the nurse came in with a child of a year old in her arms, who immediately spied me, and began a squall that you might have heard from London-Bridge to Chelsea, after the usual oratory of infants, to get me for a plaything. The mother, out of pure indulgence, took me up, and put me towards the child, who presently seized me by the middle, and got my head into his mouth, where I roared so loud that the urchin was frighten, and let me drop, and I should infallibly have broken my neck, if the mother had not held her apron under me. The nurse, to quiet her babe, made use of a rattle which was a kind of hollow vessel filled with great stones, and fastened by a cable to the child's waist: but all in vain; so that she was forced to apply the last remedy by giving it suck. I must confess no object ever disgusted me so much as the sight of her monstrous breast, which I cannot tell what to compare with, so as to give the curious reader an idea of its bulk, shape, and colour. It stood prominent six feet, and could not be less than sixteen in circumference. The nipple was about half the bigness of my head, and the hue both of that and the dug, so varied with spots, pimples, and freckles, that nothing could appear more nauseous: for I had a near sight of her, she sitting down, the more conveniently to give suck, and I standing on the table. This made me reflect upon the fair skins of our English ladies, who appear so beautiful to us, only because they are of our own size, and their defects not to be seen but through a magnifying glass; where we find by experiment that the smoothest and whitest skins look rough, and coarse, and ill-coloured.

I remember when I was at Lilliput, the complexion of those diminutive people appeared to me the fairest in the world; and talking upon this subject with a person of learning there, who was an intimate friend of mine, he said that my face appeared much fairer and smoother when he looked on me from the ground, than it did upon a nearer view, when I took him up in my hand, and brought him close, which he confessed was at first a very shocking sight. He said, he could discover great holes in my skin; that the stumps of my beard were ten times stronger than the bristles of a boar, and my complexion made up of several colours altogether disagreeable: Although I must beg leave to say for myself, that I am as fair as most of my sex and country, and very little sunburnt by all my travels. On the other side, discoursing of the ladies in that emperor's court, he used to tell me, one had freckles; another too wide a mouth; a third too large a nose; nothing of which I was able to distinguish. I confess this reflection was obvious enough; which, however, I could not forbear, lest the reader might think those vast creatures were actually deformed; for I must do them the justice to say, they are a comely race of people, and particularly the features of my master's countenance, although he was but a farmer, when I beheld him from the height of sixty feet, appeared very well proportioned.

When dinner was done, my master went out to his labourers, and, as I could discover by his voice and gesture, gave his wife strict charge to take care of me. I was very much tired, and disposed to sleep, which my mistress perceiving, she put me on her own bed, and covered me with a clean white handkerchief, but larger and coarser than the mainsail of a man-of-war.

I slept about two hours, and dreamt I was at home with my wife and children, which aggravated my sorrows when I awaked, and found myself alone in a vast room, between two and three hundred feet wide, and above two hundred high, lying in a bed twenty yards wide. My mistress was gone about her household affairs, and had locked me in. The bed was eight yards from the floor. Some natural necessities required me to get down; I durst not presume to call; and if I had, it would have been in vain, with such a voice as mine, at so great a distance from the room where I lay to the kitchen where the family kept. While I was under these circumstances, two rats crept up the curtains, and ran smelling backwards and forwards on the bed. One of them came up almost to my face, whereupon I rose in a fright, and drew out my hanger to defend myself. These horrible animals had the boldness to attack me on both sides, and one of them held his fore-feet at my collar; but I had the good fortune to rip up his belly before he could do me any mischief. He fell down at my feet; and the other, seeing the fate of his comrade, made his escape, but not without one good wound on the back, which I gave him as he fled, and made the blood run trickling from him. After this exploit, I walked gently to and fro on the bed, to recover my breath and loss of spirits. These creatures were of the size of a large mastiff, but infinitely more nimble and fierce; so that if I had taken off my belt before I went to sleep, I must have infallibly been torn to pieces and devoured. I measured the tail of the dead rat, and found it to be two yards long, wanting an inch; but it went against my stomach to drag the carcass off the bed, where it lay still bleeding; I observed it had yet some life, but with a strong slash across the neck, I thoroughly dispatched it.

Soon after my mistress came into the room, who seeing me all bloody, ran and took me up in her hand. I pointed to the dead rat, smiling, and making other signs to show I was not hurt; whereat she was extremely rejoiced, calling the maid to take up the dead rat with a pair of tongs, and throw it out of the window. Then she set me on a table, where I showed her my hanger all bloody, and wiping it on the lappet of my coat, returned it to the scabbard. I was pressed to do more than one thing which another could not do for me, and therefore endeavoured to make my mistress understand, that I desired to be set down on the floor; which after she had done, my bashfulness would not suffer me to express myself farther, than by pointing to the door, and bowing several times. The good woman, with much difficulty, at last perceived what I would be at, and taking me up again in her hand, walked into the garden, where she set me down. I went on one side about two hundred yards, and beckoning to her not to look or to follow me, I hid myself between two leaves of sorrel, and there discharged the necessities of nature.

I hope the gentle reader will excuse me for dwelling on these and the like particulars, which, however insignificant they may appear to groveling vulgar minds, yet will certainly help a philosopher to enlarge his thoughts and imagination, and apply them to the benefit of public as well as private life, which was my sole design in presenting this and other accounts of my travels to the world; wherein I have been chiefly studious of truth, without affecting any ornaments of learning or of style. But the whole scene of this voyage made so strong an impression on my mind, and is so deeply fixed in my memory, that, in committing it to paper I did not omit one material circumstance; however, upon a strict review, I blotted out several passages of less moment which were in my first copy, for fear of being censured as tedious and trifling, whereof travellers are often, perhaps not without justice, accused.

⁓ **Chapter II** ⁓

A description of the farmer's daughter. The author carried to a market-town, and then to the metropolis. The particulars of his journey.

My mistress had a daughter of nine years old, a child of towardly parts for her age, very dexterous at her needle, and skilful in dressing her baby. Her mother and she contrived to fit up the baby's cradle for me against night: the cradle was put into a small drawer of a cabinet, and the drawer placed upon a hanging shelf for fear of the rats. This was my bed all the time I stayed with those people, though made more convenient by degrees, as I began to learn their language and make my wants known. This young girl was so handy, that after I had once or twice pulled off my clothes before her, she was able to dress and undress me, though I never gave her that trouble when she would let me do either myself. She made me seven shirts, and some other linen, of as fine cloth as could be got, which indeed was coarser than sackcloth; and these she constantly washed for me with her own hands. She was likewise my school-mistress, to teach me the language: when I pointed to anything, she told me the name of it in her own tongue, so that in a few days I was able to call for whatever I had a mind to. She was very good-natured, and not above forty feet high, being little for her age. She gave me the name of *Grildrig*, which the family took up, and afterwards the whole kingdom. The word imports what the Latins call *nanunculus*, the Italians *homunceletino*, and the English *mannikin*. To her I chiefly owe my preservation in that country: we never parted while I was there; I called her my Glumdalclitch, or little nurse; and should be guilty of great ingratitude, if I omitted this honourable mention of her care and affection towards me, which I heartily wish it lay in my power to requite as she deserves, instead of being the innocent, but unhappy instrument of her disgrace, as I have too much reason to fear.

It now began to be known and talked of in the neighbourhood, that my master had found a strange animal in the field, about the bigness of a splacknuck, but exactly shaped in every part like a human creature; which it likewise imitated in all its actions; seemed to speak in a little language of its own, had already learned several words of theirs, went erect upon two legs, was tame and gentle, would come when it was called, do whatever it was bid, had the finest limbs in the world, and a complexion fairer than a nobleman's daughter of three years old. Another farmer, who lived hard by, and was a particular friend of my master, came on a visit on purpose to inquire into the truth of this story. I was immediately produced, and placed upon a table, where I walked as I was commanded, drew my hanger, put it up again, made my reverence to my master's guest, asked him in his own language how he did, and told him he was welcome, just as my little nurse had instructed me. This man, who was old and dim-sighted, put on his spectacles to behold me better; at which I could not forbear laughing very heartily, for his eyes appeared like the full moon shining into a chamber at two windows. Our people, who discovered the cause of my mirth, bore me company in laughing, at which the old fellow was fool enough to be angry and out of countenance. He had the character of a great miser; and, to my misfortune, he well deserved it, by the cursed advice he gave my master, to show me as a sight upon a market-day in the next town, which was half an hour's riding, about two-and-twenty miles from our house. I guessed there was some mischief when I observed my master and his friend whispering together, sometimes pointing at me; and my fears made me fancy that I overheard and understood some of their words. But the next morning Glumdalclitch, my little nurse, told me the whole matter, which she had cunningly picked out from her mother. The poor girl laid me on her bosom, and fell a weeping with shame and grief. She apprehended some mischief would happen to me from rude vulgar folks, who might squeeze me to death, or break one of my limbs by taking me in their hands. She had also observed how modest I was in my nature, how nicely I regarded my honour, and what an indignity I should conceive it, to be exposed for money as a public spectacle, to the meanest of the people. She said, her papa and mamma had promised that Grildrig should be hers; but now she found they meant to serve her as they did last year, when they pretended to give her a lamb, and yet, as soon as it was fat, sold it to a butcher. For my own part, I may truly affirm, that I was less concerned than my nurse. I had a strong hope, which never left me, that I should one day recover my liberty; and as to the ignominy of being carried about for a monster, I considered myself to be a perfect stranger in the country, and that such a misfortune could never be charged upon me as a reproach, if ever I should return to England, since the king of Great Britain himself, in my condition, must have undergone the same distress.

My master, pursuant to the advice of his friend, carried me in a box the next market-day to the neighbouring town, and took along with him his little daughter, my nurse, upon a pillion behind him. The box was close on every side, with a little door for me to go in and out, and a few gimlet holes to let in air. The girl had been so careful as to put the quilt of her baby's bed into it, for me to lie down on. However, I was terribly shaken and discomposed in this journey, though it was but of half an hour. For the horse went about forty feet at every step and trotted so high, that the agitation was equal to the rising and falling of a ship in a great storm, but much more frequent. Our journey was somewhat farther than from London to St Albans. My master alighted at an inn which he used to frequent; and after consulting awhile with the inn-keeper, and making some necessary preparations, he hired the grultrud, or crier, to give notice through the town of a strange creature to be seen at the sign of the Green Eagle, not so big as a *splacknuck* (an animal in that country very finely shaped, about six feet long,) and in every part of the body resembling a human creature, could speak several words, and perform a hundred diverting tricks.

I was placed upon a table in the largest room of the inn, which might be near three hundred feet square. My little nurse stood on a low stool close to the table, to take care of me, and direct what I should do. My master, to avoid a crowd, would suffer only thirty people at a time to see me. I walked about on the table as the girl commanded; she asked me questions, as far as she knew my understanding of the language reached, and I answered them as loud as I could. I turned about several times to the company, paid my humble respects, said they were welcome, and used some other speeches I had been taught. I took up a thimble filled with liquor, which Glumdalclitch had given me for a cup, and drank their health, I drew out my hanger, and flourished with it after the manner of fencers in England. My nurse gave me a part of a straw, which I exercised as a pike, having learnt the art in my youth. I was that day shown to twelve sets of company, and as often forced to act over again the same fopperies, till I was half dead with weariness and vexation; for those who had seen me made such wonderful reports, that the people were ready to break down the doors to come in. My master, for his own interest, would not suffer any one to touch me except my nurse; and to prevent danger, benches were set round the table at such a distance as to put me out of every body's reach. However, an unlucky school-boy aimed a hazel nut directly at my head, which very narrowly missed me; otherwise it came with so much violence, that it would have infallibly knocked out my brains, for it was almost as large as a small pumpkin, but I had the satisfaction to see the young rogue well beaten, and turned out of the room.

My master gave public notice that he would show me again the next market-day; and in the meantime he prepared a convenient vehicle for me, which he had reason enough to do; for I was so tired with my first journey, and with entertaining company for eight hours together, that I could hardly stand upon my legs, or speak a word. It was at least three days before I recovered my strength; and that I might have no rest at home, all the neighbouring gentlemen from a hundred miles round, hearing of my fame, came to see me at my master's own house. There could not be fewer than thirty persons with their wives and children (for the country is very populous;) and my master demanded the rate of a full room whenever he showed me at home, although it were only to a single family; so that for some time I had but little ease every day of the week (except Wednesday, which is their Sabbath,) although I were not carried to the town.

My master, finding how profitable I was likely to be, resolved to carry me to the most considerable cities of the kingdom. Having therefore provided himself with all things necessary for a long journey, and settled his affairs at home, he took leave of his wife, and upon the 17th of August, 1703, about two months after my arrival, we set out for the metropolis, situate near the middle of that empire, and about three thousand miles distance from our house. My master made his daughter Glumdalclitch ride behind him. She carried me on her lap, in a box tied about her waist. The girl had lined it on all sides with the softest cloth she could get, well quilted underneath, furnished it with her baby's bed, provided me with linen and other necessaries, and made everything as convenient as she could. We had no other company but a boy of the house, who rode after us with the luggage.

My master's design was to show me in all the towns by the way, and to step out of the road for fifty or a hundred miles, to any village, or person of quality's house, where he might expect custom. We made easy journeys, of not above seven or eight score miles a day; for Glumdalclitch, on purpose to spare me, complained she was tired with the trotting of the horse. She often took me out of my box, at my own desire, to give me air, and show me the country, but always held me fast by a leading-string. We passed over five or six rivers, many degrees broader and deeper than the Nile or the Ganges; and there was hardly a rivulet so small as the Thames at London-bridge. We were ten weeks in our journey, and I was shown in eighteen large towns, besides many villages, and private families.

On the 26th day of October we arrived at the metropolis, called in their language *Lorbrulgrud*, or Pride of the Universe. My master took a lodging in the principal street of the city, not far from the royal palace, and put out bills in the usual form, containing an exact description of my person and parts. He hired a large room between three and four hundred feet wide. He provided a table sixty feet in diameter, upon which I was to act my part, and pallisadoed it round three feet from the edge, and as many high, to prevent my falling over. I was shown ten times a day, to the wonder and satisfaction of all people. I could now speak the language tolerably well, and perfectly understood every word, that was spoken to me. Besides, I had learnt their alphabet, and could make a shift to explain a sentence here and there; for Glumdalclitch had been my instructor while we were at home, and at leisure hours during our journey. She carried a little book in her pocket, not much larger than a Sanson's Atlas; it was a common treatise for the use of young girls, giving a short account of their religion; out of this she taught me my letters, and interpreted the words.

✑~ **Chapter III** ~✑

The author sent for to court. The queen buys him of his master the farmer, and presents him to the king. He disputes with his Majesty's great scholars. An apartment at court provided for the author. He is in high favour with the queen. He stands up for the honour of his own country. His quarrels with the queen's dwarf.

The frequent labours I underwent every day, made in a few weeks a very considerable change in my health: the more my master got by me, the more insatiable he grew. I had quite lost my stomach, and was almost reduced to a skeleton. The farmer observed it, and concluding I must soon die, resolved to make as good a hand of me as he could. While he was thus reasoning and resolving with himself, a *Sardral*, or Gentleman Usher, came from court, commanding my master to carry me immediately thither for the diversion of the queen and her ladies. Some of the latter had already been to see me, and reported strange things of my beauty, behaviour, and good sense. Her Majesty, and those who attended her, were beyond measure delighted with my demeanour. I fell on my knees, and begged the honour of kissing her imperial foot; but this gracious princess held out her little finger towards me, after I was set on the table, which I embraced in both my arms, and put the tip of it with the utmost respect to my lip. She made me some general questions about my country and my travels, which I answered as distinctly, and in as few words as I could. She asked, Whether I could be content to live at court. I bowed down to the board of the table, and humbly answered that I was my master's slave; but, if I were at my own disposal, I should be proud to devote my life to her Majesty's service. She then asked my master, Whether he was willing to sell me at a good price. He, who apprehended I could not live a month, was ready enough to part with me, and demanded a thousand pieces of gold, which were ordered him on the spot, each piece being about the bigness of eight hundred moidores; but allowing for the proportion of all things between that country and Europe, and the high price of gold among them, was hardly so great a sum as a thousand guineas would be in England. I then said to the queen, Since I was now her Majesty's most humble creature and vassal, I must beg the favour, that Glumdalclitch, who had always tended me with so much care and kindness, and understood to do it so well, might be admitted into her service, and continue to be my nurse and instructor.

Her Majesty agreed to my petition, and easily got the farmer's consent, who was glad enough to have his daughter preferred at court, and the poor girl herself was not able to hide her joy. My late master withdrew, bidding me farewell, and saying he had left me in a good service; to which I replied not a word, only making him a slight bow.

The queen observed my coldness; and, when the farmer was gone out of the apartment, asked me the reason. I made bold to tell her Majesty, that I owed no other obligation to my late master, than his not dashing out the brains of a poor harmless creature, found by chance in his fields; which obligation was amply recompensed, by the gain he had made in showing me through half the kingdom, and the price he had now sold me for. That the life I had since led was laborious enough to kill an animal of ten times my strength. That my health was much impaired, by the continual drudgery of entertaining the rabble every hour of the day; and that, if my master had not thought my life in danger, her Majesty would not have got so cheap a bargain. But as I was out of all fear of being ill-treated under the protection of so great and good an empress, the ornament of nature, the darling of the world, the delight of her subjects, the phoenix of the creation, so I hoped my late master's apprehensions would appear to be groundless; for I already found my spirits revive, by the influence of her most August Presence.

This was the sum of my speech, delivered with great improprieties and hesitation. The latter part was altogether framed in the style peculiar to that people, whereof I learned some phrases from Glumdalclitch, while she was carrying me to court.

The queen, giving great allowance for my defectiveness in speaking, was, however, surprised at so much wit and good sense in so diminutive an animal. She took me in her own hand, and carried me to the king, who was then retired to his cabinet. His Majesty, a prince of much gravity and austere countenance, not well observing my shape at first view, asked the queen after a cold manner how long it was since she grew fond of a *splacknuck*; for such it seems he took me to be, as I lay upon my breast in her Majesty's right hand. But this princess, who has an infinite deal of wit and humour, set me gently on my feet upon the scrutore, and commanded me to give his Majesty an account of myself, which I did in a very few words; and Glumdalclitch who attended at the cabinet door, and could not endure I should be out of her sight, being admitted, confirmed all that had passed from my arrival at her father's house.

The king, although he be as learned a person as any in his dominions, had been educated in the study of philosophy, and particularly mathematics; yet when he observed my shape exactly, and saw me walk erect, before I began to speak, conceived I might be a piece of clock-work (which is in that country arrived to a very great perfection) contrived by some ingenious artist. But when he heard my voice, and found what I delivered to be regular and rational, he could not conceal his astonishment. He was by no means satisfied with the relation I gave him of the manner I came into his kingdom, but thought it a story concerted between Glumdalclitch and her father, who had taught me a set of words to make me sell at a better price. Upon this imagination, he put several other questions to me, and still received rational answers, no otherwise defective than by a foreign accent, and an imperfect knowledge in the language, with some rustic phrases which I had learned at the farmer's house, and did not suit the polite style of a court.

His Majesty sent for three great scholars, who were then in their weekly waiting, according to the custom in that country. These gentlemen, after they had a while examined my shape with much nicety, were of different opinions concerning me. They all agreed that I could not be produced according to the regular laws of nature, because I was not framed with a capacity of preserving my life, either by swiftness, or climbing of trees, or digging holes in the earth. They observed by my teeth, which they viewed with great exactness, that I was a carnivorous animal; yet most quadrupeds being an overmatch for me, and field mice, with some others, too nimble, they could not imagine how I should be able to support myself, unless I fed upon snails and other insects, which they offered, by many learned arguments, to evince that I could not possibly do. One of these virtuosi seemed to think that I might be an Embryo, or abortive birth. But this opinion was rejected by the other two, who observed my limbs to be perfect and finished; and that I had lived several years, as it was manifest from my beard, the stumps whereof they plainly discovered through a magnifying glass. They would not allow me to be a dwarf, because my littleness was beyond all degrees of comparison; for the queen's favourite dwarf, the smallest ever known in that kingdom, was near thirty feet high. After much debate, they concluded unanimously, that I was only relplum scalcath, which is interpreted literally lusus naturæ; a determination exactly agreeable to the modern philosophy of Europe, whose professors, disdaining the old evasion of occult causes, whereby the followers of Aristotle endeavoured in vain to disguise their ignorance, have invented this wonderful solution of all difficulties, to the unspeakable advancement of human knowledge.

After this decisive conclusion, I entreated to be heard a word or two. I applied myself to the king, and assured his Majesty, that I came from a country which abounded with several millions of both sexes, and of my own stature; where the animals, trees, and houses, were all in proportion, and where, by consequence, I might be as able to defend myself, and to find sustenance, as any of his Majesty's subjects could do here; which I took for a full answer to those gentlemen's arguments. To this they only replied with a smile of contempt, saying, That the farmer had instructed me very well in my lesson. The king, who had a much better understanding, dismissing his learned men, sent for the farmer, who by good fortune was not yet gone out of town. Having therefore first examined him privately, and then confronted him with me and the young girl, his Majesty began to think that what we told him might possibly be true. He desired the queen to order that a particular care should be taken of me; and was of opinion that Glumdalclitch should still continue in her office of tending me, because he observed we had a great affection for each other. A convenient apartment was provided for her at court; she had a sort of governess appointed to take care of her education, a maid to dress her, and two other servants for menial offices; but the care of me was wholly appropriated to herself. The queen commanded her own cabinet-maker to contrive a box, that might serve me for a bedchamber, after the model that Glumdalclitch and I should agree upon. This man was a most ingenious artist, and according to my direction, in three weeks finished for me a wooden chamber of sixteen feet square, and twelve high, with sash-windows, a door, and two closets, like a London bed-chamber. The board, that made the ceiling, was to be lifted up and down by two hinges, to put in a bed ready furnished by her Majesty's upholsterer, which Glumdalclitch took out every day to air, made it with her own hands, and letting it down at night, locked up the roof over me. A nice workman, who was famous for little curiosities, undertook to make me two chairs, with backs and frames, of a substance not unlike ivory, and two tables, with a cabinet to put my things in. The room was quilted on all sides, as well as the floor and the ceiling, to prevent any accident from the carelessness of those who carried me, and to break the force of a jolt, when I went in a coach. I desired a lock for my door, to prevent rats and mice from coming in. The smith, after several attempts, made the smallest that ever was seen among them, for I have known a larger at the gate of a gentleman's house in England. I made a shift to keep the key in a pocket of my own, fearing Glumdalclitch might lose it. The queen likewise ordered the thinnest silks that could be gotten, to make me clothes, not much thicker than an English blanket, very cumbersome till I was accustomed to them. They were after the fashion of the kingdom, partly resembling the Persian, and partly the Chinese, and are a very grave and decent habit.

The queen became so fond of my company, that she could not dine without me. I had a table placed upon the same at which her Majesty ate, just at her left elbow, and a chair to sit on. Glumdalclitch stood on a stool on the floor near my table, to assist and take care of me. I had an entire set of silver dishes and plates, and other necessaries, which, in proportion to those of the queen, were not much bigger than what I have seen in a London toy-shop for the furniture of a baby-house: these my little nurse kept in her pocket in a silver box, and gave me at meals as I wanted them, always cleaning them herself. No person dined with the queen but the two princesses royal, the eldest sixteen years old, and the younger at that time thirteen and a month. Her Majesty used to put a bit of meat upon one of my dishes, out of which I carved for myself, and her diversion was to see me eat in miniature. For the queen (who had indeed but a weak stomach) took up, at one mouthful, as much as a dozen English farmers could eat at a meal, which to me was for some time a very nauseous sight. She would craunch the wing of a lark, bones and all, between her teeth, although it were nine times as large as that of a full-grown turkey; and put a bit of bread into her mouth as big as two twelve-penny loaves. She drank out of a golden cup, above a hogshead at a draught. Her knives were twice as long as a scythe, set straight upon the handle. The spoons, forks, and other instruments, were all in the same proportion. I remember when Glumdalclitch carried me, out of curiosity, to see some of the tables at court, where ten or a dozen of those enormous knives and forks were lifted up together, I thought I had never till then beheld so terrible a sight.

It is the custom, that every Wednesday (which, as I have observed, is their Sabbath) the king and queen, with the royal issue of both sexes, dine together in the apartment of his Majesty, to whom I was now become a great favourite; and at these times, my little chair and table were placed at his left hand, before one of the salt-cellars. This prince took a pleasure in conversing with me, inquiring into the manners, religion, laws, government, and learning of Europe; wherein I gave him the best account I was able. His apprehension was so clear, and his judgment so exact, that he made very wise reflections and observations upon all I said. But I confess, that, after I had been a little too copious in talking of my own beloved country, of our trade and wars by sea and land, of our schisms in religion, and parties in the state; the prejudices of his education prevailed so far, that he could not forbear taking me up in his right hand, and stroking me gently with the other, after a hearty fit of laughing, asked me, whether I was a whig or tory? Then turning to his first minister, who waited behind him with a white staff, near as tall as the mainmast of the Royal Sovereign, he observed, how contemptible a thing was human grandeur, which could be mimicked by such diminutive insects as I; and yet, says he, I dare engage these creatures have their titles and distinctions of honour; they contrive little nests and burrows, that they call houses and cities; they make a figure in dress and equipage; they love, they fight, they dispute, they cheat, they betray. And thus he continued on, while my colour came and went several times, with indignation, to hear our noble country, the mistress of arts and arms, the scourge of France, the arbitress of Europe, the seat of virtue, piety, honour, and truth, the pride and envy of the world, so contemptuously treated.

But, as I was not in a condition to resent injuries, so upon mature thoughts I began to doubt whether I was injured or no. For, after having been accustomed several months to the sight and converse of this people, and observed every object upon which I cast mine eyes to be of proportionable magnitude, the horror I had at first conceived from their bulk and aspect was so far worn off, that if I had then beheld a company of English lords and ladies in their finery and birth-day clothes, acting their several parts in the most courtly manner of strutting, and bowing, and prating, to say the truth, I should have been strongly tempted to laugh as much at them as the king and his grandees did at me. Neither, indeed, could I forbear smiling at myself, when the queen used to place me upon her hand towards a looking-glass, by which both our persons appeared before me in full view together; and there could be nothing more ridiculous than the comparison; so that I really began to imagine myself dwindled many degrees below my usual size.

Nothing angered and mortified me so much as the queen's dwarf; who being of the lowest stature that was ever in that country (for I verily think he was not full thirty feet high), became so insolent at seeing a creature so much beneath him, that he would always affect to swagger and look big as he passed by me in the queen's antechamber, while I was standing on some table talking with the lords or ladies of the court, and he seldom failed of a smart word or two upon my littleness; against which I could only revenge myself by calling him brother, challenging him to wrestle, and such repartees as are usually in the mouths of court pages. One day, at dinner, this malicious little cub was so nettled with something I had said to him, that, raising himself upon the frame of her Majesty's chair, he took me up by the middle, as I was sitting down, not thinking any harm, and let me drop into a large silver bowl of cream, and then ran away as fast as he could. I fell over head and ears, and, if I had not been a good swimmer, it might have gone very hard with me; for Glumdalclitch in that instant happened to be at the other end of the room, and the queen was in such a fright, that she wanted presence of mind to assist me. But my little nurse ran to my relief, and took me out, after I had swallowed above a quart of cream. I was put to bed; however, I received no other damage than the loss of a suit of clothes, which was utterly spoiled. The dwarf was soundly whipt, and as a farther punishment, forced to drink up the bowl of cream into which he had thrown me; neither was he ever restored to favour; for soon after the queen bestowed him on a lady of high quality, so that I saw him no more, to my very great satisfaction; for I could not tell to what extremities such a malicious urchin might have carried his resentment.

He had before served me a scurvy trick, which set the queen a-laughing, although at the same time she was heartily vexed, and would have immediately cashiered him, if I had not been so generous as to intercede. Her Majesty had taken a marrow-bone upon her plate, and, after knocking out the marrow, placed the bone again in the dish erect, as it stood before; the dwarf, watching his opportunity, while Glumdalclitch was gone to the side-board, mounted the stool that she stood on to take care of me at meals, took me up in both hands, and squeezing my legs together, wedged them into the marrow bone above my waist, where I stuck for some time, and made a very ridiculous figure. I believe it was near a minute before anyone knew what was become of me; for I thought it below me to cry out. But, as princes seldom get their meat hot, my legs were not scalded, only my stockings and breeches in a sad condition. The dwarf, at my entreaty, had no other punishment than a sound whipping.

I was frequently rallied by the queen upon account of my fearfulness; and she used to ask me whether the people of my country were as great cowards as myself? The occasion was this: the kingdom is much pestered with flies in summer; and these odious insects, each of them as big as a Dunstable lark, hardly gave me any rest while I sat at dinner, with their continual humming and buzzing about my ears. They would sometimes alight upon my victuals, and leave their loathsome excrement, or spawn behind, which to me was very visible, though not to the natives of that country, whose large optics were not so acute as mine, in viewing smaller objects. Sometimes they would fix upon my nose, or forehead, where they stung me to the quick, smelling very offensively; and I could easily trace that viscous matter, which, our naturalists tell us, enables those creatures to walk with their feet upwards upon a ceiling. I had much ado to defend myself against these detestable animals, and could not forbear starting when they came on my face. It was the common practice of the dwarf, to catch a number of these insects in his hand, as schoolboys do among us, and let them out suddenly under my nose, on purpose to frighten me, and divert the queen. My remedy was to cut them in pieces with my knife, as they flew in the air, wherein my dexterity was much admired.

I remember, one morning, when Glumdalclitch had set me in a box upon a window, as she usually did in fair days to give me air (for I durst not venture to let the box be hung on a nail out of the window, as we do with cages in England), after I had lifted up one of my sashes, and sat down at my table to eat a piece of sweet cake for my breakfast, above twenty wasps, allured by the smell, came flying into the room, humming louder than the drones of as many bagpipes. Some of them seized my cake, and carried it piecemeal away; others flew about my head and face, confounding me with the noise, and putting me in the utmost terror of their stings. However, I had the courage to rise and draw my hanger, and attack them in the air. I dispatched four of them, but the rest got away, and I presently shut my window. These insects were as large as partridges; I took out their stings, found them an inch and a half long, and as sharp as needles. I carefully preserved them all; and having since shown them, with some other curiosities, in several parts of Europe, upon my return to England I gave three of them to Gresham College, and kept the fourth for myself.

Chapter IV

The country described. A proposal for correcting modern maps. The king's palace; and some account of the metropolis. The author's way of travelling. The chief temple described.

I now intend to give the reader a short description of this country, as far as I travelled in it, which was not above two thousand miles round Lorbrulgrud, the metropolis. For the queen, whom I always attended, never went farther when she accompanied the king in his progresses, and there staid till his Majesty returned from viewing his frontiers. The whole extent of this prince's dominions reaches about six thousand miles in length, and from three to five in breadth. Whence I cannot but conclude, that our geographers of Europe are in a great error, by supposing nothing but sea between Japan and California; for it was ever my opinion, that there must be a balance of earth to counterpoise the great continent of Tartary; and therefore they ought to correct their maps and charts, by joining this vast tract of land to the north-west parts of America, wherein I shall be ready to lend them my assistance.

The kingdom is a peninsula, terminated to the north-east by a ridge of mountains thirty miles high, which are altogether impassable, by reason of the volcanoes upon the tops. Neither do the most learned know what sort of mortals inhabit beyond those mountains, or whether they be inhabited at all. On the three other sides, it is bounded by the ocean. There is not one seaport in the whole kingdom; and those parts of the coasts into which the rivers issue, are so full of pointed rocks, and the sea generally so rough, that there is no venturing with the smallest of their boats; so that these people are wholly excluded from any commerce with the rest of the world. But the large rivers are full of vessels, and abound with excellent fish; for they seldom get any from the sea, because the sea fish are of the same size with those in Europe, and consequently not worth catching; whereby it is manifest, that nature, in the production of plants and animals of so extraordinary a bulk, is wholly confined to this continent, of which I leave the reasons to be determined by philosophers. However, now and then they take a whale that happens to be dashed against the rocks, which the common people feed on heartily. These whales I have known so large, that a man could hardly carry one upon his shoulders; and sometimes, for curiosity, they are brought in hampers to Lorbrulgrud; I saw one of them in a dish at the king's table, which passed for a rarity, but I did not observe he was fond of it; for I think, indeed, the bigness disgusted him, although I have seen one somewhat larger in Greenland.

The country is well inhabited, for it contains fifty-one cities, near a hundred walled towns, and a great number of villages. To satisfy my curious reader, it may be sufficient to describe Lorbrulgrud. This city stands upon almost two equal parts, on each side the river that passes through. It contains above eighty thousand houses, and about six hundred thousand inhabitants. It is in length three *glomglungs* (which make about fifty-four English miles,) and two and a half in breadth; as I measured it myself in the royal map made by the king's order, which was laid on the ground on purpose for me, and extended a hundred feet; I paced the diameter and circumference several times barefoot, and, computing by the scale, measured it pretty exactly.

The king's palace is no regular edifice, but a heap of buildings, about seven miles round. The chief rooms are generally two hundred and forty feet high, and broad and long in proportion. A coach was allowed to Glumdalclitch and me, wherein her governess frequently took her out to see the town, or go among the shops; and I was always of the party, carried in my box; although the girl, at my own desire, would often take me out, and hold me in her hand, that I might more conveniently view the houses and the people, as we passed along the streets. I reckoned our coach to be about a square of Westminster-hall, but not altogether so high; however, I cannot be very exact. One day the governess ordered our coachman to stop at several shops, where the beggars, watching their opportunity, crowded to the sides of the coach, and gave me the most horrible spectacle that ever a European eye beheld. There was a woman with a cancer in her breast, swelled to a monstrous size, full of holes, in two or three of which I could have easily crept, and covered my whole body. There was a fellow with a wen in his neck, larger than five wool-packs; and another, with a couple of wooden legs, each about twenty feet high. But the most hateful sight of all, was the lice crawling on their clothes. I could see distinctly the limbs of these vermin with my naked eye, much better than those of a European louse through a microscope, and their snouts with which they rooted like swine. They were the first I had ever beheld, and I should have been curious enough to dissect one of them, if I had proper instruments, which I unluckily left behind me in the ship, although indeed, the sight was so nauseous, that it perfectly turned my stomach.

Besides the large box in which I was usually carried, the queen ordered a smaller one to be made for me, of about twelve feet square, and ten high, for the convenience of travelling; because the other was somewhat too large for Glumdalclitch's lap, and cumbersome in the coach; it was made by the same artist, whom I directed in the whole contrivance. This travelling-closet was an exact square, with a window in the middle of three of the squares, and each window was latticed with iron wire on the outside, to prevent accidents in long journeys. On the fourth side, which had no window, two strong staples were fixed, through which the person that carried me, when I had a mind to be on horseback, put a leather belt, and buckled it about his waist. This was always the office of some grave trusty servant, in whom I could confide, whether I attended the king and queen in their progresses, or were disposed to see the gardens, or pay a visit to some great lady or minister of state in the court, when Glumdalclitch happened to be out of order; for I soon began to be known and esteemed among the greatest officers, I suppose more upon account of their majesties' favour, than any merit of my own. In journeys, when I was weary of the coach, a servant on horseback would buckle on my box, and place it upon a cushion before him; and there I had a full prospect of the country on three sides, from my three windows. I had, in this closet, a field-bed and a hammock, hung from the ceiling, two chairs and a table, neatly screwed to the floor, to prevent being tossed about by the agitation of the horse or the coach. And having been long used to sea-voyages, those motions, although sometimes very violent, did not much discompose me.

Whenever I had a mind to see the town, it was always in my travelling-closet; which Glumdalclitch held in her lap in a kind of open sedan, after the fashion of the country, borne by four men, and attended by two others in the queen's livery. The people, who had often heard of me, were very curious to crowd about the sedan, and the girl was complaisant enough to make the bearers stop, and to take me in her hand, that I might be more conveniently seen.

I was very desirous to see the chief temple, and particularly the tower belonging to it, which is reckoned the highest in the kingdom. Accordingly one day my nurse carried me thither, but I may truly say I came back disappointed; for the height is not above three thousand feet, reckoning from the ground to the highest pinnacle top; which, allowing for the difference between the size of those people and us in Europe, is no great matter for admiration, nor at all equal in proportion (if I rightly remember) to Salisbury steeple. But, not to detract from a nation, to which, during my life, I shall acknowledge myself extremely obliged, it must be allowed, that whatever this famous tower wants in height, is amply made up in beauty and strength. For the walls are near a hundred feet thick, built of hewn stone, whereof each is about forty feet square, and adorned on all sides with statues of gods and emperors, cut in marble, larger than the life, placed in their several niches. I measured a little finger which had fallen down from one of these statues, and lay unperceived among some rubbish, and found it exactly four feet and an inch in length. Glumdalclitch wrapped it up in her handkerchief, and carried it home in her pocket, to keep among other trinkets, of which the girl was very fond, as children at her age usually are.

The king's kitchen is indeed a noble building, vaulted at top, and about six hundred feet high. The great oven is not so wide, by ten paces, as the cupola at St. Paul's: for I measured the latter on purpose, after my return. But if I should describe the kitchen grate, the prodigious pots and kettles, the joints of meat turning on the spits, with many other particulars, perhaps I should be hardly believed; at least a severe critic would be apt to think I enlarged a little, as travellers are often suspected to do. To avoid which censure, I fear I have run too much into the other extreme; and that if this treatise should happen to be translated into the language of Brobdingnag (which is the general name of that kingdom) and transmitted thither, the king and his people would have reason to complain that I had done them an injury, by a false and diminutive representation.

His Majesty seldom keeps above six hundred horses in his stables: they are generally from fifty-four to sixty feet high. But, when he goes abroad on solemn days, he is attended, for state, by a military guard of five hundred horse, which, indeed, I thought was the most splendid sight that could be ever beheld, till I saw part of his army in battalia, whereof I shall find another occasion to speak.

⌒ **Chapter V** ⌒

Several adventurers that happened to the author. The execution of a criminal. The author shows his skill in navigation.

I should have lived happy enough in that country, if my littleness had not exposed me to several ridiculous and troublesome accidents; some of which I shall venture to relate. Glumdalclitch often carried me into the gardens of the court in my smaller box, and would sometimes take me out of it, and hold me in her hand, or set me down to walk. I remember, before the dwarf left the queen, he followed us one day into those gardens, and my nurse having set me down, he and I being close together, near some dwarf apple trees, I must needs show my wit, by a silly allusion between him and the trees, which happens to hold in their language as it does in ours. Whereupon, the malicious rogue, watching his opportunity, when I was walking under one of them, shook it directly over my head, by which a dozen apples, each of them near as large as a Bristol barrel, came tumbling about my ears; one of them hit me on the back as I chanced to stoop, and knocked me down flat on my face; but I received no other hurt, and the dwarf was pardoned at my desire, because I had given the provocation.

Another day, Glumdalclitch left me on a smooth grass-plot to divert myself, while she walked at some distance with her governess. In the meantime, there suddenly fell such a violent shower of hail, that I was immediately by the force of it, struck to the ground; and when I was down, the hailstones gave me such cruel bangs all over the body, as if I had been pelted with tennis-balls; however, I made a shift to creep on all fours, and shelter myself, by lying flat on my face on the lee-side of a border of lemon-thyme, but so bruised from head to foot, that I could not go abroad in ten days. Neither is this at all to be wondered at, because nature, in that country, observing the same proportion through all her operations, a hailstone is near eighteen hundred times as large as one in Europe; which I can assert upon experience, having been so curious as to weigh and measure them.

But a more dangerous accident happened to me in the same garden, when my little nurse, believing she had put me in a secure place (which I often entreated her to do, that I might enjoy my own thoughts) and having left my box at home, to avoid the trouble of carrying it, went to another part of the garden with her governess and some ladies of her acquaintance. While she was absent, and out of hearing, a small white spaniel that belonged to one of the chief gardeners, having got by accident into the garden, happened to range near the place where I lay. The dog, following the scent, came directly up, and taking me in his mouth, ran straight to his master wagging his tail, and set me gently on the ground. By good fortune he had been so well taught, that I was carried between his teeth without the least hurt, or even tearing my clothes. But the poor gardener, who knew me well, and had a great kindness for me, was in a terrible fright. He gently took me up in both his hands, and asked me how I did; but I was so amazed and out of breath, that I could not speak a word. In a few minutes I came to myself, and he carried me safe to my little nurse, who, by this time, had returned to the place where she left me, and was in cruel agonies when I did not appear, nor answer when she called. She severely reprimanded the gardener on account of his dog. But the thing was hushed up, and never known at court, for the girl was afraid of the queen's anger; and truly, as to myself, I thought it would not be for my reputation, that such a story should go about.

This accident absolutely determined Glumdalclitch never to trust me abroad for the future out of her sight. I had been long afraid of this resolution, and therefore concealed from her some little unlucky adventures, that happened in those times when I was left by myself. Once a kite, hovering over the garden, made a stoop at me, and if I had not resolutely drawn my hanger, and run under a thick espalier, he would have certainly carried me away in his talons. Another time, walking to the top of a fresh mole-hill, I fell to my neck in the hole, through which that animal had cast up the earth, and coined some lie, not worth remembering, to excuse myself for spoiling my clothes. I likewise broke my right shin against the shell of a snail, which I happened to stumble over, as I was walking alone and thinking on poor England.

I cannot tell whether I were more pleased or mortified to observe, in those solitary walks, that the smaller birds did not appear to be at all afraid of me, but would hop about within a yard's distance, looking for worms and other food, with as much indifference and security as if no creature at all were near them. I remember, a thrush had the confidence to snatch out of my hand, with his bill, a of cake that Glumdalclitch had just given me for my breakfast. When I attempted to catch any of these birds, they would boldly turn against me, endeavouring to peck my fingers, which I durst not venture within their reach; and then they would hop back unconcerned, to hunt for worms or snails, as they did before. But one day, I took a thick cudgel, and threw it with all my strength so luckily, at a linnet, that I knocked him down, and seizing him by the neck with both my hands, ran with him in triumph to my nurse. However, the bird, who had only been stunned, recovering himself gave me so many boxes with his wings, on both sides of my head and body, though I held him at arms length, and was out of the reach of his claws, that I was twenty times thinking to let him go. But I was soon relieved by one of our servants, who wrung off the bird's neck, and I had him next day for dinner, by the queen's command. This linnet, as near as I can remember, seemed to be somewhat larger than an English swan.

The maids of honour often invited Glumdalclitch to their apartments, and desired she would bring me along with her, on purpose to have the pleasure of seeing and touching me. They would often strip me naked from top to toe, and lay me at full length in their bosoms; wherewith I was much disgusted because, to say the truth, a very offensive smell came from their skins; which I do not mention, or intend, to the disadvantage of those excellent ladies, for whom I have all manner of respect; but I conceive that my sense was more acute in proportion to my littleness, and that those illustrious persons were no more disagreeable to their lovers, or to each other, than people of the same quality are with us in England. And, after all, I found their natural smell was much more supportable, than when they used perfumes, under which I immediately swooned away. I cannot forget, that an intimate friend of mine in Lilliput, took the freedom in a warm day, when I had used a good deal of exercise, to complain of a strong smell about me, although I am as little faulty that way, as most of my sex, but I suppose his faculty of smelling was as nice with regard to me, as mine was to that of this people. Upon this point, I cannot forbear doing justice to the queen my mistress, and Glumdalclitch my nurse, whose persons were as sweet as those of any lady in England.

That which gave me most uneasiness among these maids of honour, when my nurse carried me to visit them, was to see them use me without any manner of ceremony, like a creature who had no sort of consequence. For they would strip themselves to the skin, and put on their smocks in my presence, while I was placed on their toilet, directly before their naked bodies, which I am sure to me was very far from being a tempting sight, or from giving me any other emotions than those of horror and disgust; their skins appeared so coarse and uneven, so variously coloured, when I saw them near, with a mole here and there as broad as a trencher, and hairs hanging from it thicker than pack-threads, to say nothing farther concerning the rest of their persons. Neither did they at all scruple, while I was by, to discharge what they had drank, to the quantity of at least two hogsheads, in a vessel that held above three tons. The handsomest among these maids of honour, a pleasant, frolicsome girl of sixteen, would sometimes set me astride upon one of her nipples, with many other tricks, wherein the reader will excuse me for not being over particular. But I was so much displeased, that I entreated Glumdalclitch to contrive some excuse for not seeing that young lady any more.

One day, a young gentleman, who was nephew to my nurse's governess, came and pressed them both to see an execution. It was of a man, who had murdered one of that gentleman's intimate acquaintance. Glumdalclitch was prevailed on to be of the company, very much against her inclination, for she was naturally tender-hearted; and, as for myself, although I abhorred such kind of spectacles, yet my curiosity tempted me to see something that I thought must be extraordinary. The malefactor was fixed in a chair upon a scaffold erected for that purpose, and his head cut off at one blow, with a sword of about forty feet long. The veins and arteries spouted up such a prodigious quantity of blood, and so high in the air, that the great Jet d'Eau at Versailles was not equal to it for the time it lasted; and the head, when it fell on the scaffold floor, gave such a bounce as made me start, although I was at least half an English mile distant.

The queen, who often used to hear me talk of my sea-voyages, and took all occasions to divert me when I was melancholy, asked me whether I understood how to handle a sail or an oar, and whether a little exercise of rowing might not be convenient for my health. I answered, that I understood both very well; for although my proper employment had been to be surgeon or doctor to the ship, yet often, upon a pinch, I was forced to work like a common mariner. But I could not see how this could be done in their country, where the smallest wherry was equal to a first-rate man of war among us; and such a boat as I could manage would never live in any of their rivers. Her Majesty said, if I would contrive a boat, her own joiner should make it, and she would provide a place for me to sail in. The fellow was an ingenious workman, and by my instructions, in ten days, finished a pleasure-boat with all its tackling, able conveniently to hold eight Europeans. When it was finished, the queen was so delighted, that she ran with it in her lap to the king, who ordered it to be put into a cistern full of water, with me in it, by way of trial, where I could not manage my two sculls, or little oars, for want of room. But the queen had before contrived another project. She ordered the joiner to make a wooden trough of three hundred feet long, fifty broad, and eight deep; which, being well pitched, to prevent leaking, was placed on the floor, along the wall, in an outer room of the palace. It had a cock near the bottom to let out the water, when it began to grow stale; and two servants could easily fill it in half an hour. Here I often used to row for my own diversion, as well as that of the queen and her ladies, who thought themselves well entertained with my skill and agility. Sometimes I would put up my sail, and then my business was only to steer, while the ladies gave me a gale with their fans; and, when they were weary, some of their pages would blow my sail forward with their breath, while I showed my art by steering starboard or larboard as I pleased. When I had done, Glumdalclitch always carried back my boat into her closet, and hung it on a nail to dry.

In this exercise I once met an accident, which had like to have cost me my life; for, one of the pages having put my boat into the trough, the governess who attended Glumdalclitch very officiously lifted me up, to place me in the boat; but I happened to slip through her fingers, and should infallibly have fallen down forty feet upon the floor, if, by the luckiest chance in the world, I had not been stopped by a corking-pin that stuck in the good gentlewoman's stomacher; the head of the pin passing between my shirt and the waistband of my breeches, and thus I was held by the middle in the air, till Glumdalclitch ran to my relief.

Another time, one of the servants, whose office it was to fill my trough every third day with fresh water, was so careless as to let a huge frog (not perceiving it) slip out of his pail. The frog lay concealed till I was put into my boat, but then, seeing a resting-place, climbed up, and made it lean so much on one side, that I was forced to balance it with all my weight on the other, to prevent overturning. When the frog was got in, it hopped at once half the length of the boat, and then over my head, backward and forward, daubing my face and clothes with its odious slime. The largeness of its features made it appear the most deformed animal that can be conceived. However, I desired Glumdalclitch to let me deal with it alone. I banged it a good while with one of my sculls, and at last forced it to leap out of the boat.

But the greatest danger I ever underwent in that kingdom, was from a monkey, who belonged to one of the clerks of the kitchen. Glumdalclitch had locked me up in her closet, while she went somewhere upon business, or a visit. The weather being very warm, the closet-window was left open, as well as the windows and the door of my bigger box, in which I usually lived, because of its largeness and convenience. As I sat quietly meditating at my table, I heard something bounce in at the closet-window, and skip about from one side to the other; whereat, although I was much alarmed, yet I ventured to look out, but not stirring from my seat; and then I saw this frolicsome animal frisking and leaping up and down, till at last he came to my box, which he seemed to view with great pleasure and curiosity, peeping in at the door and every window. I retreated to the farther corner of my room, or box; but the monkey looking in at every side, put me in such a fright, that I wanted presence of mind to conceal myself under the bed, as I might easily have done. After some time spent in peeping, grinning, and chattering, he at last espied me; and reaching one of his paws in at the door, as a cat does when she plays with a mouse, although I often shifted place to avoid him, he at length seized the lappet of my coat (which being made of that country silk, was very thick and strong), and dragged me out. He took me up in his right fore-foot and held me as a nurse does a child she is going to suckle, just as I have seen the same sort of creature do with a kitten in Europe; and when I offered to struggle he squeezed me so hard, that I thought it more prudent to submit. I have good reason to believe, that he took me for a young one of his own species, by his often stroking my face very gently with his other paw. In these diversions he was interrupted by a noise at the closet door, as if somebody were opening it; whereupon he suddenly leaped up to the window at which he had come in, and thence upon the leads and gutters, walking upon three legs, and holding me in the fourth, till he clambered up to a roof that was next to ours. I heard Glumdalclitch give a shriek at the moment he was carrying me out. The poor girl was almost distracted: that quarter of the palace was all in an uproar; the servants ran for ladders; the monkey was seen by hundreds in the court, sitting upon the ridge of a building, holding me like a baby in one of his forepaws, and feeding me with the other, by cramming into my mouth some victuals he had squeezed out of the bag on one side of his chaps, and patting me when I would not eat; whereat many of the rabble below could not forbear laughing; neither do I think they justly ought to be blamed, for, without question, the sight was ridiculous enough to everybody but myself. Some of the people threw up stones, hoping to drive the monkey down; but this was strictly forbidden, or else, very probably, my brains had been dashed out.

The ladders were now applied, and mounted by several men; which the monkey observing, and finding himself almost encompassed, not being able to make speed enough with his three legs, let me drop on a ridge tile, and made his escape. Here I sat for some time, five hundred yards from the ground, expecting every moment to be blown down by the wind, or to fall by my own giddiness, and come tumbling over and over from the ridge to the eaves; but an honest lad, one of my nurse's footmen, climbed up, and putting me into his breeches pocket, brought me down safe.

I was almost choked with the filthy stuff the monkey had crammed down my throat; but my dear little nurse picked it out of my mouth with a small needle, and then I fell a-vomiting, which gave me great relief. Yet I was so weak and bruised in the sides with the squeezes given me by this odious animal, that I was forced to keep my bed a fortnight. The king, queen, and all the court, sent every day to inquire after my health; and her Majesty made me several visits during my sickness. The monkey was killed, and an order made, that no such animal should be kept about the palace.

When I attended the king after my recovery, to return him thanks for his favours, he was pleased to rally me a good deal upon this adventure. He asked me what my thoughts and speculations were, while I lay in the monkey's paw; how I liked the victuals he gave me; his manner of feeding; and whether the fresh air on the roof had sharpened my stomach. He desired to know what I would have done upon such an occasion in my own country. I told his Majesty that in Europe we had no monkeys, except such as were brought for curiosity from other places, and so small, that I could deal with a dozen of them together, if they presumed to attack me. And as for that monstrous animal with whom I was so lately engaged (it was indeed as large as an elephant), if my fears had suffered me to think so far as to make use of my hanger (looking fiercely, and clapping my hand on the hilt as I spoke) when he poked his paw into my chamber, perhaps I should have given him such a wound, as would have made him glad to withdraw it with more haste than he put it in. This I delivered in a firm tone, like a person who was jealous lest his courage should be called in question. However, my speech produced nothing else beside a laud laughter, which all the respect due to his Majesty from those about him could not make them contain. This made me reflect, how vain an attempt it is for a man to endeavour to do himself honour among those who are out of all degree of equality or comparison with him. And yet I have seen the moral of my own behaviour very frequent in England since my return; where a little contemptible varlet, without the least title to birth, person, wit, or common sense, shall presume to look with importance, and put himself upon a foot with the greatest persons of the kingdom.

I was every day furnishing the court with some ridiculous story; and Glumdalclitch, although she loved me to excess, yet was arch enough to inform the queen, whenever I committed any folly that she thought would be diverting to her Majesty. The girl, who had been out of order, was carried by her governess to take the air about an hour's distance, or thirty miles from town. They alighted out of the coach near a small foot-path in a field, and Glumdalclitch setting down my travelling box, I went out of it to walk. There was a cow-dung in the path, and I must need try my activity by attempting to leap over it. I took a run, but unfortunately jumped short, and found myself just in the middle up to my knees. I waded through with some difficulty, and one of the footmen wiped me as clean as he could with his handkerchief, for I was filthily bemired; and my nurse confined me to my box, till we returned home; where the queen was soon informed of what had passed, and the footmen spread it about the court; so that all the mirth for some days was at my expense.

⌒〜 **Chapter VI** 〜⌒

Several contrivances of the author to please the king and queen. He shows his skill in music. The king inquiries into the state of England, which the author relates to him. The king's observations thereon.

I used to attend the king's levee once or twice a week, and had often seen him under the barber's hand, which indeed was at first very terrible to behold; for the razor was almost twice as long as an ordinary scythe. His Majesty, according to the custom of the country, was only shaved twice a week. I once prevailed on the barber to give me some of the suds or lather, out of which I picked forty or fifty of the strongest stumps of hair. I then took a piece of fine wood, and cut it like the back of a comb, making several holes in it at equal distances with as small a needle as I could get from Glumdalclitch. I fixed in the stumps so artificially, scraping and sloping them with my knife toward the points, that I made a very tolerable comb; which was a seasonable supply, my own being so much broken in the teeth, that it was almost useless; neither did I know any artist in that country so nice and exact, as would undertake to make me another.

And this puts me in mind of an amusement, wherein I spent many of my leisure hours. I desired the queen's woman to save for me the combings of her Majesty's hair, whereof in time I got a good quantity; and consulting with my friend the cabinet-maker, who had received general orders to do little jobs for me, I directed him to make two chair-frames, no larger than those I had in my box, and to bore little holes with a fine awl, round those parts where I designed the backs and seats; through these holes I wove the strongest hairs I could pick out, just after the manner of cane chairs in England. When they were finished, I made a present of them to her Majesty; who kept them in her cabinet, and used to show them for curiosities, as indeed they were the wonder of every one that beheld them. The queen would have me sit upon one of these chairs, but I absolutely refused to obey her, protesting I would rather die than place a dishonourable part of my body on those precious hairs, that once adorned her Majesty's head. Of these hairs (as I had always a mechanical genius) I likewise made a neat little purse, about five feet long, with her Majesty's name deciphered in gold letters, which I gave to Glumdalclitch, by the queen's consent. To say the truth, it was more for show than use, being not of strength to bear the weight of the larger coins, and therefore she kept nothing in it but some little toys that girls are fond of.

The king, who delighted in music, had frequent concerts at court, to which I was sometimes carried, and set in my box on a table to hear them: but the noise was so great that I could hardly distinguish the tunes. I am confident that all the drums and trumpets of a royal army, beating and sounding together just at your ears, could not equal it. My practice was to have my box removed from the place where the performers sat, as far as I could, then to shut the doors and windows of it, and draw the window curtains; after which I found their music not disagreeable.

I had learned in my youth to play a little upon the spinet. Glumdalclitch kept one in her chamber, and a master attended twice a week to teach her: I called it a spinet, because it somewhat resembled that instrument, and was played upon in the same manner. A fancy came into my head, that I would entertain the king and queen with an English tune upon this instrument. But this appeared extremely difficult: for the spinet was near sixty feet long, each key being almost a foot wide, so that with my arms extended I could not reach to above five keys, and to press them down required a good smart stroke with my fist, which would be too great a labour, and to no purpose. The method I contrived was this: I prepared two round sticks, about the bigness of common cudgels; they were thicker at one end than the other, and I covered the thicker ends with pieces of a mouse's skin, that by rapping on them I might neither damage the tops of the keys nor interrupt the sound. Before the spinet a bench was placed, about four feet below the keys, and I was put upon the bench. I ran sideling upon it, that way and this, as fast as I could, banging the proper keys with my two sticks, and made a shift to play a jig, to the great satisfaction of both their majesties; but it was the most violent exercise I ever underwent; and yet I could not strike above sixteen keys, nor consequently play the bass and treble together, as other artists do; which was a great disadvantage to my performance.

The king, who as I before observed, was a prince of excellent understanding, would frequently order that I should be brought in my box, and set upon the table in his closet. He would then command me to bring one of my chairs out of the box, and sit down within three yards distance upon the top of the cabinet, which brought me almost to a level with his face. In this manner I had several conversations with him. I one day took the freedom to tell his Majesty, that the contempt he discovered towards Europe, and the rest of the world, did not seem answerable to those excellent qualities of mind that he was master of; that reason did not extend itself with the bulk of the body; on the contrary, we observed in our country, that the tallest persons were usually the least provided with it; that among other animals, bees and ants had the reputation of more industry, art, and sagacity, than many of the larger kinds; and that, as inconsiderable as he took me to be, I hoped I might live to do his Majesty some signal service. The king heard me with attention, and began to conceive a much better opinion of me than he had ever before. He desired I would give him as exact an account of the government of England as I possibly could; because, as fond as princes commonly are of their own customs (for so he conjectured of other monarchs, by my former discourses), he should be glad to hear of anything that might deserve imitation.

Imagine with thyself, courteous reader, how often I then wished for the tongue of Demosthenes or Cicero, that might have enabled me to celebrate the praise of my own dear native country in a style equal to its merits and felicity.

I began my discourse by informing his Majesty, that our dominions consisted of two islands, which composed three mighty kingdoms, under one sovereign, beside our plantations in America. I dwelt long upon the fertility of our soil, and the temperature of our climate. I then spoke at large upon the constitution of an English parliament; partly made up of an illustrious body called the House of Peers; persons of the noblest blood, and of the most ancient and ample patrimonies. I described that extraordinary care always taken of their education in arts and arms, to qualify them for being counsellors both to the king and kingdom; to have a share in the legislature; to be members of the highest court of judicature, whence there can be no appeal; and to be champions always ready for the defence of their prince and country, by their valour, conduct, and fidelity. That these were the ornament and bulwark of the kingdom, worthy followers of their most renowned ancestors, whose honour had been the reward of their virtue, from which their posterity were never once known to degenerate. To these were joined several holy persons, as part of that assembly, under the title of bishops, whose peculiar business is to take care of religion, and of those who instruct the people therein. These were searched and sought out through the whole nation, by the prince and his wisest counsellors, among such of the priesthood as were most deservedly distinguished by the sanctity of their lives, and the depth of their erudition; who were indeed the spiritual fathers of the clergy and the people.

That the other part of the parliament consisted of an assembly called the House of Commons, who were all principal gentlemen, freely picked and culled out by the people themselves, for their great abilities and love of their country, to represent the wisdom of the whole nation. And that these two bodies made up the most august assembly in Europe; to whom, in conjunction with the prince, the whole legislature is committed.

I then descended to the courts of justice; over which the judges, those venerable sages and interpreters of the law, presided, for determining the disputed rights and properties of men, as well as for the punishment of vice and protection of innocence. I mentioned the prudent management of our treasury; the valour and achievements of our forces, by sea and land. I computed the number of our people, by reckoning how many millions there might be of each religious sect, or political party among us. I did not omit even our sports and pastimes, or any other particular which I thought might redound to the honour of my country. And I finished all with a brief historical account of affairs and events in England for about a hundred years past.

This conversation was not ended under five audiences, each of several hours; and the king heard the whole with great attention, frequently taking notes of what I spoke, as well as memorandums of what questions he intended to ask me.

When I had put an end to these long discourses, his Majesty, in a sixth audience, consulting his notes, proposed many doubts, queries, and objections, upon every article. He asked, What methods were used to cultivate the minds and bodies of our young nobility, and in what kind of business they commonly spent the first and teachable parts of their lives? What course was taken to supply that assembly, when any noble family became extinct? What qualifications were necessary in those who are to be created new lords? Whether the humour of the prince, a sum of money to a court lady, or a design of strengthening a party opposite to the public interest, ever happened to be the motive in those advancements? What share of knowledge these lords had in the laws of their country, and how they came by it, so as to enable them to decide the properties of their fellow-subjects in the last resort? Whether they were always so free from avarice, partialities, or want, that a bribe, or some other sinister view, could have no place among them? Whether those holy lords I spoke of were always promoted to that rank upon account of their knowledge in religious matters, and the sanctity of their lives, had never been compliers with the times, while they were common priests; or slavish prostitute chaplains to some nobleman, whose opinions they continued servilely to follow, after they were admitted into that assembly?

He then desired to know, What arts were practised in electing those whom I called commoners: whether a stranger, with a strong purse, might not influence the vulgar voters to choose him before their own landlord, or the most considerable gentleman in the neighbourhood? How it came to pass, that people were so violently bent upon getting into this assembly, which I allowed to be a great trouble and expense, often to the ruin of their families, without any salary or pension? Because this appeared such an exalted strain of virtue and public spirit, that his Majesty seemed to doubt it might possibly not be always sincere. And he desired to know, Whether such zealous gentlemen could have any views of refunding themselves for the charges and trouble they were at by sacrificing the public good to the designs of a weak and vicious prince, in conjunction with a corrupted ministry? He multiplied his questions, and sifted me thoroughly upon every part of this head, proposing numberless inquiries and objections, which I think it not prudent or convenient to repeat.

Upon what I said in relation to our courts of justice, his Majesty desired to be satisfied in several points: and this I was the better able to do, having been formerly almost ruined by a long suit in chancery, which was decreed for me with costs. He asked, What time was usually spent in determining between right and wrong, and what degree of expense? Whether advocates and orators had liberty to plead in causes manifestly known to be unjust, vexatious, or oppressive? Whether party, in religion or politics, were observed to be of any weight in the scale of justice? Whether those pleading orators were persons educated in the general knowledge of equity, or only in provincial, national, and other local customs? Whether they or their judges had any part in penning those laws, which they assumed the liberty of interpreting, and glossing upon at their pleasure? Whether they had ever, at different times, pleaded for and against the same cause, and cited precedents to prove contrary opinions? Whether they were a rich or a poor corporation? Whether they received any pecuniary reward for pleading, or delivering their opinions? And particularly, whether they were ever admitted as members in the lower senate?

He fell next upon the management of our treasury; and said, he thought my memory had failed me, because I computed our taxes at about five or six millions a year, and when I came to mention the issues, he found they sometimes amounted to more than double; for the notes he had taken were very particular in this point, because he hoped, as he told me, that the knowledge of our conduct might be useful to him, and he could not be deceived in his calculations. But, if what I told him were true, he was still at a loss how a kingdom could run out of its estate, like a private person. He asked me, who were our creditors; and where we found money to pay them? He wondered to hear me talk of such chargeable and expensive wars; that certainly we must be a quarrelsome people, or live among very bad neighbours, and that our generals must needs be richer than our kings. He asked, what business we had out of our own islands, unless upon the score of trade, or treaty, or to defend the coasts with our fleet? Above all, he was amazed to hear me talk of a mercenary standing army, in the midst of peace, and among a free people. He said, if we were governed by our own consent, in the persons of our representatives, he could not imagine of whom we were afraid, or against whom we were to fight; and would hear my opinion, whether a private man's house might not be better defended by himself, his children, and family, than by half-a-dozen rascals, picked up at a venture in the streets for small wages, who might get a hundred times more by cutting their throats?

He laughed at my "odd kind of arithmetic", as he was pleased to call it, in reckoning the numbers of our people, by a computation drawn from the several sects among us, in religion and politics. He said he knew no reason why those, who entertain opinions prejudicial to the public, should be obliged to change, or should not be obliged to conceal them. And as it was tyranny in any government to require the first, so it was weakness not to enforce the second: for a man may be allowed to keep poisons in his closet, but not to vend them about for cordials.

He observed, that among the diversions of our nobility and gentry, I had mentioned gaming; he desired to know at what age this entertainment was usually taken up, and when it was laid down; how much of their time it employed; whether it ever went so high as to affect their fortunes; whether mean, vicious people, by their dexterity in that art, might not arrive at great riches, and sometimes keep our very nobles in dependence, as well as habituate them to vile companions, wholly take them from the improvement of their minds, and force them, by the losses they received, to learn and practise that infamous dexterity upon others?

He was perfectly astonished with the historical account gave him of our affairs during the last century; protesting it was only a heap of conspiracies, rebellions, murders, massacres, revolutions, banishments, the very worst effects that avarice, faction, hypocrisy, perfidiousness, cruelty, rage, madness, hatred, envy, lust, malice, and ambition, could produce.

His Majesty, in another audience, was at the pains to recapitulate the sum of all I had spoken; compared the questions he made with the answers I had given; then taking me into his hands, and stroking me gently, delivered himself in these words, which I shall never forget, nor the manner he spoke them in: "My little friend Grildrig, you have made a most admirable panegyric upon your country; you have clearly proved, that ignorance, idleness, and vice, are the proper ingredients for qualifying a legislator; that laws are best explained, interpreted, and applied, by those whose interest and abilities lie in perverting, confounding, and eluding them. I observe among you some lines of an institution, which, in its original, might have been tolerable, but these half erased, and the rest wholly blurred and blotted by corruptions. It does not appear, from all you have said, how any one perfection is required toward the procurement of any one station among you; much less, that men are ennobled on account of their virtue; that priests are advanced for their piety or learning; soldiers, for their conduct or valour; judges, for their integrity; senators, for the love of their country; or counsellors for their wisdom. As for yourself," continued the king, "who have spent the greatest part of your life in travelling, I am well disposed to hope you may hitherto have escaped many vices of your country. But by what I have gathered from your own relation, and the answers I have with much pains wrung and extorted from you, I cannot but conclude the bulk of your natives to be the most pernicious race of little odious vermin that nature ever suffered to crawl upon the surface of the earth."

⌒ **Chapter VII** ⌒

The author's love of his country. He makes a proposal of much advantage to the king, which is rejected. The king's great ignorance in politics. The learning of that country very imperfect and confined. The laws, and military affairs, and parties in the state.

Nothing but an extreme love of truth could have hindered me from concealing this part of my story. It was in vain to discover my resentments, which were always turned into ridicule; and I was forced to rest with patience, while my noble and beloved country was so injuriously treated. I am as heartily sorry as any of my readers can possibly be, that such an occasion was given; but this prince happened to be so curious and inquisitive upon every particular, that it could not consist either with gratitude or good manners, to refuse giving him what satisfaction I was able. Yet thus much I may be allowed to say in my own vindication, that I artfully eluded many of his questions, and gave to every point a more favourable turn, by many degrees, than the strictness of truth would allow. For I have always borne that laudable partiality to my own country, which Dionysius Halicarnassensis, with so much justice, recommends to an historian: I would hide the frailties and deformities of my political mother, and place her virtues and beauties in the most advantageous light. This was my sincere endeavour in those many discourses I had with that monarch, although it unfortunately failed of success.

But great allowances should be given to a king, who lives wholly secluded from the rest of the world, and must therefore be altogether unacquainted with the manners and customs that most prevail in other nations: the want of which knowledge will ever produce many prejudices, and a certain narrowness of thinking, from which we, and the politer countries of Europe, are wholly exempted. And it would be hard indeed, if so remote a prince's notions of virtue and vice were to be offered as a standard for all mankind.

To confirm what I have now said, and further to show the miserable effects of a confined education, I shall here insert a passage, which will hardly obtain belief. In hopes to ingratiate myself further into his Majesty's favour, I told him of an invention, discovered between three and four hundred years ago, to make a certain powder, into a heap of which, the smallest spark of fire falling, would kindle the whole in a moment, although it were as big as a mountain, and make it all fly up in the air together, with a noise and agitation greater than thunder. That a proper quantity of this powder rammed into a hollow tube of brass or iron, according to its bigness, would drive a ball of iron or lead, with such violence and speed, as nothing was able to sustain its force. That the largest balls thus discharged, would not only destroy whole ranks of an army at once, but batter the strongest walls to the ground, sink down ships, with a thousand men in each, to the bottom of the sea, and when linked together by a chain, would cut through masts and rigging, divide hundreds of bodies in the middle, and lay all waste before them. That we often put this powder into large hollow balls of iron, and discharged them by an engine into some city we were besieging, which would rip up the pavements, tear the houses to pieces, burst and throw splinters on every side, dashing out the brains of all who came near. That I knew the ingredients very well, which were cheap and common; I understood the manner of compounding them, and could direct his workmen how to make those tubes, of a size proportionable to all other things in his Majesty's kingdom, and the largest need not be above a hundred feet long; twenty or thirty of which tubes, charged with the proper quantity of powder and balls, would batter down the walls of the strongest town in his dominions in a few hours, or destroy the whole metropolis, if ever it should pretend to dispute his absolute commands. This I humbly offered to his Majesty, as a small tribute of acknowledgment, in turn for so many marks that I had received, of his royal favour and protection.

The king was struck with horror at the description I had given of those terrible engines, and the proposal I had made. He was amazed, how so impotent and grovelling an insect as I (these were his expressions) could entertain such inhuman ideas, and in so familiar a manner, as to appear wholly unmoved at all the scenes of blood and desolation which I had painted as the common effects of those destructive machines; whereof, he said, some evil genius, enemy to mankind, must have been the first contriver. As for himself, he protested, that although few things delighted him so much as new discoveries in art or in nature, yet he would rather lose half his kingdom, than be privy to such a secret; which he commanded me, as I valued any life, never to mention any more.

A strange effect of narrow principles and views! that a prince possessed of every quality which procures veneration, love, and esteem; of strong parts, great wisdom, and profound learning, endowed with admirable talents, and almost adored by his subjects, should, from a nice, unnecessary scruple, whereof in Europe we can have no conception, let slip an opportunity put into his hands that would have made him absolute master of the lives, the liberties, and the fortunes of his people! Neither do I say this, with the least intention to detract from the many virtues of that excellent king, whose character I am sensible will on this account be very much lessened in the opinion of an English reader: but I take this defect among them to have risen from their ignorance, by not having hitherto reduced politics into a science, as the more acute wits of Europe have done. For, I remember very well, in a discourse one day with the king, when I happened to say, there were several thousand books among us written upon the art of government; it gave him (directly contrary to my intention) a very mean opinion of our understandings. He professed both to abominate and despise all mystery, refinement, and intrigue, either in a prince or a minister. He could not tell what I meant by secrets of state, where an enemy, or some rival nation, were not in the case. He confined the knowledge of governing within very narrow bounds, to common sense and reason, to justice and lenity, to the speedy determination of civil and criminal causes; with some other obvious topics, which are not worth considering. And he gave it for his opinion, that whoever could make two ears of corn, or two blades of grass, to grow upon a spot of ground where only one grew before, would deserve better of mankind, and do more essential service to his country, than the whole race of politicians put together.

The learning of this people is very defective, consisting only in morality, history, poetry, and mathematics, wherein they must be allowed to excel. But the last of these is wholly applied to what may be useful in life, to the improvement of agriculture, and all mechanical arts; so that among us, it would be little esteemed. And as to ideas, entities, abstractions, and transcendentals, I could never drive the least conception into their heads.

No law in that country must exceed in words the number of letters in their alphabet, which consists only of two and twenty. But indeed few of them extend even to that length. They are expressed in the most plain and simple terms, wherein those people are not mercurial enough to discover above one interpretation; and to write a comment upon any law, is a capital crime. As to the decision of civil causes, or proceedings against criminals, their precedents are so few, that they have little reason to boast of any extraordinary skill in either.

They have had the art of printing, as well as the Chinese, time out of mind; but their libraries are not very large; for that of the king, which is reckoned the largest, does not amount to above a thousand volumes, placed in a gallery of twelve hundred feet long, whence I had liberty to borrow what books I pleased. The queen's joiner had contrived in one of Glumdalclitch's rooms, a kind of wooden machine five-and-twenty feet high, formed like a standing ladder; the steps were each fifty feet long. It was indeed a moveable pair of stairs, the lowest end placed at ten feet distance from the wall of the chamber. The book I had a mind to read, was put up leaning against the wall. I first mounted to the upper step of the ladder, and turning my face towards the book, began at the top of the page, and so walking to the right and left about eight or ten paces, according to the length of the lines, till I had gotten a little below the level of mine eyes, and then descending gradually till I came to the bottom; after which I mounted again, and began the other page in the same manner, and so turned over the leaf, which I could easily do with both my hands, for it was as thick and stiff as a pasteboard, and in the largest folios not above eighteen or twenty feet long.

Their style is clear, masculine, and smooth, but not florid; for they avoid nothing more than multiplying unnecessary words, or using various expressions. I have perused many of their books, especially those in history and morality. Among the rest, I was much diverted with a little old treatise, which always lay in Glumdalclitch's bed chamber, and belonged to her governess, a grave elderly gentlewoman, who dealt in writings of morality and devotion. The book treats of the weakness of human kind, and is in little esteem, except among the women and the vulgar. However, I was curious to see what an author of that country could say upon such a subject. This writer went through all the usual topics of European moralists, showing how diminutive, contemptible, and helpless an animal was man in his own nature; how unable to defend himself from inclemencies of the air, or the fury of wild beasts; how much he was excelled by one creature in strength, by another in speed, by a third in foresight, by a fourth in industry. He added, that nature was degenerated in these latter declining ages of the world, and could now produce only small abortive births, in comparison of those in ancient times. He said it was very reasonable to think, not only that the species of men were originally much larger, but also that there must have been giants in former ages; which, as it is asserted by history and tradition, so it has been confirmed by huge bones and skulls, casually dug up in several parts of the kingdom, far exceeding the common dwindled race of men in our days. He argued, that the very laws of nature absolutely required we should have been made, in the beginning of a size more large and robust; not so liable to destruction from every little accident, of a tile falling from a house, or a stone cast from the hand of a boy, or being drowned in a little brook. From this way of reasoning, the author drew several moral applications, useful in the conduct of life, but needless here to repeat. For my own part, I could not avoid reflecting how universally this talent was spread, of drawing lectures in morality, or indeed rather matter of discontent and repining, from the quarrels we raise with nature. And I believe, upon a strict inquiry, those quarrels might be shown as ill-grounded among us as they are among that people.

As to their military affairs, they boast that the king's army consists of a hundred and seventy-six thousand foot, and thirty-two thousand horse: if that may be called an army, which is made up of tradesmen in the several cities, and farmers in the country, whose commanders are only the nobility and gentry, without pay or reward. They are indeed perfect enough in their exercises, and under very good discipline, wherein I saw no great merit; for how should it be otherwise, where every farmer is under the command of his own landlord, and every citizen under that of the principal men in his own city, chosen after the manner of Venice, by ballot?

I have often seen the militia of Lorbrulgrud drawn out to exercise, in a great field near the city of twenty miles square. They were in all not above twenty-five thousand foot, and six thousand horse; but it was impossible for me to compute their number, considering the space of ground they took up. A cavalier, mounted on a large steed, might be about ninety feet high. I have seen this whole body of horse, upon a word of command, draw their swords at once, and brandish them in the air. Imagination can figure nothing so grand, so surprising, and so astonishing! It looked as if ten thousand flashes of lightning were darting at the same time from every quarter of the sky.

I was curious to know how this prince, to whose dominions there is no access from any other country, came to think of armies, or to teach his people the practice of military discipline. But I was soon informed, both by conversation and reading their histories; for, in the course of many ages, they have been troubled with the same disease to which the whole race of mankind is subject; the nobility often contending for power, the people for liberty, and the king for absolute dominion. All which, however happily tempered by the laws of that kingdom, have been sometimes violated by each of the three parties, and have more than once occasioned civil wars; the last whereof was happily put an end to by this prince's grand-father, in a general composition; and the militia, then settled with common consent, has been ever since kept in the strictest duty.

◠◠ **Chapter VIII** ◠◠

The king and queen make a progress to the frontiers. The author attends them. The manner in which he leaves the country very particularly related. He returns to England.

I had always a strong impulse that I should some time recover my liberty, though it was impossible to conjecture by what means, or to form any project with the least hope of succeeding. The ship in which I sailed, was the first ever known to be driven within sight of that coast, and the king had given strict orders, that if at any time another appeared, it should be taken ashore, and with all its crew and passengers brought in a tumbril to Lorbrulgrud. He was strongly bent to get me a woman of my own size, by whom I might propagate the breed: but I think I should rather have died than undergone the disgrace of leaving a posterity to be kept in cages, like tame canary-birds, and perhaps, in time, sold about the kingdom, to persons of quality, for curiosities. I was indeed treated with much kindness: I was the favourite of a great king and queen, and the delight of the whole court; but it was upon such a foot as ill became the dignity of humankind. I could never forget those domestic pledges I had left behind me. I wanted to be among people, with whom I could converse upon even terms, and walk about the streets and fields without being afraid of being trod to death like a frog or a young puppy. But my deliverance came sooner than I expected, and in a manner not very common; the whole story and circumstances of which I shall faithfully relate.

I had now been two years in this country; and about the beginning of the third, Glumdalclitch and I attended the king and queen, in a progress to the south coast of the kingdom. I was carried, as usual, in my travelling-box, which as I have already described, was a very convenient closet, of twelve feet wide. And I had ordered a hammock to be fixed, by silken ropes from the four corners at the top, to break the jolts, when a servant carried me before him on horseback, as I sometimes desired; and would often sleep in my hammock, while we were upon the road. On the roof of my closet, not directly over the middle of the hammock, I ordered the joiner to cut out a hole of a foot square, to give me air in hot weather, as I slept; which hole I shut at pleasure with a board that drew backward and forward through a groove.

When we came to our journey's end, the king thought proper to pass a few days at a palace he has near Flanflasnic, a city within eighteen English miles of the seaside. Glumdalclitch and I were much fatigued: I had gotten a small cold, but the poor girl was so ill as to be confined to her chamber. I longed to see the ocean, which must be the only scene of my escape, if ever it should happen. I pretended to be worse than I really was, and desired leave to take the fresh air of the sea, with a page, whom I was very fond of, and who had sometimes been trusted with me. I shall never forget with what unwillingness Glumdalclitch consented, nor the strict charge she gave the page to be careful of me, bursting at the same time into a flood of tears, as if she had some forboding of what was to happen. The boy took me out in my box, about half an hours walk from the palace, towards the rocks on the sea-shore. I ordered him to set me down, and lifting up one of my sashes, cast many a wistful melancholy look towards the sea. I found myself not very well, and told the page that I had a mind to take a nap in my hammock, which I hoped would do me good. I got in, and the boy shut the window close down, to keep out the cold. I soon fell asleep, and all I can conjecture is, while I slept, the page, thinking no danger could happen, went among the rocks to look for birds' eggs, having before observed him from my window searching about, and picking up one or two in the clefts. Be that as it will, I found myself suddenly awaked with a violent pull upon the ring, which was fastened at the top of my box for the convenience of carriage. I felt my box raised very high in the air, and then borne forward with prodigious speed. The first jolt had like to have shaken me out of my hammock, but afterward the motion was easy enough. I called out several times, as loud as I could raise my voice, but all to no purpose. I looked towards my windows, and could see nothing but the clouds and sky. I heard a noise just over my head, like the clapping of wings, and then began to perceive the woeful condition I was in; that some eagle had got the ring of my box in his beak, with an intent to let it fall on a rock, like a tortoise in a shell, and then pick out my body, and devour it: for the sagacity and smell of this bird enables him to discover his quarry at a great distance, though better concealed than I could be within a two-inch board.

In a little time, I observed the noise and flutter of wings to increase very fast, and my box was tossed up and down, like a sign in a windy day. I heard several bangs or buffets, as I thought given to the eagle (for such I am certain it must have been that held the ring of my box in his beak), and then, all on a sudden, felt myself falling perpendicularly down, for above a minute, but with such incredible swiftness, that I almost lost my breath. My fall was stopped by a terrible squash, that sounded louder to my ears than the cataract of Niagara; after which, I was quite in the dark for another minute, and then my box began to rise so high, that I could see light from the tops of the windows. I now perceived I was fallen into the sea. My box, by the weight of my body, the goods that were in, and the broad plates of iron fixed for strength at the four corners of the top and bottom, floated about five feet deep in water. I did then, and do now suppose, that the eagle which flew away with my box was pursued by two or three others, and forced to let me drop, while he defended himself against the rest, who hoped to share in the prey. The plates of iron fastened at the bottom of the box (for those were the strongest) preserved the balance while it fell, and hindered it from being broken on the surface of the water. Every joint of it was well grooved; and the door did not move on hinges, but up and down like a sash, which kept my closet so tight that very little water came in. I got with much difficulty out of my hammock, having first ventured to draw back the slip-board on the roof already mentioned, contrived on purpose to let in air, for want of which I found myself almost stifled.

How often did I then wish myself with my dear Glumdalclitch, from whom one single hour had so far divided me! And I may say with truth, that in the midst of my own misfortunes I could not forbear lamenting my poor nurse, the grief she would suffer for my loss, the displeasure of the queen, and the ruin of her fortune. Perhaps many travellers have not been under greater difficulties and distress than I was at this juncture, expecting every moment to see my box dashed to pieces, or at least overset by the first violent blast, or rising wave. A breach in one single pane of glass would have been immediate death: nor could anything have preserved the windows, but the strong lattice wires placed on the outside, against accidents in travelling. I saw the water ooze in at several crannies, although the leaks were not considerable, and I endeavoured to stop them as well as I could. I was not able to lift up the roof of my closet, which otherwise I certainly should have done, and sat on the top of it; where I might at least preserve myself some hours longer, than by being shut up (as I may call it) in the hold. Or if I escaped these dangers for a day or two, what could I expect but a miserable death of cold and hunger? I was four hours under these circumstances, expecting, and indeed wishing, every moment to be my last.

I have already told the reader that there were two strong staples fixed upon that side of my box which had no window, and into which the servant, who used to carry me on horseback, would put a leather belt, and buckle it about his waist. Being in this disconsolate state, I heard, or at least thought I heard, some kind of grating noise on that side of my box where the staples were fixed; and soon after I began to fancy that the box was pulled or towed along the sea; for I now and then felt a sort of tugging, which made the waves rise near the tops of my windows, leaving me almost in the dark. This gave me some faint hopes of relief, although I was not able to imagine how it could be brought about. I ventured to unscrew one of my chairs, which were always fastened to the floor; and having made a hard shift to screw it down again, directly under the slipping-board that I had lately opened, I mounted on the chair, and putting my mouth as near as I could to the hole, I called for help in a loud voice, and in all the languages I understood. I then fastened my handkerchief to a stick I usually carried, and thrusting it up the hole, waved it several times in the air, that if any boat or ship were near, the seamen might conjecture some unhappy mortal to be shut up in the box.

I found no effect from all I could do, but plainly perceived my closet to be moved along; and in the space of an hour, or better, that side of the box where the staples were, and had no windows, struck against something that was hard. I apprehended it to be a rock, and found myself tossed more than ever. I plainly heard a noise upon the cover of my closet, like that of a cable, and the grating of it as it passed through the ring. I then found myself hoisted up, by degrees, at least three feet higher than I was before. Whereupon I again thrust up my stick and handkerchief, calling for help till I was almost hoarse. In return to which, I heard a great shout repeated three times, giving me such transports of joy as are not to be conceived but by those who feel them. I now heard a trampling over my head, and somebody calling through the hole with a loud voice, in the English tongue, "If there be any body below, let them speak." I answered, I was an Englishman, drawn by ill fortune into the greatest calamity that ever any creature underwent, and begged, by all that was moving, to be delivered out of the dungeon I was in. The voice replied, I was safe, for my box was fastened to their ship; and the carpenter should immediately come and saw a hole in the cover, large enough to pull me out. I answered, that was needless, and would take up too much time; for there was no more to be done, but let one of the crew put his finger into the ring, and take the box out of the sea into the ship, and so into the captain's cabin. Some of them, upon hearing me talk so wildly, thought I was mad; others laughed; for indeed it never came into my head, that I was now got among people of my own stature and strength. The carpenter came, and in a few minutes sawed a passage about four feet square, then let down a small ladder, upon which I mounted, and thence was taken into the ship in a very weak condition.

The sailors were all in amazement, and asked me a thousand questions, which I had no inclination to answer. I was equally confounded at the sight of so many pigmies, for such I took them to be, after having so long accustomed mine eyes to the monstrous objects I had left. But the captain, Mr. Thomas Wilcocks, an honest worthy Shropshire man, observing I was ready to faint, took me into his cabin, gave me a cordial to comfort me, and made me turn in upon his own bed, advising me to take a little rest, of which I had great need. Before I went to sleep, I gave him to understand that I had some valuable furniture in my box, too good to be lost: a fine hammock, a handsome field-bed, two chairs, a table, and a cabinet; that my closet was hung on all sides, or rather quilted, with silk and cotton; that if he would let one of the crew bring my closet into his cabin, I would open it there before him, and show him my goods. The captain, hearing me utter these absurdities, concluded I was raving; however (I suppose to pacify me) he promised to give order as I desired, and going upon deck, sent some of his men down into my closet, whence (as I afterwards found) they drew up all my goods, and stripped off the quilting; but the chairs, cabinet, and bedstead, being screwed to the floor, were much damaged by the ignorance of the seamen, who tore them up by force. Then they knocked off some of the boards for the use of the ship, and when they had got all they had a mind for, let the hull drop into the sea, which by reason of many breaches made in the bottom and sides, sunk to rights. And, indeed, I was glad not to have been a spectator of the havoc they made, because I am confident it would have sensibly touched me, by bringing former passages into my mind, which I would rather have forgot.

I slept some hours, but perpetually disturbed with dreams of the place I had left, and the dangers I had escaped. However, upon waking, I found myself much recovered. It was now about eight o'clock at night, and the captain ordered supper immediately, thinking I had already fasted too long. He entertained me with great kindness, observing me not to look wildly, or talk inconsistently; and, when we were left alone, desired I would give him a relation of my travels, and by what accident I came to be set adrift, in that monstrous wooden chest. He said that about twelve o'clock at noon, as he was looking through his glass, he spied it at a distance, and thought it was a sail, which he had a mind to make, being not much out of his course, in hopes of buying some biscuit, his own beginning to fall short. That upon coming nearer, and finding his error, he sent out his long-boat to discover what it was; that his men came back in a fright, swearing they had seen a swimming house. That he laughed at their folly, and went himself in the boat, ordering his men to take a strong cable along with them. That the weather being calm, he rowed round me several times, observed my windows and wire lattices that defended them. That he discovered two staples upon one side, which was all of boards, without any passage for light. He then commanded his men to row up to that side, and fastening a cable to one of the staples, ordered them to tow my chest, as they called it, toward the ship. When it was there, he gave directions to fasten another cable to the ring fixed in the cover, and to raise up my chest with pulleys, which all the sailors were not able to do above two or three feet. He said, they saw my stick and handkerchief thrust out of the hole, and concluded that some unhappy man must be shut up in the cavity. I asked, whether he or the crew had seen any prodigious birds in the air, about the time he first discovered me. To which he answered, that discoursing this matter with the sailors while I was asleep, one of them said, he had observed three eagles flying towards the north, but remarked nothing of their being larger than the usual size, which I suppose must be imputed to the great height they were at; and he could not guess the reason of my question. I then asked the captain, how far he reckoned we might be from land? He said, by the best computation he could make, we were at least a hundred leagues. I assured him, that he must be mistaken by almost half, for I had not left the country whence I came above two hours before I dropped into the sea. Whereupon he began again to think that my brain was disturbed, of which he gave me a hint, and advised me to go to bed in a cabin he had provided. I assured him, I was well refreshed with his good entertainment and company, and as much in my senses as ever I was in my life. He then grew serious, and desired to ask me freely whether I were not troubled in my mind by the consciousness of some enormous crime, for which I was punished, at the command of some prince, by exposing me in that chest; as great criminals, in other countries, have been forced to sea in a leaky vessel, without provisions; for although he should be sorry to have taken so ill a man into his ship, yet he would engage his word to set me safe ashore, in the first port where we arrived. He added, that his suspicions were much increased by some very absurd speeches I had delivered at first to his sailors, and afterwards to himself, in relation to my closet or chest, as well as by my odd looks and behaviour while I was at supper.

I begged his patience to hear me tell my story, which I faithfully did, from the last time I left England, to the moment he first discovered me. And, as truth always forces its way into rational minds, so this honest worthy gentleman, who had some tincture of learning, and very good sense, was immediately convinced of my candour and veracity. But further to confirm all I had said, I entreated him to give order that my cabinet should be brought, of which I had the key in my pocket; for he had already informed me how the seamen disposed of my closet. I opened it in his own presence, and showed him the small collection of rarities I made in the country from which I had been so strangely delivered. There was the comb I had contrived out of the stumps of the king's beard, and another of the same materials, but fixed into a paring of her Majesty's thumb-nail, which served for the back. There was a collection of needles and pins, from a foot to half a yard long; four wasp stings, like joiner's tacks; some combings of the queen's hair; a gold ring, which one day she made me a present of, in a most obliging manner, taking it from her little finger, and throwing it over my head like a collar. I desired the captain would please to accept this ring in return for his civilities; which he absolutely refused. I showed him a corn that I had cut off with my own hand, from a maid of honour's toe; it was about the bigness of Kentish pippin, and grown so hard, that when I returned England, I got it hollowed into a cup, and set in silver. Lastly, I desired him to see the breeches I had then on, which were made of a mouse's skin.

I could force nothing on him but a footman's tooth, which I observed him to examine with great curiosity, and found he had a fancy for it. He received it with abundance of thanks, more than such a trifle could deserve. It was drawn by an unskilful surgeon, in a mistake, from one of Glumdalclitch's men, who was afflicted with the tooth-ache, but it was as sound as any in his head. I got it cleaned, and put it into my cabinet. It was about a foot long, and four inches in diameter.

The captain was very well satisfied with this plain relation I had given him, and said, he hoped, when we returned to England, I would oblige the world by putting it on paper, and making it public. My answer was, that we were overstocked with books of travels: that nothing could now pass which was not extraordinary; wherein I doubted some authors less consulted truth, than their own vanity, or interest, or the diversion of ignorant readers; that my story could contain little beside common events, without those ornamental descriptions of strange plants, trees, birds, and other animals; or of the barbarous customs and idolatry of savage people, with which most writers abound. However, I thanked him for his good opinion, and promised to take the matter into my thoughts.

He said he wondered at one thing very much, which was, to hear me speak so loud; asking me whether the king or queen of that country were thick of hearing? I told him it was what I had been used to for above two years past, and that I admired as much at the voices of him and his men, who seemed to me only to whisper, and yet I could hear them well enough. But, when I spoke in that country, it was like a man talking in the streets, to another looking out from the top of a steeple, unless when I was placed on a table, or held in any person's hand. I told him, I had likewise observed another thing, that, when I first got into the ship, and the sailors stood all about me, I thought they were the most little contemptible creatures I had ever beheld. For indeed, while I was in that prince's country, I could never endure to look in a glass, after mine eyes had been accustomed to such prodigious objects, because the comparison gave me so despicable a conceit of myself. The captain said, that while we were at supper, he observed me to look at everything with a sort of wonder, and that I often seemed hardly able to contain my laughter, which he knew not well how to take, but imputed it to some disorder in my brain. I answered, it was very true; and I wondered how I could forbear, when I saw his dishes of the size of a silver three-pence, a leg of pork hardly a mouthful, a cup not as big as a nut-shell; and so I went on, describing the rest of his household-stuff and provisions, after the same manner. For, although the queen had ordered a little equipage of all things necessary for me, while I was in her service, yet my ideas were wholly taken up with what I saw on every side of me, and I winked at my own littleness, as people do at their own faults. The captain understood my raillery very well, and merrily replied with the old English proverb, that he doubted mine eyes were bigger than my belly, for he did not observe my stomach so good, although I had fasted all day; and, continuing in his mirth, protested he would have gladly given a hundred pounds, to have seen my closet in the eagle's bill, and afterwards in its fall from so great a height into the sea; which would certainly have been a most astonishing object, worthy to have the description of it transmitted to future ages; and the comparison of Phaeton was so obvious, that he could not forbear applying it, although I did not much admire the conceit.

The captain having been at Tonquin, was, in his return to England, driven north-eastward to the latitude of 44 degrees, and longitude of 143. But meeting a trade-wind two days after I came on board him, we sailed southward a long time, and coasting New Holland, kept our course west-south-west, and then south-south-west, till we doubled the Cape of Good Hope. Our voyage was very prosperous, but I shall not trouble the reader with a journal of it. The captain called in at one or two ports, and sent in his long-boat for provisions and fresh water; but I never went out of the ship till we came into the Downs, which was on the third day of June, 1706, about nine months after my escape. I offered to leave my goods in security for payment of my freight; but the captain protested he would not receive one farthing. We took a kind leave of each other, and I made him promise he would come to see me at my house in Redriff. I hired a horse and guide for five shillings, which I borrowed of the captain.

As I was on the road, observing the littleness of the houses, the trees, the cattle, and the people, I began to think myself in Lilliput. I was afraid of trampling on every traveller I met, and often called aloud to have them stand out of the way, so that I had like to have gotten one or two broken heads for my impertinence.

When I came to my own house, for which I was forced to inquire, one of the servants opening the door, I bent down to go in (like a goose under a gate), for fear of striking my head. My wife run out to embrace me, but I stooped lower than her knees, thinking she could otherwise never be able to reach my mouth. My daughter kneeled to ask my blessing, but I could not see her till she arose, having been so long used to stand with my head and eyes erect to above sixty feet; and then I went to take her up with one hand by the waist. I looked down upon the servants, and one or two friends who were in the house, as if they had been pigmies and I a giant. I told my wife, she had been too thrifty, for I found she had starved herself and her daughter to nothing. In short, I behaved myself so unaccountably, that they were all of the captain's opinion when he first saw me, and concluded I had lost my wits. This I mention as an instance of the great power of habit and prejudice.

In a little time, I and my family and friends came to a right understanding, but my wife protested I should never go to sea any more; although my evil destiny so ordered, that she had not power to hinder me, as the reader may know hereafter. In the meantime, I here conclude the second part of my unfortunate voyages.

Part III
A Voyage to Laputa, Balnibarbi, Luggnagg, Glubbdubdrib, and Japan

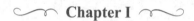

∽ **Chapter I** ∾

The author sets out on his third voyage. Is taken by pirates. The malice of a Dutchman. His arrival at an island. He is received into Laputa.

I had not been at home above ten days, when Captain William Robinson, a Cornish man, commander of the Hopewell, a stout ship of three hundred tons, came to my house. I had formerly been surgeon of another ship where he was master, and a fourth part owner, in a voyage to the Levant. He had always treated me more like a brother, than an inferior officer; and, hearing of my arrival, made me a visit, as I apprehended only out of friendship, for nothing passed more than what is usual after long absences. But repeating his visits often, expressing his joy to find I me in good health, asking whether I were now settled for life? adding that he intended a voyage to the East Indies in two months, at last he plainly invited me, though with some apologies, to be surgeon of the ship; that I should have another surgeon under me, beside our two mates; that my salary should be double to the usual pay; and that having experienced my knowledge in sea-affairs to be at least equal to his, he would enter into any engagement to follow my advice, as much as if I had shared in the command.

He said so many other obliging things, and I knew him to be so honest a man, that I could not reject this proposal; the thirst I had of seeing the world, notwithstanding my past misfortunes, continuing as violent as ever. The only difficulty that remained, was to persuade my wife, whose consent however I at last obtained, by the prospect of advantage she proposed to her children.

We set out the 5th day of August, 1706, and arrived at Fort St. George the 11th of April, 1707. We stayed there three weeks to refresh our crew, many of whom were sick. From thence we went to Tonquin, where the captain resolved to continue some time, because many of the goods he intended to buy were not ready, nor could he expect to be dispatched in several months. Therefore, in hopes to defray some of the charges he must be at, he bought a sloop, loaded it with several sorts of goods, wherewith the Tonquinese usually trade to the neighbouring islands, and putting fourteen men on board, whereof three were of the country, he appointed me master of the sloop, and gave me power to traffic, while he transacted his affairs at Tonquin.

We had not sailed above three days, when a great storm arising, we were driven five days to the north-north-east, and then to the east; after which we had fair weather, but still with a pretty strong gale from the west. Upon the tenth day we were chased by two pirates, who soon overtook us; for my sloop was so deep laden, that she sailed very slow, neither were we in a condition to defend ourselves.

We were boarded about the same time by both the pirates, who entered furiously at the head of their men; but finding us all prostrate upon our faces (for so I gave order), they pinioned us with strong ropes, and setting guard upon us, went to search the sloop.

I observed among them a Dutchman, who seemed to be of some authority, though he was not commander of either ship. He knew us by our countenances to be Englishmen, and jabbering to us in his own language, swore we should be tied back to back and thrown into the sea. I spoke Dutch tolerably well; I told him who we were, and begged him, in consideration of our being Christians and Protestants, of neighbouring countries in strict alliance, that he would move the captains to take some pity on us. This inflamed his rage; he repeated his threatenings, and turning to his companions, spoke with great vehemence in the Japanese language, as I suppose, often using the word Christianos.

The largest of the two pirate ships was commanded by a Japanese captain, who spoke a little Dutch, but very imperfectly. He came up to me, and after several questions, which I answered in great humility, he said, We should not die. I made the captain a very low bow, and then, turning to the Dutchman, said, I was sorry to find more mercy in a heathen, than in a brother Christian. But I had soon reason to repent those foolish words: for that malicious reprobate, having often endeavoured in vain to persuade both the captains that I might be thrown into the sea (which they would not yield to, after the promise made me that I should not die), however, prevailed so far, as to have a punishment inflicted on me, worse, in all human appearance, than death itself. My men were sent by an equal division into both the pirate ships, and my sloop new manned. As to myself, it was determined that I should be set adrift in a small canoe, with paddles and a sail, and four days' provisions; which last, the Japanese captain was so kind to double out of his own stores, and would permit no man to search me. I got down into the canoe, while the Dutchman, standing upon the deck, loaded me with all the curses and injurious terms his language could afford.

About an hour before we saw the pirates I had taken an observation, and found we were in the latitude of 46 N. and longitude of 183. When I was at some distance from the pirates, I discovered, by my pocket-glass, several islands to the south-east. I set up my sail, the wind being fair, with a design to reach the nearest of those islands, which I made a shift to do, in about three hours. It was all rocky; however I got many birds' eggs; and, striking fire, I kindled some heath and dry sea-weed, by which I roasted my eggs. I ate no other supper, being resolved to spare my provisions as much as I could. I passed the night under the shelter of a rock, strewing some heath under me, and slept pretty well.

The next day I sailed to another island, and thence to a third and fourth, sometimes using my sail, and sometimes my paddles. But, not to trouble the reader with a particular account of my distresses, let it suffice, that on the fifth day I arrived at the last island in my sight, which lay south-south-east to the former.

This island was at a greater distance than I expected, and I did not reach it in less than five hours. I encompassed it almost round, before I could find a convenient place to land in; which was a small creek, about three times the wideness of my canoe. I found the island to be all rocky, only a little intermingled with tufts of grass, and sweet-smelling herbs. I took out my small provisions and after having refreshed myself, I secured the remainder in a cave, whereof there were great numbers; I gathered plenty of eggs upon the rocks, and got a quantity of dry sea-weed, and parched grass, which I designed to kindle the next day, and roast my eggs as well as I could, for I had about me my flint, steel, match, and burning-glass. I lay all night in the cave where I had lodged my provisions. My bed was the same dry grass and sea-weed which I intended for fuel. I slept very little, for the disquiets of my mind prevailed over my weariness, and kept me awake. I considered how impossible it was to preserve my life in so desolate a place, and how miserable my end must be: yet found myself so listless and desponding, that I had not the heart to rise; and before I could get spirits enough to creep out of my cave, the day was far advanced. I walked awhile among the rocks; the sky was perfectly clear, and the sun so hot, that I was forced to turn my face from it; when all on a sudden it became obscure, as I thought, in a manner very different from what happens by the interposition of a cloud. I turned back, and perceived a vast opaque body between me and the sun moving forwards towards the island; it seemed to be about two miles high, and hid the sun six or seven minutes; but I did not observe the air to be much colder, or the sky more darkened, than if I had stood under the shade of a mountain. As it approached nearer over the place where I was, it appeared to be a firm substance, the bottom flat, smooth, and shining very bright, from the reflection of the sea below. I stood upon a height about two hundred yards from the shore, and saw this vast body descending almost to a parallel with me, at less than an English mile distance. I took out my pocket perspective, and could plainly discover numbers of people moving up and down the sides of it, which appeared to be sloping; but what those people were doing I was not able to distinguish.

The natural love of life gave me some inward motion of joy, and I was ready to entertain a hope that this adventure might, some way or other, help to deliver me from the desolate place and condition I was in. But at the same time the reader can hardly conceive my astonishment, to behold an island in the air, inhabited by men, who were able (as it should seem) to raise or sink, or put it into progressive motion, as they pleased. But not being at that time in a disposition to philosophise upon this phenomenon, I rather chose to observe what course the island would take, because it seemed for a while to stand still. Yet soon after, it advanced nearer, and I could see the sides of it encompassed with several gradations of galleries, and stairs, at certain intervals, to descend from one to the other. In the lowest gallery, I beheld some people fishing with long angling rods, and others looking on. I waved my cap (for my hat was long since worn out) and my handkerchief toward the island; and upon its nearer approach, I called and shouted with the utmost strength of my voice; and then looking circumspectly, I beheld a crowd gather to that side which was most in my view. I found by their pointing towards me and to each other, that they plainly discovered me, although they made no return to my shouting. But I could see four or five men running in great haste, up the stairs, to the top of the island, who then disappeared. I happened rightly to conjecture, that these were sent for orders to some person in authority upon this occasion.

The number of people increased, and, in less than half all hour, the island was moved and raised in such a manner, that the lowest gallery appeared in a parallel of less than a hundred yards distance from the height where I stood. I then put myself in the most supplicating posture, and spoke in the humblest accent, but received no answer. Those who stood nearest over against me, seemed to be persons of distinction, as I supposed by their habit. They conferred earnestly with each other, looking often upon me. At length one of them called out in a clear, polite, smooth dialect, not unlike in sound to the Italian: and therefore I returned an answer in that language, hoping at least that the cadence might be more agreeable to his ears. Although neither of us understood the other, yet my meaning was easily known, for the people saw the distress I was in.

They made signs for me to come down from the rock, and go towards the shore, which I accordingly did; and the flying island being raised to a convenient height, the verge directly over me, a chain was let down from the lowest gallery, with a seat fastened to the bottom, to which I fixed myself, and was drawn up by pulleys.

⁓ **Chapter II** ⁓

The humors and dispositions of the Laputians described. An account of their learning. Of the king and his court. The author's reception there. The inhabitants subject to fear and disquietudes. An account of the women.

At my alighting, I was surrounded with a crowd of people, but those who stood nearest seemed to be of better quality. They beheld me with all the marks and circumstances of wonder; neither indeed was I much in their debt, having never till then seen a race of mortals so singular in their shapes, habits, and countenances. Their heads were all reclined, either to the right, or the left; one of their eyes turned inward, and the other directly up to the zenith. Their outward garments were adorned with the figures of suns, moons, and stars; interwoven with those of fiddles, flutes, harps, trumpets, guitars, harpsichords, and many other instruments of music, unknown to us in Europe. I observed, here and there, many in the habit of servants, with a blown bladder, fastened like a flail to the end of a stick, which they carried in their hands. In each bladder was a small quantity of dried peas, or little pebbles, as I was afterwards informed. With these bladders, they now and then flapped the mouths and ears of those who stood near them, of which practice I could not then conceive the meaning. It seems the minds of these people are so taken up with intense speculations, that they neither can speak, nor attend to the discourses of others, without being roused by some external taction upon the organs of speech and hearing; for which reason, those persons who are able to afford it always keep a flapper (the original is climenole) in their family, as one of their domestics; nor ever walk abroad, or make visits, without him. And the business of this officer is, when two, three, or more persons are in company, gently to strike with his bladder the mouth of him who is to speak, and the right ear of him or them to whom the speaker addresses himself. This flapper is likewise employed diligently to attend his master in his walks, and upon occasion to give him a soft flap on his eyes; because he is always so wrapped up in cogitation, that he is in manifest danger of falling down every precipice, and bouncing his head against every post; and in the streets, of jostling others, or being jostled himself into the kennel.

It was necessary to give the reader this information, without which he would be at the same loss with me to understand the proceedings of these people, as they conducted me up the stairs to the top of the island, and from thence to the royal palace. While we were ascending, they forgot several times what they were about, and left me to myself, till their memories were again roused by their flappers; for they appeared altogether unmoved by the sight of my foreign habit and countenance, and by the shouts of the vulgar, whose thoughts and minds were more disengaged.

At last we entered the palace, and proceeded into the chamber of presence, where I saw the king seated on his throne, attended on each side by persons of prime quality. Before the throne, was a large table filled with globes and spheres, and mathematical instruments of all kinds. His Majesty took not the least notice of us, although our entrance was not without sufficient noise, by the concourse of all persons belonging to the court. But he was then deep in a problem; and we attended at least an hour, before he could solve it. There stood by him, on each side, a young page with flaps in their hands, and when they saw he was at leisure, one of them gently struck his mouth, and the other his right ear; at which he startled like one awaked on the sudden, and looking towards me and the company I was in, recollected the occasion of our coming, whereof he had been informed before. He spoke some words, whereupon immediately a young man with a flap came up to my side, and flapped me gently on the right ear; but I made signs, as well as I could, that I had no occasion for such an instrument; which, as I afterwards found, gave his Majesty, and the whole court, a very mean opinion of my understanding. The king, as far as I could conjecture, asked me several questions, and I addressed myself to him in all the languages I had. When it was found I could neither understand nor be understood, I was conducted by his order to an apartment in his palace (this prince being distinguished above all his predecessors for his hospitality to strangers), where two servants were appointed to attend me. My dinner was brought, and four persons of quality, whom I remembered to have seen very near the king's person, did me the honour to dine with me. We had two courses, of three dishes each. In the first course, there was a shoulder of mutton cut into an equilateral triangle, a piece of beef into a rhomboides, and a pudding into a cycloid. The second course was two ducks trussed up in the form of fiddles; sausages and puddings resembling flutes and hautboys, and a breast of veal in the shape of a harp. The servants cut our bread into cones, cylinders, parallelograms, and several other mathematical figures.

While we were at dinner, I made bold to ask the names of several things in their language, and those noble persons, by the assistance of their flappers, delighted to give me answers, hoping to raise my admiration of their great abilities if I could be brought to converse with them. I was soon able to call for bread and drink, or whatever else I wanted.

After dinner my company withdrew, and a person was sent to me by the king's order, attended by a flapper. He brought with him pen, ink, and paper, and three or four books, giving me to understand by signs that he was sent to teach me the language. We sat together four hours, in which time I wrote down a great number of words in columns, with the translations over against them; I likewise made a shift to learn several short sentences; for my tutor would order one of my servants to fetch something, to turn about, to make a bow, to sit, or to stand, or walk, and the like. Then I took down the sentence in writing. He showed me also, in one of his books, the figures of the sun, moon, and stars, the zodiac, the tropics, and polar circles, together with the denominations of many plains and solids. He gave me the names and descriptions of all the musical instruments, and the general terms of art in playing on each of them. After he had left me, I placed all my words, with their interpretations, in alphabetical order. And thus, in a few days, by the help of a very faithful memory, I got some insight into their language. The word, which I interpret the flying or floating island, is in the original Laputa, whereof I could never learn the true etymology. *Lap*, in the old obsolete language, signifies high; and *untuh*, a governor; from which they say, by corruption, was derived *Laputa*, from *Lapuntuh*. But I do not approve of this derivation, which seems to be a little strained. I ventured to offer to the learned among them a conjecture of my own, that *Laputa* was *quasi lap outed*; *lap*, signifying properly, the dancing of the sunbeams in the sea, and outed, a wing; which, however, I shall not obtrude, but submit to the judicious reader.

Those to whom the king had entrusted me, observing how ill I was clad, ordered a tailor to come next morning, and take measure for a suit of clothes. This operator did his office after a different manner from those of his trade in Europe. He first took my altitude by a quadrant, and then, with a rule and compasses, described the dimensions and outlines of my whole body, all which he entered upon paper; and in six days brought my clothes very ill made, and quite out of shape, by happening to mistake a figure in the calculation. But my comfort was, that I observed such accidents very frequent, and little regarded.

During my confinement for want of clothes, and by an indisposition that held me some days longer, I much enlarged my dictionary; and when I went next to court, was able to understand many things the king spoke, and to return him some kind of answers. His Majesty had given orders, that the island should move north-east and by east, to the vertical point over Lagado, the metropolis of the whole kingdom below, upon the firm earth. It was about ninety leagues distant, and our voyage lasted four days and a half. I was not in the least sensible of the progressive motion made in the air by the island. On the second morning, about eleven o'clock, the king himself in person, attended by his nobility, courtiers, and officers, having prepared all their musical instruments, played on them for three hours without intermission, so that I was quite stunned with the noise; neither could I possibly guess the meaning, till my tutor informed me. He said that, the people of their island had their ears adapted to hear the music of the spheres, which always played at certain periods, and the court was now prepared to bear their part, in whatever instrument they most excelled.

In our journey towards Lagado, the capital city, his Majesty ordered that the island should stop over certain towns and villages, from whence he might receive the petitions of his subjects. And to this purpose, several packthreads were let down, with small weights at the bottom. On these packthreads the people strung their petitions, which mounted up directly, like the scraps of paper fastened by school boys at the end of the string that holds their kite. Sometimes we received wine and victuals from below, which were drawn up by pulleys.

The knowledge I had in mathematics, gave me great assistance in acquiring their phraseology, which depended much upon that science, and music; and in the latter I was not unskilled. Their ideas are perpetually conversant in lines and figures. If they would, for example, praise the beauty of a woman, or any other animal, they describe it by rhombs, circles, parallelograms, ellipses, and other geometrical terms, or by words of art drawn from music, needless here to repeat. I observed in the king's kitchen all sorts of mathematical and musical instruments, after the figures of which they cut up the joints that were served to his Majesty's table.

Their houses are very ill built, the walls bevil without one right angle in any apartment; and this defect arises from the contempt they bear to practical geometry, which they despise as vulgar and mechanic; those instructions they give being too refined for the intellects of their workmen, which occasions perpetual mistakes. And although they are dexterous enough upon a piece of paper, in the management of the rule, the pencil, and the divider, yet in the common actions and behaviour of life, I have not seen a more clumsy, awkward, and unhandy people, nor so slow and perplexed in their conceptions upon all other subjects, except those of mathematics and music. They are very bad reasoners, and vehemently given to opposition, unless when they happen to be of the right opinion, which is seldom their case. Imagination, fancy, and invention, they are wholly strangers to, nor have any words in their language, by which those ideas can be expressed; the whole compass of their thoughts and mind being shut up within the two forementioned sciences.

Most of them, and especially those who deal in the astronomical part, have great faith in judicial astrology, although they are ashamed to own it publicly. But what I chiefly admired, and thought altogether unaccountable, was the strong disposition I observed in them towards news and politics, perpetually inquiring into public affairs, giving their judgments in matters of state, and passionately disputing every inch of a party opinion. I have indeed observed the same disposition among most of the mathematicians I have known in Europe, although I could never discover the least analogy between the two sciences; unless those people suppose, that because the smallest circle has as many degrees as the largest, therefore the regulation and management of the world require no more abilities than the handling and turning of a globe; but I rather take this quality to spring from a very common infirmity of human nature, inclining us to be most curious and conceited in matters where we have least concern, and for which we are least adapted by study or nature.

These people are under continual disquietudes, never enjoying a minute's peace of mind; and their disturbances proceed from causes which very little affect the rest of mortals. Their apprehensions arise from several changes they dread in the celestial bodies: for instance, that the earth, by the continual approaches of the sun towards it, must, in course of time, be absorbed, or swallowed up; that the face of the sun, will, by degrees, be encrusted with its own effluvia, and give no more light to the world; that the earth very narrowly escaped a brush from the tail of the last comet, which would have infallibly reduced it to ashes; and that the next, which they have calculated for one-and-thirty years hence, will probably destroy us. For if, in its perihelion, it should approach within a certain degree of the sun (as by their calculations they have reason to dread) it will receive a degree of heat ten thousand times more intense than that of red hot glowing iron, and in its absence from the sun, carry a blazing tail ten hundred thousand and fourteen miles long, through which, if the earth should pass at the distance of one hundred thousand miles from the nucleus, or main body of the comet, it must in its passage be set on fire, and reduced to ashes; that the sun, daily spending its rays without any nutriment to supply them, will at last be wholly consumed and annihilated; which must be attended with the destruction of this earth, and of all the planets that receive their light from it.

They are so perpetually alarmed with the apprehensions of these, and the like impending dangers, that they can neither sleep quietly in their beds, nor have any relish for the common pleasures and amusements of life. When they meet an acquaintance in the morning, the first question is about the sun's health, how he looked at his setting and rising, and what hopes they have to avoid the stroke of the approaching comet. This conversation they are apt to run into with the same temper that boys discover in delighting to hear terrible stories of spirits and hobgoblins, which they greedily listen to, and dare not go to bed for fear.

The women of the island have abundance of vivacity; they, contemn their husbands, and are exceedingly fond of strangers, whereof there is always a considerable number from the continent below, attending at court, either upon affairs of the several towns and corporations, or their own particular occasions, but are much despised, because they want the same endowments. Among these the ladies choose their gallants. But the vexation is, that they act with too much ease and security; for the husband is always so wrapped in speculation, that the mistress and lover may proceed to the greatest familiarities before his face, if he be but provided with paper and implements, and without his flapper at his side.

The wives and daughters lament their confinement to the island, although I think it the most delicious spot of ground in the world; and although they live here in the greatest plenty and magnificence, and are allowed to do whatever they please, they long to see the world, and take the diversions of the metropolis, which they are not allowed to do without a particular license from the king; and this is not easy to be obtained, because the people of quality have found, by frequent experience, how hard it is to persuade their women to return from below. I was told that a great court lady, who had several children, is married to the prime minister (the richest subject in the kingdom, a very graceful person, extremely fond of her) and lives in the finest palace of the island, went down to Lagado, on the pretense of health, there hid herself for several months, till the king sent a warrant to search for her; and she was found in an obscure eating-house all in rags, having pawned her clothes to maintain an old deformed footman, who beat her every day, and in whose company she was taken, much against her will. And although her husband received her with all possible kindness, and without the least reproach, she soon after contrived to steal down again, with all her jewels, to the same gallant, and has not been heard of since.

This may perhaps pass with the reader rather for a European or English story, than for one of a country so remote. But he may please to consider, that the caprices of womankind are not limited by any climate or nation, and that they are much more uniform, than can be easily imagined.

In about a month's time, I had made a tolerable proficiency in their language, and was able to answer most of the king's questions, when I had the honour to attend him. His Majesty discovered not the least curiosity to inquire into the laws, government, history, religion, or manners of the countries where I had been; but confined his questions to the state of mathematics, and received the account I gave him with great contempt and indifference, though often roused by his flapper on each side.

∽ **Chapter III** ∾

A phenomenon solved by modern philosophy and astronomy. The Laputians' great improvements in the latter. The king's method of suppressing insurrections.

I desired leave of this prince to see the curiosities of the island, which he was graciously pleased to grant, and ordered my tutor to attend me. I chiefly wanted to know, to what cause, in art or in nature, it owed its several motions, whereof I will now give a philosophical account to the reader.

The flying or floating island is exactly circular, its diameter 7837 yards, or about four miles and a half, and consequently contains ten thousand acres. It is three hundred yards thick. The bottom, or under surface, which appears to those who view it below, is one even regular plate of adamant, shooting up to the height of about two hundred yards. Above it lie the several minerals in their usual order, and overall is a coat of rich mould, ten or twelve feet deep. The declivity of the upper surface, from the circumference to the centre, is the natural cause why all the dews and rains, which fall upon the island, are conveyed in small rivulets toward the middle, where they are emptied into four large basins, each of about half a mile in circuit, and two hundred yards distant from the centre. From these basins the water is continually exhaled by the sun in the daytime, which effectually prevents their overflowing. Besides, as it is in the power of the monarch to raise the island above the region of clouds and vapours, he can prevent the falling of dews and rain whenever he pleases. For the highest clouds cannot rise above two miles, as naturalists agree, at least they were never known to do so in that country.

At the centre of the island there is a chasm about fifty yards in diameter, whence the astronomers descend into a large dome, which is therefore called *flandona gagnole*, or the *astronomer's cave*, situated at the depth of a hundred yards beneath the upper surface of the adamant. In this cave are twenty lamps continually burning, which from the reflection of the adamant, cast a strong light into every part. The place is stored with great variety of sextants, quadrants, telescopes, astrolabes, and other astronomical instruments. But the greatest curiosity, upon which the fate of the island depends, is a loadstone of a prodigious size, in shape resembling a weaver's shuttle. It is in length six yards, and in the thickest part at least three yards over. This magnet is sustained by a very strong axle of adamant passing through its middle, upon which it plays, and is poised so exactly that the weakest hand can turn it. It is hooped round with a hollow cylinder of adamant, four feet yards in diameter, placed horizontally, and supported by eight adamantine feet, each six yards high. In the middle of the concave side, there is a groove twelve inches deep, in which the extremities of the axle are lodged, and turned round as there is occasion.

The stone cannot be removed from its place by any force, because the hoop and its feet are one continued piece with that body of adamant which constitutes the bottom of the island.

By means of this loadstone, the island is made to rise and fall, and move from one place to another. For, with respect to that part of the earth over which the monarch presides, the stone is endued at one of its sides with an attractive power, and at the other with a repulsive. Upon placing the magnet erect, with its attracting end towards the earth, the island descends; but when the repelling extremity points downwards, the island mounts directly upwards. When the position of the stone is oblique, the motion of the island is so too: for in this magnet, the forces always act in lines parallel to its direction.

By this oblique motion, the island is conveyed to different parts of the monarch's dominions. To explain the manner of its progress, let $A\ B$ represent a line drawn across the dominions of Balnibarbi, let the line $c\ d$ represent the loadstone, of which let d be the repelling end, and c the attracting end, the island being over C; let the stone be placed in position $c\ d$, with its repelling end downwards; then the island will be driven upwards obliquely towards D. When it is arrived at D, let the stone be turned upon its axle, till its attracting end points towards E, and then the island will be carried obliquely towards E; where, if the stone be again turned upon its axle till it stands in the position $E\ F$, with its repelling point downwards, the island will rise obliquely towards F, where, by directing the attracting end towards G, the island may be carried to G, and from G to H, by turning the stone, so as to make its repelling extremity to point directly downward. And thus, by changing the situation of the stone, as often as there is occasion, the island is made to rise and fall by turns in an oblique direction, and by those alternate risings and fallings (the obliquity being not considerable) is conveyed from one part of the dominions to the other.

But it must be observed, that this island cannot move beyond the extent of the dominions below, nor can it rise above the height of four miles. For which the astronomers (who have written large systems concerning the stone) assign the following reason: that the magnetic virtue does not extend beyond the distance of four miles, and that the mineral, which acts upon the stone in the bowels of the earth, and in the sea about six leagues distant from the shore, is not diffused through the whole globe, but terminated with the limits of the king's dominions; and it was easy, from the great advantage of such a superior situation, for a prince to bring under his obedience whatever country lay within the attraction of that magnet.

When the stone is put parallel to the plane of the horizon, the island stands still; for in that case the extremities of it, being at equal distance from the earth, act with equal force, the one in drawing downwards, the other in pushing upwards, and consequently no motion can ensue.

This loadstone is under the care of certain astronomers, who, from time to time, give it such positions as the monarch directs. They spend the greatest part of their lives in observing the celestial bodies, which they do by the assistance of glasses, far excelling ours in goodness. For, although their largest telescopes do not exceed three feet, they magnify much more than those of a hundred with us, and show the stars with greater clearness. This advantage has enabled them to extend their discoveries much further than our astronomers in Europe; for they have made a catalogue of ten thousand fixed stars, whereas the largest of ours do not contain above one third part of that number. They have likewise discovered two lesser stars, or satellites, which revolve about Mars; whereof the innermost is distant from the centre of the primary planet exactly three of his diameters, and the outermost, five; the former revolves in the space of ten hours, and the latter in twenty-one and a half; so that the squares of their periodical times are very near in the same proportion with the cubes of their distance from the centre of Mars; which evidently shows them to be governed by the same law of gravitation that influences the other heavenly bodies.

They have observed ninety-three different comets, and settled their periods with great exactness. If this be true (and they affirm it with great confidence) it is much to be wished, that their observations were made public, whereby the theory of comets, which at present is very lame and defective, might be brought to the same perfection with other parts of astronomy.

The king would be the most absolute prince in the universe, if he could but prevail on a ministry to join with him; but these having their estates below on the continent, and considering that the office of a favourite has a very uncertain tenure, would never consent to the enslaving of their country.

If any town should engage in rebellion or mutiny, fall into violent factions, or refuse to pay the usual tribute, the king has two methods of reducing them to obedience. The first and the mildest course is, by keeping the island hovering over such a town, and the lands about it, whereby he can deprive them of the benefit of the sun and the rain, and consequently afflict the inhabitants with dearth and diseases. And if the crime deserve it, they are at the same time pelted from above with great stones, against which they have no defence but by creeping into cellars or caves, while the roofs of their houses are beaten to pieces. But if they still continue obstinate, or offer to raise insurrections, he proceeds to the last remedy, by letting the island drop directly upon their heads, which makes a universal destruction both of houses and men. However, this is an extremity to which the prince is seldom driven, neither indeed is he willing to put it in execution; nor dare his ministers advise him to an action, which, as it would render them odious to the people, so it would be a great damage to their own estates, which all lie below; for the island is the king's demesne.

But there is still indeed a more weighty reason, why the kings of this country have been always averse from executing so terrible an action, unless upon the utmost necessity. For, if the town intended to be destroyed should have in it any tall rocks, as it generally falls out in the larger cities, a situation probably chosen at first with a view to prevent such a catastrophe; or if it abound in high spires, or pillars of stone, a sudden fall might endanger the bottom or under surface of the island, which, although it consist, as I have said, of one entire adamant, two hundred yards thick, might happen to crack by too great a shock, or burst by approaching too near the fires from the houses below, as the backs, both of iron and stone, will often do in our chimneys. Of all this the people are well apprised, and understand how far to carry their obstinacy, where their liberty or property is concerned. And the king, when he is highest provoked, and most determined to press a city to rubbish, orders the island to descend with great gentleness, out of a pretence of tenderness to his people, but, indeed, for fear of breaking the adamantine bottom; in which case, it is the opinion of all their philosophers, that the loadstone could no longer hold it up, and the whole mass would fall to the ground.

By a fundamental law of this realm, neither the king, nor either of his two eldest sons, are permitted to leave the island; nor the queen, till she is past child-bearing.

⌒ Chapter IV ⌒

The author leaves Laputa; is conveyed to Balnibarbi; arrives at the metropolis. A description of the metropolis, and the country adjoining. The author hospitably received by a great lord. His conversation with that lord.

Although I cannot say that I was ill-treated in this island, yet I must confess I thought myself too much neglected, not without some degree of contempt; for neither prince nor people appeared to be curious in any part of knowledge, except mathematics and music, wherein I was far their inferior, and upon that account very little regarded.

On the other side, after having seen all the curiosities of the island, I was very desirous to leave it, being heartily weary of those people. They were indeed excellent in two sciences for which I have great esteem, and wherein I am not unversed; but, at the same time, so abstracted and involved in speculation, that I never met with such disagreeable companions. I conversed only with women, tradesmen, flappers, and court-pages, during two months of my abode there; by which, at last, I rendered myself extremely contemptible; yet these were the only people from whom I could ever receive a reasonable answer.

I had obtained, by hard study, a good degree of knowledge in their language; I was weary of being confined to an island where I received so little countenance, and resolved to leave it with the first opportunity.

There was a great lord at court, nearly related to the king, and for that reason alone used with respect. He was universally reckoned the most ignorant and stupid person among them. He had performed many eminent services for the crown, had great natural and acquired parts, adorned with integrity and honour; but so ill an ear for music, that his detractors reported, he had been often known to beat time in the wrong place; neither could his tutors, without extreme difficulty, teach him to demonstrate the most easy proposition in the mathematics. He was pleased to show me many marks of favour, often did me the honour of a visit, desired to be informed in the affairs of Europe, the laws and customs, the manners and learning of the several countries where I had travelled. He listened to me with great attention, and made very wise observations on all I spoke. He had two flappers attending him for state, but never made use of them, except at court and in visits of ceremony, and would always command them to withdraw, when we were alone together.

I entreated this illustrious person, to intercede in my behalf with his Majesty, for leave to depart; which he accordingly did, as he was pleased to tell me, with regret: for indeed he had made me several offers very advantageous, which, however, I refused, with expressions of the highest acknowledgment.

On the 16th of February I took leave of his Majesty and the court. The king made me a present to the value of about two hundred pounds English, and my protector, his kinsman, as much more, together with a letter of recommendation to a friend of his in Lagado, the metropolis. The island being then hovering over a mountain about two miles from it, I was let down from the lowest gallery, in the same manner as I had been taken up.

The continent, as far as it is subject to the monarch of the flying island, passes under the general name of *Balnibarbi*; and the metropolis, as I said before, is called *Lagado*. I felt some little satisfaction in finding myself on firm ground. I walked to the city without any concern, being clad like one of the natives, and sufficiently instructed to converse with them. I soon found out the person's house to whom I was recommended, presented my letter from his friend the grandee in the island, and was received with much kindness. This great lord, whose name was Munodi, ordered me an apartment in his own house, where I continued during my stay, and was entertained in a most hospitable manner.

The next morning after my arrival, he took me in his chariot to see the town, which is about half the bigness of London; but the houses very strangely built, and most of them out of repair. The people in the streets walked fast, looked wild, their eyes fixed, and were generally in rags. We passed through one of the town gates, and went about three miles into the country, where I saw many labourers working with several sorts of tools in the ground, but was not able to conjecture what they were about; neither did observe any expectation either of corn or grass, although the soil appeared to be excellent. I could not forbear admiring at these odd appearances, both in town and country; and I made bold to desire my conductor, that he would be pleased to explain to me, what could be meant by so many busy heads, hands, and faces, both in the streets and the fields, because I did not discover any good effects they produced; but, on the contrary, I never knew a soil so unhappily cultivated, houses so ill contrived and so ruinous, or a people whose countenances and habit expressed so much misery and want.

This lord Munodi was a person of the first rank, and had been some year's governor of Lagado; but, by a cabal of ministers, was discharged for insufficiency. However, the king treated him with tenderness, as a well-meaning man, but of a low contemptible understanding.

When I gave that free censure of the country and its inhabitants, he made no further answer than by telling me, that I had not been long enough among them to form a judgment; and that the different nations of the world had different customs; with other common topics to the same purpose. But, when we returned to his palace, he asked me how I liked the building, what absurdities I observed, and what quarrel I had with the dress or looks of his domestics? This he might safely do; because everything about him was magnificent, regular, and polite. I answered, that his excellency's prudence, quality, and fortune, had exempted him from those defects, which folly and beggary had produced in others. He said, if I would go with him to his country-house, about twenty miles distant, where his estate lay, there would be more leisure for this kind of conversation. I told his Excellency that I was entirely at his disposal; and accordingly we set out next morning.

During our journey he made me observe the several methods used by farmers in managing their lands, which to me were wholly unaccountable; for, except in some very few places, I could not discover one ear of corn or blade of grass. But, in three hours travelling, the scene was wholly altered; we came into a most beautiful country; farmers' houses, at small distances, neatly built; the fields enclosed, containing vineyards, corn-grounds, and meadows. Neither do I remember to have seen a more delightful prospect. His excellency observed my countenance to clear up; he told me, with a sigh, that there his estate began, and would continue the same, till we should come to his house; that his countrymen ridiculed and despised him, for managing his affairs no better, and for setting so ill an example to the kingdom; which, however, was followed by very few, such as were old, and wilful, and weak like himself.

We came at length to the house, which was indeed a noble structure, built according to the best rules of ancient architecture. The fountains, gardens, walks, avenues, and groves, were all disposed with exact judgment and taste. I gave due praises to everything I saw, whereof his excellency took not the least notice till after supper; when, there being no third companion, he told me with a very melancholy air that he doubted he must throw down his houses in town and country, to rebuild them after the present mode; destroy all his plantations, and cast others into such a form as modern usage required, and give the same directions to all his tenants, unless he would submit to incur the censure of pride, singularity, affectation, ignorance, caprice, and perhaps increase his Majesty's displeasure; that the admiration I appeared to be under would cease or diminish, when he had informed me of some particulars which, probably, I never heard of at court, the people there being too much taken up in their own speculations, to have regard to what passed here below.

The sum of his discourse was to this effect: That about forty years ago, certain persons went up to Laputa, either upon business or diversion, and, after five months continuance, came back with a very little smattering in mathematics, but full of volatile spirits acquired in that airy region. That these persons, upon their return, began to dislike the management of everything below, and fell into schemes of putting all arts, sciences, languages, and mechanics, upon a new foot. To this end, they procured a royal patent for erecting an academy of projectors in Lagado; and the humour prevailed so strongly among the people, that there is not a town of any consequence in the kingdom without such an academy. In these colleges the professors contrive new rules and methods of agriculture and building, and new instruments, and tools for all trades and manufactures; whereby, as they undertake, one man shall do the work of ten; a palace may be built in a week, of materials so durable as to last forever without repairing. All the fruits of the earth shall come to maturity at whatever season we think fit to choose, and increase a hundred fold more than they do at present; with innumerable other happy proposals. The only inconvenience is, that none of these projects are yet brought to perfection; and in the meantime, the whole country lies miserably waste, the houses in ruins, and the people without food or clothes. By all which, instead of being discouraged, they are fifty times more violently bent upon prosecuting their schemes, driven equally on by hope and despair; that as for himself, being not of an enterprising spirit, he was content to go on in the old forms, to live in the houses his ancestors had built, and act as they did, in every part of life, without innovation. That some few other persons of quality and gentry had done the same, but were looked on with an eye of contempt and ill-will, as enemies to art, ignorant, and ill common-wealth's men, preferring their own ease and sloth before the general improvement of their country.

His lordship added, that he would not, by any further particulars, prevent the pleasure I should certainly take in viewing the grand academy, whither he was resolved I should go. He only desired me to observe a ruined building, upon the side of a mountain about three miles distant, of which he gave me this account: That he had a very convenient mill within half a mile of his house, turned by a current from a large river, and sufficient for his own family, as well as a great number of his tenants; that about seven years ago, a club of those projectors came to him with proposals to destroy this mill, and build another on the side of that mountain, on the long ridge whereof a long canal must be cut, for a repository of water, to be conveyed up by pipes and engines to supply the mill, because the wind and air upon a height agitated the water, and thereby made it fitter for motion, and because the water, descending down a declivity, would turn the mill with half the current of a river whose course is more upon a level. He said, that being then not very well with the court, and pressed by many of his friends, he complied with the proposal; and after employing a hundred men for two years, the work miscarried, the projectors went off, laying the blame entirely upon him, railing at him ever since, and putting others upon the same experiment, with equal assurance of success, as well as equal disappointment.

In a few days we came back to town; and his excellency, considering the bad character he had in the academy, would not go with me himself, but recommended me to a friend of his, to bear me company thither. My lord was pleased to represent me as a great admirer of projects, and a person of much curiosity and easy belief; which, indeed, was not without truth; for I had myself been a sort of projector in my younger days.

∽ Chapter V ∽

The author permitted to see the grand academy of Lagado. The academy largely described. The arts wherein the professors employ themselves.

This academy is not an entire single building, but a continuation of several houses on both sides of a street, which growing waste, was purchased and applied to that use.

I was received very kindly by the warden, and went for many days to the academy. Every room has in it one or more projectors; and I believe I could not be in fewer than five hundred rooms.

The first man I saw was of a meagre aspect, with sooty hands and face, his hair and beard long, ragged, and singed in several places. His clothes, shirt, and skin, were all of the same colour. He has been eight years upon a project for extracting sunbeams out of cucumbers, which were to be put in phials hermetically sealed, and let out to warm the air in raw inclement summers. He told me, he did not doubt, that, in eight years more, he should be able to supply the governor's gardens with sunshine, at a reasonable rate; but he complained that his stock was low, and entreated me to give him something as an encouragement to ingenuity, especially since this had been a very dear season for cucumbers. I made him a small present, for my lord had furnished me with money on purpose, because he knew their practice of begging from all who go to see them.

I went into another chamber, but was ready to hasten back, being almost overcome with a horrible stink. My conductor pressed me forward, conjuring me in a whisper to give no offence, which would be highly resented; and therefore I durst not so much as stop my nose. The projector of this cell was the most ancient student of the academy; his face and beard were of a pale yellow; his hands and clothes daubed over with filth. When I was presented to him, he gave me a close embrace, a compliment I could well have excused. His employment, from his first coming into the academy, was an operation to reduce human excrement to its original food, by separating the several parts, removing the tincture which it receives from the gall, making the odour exhale, and scumming off the saliva. He had a weekly allowance, from the society, of a vessel filled with human ordure, about the bigness of a Bristol barrel.

I saw another at work to calcine ice into gunpowder; who likewise showed me a treatise he had written concerning the malleability of fire, which he intended to publish.

There was a most ingenious architect, who had contrived a new method for building houses, by beginning at the roof, and working downward to the foundation; which he justified to me, by the like practice of those two prudent insects, the bee and the spider.

There was a man born blind, who had several apprentices in his own condition: their employment was to mix colours for painters, which their master taught them to distinguish by feeling and smelling. It was indeed my misfortune to find them at that time not very perfect in their lessons, and the professor himself happened to be generally mistaken. This artist is much encouraged and esteemed by the whole fraternity.

In another apartment I was highly pleased with a projector who had found a device of ploughing the ground with hogs, to save the charges of ploughs, cattle, and labour. The method is this: in an acre of ground you bury, at six inches distance and eight deep, a quantity of acorns, dates, chestnuts, and other mast or vegetables, whereof these animals are fondest; then you drive six hundred or more of them into the field, where, in a few days, they will root up the whole ground in search of their food, and make it fit for sowing, at the same time manuring it with their dung. It is true, upon experiment, they found the charge and trouble very great, and they had little or no crop. However it is not doubted, that this invention may be capable of great improvement.

I went into another room, where the walls and ceiling were all hung round with cobwebs, except a narrow passage for the artist to go in and out. At my entrance, he called aloud to me not to disturb his webs. He lamented the fatal mistake the world had been so long in, of using silkworms, while we had such plenty of domestic insects who infinitely excelled the former, because they understood how to weave, as well as spin. And he proposed further, that by employing spiders, the charge of dyeing silks should be wholly saved; whereof I was fully convinced, when he showed me a vast number of flies most beautifully coloured, wherewith he fed his spiders, assuring us that the webs would take a tincture from them; and as he had them of all hues, he hoped to fit everybody's fancy, as soon as he could find proper food for the flies, of certain gums, oils, and other glutinous matter, to give a strength and consistence to the threads.

There was an astronomer, who had undertaken to place a sun-dial upon the great weathercock on the town-house, by adjusting the annual and diurnal motions of the earth and sun, so as to answer and coincide with all accidental turnings of the wind.

I was complaining of a small fit of the colic, upon which my conductor led me into a room where a great physician resided, who was famous for curing that disease, by contrary operations from the same instrument. He had a large pair of bellows, with a long slender muzzle of ivory. This he conveyed eight inches up the anus, and drawing in the wind, he affirmed he could make the guts as lank as a dried bladder. But when the disease was more stubborn and violent, he let in the muzzle while the bellows were full of wind, which he discharged into the body of the patient; then withdrew the instrument to replenish it, clapping his thumb strongly against the orifice of then fundament; and this being repeated three or four times, the adventitious wind would rush out, bringing the noxious along with it (like water put into a pump), and the patient recovered. I saw him try both experiments upon a dog, but could not discern any effect from the former. After the latter the animal was ready to burst, and made so violent a discharge as was very offensive to me and my companion. The dog died on the spot, and we left the doctor endeavouring to recover him, by the same operation.

I visited many other apartments, but shall not trouble my reader with all the curiosities I observed, being studious of brevity.

I had hitherto seen only one side of the academy, the other being appropriated to the advancers of speculative learning, of whom I shall say something, when I have mentioned one illustrious person more, who is called among them *the universal artist*. He told us he had been thirty years employing his thoughts for the improvement of human life. He had two large rooms full of wonderful curiosities, and fifty men at work. Some were condensing air into a dry tangible substance, by extracting the nitre, and letting the aqueous or fluid particles percolate; others softening marble, for pillows and pin-cushions; others petrifying the hoofs of a living horse, to preserve them from foundering. The artist himself was at that time busy upon two great designs; the first, to sow land with chaff, wherein he affirmed the true seminal virtue to be contained, as he demonstrated by several experiments, which I was not skilful enough to comprehend. The other was, by a certain composition of gums, minerals, and vegetables, outwardly applied, to prevent the growth of wool upon two young lambs; and he hoped, in a reasonable time to propagate the breed of naked sheep, all over the kingdom.

We crossed a walk to the other part of the academy, where, as I have already said, the projectors in speculative learning resided.

The first professor I saw, was in a very large room, with forty pupils about him. After salutation, observing me to look earnestly upon a frame, which took up the greatest part of both the length and breadth of the room, he said, Perhaps I might wonder to see him employed in a project for improving speculative knowledge, by practical and mechanical operations. But the world would soon be sensible of its usefulness; and he flattered himself, that a more noble, exalted thought never sprang in any other man's head. Everyone knew how laborious the usual method is of attaining to arts and sciences; whereas, by his contrivance, the most ignorant person, at a reasonable charge, and with a little bodily labour, might write books in philosophy, poetry, politics, laws, mathematics, and theology, without the least assistance from genius or study. He then led me to the frame, about the sides, whereof all his pupils stood in ranks. It was twenty feet square, placed in the middle of the room. The superficies was composed of several bits of wood, about the bigness of a die, but some larger than others. They were all linked together by slender wires. These bits of wood were covered, on every square, with paper pasted on them; and on these papers were written all the words of their language, in their several moods, tenses, and declensions; but without any order. The professor then desired me to observe; for he was going to set his engine at work. The pupils, at his command, took each of them hold of an iron handle, whereof there were forty fixed round the edges of the frame; and giving them a sudden turn, the whole disposition of the words was entirely changed. He then commanded six-and-thirty of the lads, to read the several lines softly, as they appeared upon the frame; and where they found three or four words together that might make part of a sentence, they dictated to the four remaining boys, who were scribes. This work was repeated three or four times, and at every turn, the engine was so contrived, that the words shifted into new places, as the square bits of wood moved upside down.

Six hours a day the young students were employed in this labour; and the professor showed me several volumes in large folio, already collected, of broken sentences, which he intended to piece together, and out of those rich materials, to give the world a complete body of all arts and sciences; which, however, might be still improved, and much expedited, if the public would raise a fund for making and employing five hundred such frames in Lagado, and oblige the managers to contribute in common their several collections.

He assured me that this invention had employed all his thoughts from his youth; that he had emptied the whole vocabulary into his frame, and made the strictest computation of the general proportion there is in books between the numbers of particles, nouns, and verbs, and other parts of speech.

I made my humblest acknowledgment to this illustrious person, for his great communicativeness; and promised, if ever I had the good fortune to return to my native country, that I would do him justice, as the sole inventor of this wonderful machine; the form and contrivance of which I desired leave to delineate on paper, as in the figure here annexed. I told him, although it were the custom of our learned in Europe to steal inventions from each other, who had thereby at least this advantage, that it became a controversy which was the right owner; yet I would take such caution, that he should have the honour entire, without a rival.

We next went to the school of languages, where three professors sat in consultation upon improving that of their own country.

The first project was, to shorten discourse, by cutting polysyllables into one, and leaving out verbs and participles, because, in reality, all things imaginable are but norms.

The other project was, a scheme for entirely abolishing all words whatsoever; and this was urged as a great advantage in point of health, as well as brevity. For it is plain, that every word we speak is, in some degree, a diminution of our lunge by corrosion, and, consequently, contributes to the shortening of our lives. An expedient was therefore offered, that since words are only names for things, it would be more convenient for all men to carry about them such things as were necessary to express a particular business they are to discourse on. And this invention would certainly have taken place, to the great ease as well as health of the subject, if the women, in conjunction with the vulgar and illiterate, had not threatened to raise a rebellion unless they might be allowed the liberty to speak with their tongues, after the manner of their forefathers; such constant irreconcilable enemies to science are the common people. However, many of the most learned and wise adhere to the new scheme of expressing themselves by things; which has only this inconvenience attending it, that if a man's business be very great, and of various kinds, he must be obliged, in proportion, to carry a greater bundle of things upon his back, unless he can afford one or two strong servants to attend him. I have often beheld two of those sages almost sinking under the weight of their packs, like pedlars among us, who, when they met in the street, would lay down their loads, open their sacks, and hold conversation for an hour together; then put up their implements, help each other to resume their burdens, and take their leave.

But for short conversations, a man may carry implements in his pockets, and under his arms, enough to supply him; and in his house, he cannot be at a loss. Therefore the room where company meet who practice this art, is full of all things, ready at hand, requisite to furnish matter for this kind of artificial converse.

Another great advantage proposed by this invention was, that it would serve as a universal language, to be understood in all civilized nations, whose goods and utensils are generally of the same kind, or nearly resembling, so that their uses might easily be comprehended. And thus ambassadors would be qualified to treat with foreign princes, or ministers of state, to whose tongues they were utter strangers.

I was at the mathematical school, where the master taught his pupils after a method scarce imaginable to us in Europe. The proposition, and demonstration, were fairly written on a thin wafer, with ink composed of a cephalic tincture. This, the student was to swallow upon a fasting stomach, and for three days following, eat nothing but bread and water. As the wafer digested, the tincture mounted to his brain, bearing the proposition along with it. But the success has not hitherto been answerable, partly by some error in the quantum or composition, and partly by the perverseness of lads, to whom this bolus is so nauseous, that they generally steal aside, and discharge it upwards, before it can operate; neither have they been yet persuaded to use so long an abstinence, as the prescription requires.

❧ **Chapter VI** ❧

A further account of the academy. The author proposes some improvements, which are honorably received.

In the school of political projectors, I was but ill entertained; the professors appearing, in my judgment, wholly out of their senses, which is a scene that never fails to make me melancholy. These unhappy people were proposing schemes for persuading monarchs to choose favourites upon the score of their wisdom, capacity, and virtue; of teaching ministers to consult the public good; of rewarding merit, great abilities, eminent services; of instructing princes to know their true interest, by placing it on the same foundation with that of their people; of choosing for employments persons qualified to exercise them, with many other wild, impossible chimeras, that never entered before into the heart of man to conceive; and confirmed in me the old observation, that there is nothing so extravagant and irrational, which some philosophers have not maintained for truth.

But, however, I shall so far do justice to this part of the Academy, as to acknowledge that all of them were not so visionary. There was a most ingenious doctor, who seemed to be perfectly versed in the whole nature and system of government. This illustrious person had very usefully employed his studies, in finding out effectual remedies for all diseases and corruptions to which the several kinds of public administration are subject, by the vices or infirmities of those who govern, as well as by the licentiousness of those who are to obey. For instance:

whereas all writers and reasons have agreed, that there is a strict universal resemblance between the natural and the political body; can there be any thing more evident, than that the health of both must be preserved, and the diseases cured, by the same prescriptions? It is allowed, that senates and great councils are often troubled with redundant, ebullient, and other peccant humours; with many diseases of the head, and more of the heart; with strong convulsions, with grievous contractions of the nerves and sinews in both hands, but especially the right; with spleen, flatus, vertigos, and deliriums; with scrofulous tumours, full of fetid purulent matter; with sour frothy ructations; with canine appetites, and crudeness of digestion, besides many others, needless to mention. This doctor therefore proposed, that upon the meeting of the senate, certain physicians should attend it the three first days of their sitting, and at the close of each day's debate feel the pulses of every senator; after which, having maturely considered and consulted upon the nature of the several maladies, and the methods of cure, they should on the fourth day return to the senate house, attended by their apothecaries stored with proper medicines; and before the members sat, administer to each of them lenitives, aperitives, abstersives, corrosives, restringents, palliatives, laxatives, cephalalgics, icterics, apophlegmatics, acoustics, as their several cases required; and, according as these medicines should operate, repeat, alter, or omit them, at the next meeting.

This project could not be of any great expense to the public; and might in my poor opinion, be of much use for the despatch of business, in those countries where senates have any share in the legislative power; beget unanimity, shorten debates, open a few mouths which are now closed, and close many more which are now open; curb the petulancy of the young, and correct the positiveness of the old; rouse the stupid, and damp the pert.

Again, because it is a general complaint, that the favourites of princes are troubled with short and weak memories; the same doctor proposed, that whoever attended a first minister, after having told his business, with the utmost brevity and in the plainest words, should, at his departure, give the said minister a tweak by the nose, or a kick in the belly, or tread on his corns, or lug him thrice by both ears, or run a pin into his breech; or pinch his arm black and blue, to prevent forgetfulness; and at every levee day, repeat the same operation, till the business were done, or absolutely refused.

He likewise directed, that every senator in the great council of a nation, after he had delivered his opinion, and argued in the defence of it, should be obliged to give his vote directly contrary; because if that were done, the result would infallibly terminate in the good of the public.

When parties in a state are violent, he offered a wonderful contrivance to reconcile them. The method is this: You take a hundred leaders of each party; you dispose them into couples of such whose heads are nearest of a size; then let two nice operators saw off the occiput of each couple at the same time, in such a manner that the brain may be equally divided. Let the occiputs, thus cut off, be interchanged, applying each to the head of his opposite party-man. It seems indeed to be a work that requires some exactness, but the professor assured us, that if it were dexterously performed, the cure would be infallible. For he argued thus, that the two half brains being left to debate the matter between themselves within the space of one skull, would soon come to a good understanding, and produce that moderation, as well as regularity of thinking, so much to be wished for in the heads of those, who imagine they come into the world only to watch and govern its motion: and as to the difference of brains, in quantity or quality, among those who are directors in faction, the doctor assured us, from his own knowledge, that it was a perfect trifle.

I heard a very warm debate between two professors, about the most commodious and effectual ways and means of raising money, without grieving the subject. The first affirmed, the justest method would be, to lay a certain tax upon vices and folly; and the sum fixed upon every man to be rated, after the fairest manner, by a jury of his neighbours. The second was of an opinion directly contrary; to tax those qualities of body and mind, for which men chiefly value themselves; the rate to be more or less, according to the degrees of excelling; the decision whereof should be left entirely to their own breast. The highest tax was upon men who are the greatest favourites of the other sex, and the assessments, according to the number and nature of the favours they have received; for which, they are allowed to be their own vouchers. Wit, valour, and politeness, were likewise proposed to be largely taxed, and collected in the same manner, by every person's giving his own word for the quantum of what he possessed. But as to honour, justice, wisdom, and learning, they should not be taxed at all; because they are qualifications of so singular a kind, that no man will either allow them in his neighbour or value them in himself.

The women were proposed to be taxed according to their beauty and skill in dressing, wherein they had the same privilege with the men, to be determined by their own judgment. But constancy, chastity, good sense, and good nature, were not rated, because they would not bear the charge of collecting.

To keep senators in the interest of the crown, it was proposed that the members should raffle for employment; every man first taking an oath, and giving security, that he would vote for the court, whether he won or not; after which, the losers had, in their turn, the liberty of raffling upon the next vacancy. Thus, hope and expectation would be kept alive; none would complain of broken promises, but impute their disappointments wholly to fortune, whose shoulders are broader and stronger than those of a ministry.

Another professor showed me a large paper of instructions for discovering plots and conspiracies against the government. He advised great statesmen to examine into the diet of all suspected persons; their times of eating; upon which side they lay in bed; with which hand they wipe their posteriors; take a strict view of their excrements, and, from the colour, the odour, the taste, the consistence, the crudeness or maturity of digestion, form a judgment of their thoughts and designs; because men are never so serious, thoughtful, and intent, as when they are at stool, which he found by frequent experiment; for, in such conjunctures, when he used, merely as a trial, to consider which was the best way of murdering the king, his ordure would have a tincture of green; but quite different, when he thought only of raising an insurrection, or burning the metropolis.

The whole discourse was written with great acuteness, containing many observations, both curious and useful for politicians; but, as I conceived, not altogether complete. This I ventured to tell the author, and offered, if he pleased, to supply him with some additions. He received my proposition with more compliance than is usual among writers, especially those of the projecting species, professing he would be glad to receive further information.

I told him, that in the kingdom of Tribnia, by the natives called Langden, where I had sojourned some time in my travels, the bulk of the people consist in a manner wholly of discoverers, witnesses, informers, accusers, prosecutors, evidences, swearers, together with their several subservient and subaltern instruments, all under the colours, the conduct, and the pay of ministers of state, and their deputies. The plots, in that kingdom, are usually the workmanship of those persons who desire to raise their own characters of profound politicians; to restore new vigour to a crazy administration; to stifle or divert general discontents; to fill their coffers with forfeitures; and raise, or sink the opinion of public credit, as either shall best answer their private advantage. It is first agreed and settled among them, what suspected persons shall be accused of a plot; then, effectual care is taken to secure all their letters and papers, and put the owners in chains. These papers are delivered to a set of artists, very dexterous in finding out the mysterious meanings of words, syllables, and letters. For instance, they can discover a close stool, to signify a privy council; a flock of geese, a senate; a lame dog, an invader; the plague, a standing army; a buzzard, a prime minister; the gout, a high priest; a gibbet, a secretary of state; a chamber pot, a committee of grandees; a sieve, a court lady; a broom, a revolution; a mouse-trap, an employment; a bottomless pit, a treasury; a sink, a court; a cap and bells, a favourite; a broken reed, a court of justice; an empty ton, a general; a running sore, the administration.

When this method fails, they have two others more effectual, which the learned among them call acrostics and anagrams. First, they can decipher all initial letters into political meanings. Thus N, shall signify a plot; B, a regiment of horse; L, a fleet at sea; or, secondly, by transposing the letters of the alphabet in any suspected paper, they can lay open the deepest designs of a discontented party. So, for example, if I should say, in a letter to a friend, "Our brother Tom has just got the piles," a skilful decipherer would discover, that the same letters which compose that sentence, may be analyzed into the following words, "Resist — a plot is brought home — The tour." And this is the anagrammatic method.

The professor made me great acknowledgments for communicating these observations, and promised to make honourable mention of me in his treatise.

I saw nothing in this country that could invite me to a longer continuance, and began to think of returning home to England.

 Chapter VII

The author leaves Lagado, arrives at Maldonada. No ship ready. He takes a short voyage to Glubbdubdrib. His reception by the governor.

The continent, of which this kingdom is apart, extends itself, as I have reason to believe, eastward, to that unknown tract of America westward of California; and north, to the Pacific Ocean, which is not above a hundred and fifty miles from Lagado; where there is a good port, and much commerce with the great island of Luggnagg, situated to the north-west about 29 degrees north latitude, and 140 longitude. This island of Luggnagg stands south-eastward of Japan, about a hundred leagues distant. There is a strict alliance between the Japanese emperor and the king of Luggnagg; which affords frequent opportunities of sailing from one island to the other. I determined therefore to direct my course this way, in order to my return to Europe. I hired two mules, with a guide, to show me the way, and carry my small baggage. I took leave of my noble protector, who had shown me so much favour, and made me a generous present at my departure.

My journey was without any accident or adventure worth relating. When I arrived at the port of Maldonada (for so it is called) there was no ship in the harbour bound for Luggnagg, nor likely to be in some time. The town is about as large as Portsmouth. I soon fell into some acquaintance, and was very hospitably received. A gentleman of distinction said to me, that since the ships bound for Luggnagg could not be ready in less than a month, it might be no disagreeable amusement for me to take a trip to the little island of Glubbdubdrib, about five leagues off to the south-west. He offered himself and a friend to accompany me, and that I should be provided with a small convenient bark for the voyage.

Glubbdubdrib, as nearly as I can interpret the word, signifies the island of sorcerers or magicians. It is about one third as large as the Isle of Wight, and extremely fruitful: it is governed by the head of a certain tribe, who are all magicians. This tribe marries only among each other, and the eldest in succession is prince or governor. He has a noble palace, and a park of about three thousand acres, surrounded by a wall of hewn stone twenty feet high. In this park are several small enclosures for cattle, corn, and gardening.

The governor and his family are served and attended by domestics of a kind somewhat unusual. By his skill in necromancy he has a power of calling whom he pleases from the dead, and commanding their service for twenty-four hours, but no longer; nor can he call the same persons up again in less than three months, except upon very extraordinary occasions.

When we arrived at the island, which was about eleven in the morning, one of the gentlemen who accompanied me went to the governor, and desired admittance for a stranger, who came on purpose to have the honour of attending on his highness. This was immediately granted, and we all three entered the gate of the palace between two rows of guards, armed and dressed after a very antic manner, and with something in their countenances that made my flesh creep with a horror I cannot express. We passed through several apartments, between servants of the same sort, ranked on each side as before, till we came to the chamber of presence; where, after three profound obeisances, and a few general questions, we were permitted to sit on three stools, near the lowest step of his highness's throne. He understood the language of Balnibarbi, although it was different from that of this island. He desired me to give him some account of my travels; and, to let me see that I should be treated without ceremony, he dismissed all his attendants with a turn of his finger; at which, to my great astonishment, they vanished in an instant, like visions in a dream when we awake on a sudden. I could not recover myself in some time, till the governor assured me, that I should receive no hurt; and observing my two companions to be under no concern, who had been often entertained in the same manner, I began to take courage, and related to his highness a short history of my several adventures; yet not without some hesitation, and frequently looking behind me to the place where I had seen those domestic spectres. I had the honour to dine with the governor, where a new set of ghosts served up the meat, and waited at table. I now observed myself to be less terrified than I had been in the morning. I stayed till sunset, but humbly desired his highness to excuse me for not accepting his invitation of lodging in the palace. My two friends and I lay at a private house in the town adjoining, which is the capital of this little island; and the next morning we returned to pay our duty to the governor, as he was pleased to command us.

After this manner we continued in the island for ten days, most part of every day with the governor, and at night in our lodging. I soon grew so familiarized to the sight of spirits, that after the third or fourth time they gave me no emotion at all: or, if I had any apprehensions left, my curiosity prevailed over them. For his highness the governor ordered me to call up whatever persons I would choose to name, and in whatever numbers, among all the dead from the beginning of the world to the present time, and command them to answer any questions I should think fit to ask; with this condition, that my questions must be confined within the compass of the times they lived in. And one thing I might depend upon, that they would certainly tell me the truth, for lying was a talent of no use in the lower world.

I made my humble acknowledgments to his highness for so great a favour. We were in a chamber, from whence there was a fair prospect into the park. And because my first inclination was to be entertained with scenes of pomp and magnificence, I desired to see Alexander the Great at the head of his army, just after the battle of Arbela; which, upon a motion of the governor's finger, immediately appeared in a large field, under the window where we stood. Alexander was called up into the room; it was with great difficulty that I understood his Greek, and had but little of my own. He assured me upon his honour that he was not poisoned, but died of a bad fever by excessive drinking.

Next, I saw Hannibal passing the Alps, who told me he had not a drop of vinegar in his camp.

I saw Caesar and Pompey at the head of their troops, just ready to engage. I saw the former, in his last great triumph. I desired that the senate of Rome might appear before me, in one large chamber, and an assembly of somewhat a later age in counterview, in another. The first seemed to be an assembly of heroes and demigods; the other, a knot of pedlars, pick-pockets, highwayman, and bullies.

The governor, at my request, gave the sign for Caesar and Brutus to advance towards us. I was struck with a profound veneration at the sight of Brutus, and could easily discover the most consummate virtue, the greatest intrepidity and firmness of mind, the truest love of his country, and general benevolence for mankind, in every lineament of his countenance. I observed, with much pleasure, that these two persons were in good intelligence with each other; and Caesar freely confessed to me, that the greatest actions of his own life were not equal, by many degrees, to the glory of taking it away. I had the honour to have much conversation with Brutus; and was told, that his ancestor Junius, Socrates, Epaminondas, Cato the younger, Sir Thomas More, and himself were perpetually together: A sextumvirate, to which all the ages of the world cannot add a seventh.

It would be tedious to trouble the reader with relating what vast numbers of illustrious persons were called up to gratify that insatiable desire I had to see the world in every period of antiquity placed before me. I chiefly fed mine eyes with beholding the destroyers of tyrants and usurpers, and the restorers of liberty to oppressed and injured nations. But it is impossible to express the satisfaction I received in my own mind, after such a manner as to make it a suitable entertainment to the reader.

Chapter VIII

A further account of Glubbdubdrib. Ancient and modern history corrected.

Having a desire to see those ancients who were most renowned for wit and learning, I set apart one day on purpose. I proposed that Homer and Aristotle might appear at the head of all their commentators; but these were so numerous, that some hundreds were forced to attend in the court, and outward rooms of the palace. I knew, and could distinguish those two heroes, at first sight, not only from the crowd, but from each other. Homer was the taller and comelier person of the two, walked very erect for one of his age, and his eyes were the most quick and piercing I ever beheld. Aristotle stooped much, and made use of a staff. His visage was meagre, his hair lank and thin, and his voice hollow. I soon discovered that both of them were perfect strangers to the rest of the company, and had never seen or heard of them before; and I had a whisper from a ghost who shall be nameless, that these commentators always kept in the most distant quarters from their principals, in the lower world, through a consciousness of shame and guilt, because they had so horribly misrepresented the meaning of those authors to posterity. I introduced Didymus and Eustathius to Homer, and prevailed on him to treat them better than perhaps they deserved, for he soon found they wanted a genius to enter into the spirit of a poet. But Aristotle was out of all patience with the account I gave him of Scotus and Ramus, as I presented them to him; and he asked them, whether the rest of the tribe were as great dunces as themselves?

I then desired the governor to call up Descartes and Gassendi, with whom I prevailed to explain their systems to Aristotle. This great philosopher freely acknowledged his own mistakes in natural philosophy, because he proceeded in many things upon conjecture, as all men must do; and he found that Gassendi, who had made the doctrine of Epicurus as palatable as he could, and the vortices of Descartes, were equally to be exploded. He predicted the same fate to *attraction*, whereof the present learned are such zealous asserters. He said that new systems of nature were but new fashions, which would vary in every age; and even those, who pretend to demonstrate them from mathematical principles, would flourish but a short period of time, and be out of vogue when that was determined.

I spent five days in conversing with many others of the ancient learned. I saw most of the first Roman emperors. I prevailed on the governor to call up Heliogabalus's cooks to dress us a dinner, but they could not show us much of their skill, for want of materials. A helot of Agesilaus made us a dish of Spartan broth, but I was not able to get down a second spoonful.

The two gentlemen, who conducted me to the island, were pressed by their private affairs to return in three days, which I employed in seeing some of the modern dead, who had made the greatest figure, for two or three hundred years past, in our own and other countries of Europe; and having been always a great admirer of old illustrious families, I desired the governor would call up a dozen or two of kings, with their ancestors in order for eight or nine generations.

But my disappointment was grievous and unexpected. For, instead of a long train with royal diadems, I saw in one family two fiddlers, three spruce courtiers, and an Italian prelate. In another, a barber, an abbot, and two cardinals. I have too great a veneration for crowned heads, to dwell any longer on so nice a subject. But as to counts, marquises, dukes, earls, and the like, I was not so scrupulous. And I confess, it was not without some pleasure, that I found myself able to trace the particular features, by which certain families are distinguished, up to their originals. I could plainly discover whence one family derives a long chin; why a second has abounded with knaves for two generations, and fools for two more; why a third happened to be crack-brained, and a fourth to be sharpers; whence it came, what Polydore Virgil says of a certain great house, *Nec vir fortis, nec foemina casta*; how cruelty, falsehood, and cowardice, grew to be characteristics by which certain families are distinguished as much as by their coats of arms; who first brought the pox into a noble house, which has lineally descended scrofulous tumours to their posterity. Neither could I wonder at all this, when I saw such an interruption of lineages, by pages, lackeys, valets, coachmen, gamesters, fiddlers, players, captains, and pickpockets.

I was chiefly disgusted with modern history. For having strictly examined all the persons of greatest name in the courts of princes, for a hundred years past, I found how the world had been misled by prostitute writers, to ascribe the greatest exploits in war, to cowards; the wisest counsel, to fools; sincerity, to flatterers; Roman virtue, to betrayers of their country; piety, to atheists; chastity, to sodomites; truth, to informers. How many innocent and excellent persons had been condemned to death or banishment by the practising of great ministers upon the corruption of judges, and the malice of factions. How many villains had been exalted to the highest places of trust, power, dignity, and profit. How great a share in the motions and events of courts, councils, and senates might be challenged by bawds, whores, pimps, parasites, and buffoons. How low an opinion I had of human wisdom and integrity, when I was truly informed of the springs and motives of great enterprises and revolutions in the world, and of the contemptible accidents to which they owed their success.

Here I discovered the roguery and ignorance of those who pretend to write anecdotes, or secret history; who send so many kings to their graves with a cup of poison; will repeat the discourse between a prince and chief minister, where no witness was by; unlock the thoughts and cabinets of ambassadors and secretaries of state; and have the perpetual misfortune to be mistaken. Here I discovered the true causes of many great events that have surprised the world; how a whore can govern the back-stairs, the back-stairs a council, and the council a senate. A general confessed, in my presence, that he got a victory purely by the force of cowardice and ill conduct; and an admiral, that for want of proper intelligence, he beat the enemy, to whom he intended to betray the fleet. Three kings protested to me, that in their whole reigns they never did once prefer any person of merit, unless by mistake, or treachery of some minister in whom they confided; neither would they do it if they were to live again; and they showed, with great strength of reason, that the royal throne could not be supported without corruption, because that positive, confident, restiff temper, which virtue infused into a man, was a perpetual clog to public business.

I had the curiosity to inquire in a particular manner, by what methods great numbers had procured to themselves high titles of honour, and prodigious estates; and I confined my inquiry to a very modern period: However, without grating upon present times, because I would be sure to give no offence even to foreigners (for I hope the reader need not be told, that I do not in the least intend my own country, in what I say upon this occasion,) a great number of persons concerned were called up; and, upon a very slight examination, discovered such a scene of infamy, that I cannot reflect upon it without some seriousness. Perjury, oppression, subornation, fraud, pandarism, and the like infirmities, were among the most excusable arts they had to mention; and for these I gave, as it was reasonable, great allowance. But when some confessed they owed their greatness and wealth to sodomy, or incest; others, to the prostituting of their own wives and daughters; others, to the betraying of their country or their prince; some, to poisoning; more to the perverting of justice, in order to destroy the innocent, I hope I may be pardoned, if these discoveries inclined me a little to abate of that profound veneration, which I am naturally apt to pay to persons of high rank, who ought to be treated with the utmost respect due to their sublime dignity, by us their inferiors.

I had often read of some great services done to princes and states, and desired to see the persons by whom those services were performed. Upon inquiry I was told, that their names were to be found on no record, except a few of them, whom history has represented as the vilest of rogues and traitors. As to the rest, I had never once heard of them. They all appeared with dejected looks, and in the meanest habit; most of them telling me they died in poverty and disgrace, and the rest on a scaffold or a gibbet.

Among others, there was one person, whose case appeared a little singular. He had a youth about eighteen years old standing by his side. He told me, he had for many years been commander of a ship; and in the sea fight at Actium had the good fortune to break through the enemy's great line of battle, sink three of their capital ships, and take a fourth, which was the sole cause of Antony's flight, and of the victory that ensued; that the youth standing by him, his only son, was killed in the action. He added, that upon the confidence of some merit, the war being at an end, he went to Rome, and solicited at the court of Augustus to be preferred to a greater ship, whose commander had been killed; but, without any regard to his pretensions, it was given to a boy who had never seen the sea, the son of Libertina, who waited on one of the emperor's mistresses. Returning back to his own vessel, he was charged with neglect of duty, and the ship given to a favourite page of Publicola, the vice-admiral; whereupon he retired to a poor farm at a great distance from Rome, and there ended his life. I was so curious to know the truth of this story, that I desired Agrippa might be called, who was admiral in that fight. He appeared, and confirmed the whole account, but with much more advantage to the captain, whose modesty had extenuated or concealed a great part of his merit.

I was surprised to find corruption grown so high and so quick in that empire, by the force of luxury so lately introduced; which made me less wonder at many parallel cases in other countries, where vices of all kinds have reigned so much longer, and where the whole praise, as well as pillage, has been engrossed by the chief commander, who perhaps had the least title to either.

As every person called up made exactly the same appearance he had done in the world, it gave me melancholy reflections to observe how much the race of human kind was degenerated among us within these hundred years past; how the pox, under all its consequences and denominations had altered every lineament of an English countenance; shortened the size of bodies, unbraced the nerves, relaxed the sinews and muscles, introduced a sallow complexion, and rendered the flesh loose and rancid.

I descended so low, as to desire some English yeoman of the old stamp might be summoned to appear; once so famous for the simplicity of their manners, diet, and dress; for justice in their dealings; for their true spirit of liberty; for their valour, and love of their country. Neither could I be wholly unmoved, after comparing the living with the dead, when I considered how all these pure native virtues were prostituted for a piece of money by their grand-children; who, in selling their votes and managing at elections, have acquired every vice and corruption that can possibly be learned in a court.

Chapter IX

The author returns to Maldonada. Sails to the kingdom of Luggnagg. The author confined. He is sent for to court. The manner of his admittance. The king's great lenity to his subjects.

The day of our departure being come, I took leave of his highness, the Governor of Glubbdubdrib, and returned with my two companions to Maldonada, where, after a fortnight's waiting, a ship was ready to sail for Luggnagg. The two gentlemen, and some others, were so generous and kind as to furnish me with provisions, and see me on board. I was a month in this voyage. We had one violent storm, and were under a necessity of steering westward to get into the trade wind, which holds for above sixty leagues. On the 21st of April, 1708, we sailed into the river of Clumegnig, which is a seaport town, at the south-east point of Luggnagg. We cast anchor within a league of the town, and made a signal for a pilot. Two of them came on board in less than half an hour, by whom we were guided between certain shoals and rocks, which are very dangerous in the passage, to a large basin, where a fleet may ride in safety within a cable's length of the town-wall.

Some of our sailors, whether out of treachery or inadvertence, had informed the pilots that I was a stranger, and great traveller; whereof these gave notice to a custom-house officer, by whom I was examined very strictly upon my landing. This officer spoke to me in the language of Balnibarbi, which, by the force of much commerce, is generally understood in that town, especially by seamen and those employed in the customs. I gave him a short account of some particulars, and made my story as plausible and consistent as I could; but I thought it necessary to disguise my country, and call myself a Hollander; because my intentions were for Japan, and I knew the Dutch were the only Europeans permitted to enter into that kingdom. I therefore told the officer, that having been shipwrecked on the coast of Balnibarbi, and cast on a rock, I was received up into Laputa, or the flying island (of which he had often heard), and was now endeavouring to get to Japan, whence I might find a convenience of returning to my own country. The officer said, I must be confined till he could receive orders from court, for which he would write immediately, and hoped to receive an answer in a fortnight. I was carried to a convenient lodging with a sentry placed at the door; however, I had the liberty of a large garden, and was treated with humanity enough, being maintained all the time at the king's charge. I was invited by several persons, chiefly out of curiosity, because it was reported that I came from countries very remote, of which they had never heard.

I hired a young man, who came in the same ship, to be an interpreter; he was a native of Luggnagg, but had lived some years at Maldonada, and was a perfect master of both languages. By his assistance, I was able to hold a conversation with those who came to visit me; but this consisted only of their questions, and my answers.

The despatch came from court about the time we expected. It contained a warrant for conducting me and my retinue to *Traldragdubh*, or *Trildrogdrib* (for it is pronounced both ways as near as I can remember), by a party of ten horse. All my retinue was that poor lad for an interpreter, whom I persuaded into my service, and, at my humble request, we had each of us a mule to ride on. A messenger was despatched half a day's journey before us, to give the king notice of my approach, and to desire, that his Majesty would please to appoint a day and hour, when it would by his gracious pleasure that I might have the honour to lick the dust before his footstool. This is the court style, and I found it to be more than matter of form: For, upon my admittance two days after my arrival, I was commanded to crawl upon my belly, and lick the floor as I advanced; but, on account of my being a stranger, care was taken to have it made so clean, that the dust was not offensive. However, this was a peculiar grace, not allowed to any but persons of the highest rank, when they desire an admittance. Nay, sometimes the floor is strewed with dust on purpose, when the person to be admitted happens to have powerful enemies at court; and I have seen a great lord with his mouth so crammed, that when he had crept to the proper distance from the throne; he was not able to speak a word. Neither is there any remedy; because it is capital for those, who receive an audience to spit or wipe their mouths in his Majesty's presence. There is indeed another custom, which I cannot altogether approve of: when the king has a mind to put any of his nobles to death in a gentle indulgent manner, he commands the floor to be strewed with a certain brown powder of a deadly composition, which being licked up, infallibly kills him in twenty-four hours. But in justice to this prince's great clemency, and the care he has of his subjects' lives (wherein it were much to be wished that the Monarchs of Europe would imitate him), it must be mentioned for his honour, that strict orders are given to have the infected parts of the floor well washed after every such execution, which, if his domestics neglect, they are in danger of incurring his royal displeasure. I myself heard him give directions, that one of his pages should be whipped, whose turn it was to give notice about washing the floor after an execution, but maliciously had omitted it; by which neglect a young lord of great hopes, coming to an audience, was unfortunately poisoned, although the king at that time had no design against his life. But this good prince was so gracious as to forgive the poor page his whipping, upon promise that he would do so no more, without special orders.

To return from this digression. When I had crept within four yards of the throne, I raised myself gently upon my knees, and then striking my forehead seven times against the ground, I pronounced the following words, as they had been taught me the night before, *Ickpling gloffthrobb squut serummblhiop mlashnalt zwin tnodbalkuffh slhiophad gurdlubh asht*. This is the compliment, established by the laws of the land, for all persons admitted to the king's presence. It may be rendered into English thus: May your celestial Majesty outlive the sun, eleven moons and a half! To this the king returned some answer, which, although I could not understand, yet I replied as I had been directed: *Fluft drin yalerick dwuldom prastrad mirpush*, which properly signifies, "My tongue is in the mouth of my friend;" and by this expression was meant, that I desired leave to bring my interpreter; whereupon the young man already mentioned was accordingly introduced, by whose intervention I answered as many questions as his Majesty could put in above an hour. I spoke in the Balnibarbian tongue, and my interpreter delivered my meaning in that of Luggnagg.

The king was much delighted with my company, and ordered his *bliffmarklub*, or high-chamberlain, to appoint a lodging in the court for me and my interpreter; with a daily allowance for my table, and a large purse of gold for my common expenses.

I staid three months in this country, out of perfect obedience to his Majesty; who was pleased highly to favour me, and made me very honourable offers. But I thought it more consistent with prudence and justice to pass the remainder of my days with my wife and family.

∽ **Chapter X** ∽

The Luggnaggians commended. A particular description of the Struldbrugs, with many conversations between the author and some eminent persons upon that subject.

The Luggnaggians are a polite and generous people; and although they are not without some share of that pride which is peculiar to all Eastern countries, yet they show themselves courteous to strangers, especially such who are countenanced by the court. I had many acquaintance, and among persons of the best fashion; and being always attended by my interpreter, the conversation we had was not disagreeable.

One day, in much good company, I was asked by a person of quality, whether I had seen any of their struldbrugs, or immortals? I said I had not; and desired he would explain to me what he meant by such an appellation, applied to a mortal creature. He told me that sometimes, though very rarely, a child happened to be born in a family, with a red circular spot in the forehead, directly over the left eyebrow, which was an infallible mark that it should never die. The spot, as he described it, was about the compass of a silver threepence, but in the course of time grew larger, and changed its colour; for at twelve years old it became green, so continued till five and twenty, then turned to a deep blue; at five and forty it grew coal black, and as large as an English shilling; but never admitted any further alteration. He said, these births were so rare, that he did not believe there could be above eleven hundred struldbrugs, of both sexes, in the whole kingdom; of which he computed about fifty in the metropolis, and, among the rest, a young girl born about three years ago. That, these productions were not peculiar to any family, but a mere effect of chance; and the children of the struldbrugs themselves were equally mortal with the rest of the people.

I freely own myself to have been struck with inexpressible delight, upon hearing this account; and the person who gave it me happening to understand the Balnibarbian language, which I spoke very well, I could not forbear breaking out into expressions, perhaps a little too extravagant. I cried out, as in a rapture, "Happy nation, where every child hath at least a chance for being immortal! Happy people, who enjoy so many living examples of ancient virtue, and have masters ready to instruct them in the wisdom of all former ages! but happiest, beyond all comparison, are those excellent *struldbrugs*, who, being born exempt from that universal calamity of human nature, have their minds free and disengaged, without the weight and depression of spirits caused by the continual apprehensions of death!" I discovered my admiration that I had not observed any of these illustrious persons at court; the black spot on the forehead being so remarkable a distinction, that I could not have easily overlooked it: and it was impossible that his Majesty, a most judicious prince, should not provide himself with a good number of such wise and able counsellors. Yet perhaps the virtue of those reverend sages was too strict for the corrupt and libertine manners of a court. And we often find by experience, that young men are too opinionated and volatile to be guided by the sober dictates of their seniors. However, since the king was pleased to allow me access to his royal person, I was resolved, upon the very first occasion, to deliver my opinion to him on this matter freely and at large, by the help of my interpreter; and whether he would please to take my advice or not, yet in one thing I was determined, that his Majesty having frequently offered me an establishment in this country, I would, with great thankfulness, accept the favour, and pass my life here in the conversation of those superior beings the struldbrugs, if they would please to admit me.

The gentleman to whom I addressed my discourse, because (as I have already observed) he spoke the language of Balnibarbi, said to me, with a sort of a smile which usually arises from pity to the ignorant, that he was glad of any occasion to keep me among them, and desired my permission to explain to the company what I had spoke. He did so, and they talked together for some time in their own language, whereof I understood not a syllable, neither could I observe by their countenances, what impression my discourse had made on them. After a short silence, the same person told me, that his friends and mine (so he thought fit to express himself) were very much pleased with the judicious remarks I had made on the great happiness and advantages of immortal life, and they were desirous to know, in a particular manner, what scheme of living I should have formed to myself, if it had fallen to my lot to have been born a struldbrug.

I answered, "it was easy to be eloquent on so copious and delightful a subject, especially to me, who had been often apt to amuse myself with visions of what I should do, if I were a king, a general, or a great lord: and upon this very case, I had frequently run over the whole system how I should employ myself, and pass the time, if I were sure to live for ever.

"That, if it had been my good fortune to come into the world a struldbrug, as soon as I could discover my own happiness, by understanding the difference between life and death, I would first resolve, by all arts and methods, whatsoever, to procure myself riches. In the pursuit of which, by thrift and management, I might reasonably expect, in about two hundred years, to be the wealthiest man in the kingdom. In the second place, I would, from my earliest youth, apply myself to the study of arts and sciences, by which I should arrive in time to excel all others in learning. Lastly, I would carefully record every action and event of consequence, that happened in the public, impartially draw the characters of the several successions of princes and great ministers of state, with my own observations on every point. I would exactly set down the several changes in customs, language, fashions of dress, diet, and diversions. By all which acquirements, I should be a living treasure of knowledge and wisdom, and certainly become the oracle of the nation.

"I would never marry after threescore, but live in a hospitable manner, yet still on the saving side. I would entertain myself in forming and directing the minds of hopeful young men, by convincing them, from my own remembrance, experience, and observation, fortified by numerous examples, of the usefulness of virtue in public and private life. But my choice and constant companions should be a set of my own immortal brotherhood; among whom, I would elect a dozen from the most ancient, down to my own contemporaries. Where any of these wanted fortunes, I would provide them with convenient lodges round my own estate, and have some of them always at my table; only mingling a few of the most valuable among you mortals, whom length of time would harden me to lose with little or no reluctance, and treat your posterity after the same manner; just as a man diverts himself with the annual succession of pinks and tulips in his garden, without regretting the loss of those which withered the preceding year.

"These struldbrugs and I would mutually communicate our observations and memorials, through the course of time; remark the several gradations by which corruption steals into the world, and oppose it in every step, by giving perpetual warning and instruction to mankind; which, added to the strong influence of our own example, would probably prevent that continual degeneracy of human nature so justly complained of in all ages.

"Add to this, the pleasure of seeing the various revolutions of states and empires; the changes in the lower and upper world; ancient cities in ruins, and obscure villages become the seats of kings; famous rivers lessening into shallow brooks; the ocean leaving one coast dry, and overwhelming another; the discovery of many countries yet unknown; barbarity overrunning the politest nations, and the most barbarous become civilized. I should then see the discovery of the longitude, the perpetual motion, the universal medicine, and many other great inventions, brought to the utmost perfection.

"What wonderful discoveries should we make in astronomy, by outliving and confirming our own predictions; by observing the progress and return of comets, with the changes of motion in the sun, moon, and stars!"

I enlarged upon many other topics, which the natural desire of endless life, and sublunary happiness, could easily furnish me with. When I had ended, and the sum of my discourse had been interpreted, as before, to the rest of the company, there was a good deal of talk among them in the language of the country, not without some laughter at my expense. At last, the same gentleman who had been my interpreter, said, he was desired by the rest to set me right in a few mistakes, which I had fallen into through the common imbecility of human nature, and upon that allowance was less answerable for them. That this breed of struldbrugs was peculiar to their country, for there were no such people either in Balnibarbi or Japan, where he had the honour to be ambassador from his Majesty, and found the natives in both those kingdoms very hard to believe that the fact was possible; and it appeared from my astonishment when he first mentioned the matter to me, that I received it as a thing wholly new, and scarcely to be credited. That in the two kingdoms above mentioned, where, during his residence, he had conversed very much, he observed long life to be the universal desire and wish of mankind. That whoever had one foot in the grave was sure to hold back the other as strongly as he could. That the oldest had still hopes of living one day longer, and looked on death as the greatest evil, from which nature always prompted him to retreat. Only in this island of Luggnagg the appetite for living was not so eager, from the continual example of the struldbrugs before their eyes.

That the system of living contrived by me, was unreasonable and unjust; because it supposed a perpetuity of youth, health, and vigour, which no man could be so foolish to hope, however extravagant he may be in his wishes. That the question therefore was not, whether a man would choose to be always in the prime of youth, attended with prosperity and health; but how he would pass a perpetual life under all the usual disadvantages which old age brings along with it. For although few men will avow their desires of being immortal, upon such hard conditions, yet in the two kingdoms before mentioned, of Balnibarbi and Japan, he observed that every man desired to put off death some time longer, let it approach ever so late: and he rarely heard of any man who died willingly, except he were incited by the extremity of grief or torture. And he appealed to me, whether in those countries I had travelled, as well as my own, I had not observed the same general disposition.

After this preface, he gave me a particular account of the struldbrugs among them. He said, they commonly acted like mortals till about thirty years old; after which, by degrees, they grew melancholy and dejected, increasing in both till they came to fourscore. This he learned from their own confession; for otherwise, there not being above two or three of that species born in an age, they were too few to form a general observation by. When they came to fourscore years, which is reckoned the extremity of living in this country, they had not only all the follies and infirmities of other old men, but many more which arose from the dreadful prospect of never dying. They were not only opinionative, peevish, covetous, morose, vain, talkative, but incapable of friendship, and dead to all natural affection, which never descended below their grandchildren. Envy and impotent desires are their prevailing passions. But those objects against which their envy seems principally directed, are the vices of the younger sort and the deaths of the old. By reflecting on the former, they find themselves cut off from all possibility of pleasure; and whenever they see a funeral, they lament and repine that others have gone to a harbour of rest to which they themselves never can hope to arrive. They have no remembrance of anything but what they learned and observed in their youth and middle-age, and even that is very imperfect; and for the truth or particulars of any fact, it is safer to depend on common tradition, than upon their best recollections. The least miserable among them appear to be those who turn to dotage, and entirely lose their memories; these meet with more pity and assistance, because they want many bad qualities which abound in others.

If a struldbrug happen to marry one of his own kind, the marriage is dissolved of course, by the courtesy of the kingdom, as soon as the younger of the two comes to be fourscore; for the law thinks it a reasonable indulgence, that those who are condemned, without any fault of their own, to a perpetual continuance in the world, should not have their misery doubled by the load of a wife.

As soon as they have completed the term of eighty years, they are looked on as dead in law; their heirs immediately succeed to their estates; only a small pittance is reserved for their support; and the poor ones are maintained at the public charge. After that period, they are held incapable of any employment of trust or profit; they cannot purchase lands, or take leases; neither are they allowed to be witnesses in any cause, either civil or criminal, not even for the decision of meers and bounds.

At ninety, they lose their teeth and hair; they have at that age no distinction of taste, but eat and drink whatever they can get, without relish or appetite. The diseases they were subject to still continue, without increasing or diminishing. In talking, they forget the common appellation of things, and the names of persons, even of those who are their nearest friends and relations. For the same reason, they never can amuse themselves with reading, because their memory will not serve to carry them from the beginning of a sentence to the end; and by this defect, they are deprived of the only entertainment whereof they might otherwise be capable.

The language of this country being always upon the flux, the struldbrugs of one age do not understand those of another; neither are they able, after two hundred years, to hold any conversation (farther than by a few general words) with their neighbours the mortals; and thus they lie under the disadvantage of living like foreigners in their own country.

This was the account given me of the struldbrugs, as near as I can remember. I afterwards saw five or six of different ages, the youngest not above two hundred years old, who were brought to me at several times by some of my friends; but although they were told, that I was a great traveller, and had seen all the world, they had not the least curiosity to ask me a question; only desired I would give them slumskudask, or a token of remembrance; which is a modest way of begging, to avoid the law, that strictly forbids it, because they are provided for by the public, although indeed with a very scanty allowance.

They are despised and hated by all sorts of people. When one of them is born, it is reckoned ominous, and their birth is recorded very particularly so that you may know their age by consulting the register, which, however, has not been kept above a thousand years past, or at least has been destroyed by time or public disturbances. But the usual way of computing how old they are, is by asking them what kings or great persons they can remember, and then consulting history; for infallibly the last prince in their mind did not begin his reign after they were fourscore years old.

They were the most mortifying sight I ever beheld; and the women more horrible than the men. Besides the usual deformities in extreme old age, they acquired an additional ghastliness, in proportion to their number of years, which is not to be described; and among half a dozen, I soon distinguished which was the eldest, although there was not above a century or two between them.

The reader will easily believe, that from what I had hear and seen, my keen appetite for perpetuity of life was much abated. I grew heartily ashamed of the pleasing visions I had formed; and thought no tyrant could invent a death into which I would not run with pleasure, from such a life. The king heard of all that had passed between me and my friends upon this occasion, and rallied me very pleasantly; wishing I could send a couple of struldbrugs to my own country, to arm our people against the fear of death; but this, it seems, is forbidden by the fundamental laws of the kingdom, or else I should have been well content with the trouble and expense of transporting them.

I could not but agree, that the laws of this kingdom relative to the struldbrugs were founded upon the strongest reasons, and such as any other country would be under the necessity of enacting, in the like circumstances. Otherwise, as avarice is the necessary consequence of old age, those immortals would in time become proprietors of the whole nation, and engross the civil power, which, for want of abilities to manage, must end in the ruin of the public.

～ Chapter XI ～

The author leaves Luggnagg, and sails to Japan. From thence he returns in a Dutch ship to Amsterdam, and from Amsterdam to England.

I thought this account of the struldbrugs might be some entertainment to the reader, because it seems to be a little out of the common way; at least I do not remember to have met the like in any book of travels that has come to my hands; and if I am deceived, my excuse must be, that it is necessary for travellers who describe the same country, very often to agree in dwelling on the same particulars, without deserving the censure of having borrowed or transcribed from those who wrote before them.

There is indeed a perpetual commerce between this kingdom and the great empire of Japan; and it is very probable, that the Japanese authors may have given some account of the struldbrugs; but my stay in Japan was so short, and I was so entirely a stranger to the language, that I was not qualified to make any inquiries. But I hope the Dutch, upon this notice, will be curious and able enough to supply my defects.

His Majesty having often pressed me to accept some employment in his court, and finding me absolutely determined to return to my native country, was pleased to give me his license to depart; and honoured me with a letter of recommendation, under his own hand, to the Emperor of Japan. He likewise presented me with four hundred and forty-four large pieces of gold (this nation delighting in even numbers), and a red diamond, which I sold in England for eleven hundred pounds.

On the 6th of May, 1709, I took a solemn leave of his Majesty, and all my friends. This prince was so gracious as to order a guard to conduct me to Glanguenstald, which is a royal port to the south-west part of the island. In six days I found a vessel ready to carry me to Japan, and spent fifteen days in the voyage. We landed at a small port-town called Xamoschi, situated on the south-east part of Japan; the town lies on the western point, where there is a narrow strait leading northward into along arm of the sea, upon the north-west part of which, Yedo, the metropolis, stands. At landing, I showed the custom-house officers my letter from the king of Luggnagg to his Imperial Majesty. They knew the seal perfectly well; it was as broad as the palm of my hand. The impression was, *A king lifting up a lame beggar from the earth.* The magistrates of the town, hearing of my letter, received me as a public minister. They provided me with carriages and servants, and bore my charges to Yedo; where I was admitted to an audience, and delivered my letter, which was opened with great ceremony, and explained to the Emperor by an interpreter, who then gave me notice, by his Majesty's order, that I should signify my request, and, whatever it were, it should be granted, for the sake of his royal brother of Luggnagg. This interpreter was a person employed to transact affairs with the Hollanders. He soon conjectured, by my countenance, that I was a European, and therefore repeated his Majesty's commands in Low Dutch, which he spoke perfectly well. I answered, as I had before determined, that I was a Dutch merchant, shipwrecked in a very remote country, whence I had travelled by sea and land to Luggnagg, and then took shipping for Japan; where I knew my countrymen often traded, and with some of these I hoped to get an opportunity of returning into Europe: I therefore most humbly entreated his royal favour, to give order that I should be conducted in safety to Nangasac. To this I added another petition, that for the sake of my patron the king of Luggnagg, his Majesty would condescend to excuse my performing the ceremony imposed on my countrymen, of trampling upon the crucifix, because I had been thrown into his kingdom by my misfortunes, without any intention of trading. When this latter petition was interpreted to the Emperor, he seemed a little surprised; and said, he believed I was the first of my countrymen who ever made any scruple in this point; and that he began to doubt, whether I was a real Hollander, or not; but rather suspected I must be a Christian. However, for the reasons I had offered, but chiefly to gratify the king of Luggnagg by an uncommon mark of his favour, he would comply with the singularity of my humour; but the affair must be managed with dexterity, and his officers should be commanded to let me pass, as it were by forgetfulness. For he assured me, that if the secret should be discovered by my countrymen the Dutch, they would cut my throat in the voyage. I returned my thanks, by the interpreter, for so unusual a favour; and some troops being at that time on their march to Nangasac, the commanding officer had orders to convey me safe thither, with particular instructions about the business of the crucifix.

On the 9th day of June, 1709, I arrived at Nangasac, after a very long and troublesome journey. I soon fell into the company of some Dutch sailors belonging to the Amboyna, of Amsterdam, a stout ship of 450 tons. I had lived long in Holland, pursuing my studies at Leyden, and I spoke Dutch well. The seamen soon knew whence I came last: they were curious to inquire into my voyages and course of life. I made up a story as short and probable as I could, but concealed the greatest part. I knew many persons in Holland. I was able to invent names for my parents, whom I pretended to be obscure people in the province of Gelderland. I would have given the captain (one Theodorus Vangrult) what he pleased to ask for my voyage to Holland; but understanding I was a surgeon, he was contented to take half the usual rate, on condition that I would serve him in the way of my calling. Before we took shipping, I was often asked by some of the crew, whether I had performed the ceremony above mentioned? I evaded the question by general answers; that I had satisfied the Emperor and court in all particulars. However, a malicious rogue of a skipper went to an officer, and pointing to me, told him, I had not yet trampled on the crucifix; but the other, who had received instructions to let me pass, gave the rascal twenty strokes on the shoulders with a bamboo; after which I was no more troubled with such questions.

Nothing happened worth mentioning in this voyage. We sailed with a fair wind to the Cape of Good Hope, where we staid only to take in fresh water. On the 10th of April, 1710, we arrived safe at Amsterdam, having lost only three men by sickness in the voyage, and a fourth, who fell from the foremast into the sea, not far from the coast of Guinea. From Amsterdam I soon after set sail for England, in a small vessel belonging to that city.

On the 16th of April, 1710, we put in at the Downs. I landed next morning, and saw once more my native country, after an absence of five years and six months complete. I went straight to Redriff, where I arrived the same day at two in the afternoon, and found my wife and family in good health.

Part IV
A Voyage to the Country of the Houyhnhnms

∽ Chapter I ∽

The author sets out as captain of a ship. His men conspire against him, confine him a long time to his cabin, and set him on shore in an unknown land. He travels up into the country. The Yahoos, a strange sort of animal, described. The author meets two Houyhnhnms.

I continued at home with my wife and children about five months, in a very happy condition, if I could have learned the lesson of knowing when I was well. I left my poor wife big with child, and accepted an advantageous offer made me to be captain of the Adventurer, a stout merchantman of 350 tons: for I understood navigation well, and being grown weary of a surgeon's employment at sea, which, however, I could exercise upon occasion, I took a skilful young man of that calling, one Robert Purefoy, into my ship. We set sail from Portsmouth upon the 7th day of September, 1710; on the 14th we met with Captain Pocock, of Bristol, at Teneriffe, who was going to the bay of Campechy to cut logwood. On the 16th, he was parted from us by a storm; I heard since my return, that his ship foundered, and none escaped but one cabin boy. He was an honest man, and a good sailor, but a little too positive in his own opinions, which was the cause of his destruction, as it has been with several others; for if he had followed my advice, he might have been safe at home with his family at this time, as well as myself.

I had several men who died in my ship of calentures, so that I was forced to get recruits out of Barbadoes and the Leeward Islands, where I touched, by the direction of the merchants who employed me; which I had soon too much cause to repent: for I found afterwards, that most of them had been buccaneers. I had fifty hands onboard; and my orders were, that I should trade with the Indians in the South-Sea, and make what discoveries I could. These rogues, whom I had picked up, debauched my other men, and they all formed a conspiracy to seize the ship, and secure me; which they did one morning, rushing into my cabin, and binding me hand and foot, threatening to throw me overboard, if I offered to stir. I told them, I was their prisoner, and would submit. This they made me swear to do, and then they unbound me, only fastening one of my legs with a chain, near my bed, and placed a sentry at my door with his piece charged, who was commanded to shoot me dead if I attempted my liberty. They sent me own victuals and drink, and took the government of the ship to themselves. Their design was to turn pirates and, plunder the Spaniards, which they could not do till they got more men. But first they resolved to sell the goods the ship, and then go to Madagascar for recruits, several among them having died since my confinement. They sailed many weeks, and traded with the Indians; but I knew not what course they took, being kept a close prisoner in my cabin, and expecting nothing less than to be murdered, as they often threatened me.

Upon the 9th day of May, 1711, one James Welch came down to my cabin, and said he had orders from the captain to set me ashore. I expostulated with him, but in vain; neither would he so much as tell me who their new captain was. They forced me into the long-boat, letting me put on my best suit of clothes, which were as good as new, and take a small bundle of linen, but no arms, except my hanger; and they were so civil as not to search my pockets, into which I conveyed what money I had, with some other little necessaries. They rowed about a league, and then set me down on a strand. I desired them to tell me what country it was. They all swore, they knew no more than myself; but said, that the captain (as they called him) was resolved, after they had sold the lading, to get rid of me in the first place where they could discover land. They pushed off immediately, advising me to make haste for fear of being overtaken by the tide, and so bade me farewell.

In this desolate condition I advanced forward, and soon got upon firm ground, where I sat down on a bank to rest myself, and consider what I had best do. When I was a little refreshed, I went up into the country, resolving to deliver myself to the first savages I should meet, and purchase my life from them by some bracelets, glass rings, and other toys, which sailors usually provide themselves with in those voyages, and whereof I had some about me. The land was divided by long rows of trees, not regularly planted, but naturally growing; there was great plenty of grass, and several fields of oats. I walked very circumspectly, for fear of being surprised, or suddenly shot with an arrow from behind, or on either side. I fell into a beaten road, where I saw many tracts of human feet, and some of cows, but most of horses. At last I beheld several animals in a field, and one or two of the same kind sitting in trees. Their shape was very singular and deformed, which a little discomposed me, so that I lay down behind a thicket to observe them better. Some of them coming forward near the place where I lay, gave me an opportunity of distinctly marking their form. Their heads and breasts were covered with a thick hair, some frizzled, and others lank; they had beards like goats, and a long ridge of hair down their backs, and the fore parts of their legs and feet; but the rest of their bodies was bare, so that I might see their skins, which were of a brown buff colour. They had no tails, nor any hair at all on their buttocks, except about the anus, which, I presume, nature had placed there to defend them as they sat on the ground, for this posture they used, as well as lying down, and often stood on their hind feet. They climbed high trees as nimbly as a squirrel, for they had strong extended claws before and behind, terminating in sharp points, and hooked. They would often spring, and bound, and leap, with prodigious agility. The females were not so large as the males; they had long lank hair on their heads, but none on their faces, nor any thing more than a sort of down on the rest of their bodies, except about the anus and pudenda. The dugs hung between their fore feet, and often reached almost to the ground as they walked. The hair of both sexes was of several colours, brown, red, black, and yellow. Upon the whole, I never beheld, in all my travels, so disagreeable an animal, or one against which I naturally conceived so strong an antipathy. So that, thinking I had seen enough, full of contempt and aversion, I got up, and pursued the beaten road, hoping it might direct me to the cabin of some Indian. I had not got far, when I met one of these creatures full in my way, and coming up directly to me. The ugly monster, when he saw me, distorted several ways, every feature of his visage, and stared, as at an object he had never seen before; then approaching nearer, lifted up his fore-paw, whether out of curiosity or mischief I could not tell; but I drew my hanger, and gave him a good blow with the flat side of it, for I durst not strike with the edge, fearing the inhabitants might be provoked against me, if they should come to know that I had killed or maimed any of their cattle. When the beast felt the smart, he drew back, and roared so loud, that a herd of at least forty came flocking about me from the next field, howling and making odious faces; but I ran to the body of a tree, and leaning my back against it, kept them off by waving my hanger. Several of this cursed brood, getting hold of the branches behind, leaped up into the tree, whence they began to discharge their excrements on my head; however, I escaped pretty well by sticking close to the stem of the tree, but was almost stifled with the filth, which fell about me on every side.

In the midst of this distress, I observed them all to run away on a sudden as fast as they could; at which I ventured to leave the tree and pursue the road, wondering what it was that could put them into this fright. But looking on my left hand, I saw a horse walking softly in the field; which my persecutors having sooner discovered, was the cause of their flight. The horse started a little, when he came near me, but soon recovering himself, looked full in my face with manifest tokens of wonder; he viewed my hands and feet, walking round me several times. I would have pursued my journey, but he placed himself directly in the way, yet looking with a very mild aspect, never offering the least violence. We stood gazing at each other for some time; at last I took the boldness to reach my hand towards his neck with a design to stroke it, using the common style and whistle of jockeys, when they are going to handle a strange horse. But this animal seemed to receive my civilities with disdain, shook his head, and bent his brows, softly raising up his right fore-foot to remove my hand. Then he neighed three or four times, but in so different a cadence, that I almost began to think he was speaking to himself, in some language of his own.

While he and I were thus employed, another horse came up; who applying himself to the first in a very formal manner, they gently struck each other's right hoof before, neighing several times by turns, and varying the sound, which seemed to be almost articulate. They went some paces off, as if it were to confer together, walking side by side, backward and forward, like persons deliberating upon some affair of weight, but often turning their eyes towards me, as it were to watch that I might not escape. I was amazed to see such actions and behaviour in brute beasts; and concluded with myself, that if the inhabitants of this country were endued with a proportionable degree of reason, they must needs be the wisest people upon earth. This thought gave me so much comfort, that I resolved to go forward, until I could discover some house or village, or meet with any of the natives, leaving the two horses to discourse together as they pleased. But the first, who was a dapple gray, observing me to steal off, neighed after me in so expressive a tone, that I fancied myself to understand what he meant; whereupon I turned back, and came near to him to expect his farther commands; but concealing my fear as much as I could, for I began to be in some pain how this adventure might terminate; and the reader will easily believe I did not much like my present situation.

The two horses came up close to me, looking with great earnestness upon my face and hands. The gray steed rubbed my hat all round with his right fore-hoof, and discomposed it so much that I was forced to adjust it better by taking it off and settling it again; whereat, both he and his companion (who was a brown bay) appeared to be much surprised; the latter felt the lappet of my coat, and finding it to hang loose about me, they both looked with new signs of wonder. He stroked my right hand, seeming to admire the softness and colour; but he squeezed it so hard between his hoof and his pastern, that I was forced to roar; after which they both touched me with all possible tenderness. They were under great perplexity about my shoes and stockings, which they felt very often, neighing to each other, and using various gestures, not unlike those of a philosopher, when he would attempt to solve some new and difficult phenomenon.

Upon the whole, the behaviour of these animals was so orderly and rational, so acute and judicious, that I at last concluded they must needs be magicians, who had thus metamorphosed themselves upon some design, and seeing a stranger in the way, resolved to divert themselves with him; or, perhaps, were really amazed at the sight of a man so very different in habit, feature, and complexion, from those who might probably live in so remote a climate. Upon the strength of this reasoning, I ventured to address them in the following manner: "Gentlemen, if you be conjurers, as I have good cause to believe, you can understand my language; therefore I make bold to let your worships know that I am a poor distressed Englishman, driven by his misfortunes upon your coast; and I entreat one of you to let me ride upon his back, as if he were a real horse, to some house or village where I can be relieved. In return of which favour, I will make you a present of this knife and bracelet," taking them out of my pocket. The two creatures stood silent while I spoke, seeming to listen with great attention, and when I had ended, they neighed frequently towards each other, as if they were engaged in serious conversation. I plainly observed that their language expressed the passions very well, and the words might, with little pains, be resolved into an alphabet more easily than the Chinese.

I could frequently distinguish the word *Yahoo*, which was repeated by each of them several times; and although it was impossible for me to conjecture what it meant, yet while the two horses were busy in conversation, I endeavoured to practise this word upon my tongue; and as soon as they were silent, I boldly pronounced *Yahoo* in a loud voice, imitating at the same time, as near as I could, the neighing of a horse; at which they were both visibly surprised; and the gray repeated the same word twice, as if he meant to teach me the right accent; wherein I spoke after him as well as I could, and found myself perceivably to improve every time, though very far from any degree of perfection. Then the bay tried me with a second word, much harder to be pronounced; but reducing it to the English orthography, may be spelt thus, *Houyhnhnm*. I did not succeed in this so well as in the former; but after two or three farther trials, I had better fortune; and they both appeared amazed at my capacity.

After some further discourse, which I then conjectured might relate to me, the two friends took their leaves, with the same compliment of striking each other's hoof; and the gray made me signs that I should walk before him; wherein I thought it prudent to comply, till I could find a better director. When I offered to slacken my pace, he would cry *hhuun hhuun*; I guessed his meaning, and gave him to understand, as well as I could, that I was weary, and not able to walk faster; upon which he would stand awhile to let me rest.

∽ **Chapter II** ∽

The author conducted by a Houyhnhnm to his house. The house described. The author's reception. The food of the Houyhnhnms. The author in distress for want of meat, is at last relieved. His manner of feeding in this country.

Having travelled about three miles, we came to a long kind of building, made of timber stuck in the ground, and wattled across; the roof was low and covered with straw. I now began to be a little comforted; and took out some toys, which travellers usually carry for presents to the savage Indians of America, and other parts, in hopes the people of the house would be thereby encouraged to receive me kindly. The horse made me a sign to go in first; it was a large room with a smooth clay floor, and a rack and manger, extending the whole length on one side. There were three nags and two mares, not eating, but some of them sitting down upon their hams, which I very much wondered at; but wondered more to see the rest employed in domestic business; these seemed but ordinary cattle. However, this confirmed my first opinion, that a people who could so far civilise brute animals, must needs excel in wisdom all the nations of the world. The gray came in just after, and thereby prevented any ill treatment which the others might have given me. He neighed to them several times in a style of authority, and received answers.

Beyond this room there were three others, reaching the length of the house, to which you passed through three doors, opposite to each other, in the manner of a vista. We went through the second room towards the third. Here the gray walked in first, beckoning me to attend: I waited in the second room, and got ready my presents for the master and mistress of the house; they were two knives, three bracelets of false pearls, a small looking-glass, and a bead necklace. The horse neighed three or four times, and I waited to hear some answers in a human voice, but I heard no other returns than in the same dialect, only one or two a little shriller than his. I began to think that this house must belong to some person of great note among them, because there appeared so much ceremony before I could gain admittance. But, that a man of quality should be served all by horses, was beyond my comprehension. I feared my brain was disturbed by my sufferings and misfortunes. I roused myself, and looked about me in the room where I was left alone: this was furnished like the first, only after a more elegant manner. I rubbed my eyes often, but the same objects still occurred. I pinched my arms and sides to awake myself, hoping I might be in a dream. I then absolutely concluded, that all these appearances could be nothing else but necromancy and magic. But I had no time to pursue these reflections; for the gray horse came to the door, and made me a sign to follow him into the third room where I saw a very comely mare, together with a colt and foal, sitting on their haunches upon mats of straw, not unartfully made, and perfectly neat and clean.

The mare soon after my entrance rose from her mat, and coming up close, after having nicely observed my hands and face, gave me a most contemptuous look; and turning to the horse, I heard the word *Yahoo* often repeated betwixt them; the meaning of which word I could not then comprehend, although it was the first I had learned to pronounce. But I was soon better informed, to my everlasting mortification; for the horse, beckoning to me with his head, and repeating the *hhuun, hhuun*, as he did upon the road, which I understood was to attend him, led me out into a kind of court, where was another building, at some distance from the house. Here we entered, and I saw three of those detestable creatures, which I first met after my landing, feeding upon roots, and the flesh of some animals, which I afterwards found to be that of asses and dogs, and now and then a cow, dead by accident or disease. They were all tied by the neck with strong withes fastened to a beam; they held their food between the claws of their fore feet, and tore it with their teeth.

The master horse ordered a sorrel nag, one of his servants, to untie the largest of these animals, and take him into the yard. The beast and I were brought close together, and by our countenances diligently compared both by master and servant, who thereupon repeated several times the word *Yahoo*. My horror and astonishment are not to be described, when I observed in this abominable animal, a perfect human figure: the face of it indeed was flat and broad, the nose depressed, the lips large, and the mouth wide; but these differences are common to all savage nations, where the lineaments of the countenance are distorted, by the natives suffering their infants to lie grovelling on the earth, or by carrying them on their backs, nuzzling with their face against the mothers' shoulders. The fore-feet of the *Yahoo* differed from my hands in nothing else but the length of the nails, the coarseness and brownness of the palms, and the hairiness on the backs. There was the same resemblance between our feet, with the same differences; which I knew very well, though the horses did not, because of my shoes and stockings; the same in every part of our bodies except as to hairiness and colour, which I have already described.

The great difficulty that seemed to stick with the two horses, was to see the rest of my body so very different from that of a *Yahoo*, for which I was obliged to my clothes, whereof they had no conception. The sorrel nag offered me a root, which he held (after their manner, as we shall describe in its proper place) between his hoof and pastern; I took it in my hand, and, having smelt it, returned it to him again as civilly as I could. He brought out of the *Yahoos'* kennel a piece of ass's flesh; but it smelt so offensively that I turned from it with loathing; he then threw it to the *Yahoo*, by whom it was greedily devoured. He afterwards showed me a wisp of hay, and a fetlock full of oats; but I shook my head, to signify that neither of these were food for me. And indeed I now apprehended that I must absolutely starve, if I did not get to some of my own species; for as to those filthy *Yahoos*, although there were few greater lovers of mankind at that time than myself, yet I confess I never saw any sensitive being so detestable on all accounts; and the more I came near them the more hateful they grew, while I stayed in that country. This the master horse observed by my behaviour, and therefore sent the *Yahoo* back to his kennel. He then put his fore-hoof to his mouth, at which I was much surprised, although he did it with ease, and with a motion that appeared perfectly natural, and made other signs, to know what I would eat; but I could not return him such an answer as he was able to apprehend; and if he had understood me, I did not see how it was possible to contrive any way for finding myself nourishment. While we were thus engaged, I observed a cow passing by, whereupon I pointed to her, and expressed a desire to go and milk her. This had its effect; for he led me back into the house, and ordered a mare-servant to open a room, where a good store of milk lay in earthen and wooden vessels, after a very orderly and cleanly manner. She gave me a large bowlful, of which I drank very heartily, and found myself well refreshed.

About noon, I saw coming towards the house a kind of vehicle drawn like a sledge by four *Yahoos*. There was in it an old steed, who seemed to be of quality; he alighted with his hind-feet forward, having by accident got a hurt in his left fore-foot. He came to dine with our horse, who received him with great civility. They dined in the best room, and had oats boiled in milk for the second course, which the old horse ate warm, but the rest cold. Their mangers were placed circular in the middle of the room, and divided into several partitions, round which they sat on their haunches, upon bosses of straw. In the middle was a large rack, with angles answering to every partition of the manger; so that each horse and mare ate their own hay, and their own mash of oats and milk, with much decency and regularity. The behaviour of the young colt and foal appeared very modest, and that of the master and mistress extremely cheerful and complaisant to their guest. The gray ordered me to stand by him; and much discourse passed between him and his friend concerning me, as I found by the stranger's often looking on me, and the frequent repetition of the word *Yahoo*.

I happened to wear my gloves, which the master gray observing, seemed perplexed, discovering signs of wonder what I had done to my fore feet. He put his hoof three or four times to them, as if he would signify, that I should reduce them to their former shape, which I presently did, pulling off both my gloves, and putting them into my pocket. This occasioned farther talk; and I saw the company was pleased with my behaviour, whereof I soon found the good effects. I was ordered to speak the few words I understood; and while they were at dinner, the master taught me the names for oats, milk, fire, water, and some others, which I could readily pronounce after him, having from my youth a great facility in learning languages.

When dinner was done, the master horse took me aside, and by signs and words made me understand the concern he was in that I had nothing to eat. Oats in their tongue are called *hlunnh*. This word I pronounced two or three times; for although I had refused them at first, yet, upon second thoughts, I considered that I could contrive to make of them a kind of bread, which might be sufficient, with milk, to keep me alive, till I could make my escape to some other country, and to creatures of my own species. The horse immediately ordered a white mare servant of his family to bring me a good quantity of oats in a sort of wooden tray. These I heated before the fire, as well as I could, and rubbed them till the husks came off, which I made a shift to winnow from the grain. I ground and beat them between two stones; then took water, and made them into a paste or cake, which I toasted at the fire and eat warm with milk. It was at first a very insipid diet, though common enough in many parts of Europe, but grew tolerable by time; and having been often reduced to hard fare in my life, this was not the first experiment I had made how easily nature is satisfied. And I cannot but observe, that I never had one hours sickness while I stayed in this island. It is true, I sometimes made a shift to catch a rabbit, or bird, by springs made of *Yahoo*'s hairs; and I often gathered wholesome herbs, which I boiled, and ate as salads with my bread; and now and then, for a rarity, I made a little butter, and drank the whey. I was at first at a great loss for salt, but custom soon reconciled me to the want of it; and I am confident that the frequent use of salt among us is an effect of luxury, and was first introduced only as a provocative to drink, except where it is necessary for preserving flesh in long voyages, or in places remote from great markets; for we observe no animal to be fond of it but man, and as to myself, when I left this country, it was a great while before I could endure the taste of it in anything that I ate.

This is enough to say upon the subject of my diet, wherewith other travellers fill their books, as if the readers were personally concerned whether we fare well or ill. However, it was necessary to mention this matter, lest the world should think it impossible that I could find sustenance for three years in such a country, and among such inhabitants.

When it grew towards evening, the master horse ordered a place for me to lodge in; it was but six yards from the house and separated from the stable of the *Yahoos*. Here I got some straw, and covering myself with my own clothes, slept very sound. But I was in a short time better accommodated, as the reader shall know hereafter, when I come to treat more particularly about my way of living.

Chapter III

The author studies to learn the language. The Houyhnhnm, his master, assists in teaching him. The language described. Several Houyhnhnms of quality come out of curiosity to see the author. He gives his master a short account of his voyage.

My principal endeavour was to learn the language, which my master (for so I shall henceforth call him), and his children, and every servant of his house, were desirous to teach me; for they looked upon it as a prodigy, that a brute animal should discover such marks of a rational creature. I pointed to every thing, and inquired the name of it, which I wrote down in my journal-book when I was alone, and corrected my bad accent by desiring those of the family to pronounce it often. In this employment, a sorrel nag, one of the under-servants, was very ready to assist me.

In speaking, they pronounced through the nose and throat, and their language approaches nearest to the High-Dutch, or German, of any I know in Europe; but is much more graceful and significant. The emperor Charles V. made almost the same observation, when he said that if he were to speak to his horse, it should be in High-Dutch.

The curiosity and impatience of my master were so great, that he spent many hours of his leisure to instruct me. He was convinced (as he afterwards told me) that I must be a *Yahoo*; but my teachableness, civility, and cleanliness, astonished him; which were qualities altogether opposite to those animals. He was most perplexed about my clothes, reasoning sometimes with himself, whether they were a part of my body; for I never pulled them off till the family were asleep, and got them on before they waked in the morning. My master was eager to learn whence I came; how I acquired those appearances of reason, which I discovered in all my actions; and to know my story from my own mouth, which he hoped he should soon do by the great proficiency I made in learning and pronouncing their words and sentences. To help my memory, I formed all I learned into the English alphabet, and writ the words down, with the translations. This last, after some time, I ventured to do in my master's presence. It cost me much trouble to explain to him what I was doing; for the inhabitants have not the least idea of books or literature.

In about ten weeks time, I was able to understand most of his questions; and in three months, could give him some tolerable answers. He was extremely curious to know from what part of the country I came, and how I was taught to imitate a rational creature; because the *Yahoos* (whom he saw I exactly resembled in my head, hands, and face, that were only visible), with some appearance of cunning, and the strongest disposition to mischief, were observed to be the most unteachable of all brutes. I answered, that I came over the sea, from a far place, with many others of my own kind, in a great hollow vessel made of the bodies of trees: that my companions forced me to land on this coast, and then left me to shift for myself. It was with some difficulty, and by the help of many signs, that I brought him to understand me. He replied, that I must needs be mistaken, or that I said the thing which was not;" for they have no word in their language to express lying or falsehood. He knew it was impossible that there could be a country beyond the sea, or that a parcel of brutes could move a wooden vessel whither they pleased upon water. He was sure no *Houyhnhnm* alive could make such a vessel, nor would trust *Yahoos* to manage it.

The word *Houyhnhnm*, in their tongue, signifies a *horse*, and, in its etymology, the *perfection of nature*. I told my master, that I was at a loss for expression, but would improve as fast as I could; and hoped, in a short time, I should be able to tell him wonders. He was pleased to direct his own mare, his colt, and foal, and the servants of the family, to take all opportunities of instructing me; and every day, for two or three hours, he was at the same pains himself. Several horses and mares of quality in the neighbourhood came often to our house, upon the report spread of a wonderful *Yahoo*, that could speak like a *Houyhnhnm*, and seemed, in his words and actions, to discover some glimmerings of reason. These delighted to converse with me: they put many questions, and received such answers as I was able to return. By all these advantages I made so great a progress, that, in five months from my arrival I understood whatever was spoken, and could express myself tolerably well.

The *Houyhnhnms*, who came to visit my master out of a design of seeing and talking with me, could hardly believe me to be a right *Yahoo*, because my body had a different covering from others of my kind. They were astonished to observe me without the usual hair or skin, except on my head, face, and hands; but I discovered that secret to my master upon an accident which happened about a fortnight before.

I have already told the reader, that every night, when the family were gone to bed, it was my custom to strip, and cover myself with my clothes. It happened, one morning early, that my master sent for me by the sorrel nag, who was his valet. When he came I was fast asleep, my clothes fallen off on one side, and my shirt above my waist. I awaked at the noise he made, and observed him to deliver his message in some disorder; after which he went to my master, and in a great fright gave him a very confused account of what he had seen. This I presently discovered, for, going as soon as I was dressed to pay my attendance upon his honour, he asked me the meaning of what his servant had reported, that I was not the same thing when I slept, as I appeared to be at other times; that his vale assured him, some part of me was white, some yellow, at least not so white, and some brown.

I had hitherto concealed the secret of my dress, in order to distinguish myself, as much as possible, from that cursed race of *Yahoos*; but now I found it in vain to do so any longer. Besides, I considered that my clothes and shoes would soon wear out, which already were in a declining condition, and must be supplied by some contrivance from the hides of *Yahoos*, or other brutes; whereby the whole secret would be known. I therefore told my master, that in the country whence I came, those of my kind always covered their bodies with the hairs of certain animals prepared by art, as well for decency as to avoid the inclemencies of air, both hot and cold; of which, as to my own person, I would give him immediate conviction, if he pleased to command me; only desiring his excuse, if I did not expose those parts that nature taught us to conceal. He said, my discourse was all very strange, but especially the last part; for he could not understand, why nature should teach us to conceal what nature had given; that neither himself nor family were ashamed of any parts of their bodies; but, however, I might do as I pleased. Whereupon I first unbuttoned my coat, and pulled it off. I did the same with my waistcoat. I drew off my shoes, stockings, and breeches. I let my shirt down to my waist, and drew up the bottom; fastening it like a girdle about my middle, to hide my nakedness.

My master observed the whole performance with great signs of curiosity and admiration. He took up all my clothes in his pastern, one piece after another, and examined them diligently; he then stroked my body very gently, and looked round me several times; after which, he said, it was plain I must be a perfect *Yahoo*; but that I differed very much from the rest of my species in the softness, whiteness, and smoothness of my skin; my want of hair in several parts of my body; the shape and shortness of my claws behind and before; and my affectation of walking continually on my two hinder feet. He desired to see no more; and gave me leave to put on my clothes again, for I was shuddering with cold.

I expressed my uneasiness at his giving me so often the appellation of *Yahoo*, an odious animal, for which I had so utter a hatred and contempt. I begged he would forbear applying that word to me, and make the same order in his family and among his friends whom he suffered to see me. I requested likewise, that the secret of my having a false covering to my body, might be known to none but himself, at least as long as my present clothing should last; for as to what the sorrel nag, his valet, had observed, his honour might command him to conceal it.

All this my master very graciously consented to; and thus the secret was kept till my clothes began to wear out, which I was forced to supply by several contrivances that shall hereafter be mentioned. In the meantime, he desired I would go on with my utmost diligence to learn their language, because he was more astonished at my capacity for speech and reason, than at the figure of my body, whether it were covered or not; adding, that he waited with some impatience to hear the wonders which I promised to tell him.

From thenceforward he doubled the pains he had been at to instruct me; he brought me into all company, and made them treat me with civility; because, as he told them, privately, this would put me into good humour, and make me more diverting.

Every day, when I waited on him, beside the trouble he was at in teaching, he would ask me several questions concerning myself, which I answered as well as I could, and by these means he had already received some general ideas, though very imperfect. It would be tedious to relate the several steps by which I advanced to a more regular conversation; but the first account I gave of myself in any order and length was to this purpose:

That I came from a very far country, as I already had attempted to tell him, with about fifty more of my own species; that we travelled upon the seas in a great hollow vessel made of wood, and larger than his honour's house. I described the ship to him in the best terms I could, and explained, by the help of my handkerchief displayed, how it was driven forward by the wind. That upon a quarrel among us, I was set on shore on this coast, where I walked forward, without knowing whither, till he delivered me from the persecution of those execrable *Yahoos*. He asked me, who made the ship, and how it was possible that the *Houyhnhnms* of my country would leave it to the management of brutes? My answer was, that I durst proceed no further in my relation, unless he would give me his word and honour that he would not be offended, and then I would tell him the wonders I had so often promised." He agreed; and I went on by assuring him, that the ship was made by creatures like myself; who, in all the countries I had travelled, as well as in my own, were the only governing rational animals; and that upon my arrival hither, I was as much astonished to see the *Houyhnhnms* act like rational beings, as he, or his friends, could be, in finding some marks of reason in a creature he was pleased to call a *Yahoo*; to which I owned my resemblance in every part, but could not account for their degenerate and brutal nature. I said farther, that if good fortune ever restored me to my native country, to relate my travels hither, as I resolved to do, everybody would believe, that I said the thing that was not, that I invented the story out of my own head; and (with all possible respect to himself, his family, and friends, and under his promise of not being offended) our countrymen would hardly think it probable that a *Houyhnhnm* should be the presiding creature of a nation, and a *Yahoo* the brute.

⌒ **Chapter IV** ⌒

The Houyhnhnm's notion of truth and falsehood. The author's discourse disapproved by his master. The author gives a more particular account of himself, and the accidents of his voyage.

My master heard me with great appearances of uneasiness in his countenance; because doubting, or not believing, are so little known in this country, that the inhabitants cannot tell how to behave themselves under such circumstances. And I remember, in frequent discourses with my master concerning the nature of manhood in other parts of the world, having occasion to talk of *lying and false representation*, it was with much difficulty that he comprehended what I meant, although he had otherwise a most acute judgment. For he argued thus: that the use of speech was to make us understand one another, and to receive information of facts; now, if any one said the thing which was not, these ends were defeated, because I cannot properly be said to understand him; and I am so far from receiving information, that he leaves me worse than in ignorance; for I am led to believe a thing black, when it is white, and short, when it is long. And these were all the notions he had concerning that faculty of lying, so perfectly well understood, and so universally practised, among human creatures.

To return from this digression. When I asserted that the *Yahoos* were the only governing animals in my country, which my master said was altogether past his conception, he desired to know, whether we had *Houyhnhnms* among us, and what was their employment? I told him, we had great numbers; that in summer they grazed in the fields, and in winter were kept in houses with hay and oats, where *Yahoo* servants were employed to rub their skins smooth, comb their manes, pick their feet, serve them with food, and make their beds. "I understand you well," said my master: "it is now very plain, from all you have spoken, that whatever share of reason the *Yahoos* pretend to, the *Houyhnhnms* are your masters; I heartily wish our *Yahoos* would be so tractable." I begged his honour would please to excuse me from proceeding any further, because I was very certain that the account he expected from me would be highly displeasing. But he insisted in commanding me to let him know the best and the worst. I told him he should be obeyed. I owned that the *Houyhnhnms* among us, whom we called horses, were the most generous and comely animals we had; that they excelled in strength and swiftness; and when they belonged to persons of quality, were employed in travelling, racing, or drawing chariots; they were treated with much kindness and care, till they fell into diseases, or became foundered in the feet; but then they were sold, and used to all kind of drudgery till they died; after which their skins were stripped, and sold for what they were worth, and their bodies left to be devoured by dogs and birds of prey. But the common race of horses had not so good fortune, being kept by farmers and carriers, and other mean people, who put them to greater labour, and fed them worse. I described, as well as I could, our way of riding; the shape and use of a bridle, a saddle, a spur, and a whip; of harness and wheels. I added, that we fastened plates of a certain hard substance, called iron, at the bottom of their feet, to preserve their hoofs from being broken by the stony ways, on which we often travelled.

My master, after some expressions of great indignation, wondered how we dared to venture upon a *Houyhnhnm's* back; for he was sure, that the weakest servant in his house would be able to shake off the strongest *Yahoo*; or by lying down and rolling on his back, squeeze the brute to death. I answered that our horses were trained up, from three or four years old, to the several uses we intended them for; that if any of them proved intolerably vicious, they were employed for carriages; that they were severely beaten, while they were young, for any mischievous tricks; that the males, designed for the common use of riding or draught, were generally castrated about two years after their birth, to take down their spirits, and make them more tame and gentle; that they were indeed sensible of rewards and punishments; but his honour would please to consider, that they had not the least tincture of reason, any more than the *Yahoos* in this country.

It put me to the pains of many circumlocutions, to give my master a right idea of what I spoke; for their language does not abound in variety of words, because their wants and passions are fewer than among us. But it is impossible to express his noble resentment at our savage treatment of the *Houyhnhnm* race; particularly after I had explained the manner and use of castrating horses among us, to hinder them from propagating their kind, and to render them more servile. He said, if it were possible there could be any country where *Yahoos* alone were endued with reason, they certainly must be the governing animal; because reason in time will always prevail against brutal strength. But, considering the frame of our bodies, and especially of mine, he thought no creature of equal bulk was so ill-contrived for employing that reason in the common offices of life; whereupon he desired to know whether those among whom I lived resembled me, or the *Yahoos* of his country? I assured him, that I was as well shaped as most of my age; but the younger, and the females, were much more soft and tender, and the skins of the latter generally as white as milk. He said, I differed indeed from other *Yahoos*, being much more cleanly, and not altogether so deformed; but, in point of real advantage, he thought I differed for the worse: that my nails were of no use either to my fore or hinder feet; as to my fore feet, he could not properly call them by that name, for he never observed me to walk upon them; that they were too soft to bear the ground; that I generally went with them uncovered; neither was the covering I sometimes wore on them of the same shape, or so strong as that on my feet behind; that I could not walk with any security, for if either of my hinder feet slipped, I must inevitably fail. He then began to find fault with other parts of my body: the flatness of my face, the prominence of my nose, mine eyes placed directly in front, so that I could not look on either side without turning my head; that I was not able to feed myself, without lifting one of my fore-feet to my mouth, and therefore nature had placed those joints to answer that necessity. He knew not what could be the use of those several clefts and divisions in my feet behind; that these were too soft to bear the hardness and sharpness of stones, without a covering made from the skin of some other brute; that my whole body wanted a fence against heat and cold, which I was forced to put on and off every day, with tediousness and trouble. And lastly, that he observed every animal in this country naturally to abhor the *Yahoos*, whom the weaker avoided, and the stronger drove from them. So that, supposing us to have the gift of reason, he could not see how it were possible to cure that natural antipathy, which every creature discovered against us; nor consequently how we could tame and render them serviceable. However, he would, as he said, debate the matter no farther, because he was more desirous to know my own story, the country where I was born, and the several actions and events of my life, before I came hither.

I assured him, how extremely desirous I was that he should be satisfied on every point; but I doubted much, whether it would be possible for me to explain myself on several subjects, whereof his honour could have no conception; because I saw nothing in his country to which I could resemble them; that, however, I would do my best, and strive to express myself by similitudes, humbly desiring his assistance when I wanted proper words; which he was pleased to promise me.

I said, my birth was of honest parents, in an island called England; which was remote from his country, as many days' journey as the strongest of his honour's servants could travel in the annual course of the sun; that I was bred a surgeon, whose trade it is to cure wounds and hurts in the body, gotten by accident or violence; that my country was governed by a female man, whom we called queen; that I left it to get riches, whereby I might maintain myself and family, when I should return; that, in my last voyage, I was commander of the ship, and had about fifty *Yahoos* under me, many of which died at sea, and I was forced to supply them by others picked out from several nations; that our ship was twice in danger of being sunk, the first time by a great storm, and the second by striking against a rock. Here my master interposed, by asking me, how I could persuade strangers, out of different countries, to venture with me, after the losses I had sustained, and the hazards I had run? I said, they were fellows of desperate fortunes, forced to fly from the places of their birth on account of their poverty or their crimes. Some were undone by lawsuits; others spent all they had in drinking, whoring, and gaming; others fled for treason; many for murder, theft, poisoning, robbery, perjury, forgery, coining false money, for committing rapes, or sodomy; for flying from their colours, or deserting to the enemy; and most of them had broken prison; none of these durst return to their native countries, for fear of being hanged, or of starving in a jail; and therefore they were under the necessity of seeking a livelihood in other places.

During this discourse, my master was pleased to interrupt me several times. I had made use of many circumlocutions in describing to him the nature of the several crimes for which most of our crew had been forced to fly their country. This labour took up several days' conversation, before he was able to comprehend me. He was wholly at a loss to know what could be the use or necessity of practising those vices. To clear up which, I endeavoured to give some ideas of the desire of power and riches; of the terrible effects of lust, intemperance, malice, and envy. All this I was forced to define and describe by putting cases and making suppositions. After which, like one whose imagination was struck with something never seen or heard of before, he would lift up his eyes with amazement and indignation. Power, government, war, law, punishment, and a thousand other things, had no terms wherein that language could express them, which made the difficulty almost insuperable, to give my master any conception of what I meant. But being of an excellent understanding, much improved by contemplation and converse, he at last arrived at a competent knowledge of what human nature, in our parts of the world, is capable to perform, and desired I would give him some particular account of that land which we call Europe, but especially of my own country.

Chapter V

The author at his master's command, informs him of the state of England. The causes of war among the princes of Europe. The author begins to explain the English constitution.

The reader may please to observe, that the following extract of many conversations I had with my master, contains a summary of the most material points which were discoursed at several times for above two years; his Honour often desiring fuller satisfaction, as I farther improved in the *Houyhnhnm* tongue. I laid before him, as well as I could, the whole state of Europe; I discoursed of trade and manufactures, of arts and sciences; and the answers I gave to all the questions he made, as they arose upon several subjects, were a fund of conversation not to be exhausted. But I shall here only set down the substance of what passed between us concerning my own country, reducing it in order as well as I can, without any regard to time or other circumstances, while I strictly adhere to truth. My only concern is, that I shall hardly be able to do justice to my master's arguments and expressions, which must needs suffer by my want of capacity, as well as by a translation into our barbarous English.

In obedience, therefore, to his honour's commands, I related to him the Revolution under the Prince of Orange; the long war with France, entered into by the said prince, and renewed by his successor, the present queen, wherein the greatest powers of Christendom were engaged, and which still continued: I computed, at his request, that about a million of *Yahoos* might have been killed in the whole progress of it; and perhaps a hundred or more cities taken, and five times as many ships burnt or sunk.

He asked me, what were the usual causes or motives that made one country go to war with another? I answered they were innumerable; but I should only mention a few of the chief. Sometimes the ambition of princes, who never think they have land or people enough to govern; sometimes the corruption of ministers, who engage their master in a war, in order to stifle or divert the clamour of the subjects against their evil administration. Difference in opinions has cost many millions of lives: for instance, whether flesh be bread, or bread be flesh; whether the juice of a certain berry be blood or wine; whether whistling be a vice or a virtue; whether it be better to kiss a post, or throw it into the fire; what is the best colour for a coat, whether black, white, red, or gray; and whether it should be long or short, narrow or wide, dirty or clean; with many more. Neither are any wars so furious and bloody, or of so long a continuance, as those occasioned by difference in opinion, especially if it be in things indifferent.

Sometimes the quarrel between two princes is to decide which of them shall dispossess a third of his dominions, where neither of them pretend to any right. Sometimes one prince quarrels with another for fear the other should quarrel with him. Sometimes a war is entered upon, because the enemy is too strong; and sometimes, because he is too weak. Sometimes our neighbours want the things which we have, or have the things which we want, and we both fight, till they take ours, or give us theirs. It is a very justifiable cause of a war, to invade a country after the people have been wasted by famine, destroyed by pestilence, or embroiled by factions among themselves. It is justifiable to enter into war against our nearest ally, when one of his towns lies convenient for us, or a territory of land, that would render our dominions round and complete. If a prince sends forces into a nation, where the people are poor and ignorant, he may lawfully put half of them to death, and make slaves of the rest, in order to civilize and reduce them from their barbarous way of living. It is a very kingly, honourable, and frequent practice, when one prince desires the assistance of another, to secure him against an invasion, that the assistant, when he has driven out the invader, should seize on the dominions himself, and kill, imprison, or banish, the prince he came to relieve. Alliance by blood, or marriage, is a frequent cause of war between princes; and the nearer the kindred is, the greater their disposition to quarrel; poor nations are hungry, and rich nations are proud; and pride and hunger will ever be at variance. For these reasons, the trade of a soldier is held the most honourable of all others; because a soldier is a *Yahoo* hired to kill, in cold blood, as many of his own species, who have never offended him, as possibly he can.

There is likewise a kind of beggarly princes in Europe, not able to make war by themselves, who hire out their troops to richer nations, for so much a day to each man; of which they keep three-fourths to themselves, and it is the best part of their maintenance: such are those in many northern parts of Europe.

"What you have told me," said my master, "upon the subject of war, does indeed discover most admirably the effects of that reason you pretend to: however, it is happy that the shame is greater than the danger; and that nature has left you utterly incapable of doing much mischief. For, your mouths lying flat with your faces, you can hardly bite each other to any purpose, unless by consent. Then as to the claws upon your feet before and behind, they are so short and tender, that one of our *Yahoos* would drive a dozen of yours before him. And therefore, in recounting the numbers of those who have been killed in battle, I cannot but think you have said the thing which is not."

I could not forbear shaking my head, and smiling a little at his ignorance. And being no stranger to the art of war, I gave him a description of cannons, culverins, muskets, carabines, pistols, bullets, powder, swords, bayonets, battles, sieges, retreats, attacks, undermines, countermines, bombardments, sea fights, ships sunk with a thousand men, twenty thousand killed on each side, dying groans, limbs flying in the air, smoke, noise, confusion, trampling to death under horses' feet, flight, pursuit, victory; fields strewed with carcases, left for food to dogs and wolves and birds of prey; plundering, stripping, ravishing, burning, and destroying. And to set forth the valour of my own dear countrymen, I assured him, that I had seen them blow up a hundred enemies at once in a siege, and as many in a ship, and beheld the dead bodies drop down in pieces from the clouds, to the great diversion of the spectators.

I was going on to more particulars, when my master commanded me silence. He said, whoever understood the nature of *Yahoos*, might easily believe it possible for so vile an animal to be capable of every action I had named, if their strength and cunning equalled their malice. But as my discourse had increased his abhorrence of the whole species, so he found it gave him a disturbance in his mind to which he was wholly a stranger before. He thought his ears, being used to such abominable words, might, by degrees, admit them with less detestation: that although he hated the *Yahoos* of this country, yet he no more blamed them for their odious qualities, than he did a *gnnayh* (a bird of prey) for its cruelty, or a sharp stone for cutting his hoof. But when a creature pretending to reason could be capable of such enormities, he dreaded lest the corruption of that faculty might be worse than brutality itself. He seemed therefore confident, that, instead of reason we were only possessed of some quality fitted to increase our natural vices; as the reflection from a troubled stream returns the image of an ill shapen body, not only larger but more distorted.

He added, that he had heard too much upon the subject of war, both in this and some former discourses. There was another point, which a little perplexed him at present. I had informed him, that some of our crew left their country on account of being ruined by law; that I had already explained the meaning of the word; but he was at a loss how it should come to pass, that the law, which was intended for every man's preservation, should be any man's ruin. Therefore he desired to be further satisfied what I meant by law, and the dispensers thereof, according to the present practice in my own country; because he thought nature and reason were sufficient guides for a reasonable animal, as we pretended to be, in showing us what he ought to do, and what to avoid.

I assured his honour, that the law was a science in which I had not much conversed, further than by employing advocates, in vain, upon some injustices that had been done me; however, I would give him all the satisfaction I was able.

I said, there was a society of men among us, bred up from their youth in the art of proving, by words multiplied for the purpose, that white is black, and black is white, according as they are paid. To this society all the rest of the people are slaves. For example, if my neighbour has a mind to my cow, he has a lawyer to prove that he ought to have my cow from me. I must then hire another to defend my right, it being against all rules of law that any man should be allowed to speak for himself. Now, in this case, I, who am the right owner, lie under two great disadvantages: first, my lawyer, being practised almost from his cradle in defending falsehood, is quite out of his element when he would be an advocate for justice, which is an unnatural office he always attempts with great awkwardness, if not with ill-will. The second disadvantage is, that my lawyer must proceed with great caution, or else he will be reprimanded by the judges, and abhorred by his brethren, as one that would lessen the practice of the law. And therefore I have but two methods to preserve my cow. The first is, to gain over my adversary's lawyer with a double fee, who will then betray his client by insinuating that he hath justice on his side. The second way is for my lawyer to make my cause appear as unjust as he can, by allowing the cow to belong to my adversary; and this, if it be skilfully done, will certainly bespeak the favour of the bench. Now your honour is to know, that these judges are persons appointed to decide all controversies of property, as well as for the trial of criminals, and picked out from the most dexterous lawyers, who are grown old or lazy; and having been biased all their lives against truth and equity, lie under such a fatal necessity of favouring fraud, perjury, and oppression, that I have known some of them refuse a large bribe from the side where justice lay, rather than injure the faculty, by doing any thing unbecoming their nature or their office.

It is a maxim among these lawyers that whatever has been done before, may legally be done again: and therefore they take special care to record all the decisions formerly made against common justice, and the general reason of mankind. These, under the name of precedents, they produce as authorities to justify the most iniquitous opinions; and the judges never fail of directing accordingly.

In pleading, they studiously avoid entering into the merits of the cause; but are loud, violent, and tedious, in dwelling upon all circumstances which are not to the purpose. For instance, in the case already mentioned; they never desire to know what claim or title my adversary has to my cow; but whether the said cow were red or black; her horns long or short; whether the field I graze her in be round or square; whether she was milked at home or abroad; what diseases she is subject to, and the like; after which they consult precedents, adjourn the cause from time to time, and in ten, twenty, or thirty years, come to an issue.

It is likewise to be observed, that this society has a peculiar cant and jargon of their own, that no other mortal can understand, and wherein all their laws are written, which they take special care to multiply; whereby they have wholly confounded the very essence of truth and falsehood, of right and wrong; so that it will take thirty years to decide, whether the field left me by my ancestors for six generations belongs to me, or to a stranger three hundred miles off.

In the trial of persons accused for crimes against the state, the method is much more short and commendable: the judge first sends to sound the disposition of those in power, after which he can easily hang or save a criminal, strictly preserving all due forms of law.

Here my master interposing, said, it was a pity, that creatures endowed with such prodigious abilities of mind, as these lawyers, by the description I gave of them, must certainly be, were not rather encouraged to be instructors of others in wisdom and knowledge. In answer to which I assured his honour, that in all points out of their own trade, they were usually the most ignorant and stupid generation among us, the most despicable in common conversation, avowed enemies to all knowledge and learning, and equally disposed to pervert the general reason of mankind in every other subject of discourse as in that of their own profession.

⌒ **Chapter VI** ⌒

A continuation of the state of England under Queen Anne. The character of a first minister of state in European courts.

My master was yet wholly at a loss to understand what motives could incite this race of lawyers to perplex, disquiet, and weary themselves, and engage in a confederacy of injustice, merely for the sake of injuring their fellow-animals; neither could he comprehend what I meant in saying, they did it for hire. Whereupon I was at much pains to describe to him the use of money, the materials it was made of, and the value of the metals; that when a *Yahoo* had got a great store of this precious substance, he was able to purchase whatever he had a mind to; the finest clothing, the noblest houses, great tracts of land, the most costly meats and drinks, and have his choice of the most beautiful females. Therefore since money alone was able to perform all these feats, our *Yahoos* thought they could never have enough of it to spend, or to save, as they found themselves inclined, from their natural bent either to profusion or avarice; that the rich man enjoyed the fruit of the poor man's labour, and the latter were a thousand to one in proportion to the former; that the bulk of our people were forced to live miserably, by labouring every day for small wages, to make a few live plentifully.

I enlarged myself much on these, and many other particulars to the same purpose; but his honour was still to seek; for he went upon a supposition, that all animals had a title to their share in the productions of the earth, and especially those who presided over the rest. Therefore he desired I would let him know, what these costly meats were, and how any of us happened to want them? Whereupon I enumerated as many sorts as came into my head, with the various methods of dressing them, which could not be done without sending vessels by sea to every part of the world, as well for liquors to drink as for sauces and innumerable other conveniences. I assured him that this whole globe of earth must be at least three times gone round before one of our better female *Yahoos* could get her breakfast, or a cup to put it in. He said that must needs be a miserable country which cannot furnish food for its own inhabitants. But what he chiefly wondered at was, how such vast tracts of ground as I described should be wholly without fresh water, and the people put to the necessity of sending over the sea for drink. I replied that England (the dear place of my nativity) was computed to produce three times the quantity of food more than its inhabitants are able to consume, as well as liquors extracted from grain, or pressed out of the fruit of certain trees, which made excellent drink, and the same proportion in every other convenience of life. But, in order to feed the luxury and intemperance of the males, and the vanity of the females, we sent away the greatest part of our necessary things to other countries, whence, in return, we brought the materials of diseases, folly, and vice, to spend among ourselves. Hence it follows of necessity, that vast numbers of our people are compelled to seek their livelihood by begging, robbing, stealing, cheating, pimping, flattering, suborning, forswearing, forging, gaming, lying, fawning, hectoring, voting, scribbling, star-gazing, poisoning, whoring, canting, libelling, freethinking, and the like occupations: every one of which terms I was at much pains to make him understand.

That wine was not imported among us from foreign countries to supply the want of water or other drinks, but because it was a sort of liquid which made us merry by putting us out of our senses, diverted all melancholy thoughts, begat wild extravagant imaginations in the brain, raised our hopes and banished our fears, suspended every office of reason for a time, and deprived us of the use of our limbs, till we fell into a profound sleep; although it must be confessed, that we always awaked sick and dispirited; and that the use of this liquor filled us with diseases which made our lives uncomfortable and short.

But beside all this, the bulk of our people supported themselves by furnishing the necessities or conveniences of life to the rich and to each other. For instance, when I am at home, and dressed as I ought to be, I carry on my body the workmanship of a hundred tradesmen; the building and furniture of my house employ as many more, and five times the number to adorn my wife.

I was going on to tell him of another sort of people, who get their livelihood by attending the sick, having, upon some occasions, informed his honour that many of my crew had died of diseases. But here it was with the utmost difficulty that I brought him to apprehend what I meant. He could easily conceive, that a *Houyhnhnm*, grew weak and heavy a few days before his death, or by some accident might hurt a limb; but that nature, who works all things to perfection, should suffer any pains to breed in our bodies, he thought impossible, and desired to know the reason of so unaccountable an evil.

I told him we fed on a thousand things which operated contrary to each other; that we ate when we were not hungry, and drank without the provocation of thirst; that we sat whole nights drinking strong liquors, without eating a bit, which disposed us to sloth, inflamed our bodies, and precipitated or prevented digestion; that prostitute female *Yahoos* acquired a certain malady, which bred rottenness in the bones of those who fell into their embraces; that this, and many other diseases, were propagated from father to son; so that great numbers came into the world with complicated maladies upon them; that it would be endless to give him a catalogue of all diseases incident to human bodies, for they would not be fewer than five or six hundred, spread over every limb and joint — in short, every part, external and intestine, having diseases appropriated to itself. To remedy which, there was a sort of people bred up among us in the profession, or pretence, of curing the sick. And because I had some skill in the faculty, I would, in gratitude to his honour, let him know the whole mystery and method by which they proceed.

Their fundamental is, that all diseases arise from repletion; whence they conclude, that a great evacuation of the body is necessary, either through the natural passage or upwards at the mouth. Their next business is from herbs, minerals, gums, oils, shells, salts, juices, sea-weed, excrements, barks of trees, serpents, toads, frogs, spiders, dead men's flesh and bones, birds, beasts, and fishes, to form a composition, for smell and taste, the most abominable, nauseous, and detestable, they can possibly contrive, which the stomach immediately rejects with loathing, and this they call a vomit; or else, from the same store-house, with some other poisonous additions, they command us to take in at the orifice above or below (just as the physician then happens to be disposed) a medicine equally annoying and disgustful to the bowels; which, relaxing the belly, drives down all before it; and this they call a *purge*, or a *clyster*. For nature (as the physicians allege) having intended the superior anterior orifice only for the intromission of solids and liquids, and the inferior posterior for ejection; these artists ingeniously considering that in all diseases nature is forced out of her seat, therefore, to replace her in it, the body must be treated in a manner directly contrary, by interchanging the use of each orifice; forcing solids and liquids in at the anus, and making evacuations at the mouth.

But, besides real diseases, we are subject to many that are only imaginary, for which the physicians have invented imaginary cures; these have their several names, and so have the drugs that are proper for them; and with these our female *Yahoos* are always infested.

One great excellency in this tribe, is their skill at prognostics, wherein they seldom fail; their predictions in real diseases, when they rise to any degree of malignity, generally portending death, which is always in their power, when recovery is not: and therefore, upon any unexpected signs of amendment, after they have pronounced their sentence, rather than be accused as false prophets, they know how to approve their sagacity to the world, by a seasonable dose.

They are likewise of special use to husbands and wives who are grown weary of their mates; to eldest sons, to great ministers of state, and often to princes.

I had formerly, upon occasion, discoursed with my master upon the nature of government in general, and particularly of our own excellent constitution, deservedly the wonder and envy of the whole world. But having here accidentally mentioned a minister of state, he commanded me, some time after, to inform him, what species of *Yahoo* I particularly meant by that appellation.

I told him, that a first or chief minister of state, who was the person I intended to describe, was the creature wholly exempt from joy and grief, love and hatred, pity and anger; at least, makes use of no other passions, but a violent desire of wealth, power, and titles; that he applies his words to all uses, except to the indication of his mind; that he never tells a truth but with an intent that you should take it for a lie; nor a lie, but with a design that you should take it for a truth; that those he speaks worst of behind their backs are in the surest way of preferment; and whenever he begins to praise you to others, or to yourself, you are from that day forlorn. The worst mark you can receive is a promise, especially when it is confirmed with an oath; after which, every wise man retires, and gives over all hopes.

There are three methods, by which a man may rise to be chief minister. The first is, by knowing how, with prudence, to dispose of a wife, a daughter, or a sister; the second, by betraying or undermining his predecessor; and the third is, by a furious zeal, in public assemblies, against the corruption's of the court. But a wise prince would rather choose to employ those who practise the last of these methods; because such zealots prove always the most obsequious and subservient to the will and passions of their master. That these ministers, having all employments at their disposal, preserve themselves in power, by bribing the majority of a senate or great council; and at last, by an expedient, called an act of indemnity (whereof I described the nature to him), they secure themselves from after-reckonings, and retire from the public laden with the spoils of the nation.

The palace of a chief minister is a seminary to breed up others in his own trade. The pages, lackeys, and porters, by imitating their master, become ministers of state in their several districts, and learn to excel in the three principal ingredients, of insolence, lying, and bribery. Accordingly, they have a subaltern court paid to them by persons of the best rank; and sometimes by the force of dexterity and impudence, arrive, through several gradations, to be successors to their lord.

He is usually governed by a decayed wench, or favourite footman, who are the tunnels through which all graces are conveyed, and may properly be called, in the last resort, the governors of the kingdom.

One day, in discourse, my master, having heard me mention the nobility of my country, was pleased to make me a compliment which I could not pretend to deserve: that he was sure I must have been born of some noble family, because I far exceeded in shape, colour, and cleanliness, all the *Yahoos* of his nation, although I seemed to fail in strength and agility, which must be imputed to my different way of living from those other brutes; and besides I was not only endowed with the faculty of speech, but likewise with some rudiments of reason, to a degree that, with all his acquaintance, I passed for a prodigy.

He made me observe, that among the *Houyhnhnms*, the white, the sorrel, and the iron-gray, were not so exactly shaped as the bay, the dapple-gray, and the black; nor born with equal talents of mind, or a capacity to improve them; and therefore continued always in the condition of servants, without ever aspiring to match out of their own race, which in that country would be reckoned monstrous and unnatural.

I made his honour my most humble acknowledgments for the good opinion he was pleased to conceive of me, but assured him at the same time, that my birth was of the lower sort, having been born of plain honest parents, who were just able to give me a tolerable education; that nobility, among us, was altogether a different thing from the idea he had of it; that our young noblemen are bred from their childhood in idleness and luxury; that, as soon as years will permit, they consume their vigour, and contract odious diseases among lewd females; and when their fortunes are almost ruined, they marry some woman of mean birth, disagreeable person, and unsound constitution (merely for the sake of money), whom they hate and despise. That the productions of such marriages are generally scrofulous, rickety, or deformed children; by which means the family seldom continues above three generations, unless the wife takes care to provide a healthy father, among her neighbours or domestics, in order to improve and continue the breed. That a weak diseased body, a meagre countenance, and sallow complexion, are the true marks of noble blood; and a healthy robust appearance is so disgraceful in a man of quality, that the world concludes his real father to have been a groom or a coachman. The imperfections of his mind run parallel with those of his body, being a composition of spleen, dullness, ignorance, caprice, sensuality, and pride.

"Without the consent of this illustrious body, no law can be enacted, repealed, or altered: and these nobles have likewise the decision of all our possessions, without appeal."

∽ **Chapter VII** ∽

The author's great love of his native country. His master's observations upon the constitution and administration of England, as described by the author, with parallel cases and comparisons. His master's observations upon human nature.

The reader may be disposed to wonder how I could prevail on myself to give so free a representation of my own species, among a race of mortals who are already too apt to conceive the vilest opinion of humankind, from that entire congruity between me and their *Yahoos*. But I must freely confess, that the many virtues of those excellent quadrupeds, placed in opposite view to human corruptions, had so far opened my eyes and enlarged my understanding, that I began to view the actions and passions of man in a very different light, and to think the honour of my own kind not worth managing; which, besides, it was impossible for me to do, before a person of so acute a judgment as my master, who daily convinced me of a thousand faults in myself, whereof I had not the least perception before, and which, with us, would never be numbered even among human infirmities. I had likewise learned, from his example, an utter detestation of all falsehood or disguise; and truth appeared so amiable to me, that I determined upon sacrificing every thing to it.

Let me deal so candidly with the reader as to confess that there was yet a much stronger motive for the freedom I took in my representation of things. I had not yet been a year in this country before I contracted such a love and veneration for the inhabitants, that I entered on a firm resolution never to return to humankind, but to pass the rest of my life among these admirable *Houyhnhnms*, in the contemplation and practice of every virtue, where I could have no example or incitement to vice. But it was decreed by fortune, my perpetual enemy, that so great a felicity should not fall to my share. However, it is now some comfort to reflect, that in what I said of my countrymen, I extenuated their faults as much as I durst before so strict an examiner; and upon every article gave as favourable a turn as the matter would bear. For, indeed, who is there alive that will not be swayed by his bias and partiality to the place of his birth?

I have related the substance of several conversations I had with my master during the greatest part of the time I had the honour to be in his service; but have, indeed, for brevity sake, omitted much more than is here set down.

When I had answered all his questions, and his curiosity seemed to be fully satisfied, he sent for me one morning early, and commanded me to sit down at some distance (an honour which he had never before conferred upon me). He said, he had been very seriously considering my whole story, as far as it related both to myself and my country; that he looked upon us as a sort of animals, to whose share, by what accident he could not conjecture, some small pittance of reason had fallen, whereof we made no other use, than by its assistance, to aggravate our natural corruptions, and to acquire new ones, which nature had not given us; that we disarmed ourselves of the few abilities she had bestowed; had been very successful in multiplying our original wants, and seemed to spend our whole lives in vain endeavours to supply them by our own inventions; that, as to myself, it was manifest I had neither the strength nor agility of a common *Yahoo*; that I walked infirmly on my hinder feet; had found out a contrivance to make my claws of no use or defence, and to remove the hair from my chin, which was intended as a shelter from the sun and the weather: lastly, that I could neither run with speed, nor climb trees like my *brethren* (as he called them) the *Yahoos* in his country.

That our institutions of government and law were plainly owing to our gross defects in reason, and by consequence in virtue; because reason alone is sufficient to govern a rational creature; which was, therefore, a character we had no pretence to challenge, even from the account I had given of my own people; although he manifestly perceived, that, in order to favour them, I had concealed many particulars, and often said the thing which was not.

He was the more confirmed in this opinion, because, he observed, that as I agreed in every feature of my body with other *Yahoos*, except where it was to my real disadvantage in point of strength, speed, and activity, the shortness of my claws, and some other particulars where nature had no part; so from the representation I had given him of our lives, our manners, and our actions, he found as near a resemblance in the disposition of our minds. He said, the *Yahoos* were known to hate one another, more than they did any different species of animals; and the reason usually assigned was, the odiousness of their own shapes, which all could see in the rest, but not in themselves. He had therefore begun to think it not unwise in us to cover our bodies, and by that invention conceal many of our deformities from each other, which would else be hardly supportable. But he now found he had been mistaken, and that the dissensions of those brutes in his country were owing to the same cause with ours, as I had described them. For if, said he, you throw among five *Yahoos* as much food as would be sufficient for fifty, they will, instead of eating peaceably, fall together by the ears, each single one impatient to have all to itself; and therefore a servant was usually employed to stand by while they were feeding abroad, and those kept at home were tied at a distance from each other; that if a cow died of age or accident, before a *Houyhnhnm* could secure it for his own *Yahoos*, those in the neighbourhood would come in herds to seize it, and then would ensue such a battle as I had described, with terrible wounds made by their claws on both sides, although they seldom were able to kill one another, for want of such convenient instruments of death as we had invented. At other times, the like battles have been fought between the *Yahoos* of several neighbourhoods, without any visible cause; those of one district watching all opportunities to surprise the next, before they are prepared. But if they find their project has miscarried, they return home, and, for want of enemies, engage in what I call a civil war among themselves.

That in some fields of his country there are certain shining stones of several colours, whereof the *Yahoos* are violently fond; and when part of these stones is fixed in the earth, as it sometimes happens, they will dig with their claws for whole days to get them out; then carry them away, and hide them by heaps in their kennels; but still looking round with great caution, for fear their comrades should find out their treasure. My master said, he could never discover the reason of this unnatural appetite, or how these stones could be of any use to a *Yahoo*; but now he believed it might proceed from the same principle of avarice which I had ascribed to mankind. That he had once, by way of experiment, privately removed a heap of these stones from the place where one of his *Yahoos* had buried it; whereupon the sordid animal, missing his treasure, by his loud lamenting brought the whole herd to the place, there miserably howled, then fell to biting and tearing the rest, began to pine away, would neither eat, nor sleep, nor work, till he ordered a servant privately to convey the stones into the same hole, and hide them as before; which, when his *Yahoo* had found, he presently recovered his spirits and good humour, but took good care to remove them to a better hiding place, and has ever since been a very serviceable brute.

My master further assured me, which I also observed myself, that in the fields where the shining stones abound, the fiercest and most frequent battles are fought, occasioned by perpetual inroads of the neighbouring *Yahoos*.

He said, it was common, when two *Yahoos* discovered such a stone in a field, and were contending which of them should be the proprietor, a third would take the advantage, and carry it away from them both; which my master would needs contend to have some kind of resemblance with our suits at law; wherein I thought it for our credit not to undeceive him; since the decision he mentioned was much more equitable than many decrees among us; because the plaintiff and defendant there lost nothing beside the stone they contended for, whereas our courts of equity would never have dismissed the cause, while either of them had any thing left.

My master, continuing his discourse, said, there was nothing that rendered the *Yahoos* more odious, than their undistinguishing appetite to devour every thing that came in their way, whether herbs, roots, berries, the corrupted flesh of animals, or all mingled together: and it was peculiar in their temper, that they were fonder of what they could get by rapine or stealth, at a greater distance, than much better food provided for them at home. If their prey held out, they would eat till they were ready to burst; after which, nature had pointed out to them a certain root that gave them a general evacuation.

There was also another kind of root, very juicy, but somewhat rare and difficult to be found, which the *Yahoos* sought for with much eagerness, and would suck it with great delight; it produced in them the same effects that wine has upon us. It would make them sometimes hug, and sometimes tear one another; they would howl, and grin, and chatter, and reel, and tumble, and then fall asleep in the mud.

I did indeed observe that the *Yahoos* were the only animals in this country subject to any diseases; which, however, were much fewer than horses have among us, and contracted, not by any ill-treatment they meet with, but by the nastiness and greediness of that sordid brute. Neither has their language any more than a general appellation for those maladies, which is borrowed from the name of the beast, and called *hnea-yahoo*, or *Yahoo's evil*; and the cure prescribed is a mixture of their own dung and urine, forcibly put down the *Yahoo*'s throat. This I have since often known to have been taken with success, and do here freely recommend it to my countrymen for the public good, as an admirable specific against all diseases produced by repletion.

As to learning, government, arts, manufactures, and the like, my master confessed, he could find little or no resemblance between the *Yahoos* of that country and those in ours; for he only meant to observe what parity there was in our natures. He had heard, indeed, some curious *Houyhnhnms* observe, that in most herds there was a sort of ruling *Yahoo* (as among us there is generally some leading or principal stag in a park), who was always more deformed in body, and mischievous in disposition, than any of the rest; that this leader had usually a favourite as like himself as he could get, whose employment was to lick his master's feet and posteriors, and drive the female *Yahoos* to his kennel; for which he was now and then rewarded with a piece of ass's flesh. This favourite is hated by the whole herd, and therefore, to protect himself, keeps always near the person of his leader. He usually continues in office till a worse can be found; but the very moment he is discarded, his successor, at the head of all the *Yahoos* in that district, young and old, male and female, come in a body, and discharge their excrements upon him from head to foot. But how far this might be applicable to our courts, and favourites, and ministers of state, my master said I could best determine.

I durst make no return to this malicious insinuation, which debased human understanding below the sagacity of a common hound, who has judgment enough to distinguish and follow the cry of the ablest dog in the pack, without being ever mistaken.

My master told me, there were some qualities remarkable in the *Yahoos*, which he had not observed me to mention, or at least very slightly, in the accounts I had given of humankind. He said, those animals, like other brutes, had their females in common; but in this they differed, that the she-*Yahoo* would admit the males while she was pregnant; and that the hes would quarrel and fight with the females, as fiercely as with each other; both which practices were such degrees of infamous brutality, as no other sensitive creature ever arrived at.

Another thing he wondered at in the *Yahoos*, was their strange disposition to nastiness and dirt; whereas there appears to be a natural love of cleanliness in all other animals. As to the two former accusations, I was glad to let them pass without any reply, because I had not a word to offer upon them in defence of my species, which otherwise I certainly had done from my own inclinations. But I could have easily vindicated humankind from the imputation of singularity upon the last article, if there had been any swine in that country (as unluckily for me there were not), which, although it may be a sweeter quadruped than a *Yahoo*, cannot, I humbly conceive, in justice, pretend to more cleanliness; and so his honour himself must have owned, if he had seen their filthy way of feeding, and their custom of wallowing and sleeping in the mud.

My master likewise mentioned another quality which his servants had discovered in several *Yahoos*, and to him was wholly unaccountable. He said, a fancy would sometimes take a *Yahoo* to retire into a corner, to lie down, and howl, and groan, and spurn away all that came near him, although he were young and fat, wanted neither food nor water, nor did the servant imagine what could possibly ail him. And the only remedy they found was, to set him to hard work, after which he would infallibly come to himself. To this I was silent out of partiality to my own kind; yet here I could plainly discover the true seeds of spleen, which only seizes on the lazy, the luxurious, and the rich; who, if they were forced to undergo the same regimen, I would undertake for the cure.

His honour had further observed, that a female *Yahoo* would often stand behind a bank or a bush, to gaze on the young males passing by, and then appear, and hide, using many antic gestures and grimaces, at which time it was observed that she had a most offensive smell; and when any of the males advanced, would slowly retire, looking often back, and with a counterfeit show of fear, run off into some convenient place, where she knew the male would follow her.

At other times, if a female stranger came among them, three or four of her own sex would get about her, and stare, and chatter, and grin, and smell her all over; and then turn off with gestures, that seemed to express contempt and disdain.

Perhaps my master might refine a little in these speculations, which he had drawn from what he observed himself, or had been told him by others; however, I could not reflect without some amazement, and much sorrow, that the rudiments of lewdness, coquetry, censure, and scandal, should have place by instinct in womankind.

I expected every moment that my master would accuse the *Yahoos* of those unnatural appetites in both sexes, so common among us. But nature, it seems, has not been so expert a school-mistress; and these politer pleasures are entirely the productions of art and reason on our side of the globe.

Chapter VIII

The author relates several particulars of the Yahoos. The great virtues of the Houyhnhnms. The education and exercise of their youth. Their general assembly.

As I ought to have understood human nature much better than I supposed it possible for my master to do, so it was easy to apply the character he gave of the *Yahoos* to myself and my countrymen; and I believed I could yet make further discoveries, from my own observation. I therefore often begged his honour to let me go among the herds of *Yahoos* in the neighbourhood; to which he always very graciously consented, being perfectly convinced that the hatred I bore these brutes would never suffer me to be corrupted by them; and his honour ordered one of his servants, a strong sorrel nag, very honest and good-natured, to be my guard; without whose protection I durst not undertake such adventures. For I have already told the reader how much I was pestered by these odious animals, upon my first arrival; and I afterwards failed very narrowly, three or four times, of falling into their clutches, when I happened to stray at any distance without my hanger. And I have reason to believe they had some imagination that I was of their own species, which I often assisted myself by stripping up my sleeves, and showing my naked arms and breasts in their sight, when my protector was with me. At which times they would approach as near as they durst, and imitate my actions after the manner of monkeys, but ever with great signs of hatred; as a tame jackdaw with cap and stockings is always persecuted by the wild ones, when he happens to be got among them.

They are prodigiously nimble from their infancy. However, I once caught a young male of three years old, and endeavoured, by all marks of tenderness, to make it quiet; but the little imp fell a squalling, and scratching, and biting with such violence, that I was forced to let it go; and it was high time, for a whole troop of old ones came about us at the noise, but finding the cub was safe (for away it ran), and my sorrel nag being by, they durst not venture near us. I observed the young animal's flesh to smell very rank, and the stink was somewhat between a weasel and a fox, but much more disagreeable. I forgot another circumstance (and perhaps I might have the reader's pardon if it were wholly omitted), that while I held the odious vermin in my hands, it voided its filthy excrements of a yellow liquid substance all over my clothes; but by good fortune there was a small brook hard by, where I washed myself as clean as I could; although I durst not come into my master's presence until I were sufficiently aired.

By what I could discover, the *Yahoos* appear to be the most unteachable of all animals: their capacity never reaching higher than to draw or carry burdens. Yet I am of opinion, this defect arises chiefly from a perverse, restive disposition; for they are cunning, malicious, treacherous, and revengeful. They are strong and hardy, but of a cowardly spirit, and, by consequence, insolent, abject, and cruel. It is observed, that the red haired of both sexes are more libidinous and mischievous than the rest, whom yet they much exceed in strength and activity.

The *Houyhnhnms* keep the Yahoos for present use in huts not far from the house; but the rest are sent abroad to certain fields, where they dig up roots, eat several kinds of herbs, and search about for carrion, or sometimes catch weasels and luhimuhs (a sort of wild rat), which they greedily devour. Nature has taught them to dig deep holes with their nails on the side of a rising ground, wherein they lie by themselves; only the kennels of the females are larger, sufficient to hold two or three cubs.

They swim from their infancy like frogs, and are able to continue long under water, where they often take fish, which the females carry home to their young. And, upon this occasion, I hope the reader will pardon my relating an odd adventure.

Being one day abroad with my protector the sorrel nag, and the weather exceeding hot, I entreated him to let me bathe in a river that was near. He consented, and I immediately stripped myself stark naked, and went down softly into the stream. It happened that a young female *Yahoo*, standing behind a bank, saw the whole proceeding, and inflamed by desire, as the nag and I conjectured, came running with all speed, and leaped into the water, within five yards of the place where I bathed. I was never in my life so terribly frightened. The nag was grazing at some distance, not suspecting any harm. She embraced me after a most fulsome manner. I roared as loud as I could, and the nag came galloping towards me, whereupon she quitted her grasp, with the utmost reluctancy, and leaped upon the opposite bank, where she stood gazing and howling all the time I was putting on my clothes.

This was a matter of diversion to my master and his family, as well as of mortification to myself. For now I could no longer deny that I was a real *Yahoo* in every limb and feature, since the females had a natural propensity to me, as one of their own species. Neither was the hair of this brute of a red colour (which might have been some excuse for an appetite a little irregular), but black as a sloe, and her countenance did not make an appearance altogether so hideous as the rest of her kind; for I think she could not be above eleven years old.

Having lived three years in this country, the reader, I suppose, will expect that I should, like other travellers, give him some account of the manners and customs of its inhabitants, which it was indeed my principal study to learn.

As these noble *Houyhnhnms* are endowed by nature with a general disposition to all virtues, and have no conceptions or ideas of what is evil in a rational creature, so their grand maxim is, to cultivate reason, and to be wholly governed by it. Neither is reason among them a point problematical, as with us, where men can argue with plausibility on both sides of the question, but strikes you with immediate conviction; as it must needs do, where it is not mingled, obscured, or discoloured, by passion and interest. I remember it was with extreme difficulty that I could bring my master to understand the meaning of the word opinion, or how a point could be disputable; because reason taught us to affirm or deny only where we are certain; and beyond our knowledge we cannot do either. So that controversies, wranglings, disputes, and positiveness, in false or dubious propositions, are evils unknown among the *Houyhnhnms*. In the like manner, when I used to explain to him our several systems of natural philosophy, he would laugh, that a creature pretending to reason, should value itself upon the knowledge of other people's conjectures, and in things where that knowledge, if it were certain, could be of no use. Wherein he agreed entirely with the sentiments of Socrates, as Plato delivers them; which I mention as the highest honour I can do that prince of philosophers. I have often since reflected, what destruction such doctrine would make in the libraries of Europe; and how many paths of fame would be then shut up in the learned world.

Friendship and benevolence are the two principal virtues among the *Houyhnhnms*; and these not confined to particular objects, but universal to the whole race; for a stranger from the remotest part is equally treated with the nearest neighbour, and wherever he goes, looks upon himself as at home. They preserve decency and civility in the highest degrees, but are altogether ignorant of ceremony. They have no fondness for their colts or foals, but the care they take in educating them proceeds entirely from the dictates of reason. And I observed my master to show the same affection to his neighbour's issue, that he had for his own. They will have it that nature teaches them to love the whole species, and it is reason only that makes a distinction of persons, where there is a superior degree of virtue.

When the matron *Houyhnhnms* have produced one of each sex, they no longer accompany with their consorts, except they lose one of their issue by some casualty, which very seldom happens; but in such a case they meet again; or when the like accident befalls a person whose wife is past bearing, some other couple bestow on him one of their own colts, and then go together again until the mother is pregnant. This caution is necessary, to prevent the country from being overburdened with numbers. But the race of inferior *Houyhnhnms*, bred up to be servants, is not so strictly limited upon this article: these are allowed to produce three of each sex, to be domestics in the noble families.

In their marriages, they are exactly careful to choose such colours as will not make any disagreeable mixture in the breed. Strength is chiefly valued in the male, and comeliness in the female; not upon the account of love, but to preserve the race from degenerating; for where a female happens to excel in strength, a consort is chosen, with regard to comeliness. Courtship, love, presents, jointures, settlements have no place in their thoughts, or terms whereby to express them in their language. The young couple meet, and are joined, merely because it is the determination of their parents and friends; it is what they see done every day, and they look upon it as one of the necessary actions of a reasonable being. But the violation of marriage, or any other unchastity, was never heard of; and the married pair pass their lives with the same friendship and mutual benevolence, that they bear to all others of the same species who come in their way, without jealousy, fondness, quarrelling, or discontent.

In educating the youth of both sexes, their method is admirable, and highly deserves our imitation. These are not suffered to taste a grain of oats, except upon certain days, till eighteen years old; nor milk, but very rarely; and in summer they graze two hours in the morning, and as many in the evening, which their parents likewise observe; but the servants are not allowed above half that time, and a great part of their grass is brought home, which they eat at the most convenient hours, when they can be best spared from work.

Temperance, industry, exercise, and cleanliness, are the lessons equally enjoined to the young ones of both sexes: and my master thought it monstrous in us, to give the females a different kind of education from the males, except in some articles of domestic management; whereby, as he truly observed, one half of our natives were good for nothing but bringing children into the world; and to trust the care of our children to such useless animals, he said, was yet a greater instance of brutality.

But the *Houyhnhnms* train up their youth to strength, speed, and hardiness, by exercising them in running races up and down steep hills, and over hard stony grounds; and when they are all in a sweat, they are ordered to leap over head and ears into a pond or river. Four times a year the youth of a certain district meet to show their proficiency in running and leaping, and other feats of strength and agility; where the victor is rewarded with a song in his or her praise. On this festival, the servants drive a herd of *Yahoos* into the field, laden with hay, and oats, and milk, for a repast to the *Houyhnhnms*; after which, these brutes are immediately driven back again, for fear of being noisome to the assembly.

Every fourth year, at the vernal equinox, there is a representative council of the whole nation, which meets in a plain about twenty miles from our house, and continues about five or six days. Here they inquire into the state and condition of the several districts; whether they abound or be deficient in hay or oats, or cows, or *Yahoos*; and wherever there is any want (which is but seldom) it is immediately supplied by unanimous consent and contribution. Here likewise the regulation of children is settled: as for instance, if a *Houyhnhnm* has two males, he changes one of them with another that has two females; and when a child has been lost by any casualty, where the mother is past breeding, it is determined what family in the district shall breed another to supply the loss.

∽ **Chapter IX** ∽

A grand debate at the general assembly of the Houyhnhnms, and how it was determined. The learning of the Houyhnhnms. Their buildings. Their manner of burials. The defectiveness of their language.

One of these grand assemblies was held in my time, about three months before my departure, whither my master went as the representative of our district. In this council was resumed their old debate, and indeed the only debate that ever happened in their country; whereof my master, after his return, give me a very particular account.

The question to be debated was, whether the *Yahoos* should be exterminated from the face of the earth? One of the members for the affirmative offered several arguments of great strength and weight, alleging, that as the *Yahoos* were the most filthy, noisome, and deformed animals which nature ever produced, so they were the most restive and indocible, mischievous and malicious; they would privately suck the teats of the *Houyhnhnms*' cows, kill and devour their cats, trample down their oats and grass, if they were not continually watched, and commit a thousand other extravagancies. He took notice of a general tradition, that *Yahoos* had not been always in their country; but that many ages ago, two of these brutes appeared together upon a mountain; whether produced by the heat of the sun upon corrupted mud and slime, or from the ooze and froth of the sea, was never known; that these *Yahoos* engendered, and their brood, in a short time, grew so numerous as to overrun and infest the whole nation; that the *Houyhnhnms*, to get rid of this evil, made a general hunting, and at last enclosed the whole herd; and destroying the elder, every *Houyhnhnm* kept two young ones in a kennel, and brought them to such a degree of tameness, as an animal, so savage by nature, can be capable of acquiring, using them for draught and carriage; that there seemed to be much truth in this tradition, and that those creatures could not be *yinhniamshy* (or *aborigines* of the land), because of the violent hatred the *Houyhnhnms*, as well as all other animals, bore them, which, although their evil disposition sufficiently deserved, could never have arrived at so high a degree if they had been aborigines, or else they would have long since been rooted out; that the inhabitants, taking a fancy to use the service of the *Yahoos*, had, very imprudently, neglected to cultivate the breed of asses, which are a comely animal, easily kept, more tame and orderly, without any offensive smell, strong enough for labour, although they yield to the other in agility of body, and if their braying be no agreeable sound, it is far preferable to the horrible howlings of the *Yahoos*.

Several others declared their sentiments to the same purpose, when my master proposed an expedient to the assembly, whereof he had indeed borrowed the hint from me. He approved of the tradition mentioned by the honourable member who spoke before, and affirmed, that the two *Yahoos* said to be seen first among them, had been driven thither over the sea; that coming to land, and being forsaken by their companions, they retired to the mountains, and degenerating by degrees, became in process of time much more savage than those of their own species in the country whence these two originals came. The reason of this assertion was, that he had now in his possession a certain wonderful *Yahoo* (meaning myself) which most of them had heard of, and many of them had seen. He then related to them how he first found me; that my body was all covered with an artificial composure of the skins and hairs of other animals; that I spoke in a language of my own, and had thoroughly learned theirs; that I had related to him the accidents which brought me thither; that when he saw me without my covering, I was an exact *Yahoo* in every part, only of a whiter colour, less hairy, and with shorter claws. He added, how I had endeavoured to persuade him, that in my own and other countries, the *Yahoos* acted as the governing, rational animal, and held the *Houyhnhnms* in servitude; that he observed in me all the qualities of a *Yahoo*, only a little more civilized by some tincture of reason, which, however, was in a degree as far inferior to the *Houyhnhnm* race, as the *Yahoos* of their country were to me; that, among other things, I mentioned a custom we had of castrating *Houyhnhnms* when they were young, in order to render them tame; that the operation was easy and safe; that it was no shame to learn wisdom from brutes, as industry is taught by the ant, and building by the swallow (for so I translate the word *lyhannh*, although it be a much larger fowl); that this invention might be practised upon the younger *Yahoos* here, which besides rendering them tractable and fitter for use, would in an age put an end to the whole species, without destroying life; that in the mean time the *Houyhnhnms* should be exhorted to cultivate the breed of asses, which, as they are in all respects more valuable brutes, so they have this advantage, to be fit for service at five years old, which the others are not till twelve.

This was all my master thought fit to tell me, at that time, of what passed in the grand council. But he was pleased to conceal one particular, which related personally to myself, whereof I soon felt the unhappy effect, as the reader will know in its proper place, and whence I date all the succeeding misfortunes of my life.

The *Houyhnhnms* have no letters, and consequently their knowledge is all traditional. But there happening few events of any moment among a people so well united, naturally disposed to every virtue, wholly governed by reason, and cut off from all commerce with other nations, the historical part is easily preserved without burdening their memories. I have already observed that they are subject to no diseases, and therefore can have no need of physicians. However, they have excellent medicines, composed of herbs, to cure accidental bruises and cuts in the pastern or frog of the foot, by sharp stones, as well as other maims and hurts in the several parts of the body.

They calculate the year by the revolution of the sun and moon, but use no subdivisions into weeks. They are well enough acquainted with the motions of those two luminaries, and understand the nature of eclipses; and this is the utmost progress of their astronomy.

In poetry, they must be allowed to excel all other mortals; wherein the justness of their similes, and the minuteness as well as exactness of their descriptions, are indeed inimitable. Their verses abound very much in both of these, and usually contain either some exalted notions of friendship and benevolence or the praises of those who were victors in races and other bodily exercises. Their buildings, although very rude and simple, are not inconvenient, but well contrived to defend them from all injuries of and heat. They have a kind of tree, which at forty years old loosens in the root, and falls with the first storm; it grows very straight, and being pointed like stakes with a sharp stone (for the *Houyhnhnms* know not the use of iron), they stick them erect in the ground, about ten inches asunder, and then weave in oat straw, or sometimes wattles, between them. The roof is made after the same manner, and so are the doors.

The *Houyhnhnms* use the hollow part, between the pastern and the hoof of their fore-foot, as we do our hands, and this with greater dexterity than I could at first imagine. I have seen a white mare of our family thread a needle (which I lent her on purpose) with that joint. They milk their cows, reap their oats, and do all the work which requires hands, in the same manner. They have a kind of hard flints, which, by grinding against other stones, they form into instruments, that serve instead of wedges, axes, and hammers. With tools made of these flints, they likewise cut their hay, and reap their oats, which there grow naturally in several fields; the *Yahoos* draw home the sheaves in carriages, and the servants tread them in certain covered huts to get out the grain, which is kept in stores. They make a rude kind of earthen and wooden vessels, and bake the former in the sun.

If they can avoid casualties, they die only of old age, and are buried in the obscurest places that can be found, their friends and relations expressing neither joy nor grief at their departure; nor does the dying person discover the least regret that he is leaving the world, any more than if he were upon returning home from a visit to one of his neighbours. I remember my master having once made an appointment with a friend and his family to come to his house, upon some affair of importance; on the day fixed, the mistress and her two children came very late; she made two excuses, first for her husband, who, as she said, happened that very morning to *shnuwnh*. The word is strongly expressive in their language, but not easily rendered into English; it signifies, "to retire to his first mother." Her excuse for not coming sooner, was, that her husband dying late in the morning, she was a good while consulting her servants about a convenient place where his body should be laid; and I observed, she behaved herself at our house as cheerfully as the rest. She died about three months after.

They live generally to seventy, or seventy-five years, very seldom to fourscore. Some weeks before their death, they feel a gradual decay; but without pain. During this time they are much visited by their friends, because they cannot go abroad with their usual ease and satisfaction. However, about ten days before their death, which they seldom fail in computing, they return the visits that have been made them by those who are nearest in the neighbourhood, being carried in a convenient sledge drawn by *Yahoos*; which vehicle they use, not only upon this occasion, but when they grow old, upon long journeys, or when they are lamed by any accident: and therefore when the dying *Houyhnhnms* return those visits, they take a solemn leave of their friends, as if they were going to some remote part of the country, where they designed to pass the rest of their lives.

I know not whether it may be worth observing, that the *Houyhnhnms* have no word in their language to express any thing that is evil, except what they borrow from the deformities or ill qualities of the *Yahoos*. Thus they denote the folly of a servant, an omission of a child, a stone that cuts their feet, a continuance of foul or unseasonable weather, and the like, by adding to each the epithet of *Yahoo*. For instance, *hhnm Yahoo; whnaholm Yahoo, ynlhmndwihlma Yahoo*, and an ill-contrived house *ynholmhnmrohlnw Yahoo*.

I could, with great pleasure, enlarge further upon the manners and virtues of this excellent people; but intending in a short time to publish a volume by itself, expressly upon that subject, I refer the reader thither; and, in the mean time, proceed to relate my own sad catastrophe.

ᑐᔦ **Chapter X** ᔧᔤᑐ

The author's economy, and happy life, among the Houyhnhnms. His great improvement in virtue by conversing with them. Their conversations. The author has notice given him by his master, that he must depart from the country. He falls into a swoon for grief; but submits. He contrives and finishes a canoe by the help of a fellow-servant, and puts to sea at a venture.

I had settled my little economy to my own heart's content. My master had ordered a room to be made for me, after their manner, about six yards from the house; the sides and floors of which I plastered with clay, and covered with rush-mats of my own contriving. I had beaten hemp, which there grows wild, and made of it a sort of ticking; this I filled with the feathers of several birds I had taken with springes made of *Yahoos*' hairs, and were excellent food. I had worked two chairs with my knife, the sorrel nag helping me in the grosser and more laborious part. When my clothes were worn to rags, I made myself others with the skins of rabbits, and of a certain beautiful animal, about the same size, called *nnuhnoh*, the skin of which is covered with a fine down. Of these I also made very tolerable stockings. I soled my shoes with wood, which I cut from a tree, and fitted to the upper-leather; and when this was worn out, I supplied it with the skins of *Yahoos* dried in the sun. I often got honey out of hollow trees, which I mingled with water, or ate with my bread. No man could more verify the truth of these two maxims, "That nature is very easily satisfied." and "That necessity is the mother of invention." I enjoyed perfect health of body, and tranquillity of mind; I did not feel the treachery or inconstancy of a friend, nor the injuries of a secret or open enemy. I had no occasion of bribing, flattering, or pimping, to procure the favour of any great man, or of his minion; I wanted no fence against fraud or oppression: here was neither physician to destroy my body, nor lawyer to ruin my fortune; no informer to watch my words and actions, or forge accusations against me for hire; here were no gibers, censurers, backbiters, pickpockets, highwaymen, housebreakers, attorneys, bawds, buffoons, gamesters, politicians, wits, splenetics, tedious talkers, controvertists, ravishers, murderers, robbers, virtuosos; no leaders, or followers, of party and faction; no encouragers to vice, by seducement or examples; no dungeon, axes, gibbets, whipping-posts, or pillories; no cheating shopkeepers or mechanics; no pride, vanity, or affectation; no fops, bullies, drunkards, strolling whores, or poxes; no ranting, lewd, expensive wives; no stupid, proud pedants; no importunate, overbearing, quarrelsome, noisy, roaring, empty, conceited, swearing companions; no scoundrels raised from the dust upon the merit of their vices, or nobility thrown into it on account of their virtues; no lords, fiddlers, judges, or dancing-masters.

I had the favour of being admitted to several *Houyhnhnms*, who came to visit or dine with my master; where his honour graciously suffered me to wait in the room, and listen to their discourse. Both he and his company would often descend to ask me questions, and receive my answers. I had also sometimes the honour of attending my master in his visits to others. I never presumed to speak, except in answer to a question; and then I did it with inward regret, because it was a loss of so much time for improving myself; but I was infinitely delighted with the station of an humble auditor in such conversations, where nothing passed but what was useful, expressed in the fewest and most significant words; where, as I have already said, the greatest decency was observed, without the least degree of ceremony; where no person spoke without being pleased himself, and pleasing his companions; where there was no interruption, tediousness, heat, or difference of sentiments. They have a notion, that when people are met together, a short silence does much improve conversation: this I found to be true; for during those little intermissions of talk, new ideas would arise in their minds, which very much enlivened the discourse. Their subjects are, generally on friendship and benevolence, on order and economy; sometimes upon the visible operations of nature, or ancient traditions; upon the bounds and limits of virtue; upon the unerring rules of reason, or upon some determinations to be taken at the next great assembly; and often upon the various excellences of poetry. I may add, without vanity, that my presence often gave them sufficient matter for discourse, because it afforded my master an occasion of letting his friends into the history of me and my country, upon which they were all pleased to descant, in a manner not very advantageous to humankind; and for that reason I shall not repeat what they said; only I may be allowed to observe, that his honour, to my great admiration, appeared to understand the nature of *Yahoos* much better than myself. He went through all our vices and follies, and discovered many, which I had never mentioned to him, by only supposing what qualities a *Yahoo* of their country, with a small proportion of reason, might be capable of exerting; and concluded, with too much probability: how vile, as well as miserable, such a creature must be.

I freely confess, that all the little knowledge I have of any value, was acquired by the lectures I received from my master, and from hearing the discourses of him and his friends; to which I should be prouder to listen, than to dictate to the greatest and wisest assembly in Europe. I admired the strength, comeliness, and speed of the inhabitants; and such a constellation of virtues, in such amiable persons, produced in me the highest veneration. At first, indeed, I did not feel that natural awe, which the Yahoos and all other animals bear toward them; but it grew upon me by decrees, much sooner than I imagined, and was mingled with a respectful love and gratitude, that they would condescend to distinguish me from the rest of my species.

When I thought of my family, my friends, my countrymen, or the human race in general, I considered them, as they really were, *Yahoos* in shape and disposition, perhaps a little more civilized, and qualified with the gift of speech; but making no other use of reason, than to improve and multiply those vices whereof their brethren in this country had only the share that nature allotted them. When I happened to behold the reflection of my own form in a lake or fountain, I turned away my face in horror and detestation of myself, and could better endure the sight of a common *Yahoo* than of my own person. By conversing with the *Houyhnhnms*, and looking upon them with delight, I fell to imitate their gait and gesture, which is now grown into a habit; and my friends often tell me, in a blunt way, that I trot like a horse; which, however, I take for a great compliment. Neither shall I disown, that in speaking I am apt to fall into the voice and manner of the *Houyhnhnms*, and hear myself ridiculed on that account, without the least mortification.

In the midst of all this happiness, and when I looked upon myself to be fully settled for life, my master sent for me one morning a little earlier than his usual hour. I observed by his countenance that he was in some perplexity, and at a loss how to begin what he had to speak. After a short silence, he told me, he did not know how I would take what he was going to say: that in the last general assembly, when the affair of the *Yahoos* was entered upon, the representatives had taken offence at his keeping a *Yahoo* (meaning myself) in his family, more like a *Houyhnhnm* than a brute animal; that he was known frequently to converse with me, as if he could receive some advantage or pleasure in my company; that such a practice was not agreeable to reason or nature, or a thing ever heard of before among them; the assembly did therefore exhort him either to employ me like the rest of my species, or command me to swim back to the place whence I came; that the first of these expedients was utterly rejected by all the *Houyhnhnms* who had ever seen me at his house or their own; for they alleged, that because I had some rudiments of reason, added to the natural pravity of those animals, it was to be feared I might be able to seduce them into the woody and mountainous parts of the country, and bring them in troops by night to destroy the *Houyhnhnms'* cattle, as being naturally of the ravenous kind, and averse from labour.

My master added, that he was daily pressed by the *Houyhnhnms* of the neighbourhood to have the assembly's exhortation executed, which he could not put off much longer. He doubted it would be impossible for me to swim to another country; and therefore wished I would contrive some sort of vehicle, resembling those I had described to him, that might carry me on the sea; in which work I should have the assistance of his own servants, as well as those of his neighbours. He concluded, that for his own part, he could have been content to keep me in his service as long as I lived; because he found I had cured myself of some bad habits and dispositions, by endeavouring, as far as my inferior nature was capable, to imitate the *Houyhnhnms*.

I should here observe to the reader, that a decree of the general assembly in this country is expressed by the word *hnhloayn*, which signifies an exhortation, as near as I can render it; for they have no conception how a rational creature can be compelled, but only advised, or exhorted; because no person can disobey reason, without giving up his claim to be a rational creature.

I was struck with the utmost grief and despair at my master's discourse; and being unable to support the agonies I was under, I fell into a swoon at his feet. When I came to myself, he told me that he concluded I had been dead; for these people are subject to no such imbecilities of nature. I answered in a faint voice, that death would have been too great a happiness; that although I could not blame the assembly's exhortation, or the urgency of his friends; yet, in my weak and corrupt judgment, I thought it might consist with reason to have been less rigorous; that I could not swim a league, and probably the nearest land to theirs might be distant above a hundred: that many materials, necessary for making a small vessel to carry me off, were wholly wanting in this country; which, however, I would attempt, in obedience and gratitude to his honour, although I concluded the thing to be impossible, and therefore looked on myself as already devoted to destruction; that the certain prospect of an unnatural death was the least of my evils; for, supposing I should escape with life by some strange adventure, how could I think with temper of passing my days among *Yahoos*, and relapsing into my old corruptions, for want of examples to lead and keep me within the paths of virtue? that I knew too well upon what solid reasons all the determinations of the wise *Houyhnhnms* were founded, not to be shaken by arguments of mine, a miserable *Yahoo*; and therefore, after presenting him with my humble thanks for the offer of his servants' assistance in making a vessel, and desiring a reasonable time for so difficult a work, I told him I would endeavour to preserve a wretched being; and if ever I returned to England, was not without hopes of being useful to my own species, by celebrating the praises of the renowned *Houyhnhnms*, and proposing their virtues to the imitation of mankind.

My master, in a few words, made me a very gracious reply; allowed me the space of two months to finish my boat; and ordered the sorrel nag, my fellow-servant (for so, at this distance, I may presume to call him), to follow my instruction; because I told my master, that his help would be sufficient, and I knew he had a tenderness for me.

In his company, my first business was to go to that part of the coast where my rebellious crew had ordered me to be set on shore. I got upon a height, and looking on every side into the sea; fancied I saw a small island toward the north-east. I took out my pocket glass, and could then clearly distinguish it above five leagues off, as I computed; but it appeared to the sorrel nag to be only a blue cloud: for as he had no conception of any country beside his own, so he could not be as expert in distinguishing remote objects at sea, as we who so much converse in that element.

After I had discovered this island, I considered no further; but resolved it should if possible, be the first place of my banishment, leaving the consequence to fortune.

I returned home, and consulting with the sorrel nag, we went into a copse at some distance, where I with my knife, and he with a sharp flint, fastened very artificially after their manner, to a wooden handle, cut down several oak wattles, about the thickness of a walking-staff, and some larger pieces. But I shall not trouble the reader with a particular description of my own mechanics; let it suffice to say, that in six weeks time with the help of the sorrel nag, who performed the parts that required most labour, I finished a sort of Indian canoe, but much larger, covering it with the skins of *Yahoos*, well stitched together with hempen threads of my own making. My sail was likewise composed of the skins of the same animal; but I made use of the youngest I could get, the older being too tough and thick; and I likewise provided myself with four paddles. I laid in a stock of boiled flesh, of rabbits and fowls, and took with me two vessels, one filled with milk and the other with water.

I tried my canoe in a large pond, near my master's house, and then corrected in it what was amiss; stopping all the chinks with *Yahoos*' tallow, till I found it staunch, and able to bear me and my freight; and, when it was as complete as I could possibly make it, I had it drawn on a carriage very gently by *Yahoos* to the sea-side, under the conduct of the sorrel nag and another servant.

When all was ready, and the day came for my departure, I took leave of my master and lady and the whole family, my eyes flowing with tears, and my heart quite sunk with grief. But his honour, out of curiosity, and, perhaps (if I may speak without vanity) partly out of kindness, was determined to see me in my canoe, and got several of his neighbouring friends to accompany him. I was forced to wait above an hour for the tide; and then observing the wind very fortunately bearing toward the island to which I intended to steer my course, I took a second leave of my master; but as I was going to prostrate myself to kiss his hoof, he did me the honour to raise it gently to my mouth. I am not ignorant how much I have been censured for mentioning this last particular. Detractors are pleased to think it improbable, that so illustrious a person should descend to give so great a mark of distinction to a creature so inferior as I. Neither have I forgotten how apt some travellers are to boast of extraordinary favours they have received. But, if these censurers were better acquainted with the noble and courteous disposition of the *Houyhnhnms*, they would soon change their opinion.

I paid my respects to the rest of the *Houyhnhnms* in his honour's company; then getting into my canoe, I pushed off from shore.

⌒⌒ **Chapter XI** ⌒⌒

The author's dangerous voyage. He arrives at New Holland, hoping to settle there. Is wounded with an arrow by one of the natives. Is seized and carried by force into a Portuguese ship. The great civilities of the captain. The author arrives at England.

I began this desperate voyage on February 15, 1714-15, at nine o'clock in the morning. The wind was very favourable; however, I made use at first only of my paddles; but considering I should soon be weary, and that the wind might chop about, I ventured to set up my little sail; and thus, with the help of the tide, I went at the rate of a league and a half an hour, as near as I could guess. My master and his friends continued on the shore till I was almost out of sight; and I often heard the sorrel nag (who always loved me) crying out, "*Hnuy illa nyha, majah Yahoo*;" "Take care of thyself, gentle *Yahoo*."

My design was, if possible, to discover some small island uninhabited, yet sufficient, by my labour, to furnish me with the necessaries of life, which I would have thought a greater happiness, than to be first minister in the politest court of Europe; so horrible was the idea I conceived of returning to live in the society, and under the government of *Yahoos*. For in such a solitude as I desired, I could at least enjoy my own thoughts, and reflect with delight on the virtues of those inimitable *Houyhnhnms*, without an opportunity of degenerating into the vices and corruptions of my own species.

The reader may remember what I related, when my crew conspired against me, and confined me to my cabin; how I continued there several weeks without knowing what course we took; and when I was put ashore in the long-boat, how the sailors told me, with oaths, whether true or false, that they knew not in what part of the world we were. However, I did then believe us to be about 10 degrees southward of the Cape of Good Hope, or about 45 degrees southern latitude, as I gathered from some general words I overheard among them, being I supposed to the south-east in their intended voyage to Madagascar. And although this were little better than conjecture, yet I resolved to steer my course eastward, hoping to reach the south-west coast of New Holland, and perhaps some such island as I desired lying westward of it. The wind was full west, and by six in the evening I computed I had gone eastward at least eighteen leagues; when I spied a very small island about half a league off, which I soon reached. It was nothing but a rock, with one creek naturally arched by the force of tempests. Here I put in my canoe, and climbing a part of the rock, I could plainly discover land to the east, extending from south to north. I lay all night in my canoe; and repeating my voyage early in the morning, I arrived in seven hours to the south-east point of New Holland. This confirmed me in the opinion I have long entertained, that the maps and charts place this country at least three degrees more to the east than it really is; which thought I communicated many years ago to my worthy friend, Mr. Herman Moll, and gave him my reasons for it, although he has rather chosen to follow other authors.

I saw no inhabitants in the place where I landed, and being unarmed, I was afraid of venturing far into the country. I found some shellfish on the shore, and ate them raw, not daring to kindle a fire, for fear of being discovered by the natives. I continued three days feeding on oysters and limpets, to save my own provisions; and I fortunately found a brook of excellent water, which gave me great relief.

On the fourth day, venturing out early a little too far, I saw twenty or thirty natives upon a height not above five hundred yards from me. They were stark naked, men, women, and children, round a fire, as I could discover by the smoke. One of them spied me, and gave notice to the rest; five of them advanced toward me, leaving the women and children at the fire. I made what haste I could to the shore, and, getting into my canoe, shoved off: the savages, observing me retreat, ran after me; and before I could get far enough into the sea, discharged an arrow which wounded me deeply on the inside of my left knee: I shall carry the mark to my grave. I apprehended the arrow might be poisoned, and paddling out of the reach of their darts (being a calm day), I made a shift to suck the wound, and dress it as well as I could.

I was at a loss what to do, for I durst not return to the same landing-place, but stood to the north, and was forced to paddle, for the wind, though very gentle, was against me, blowing north-west. As I was looking about for a secure landing-place, I saw a sail to the north-north-east, which appearing every minute more visible, I was in some doubt whether I should wait for them or not; but at last my detestation of the *Yahoo* race prevailed; and turning my canoe, I sailed and paddled together to the south, and got into the same creek whence I set out in the morning, choosing rather to trust myself among these barbarians, than live with European *Yahoos*. I drew up my canoe as close as I could to the shore, and hid myself behind a stone by the little brook, which, as I have already said, was excellent water.

The ship came within half a league of this creek, and sent her long boat with vessels to take in fresh water (for the place, it seems, was very well known); but I did not observe it, till the boat was almost on shore; and it was too late to seek another hiding-place. The seamen at their landing observed my canoe, and rummaging it all over, easily conjectured that the owner could not be far off. Four of them, well armed, searched every cranny and lurking-hole, till at last they found me flat on my face behind the stone. They gazed awhile in admiration at my strange uncouth dress; my coat made of skins, my wooden-soled shoes, and my furred stockings; whence, however, they concluded, I was not a native of the place, who all go naked. One of the seamen, in Portuguese, bid me rise, and asked who I was. I understood that language very well, and getting upon my feet, said, I was a poor *Yahoo* banished from the *Houyhnhnms*, and desired they would please to let me depart. They admired to hear me answer them in their own tongue, and saw by my complexion I must be a European; but were at a loss to know what I meant by *Yahoos* and *Houyhnhnms*; and at the same time fell a-laughing at my strange tone in speaking, which resembled the neighing of a horse. I trembled all the while betwixt fear and hatred. I again desired leave to depart, and was gently moving to my canoe; but they laid hold of me, desiring to know, what country I was of? whence I came? with many other questions. I told them I was born in England, whence I came about five years ago, and then their country and ours were at peace. I therefore hoped they would not treat me as an enemy, since I meant them no harm, but was a poor *Yahoo* seeking some desolate place where to pass the remainder of his unfortunate life.

When they began to talk, I thought I never heard or saw any thing more unnatural; for it appeared to me as monstrous as if a dog or a cow should speak in England, or a *Yahoo* in *Houyhnhnmland*. The honest Portuguese were equally amazed at my strange dress, and the odd manner of delivering my words, which, however, they understood very well. They spoke to me with great humanity, and said, they were sure the captain would carry me gratis to Lisbon, whence I might return to my own country; that two of the seamen would go back to the ship, inform the captain of what they had seen, and receive his orders; in the mean time, unless I would give my solemn oath not to fly, they would secure me by force. I thought it best to comply with their proposal. They were very curious to know my story, but I gave them very little satisfaction, and they all conjectured that my misfortunes had impaired my reason. In two hours the boat, which went laden with vessels of water, returned, with the captain's command to fetch me on board. I fell on my knees to preserve my liberty; but all was in vain; and the men, having tied me with cords, heaved me into the boat, whence I was taken into the ship, and thence into the captain's cabin.

His name was Pedro de Mendez; he was a very courteous and generous person. He entreated me to give some account of myself, and desired to know what I would eat or drink;

said, I should be used as well as himself; and spoke so many obliging things, that I wondered to find such civilities from a *Yahoo*. However, I remained silent and sullen; I was ready to faint at the very smell of him and his men. At last I desired something to eat out of my own canoe; but he ordered me a chicken, and some excellent wine, and then directed that I should be put to bed in a very clean cabin. I would not undress myself, but lay on the bed-clothes, and in half an hour stole out, when I thought the crew was at dinner, and getting to the side of the ship, was going to leap into the sea, and swim for my life, rather than continue among *Yahoos*. But one of the seamen prevented me, and having informed the captain, I was chained to my cabin.

After dinner, Don Pedro came to me, and desired to know my reason for so desperate an attempt; assured me, he only meant to do me all the service he was able; and spoke so very movingly, that at last I descended to treat him like an animal which had some little portion of reason. I gave him a very short relation of my voyage; of the conspiracy against me by my own men; of the country where they set me on shore, and of my five years residence there. All which he looked upon as if it were a dream or a vision; whereat I took great offence; for I had quite forgot the faculty of lying, so peculiar to *Yahoos*, in all countries where they preside, and, consequently, their disposition of suspecting truth in others of their own species. I asked him, whether it were the custom in his country to say the thing which was not? I assured him, I had almost forgot what he meant by falsehood, and if I had lived a thousand years in *Houyhnhnmland*, I should never have heard a lie from the meanest servant; that I was altogether indifferent whether he believed me or not; but, however, in return for his favours, I would give so much allowance to the corruption of his nature, as to answer any objection he would please to make, and then he might easily discover the truth.

The captain, a wise man, after many endeavours to catch me tripping in some part of my story, at last began to have a better opinion of my veracity. But he added, that since I professed so inviolable an attachment to truth, I must give him my word and honour to bear him company in this voyage, without attempting any thing against my life; or else he would continue me a prisoner till we arrived at Lisbon. I gave him the promise he required; but at the same time protested, that I would suffer the greatest hardships, rather than return to live among *Yahoos*.

Our voyage passed without any considerable accident. In gratitude to the captain, I sometimes sat with him, at his earnest request, and strove to conceal my antipathy against human kind, although it often broke out; which he suffered to pass without observation. But the greatest part of the day I confined myself to my cabin, to avoid seeing any of the crew. The captain had often entreated me to strip myself of my savage dress, and offered to lend me the best suit of clothes he had. This I would not be prevailed on to accept, abhorring to cover myself with any thing that had been on the back of a *Yahoo*. I only desired he would lend me two clean shirts, which, having been washed since he wore them, I believed would not so much defile me. These I changed every second day, and washed them myself.

We arrived at Lisbon, Nov. 5, 1715. At our landing, the captain forced me to cover myself with his cloak, to prevent the rabble from crowding about me. I was conveyed to his own house; and at my earnest request he led me up to the highest room backwards. I conjured him to conceal from all persons what I had told him of the *Houyhnhnms*; because the least hint of such a story would not only draw numbers of people to see me, but probably put me in danger of being imprisoned, or burnt by the Inquisition. The captain persuaded me to accept a suit of clothes newly made; but I would not suffer the tailor to take my measure; however, Don Pedro being almost of my size, they fitted me well enough. He accoutred me with other necessaries, all new, which I aired for twenty-four hours before I would use them.

The captain had no wife, nor above three servants, none of which were suffered to attend at meals; and his whole deportment was so obliging, added to very good human understanding, that I really began to tolerate his company. He gained so far upon me, that I ventured to look out of the back window. By degrees I was brought into another room, whence I peeped into the street, but drew my head back in a fright. In a week's time he seduced me down to the door. I found my terror gradually lessened, but my hatred and contempt seemed to increase. I was at last bold enough to walk the street in his company, but kept my nose well stopped with rue, or sometimes with tobacco.

In ten days, Don Pedro, to whom I had given some account of my domestic affairs, put it upon me, as a matter of honour and conscience, that I ought to return to my native country, and live at home with my wife and children. He told me, there was an English ship in the port just ready to sail, and he would furnish me with all things necessary. It would be tedious to repeat his arguments, and my contradictions. He said, it was altogether impossible to find such a solitary island as I desired to live in; but I might command in my own house, and pass my time in a manner as recluse as I pleased.

I complied at last, finding I could not do better. I left Lisbon the 24th day of November, in an English merchantman, but who was the master I never inquired. Don Pedro accompanied me to the ship, and lent me twenty pounds. He took kind leave of me, and embraced me at parting, which I bore as well as I could. During this last voyage I had no commerce with the master or any of his men; but, pretending I was sick, kept close in my cabin. On the fifth of December, 1715, we cast anchor in the Downs, about nine in the morning, and at three in the afternoon I got safe to my house at Redriff.

My wife and family received me with great surprise and joy, because they concluded me certainly dead; but I must freely confess the sight of them filled me only with hatred, disgust, and contempt; and the more, by reflecting on the near alliance I had to them. For although, since my unfortunate exile from the *Houyhnhnm* country, I had compelled myself to tolerate the sight of *Yahoos*, and to converse with Don Pedro de Mendez, yet my memory and imagination were perpetually filled with the virtues and ideas of those exalted *Houyhnhnms*. And when I began to consider that, by copulating with one of the *Yahoo* species I had become a parent of more, it struck me with the utmost shame, confusion, and horror.

As soon as I entered the house, my wife took me in her arms, and kissed me; at which, having not been used to the touch of that odious animal for so many years, I fell into a swoon for almost an hour. At the time I am writing, it is five years since my last return to England. During the first year, I could not endure my wife or children in my presence; the very smell of them was intolerable; much less could I suffer them to eat in the same room. To this hour they dare not presume to touch my bread, or drink out of the same cup, neither was I ever able to let one of them take me by the hand. The first money I laid out was to buy two young stone-horses, which I keep in a good stable; and next to them, the groom is my greatest favourite, for I feel my spirits revived by the smell he contracts in the stable. My horses understand me tolerably well; I converse with them at least four hours every day. They are strangers to bridle or saddle; they live in great amity with me and friendship to each other.

Chapter XII

The author's veracity. His design in publishing this work. His censure of those travellers who swerve from the truth. The author clears himself from any sinister ends in writing. An objection answered. The method of planting colonies. His native country commended. The right of the crown to those countries described by the author is justified. The difficulty of conquering them. The author takes his last leave of the reader; proposes his manner of living for the future; gives good advice, and concludes.

Thus, gentle reader, I have given thee a faithful history of my travels for sixteen years and above seven months: wherein I have not been so studious of ornament as of truth. I could, perhaps, like others, have astonished thee with strange improbable tales; but I rather chose to relate plain matter of fact, in the simplest manner and style; because my principal design was to inform, and not to amuse thee.

It is easy for us who travel into remote countries, which are seldom visited by Englishmen or other Europeans, to form descriptions of wonderful animals both at sea and land. Whereas a traveller's chief aim should be to make men wiser and better, and to improve their minds by the bad, as well as good, example of what they deliver concerning foreign places.

I could heartily wish a law was enacted, that every traveller, before he were permitted to publish his voyages, should be obliged to make oath before the Lord High Chancellor, that all he intended to print was absolutely true to the best of his knowledge; for then the world would no longer be deceived, as it usually is, while some writers, to make their works pass the better upon the public, impose the grossest falsities on the unwary reader. I have perused several books of travels with great delight in my younger days; but having since gone over most parts of the globe, and been able to contradict many fabulous accounts from my own observation, it has given me a great disgust against this part of reading, and some indignation to see the credulity of mankind so impudently abused. Therefore, since my acquaintance were pleased to think my poor endeavours might not be unacceptable to my country, I imposed on myself, as a maxim never to be swerved from, that I would strictly adhere to truth; neither indeed can I be ever under the least temptation to vary from it, while I retain in my mind the lectures and example of my noble master and the other illustrious *Houyhnhnms* of whom I had so long the honour to be an humble hearer.

— *Nec si miserum Fortuna Sinonem*

Finxit, vanum etiam, mendacemque improba finget.

I know very well, how little reputation is to be got by writings which require neither genius nor learning, nor indeed any other talent, except a good memory, or an exact journal. I know likewise, that writers of travels, like dictionary-makers, are sunk into oblivion by the weight and bulk of those who come last, and therefore lie uppermost. And it is highly probable, that such travellers, who shall hereafter visit the countries described in this work of mine, may, by detecting my errors (if there be any), and adding many new discoveries of their own, justle me out of vogue, and stand in my place, making the world forget that ever I was an author. This indeed would be too great a mortification, if I wrote for fame: but as my sole intention was the public good, I cannot be altogether disappointed. For who can read of the virtues I have mentioned in the glorious *Houyhnhnms*, without being ashamed of his own vices, when he considers himself as the reasoning, governing animal of his country? I shall say nothing of those remote nations where *Yahoos* preside; among which the least corrupted are the *Brobdingnagians*; whose wise maxims in morality and government it would be our happiness to observe. But I forbear descanting further, and rather leave the judicious reader to his own remarks and application.

I am not a little pleased that this work of mine can possibly meet with no censurers: for what objections can be made against a writer, who relates only plain facts, that happened in such distant countries, where we have not the least interest, with respect either to trade or negotiations? I have carefully avoided every fault with which common writers of travels are often too justly charged. Besides, I meddle not the least with any party, but write without passion, prejudice, or ill-will against any man, or number of men, whatsoever. I write for the noblest end, to inform and instruct mankind; over whom I may, without breach of modesty, pretend to some superiority, from the advantages I received by conversing so long among the most accomplished *Houyhnhnms*. I write without any view to profit or praise. I never suffer a word to pass that may look like reflection, or possibly give the least offence, even to those who are most ready to take it. So that I hope I may with justice pronounce myself an author perfectly blameless; against whom the tribes of Answerers, Considerers, Observers, Reflectors, Detectors, Remarkers, will never be able to find matter for exercising their talents.

I confess, it was whispered to me, that I was bound in duty, as a subject of England, to have given in a memorial to a secretary of state at my first coming over; because, whatever lands are discovered by a subject belong to the crown. But I doubt whether our conquests in the countries I treat of would be as easy as those of Ferdinando Cortez over the naked Americans. The Lilliputians, I think, are hardly worth the charge of a fleet and army to reduce them; and I question whether it might be prudent or safe to attempt the *Brobdingnagians*; or whether an English army would be much at their ease with the Flying Island over their heads. The *Houyhnhnms* indeed appear not to be so well prepared for war, a science to which they are perfect strangers, and especially against missive weapons. However, supposing myself to be a minister of state, I could never give my advice for invading them. Their prudence, unanimity, unacquaintedness with fear, and their love of their country, would amply supply all defects in the military art. Imagine twenty thousand of them breaking into the midst of an European army, confounding the ranks, overturning the carriages, battering the warriors' faces into mummy by terrible yerks from their hinder hoofs; for they would well deserve the character given to *Augustus, Recalcitrat undique tutus*. But, instead of proposals for conquering that magnanimous nation, I rather wish they were in a capacity, or disposition, to send a sufficient number of their inhabitants for civilizing Europe, by teaching us the first principles of honour, justice, truth, temperance, public spirit, fortitude, chastity, friendship, benevolence, and fidelity. The names of all which virtues are still retained among us in most languages, and are to be met with in modern, as well as ancient authors; which I am able to assert from my own small reading.

But I had another reason, which made me less forward to enlarge his Majesty's dominions by my discoveries. To say the truth, I had conceived a few scruples with relation to the distributive justice of princes upon those occasions. For instance, a crew of pirates are driven by a storm they know not whither; at length a boy discovers land from the topmast; they go on shore to rob and plunder, they see a harmless people, are entertained with kindness; they give the country a new name; they take formal possession of it for their king; they set up a rotten plank, or a stone, for a memorial; they murder two or three dozen of the natives, bring away a couple more, by force, for a sample; return home, and get their pardon. Here commences a new dominion acquired with a title by divine right. Ships are sent with the first opportunity; the natives driven out or destroyed; their princes tortured to discover their gold; a free license given to all acts of inhumanity and lust, the earth reeking with the blood of its inhabitants: and this execrable crew of butchers, employed in so pious an expedition, is a modern colony, sent to convert and civilize an idolatrous and barbarous people!

But this description, I confess, does by no means affect the British nation, who may be an example to the whole world for their wisdom, care, and justice in planting colonies; their liberal endowments for the advancement of religion and learning; their choice of devout and able pastors to propagate Christianity; their caution in stocking their provinces with people of sober lives and conversations from this the mother kingdom; their strict regard to the distribution of justice, in supplying the civil administration through all their colonies with officers of the greatest abilities, utter strangers to corruption; and, to crown all, by sending the most vigilant and virtuous governors, who have no other views than the happiness of the people over whom they preside, and the honour of the king their master.

But as those countries which I have described do not appear to have any desire of being conquered and enslaved, murdered or driven out by colonies, nor abound either in gold, silver, sugar, or tobacco, I did humbly conceive, they were by no means proper objects of our zeal, our valour, or our interest. However, if those whom it more concerns think fit to be of another opinion, I am ready to depose, when I shall be lawfully called, that no European did ever visit those countries before me. I mean, if the inhabitants ought to be believed, unless a dispute may arise concerning the two *Yahoos*, said to have been seen many years ago upon a mountain in *Houyhnhnmland*, from whence the opinion is, that the race of those brutes hath descended; and these, for anything I know, may have been English, which indeed I was apt to suspect from the lineaments of their posterity's countenances, Although very much defaced. But, how far that will go to make out a title, I leave to learned in colony-law.

But, as to the formality of taking possession in my sovereign's name, it never came once into my thoughts; and if it had, yet, as my affairs then stood, I should perhaps, in point of prudence and self-preservation, have put it off to a better opportunity.

Having thus answered the only objection that can ever be raised against me as a traveller, I here take a final leave of all my courteous readers, and return to enjoy my own speculations in my little garden at Redriff; to apply those excellent lessons of virtue which I learned among the *Houyhnhnms*; to instruct the *Yahoos* of my own family, is far as I shall find them docible animals; to behold my figure often in a glass, and thus, if possible, habituate myself by time to tolerate the sight of a human creature; to lament the brutality to *Houyhnhnms* in my own country, but always treat their persons with respect, for the sake of my noble master, his family, his friends, and the whole *Houyhnhnm* race, whom these of ours have the honour to resemble in all their lineaments, however their intellectuals came to degenerate.

I began last week to permit my wife to sit at dinner with me, at the farthest end of a long table; and to answer (but with the utmost brevity) the few questions I asked her. Yet, the smell of a *Yahoo* continuing very offensive, I always keep my nose well stopped with rue, lavender, or tobacco leaves. And, although it be hard for a man late in life to remove old habits, I am not altogether out of hopes, in some time, to suffer a neighbour *Yahoo* in my company, without the apprehensions I am yet under of his teeth or his claws.

My reconcilement to the *Yahoo* kind in general might not be so difficult, if they would be content with those vices and follies only which nature has entitled them to. I am not in the least provoked at the sight of a lawyer, a pickpocket, a colonel, a fool, a lord, a gamester, a politician, a whoremonger, a physician, an evidence, a suborner, an attorney, a traitor, or the like; this is all according to the due course of things: but when I behold a lump of deformity and diseases, both in body and mind, smitten with pride, it immediately breaks all the measures of my patience; neither shall I be ever able to comprehend how such an animal, and such a vice, could tally together. The wise and virtuous *Houyhnhnms*, who abound in all excellences that can adorn a rational creature, have no name for this vice in their language, which has no terms to express any thing that is evil, except those whereby they describe the detestable qualities of their *Yahoos*, among which they were not able to distinguish this of pride, for want of thoroughly understanding human nature, as it shows itself in other countries where that animal presides. But I, who had more experience, could plainly observe some rudiments of it among the wild *Yahoos*.

But the *Houyhnhnms*, who live under the government of reason, are no more proud of the good qualities they possess, than I should be for not wanting a leg or an arm; which no man in his wits would boast of, although he must be miserable without them. I dwell the longer upon this subject from the desire I have to make the society of an English *Yahoo* by any means not insupportable; and therefore I here entreat those who have any tincture of this absurd vice, that they will not presume to come in my sight.

格列佛游记

[英] 乔纳森·斯威夫特

给读者的话

这部游记的作者，莱米尔·格列佛先生，是我很亲密的一位老友。我们俩甚至还有一点亲属关系，应该是我们各自的母亲那边的关系。大约三年前，格列佛先生厌烦了他在雷德里夫的住所，因为那儿总是有大批怀着好奇心的客人前来造访。于是，他在诺丁汉郡的纽瓦克买下了一块地，还有一幢房子。诺丁汉郡是他出生的地方，也是他现在颐养天年的地方，他和邻居们过着和睦的生活。

虽然格列佛先生是在诺丁汉郡出生的，但是我曾听他说过他们一家子其实来自牛津郡。为了证实这一点，我到牛津郡班伯里的一个教堂墓园看过，发现了格列佛家族的几座墓穴和墓碑。

在他离开雷德里夫之前，他把所有的手稿都托付给了我，并且授权我随意处置。我把这些手稿仔仔细细地读了三遍，文章风格相当平淡而简洁，唯一的缺点是描述得过于详尽了，不过这也是旅行家们的通病。字里行间透露着一种详尽可靠的气息，作者也因为这种诚实的作风而受到好评。在他的家乡雷德里夫甚至还有这样的说法：如果想证明一件事情是真的，除非格列佛先生亲口讲过。

经过作者的允许，我曾把这些手稿交给几位德高望重的前辈审阅。在他们的建议之下，我才决定将其公之于众，希望本书能成为年轻贵族的有趣读物。至少从现在的情况来看，这本书要比寻常的那些空谈政治和政党的书籍有趣多了。

如果我没有大胆地删去一些有关风向、潮汐，以及几次旅行中的定位和方向之类的内容，没有删去那些关于如何在暴风雨中操控船只的详细描述，没有删去那些辨识经纬度的知识的话，这本书的篇幅可能会比现在多出一倍。我能够预见格列佛先生对此颇有微词，但我下定决心，要使这本书尽可能地适合广大读者阅读。如果由于我本人的疏忽，而使书中出现了有关航海的低级错误的话，我在此声明，对此负全部责任。如果有热衷旅行的人对原稿表示好奇，想要一睹为快的话，我随时都会满足他的要求。

如果想了解有关作者生平的更多细节，读者可以通过仔细阅读本书起始的几页得到满意的答案。

理查德·辛普森

格列佛船长
致其表兄辛普森的一封信

　　我是在你的不断催促和热情鼓励之下才决定出版这本内容松散、记叙混乱的游记的；如果有人就这个问题质疑你，希望你能够公开这一点。我曾叮嘱你聘请几位大学里的年轻绅士帮忙整理一下稿子，矫正一下文体；我的堂兄丹皮尔出版他的那本《环球航行记》时，就是听从我的意见这么办的。但是我并不记得我赋予过你任意删减其中内容的权利，更不要说同意你增添任何内容。因此，我在此郑重声明，对于你后来增添的文字，我表示坚决反对，特别是那段有关安妮女王陛下的文字。虽然我对她致以最为崇高的敬意，但这样的文字我是不可能接受的。但是你，或者你聘用的那些家伙，应该考虑到这不是我的本意，在我的主人"慧骃"面前赞美我们这个物种中的任何一位都是不合适的。更何况那段文字本身就是捏造的。据我所知，伟大的英国女王安妮在位期间，的确任命过国家首相，而且接连任命过两位，第一位是戈多尔芬伯爵，随后是牛津伯爵。因此，是你把错误的事情推到了我的身上。同样，在描述有关科学院的篇章中，以及我和我的主人"慧骃"的几次谈话中，你要么删掉了一些重要的细节，要么篡改了其中的内容，导致我自己都快读不懂自己写的内容了。我曾写信给你，表达过类似的意思，而你却告诉我，自己之所以这样做是为了避免我冒犯高层，因为他们对出版行业十分重视。他们不仅擅长曲解内容，而且还会对所有与"讽刺"（我记得你用的是这个词）有关的作品加以惩罚。但是恕我直言，那么多年前，我在距离这个国家五千里格以外另一个君王的领地说过的一些话，和现在统治着一群野兽的"野猢"有什么关系呢？那时候的我对于他们统治下的生活的痛苦和不幸没有一点点概念，所以更谈不上有什么畏惧了！难道我看到那些"慧骃"成了拉车的，而那些"野猢"就端坐在车里，就像前者变成了畜生，而"野猢"则变得人模狗样的时候，我不能抱怨几句吗？说实话，我正是为了躲开这样恐怖而荒谬的不堪场景，才选择离开这个地方的。

　　正是出于对你的信任，我才觉得自己应该把最真实的想法告诉你。

　　但是从另外一个方面来讲，我还是应该怪自己没有主见，竟然在你和其他人的劝说之下轻易听信了你们的话，同意出版我的这本游记，而这本身就违背了我自己的意愿。请你好好想想，当你打着为了公众利益的旗号坚持出版我的游记时，我有没有请你好好考虑一下，那些"野猢"是不可能通过讲道理或者举例子之类的办法来认识到自己的错误的。这一点已经得到了证明，我原本对这个小岛还是有一点期望的，还希望岛上的腐败和弊端能够得到改善。但是六个月过去之后，我通过这本书发出的警示并没有得到哪怕一丁点的效果。我原本还盼望着你能写封信给我，让我知道那些只知道纷争和内讧的政党团体已经销声匿迹；法官变得博学正直；律师开始明白事理，同时变得谦逊而诚实。原本我希望有无数法律文书在史密斯菲尔德广场付之一炬；那些年轻贵族也已经洗心革面；招摇撞骗的庸医没有了立足之地；而那些女性"野猢"变得重视名誉和道德；部长们的院落被打扫得干干净净；那些拥有智慧、美德、学识的普通人会受到嘉奖；而那些酸腐文人会得到惩罚，只准食用自己的衣服充饥，喝自己的墨水解渴。从你鼓励我出版的言辞中，我坚信这一切，以及上千个改良措施能够得以实行，因为我的书里记载着可行的改良办法。如果那些"野猢"的天性中还有那么一点点对美德和智慧的渴望的话，在这七个月的时间里，他们早已纠正了自己的恶习。然而你的来信中并没有任何相关的答复。恰恰相反，每周的信中只有各种夹杂着侮辱和诽谤的内容，甚至还有许多莫名其妙的指责。在这些文字中，我看到他们控诉我污蔑大臣、贬低人性（亏他们还能理直气壮地说出这个词），还指责我辱骂妇女。我发现这些人的意见还不太统一，有些人宣称我不可能是此书的作者，有些人则坚信许多与我无关的著作是我写的。

　　我还发现你找的印刷商人十分粗心，他们把整个游记的顺序、日期，还有我几次航程的出发和返航时间都搞错了，那些年份、月份和日子也没有一个是正确的。我还听说出版之后原稿就被毁掉了，而我自己也没有留下任何副本，但我还是送去了一份勘误表。如果以后还会再版的话，我希望你能够改正过来。然而我不是一个固执的人，我想这一切还是交由明智、坦诚的读者们来判断吧。

　　我听说有好几个"野猢"在我的书中鸡蛋里挑骨头，不是认为航海语言使用不当，就是说这些语言已经过时了。对此我也无能为力，在我最初的几次航行中，我还是一个初出茅庐的家伙，全凭一些老水手的教导，一言一行都是亦步亦趋。不过我很快就发现那些海上的"野猢"和陆地上的一样，都喜欢在用词上标新立异——这也导致他们的语言每年都在变化。正是因为这样，我每次回国都听不懂他们的新语言。我还发现，每当有"野猢"出于好奇从伦敦跑来我家看望我时，我们双方都无法使对方明白自己所表达的意思。

　　如果说这些"野猢"的指责有哪里让我不痛快的话，那就是其中几位指责我的游记是凭空想象所得，这样的言论让我出离愤怒。甚至还有人认为"慧骃"和"野猢"只是虚构的乌托邦的产物。

　　对此我必须承认，关于利立浦特、布罗丁格拉格（这才是正确写法，那个布罗丁格奈格的写法是错误的）和拉普塔的人民，我从未听说有"野猢"敢自以为是地怀疑他们的真实性，或者怀疑我讲述的和他们有关的事情，因为事实会让每一位读者信服。但是为什么在我讲到"慧骃"和"野猢"的时候，总会有人跑出来质疑呢？就以后者为例，我们这个国家就有数不清的"野猢"。和生活在"慧骃"国的同类相比，他们除了更加吵闹，身上裹着一些遮羞布，两者又有什么区别呢？我之所以写下这本游记，是为了让他们改邪归正，而不是得到他们的赞许。那些"野猢"的溢美之词，在我听来还不如我养在马厩里的那两匹已经退化的"慧骃"的嘶鸣，毕竟从它们那已经退化的天性中，我还能学习到一些纯正的、不掺杂一丝邪气的美德。

　　难道这些不堪的动物以为我会为这本游记的真实性去辩护吗？我本人就是一只"野猢"，但我生活在"慧骃"国的两年时间里，亲眼看到我的那些坦荡的主人们的一举一动。在它们潜移默化地教导下，我已经摆脱了撒谎、拖延、欺骗、推诿等坏习惯（我承认这很难），尽管这些恶习已经在我们的内心深处深深扎根，特别是那些欧洲的"野猢"。

　　有关这本书的出版，我还有许多抱怨之处，但是我不想给自己找麻烦了，也不想再给你添麻烦了。还有一点我必须坦白，那就是自从我上次旅行结束回国之后，我不得不和你们进行交流，特别是我的家庭成员，这也是不可避免的。但这样一来我身上那些属于"野猢"的堕落性格又死灰复燃了，不然的话我也不可能产生企图改变"野猢"这个种群的荒唐念头。不过现在我已经彻底放弃了这样的念头。

1727 年 4 月 2 日

第一卷
利立浦特游记

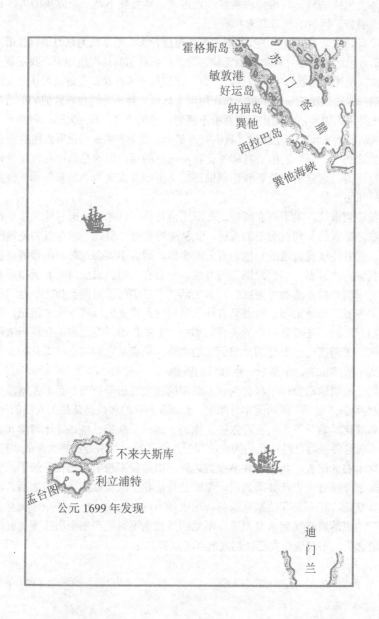

霍格斯岛

苏门答腊

敏敦港

好运岛

纳福岛

巽他

西拉巴岛

巽他海峡

不来夫斯库

孟台图

利立浦特

公元 1699 年发现

迪门兰

第一章

作者简要叙述了自己的家世，以及自己最初的外出动机。由于货船失事，他不得不泅水逃生，随后在利立浦特的海岸登陆。他被俘虏了，然后被带到首都。

我的父亲在诺丁汉郡拥有一块小小的庄园，他一共有五个儿子，我排行第三。在我十四岁的时候，他就把我送去了剑桥的伊曼纽尔学院上学，我在那儿研读了三年时间；不过由于经费有限，高昂的学费给我的家庭带来了很大的负担，于是我就去詹姆斯·贝茨医生那儿当学徒，借此补贴家用。贝茨先生是伦敦有名的外科医生，我在他手下干了四年活。我的父亲时不时会寄给我几笔小额的补助，而我把这些钱都投入了航海和一些数学科目，因为我一直觉得自己是要出去旅行的，而这些知识对我的旅行生涯是很有帮助的。离开贝茨先生后，我就回家去见了父亲。在他和我的叔叔约翰及其他亲戚的帮助下，凑齐了四十英镑，我的父亲还答应每年都给我三十英镑，供我到莱顿念书；我在莱顿学习了两年零七个月的医学知识，我知道这也会给我的旅行生涯带来不小的助益。

我从莱顿回到伦敦后不久，我的恩师贝茨先生就举荐我去亚伯拉罕·潘内尔船长手下的"燕子号"商船做外科医生，我在那儿整整干了三年半，也曾去过黎凡特和其他地方两次。回来之后，我就决定在伦敦定居了。我的导师贝茨先生十分支持我的决定，并且给我介绍了好几位病人。我在犹太人街区租了一套小房子，然后听从朋友的建议，改善一下我的生活状况，和在新门街做针织品生意的艾德蒙·波顿家的二女儿玛丽·波顿成亲了。妻子还给我带来了四百英镑的嫁妆。

两年之后，我的恩师贝茨先生去世了，由于没有朋友的扶助，而我又不允许自己像其他同行一样去干那些欺上瞒下的勾当，生意因此日渐萧条。在和我的妻子以及一些熟人商量了一番之后，我决定再次出海。在接下来的六年时间里，我先后在两艘船上担任外科医生的职务，出了好几次海，去过东印度和西印度群岛，这也给我带来了一笔丰厚的收入。闲暇时光里，我阅读了好些古代和现代的名作；当我上岸的时候，就考察当地的风土人情，还抽空学习了他们的语言。我的记忆力不错，所以这样的学习还是相对轻松的。

但是最后一趟旅程并不顺心，让我对航海生涯产生了一丝厌倦，我甚至打算从此以后待在家里和我的妻儿一起安享平静的生活了。我从老犹太街搬到了费达巷，然后又搬到了距离码头比较近的沃平，盘算着能接到一些水手的生意，但实际上却事与愿违。三年过去了，生活还是没有希望，这时候我接受了"羚羊号"的船长威廉·普利查德的邀请，和他一起前往南太平洋，因为他给了我丰厚的待遇。于是，在 1699 年 5 月 4 日，我们从布里斯托尔启程。旅程一开始是相当顺利的。

但是出于某些原因，将航海过程中的冒险经历事无巨细地描述给读者听显然有些不太合适，所以我只要把旅途中重要的事情讲一讲就好。我们的船只在东印度洋航行的途中遭遇了超强的暴风雨，把我们刮到了位于范迪门地西北方的海域。我们观测了一番，发现自己位于南纬三十度零二分的海面上。由于繁重的劳动和有限的食物，十二位海员在海上去世了，剩下的也个个虚弱不堪。11 月 5 日正值当地初夏时节，海面上升腾起浓厚的雾气，当海员们发现前方的礁石时，狂风中的船已经无力躲避了。整艘船向着礁石冲去，船体一下子被撞得支离破碎。包括我在内的六个人放下了一只救生艇，用尽吃奶的力气才把救生艇划离礁石和船只所在的范围。我们一口气划出了大约三里格远，然后就累得没了力气，因为之前在船上就已经耗费了大部分体力。我们只能祈祷海浪能够拯救我们。差不多半个小时之后，突然刮起了一阵北风，把救生艇吹翻了。救生艇上的其他人，包括逃到礁石上的和留在船上的人的命运如何我就不得而知了，不过他们生还的希望很渺茫。至于落入海中的我，只能任凭风浪吹打，这条命都只能看天意了。我时不时地把双腿沉下去，但却怎么都感觉不到坚实的大地。就在我快要支撑不住，打算放弃的时候，我发现自己的双脚碰到了地面。这时候风暴小了下去，于是我就沿着平坦的岸线走了差不多一英里，这才上了岸。据我估计当时应该是晚上八点左右。我继续朝内陆走了大约半英里，没发现一点人烟；由于当时的我过于虚弱，就算有也发现不了。当时的我筋疲力尽，再加上气候炎热，我离开大船时还喝了差不多半品脱的白兰地，整个人都昏昏欲睡。脚下的草地十分柔软，于是，我一头栽在地上呼呼大睡起来，我敢说这辈子还没睡过那么香甜的一觉。大约九个小时之后我才醒过来，这会儿天仿佛刚刚亮。我想爬起来，但却无法动弹，因为我正好面朝天躺着，我发现自己的胳膊和腿都被牢牢固定在了地上，我那又长又浓密的头发也被绑在了地上。我感觉到自己的身体，从腋窝到大腿绑着好几根细细的绳子。我只能维持向上看的姿势。太阳变得火热起来，阳光刺痛了眼睛。我听到身边有说话的声音，但是我当时的姿势就只能抬头向天。很快我就感觉到有个什么东西爬上了我的左腿，然后慢慢走到我的胸口，爬上了我的下巴。我努力向下看，发现眼前是一个身高不足六英寸的小人，手里拿着弓箭，背后还有箭袋。同时我也看到了他的身后有差不多四十个一样身材的小人，这样的场面让我十分惊讶，于是我大声咆哮起来；小人们听到了我的可怕声音，一个个害怕得转身就跑。我事后才知道，还有好几个人在从我身上跳下去的过程中受伤了。不过他们很快又聚拢回来了。其中一个胆子特别大的甚至还凑上前来端详了我的脸庞。只见他高高举起自己的双手，眼里满是羡慕的眼神。他的嘴里高喊着"海琴那·德古尔"，周围的小人们也重复了好几次这个词语，但是我并不知道这到底是什么意思。各位读者想必也能想到，这时候的我被固定在地上，是有多么不舒服了。一心挣扎的我终于把那些绳子挣断了，然后把固定我左胳膊的木桩子拔了出来。我仔细端详自己的左臂，发现了他们绑缚我的方法。我用力一挣，就把左侧的头发拉了出来；虽然拔出头发的时候感觉到一阵疼痛，但是我已经可以转动自己的脑袋了。这些家伙在我抓住他们之前就机灵地跑开了，然后就响起了一阵尖锐的叫喊声，之后就是一个响亮的声音"拓尔古·芬纳克"。刹那间，我就感觉到有一百支箭射进了我的左手臂，像被无数根针扎了一般。随后他们又来了一轮抛射，就像我们在欧洲扔炸弹的姿势一般。许多支箭落在我的身上（虽然我并没有感觉到疼痛），还有一些落在了我的脸上，吓得我赶紧拿左手去遮挡。箭雨过后，我感到一阵难以忍受的疼痛。我再一次挣扎着想要脱身，他们就更加猛烈地向我齐射，还有几个试图用长矛捅我的腰部；幸运的是我穿了一身牛皮背心，他们没法扎破。我想这时候最适合我的办法就是静静躺下，毕竟现在我的左手已经恢复了自由。只要等到夜幕降临，我就能轻轻松松地挣脱束缚。至于我眼前的这些原住民，如果他们都是这样的身材的话，不管多少人都不可能是我的对手。但是命运却给了我截然不同的安排。当我安静下来之后，他们也停止了射箭；从我身边的响声来看，他们的人数又增加了，就在距离我四码的位置响起了一阵敲打声，好像在忙着建什么东西。我努力转过脑袋，发现他们修建起了一座大约一英尺半高的台子，边上还有两三个供他们攀爬的梯子。这个台子大约可以容纳四个小人。台子上的四个人当中有一个看上去地位较高，他发表了一大篇演讲，可惜我根本就听不懂。不过说到这儿，我得先提一句，那就是他在发表演讲之前，还大喊了三声"兰格罗·德古尔·桑"（这几个词和先前的几个词语的意思会在后文有解释）。他一喊完就有大约五十个小人冲上前来，把固定在我脑袋左边的绳索割断了，这样我就可以自由地把脑袋转向右边，好好观察台子上那位准备演讲的小人的言行举止。这是个中年人，身高比旁边的三个人都要高一些。三个人当中有一个看上去像仆人，托着他的裙摆，只比我的中指长那么一点点；旁边的两个小人一左一右护卫在他的身边。他的一举一动都像个演说家，可以看出他说了不少威胁的话，当然还有承诺、同情和友好的话。我也回答了几句，尽量装出一副恭敬的模样。我举起左手，看着太阳，请太阳给我作证。这会儿的我其实已经好长时间没有吃东西了，饥肠辘辘，我感到这种生理需求是如此强烈，于是就把手指放在嘴巴旁边，表示要吃东西。虽然这样的举动可能违背了礼节，但是这位"赫够"（后来我才知道，他们都是这么称呼领主的）很快就明白了我的意思。他从台子上爬了下去，命令手下把那几架梯子搬到我的身边。差不多一百个小人爬上了梯子，把一篮篮肉食送到我的嘴边。原来是皇帝听说了我的到来，特意准备了这些食物。我注意到篮子里有好几种动物的肉，但是我没法通过味道判断出来。从形状上看有些可能是羊肉，主要是前腿、后腿和后腰的肉，每一块肉就只有云雀翅膀那么小，一口就可以吃下两三块。还有和子弹差不多大小的面包，我一口可以吃下三个。他们飞快地供应着食物，对我的食量感到万分惊讶。我又做了个手势，表示自己想要喝点什么；他们从我吃东西的样子看出，少量的水是不够我喝的。这些人非常聪明，他们十分熟练地吊起一只头号大桶，然后把它滚到我手边，撬开桶盖。我一饮而尽，这我很容易做到，因为一桶酒还不到半品脱。酒的味道很像勃艮第产的淡味葡萄酒，但是闻起来却香得多。接着他们又给我弄来了一桶，我也是一口气喝个精光，并表示还想喝，可他们已拿不出来了。我表演完这些奇迹之后，他们欢呼雀跃，在我的胸脯上手舞足蹈，像起先那样一遍又一遍地高喊"海琴那·德古尔"。他们示意我把那两个酒桶扔下去，不过事先还是让底下的那些看热闹的人散开，嘴里喊着"博拉奇·麦福拉"；当他们看到两个酒桶被我扔上了天空之后，一齐大喊"海琴那·德古尔"。我必须承认，当我看到身边的那些小人在走动的时候，内心有一种冲动，那就是抓住手边那四五十个小人，然后把他们扔在地上。但我想起了刚才吃过的苦头，怀疑这并不是他们最厉害的手段；更何况我曾经发过誓（我是这样解释刚才的那种恭顺的态度的），所以我很快就打消了这样的念头。更何况，他们既然这样隆重地款待我，我也应该礼尚往来。但私底下我还是对这些小家伙的无知无畏感到惊讶，毕竟我的一只手已经自由了，而他们竟然还敢在我身边走来走去；我是他们眼中的庞然大物，但是他们却没有一点害怕或者畏惧的表现。过了一会儿，他们发现我不需要吃肉了，我的面前就出现了一位由皇帝委派而来的高官。他的身后带着十二三个随从，一起沿着我的右小腿爬了上来，出现在我的面前。他拿出了一份盖有印玺的圣旨，对着我念叨了差不多有十分钟。虽然没有任何愤怒的意思，但却带着一股子坚决劲儿。他时不时地用手指向前方，后来我才知道，那是他们的首都的方向，距离这儿不过半英里的距离。这儿的皇帝已经下了命令，要把我运送到首都去。我回答了几句话，可是毫无意义。我用自由的左手做了一个手势，然后滑到右手上（当然我十分小心，没有碰到这些脆弱的家伙），接着又指了指我的脑袋和身体，示意自己想要获得自由。他仿佛明白了我的意思，因为他摇了摇头，表示不同意，同时举起手来做了个手势，表明我必须被当作俘虏押送去皇宫。不过他也用手势让我明白，我少不了好酒好肉的招待。我又一次试图挣脱身上的束缚，但扎在我脸上和手上的那些小箭弄得我生疼，很多伤口都已经起了疱，而箭头却仍然深陷其中。同时我的敌人的数目已经多了不少，无奈之下，我只能做手势表明自己任由他们处置。看到我的反应之后，那位"赫够"和他的随从才满意地离开了。很快我就听到边上的小人们一起反复喊着"派布隆·赛兰"；我感觉到左侧有很多人在帮我松绑，这样我整个人就可以向右翻过去，并且可以小解了。我尿了不少，这让在场的小人们感到十分惊讶，纷纷向两旁散去，躲避那一股凶猛的"洪流"。与此同时，他们在我身上抹了一种很香的药膏，我的伤口一下子就痊愈了。这样的待遇再加上我享用的美食，让我一下子就恢复了精力，然后又沉沉睡去。我大约睡了八个小时（这是事后才知道的），因为那些医生奉皇帝的命令，在我的酒里掺杂了一些安眠药水。

格列佛挣脱了绳索的束缚，
忍不住伸了个懒腰

看来在我上岸之后就被发现了，那时候我还在睡觉，而这些人就去报告了皇帝；他们通过商议决定用之前我说过的办法把我捆绑起来（这一定是趁着晚上做的），同时他也安排了足够多的肉和酒水防止我饿死。当然还少不了一架能够把我拉到首都的巨大机器。

皇帝的这个安排也许是大胆而危险的，因为我敢肯定，如果是欧洲的皇室遇到了同样的情况，是不可能有这样的举措的。不过在我看来，这样的安排虽然是慷慨的，但同样也是欠考虑的。因为假如这些人趁我睡着的时候企图用长矛和弓箭偷袭我，那么我一定会被惊醒。盛怒之下，我会用力挣断绳索。到那时，他们就无法和我对抗了，自然也别指望我放过他们了。

这些小人都是十分出色的数学家，而这位皇帝也以鼓励学术发展而受到称赞。在皇帝的鼓励之下，这个国家的机械制造能力堪称完美。皇帝有好几架装有轮子的机器，可以用来搬运大树和其他重物。他们经常选用最粗壮的大树打造战舰，成品有整整九英尺那么长，然后用这些机器把战舰运到三四百码以外的海面上去。整整五百名木工和机械师很快就投入了工作，为的是运送我这个庞然大物。他们打造了一个三英寸高的木架子，整整有七英尺那么长，四英尺那么宽，下面组装着二十二个轮子。这么看来，这架机器在我上岸四个小时之后就开始往这个地方运送了。我刚醒过来的时候听到的欢呼声，应该就是因为这架机器顺利抵达了。他们把这架机器推到我身边和我齐平的位置，不过最大的难题在于如何把我抬起来放到那个架子上面。于是他们准备了八十根一英尺高的木柱子，那些工人们用绷带把我的脖子、双手、双脚和身体都牢牢地固定住，然后用我们平时捆货物用的绳子，一端用钩子钩住绷带，另一端则绕过那些木桩顶端的滑轮。最后，由九百名最强壮的小人用了将近 3 个小时把我拉上架子，又用绳子把我牢牢捆住。这一切都是他们后来告诉我的，因为他们在忙活的时候，掺在我酒里的催眠药药性发作，我在那儿睡得正香甜呢！皇帝派出了整整五百匹骏马来拉这个木架子，每一匹骏马都有四英寸半那么高。浩浩荡荡的队伍就这样向着京城出发了。

我们在路上走了差不多四个小时，我被一件特别滑稽的事情给弄醒了。那时马车恰好停下来休整，两三个好奇心特别强的士兵想看看我睡着是什么模样，于是就悄悄爬上了那个架子，来到我的脸上。其中一个军官把手里的长枪往我的鼻子里伸，我感觉鼻子里像进了一根稻草那样发痒，于是就狠狠打了一个喷嚏。见势不妙的几个调皮鬼就这样悄悄逃跑了。三个星期之后我才知道我那时为什么会突然醒来。那天我们又走了很长的路，到了晚上休息的时候，身子每一侧有整整五百名卫兵看守着我，他们中的一半举着火把，另外一半拿着弓箭；如果我有什么危险举动的话，他们就会毫不犹豫地朝我放箭。

第二天天一亮，我们又继续赶路，差不多到了中午的时候，我们已经来到了距离城门不到两百码的地方。皇帝率领满城的文武百官前来迎接，只不过那些官员们怎么都不同意皇帝冒险走上我的身体。

马车停下的地方是全国最大的一座古庙。前几年在这儿发生过一起惨绝人寰的凶杀案，当地人都认为这座古庙被亵渎了，于是他们就把古庙里的所有东西都搬走了，只把这里当成一般的公共场所。恰好这个地方可以做我的住所。大门朝北，差不多有四英尺高，两英尺宽，我能够轻松地爬进去。在大门的两边各有一扇离地不过六英寸的小窗户。皇帝的铁匠特意打造了九十一条和我们的表链差不多粗细的铁链，铁链的一头固定在古庙里，还有一头则用三十六把铁锁固定在我的左腿上。这座古庙的对面，隔着一条马路大约20英尺远的地方是一座五英尺高的塔楼。皇帝和他的官员就爬上这座塔楼来观察我；这些都是后来才告诉我的，我那时候根本看不到他们。据说有大约十万以上的居民前来目睹我的风采；虽然我有卫兵守护，可我还是能够感觉到很多人爬上梯子，踩在我的身体上。很快皇帝就颁布了禁令，禁止任何人爬上我的身体，违令者将被处斩。那些工人觉得我已经被牢牢束缚了，就把我身上的绳索砍断了，这样我就可以站起来了。当时的我真是苦不堪言。周围的那些小人看到我站了起来，惊讶之情溢于言表。拴在我左腿上的铁链大概有两码长，这就是我的活动范围；而且铁链是固定在离大门不到四英寸的地方，所以我可以爬进古庙，然后伸直身体在里面休息。

第二章

利立浦特皇帝在好几位贵族的陪同下前来看望身陷囹圄的作者。作者对皇帝的样貌和服饰进行了描述。一些博学之士奉命教授作者当地语言。作者温和的性格赢得了皇帝的赞赏。皇帝派人搜查他的口袋，贴身的宝剑和手枪都被没收了。

我站了起来，环顾四周。必须承认的一点是，我从未见过那么美丽的景色。周围的田野像巨大的花园一般，围起来的田地有差不多四十英尺见方，看上去就像五彩缤纷的花坛。这些田地间还夹杂着树木，最高的可能有七英尺。我看了看位于我左手边的城池，看上去就像我们的剧院的背景墙上的那种城市布景一样。

我憋了好几个小时了，这一点也不奇怪，毕竟我已经连续两天没有大便了。但是这会儿的处境让我感觉到分外窘迫；我能想到的最好的办法就是钻进属于我的房间，然后关上门。实际上我也是这么做的。我拼命往里爬，一直爬到脚上的铁链长度所能允许的最深处，然后才蹲在那里畅快地排出了体内那让人难受的负担。不过这还是我第一次如此难堪地做出这样的事情，这让我感到分外不安。在此我希望公正的读者能够多多包涵，考虑一下我当时的处境与内心的痛苦。从那以后，每当我有这方面的冲动的时候，我都会跑到最远的地方去解决，而我的排泄物也有了处理的办法：皇帝安排了两个仆人，专门负责在国人前来围观我之前把排泄物处理掉。这虽然是一件小事，但我还是有必要写出来；为的是交代我略微有点洁癖的性格，毕竟正如我先前所说，总有人在这样的小事情上揪着我不放。

当我解决了自己的生理需求之后，我又走出房间，呼吸一下外面的新鲜空气。皇帝已经爬下了塔楼，骑着一匹骏马向我走来。那匹马一定花费不少，虽然受过良好训练，但是从来没见过我这样的庞然大物。我像一座山一般横亘在它的面前，吓得这匹马前蹄腾空，差点就把皇帝摔了下去。幸好皇帝本人也是一位技艺出众的骑手，赶紧控制住了这匹马。他身后的随从们赶紧上前勒住缰绳，皇帝这才安全下了马。当他站在地面上之后，他先是带着无比惊奇的神态绕着我走了一圈，当然他没有走进我的铁链范围之内。他命令厨师和仆人为我端上酒菜，他们把早已准备好的食物用小推车推到我能够得着的地方。我拿起那些小推车，一下子就把酒菜吃了个精光。一共有二十辆装肉的车子和十辆装酒的车子；每辆车上的肉只够我吃两三口，而每辆车上都放着十坛美酒。我把十坛酒放在一起，一口就喝了下去。剩下的几车也是如此。陪着皇帝一起来的还有皇后和年轻的王子、公主，他们在一排贵妇人的簇拥下坐在椅子上远远看着我。但是皇帝的坐骑出了点意外，于是他们全部围到了皇帝身边。现在我要给读者描述一下皇帝的模样。他的个子要比所有的大臣都高出大概一个指甲盖，所以他看上去特别威严。他长着一张威武的面孔，有着奥地利人的嘴唇和鹰钩鼻，他的皮肤是那种健康的橄榄色，体格匀称，体态健硕，举止文雅，态度庄严。皇帝当年二十八岁零九个月，而且已经在位七年了。在他的治理之下，这个国家的人民富足，国泰民安。为了更好地观察他，我特意侧躺下来，这样我的脸就和他的脸在同一高度了。我们之间只有三码的距离，之后我曾多次把他捧在手心，所以我对他的描述是绝对正确的。他的穿着简单而又大方，穿衣风格兼具亚洲和欧洲的风格。他头戴一顶镶嵌着珠宝的金皇冠，盔顶上插着一根羽毛。他手握着剑，万一我挣脱束缚，他就用剑来防身。这剑大约三英寸长，剑柄和剑鞘全是金子做的，上面镶满了钻石。他的嗓音很尖，但嘹亮清晰，我站起来也可以听得清清楚楚。贵妇人和廷臣们全都穿得非常华丽，他们站在那里看起来仿佛地上铺了一条绣满了金人和银人的衬裙。皇帝时不时地跟我说话，我也回答他，但彼此一个字都听不懂。在场的还有他的几个牧师和律师（我从他们的服装推断），也奉命跟我谈话。我就用我一知半解的各种语言与他们对话，其中包括高地荷兰语和低地荷兰语（高地荷兰语指德语，低地荷兰语指荷兰语），拉丁语，法语，西班牙语，意大利语，以及通行于地中海一些港口地区的意、西、法、希腊、阿拉伯等的混合语，可是却没起到一点作用。过了大约两个小时，宫廷的人才全部离去，只留下一支强大的卫队，防止乱民们做出无礼或者恶意的举动；这些人出于好奇，急不可耐地往我周围挤，大着胆子尽可能地挨近我；我在房门口地上坐着的时候，竟有人无礼地向我放箭，有一支射在我的左眉上，差点儿射中了我的左眼。领队的上校下令逮捕了六个罪魁祸首，他觉得最合适的惩罚莫过于将他们捆绑着送到我手中。他的几个兵照办了，用枪托将他们推到我手可以够得着的地方。我用右手一把把他们全部抓住，五个放入上衣口袋，至于第六个，我做出要生吃他的样子。那可怜虫号啕大哭，上校和军官们也都痛苦万状，尤其当他们看见我掏出小刀的时候。不过我很快就让他们放心了下来，因为我温和地用小刀把捆在他身上的绳子割断了，然后又轻柔地把他放在了地上。他的双脚刚一落地就飞快地逃跑了。剩下的五个人的待遇也是一样的，我一个一个把他们从口袋里掏出来，然后把他们放走。这种仁慈的行为让在场的所有士兵和百姓都万分感激。后来有人把这件事情禀告给了皇帝，我也因此受到了嘉奖。

到了晚上，我要花费好大一番力气才能爬进我的房间，然后躺在地上睡觉。这样的日子差不多过了半个月。在这期间，皇帝命令手下为我准备一张床。他们先是准备了整整六百张普通尺寸的床铺，放在我的房间里面；随后他们把整整一百五十张床拼在一起，一共叠了四层，这才拼成了一张符合我的尺寸要求的床铺。但我还是觉得这样的床铺睡着不舒服。随后他们又按照我的尺寸为我准备了床单、毛毯和被褥。对于我这么一个习惯了艰苦生活的人来说，这样的待遇让我心满意足。

随着我来到的消息传遍整个王国，引得无数富人、闲人和好奇的人前来观看。乡村里人差不多都走空了，要不是皇帝特意下敕令颁公告禁止这种骚乱，那么就会出现无人耕种，无人理家的严重后果。皇帝命令那些看过我的人必须回家，不经过朝廷的许可任何人不得擅自进入离我房子五十码以内的地方，廷臣们倒还因此获得了数量可观的税款。

与此同时，皇帝频繁召开会议，商量处置我的办法。直到后来才有一位好朋友告诉我，他们对于这个问题感觉到非常棘手。我的朋友是一个颇有地位的家伙，他也参加过几次这样的会议。他们一方面担心我会逃跑，另外一方面又觉得我的开销过于昂贵，也许会造成饥荒。他们甚至还决定把我饿死，或者拿毒箭射我的脸和手，这样一来很快就能杀死我。但与此同时，他们又担忧这样庞大的尸体会给整个京城造成瘟疫，甚至可能影响整个国家。正当他们在讨论的时候，有好几个军官走进了会议室的大门；其中两位奉命汇报我对待之前说过的那六个调皮鬼的举动，这无疑给皇帝以及他的重臣们留下了很好的印象。于是，他们特意颁布了旨意，要求方圆九百码内的村庄，每天早上都要上交六头牛和四十只羊，还有其他各类的食品作为我的口粮；他们还要提供相当数量的面包、葡萄酒和其他饮料。这些费用就由皇室承担，因为这位皇帝的花费主要还是依靠自己的农庄，很少会向平民征税。当然如果起了战事，那么所有的居民都要自费参加战争。皇帝又指令组成一个六百人的队伍做我的听差，发给他们伙食费以维持生计；为方便服务，又在我的门两旁搭建帐篷供他们居住。还下令三百个裁缝做一套本国样式的衣服给我，雇六名最伟大的学者教我学习他们的语言；最后，他还要他的御马、贵族们的马以及卫队的马时常在我跟前操练，使它们对我习惯起来。所有这些命令都得到了及时执行。大约过了三个星期，我在学习他们的语言方面大有进步，在这期间，皇帝经常来光顾，并且很乐意帮助我的老师一起教我。我已经可以与他们进行某些方面的交谈了。我学会的第一句话就是向他表达我的愿望，他是否可以让我获得自由。"路莫斯·凯尔民·派索·德斯马尔·隆·艾姆泊索"，这句话每天我都跪在地上不停地念叨。据我理解，他回答的是：这得经过时间的考验，不征求内阁会议的意见，是不予考虑的，而且首先我要宣誓与他及他的王国和平相处。当然，他们待我是很好的；他还劝我要耐心谨慎，以此来赢得他及他的臣民的好感。他还希望，假如他命令几个官员专门来搜我的身，我不要见怪，因为我身上很可能带着几件武器，要是这些武器的大小配得上我这么一个庞然大物，那一定是很危险的东西。我一边说话一边用手势表达，我可以满足陛下的要求，我随时可以脱下衣服，翻出口袋让他检查。他回答说，根据王国的法律，我必须经过两位官员的搜查；他也知道，没有我的同意和协作，他们是办不到这件事的，但是他对我的大度和正直极有好感，很放心将他们的安全托付给我；并且无论他们从我身上取走什么，我离开这个国家时自当奉还，或者按我规定的价格如数赔偿。我把那两位负责检查的官员托在手里，先把他们放进了我的上衣口袋，然后又依次放进了我所有的口袋。不过我并没有让他们搜查我的两个表袋和放着几个硬币的衣袋，因为我觉得没有必要搜查这些东西，而且里面有一些在我看来很有意义，但是对别人来说却一文不值的东西。其中一个表袋里装着一只银表，而另外一个装着一个钱包，钱包里有一点点金子。这两位官员随身带纸笔，看到什么就记在那张清单上。当他们检查完毕之后就让我把他们放下，然后把那张清单交给了皇帝。后来，我把这份清单翻译成了英文，是这样写的：

经过最严格的搜查，在山巨人的右侧上衣口袋里（他们的原文是"昆布斯·弗莱斯丁"，我翻译成了山巨人）发现了一块粗布，大小刚好和皇宫大殿的地毯一样。左侧口袋里面有一个巨大的银色箱子，就连箱子的盖都是银子打造的，我们打不开。我们要求山巨人把这个箱子打开，然后跳进去看了一下，发现里边某种和灰尘很像的东西一下子就没了小腿；还有一些尘土飘了起来，落在我们的脸上，害得我们打了好几个喷嚏。在他马甲的右边口袋里有一大捆白色的东西，叠在一起，差不多有三个我们的人那么高，而且是用一根结实的绳子捆在一起的，那些白色的东西上面还有黑色的图案。我们推测这就是他们的文字。每一个字母差不多有我们的半个手掌那么大。在左边的口袋里面有一个好像机器的东西，延伸出去二十根长长的柱子，就像陛下您殿前的栏杆一样，我们认为这应该是山巨人的梳子。由于和他交流实在是太困难了，所以我们并没有询问他太多的问题。在他的右侧的最大的口袋里（当时他们的原话是"兰弗洛"，意思应该是指我的马裤），我们发现了一根竖立着的空心铁柱子，差不多有我们一个人那么高，其中一头固定在比铁柱子还要大一些的坚硬木头上，另外一头连着几个硕大的铁片，形状十分奇怪，我们都搞不清楚这到底是干什么用的。在左边的一个口袋里还有一个同样的机器。右边的小口袋里有好几块扁扁的金属，各种颜色都有，大小各异，其中白色的可能是银子，但是太重了，我们根本就拿不起来。在左边的口袋里有两根形状不规则的黑色柱子。当我们站在口袋底部的时候，想要碰到柱子的顶端可不是一件省力的事情。其中一个柱子是有盖子的，和柱子连在一起；而另外一个柱子的顶端有一个相当我们两个脑袋大小的白色圆形物体。这两根柱子都包裹着一块巨大的钢板。我们担心这些东西是有危险的，于是我们命令他拿出来给我们看。他把那两个东西给拿了出来，告诉我们，在他的国家，一个用来刮胡子，一个用来切肉。还有两个口袋我们进不去，他说那是表袋。右边表袋挂着一条又大又沉的银链子，连着一架十分神奇的机器。我们命令他，不管链子那头是什么东西，都要拿出来给我们看看。他拿出了一个球形的东西，一半是银子做的，另外一半是透明的。透明的那一面还刻着很多奇怪的呈圆形排列的数字，我们本来想去摸一摸，但是却被那种透明的物质给挡住了。他把那个机器凑到我们的耳边，我们听到了那机器不停地发出的噪声，听上去像水磨的声音。我们推测这要么就是一种我们都不认识的动物，要么就是他们崇拜的神灵。我们都倾向于后面那种看法，因为他告诉我，不管他们做什么都要事先端详一番那台机器（如果我们的理解没有错误的话，毕竟他说的话都是那么含糊不清）。他称它为先知，还说所有的行动都需要在合适的时间进行。左边的表袋里有一个像渔夫用的大网一样的东西，这个东西还能像钱包一样开合，实际上那就是他的钱包。我们还在钱包里找到了好几块黄色的金属，如果这些金属是黄金的话，那么肯定价值不菲。

　　我们遵从陛下的命令，认真检查了他所有的口袋。我们还发现他的腰间系着一条腰带，是用某种巨大的动物的皮革做成的。在腰带的左边挂着一把有我们五个人那么长的宝剑；右边则是一个皮囊，里面分成了两个小袋子，每个袋子里都能放下三个我们的子民。其中一个口袋里放着好几个金属圆球，差不多有我们的脑袋那么大，只有特别有力气的人才能拿起来。另外一个口袋里装着很多黑色的颗粒，个头不大，重量也很轻，我们一手就能抓起来五十多个。

　　这就是我们从山巨人身上搜出来的所有物品。山巨人对我们十分有礼貌，也对皇帝陛下的命令表现出了应有的尊重。

　　陛下登基的第八十九个月，第四天。

克莱夫林·福莱洛克
马尔西·福莱洛克

当皇帝陛下看完了这份清单之后，就委婉地命令我把这些物品交出来。首先，他要求我把随身的弯刀交给他，于是，我就把弯刀和刀鞘一起交给他。当然在这个过程中，他命令那三千名士兵一直挽着弓在边上随时戒备；当时因为我两眼一直盯在陛下身上，所以根本就没有察觉。他要求我把弯刀拔出来，那把刀虽然被海水泡过了，显得有些生锈，但整体上还是闪着光的。当我把弯刀抽出刀鞘的时候，所有的士兵都惊恐地大叫起来。此时正烈日当空，我手拿弯刀舞来舞去，那刀光使他们眼花缭乱。陛下毕竟是位气概不凡的君王，并没有像我所料想的那么惊恐；他命令我将刀收回刀鞘，轻轻地放到离拴着我的链子的末端约六英尺的地方。他要我交出的第二件东西是那两根中空的铁柱之一，他指的是我的袖珍手枪。我把枪拔出来，按照他的要求，尽可能清楚地向他说明了枪的用途。因为皮囊裹得很紧，其中的火药也幸运地没有被海水浸湿（所有谨慎的航海家都会特别小心以免火药被海水浸湿这种不愉快的事情发生）；我装上火药，并且事先告诉皇帝不要害怕，然后向空中放了一枪。他们这一次所受的惊吓，大大超过了刚才看见我腰刀时的惊吓，几百人倒地，好像被震死了一样，就是皇帝，虽然依旧站着没有倒下，却也半天不能恢复常态。我像交出腰刀那样，交出了两把手枪以及弹药包；我告诉他千万要注意，不要让火药接近火，因为一丁点儿火星就会引起燃烧，把他的皇宫轰上天去。同样我把手表也交了出去，皇帝看了十分好奇，命令两个个子最高的卫兵用杠子抬在肩上，就像英格兰的运货车夫抬着一桶淡啤酒一样。对于表所发出的连续不断的声音和分针的走动，他大为惊奇；由于他们的视力远比我们敏锐，所以很容易就看得出分针是在走动着。他询问王国里最博学的学者，想要让他解释一下到底是怎么一回事。国内的学者产生了很大的分歧，不用我赘述，读者们能够想象到他们那争论不休的样子。不过说实在的我也完全听不明白他们的话。随后我就把这些银币和铜板交给他们，当然还有钱包里的九枚大金币和一些小金币。之后我又拿出了我的小刀、剃刀、梳子、烟盒、手绢和日记。最后我的弯刀、手枪、枪套都装进车子，送到了皇帝的仓库里，而其他的都还给了我。

我之前说过，我有一个秘密口袋躲过了他们的检查。那个口袋里放着一副眼镜（因为我的视力不太好），还有一架小型望远镜和其他实用的小东西。我觉得这些东西对他们来说也没有什么用，同时也担心他们把我的东西弄坏或者弄丢，所以我并没有上交，而是选择自己私藏下来。

第三章

作者给皇帝和贵族们表演了非同一般的节目。作者还描述了利立浦特宫廷中的各种消遣活动。在答应了某些条件的前提下，作者获得了自由。

我温和的性格和良好的表现无疑赢得了皇帝和大臣们的好感，士兵和普通百姓也很喜欢我，所以我涌起了希望，觉得自己很快就能够获得自由了。我想尽一切办法来赢得他们的喜爱，他们慢慢地就不觉得我很危险了。有的时候我会躺在地上，让五六个人在我的手上跳舞，到最后那些男孩和女孩都可以在我的头发里玩捉迷藏了。我学这个国家的语言也有了长足的进步，不仅能够更好地听懂他们的话，甚至还能和他们对话了。皇帝有一天突发奇想，邀请我欣赏这个国家的一些表演。我觉得他们的表演非常有趣，比我看过的任何国家的任何表演都要优秀。让我最为津津乐道的是秋千舞。这是一根差不多两英尺长的绳子，被固定在距离地面十二英寸高的地方。我希望读者朋友们能够耐心地听我把这件事情仔细地说一说。

这个技艺只有担任要职的重臣和深受皇帝器重的人才有资格表演。他们从小就接受这样的训练，但他们并不一定有高贵的血统或者良好的学识。如果有重要的职位出现了空缺（无论是死亡还是被罢免，后者也是经常发生的事情），就会有五六位候选人请求表演这种秋千舞。哪个跳得最高，而且没有从绳子上掉下来就算是赢得了这个职位。皇帝也会时常让他手下的大臣来表演，为的是证明他们仍然是称职的。财政大臣弗里木纳普是公认跳得最好的，比整个国家的任何人都高至少一英寸。我曾经亲眼看到他在那个拴在绳子上的一块踏板上表演了好几个筋斗，而那根绳子也不比英国人拿来包扎东西用的绳子粗多少。我的朋友雷德瑞萨，也就是这个国家的内务大臣，跳得仅次于财政大臣。其余的大臣们的表现也难分秋色。

当然这些娱乐活动经常会伴随着致命的意外，许多次这样的意外都被记录了下来。就连我本人都见过两三个候选人跌断了脖子。特别是当大臣们奉皇帝的命令表演的时候，危险就更大了。因为所有的大臣都想展示自己过人的技艺，都想表明自己比其他同僚要厉害。几乎每个大臣都跌落下来过，有些人甚至还摔过两三次。有人告诉过我，在我来到这儿一两年之前，财政大臣弗里木纳普就差点摔断了脖子。要不是皇帝的坐垫恰好减轻了下落的力量，他的脖子肯定就断了。

除此之外还有一个节目，而且是在特别重大的节日才会表演的，观众就只有皇帝、皇后和首相。皇帝会把三根六英尺长的精美丝带放在桌子上，一根是蓝色的，一根是红色的，还有一根是绿色的。这三根丝带就是皇帝专门用来奖赏那些他认为特别出色的家伙的。这种典礼是在皇宫大殿举行的，候选人要表演一种与前面完全不同的技艺。不管是在新大陆还是在旧大陆都不会有类似的表演。皇帝会手拿一根棍子，与地面齐平，候选人会一个个跑到棍子前边，根据棍子的高矮变动，或是跳过去，或是从底下爬过去，来来回回好几遍。有的时候是由皇帝和首相一人拿一头，有的时候则是由首相一个人拿着。谁的动作最敏捷，坚持的时间越长，就会被授予蓝色丝带，第二名会得到红色丝带，第三名则是绿色的。他们会把丝带绕两圈缠在腰间，宫廷中有地位的人都拿这种彩色丝带作为装饰。

由于战马和皇家御马每天都被带到我的跟前，经过时间的考验它们已经不再胆怯，一直走到我的脚边也不会惊吓。我把手放在地下，骑手们就纵马从上面跃过去；其中有一名猎手是皇帝的狩猎队的，骑一匹高大的骏马从我穿着鞋子的脚面跳了过去。这确是惊人的一跳。一天，我很荣幸有机会表演一种非常特别的游戏供皇帝消遣。我请求他吩咐人给我弄几根两英尺长的棍子来，像普通手杖一样粗细的就行。皇帝命令管理森林的官员前去照办。第二天清晨，六个伐木工人驾着六辆马车来了，每辆车都由八匹马拉着。我从车上取下九根木棍并把它们牢牢地插在地上，摆成一个二点五平方英尺的四边形。然后，我又取了四根木棍，横绑在四边形的四角，离地高约两英尺。接着我把手帕平铺在九根直立的木棍上并绑紧，四面绷紧就像鼓面一样。那四根横绑的木棍高出手帕约五英寸当作四边的栏杆。这活干完之后，我就请皇帝让一支由二十四人组成的精骑兵上这块平台来操演。皇帝同意了我的这一建议，我用手将这些马一匹匹拿起来放到手帕上，马上骑着全副武装的军官，准备操练。他们一站整齐就马上分成两队，进行小规模的军事演习，一时钝箭齐发，刀剑出鞘，跑的跑，追的追，攻的攻，退的退，总之表现出了我从未见过的严明的军事纪律。由于四根横木的保护，他们没有从平台上跌下来。皇帝高兴至极，命令这个游戏几天内反复表演。有一次他竟然让我把他举到平台上去发号施令。他甚至费尽口舌说动皇后，让我把她连人带轿同时举到离平台不到两码的高处，从那里她得以饱览操练的全景。也算我运气好，几次表演都没有什么不幸的事故发生。只有一次，一位队长骑的一匹性情暴烈的马用蹄子乱踢，在手帕上踹出了一个洞，马腿一滑，人仰马翻。但我马上就将人和马都救了起来，一手遮住洞，一手像原先送他们上台时那样连人带马放回地上。失足马的左肩胛扭伤了，骑手什么事也没有。我尽量将手帕补好，不过我再也不相信这手帕有多坚牢，能经得起这种危险的游戏了。

在我获得自由的两三天前，我正在给朝廷表演这种技艺的时候，忽然有一位特使进宫向皇帝禀报，说在当初俘获我的地方发现了一个又大又黑的东西。那东西落在地上，看上去十分古怪，边缘是圆形的，差不多和皇帝的寝宫一样大，中间高起来的部分差不多有一个人那么高。一开始他们还担心那是个活生生的动物，后来发现它待在草地里一动不动，是个完全没有生命的东西。有好几个人绕着那个东西看了好几圈，之后又有人踩在别人的肩膀上，慢慢爬到了那个东西的顶部。那个顶部原本是平坦的，但是踩上去之后才发现里面是空的。他们猜测这个东西可能是山巨人的。如果皇帝允许的话，他们可以马上把那东西带回来，只需要五匹马就可以拉动它。我马上就明白他们在讲什么东西了，这个消息让我感到分外高兴。轮船出事之后，我只顾着仓皇逃命，上岸的时候心慌意乱的，还没走到我睡觉的地方，帽子就不见了。那帽子我划船时曾用绳子系在头上，泅水时也一直戴着，估计是到了后来发生了意外，绳子断了，而我却一无所知，还以为帽子掉在海里了呢。我请求皇帝让他们把帽子帮我拉回来，同时向他说明了帽子的用途和特性。第二天，车夫将帽子运来了，可是已经破旧了许多。他们在离帽檐边不到一英寸半的地方钻了两个孔，孔上扎了两个钩子，再用一根长绳系住钩子一头接到马具上，就这样将我的帽子拖了半英里多。不过这个国家的地面极为平整光滑，所以帽子所受的损伤比我预想的要轻许多。

两天之后，皇帝又想出了一个新奇的点子。他命令驻扎在京城周边的军队都做好准备，参加这场演出。他要我像一座巨像那样站在那儿，两腿尽可能地分开，然后命令他的将军（一位经验丰富的老将，也是我的一位大恩人）集合队伍排成密集队形，从我的胯下行军。步兵二十四人一排，骑兵十六人一排，擂鼓扬旗，手持长枪向前进。这是一支由三千步兵和一千骑兵组成的军队。皇帝命令，前进中每一名士兵必须严守纪律，尊敬我个人，违者处死。不过这道命令并没有禁止住几位年轻军官在我胯下经过时抬起头来朝我看。说实话，我的裤子那时已经破得不成样子了，所以会引起那些军官的哄笑与惊奇。

格列佛像巨人一样站在那儿

我向皇帝递交了很多本奏章，请求他给予我自由。皇帝在内阁会议上提到这件事情，然后命令全体官员商议这件事情。除了斯基雷什·伯格拉姆，没有人提出反对意见。我以前从来没有得罪过伯格拉姆，不知道他到底为什么要这么做。不过其他人都持有不同意见，所以皇帝便答应了我的请求。用这个国家的语言来说，伯格拉姆就是"家贝特"，也就是我们的海军上将。他深得皇帝的信任，工作上也得心应手，但总是一副苦瓜脸，给人一种阴郁的感觉。最后他还是被其他人说服了，但是他坚持要亲自起草我必须遵守的条款，只有遵从这些条款，我才能够获得自由。起草（文件）完毕之后，斯基雷什·伯格拉姆就带着两个秘书和其他官员，亲自把文件交给了我。之后我宣誓遵从他们的条件。我先是按照我所在国家的方式，然后再按照他们的法律所规定的方式宣誓。他们的方式是：用左手拿住右脚，右手中指置于头顶，大拇指放在右耳尖。读者可能好奇想了解一下这个民族特有的文章风格和表达方式，以及我恢复自由所应该遵守的条款，我就将整个文件尽可能地逐字逐句地在此翻译出来，供大家一看：

尊敬的利立浦特的皇帝，威震寰宇、受人爱戴的高乐巴斯图·摩玛雷姆·伊芙拉姆·戈尔迪洛·石芬因·穆雷·尤里·古尔，统治着五千布勒司徒格斯（周界约十二英里）的大国，覆盖着整个宇宙。他是至高无上的万王之王，他的威猛身材超过所有人类！他的双足踏着宇宙的中心，他头顶着太阳；他轻轻点头，全世界的王子都会颤抖。他像春天一般温暖，像夏天一般舒适，像秋天一般富饶，像冬天一般令人生畏。最为尊贵的皇帝陛下，向最近来到我们国家的山巨人提出以下要求，山巨人必须起誓，一定会遵守这些要求。

第一条　没有加盖皇帝陛下的国玺的通行证，山巨人不能离开国境。

第二条　没有得到我们的命令，山巨人不能擅自进入我们的京城。如果接到进京的命令的话，京城的百姓会在两个小时之内收到通知，然后关上门，足不出户。

第三条　山巨人只能在国家的大路上行走，不准踩踏或者躺倒在我们的农田里。

第四条　山巨人在主干道上行走的时候必须特别小心，不能踩踏我们的百姓和马匹，没有经过居民本人同意，山巨人不能随意把他们拿在手里。

第五条　如果有需要紧急传递的公文，山巨人有义务将信使连人带马放在口袋里传递，走完六天的路程，每月一次。如果有必要，还需要将信使平安送回到皇帝陛下面前。

第六条　山巨人必须和我们共同抵抗布莱福斯库岛的敌人，必须尽力摧毁他们准备入侵的舰队。

第七条　山巨人有空的时候必须帮助我们的工匠运送建造国家公园围墙和皇家建筑的大石头。

第八条　山巨人必须在两个月之内，沿海岸用步测的方法亲自丈量出我国领土的精确疆域。

如果山巨人能够严格遵守上述条款，就可以得到足以维持我国一千七百二十四位居民生活的肉食和饮料，并且能够自由进入我们的皇宫，随时面见皇帝。

此榜文发布于皇帝登基以来的第九十一月十二日，于贝尔法波拉克皇宫。

尽管上述条款中有一部分和我的预期不符，但总体上我还是能够接受的，于是，我在上面签字了。至于那些心怀不轨的条款，肯定是海军上将斯基雷什·伯格拉姆捣鬼的结果。但是当我腿上的锁被打开之后，我还是恢复了自由。皇帝本人也特意赏脸参加了我的释放典礼。我拜倒在皇帝面前，表达了我最深的谢意。随后他就命令我站起来，还说了很多赞美我的话，在这里我就不多说了，免得有人指责我虚荣。最后，皇帝说希望我能够成为一位有用的仆人，不要辜负他的期望。如果表现得好的话，还会赏赐给我更多的恩典。

读者们也许已经注意到了，在释放我的附加条款的最后一条中，皇帝规定每天都会给我提供利立浦特一千七百二十四位居民所需要的肉食和饮料。后来我询问一位朋友，他们是如何算出这个数字的。那位朋友告诉我，皇帝的数学家们用四分仪测出我的身高，发现和他们的比例是十二比一，然后根据我和他们的体型完全相似，得出我的体积是他们的一千七百二十四倍，所以我的食量应该也和这个比例相当。看到这儿，读者们应该可以想象到这个民族是多么聪明，这位皇帝的行事是多么严谨。

第四章

描述了利立浦特首都米尔登多和皇宫。作者与机要大臣密谈了一些国家大事，作者表示愿意为了皇帝一战。

在我获得自由之后的第一个要求就是参观利立浦特的首都米尔登多。皇帝很痛快地答应了我的请求，只是叮嘱我不能伤害当地的居民，也不能毁坏他们的房屋。附近的居民事先得到了通知，知道我要访问京城了。京城的城墙差不多有两英尺半高，十一英寸宽，能够容纳马车在上面驰骋。每隔十英尺，就会有一座坚固的塔楼。我小心翼翼地迈过西大门，走进了京城。我的步子十分谨慎，偶尔还得侧着身体才能穿过两条主要的街道。我只穿着一件齐腰背心，因为如果穿着衬衫的话，偶尔转身就可能把边上的屋顶和屋檐碰坏。皇帝已经下了命令，禁止任何人走出自己的房子，以免发生什么意外。尽管如此，我还是得十分小心，万一路上有人而我没有留意到的话，就糟糕了。阁楼的窗口和屋顶都挤满了看热闹的人，我敢说这是我见过的人口最为稠密的地方。京城是正方形的，每一边城墙有五百英尺那么长。有两条交叉的大街把城市分割成了四个部分，每条大街都有整整五英尺那么宽。普通的街道应该只有十二英寸到十八英寸宽，我肯定是进不去的，只能在路过的时候看看。整个城市的人口差不多有五十万，房子大多是三层到五层的，还有许许多多的商店和市场。

皇帝的宫殿就在那两条大街交汇的地方。皇宫的宫墙差不多有两英尺那么高，与里面的皇宫建筑物距离十二英尺。皇帝允许我跨过宫墙，而且宫墙和宫殿之间的间距特别宽阔，所以我可以绕着宫殿好好参观。外殿是一个四十英尺见方的院落，里面有两层宫殿。最里面的就是皇室的住所，我很想上前看个仔细，但是这很难。因为从一个院落的大门到另外一个大门只有十八英寸高，七英寸宽，但是那些外院的建筑物却至少有五英尺高。如果我强行跨过的话，肯定会把建筑物弄得乱七八糟的。虽然宫墙有差不多四英寸厚，而且都是石头打造的，但也不可能经受得住我的重量。但是皇帝却特别希望我能够看看他那富丽堂皇的宫殿。于是我花了整整三天时间，用我的小刀在距离京城一百码的御花园里砍下了几棵最大的树木，做成了两把凳子。这两把凳子足足有三英尺高，而且能够支撑我的重量。市民们得到第二次通告后，我又进城了，手拿着两张凳子前往皇宫。到达外院旁边，我站上一张凳子之后将另一张举过屋顶，轻轻地放到一院和二院之间那块宽约八英尺的空地上。这样从一张凳子到另一张凳子，我很轻松就跨过了外院的楼群，之后我再用带弯钩的棍棒把第一张凳子钩过来。我用这样的方法来到了皇家内院。我侧着身子躺下来，脸挨到中间几层楼那扇特地为我打开的窗子前，由此看到了人们所能想象到的最辉煌壮丽的内宫。我看到了皇后和年轻的王子们各自的寝宫里都有一些主要的侍从相随。皇后很高兴，对我十分和蔼地笑了笑，又从窗子里伸出手来赐我亲吻。

但是我不想读者过多地听这一类的描述了，因为我把它们留给了另一部篇幅更大的书，那书差不多就要出版了，里边概括地叙述了这个帝国从创建开始，历经各代君王的整个历史，特别叙述了该帝国的战争、政治、法律、学术、宗教、动植物、特殊的风俗习惯以及其他稀奇而有益的事情。眼下我主要想描述一下我住在这个帝国约九个月的时间里发生在我身上以及全国上下的种种事件。

一天早上，差不多在我获得自由之后的两个星期，机要大臣雷德瑞萨前来拜访。由于这次商量的是私事，所以他只带了一个仆人。他命令他的马车在远处等候，希望我能够抽出一个小时的时间来和他说说话。说实话我一向尊敬他的品格和个性，也很感激当初他为我求情，所以我很爽快地答应了。原本我是打算躺在地上，这样他就能在我的耳边说话了，但他却希望我把他放在手心里。他首先祝贺我获得了自由，他说他自以为在这件事情上有些功劳，但是后来他又说，"如果不是现在有些状况发生，你可能不会那么快获得自由，因为，"他说，"在外人看来我们也许很强大，但是实际上我们国家正面临两大威胁。其一是来自国内的冲突，其二是外敌入侵。国内的冲突不知道你是否有所了解，我们国家一直存在两大政党，已经明争暗斗了大约七十个月了。其中一个政党叫特拉梅克山，另外一个是斯拉梅克山；两党最大的分歧就在于鞋跟的高低。据说高跟党是推崇传统制度的党派，但是殿下还是决定在政府管理中心只用低跟党人，所有重要职位都留给他们。也许你已经发现了，所有的官员的鞋跟都很低，我们的皇帝的鞋跟尤其低，比所有官员的鞋跟都要低一个德尔（这是他们的计量单位，差不多是一英寸的十四分之一）。两党明争暗斗得很厉害，平时断绝了一切往来。从人数上来看，高跟党的人数最为庞大，但是权力却掌握在我们手里。最让我们担心的就是我们的太子殿下，因为他很明显更倾向于高跟党。我们一眼就能够看出，他的鞋跟一只高一只低，所以走起路来不是很稳。内部的斗争已经够麻烦了，更何况我们还面临外敌入侵，那就是布莱福斯库岛的敌人。那是另外一个巨大的帝国，和我们的国家不相上下。虽然我们也听你说过，外面有许多帝国住着和你一般大小的人类。但是我们国家的哲学家却认为这不太可能，他们更倾向于你是从月球或者别的星球来的。因为身躯像你这样巨大的人，只需要一百个就能把我国境内的所有东西给吃光。而且就我们六千个月的悠久历史来看，除了利立浦特和布莱福斯库，还从未提到过别的国家。我想说的是，两个国家已经交战了三十六个月，战况惨烈。战争的导火索是这样的，所有人都认为吃鸡蛋的时候应该敲大的那一头，因为这是自古以来的传统。但是皇帝的祖父小的时候，有一次吃蛋不小心割破了手指，于是当时的皇帝，也就是他的父亲，就命令所有的子民都要从鸡蛋的小头开始敲，违令者予以重罚。人们对此十分愤恨，并且发动了整整六次叛乱。有一个皇帝因此丢了性命，还有一位丢了皇位，而这些叛乱都是由我们的老对头布莱福斯库国煽动的。这些叛乱被镇压之后，有些反叛者偷渡到了布莱福斯库寻求帮助。据我们估计，前后数次大约有一万一千人情愿受死，也不想忍受敲鸡蛋小头的法令。关于这场纠纷出版了几百部巨著，但是有关大头派的著作都被禁止发行了。法律还规定，所有赞同大头派的都不许做官。布莱福斯库的大使经常来我国表示抗议，指责我们分裂宗教，声称我们的做法违背了伟大的先知路斯特罗格在《布兰德克拉尔》第五十四章里一条最基本的教义。不过我们认为这只是他们的曲解，因为原文是这样的，'所有的信徒都应该在方便的那一端敲碎鸡蛋'。所以到底哪一端才是方便的呢？在我看来，这只能让每个人自己来决定，至少也应该让当地行政长官来决定。但是现在大头派的狂热分子却得到了布莱福斯库皇帝的支持，又得到国内同党私下的帮助和怂恿，因此挑起了两个国家之间长达三十六个月的血腥战斗，各有胜败。这期间我们损失了四十艘主要战舰和数目更多的小艇，我们还折损了三万最精锐的水兵和陆军。据我们估计，敌人所受的损失比我们的还要大些。可是他们现在已经装备好了一支庞大的舰队，正准备向我们发起进攻。陛下深信你的勇气和力量，所以才命我来把这件事说与你听。"

我请求他帮我转达自己的意见：我作为一个外来人，不应该介入你们的党派之争。但是，如果你们面临外敌入侵，那么我哪怕是要冒生命危险，都会保卫皇上和这个国家。

第五章

作者采取了非凡的战略阻止敌军侵略，并因此获得了荣宠和爵位。布莱福斯库的皇帝前来议和。皇后的寝宫失火了，作者救下了精美的宫殿。

　　布莱福斯库坐落在利立浦特东北部的一个岛上，两个国家之间隔着八百码的海峡。我还从未见过那座岛，而且自从得到对方即将入侵的消息之后，就避免我在海岸边出现，以免被对方发现。海面上时不时会有敌军的舰船出现，但是他们并不知道我的存在。在交战期间，两国之间禁止任何往来，违者要被处死。皇帝还下令不许任何船只出海。我向皇帝谈到了我的计划，告诉他我打算如何俘获敌方所有的船只。根据我们的哨兵报告，敌军的船只全部停泊在港口，一旦有顺风出现，就会马上出发。我向最有经验的海员询问海峡的深度，他们曾经用铅锤测量过很多次。他们说在涨潮的时候，深度为七十格拉姆格拉芙，大约是欧洲的六英尺，而平时最深的地方就只有五十格拉姆格拉芙。我在东北部的海岸边遥望坐落在一座小山后面的布莱福斯库，拿出我的望远镜观察停泊在港口的舰队，数量差不多是五十艘，当然还有很多补给舰队。之后我回到住所，下令（我有委任状）让人准备大量最结实的绳索和铁棍，绳索和我们用来包裹货物的差不多，而铁棍则像毛衣针一样粗细。我把三根绳索搓在一起，这样就更加结实了。而为了让铁棍更加结实，我也把三根铁棍绞在一起，然后把两端弄成了钩子状。我准备了整整五十个钩子，后边系着绳索，然后就朝着东北方的海岸出发了。到了岸边之后，我脱下了鞋子和袜子，只穿一件牛皮背心，走下海去，这时离满潮还有半小时。我飞快地前进，我在海中游了大约 30 码，直到脚能踩着海底。不到半小时，我就来到了敌军停泊战舰的地方。敌人看到我之后，吓得惊慌失措，一个个慌忙从船上跳进海里，然后朝着岸边游去。粗粗一看，在海水里的敌军差不多有三万人。我赶紧拿出了我的绳索和钩子，紧紧固定在那些大船的船孔上边，另外一端抓在手里。当我忙着干活的时候，敌军冲着我射箭，一瞬间万箭齐发，很多箭都射在了我的脸上和手上，除了极度疼痛，还大大干扰了我的行动。幸亏我想到了一个好主意，要不我的眼睛肯定会被射瞎。之前我说过，我在衣袋里面藏了一副眼镜，而且躲过了检察官的搜查。我掏出眼镜，固定在眼睛上面，这样就可以放心大胆地干活了。那些箭矢砸在我的眼镜片上，除了对眼镜片有点损伤，就没有别的危险了。很快我就把所有的钩子都挂在了船上，然后拾起绳索开始往回拉。但是那些船纹丝不动，原来是被船锚固定住了。看来我还要经历一番考验。我把绳索放下，让铁钩依旧钩在船上，然后用小刀把船锚割断了，当然付出的代价是我的脸上和手上又多了两百多支箭。一切都完成之后，我把系着铁钩的绳结攥在手里，拉着最大的五十艘船就回去了。

格列佛俘虏了敌军舰队

　　布莱福斯库的军官们根本没有想到我到底

要做什么，他们早已被我的出现给吓坏了。他们看到我砍断了绳索，还以为我只是想让那些没人的船只随波漂走，或者是让船只互相碰撞，让船只沉没。但是当他们看到整支舰队都在我的拉扯之下开始移动，便发出了凄厉的尖叫声，我可以感觉到他们心中的伤心和绝望，这可真是难以形容。等我走出了危险地带之后，我就先停了下来，把扎在我的脸上和手上的箭取出来，然后涂了好些药膏。之前我提到过，这种药膏是我刚到利立浦特的时候他们给我的。然后我又把眼镜摘下放好，等了差不多一个小时之后海浪稍稍退下，就带着我的战利品又一次渡过了海峡，回到了利立浦特的海岸上。

皇帝和所有的大臣都站在海岸边上，期待着这次冒险行动的成功。他们只看到敌国的舰队冲着他们漂来，却没有看到我，因为那会儿海水没过了我的胸膛。当我走到海峡中间的时候，他们越发悲痛了，因为那里的海水都没过了我的脖子。皇帝断定我被淹死了，而敌军却来势汹汹。但是很快他的恐惧就消失了，因为海水越来越浅，露出了我的身体。不一会儿，我就听到了岸上的呼喊声。我举着系着舰队的绳子的一端，大声喊道："最强大的利立浦特的皇帝万岁！"皇帝亲自送我上岸，好好夸了我一通，并且当场封我为"纳达克"，这是这个国家最为崇高的荣耀。

皇帝陛下希望我能找机会把敌国的其他船只也拉到这儿来。不得不说皇帝的野心是深不可测的，他大概觉得毁灭布莱福斯库也不是不可能的吧，然后他就可以占领布莱福斯库，使其成为他治下的一个省。之后他还想把那些异端铲除，命令治下的所有人都必须从鸡蛋的小头开始打破鸡蛋。这样一来他就能够成为这个世界上独一无二的君王。但我还是极力反对这个计划，并且从政策和正义两个方面提出了这么做的弊端。最后我坦白地说："我不会成为你的工具，奴役这群自由勇敢的人民。"后来在朝廷上，最具智慧的那批官员也赞同我的意见。

我这样公然表达自己的想法，实际上是和皇帝的想法相违背的，所以他不可能原谅我。在朝廷上他当然也提及了这个想法，但是后来有人告诉我，最为睿智的那批官员婉转地表达了对我的支持，至少以沉默做了表态。这样一来那些暗地里对我心怀不满的那批人却因此旁敲侧击地中伤我。所以皇帝和这批人就一起策划了阴谋，不到两个月差点把我给摧毁了。这一事件也说明，不管你曾经为皇帝做出了怎样的功绩，只要你未能赞同他的一次看法，你所有的业绩都变得一文不值。

在这次伟大行动之后的大约三个星期，布莱福斯库派遣了使者，前来求和。他们的态度很好，所以两国很快就达成了协议。协议的条件自然对我们很有利，我在此也不多讲了。他们的使团一共有六位使者，还有大约五百个随从。入境仪式十分隆重，既表达了他们国家皇帝的尊贵，又点明了此行的重要意义。签订了协议之后，他们还特意来拜访我。由于我当时的地位很高，所以我就为他们说了一些好话。他们对我的英勇行为和宽宏大量的气概极尽赞美，还邀请我去他们国家做客。他们自然对我的无穷的力量感到十分不可思议，希望我能够表演一下。这样的要求我自然没有拒绝，具体我就不多讲了。

当我招待了这些尊贵的客人之后，他们感到很满意，也十分惊讶，而我也希望他们能够转达我对他们的皇帝的敬意。我称赞他们的皇帝的良好品格，并且许诺在回到自己的国家之前会去拜访。后来我去面见利立浦特的皇帝的时候自然也提出了前去拜见布莱福斯库的皇帝。他看上去很高兴，但是，我能够感觉到他内心的冷淡。我猜不出其中的原因，有人告诉我，先前弗里木纳普和伯格拉姆就已经把我和特使见面的事情告诉了皇帝，所以皇帝有理由相信我可能心怀不轨。但我的确问心无愧，这是我第一次认识到皇帝和宫廷并没有我想象得那么好。

有一点值得注意，这些大使是通过翻译与我交谈的。两帝国的语言和欧洲任何两个国家的语言一样，彼此差别很大。每一国都夸耀自己民族的语言美丽、有力、历史悠久，而对邻国的语言公然蔑视。可是，我们皇帝仗着夺了人家舰队的优势，强硬地要求布莱福斯库国的人用利立浦特语递交国书并致辞。同时也承认，因为两国间的商贸往来很多，彼此都不断接受对方的流亡人员，又因为两个帝国都有互派贵族及富家子弟到对方国家留学，以增长见识，了解异域风土人情的风尚，所以名门望族和住在沿海地区的商人、海员，几乎没有人不会说两国的语言的。这一点我在几个星期后去朝见布莱福斯库皇帝时就发现了。由于我的敌人们不怀好意，当时我正身处种种不幸之中，但这次朝见还是一件让人开心的事。这件事，我以后还要在适当的地方加以叙述。

　　读者也许还记得，在我当初获得自由的时候，还签署过几条协议。当时我对此十分不满，因为我觉得这样的条款十分屈辱。那时的我急于获得自由，所以才委曲求全。现在既然我已经是王国里地位崇高的人，再谈这些条约就显得有失身份了。而且皇帝本人也不再和我提那些条约了。没过多久，我就又有了一个为皇帝效力的机会。某天夜里，当我在睡觉的时候，听见外面响起几百个人的大喊声，因为突然被惊醒不由让我有些害怕。我听到人们嘴里喊着"布格拉姆"，还有几个来自宫内的人从人群中挤过来急切地恳求我去趟皇宫。后来我才了解到，原来是皇后宫中的一位侍女晚上看传奇小说的时候不小心睡着了，然后就引发了火灾。我马上就走出了自己的屋子，前往宫中的道路也早已为我准备了出来。这个晚上月亮很圆，而且我走路的时候也十分小心，所以并没有伤害到任何人。我看到他们已把梯子竖到了宫墙上，梯子和水桶也已经准备妥当。但是，由于水源很远，而且那些水桶在我看来并不比顶针大多少，所以虽然人们拼命地把水桶递给我，但对于这火势来说仍然是杯水车薪。如果我当时穿着外套的话，自然可以轻松地把火扑灭，但是现在我身上只有一件皮背心，慌乱之中忘了穿外套。火势越来越大，仿佛只能听天由命了。如果不是我灵机一动，壮丽的宫殿就一定被烧成灰烬了。恰好那天晚上我喝了不少美酒（这种酒被布莱福斯库的人称为"弗隆耐克"，但是利立浦特人的酿造水平更好），喝了这种酒很容易尿尿，而那天晚上我恰好没有小便。当时火焰烤得我有些热，所以我就直接冲着燃烧的宫殿来了一泡尿。不到三分钟，大火就被扑灭了。精美的宫殿就这样得以保存。

　　天差不多快亮了，我并没有留下来等待皇帝的嘉奖。因为虽然我保住了宫殿，但是这样的做法可能会招致皇帝的厌恶。因为这个国家有一条法律，那就是无论是谁，只要在皇宫里撒尿，都会被判处死刑。不过皇帝很快就派人传信，说他会下令给司法部门，饶恕我的罪过。但是最后我却没有收到正式的诏书。后来有人偷偷告诉我，皇后对我的所作所为十分痛恨，她现在已经搬到了另外一个地方去住了。她还下令不准修建那座宫殿，因为她再也不会回去了。她还对随从们赌咒发誓，说她一定会报复我的。

第六章

作者介绍了利立浦特的日常生活，以及他们在学术、法律上的成就，当然也少不了风俗习惯和教育模式。作者在这个国家的生活。作者还为一位贵妇进行了辩护。

　　虽然我很想对这个国家的风俗习惯做专门描述，但是我又想先大致介绍一下，以满足读者的好奇心。这个国家的大多数人的身高只有六英寸，其他所有的动物和植物的比例都和这个尺寸相当。举例来说，牛和马的身高在四到五英寸，羊可能只有一英寸半左右，鹅和我们的麻雀差不多大，按照这样的顺序和比例，最小的东西我基本上就看不见了。

不过利立浦特人的眼神自然比我们要好。只要距离合适，他们能够看到在我们看来很小的东西。我可以对此举例说明。我曾经见过厨师在拔一只比苍蝇大不了多少的云雀的毛，一位小姑娘也可以轻松地拿针线穿过我几乎无法看到的针眼，这样的事例数不胜数。这儿最高的树木也就只有七英尺高，大部分都分布在皇家园林当中；我攥着拳头几乎就能够得着树梢了。其他所有的蔬菜的比例也与此相当，这一点就留给读者去想象吧。

接下来我要说的是他们的学术成果。经过多年的研究，这个国家在各个领域都取得了惊人的成就。但他们的书写方向却很奇怪，不像欧洲人那样从左向右，也不像阿拉伯人那样从右到左，更不像中国人那样从上到下，而是和英国的某些太太们一样，从一个角落写到另外一个角落。

他们埋葬死者的方式是脑袋朝下的，因为有一个古老的传说，在一万一千个月之后，所有的死者都会死而复生。到那时地球（他们认为地球是平的）就会上下颠倒，这样一来那些死者就可以轻松地站起来了。当然这个说法受到了很多博学之士的批评，但由于这是传统，所以他们也只能尊重这样的现象。

这个国家还有不少法律和习惯是很特别的，这些法律和我亲爱的祖国的法律是完全相反的，不然我真想讲讲这些法律的合理性，也很希望这样的法律能够在我们国家施行。首先我想说的是有关告密者的条款。一切背叛国家的行为都要受到最严厉的惩罚，但是如果被告能够证明自己的清白，那么原告就要受到惩罚。无辜的被告还能得到大约四倍的赔偿金，以弥补自己损失的时间、经历的危险、被关押的痛苦以及在辩护过程中花费的费用。如果原告无法弥补赔偿金的话，那么就要由皇帝负担大部分赔款。皇帝还要负责公开为被告恢复名誉。

利立浦特人认为欺骗要比偷窃严重很多，所以欺骗别人的罪犯一般会被处以死刑。利立浦特人认为，一个人只要小心一些，并且具备一些生活常识的话，就可以防备那些偷窃的贼人。但是诚实的人却无法防范那些精心设计的陷阱，而商业行为在社会生活中是不可避免的。如果欺诈没有得到严惩，那么诚实的商人就会破产，而流氓恶棍却会大发横财。我记得有一次，我曾在皇帝面前替一个拐骗了主人一大笔钱的罪犯说情，那人奉主人之命去收款，随后竟携款潜逃。我对皇帝说，这只是一种背信弃义的行为，希望能减轻对他的量刑。皇帝觉得我荒谬到了极点，竟会将最能加重其罪行的理由提出来替他辩护。说真的，我当时无言以对，只好泛泛地回答说，也许是各国有各国不同的习俗吧。必须承认，我那时确实羞愧难当。

虽然我们都认为奖赏和惩罚是所有政府得以正常运行的两个重要因素，但是我却从未见过有哪个国家能像利立浦特这般将此应用到极致的。在利立浦特，只要有人能够证明在过去七十三个月里严格遵从了国家法律，就可以申请得到某种特权。根据其生活习惯和社会地位，他就能够得到一笔相应的奖金，同时还能得到一个"斯尼帕尔"的称号，也就是所谓的"守法标兵"。不过这个称号只能由本人享有，不能世袭。我告诉他们，在我们的国家，只有相应的惩罚，却没有任何奖励，他们觉得我们的法律是有缺陷的。在他们的法院里竖着正义女神的雕像。这个雕像上有六只眼睛，前面两只，后面两只，左右各有一只，眼睛象征着正义女神的周全和慎重。神像的右手拿着一袋打开的金子，而左手则握着一把插在剑鞘里的利剑，这象征着女神更喜欢奖励而非惩罚。

在选拔政府官员的标准上，他们更看重道德修养，而非专业技能。因为他们相信，既然政府是必不可少的，那么这些岗位具备普通才能的人就能够胜任。这类事务性的管理工作不可能是难以理解的神秘的事情，也不可能只有少数一部分人能够领悟，毕竟天才在一个时代可能不多于三个。但是他们相信，大多数人都能够理解正直、公正和节制等美德。如果能够践行这些美德，同时拥有一定的工作经验，再加上对服务大众的良好期愿，这样的人就能够成为为国效力的人才。但是如果一个人道德缺失，那么哪怕拥有再卓越的能力，都不能承担这样的工作。因为具备美德的人就算才能不佳，也不会给公众利益造成不可挽回的巨大损失。而具有恶劣品格的人如果还有了巧妙的手腕，对于社会的危害更大，更为可怕的是他们还能够为自己不道德的行为找到掩饰的办法。

与此同时，不信任权威的人也无法担任这样的工作。当地人认为皇帝就是权威的化身，所以如果皇帝任命的人否认皇帝的权威，那简直就是最为荒唐的事情了。

之所以要描述这些法律和规定，只不过是想把这个国家的特色介绍给读者，希望你们能够理解。对于那些随着人性的堕落而出现的丑陋的腐败制度，我本人是十分不赞同的。希望我的读者们能够明白，像这种通过跳绳来赢得官位，或者在棍子上上蹿下跳来邀宠的行为，都是从当今皇帝的祖父那一辈开始的。随着党派之间的斗争愈演愈烈，这种歪风邪气得到了助长。

对于他们来说，忘恩负义也是一种死罪。当然很多国家也有类似的规定，他们是这样解释的：以怨报德的人对于他们的恩人都能做出这样的事情，对于那些未能施恩的人必将恶毒百倍。这样的人就是全人类的公敌，不配活在这个世界。

对于父母和孩子的关系，利立浦特人的观念也和我们截然不同。他们认为，男女结合是自然规律，为的是繁衍后代，因此，利立浦特人需要这种关系。但是男女之间的结合却是以情欲为动机的，而父母对子女的呵护也是出于同样的自然规律，所以子女不需要对赋予他生命的父母承担任何责任。人生是那么艰难，所以获得生命也不见得是一件好事情，而且父母在孕育生命的时候，脑袋里可能根本就在想别的事情。出于以上的逻辑关系，利立浦特人认为父母并不适合教育子女。利立浦特的每个乡镇都有公共学校。除了农夫和工人，所有人必须把年满二十个月的孩子送到那儿接受抚养和教育，因为那个年龄段的孩子算是比较听话了。学校的种类很多，可以满足不同阶层不同性别的孩子的需求。学校里有许多受过专门训练的老师，能够根据父母的地位以及孩子的天分因材施教。我要先说说男子学校，然后再谈谈女子学校。

接收名门贵族子弟的男子学校配有受人爱戴而又博才多学的教师，他们手下还有助教。孩子们的衣食简单朴素。他们受到荣誉、正义、勇敢、谦虚、仁慈、宗教、爱国等方面原则性的培养教育，除了短暂的吃饭、睡觉时间以及包括锻炼身体在内的两小时娱乐活动，他们总有些事情要做。四岁以前男仆给他们穿衣服，之后则不管身份多高，都得自己穿衣。女仆们年纪相当于我们的五十岁，只做那些最粗贱的活儿。孩子们绝不准许同仆人交谈，只许一小伙或大群地在一块儿玩耍，还总得有一位教师或者助教在旁，这样他们就不会像我们的孩子那样幼年时代染上愚顽的恶习。一年中父母亲只准看望孩子们两次，每次看望的时间只有一小时，见面和分别时可以吻一下自己的子女，但那种时候总有一位教师在旁，他们不允许父母窃窃私语或对孩子表示爱抚，也不允许他们带玩具、糖果之类的礼物。

每家必须缴纳子女的教育及娱乐费用，过期不缴的则由朝廷官吏征收。

在接收一般绅士、商人、做小买卖和手艺人子弟的学校里，也按照同样的方法进行相应的管理。不过那些预备要做生意的孩子十一岁就得放出去当学徒，而贵族子弟则继续在校学到十五岁（相当于我们的二十一岁），只是最后三年的管教比较松。

女子学校的贵族姑娘们受到的教育和男孩们差不多，只不过给她们穿衣服的是衣着整齐的女仆，而且每次都必须有一位教师或者助教在场才可以。这样的情况要一直坚持到五岁以后。如果发现有女仆擅自给女孩们讲一些恐怖或者愚蠢的故事，或是戏耍那些属于侍女的愚蠢把戏，那么女仆就要被鞭打游街三次，然后被关押一年，最后流放到这个世界的角落。所以这儿的年轻姑娘和男孩子们一样，都耻于成为懦夫和呆子，也鄙视所有不正派的打扮。男孩和女孩的教育并没有因为性别不同而有差异，除了两者在体育运动的剧烈程度不相同。她们虽然也要学一些家政，相比较男孩的研究领域也狭窄一点，但是她们永远恪守一个信念，那就是作为一个妻子，必须永远都是一个懂道理、和蔼的伴侣，因为她们不可能永远保持年轻。女孩子十二岁就到了可以结婚的年纪了，她们的父母或者监护人会把她们领回家。离别的时候自然少不了家长对老师的感激之言，以及年轻姑娘们分别时的伤感之情。

在等级稍稍低下一些的女子学校里，小姑娘们主要学习的是符合她们的性别和身份等级的工作。那些打算当学徒的小姑娘七岁的时候就退学了，其余的一般都要留到十一岁。

有孩子在这样的学校里上学的家庭除了平时微薄的学费，每个月还得上交一部分给学校的财政主管，作为赠予孩子的一份财产，所以所有父母的开支都要受到法律的限制。利立浦特人认为，孩子不过是父母一己私欲的后果，没有理由要让公众来承担抚养义务。至于那些贵族家庭，也需要保证一笔财产留给孩子，而且这份财产会永远受到公平的管理和支配。

而普通的村民和劳工则把自己的孩子养在家里，因为他们的工作就是种田，所以他们是否要受教育就没有多大关系了。当然这一类人年老体衰之后，也会有养老院来赡养，因为在利立浦特是没有乞丐的。

我在利立浦特度过了大约九个月零十三天，我想读者一定很好奇我到底是如何生活的。我用皇家花园里最为粗壮的树木给自己打造了一套桌椅。虽然有整整两百位女仆为我缝制衬衫、床单和台布，但是由于他们的布料过于纤细，所以就算是利立浦特最粗糙

利立浦特的裁缝帮格列佛丈量尺寸

强韧的布匹都得叠上好几层才能够满足我的需求。这个国家的亚麻布是三英寸宽，三英尺长算一匹。量尺寸的时候，一个女仆站在我的脖子上，另一个站在我的腿肚子上，把一根绳子拉直，然后再由第三个人拿着一把一英尺长的绳子来丈量。接着他们就只量了我的大拇指的周长，因为从数学上来说，大拇指的两周和手腕的一周是一样的，而脖子的周长和腰围也可以按照相应的比例计算出来。我把一件旧衬衫铺在地上，她们很快就做出了很合身的衣服。又有整整三百名裁缝为我缝制外衣，不过这一次他们丈量的办法却是不一样的。他们让我跪在地上，然后竖起一架梯子，靠在我的脖子上。一个人爬上梯子，把铅锤从我的领口一直挂到地面，这就是我的外衣的长度了。而腰围和手臂长度是我自己来量。这些衣服都是在我的房间里做的，因为他们的房子没法容纳那么大的衣服。最后衣服看上去就像英国太太们的百衲衣一样，只不过是同一种颜色的布料做成的。

专门负责为我做饭的厨师也有三百位，他

们拖家带口住在我的房子旁边的茅屋里面，每位厨师都为我准备两道菜。我先用手把二十位服务员托到桌子上，还有一百位服务员在地上忙碌，有些端着肉，有些扛着酒桶或饮料。我想吃什么，桌子上的服务员就用绳子把食物钓上来，就像欧洲人从水井里打水一样。他们的一盘肉只够我吃一口，一桶饮料也只够我喝一口。他们的羊肉味道一般，但是牛肉的味道却特别棒。我曾经吃到一块特别大的牛腰肉，我得分三口才能把这块肉吃掉，不过这样的事情很少见。我的仆人们看到我总是连皮带骨头一起吞下去，感到十分惊讶，但这就像我们吃下一只云雀的腿一样。他们的鹅和火鸡我也是一口吃掉的，而且我承认这些食物的味道比我们的要好多了。至于那些再小一点的家禽，我一把刀就可以串起来二三十只。

皇帝陛下听说了我生活的情形后，就想带上年轻的王子和公主一起来"享受吃饭的乐趣"。他们果然来了，我把他们放在桌子上。他们对着我坐着，旁边站满了护卫。财政大臣弗里木纳普拿着那根象征着权势的权杖站在我的旁边。我注意到他时不时用阴沉的目光盯着我，而我则装出一副毫不在意的模样。为了表现我对这个国家的敬意，也为了满足他们的羡慕之情，这一餐我吃得比平时要多很多。我隐隐约约感觉到，皇帝的这次造访给了弗里木纳普以陷害我的机会。这位财政大臣一向和我不和，虽然表面上他装出一副十分热情的模样，但是熟知他性格的我早已察觉到了不对劲。他向皇帝通报了国库紧张，他不得不将国库券以面值的百分之九十的价格进行流通。而我已经花费了皇帝整整一百五十万个斯普鲁（这是利立浦特最大面值的金币，差不多有我们的一个小纽扣一般大小），所以现在最明智的做法就是找个机会把我打发走。

既然说到这里，我不得不为一位德行高贵的夫人做一番申辩。她原本是一个清白的人，但是却因为我的缘故遭受别人的诟病。那位财政大臣异想天开，竟然怀疑起了自己的妻子。有人恶意散布谣言，说这位夫人爱上了我，这不由得让财政大臣心怀嫉妒。对于这件事情，我不得不做出声明，宣称这不过是无耻的造谣而已。那位可爱的夫人无非是在和我打交道的过程中显得天真无邪了一点。她的确经常来我住的地方，但每一次都是光明正大的，而且每次至少都是三个人一起来，一般是她的妹妹或者女儿，有几次还有她的几个闺中密友，这样的事情原本再正常不过了。我甚至可以向我的仆人们求证，有哪一次马车前来造访的时候，他们会不知道车里面坐着哪位大人物的。每次这位夫人前来拜访的时候，仆人都会通报给我，而我就会亲自到门口去迎接。在向她们问好之后，我会小心地把马车和马放在手里（如果是六匹马的话，车夫会先把四匹马卸下来），然后把马车放在桌子上。这张桌子的边缘我设置了大约五英寸高的边框，这样就不会发生意外了。我的桌子上时常会有四辆马车，里面坐满了客人。而我则坐在椅子上，把脸凑过去。当我和其中一辆马车里的客人说话的时候，车夫就会赶着其他马车在桌子边上打转转。我和客人们度过了很多个惬意的下午。但是我要正告财政大臣和那两个告密者（我会说出他们的名字，让他们知道后果），他们是克拉斯特鲁尔和德伦罗。我要向他们证明，除了机要大臣雷德瑞萨奉皇帝的命令一个人前来和我会面，我就再也没有单独接待过某位客人，而这件事情我已经在之前交代过了。如果不是事关一位高贵的夫人的名誉，我是不会在这儿长篇大论的。如果只影响我的名誉，那我倒是丝毫不觉得有什么关系，因为我已经有了"纳达克"的封号，而财政大臣并没有。所有人都知道，他只是个"格鲁姆格鲁姆"，比我要低一级，就好像在英国的侯爵要比公爵的地位低一样。但是论职务，他显然比我要重要一些。后来我无意中得知，由于这个谣言，财政大臣一度对自己的太太态度非常粗暴，连带着对我也没有什么好脸色。至于我是如何知道这件事情的，这儿就不详细讲了。虽然最后他还是醒悟过来，和他夫人和好如初，但是我却永远失去了他的信任。很快，我就感觉到皇帝对我也越发冷淡，看来他的确是听信自己宠臣的谗言了。

第七章

作者得到消息，有人密谋控诉他犯了叛国罪，所以作者只能逃往布莱福斯库。他在布莱福斯库得到了热情款待。

在我叙述自己离开这个国家的情形之前，有必要给读者们讲一讲已经准备了两个月的一桩针对我的阴谋。

直到那之前，我都对朝廷里的事情不是很清楚，这是我的地位使然。我也听说过许多皇帝和大臣的阴暗做法，但是我从来没有想到，在如此偏远的一个国家都会有这么可怕的政治斗争，我原本以为这儿的统治者和欧洲的不一样呢！

当我准备去拜访布莱福斯库的皇帝的时候，朝廷里的一位重要人物（他曾经触怒过皇帝，是我帮了他的忙）趁着夜色悄悄来到了我的家。一开始他并没有通报姓名，只是要求见我。他把那些轿夫打发走后，我就把他和那顶轿子一起放进了上衣口袋，随后吩咐我的心腹，说我有点不舒服，今天打算早早睡下。我关上了大门，把那顶轿子放在桌子上，然后坐在旁边的凳子上。一番寒暄之后，我发现这位官老爷一脸忧虑，就询问他到底是为什么。他说他希望我能够耐心地听他讲，因为接下来要讲的事情事关我的荣誉和生命。我把他的谈话内容记了下来，大致是这样的：

"你要知道，"他说，"最近已经召开了好几次关于你机密的会议，而且就在这两天，皇帝终于做了决定。

"你应该很清楚，斯基雷什·伯格拉姆（就是那个海军上将）一直是你的死对头，他从你来到这儿的第一天起就看你不顺眼了。最初的原因我也不清楚，但是自从你打败了布莱福斯库的海军之后，他对你的恨意就与日俱增了，因为他认为你抢走了属于他的荣誉。他和财政大臣弗里木纳普（因为他夫人的事情，他对你怀恨在心），还有司令员里木托克、礼仪大臣拉尔孔、大法官巴尔莫夫密谋准备了一份弹劾书，控诉你犯了叛国罪和其他重大罪行。"

这一番啰唆的说辞让我很是不耐烦，我忍不住想要打断他，毕竟我自认为是有功无过的。不过他却请我安静下来，然后说：

"为了报答你对我的恩情，我冒着被处死的危险探听到了这件事情，同时还弄到了一份弹劾书的副本。

对昆布斯·弗莱斯丁（山巨人）的弹劾书

第一条

先皇卡林·德法尔·普鲁斯曾经制订过一条法律，规定在皇宫范围之内不得小便，否则将以叛国罪论处。而昆布斯·弗莱斯丁却无视这一条法令，借口扑灭皇后寝宫的火灾，竟然敢对着宫殿撒尿，居心叵测！同时他未经允许，就擅自进入皇宫内院，不仅触犯了法律，而且大大越权。

第二条

昆布斯·弗莱斯丁曾经将布莱福斯库的舰队押送到我国的港口，但是当皇帝命令他俘获布莱福斯库的剩余船只，将布莱福斯库彻底占领吞并的时候，他竟然以不愿违背良心去摧残一个无辜民族的自由和生命为借口，恳求皇帝收回成命，致使流亡在布莱福斯库的大头派异端逍遥法外。

第三条

当布莱福斯库派遣使者来向我朝求和的时候，弗莱斯丁与一般狡诈忤逆之徒毫无区别，竟然敢公然帮助、安慰、款待敌国的使臣，丝毫不思考对方是与我国皇帝陛下公然为敌的敌国臣子。

第四条

昆布斯·弗莱斯丁不履行我国子民的责任，仅仅在陛下的口头许诺之下就打算前往布莱福斯库，并且还打算和布莱福斯库的皇帝会面。昆布斯公然背信弃义，试图前往辅助甚至教唆布莱福斯库的皇帝；这一点尤为不可饶恕。

"当然还有许多别的罪状，但是上述几条是最重要的，而我也简要为你念过了。不得不说，在之前的几次辩论中，皇帝陛下还是显现出宽大的一面，他多次强调了你的功绩，试图减轻你的罪行。但是海军大臣和财政大臣却坚持要把你处死。他们打算趁着晚上放火烧你的房子，让你在痛苦中死去。司令官建议派出两万弓箭手，用毒箭射你的脸和手。他们甚至还打算派几位心腹，趁你睡着的时候在你的衬衣上撒毒药，让你把自己的皮肉抓烂，在痛苦中死去。司令官等人对于上述做法都欣然同意。在很长一段时间里，大多数人都是站在反对你的立场上的。但是皇帝却想要保住你的性命，同时还劝住了礼仪大臣。

"在这件事情上，机要大臣雷德瑞萨也奉命发表自己的看法。他一向被认为是你真正的朋友，这一点也在他的意见中得以体现。他承认你罪行深重，但是仍有被宽恕的可能性，而宽恕是君王最可贵的品格。他自称和你是最好的朋友，所以为你辩护显得有偏袒之嫌。但是既然皇帝陛下有命令，那么他也愿意坦率地表达自己的看法。他希望皇帝陛下能够念在你先前的功劳，赦免你的性命，只要戳瞎你的一对眼睛就算是惩罚了。他觉得这样的办法既能够展示皇帝的公正严明，也能够体现皇帝的仁慈。失去双眼的你并不会因此而失去力量，一样可以为皇帝效力；而看不见的你会越发勇敢，因为你看不见危险。当初你也是因为担心眼睛被弄瞎，才没能去把敌人剩下的战舰俘获。所以今后由大臣们帮你观察敌情是很合适的，伟大的君王当如是！

"但是这个建议却遭到了全体成员的反对。海军大臣伯格拉姆甚至还怒气冲冲地站了起来，说他感到很奇怪，机要大臣为什么会主张留下一个叛徒的性命。不管从什么理由来看，你所做的功绩只会加重罪行。既然你用一泡尿就可以扑灭大火，那么同样你也可以用这样的办法引来洪灾，把整座皇宫淹没。既然你可以俘获舰队，那么同样你也可以把舰队送回去。叛逆的人总是先盘算清楚然后再付诸实践的。因此他坚持处死你。

"财政大臣的意见同他是一样的。他指出，你的生活开支巨大皇家财政已经到了十分窘迫的地步，如果再这样下去，很快就要供不起了。内务大臣提出弄瞎你的眼睛远不是消灭这一祸害的良策，说不定反会使祸害加重。从弄瞎某类家禽的一般情形来看，很明显，这些家禽眼瞎之后吃得更多，很快发胖。神圣的皇帝和阁员们就是你的审判官，他们凭着各自的是非心完全可以认为你有罪，这就足以判你死刑，并不需要有法律明文规定的正式证据。

"但是皇帝陛下拿定主意反对把你处死，他仁慈地说，既然阁员们觉得弄瞎眼睛的刑罚太轻了点，以后还可以加其他刑嘛。这时你的朋友机要大臣谦恭地要求再次得到发言的机会，来答复财政大臣提出的反对他的理由：皇帝为了维持你的生活耗资巨大。他说既然阁下全权处理皇帝的财政，不妨逐渐减少你的份例，这样这个祸害很容易就可以得到解决。吃不到足够的食物，你就会因身体虚弱而昏死过去，没有胃口，很快你就会被饿死。到那时你的体重轻了一大半，尸体发出的臭气也就不会有太大危害了。你一死，五六千个老百姓两三天就可以把你的肉从骨头上割下来，用货车运走，埋得远远的，免得传染，留下你的骨架作为纪念，供后人瞻仰。

"在机要大臣的伟大友谊之下，判决结果也因此有了一个折中的结果。皇帝密令将饿死你的计划悄悄进行，但是把你的眼睛弄瞎的判决却写在了弹劾书当中。除了海军大将伯格拉姆，所有人都表示同意。伯格拉姆是皇后的人，而皇后打心眼里想要把你处死。自从你用那种可耻的手法扑灭了她皇宫的大火之后，她就对你怀恨在心。

"大约三天后，你的朋友机要大臣就会来此宣读弹劾书，同时还要向你阐述一番皇帝和内阁的宽大胸怀，正是由于他们的宽大胸怀，你才会被判失去双眼。皇帝相信你会感激涕零地接受。之后会有二十位御医前来监督，保证手术顺利进行。到时候你会躺在地上，而他们会用利箭刺入你的眼球。

"至于你到底如何应对，就由你自己考虑吧！为了不让人怀疑，我得马上离开了。"

这位老爷走了，留下我一个人一片茫然。

这位皇帝和他的内阁有一种惯例（以前有人告诉我，这样的做法和先前是不一样的），那就是，如果朝廷要颁布一项严酷的判决，那么不管是为了替皇帝出气，还是为了满足宠臣的报复心，皇帝都要在全体会议上发表一通演说，强调自己的宽大仁慈，并且强调这些品质是举世闻名的。这一番说辞很快就会刊发到全国。老百姓们对此十分恐惧，因为所有人都很清楚，这样的自夸越是厉害，接下来的刑罚就会越发可怕，而受害者的冤屈也就更加沉重。就拿我自己来看，我不得不承认，无论是我的出身还是我所受的教育，都不足以成为内阁的一员。但是我觉得这样的判决对我来说毫无宽大可言，而且是不能再严苛了。有的时候我就想自己何不乖乖受审呢，毕竟弹劾书上的几条刑罚我也是供认不讳的，只是我希望他们能够减轻我的刑罚。不过我这一生也是仔细研究过各种政治案件的审判的，我的一个结论就是，许多的案件最后都是由判官自以为是地结案。所以面对这样的敌手，逆来顺受也是很有风险的。这时候我又想到了反抗，毕竟我现在拥有自由；哪怕是整个国家都不一定能够敌过我的力量。我只需要几块石头就可以把整个京城砸坏。但是我毕竟对皇帝宣过誓，他曾经赐予我恩典，也曾授予我"纳达克"的称号，这样以怨报德的做法是不可取的。但是我也没有学会他们的那种感恩戴德的做派，所以我对自己说，既然皇帝决定如此残忍地对待我，那么所谓应尽的义务自然也一笔勾销了。

最后我做出了一个决定。也许这会让我招致非议，但是这样的决定也并非毫无道理，毕竟由于这个决定，我保住了自己的双眼，同时捍卫了我的自由。如果我当时就知道皇帝和大臣的性格，以及他们对待那些凡人的手段的话，我一定愿意服从这样简单的刑罚。但是那时候我太年轻了，就趁着自己有了皇帝的口头许诺，抓紧写了一封信给我的朋友机要大臣，告诉他我已经得到了许诺，决定前往布莱福斯库。没等他回信答复，我就来到了舰队停泊的港口，抓起一艘大船，解下船锚，脱下衣服，然后把衣服和被子放在了那条船上。随后我就抱着那条船，来到了布莱福斯库的港口。那里的人民早就在海边迎接我了。他们给我派了两名向导带我前往首都布莱福斯库。我把两人拿在手里，一直走到离城门不到两百码的地方。我让他们去通报一位大臣，就说我到了，让他知道我在此等候皇帝的命令。过了大约有一个钟头，我得到回报，说皇帝陛下已经率皇室及朝廷重臣出来迎接我了。我又往前走了一百码。皇帝及其随从从马上下来，皇后和贵妇们也都下了车，看不出他们有任何害怕或忧虑的表现，我卧在地上吻了皇帝和皇后的手。我告诉皇帝，我是来践约的，为我能征得皇帝的许可前来拜见他这么一位伟大的君主，而感到不胜荣幸。我愿尽力为他效劳，这也与我为自己君王尽义务完全一致。我对我失宠的事一个字也没提，因为到那时为止我并没有接到正式通知，可以完全装作对这事一无所知。我现在不在他的势力范围之内，推想皇帝也不可能公开那件密谋的。然而不久我就发现这种想法错了。

我不想把这个朝廷如何接待我的详细情形再来说给读者听了，总之，这种接待是和这么一位伟大君王的慷慨气度相称的。我也不想再多说我怎么没有房子没有床，被迫裹了被子睡在地上等困难情形了。

第八章

作者幸运地找到了离开布莱福斯库的办法，在经历了一些困难之后，他安全地回到了自己的祖国。

抵达布莱福斯库三天之后，我出于好奇信步到这个小岛的东北海岸。我发现在距离海岸半里格的地方好像有一条小船。我脱下了鞋子和袜子，朝海里走了两三百码，发现那东西在海浪的作用下越发靠近了，看模样还真是一条小船，我估计应该是从某条大船上被吹下来的。于是我赶紧回到布莱福斯库的京城，请求皇帝陛下借给我最大的二十艘舰船，还有三千军士；毕竟先前的惨败让他的舰队有些捉襟见肘。当我以最快的速度回到海岸的时候，我发现海浪把那条小船冲近了不少。那些大船上都配备了最结实的绳索，这是我先前就准备好的。当那些舰船准备就绪之后，我脱下了衣服，朝着那条小船走去。往前走了大约一百码，海水就很深了，所以我不得不朝着小船游去。我让舰船上的水手把绳索的一头扔给我，然后我把绳索系在那条小船上。可是我忙了很久却没有多大成效，因为海水太深了，我根本就碰不到海底，所以也就没法用力了。我只好游到小船的后面，用一只手推着那艘小船前进。不得不说潮水帮了我很大的忙，小船前进的速度很快，不久我的双脚就能够站在海底了，这时下巴刚好能露出水面。我休息了两三分钟，又继续推着小船前进，直到海水漫不过我的腋窝。最费力的阶段就算是结束了，这时候我拿起其中一根绳索，系在小船上，然后又把这绳索分给剩下的那些军舰。风向帮了我大忙，那些舰船在前边拉，我在后面推，很快我们就把小船拖到了距离海岸不到四十码的地方。潮水退去之后，小船就露出了模样。在那两千军士的帮助下，我们使用了绳索和机械把小船翻了过来，发现这条小船几乎没有什么损伤。

我本不该和读者们絮叨之后发生的那些麻烦事儿，总之我花费了整整十天时间才做成了好几把船桨，然后我就划船去了布莱福斯库的皇家港口。港口已经聚满了人，都在等待着我的到来。当他们看到如此巨大的一艘小船的时候，他们内心的激动之情显而易见。我对布莱福斯库的皇帝说，我的运气太好了，这样的一艘船可以带我去很多地方，甚至还可以带我回国。我请求皇帝陛下能够给我一些材料，让我彻底修好这艘船，同时我也请求一张通行证。虽然他善意地挽留了我一会儿，不过最终他还是欣然同意了。

在这段时间里，我也很纳闷，为什么利立浦特的皇帝没有向布莱福斯库皇帝送来关于我的紧急文书。后来有人告诉我，利立浦特的皇帝根本就没有意识到我事先察觉到了他们的计划，他还以为我不过是在他的允诺之下前来布莱福斯库做客。毕竟他的口头承诺也是人尽皆知的，他相信过几天我就会回去了。但是看我那么久还没有回去，他忍不住有些不安。皇帝再次和财政大臣以及其他党羽商议了一番后，派遣了一位官员带着弹劾书来到布莱福斯库。特使对布莱福斯库君主说："皇帝陛下是如此的仁慈，只同意刺瞎山巨人的眼睛；但是面对如此公正的惩罚，山巨人竟然敢逃跑。如果在两个小时之内，他不回到利立浦特的话，皇帝就要剥夺他'纳达克'的封号，并且公开宣布他为国家叛徒。"特使又补充了一句："为了维持我们两个国家的友好关系，希望布莱福斯库的皇帝能够下令将山巨人遣返回国，并且希望在遣返时能够像对待俘虏一般将他捆绑起来。"

布莱福斯库的皇帝花了整整三天时间和朝臣商议，然后做出了回应。回信的口气十分有礼，他不断请求谅解，说："皇帝陛下您应该知道，尽管他摧毁了我的舰队，但是想要把他捆绑起来遣返回利立浦特根本就是一件做不到的事情，更何况他在两国议和的过程中曾经鼎力相助，所以我对他还是心怀感激的。不过我们两个国家很快就会摆脱这个烦恼，因为山巨人在我们的海岸边发现了一艘巨轮，他自称能够乘坐这艘巨轮出海。我已经下令帮助他修缮这条船，我有理由相信，几个星期之后我们都能够摆脱这个沉重的负担。"

特使带着这封回信回到利立浦特，布莱福斯库的皇帝也把这一切通通告诉我了。同时他还表示说，如果我愿意留下来帮助他，那么他一定会保护我的。当然这些话只能在私下里说。虽然我很相信他的诚意，但是经过利立浦特的事情之后，我已经不想对任何皇帝、大臣们推心置腹了。因此我先是对他的善意表示感谢，然后就诚挚地表达了自己内心的歉意。我说："命运既然赐给了我一个机会，那么不管结果如何，我都要乘船出海，去迎接那未知的命运。我也不希望你们两个国家再起什么冲突了。"我发现这一番表态并没有惹得皇帝有什么不高兴。甚至一次非常偶然的机会，我听说他对我的决定十分赞赏，他的臣子也十分开心。

这些因素都促使我赶紧离开，布莱福斯库的人巴不得我快点走，所以他们给了我很大帮助。我先是指挥了五百个工人把十三层最结实的亚麻布缝在一起，做成了两个船帆；我把几十根国内最粗的绳索给拧成了一根特别结实的绳索。我在海岸边找了好久，这才找到了一块足够充当船锚的大石头。他们送给我三百头牛身上提炼出来的牛油，让我用来涂抹船身。随后我又砍断了好几棵最大的树木，用来制作船桨和桅杆。皇家工匠给了我很大帮助，在我把粗重的活计干完之后，他们就负责帮我打磨。

差不多一个月的时间里，我把一切都准备好了。随后我就去面见皇帝，希望他允许我离开。皇帝和他的皇室成员全部送出了皇宫。我匍匐在地上，亲吻着他的手，皇后和那些年轻的王子也是一样。皇帝送给我五十个钱袋子，每个袋子里面都放着两百个斯普鲁，他还送给我一幅他的全身画像。我赶紧把这幅珍贵的画像藏在了自己的手套里。送行仪式相当烦琐，我也就不再赘述了。

我在船上装了一百头牛和三百只羊，尽可能多的面包和饮料，还有四百位厨师为我准备了许许多多的肉食。我带了六头活的母牛，两头公牛，六只母羊和两只山羊，希望能够把这些稀奇的品种带回我的祖国。为了保证他们能够存活，我在船上准备了一大捆干草和一口袋玉米。其实我还想带十几个人回去，但是皇帝陛下并不赞同。他不但对我的口袋严加搜查，还让我发誓不能带走任何一个子民，哪怕他们是出于自愿的。

一切都准备就绪之后，我在 1701 年 9 月 24 日那一天的早晨六点钟扬帆起航。我向北走了大约二十公里，在下午六点钟左右的时候我发现了一个小岛，距离我不到两公里远。恰好这会儿在吹东南风，所以我继续航行，一直转到了小岛的背阴处才抛锚休息。

这个岛上好像没有人烟。我吃了点东西，然后就草草睡去。我大概睡了六个小时，因为第二天我醒来两个小时之后天就亮了。这是个晴朗的夜晚，太阳还没升起来的时候我就吃了早饭，然后继续出发。当时是顺风，所以在指南针的指引下，我沿着前一天的航线继续前进。我当时打算前往范迪门的东北部的一个小岛，这个方向应该不会有错。但是一整天下来我什么也没有发现，可是第二天下午三点钟左右，我估计那时驶离布莱福斯库已有二十四里格，我正朝正东方向行驶，忽然发现一艘帆船正在向东南方向开去。我向那船呼叫，但没有反应，不过风势已弱，我发现我已在逼近那艘帆船。我扬帆全速前进，大约过了半个小时，那船发现了我，就拉起了一面旗，同时放了一枪。没想到我还有希望再次见到我亲爱的祖国和我留在那里的我的亲人，那样的快乐真是难以表达！那艘船降帆慢行，我就在 9 月 26 日傍晚的五六点钟终于赶上了它。看到那船上的英国国旗，我的心直跳。我把牛羊都装入了我的上衣口袋，带着我所有的给养和货物上了那艘船。这是一艘英国商船，经北太平洋和南太平洋由日本返航。船长是戴浦特津（戴浦特津是印度孟买以北的一个城市）的约翰·毕得尔先生，是位彬彬有礼而且十分出色的海员。

这时我们的位置是在南纬三十度，船上大约有五十个人，在这里我竟然还碰到了我的一个老同事，叫彼得·威廉姆斯，他向船长称赞我人不错。这位先生对我很友好，他要我告诉他我从哪里来又到哪里去。我答了几句，可他以为我是在说胡话，是我经历的种种危险使我的大脑出了问题。我从口袋里掏出牛羊，他见了无比惊讶，这才完全相信我说的是实话。接着我又给他看了布莱福斯库皇帝送我的金币、皇帝的全身画像以及那个国家的其他一些稀罕玩意儿。我送了他两袋钱，每只袋里装有两百个“斯普鲁”，并向他许诺回到英国以后，再送他一头怀孕的母牛和一只怀孕的母羊。

关于这次回程的细节我就不多讲了，总之这也算是一次顺利的旅程。1702 年 4 月 13 日，我们顺利地回到了唐兹港。在这次旅行中只有一个小小的不幸，那就是船上的老鼠偷走了我的一头羊。我在一个老鼠洞里发现了羊的尸骨，所有的肉都被吃完了。其他的牲畜都被我安全带上了岸，放在格林威治的草地上吃草。那儿的青草分外鲜嫩，它们都吃得津津有味，但是我却总是担心它们。在那漫长的旅途中，如果不是船长拿出自己最精美的饼干，让我碾碎了喂给它们充当食粮，它们根本不可能活到现在。在短暂停留的过程中，我把这些小巧的玩意展示给当地的显贵，借此赚到了一笔钱。第二次航行开始之前，我就以六百英镑的价格把它们卖掉了。后来我发现它们繁衍得不错，特别是那些羊。我希望它们那柔软的羊毛能够为纺织行业做出贡献。

我和我的家人只待了两个月，就又不安分起来，迫切地想要去国外探险。我给我的妻子留下了一千五百英镑，然后把她安顿在雷德里夫的一幢不错的房子里。剩下的家当都被我给带去了，有现钱，也有货物，因为我指望这一次能够赚一笔钱。我的大伯父留给我一份田产，每年有三十六英镑的收入，我把菲达巷的黑牛旅馆也给租了出去，每年也能有一笔收入。这样一来我就不用担心我离开之后家人需要依靠教会接济了。我的儿子约翰已经在上小学了，他的名字还是根据他叔叔的名字来起的，这是个温和的孩子。而我的女儿贝蒂（现在她已经结婚生子）就在家里忙一些针线活。我和我的家人分别之后，就踏上了三百吨的“探险号”商船，准备前往苏拉特。船长是约翰·尼古拉斯，是利物浦人。关于这一趟旅行，我就在游记的第二卷详细描述了。

第二卷
布罗丁格奈格游记

布罗丁奈格

弗兰夫拉斯尼克

劳不鲁格鲁

公元 1703 年发现

北美洲

安曼海峡

勃兰科角

圣西巴新

新阿尔宾

门德西诺角

圣法兰西·德莱克港

圣马丁山

孟特西港

第一章

作者所在的船只遇到了暴风雨，他们派出了一条小船去取水，作者也跟着一起去了，想要去看看那座小岛。结果他被抛弃了，而且还被土著抓住，带到了一个农夫的家里。作者在那儿经历了好几次危险。作者还描述了一下当地人的模样。

　　我在上文中已经交代了，在我平安返回祖国的两个月之后，就再次离开了那里，在1702年6月20日，登上了从唐兹出发的商船，前往苏拉特。这艘船是"冒险号"，船长是来自康沃尔郡的约翰·尼古拉斯。我们的前半段旅程顺风顺水，很快就抵达了好望角，在那儿停下来补充淡水。这时我们发现船身有些破损，于是不得不把所有的货物卸下来，然后在好望角过冬。由于船长得了疟疾，所以我们一直在好望角待到了第二年的三月底才再次出发，并且顺利渡过了马达加斯加海峡。但是当轮船行驶到马达加斯加岛的北部，大约北纬五度的时候，风势却突然发生了变化。一般来说，这一带在每年的十二月初到第二年的五月份都是刮西北风的，但是在4月19日那天风势却格外大，而且风向偏西，这样的天气一直持续了二十天。于是我们的船只被吹到了莫璐卡群岛的东边。船长在5月2日简单观测了一下，发现我们位于北纬三度的位置。虽然风平浪静，但是船长却警告欣喜万分的我们。他在这一带跑了很多年的船，经验丰富，他警告我们暴风雨马上就要来了。果然第二天南风就呼啸而至。

　　之后的天气越来越差，我们担心季风太大，就把斜帆收了下来，并且随时准备把尾帆也收起来。风越来越大，我们只好检查所有的大炮，并且把其余的船帆都收了起来。由于天气实在太差，冒险号在狂风中逐渐偏离了航道。无可奈何的我们思索着与其和狂风抗争，不如顺其自然地扬帆起航，好过船只在风浪中随波逐流。于是我们卷起前桅帆把它定住，随后将前桅帆下端索拉向船尾。船舵吃风很紧，船尾猛地转向风的一面。我们把前桅的落帆索拴在套索桩上，但是船帆碎裂了，我们就把帆桁收下来，将帆收进船内，解掉了上面所有的东西。这是一场十分凶猛的风暴，大海就像变了脸一样非常惊险。我们紧拉舵柄上的绳索以改变航向，避开风浪，接着帮助舵工一起掌舵。我们不想把中桅降下来，而是让它照旧直立着，因为船在海上行驶得很好。我们也知道，中桅这么直立在那里，船也更安全一些，既然在海上有操纵的余地，船就可以更顺利地向前行驶。猛烈的风暴过去以后，我们扯起了前帆和主帆，把船停了下来。之后我们又忙着挂起后帆、中桅的主帆和中桅的前帆。此时我们的航向是东北偏东，风向西南。右舷的上下角索也被我们收到船边，同时解开迎风一面的转帆索和空中供应线，背风一面的转帆索则通过上风滚筒朝前拉紧、套牢，再把后帆的上下角索拉过来迎着风，这样使船尽可能沿着航道满帆前进。

　　暴风雨过去之后，又是一阵西南偏西的强风。我们测算了一下，大概又被吹到了偏东五百里格的海域上，就连甲板上经验最丰富的老水手都不知道我们到底在什么位置了。那时候我们的船上的物资储备充足，船只也完好无损，船员的身体状况也不错，但我们面临的最大问题就是缺水。我们决定沿着现在的方向继续前进，毕竟如果我们一路向北的话，也许会把我们带到大鞑靼的西北部，到时候就会进入冰海了。

　　1703年6月16日，一个男孩在桅杆上发现了陆地。第二天，一座巨大的岛屿，或者是一块陆地（我们当时根本就判断不出来）出现了，而且有一小串小岛延伸到了海洋。这个港湾很小，只能容纳大约一百吨的商船。于是，我们就在距离港湾大约一里格的地方抛锚。船长派出了一队全副武装的船员，乘坐一条小船去寻找淡水。我也想和他们一起去，这样还能见识一下这片未知的土地。当我们来到陆地上之后，却发现根本就没有什么河流或者泉水，也没有任何生物居住的迹象。于是我们就沿着海岸巡视了一圈，想要看看海边有没有淡水，而我一个人沿着相反的方向走了大约一英里，但是周围寸草不生，怪石嶙峋，这不由得让我很扫兴，于是我就转身朝着港湾走去。当我走到海边，欣赏大海美景的时候，却发现那些上岸来取水的水手都已经跳上了小船，飞快地朝着大船所在的方向划去。正当我准备高声呼喊的时候，虽然这可能并没有什么用处，我发现有一个仿佛怪兽一般的巨人在后面快步追赶，海水竟然淹不到他的膝盖。幸好水手们已经和那个怪物有了半里格的距离，再加上这一片海域的礁石也足够锋利，那个巨人才放弃了追赶，而他们也就逃出生天了。这一切都是他们之后告诉我的。当时的我一点都不想待在原地了，于是就沿着原路往回跑，跑上了一座小山。当我在山上俯瞰的时候，发现这竟然是一片耕地。但最让我感到惊讶的是这儿的干草的长度，竟然有二十英尺那么高，而这仅仅是用来做饲料的干草。

格列佛看到了二十英尺高的干草

随后我就走上了一条看上去很宽阔的大路，后来我才知道，这不过是当地人的一条麦田里的小路而已。这时节恰好是收割麦子的好时候，两旁的麦子至少有四十英尺那么高。我在麦田里走了大约一个小时，这才发现麦田的尽头。当我回头张望的时候，发现麦田的周围是有篱笆的，篱笆的高度至少有一百二十英尺。在麦田旁边还长着树，只不过我根本就搞不清楚这树到底有多高。两块麦田之间还有四级台阶，只有爬上最高的那级台阶，然后再跳上一块大石头，才能走到另外一块麦田。每一级台阶差不多有六英尺那么高，而台阶上的石头有整整二十英尺，所以我是绝对不可能爬上那些台阶的，更别提翻过那块大石头了。如果我想要穿过麦田的话，唯一的办法就是穿过那些篱笆。正当我忙着在篱笆中间寻找缝隙的时候，发现有个土著朝着我的方向走来。正当我在寻找篱笆上可能有缝隙的时候，我看到一个巨人跨过了旁边的麦田，朝着我这边的台阶走来。他的体型和之前在大海里追逐我们的小船的那个巨人差不多，差不多和欧洲的教堂的尖塔一样高。他的步子迈得很大，初步估计一步就能够走过十几码。看到这样的巨人逐渐靠近，惊慌失措的我赶紧躲进了麦田。只见这个巨人站在台阶的最高处，然后冲着右手边的麦田大喊一声，声音就好像是平地里的炸雷一般。听到他的喊声，从那边的麦田里出现了七个和他身材差不多的巨人，纷纷围拢过来。他们每人的手里都握着一把镰刀，镰刀差不多有我们国家的六把镰刀拼起来那么大。这些人的衣着稍显朴素，看上去像是第一个人的佣人或者是长工。当他说了几句话之后，那些人就开始收割起我藏身的这块麦田。我试图远离他们，但是麦秆之间的缝隙只有一英尺不到，所以我想要转移还是很困难的。处于如此危急关头的我还是想方设法地前进。不知道是不是因为曾经有暴风雨侵袭的缘故，一小株麦子被吹倒了，而且还和旁边的麦子黏在了一起，阻挡了我前进的道路。我在麦田里穿梭的过程中，还时不时有些麦芒掉下来，戳进了我的衣服。这时候那些割麦人已经距离我不到一百码了。绝望无助的我徒劳地躺在地上，心想着这可能就是我这一生的结局了。我想起了远在故土的妻子，她可能就要成为寡妇了；而我那尚在襁褓的孩子也将永远失去他的父亲，这一切不由得让我悲从中来。当初我不听亲友的劝告，执意要再次出海；现在我却追悔莫及，骨子里的那种不安分的性格让我感到十分羞愧。悲痛不安的我不由得想起了利立浦特。在那儿，所有的居民都视我如天神一般，我也曾立下丰功伟绩，我一个人就能够俘获一支皇家舰队。我的功绩将被载入利立浦特的史册，这样的功劳可能难以被他们的后辈所相信，但的确是真实存在的。就好像那些利立浦特人在我眼中是那么微不足道一般，现在的我在这群巨人中当中同样是微不足道的，这不能不说是一种耻辱。因为据说人类的野蛮和残暴与他们的身材是成比例的，身材越高大，就越野蛮越残暴。那么，要是这帮巨大的野人中有一个碰巧发现我，我只能是他们口中的一块美食了，不会有别的出路的。毫无疑问，哲学家们的话还是对的，他们告诉我们：万事万物只有比较才能有大小之分。命运真能捉弄人，利立浦特人也一定能够找到一个民族，那里的人比他们还要小，就像他们比我们小一样。谁又知道，就是这么高大的一族巨人，不会同样被世界上某个遥远地方的更高大的人比下去呢？只不过我们还没有见到过那样的巨人罢了。

惊恐万分的我忍不住开始胡思乱想，根本就没有意识到其中一个割麦的巨人已经走到了距离我所在的田垄不到十码的距离。我很担心他再走一步就会把我踩成烂泥，或者被他手里的镰刀给斩断。正当他迈出那一步的时候，我忍不住尖叫了起来。听到我的喊声，他停下了脚步，弯下腰来仔细打量着周围，很快就发现了在地上瑟瑟发抖的我。他并没有马上弯腰把我捡起来，而是犹豫了一会儿，仿佛面对的是一只可能有危险的小动物，担心自己被咬伤或者被抓伤，那副模样就像我在英国捉鼬鼠时一样。最后他还用食指和拇指夹着我的脊背，然后把我提到他眼前大约三码的距离，以便更好地观察我。幸好当时的我理会了他的意图，并没有挣扎，毕竟当时我距离地面已经有整整六十英尺了。而这个巨人也担心我从他手里滑落，两指间的力道也有点加强，把我捏得很疼，但是我却忍着没有动弹。我当时唯一的举动就是抬头看着太阳，双手合十，做出了一副苦苦哀求的可怜样子。之后我又好言相劝，因为我很担心他会把我摔死在地上，就像我们对付那

当格列佛第一次见到布罗丁格奈格的居民的时候，他实在是太过于惊慌了

些狡猾的小动物一样。不过我的运气好像不差，这个巨人仿佛对我的声音和表现十分满意，眼神里充满了好奇，而且嘴里还念叨着一句我完全听不懂的话。这时候我实在是忍不了腰部的疼痛了，忍不住呻吟起来，同时也流下了泪水。我努力把自己的脑袋伸向我的腰部，尽可能向他示意，他的两个手指已经压得我受不了了。幸好他很快就明白了我的意思，因为他很快就拉起了自己衣服的下摆，温柔地把我放在里面，然后就飞快地跑到了自己的主人身边。他的主人就是先前我看到的那位农夫，看上去家境不错。

　　这位雇工先是把这件事情和他的主人讲了一遍（这是我从他们的谈话过程中推测出来的），他的主人随手捡起了一根小稻草（在我看来这几乎有一根手杖大小了），拨弄了一下我的上衣下摆，也许他以为这衣服是我天生的外壳呢！他把我的头发吹到一边，这样就可以清楚地看到我的脸了。他把雇工们召集过来，询问他们是否有看到和我差不多的家伙。随后他就温和地把我放在了地上，让我的手脚都在地上。但是我很快就站了起来，在他们面前走来走去，我又很好地控制了我的方向，以免让他们以为我要逃跑。他们纷纷坐了下来，绕着我围成了一个圆圈，观察着我的举动。我摘下帽子，冲着这些巨人团团作揖，然后跪在地上，双手高举，大声地冲着他们说了几句话。随后我又从口袋里掏出了一袋金币，毕恭毕敬地递给他。他接过了那个钱袋，放在眼前看了半天也没搞清楚这到底是什么东西，甚至还拿出了一枚别针，拨弄了半天。我只好冲着他做手势，让他把钱袋放在地上。随后我就拿起钱袋，打开以后掏出了所有的金币，一共有二三十个小金币，还有价值四个皮斯托的六枚西班牙金币。他舔了舔自己的小拇指，捻起了最大的一块金币，然后又拿起另外一块仔细端详，却还是不清楚这到底是个什么东西。随后他就比画了几下，让我把金币放进自己的钱袋，把钱袋塞回了我的口袋。虽然我推辞了好几次，但是他坚持这么做，所以我只好照办。

　　这会儿这位农夫才相信我是具有思维的。他和我说了好多话，但是他的声音震耳欲聋，就像站在水磨边上的刺耳声，不过很明显这是他们的语言。我用好几种语言回答了他的提问，而他也把自己的耳朵凑到距离我两码不到的位置，想要好好听听我讲了什么；但这一切都是徒劳，因为我们俩的语言不通。他让仆人继续去干活，然后掏出了他的手帕，折叠了一下，摊在左手上，手心朝上放在地上，示意我走上去。我轻松地爬上了他的左手，因为他的左手还没有一英尺厚。我觉得此时最适合我的做法还是顺从，而且我也担心会掉下去，于是我整个人就躺在手帕里一动不动；而他也小心翼翼地用手帕把我包裹起来，免得发生什么不测。就这样他端着我回到了家里，然后喊着自己的妻子前来观看。不过他的妻子看到我的第一眼就发出了一阵尖叫声，然后跑回了屋子；这样的反应和英国的妇女看到蟾蜍或者蜘蛛的反应没有多大区别。过了一会儿，她又回来仔细端详我了，而且她的丈夫不管做了什么手势，我都能很好地做出回应，所以她很快就接受了我，并且喜欢上了我。

　　差不多是中午十二点，仆人送上了午餐。午餐不过是一盘肉（这是农民的日常伙食），放在一个直径二十四英尺的巨大盘子里。餐桌上的就只有农夫和他的妻子、三个孩子以及一位老奶奶。当他们坐下吃饭的时候，农夫把我放在桌子上，这张桌子距离地面有整整三十英尺。我被吓得不轻，赶紧离开桌子的边缘。农夫的妻子切下了一小块肉，放在一个木头碟子上，然后又撕下了一小块面包，同样放在那个碟子上，然后把碟子推到我的面前。我冲着她鞠了一躬表示感谢，然后从身上拿出刀叉，开始享用起来。他们饶有兴趣地看着我吃饭。随后女主人又命人拿来了一个小酒杯，在里面倒上了大约两加仑的酒，然后递给我。我十分吃力地用双手把这个酒杯抬了起来，然后恭敬地喝下。随后我又用最大的音调向她表示了感谢，他们看到我的模样，哄堂大笑起来，差点就把我的耳朵给震聋了。这杯酒的味道和我们的苹果酒差不多，味道还有点淡。随后主人就示意我去那个碟子边上享用自己的美食。我顺从地向碟子走去，但是突然发生了一个意外。我想宽容的读者们能够理解我，并且原谅我。原来我一不留神被桌上的面包屑绊倒了，脸朝下就这么摔在了桌子上，幸好没有受伤。我马上爬了起来，看到边上的人都是一脸关切，心里不由得涌起一阵感激。我拿起自己的帽子（之前我一直很有礼貌地把帽子夹在自己的胳膊下面），举过头顶，然后连说了三声"没关系"，表示自己并没有受伤。但是当我继续向前快要走到我的主人（以后我就这么称呼他了）那里的时候，坐在他边上的那个调皮的小儿子，大约是个十岁的小男孩，一把抓住了我的腿，把我提到了空中，这让我吓了个半死。不过他的父亲一把就夺过了我，然后狠狠给了他儿子一个耳光，命令下人把他带走。这记耳光的声音特别大，简直能把一队欧洲骑兵给震下马。我却很担心这个小孩因此迁怒于我，那就糟糕了。而且我也很理解小孩子是天生喜欢捉弄小动物的，像是麻雀、兔子、小猫、小狗之类的动物是他们经常捉弄的对象，于是我跪倒在地，指着那个小男孩，希望我的主人能够原谅那孩子。父亲原谅了他，小家伙重新坐回到自己的位子上。我走到他的身边，亲吻着他的手，表示我的善意。而他的父亲也拉着他的手，让他温柔地抚摸我。

吃饭时，女主人宠爱的猫跳到她膝盖上来了。我听到身后闹哄哄像是十几个织袜工人干活的声音，掉头一看，发现原来是那只猫在打呼噜，女主人正在边抚摸边喂它吃东西呢。我看到它的头和一只爪子，估计这猫足有我们国家的三头公牛那么大。我老远地站在桌子的另一边，与猫相距五十多英尺，女主人也怕它万一跳过来伤害我，所以紧紧地抱住它，即使这样，那畜生狰狞的面相还是让我感到十分不安。可是什么危险都没有发生，我的主人把我放到离它不足三码的地方，它连理都没理我一下。我常听人说，自己旅行中的亲身经历也证明是这样，当着猛兽的面逃跑或者表现出恐惧，它就肯定会来追你或者向你进攻。因此，在这危险关头，我是拿定主意要表现得满不在乎。我在猫的面前毫无惧色地踱了五六次，有时离它还不到半码远。那猫好像更怕我似的，把身子缩了回去。至于狗，我就更是一点也不害怕了。这时有三四条狗进了屋子，这在农民家里是常见的事，其中有一条是獒犬，身躯抵得上四头大象，还有一只灵提，没有獒犬大，却更高些。

午饭就要用完的时候，保姆抱着个一岁的小孩走了进来。他一见我就大声喊叫起来，那喊叫从伦敦桥到切尔西（切尔西是伦敦西南部的一个住宅区，从伦敦桥到切尔西约有五英里）那么远也能听得到。他像平常孩子那样咿呀了半天要拿我去当玩具。母亲也真是一味地溺爱孩子，就把我拿起来送到了孩子跟前。他立刻一把拦腰将我抓住，把我的头直往嘴里塞。我大吼起来，吓得这小淘气一松手把我扔了。要不是他母亲用围裙在下面接住我，我肯定摔死在地上了。保姆为了哄孩子不哭，就用了一支拨浪鼓。那是一种中间空的盒子，里边装上几块大石头，用一根缆绳拴在孩子的腰间。但所有这一切都没起作用，她只有使出最后一招，给孩子喂奶。我得承认，还从没见过什么东西比这乳房更让我恶心的，它长得特别奇怪，我真不知道拿什么来和它相比，所以也无法对好奇的读者详细说明这乳房的大小、形状和颜色。乳房挺起来大约有六英尺高，周长少说也有十六英尺，乳头大概有我半个头那么大。乳房上布满了黑点、丘疹和雀斑，那颜色那样子真是再没有什么比它更叫人作呕的了。因为她坐着喂奶比较方便，而我是站在桌上，离得近，所以这一切我看得清清楚楚。这使我想起我们英国的太太们皮肤白皙细嫩，在我们眼中是多么的漂亮。不过那也只是因为她们身材和我们是一般大小罢了，有什么缺点瑕疵，还得借助于放大镜才能看得清。我们做过试验，从放大镜里看，最光滑洁白的皮肤也是粗糙不平、颜色难看的。

记得之前在利立浦特的时候，我觉得那些人的皮肤是我见过的最滑嫩、最美丽的，当时我也和那儿的一个学者讨论过这样的话题。他说如果我站在地上，他会觉得我的皮肤也是相当光滑白皙的。但是如果我把他托在手里，那么他也会被我的皮肤给吓坏。因为他能够看清我皮肤上的坑坑洼洼，我的胡子比野猪的鬃毛还要粗硬，更别提我的皮肤其实是不同颜色的，看上去格外别扭。当时的我还反驳说我的皮肤和我们国家的大多数人一样好，虽然我经常在外面跑，但是并没有留下太多被太阳晒伤的痕迹。当我们谈及利立浦特的妇女时，他常常会说，这个人脸上有雀斑，那个人嘴巴太宽，这个人鼻子太大，都不好看。但是这一切我都分辨不出来。我想大家应该能明白其中的原因，我还是想多说几句，免得大家以为这儿的巨人长得非常丑陋。在这儿我必须要说一句公道话，那就是这个民族的长相算是非常英俊，特别是我的主人。如果能够在六十英尺开外观察他，就会发现他也是个英俊的小伙子呢！

午餐结束之后，主人就出去监工了，从他的声音和手势中我就能够明白，他一直嘱咐他的妻子好好照顾我。我那时特别疲惫，很想好好睡一觉。女主人很快就领会了我的意思，把我放在她的床上，用一块干净的白色手帕盖在我的身上。这块手帕比我们的战舰的船帆还要大不少，也粗糙不少。

我睡了差不多两个小时，梦到自己回家和妻子孩子团聚，所以醒来之后我十分悲伤。这时候我发现自己孤零零地身处一个巨大的房间，有两三百英尺宽，两百英尺高。而我所在的大床也有二十多码宽，距离地面也有差不多八码。恰好我又想上厕所，所以就只好尝试着爬下床。我知道大喊是没有用处的，因为以我的嗓门，在这么长的距离之下，是不可能让那些在厨房里忙活的人听到的。但是就在这时候，有两只老鼠沿着窗帘爬了上来，跳到了床上，一阵乱闻，其中一只还差点踩在了我的脸上。这可把我吓了一跳，我赶紧拿出了自己防身的腰刀。两只老鼠已经形成了夹击的态势，其中一只抬起前爪，抓住了我的衣领。反应快速的我挥舞着手里的刀，划开了它的肚子，一下子就杀死了它，留下了一具尸体。而另外一只老鼠见势不妙，转身就想要逃跑。我飞快地冲着老鼠的后背刺出一刀，鲜血喷涌而出。大功告成以后，我慢慢地在床上来回走动以平定呼吸，恢复精神。两只畜生有一条大獒犬那么大，但要灵活、凶猛得多，所以要是我睡觉前解去了皮带，我肯定就被它们撕成碎片吞吃了。我量了一下死老鼠的尾巴，发现差一英寸就有两码长了。老鼠的尸身还躺在那里淌血，我感到恶心，但却没有办法把它扔下床去。我见它还有点气息，就在它脖子上猛砍了一刀，这才彻底结果了它的性命。

过了一会儿，我的女主人回到房间，发现我浑身是血，赶紧跑过来把我托在她的手里。我指了指死去的老鼠，一边笑一边做着手势，表示我并没有受伤。她明白了我的意思之后显得分外高兴，忙着招呼自己的仆人把死老鼠扔出去，然后她又把我放在桌子上，我把自己的腰刀拿给她看。由于时间过得并不长，所以我的腰刀上沾满了鲜血，不过我很快就用上衣下摆把腰刀擦干净了，然后放回了刀鞘。现在我最想做的那件事情就快要憋不住了。所以我赶紧做手势让我的女主人明白，我现在想要下地。当她把我放在地上之后，我的生理需求让我没法再进一步表达我的意思，于是我就指了指门口，然后鞠了几躬。我的好主人终于明白了我的意思，就把我带去了花园再把我放下来。我走了大约两百码的距离，恳求她不要跟着我或者偷看我，然后就在两片酸枣叶子中间解决了生理需求。

我希望温柔的读者能够原谅我在这些微不足道的小事情上花费那么多的篇幅。对于一些没什么脑子的人来说，这样的事情自然是够无聊的；但是在那些哲学家看来，这样的事情可以帮助他们发挥想象，并且从这些事情中总结经验，进而更好地服务公共事业，或者是为个人的生活提供助力。这也是我为什么要详细描述这些细节，并且同意把这几篇游记公之于众。这些细节都真实存在，每一个细节和场景都历历在目，而且我没有做任何删减和隐瞒。不过我在整理过程中还是删掉了几处不是很重要的细节，唯恐有人指责我的游记太过冗长琐碎。旅行家们在写游记的过程中经常会受到这样的苛责，而这样的指责也不是完全没有道理。

第二章

作者描述了农夫的女儿。作者被带到集市上，然后又被带去了首都。他详细描述了旅途中的情形。

　　我的女主人有一个九岁的女儿，和她的同龄人相比，这是个心灵手巧的姑娘，她的针线活做得特别好，也特别擅长打扮自己的洋娃娃。她和她的母亲打算给我准备一个婴儿摇篮，作为我晚上睡觉的地方。她们起先准备把摇篮放在衣橱的抽屉里，又担心会有老鼠来伤害我，就把整个抽屉悬挂在一块吊板上面。我和这户人家住在一起的时候，这儿就是我的床了。之后我开始学习当地语言，在慢慢地学会表达自己的意思之后，她们也就把我的摇篮改得更加舒适了。小姑娘的手十分巧，我只当着她的面换了一两次衣服，她就会为我做衣服了。她一共帮我做了七件衬衫，还有许多的床单。用的料子虽然已经是他们国内最精细的，但是在我看来却仍比麻布还要粗糙，这当然是因为这些布料在我看来特别大的缘故。我所有的衣服也都是她亲自帮我洗的。她同时也是我的老师，在教授我当地的语言的时候极为耐心。我指着一种东西，她就会告诉我用当地的语言该如何说。几天以后我就能够熟练地表达自己的意思了。她天生是个好脾气的人，虽然有接近四十英尺的身高，但和同龄人相比，她算是比较矮的了。她给我取名"格里德里格"，后来全家人乃至这个国家的所有人都这么称呼我。这个词语和我们的小不点的意思差不多。我之所以能够在这个国家幸存下来，多亏了她的功劳。我们一直都是形影不离的，而我也称呼她为"格兰姆达尔克里奇"，意思就是小保姆。如果我不在这儿详细描述一下她对我的关注，那我就是忘恩负义之徒了。我希望有一天能够报答她对我的宠爱，虽然我也很担心她因为我的缘故惹得她的家人不开心。虽然这一切也不是我能够决定的。

　　这件事很快就传到了邻里们的家中，他们纷纷开始谈论我的主人在地里发现了一头怪兽，大小相当于一只"斯没拉克那克"，形状却处处像人。它还能模仿人的一举一动，好像有它自己的语言，也学会了几句他们的话。它用两条腿挺着身走路，性情驯良，懂礼貌，怎样指挥它，它就怎样去做。它长着世上最漂亮的四肢，面孔比贵族家中三岁的女儿还要白嫩。有一个住在附近的农民，他是我主人的一位好朋友，听闻了这件事情之后特地来拜访，想弄清事情的真相。我主人立即把我拿了出来放到桌上，我按照他的命令在桌上走路，抽出腰刀又放回刀鞘。我向主人的朋友致敬，用他们自己的话向他问好，又说欢迎他的到来，一切全是按照我的小保姆教我的话说的。这个人老眼昏花，戴上眼镜想把我看个仔细。这一戴，却叫我忍不住大笑起来，因为他的眼镜就像两个从窗户照进房间来的满月。这一家人弄清楚我为什么而发笑时，也和我一同大笑起来。老头子傻头傻脑，竟气得脸色都变了。就我不幸的遭遇来说，说他是个守财奴真是一点也不冤枉他。他给我的主人出了一个馊点子，让我主人趁赶集的日子把我带到邻近的镇上去展览。那镇子在离我主人家约二十二英里的地方，骑马半个钟头就到了。我看到主人和他的朋友在那儿窃窃私语老半天，有时还指指我，就猜想他们是在打什么坏主意了。我偷听到了他们的一些话，有几句还听懂了。我一害怕就胡思乱想起来。可是第二天早上，我的小保姆格兰姆达尔克里奇就将整个事情一五一十地告诉了我，她是从她母亲那里巧妙地探听得来的。可怜的小姑娘把我抱在怀里，又羞又悲地哭了起来。她担心那些粗鲁的俗人会伤害我。他们把我拿在手里时说不定会把我捏死或者弄断我的手脚。她又说我的性情是那么朴实温和，对自己的面子又是那么顾惜，现在要拿我去赚钱，给一帮最下流的人当把戏耍，我该认为那是多么大的耻辱啊。她说爸爸妈妈都已答应她，"格里德里格"

是她的，可如今她看得出来，他们又要像去年那样来对待她了。去年他们假装给她一只小羊羔，但等到羊长得膘肥体壮时，他们就把它卖给了屠户。至于我自己，反倒没有我的小保姆那样担心。一直以来我都抱着一个强烈的愿望，总有一天我会恢复自由的。至于被人当作怪物带着到处跑这般不光彩的事，我就把自己当作是这个国家里的一个地道的异乡人，有朝一日我回到英国，人们也绝不可能因为我有过这样的不幸遭遇来羞辱我，因为就是大不列颠国王自己，处在我的位置，也同样要遭遇这不幸的。

我的主人听从了他的朋友的建议，在下一次赶集的时候把我装在一个盒子里带到了邻近的镇子，当然他也带上了我的小保姆也就是他的女儿。她就坐在马车的后边。这个盒子的四面都是密封的，只给我留下了一个能够进出的小门，还有几个通气的小孔。小姑娘很细心地带上了我的婴儿床，让我可以在旅途中休息。但是这趟旅行仍然是说不出的惊险而又可怕，虽然这只是一趟不到半个小时的旅程。拉车的马一步就要走上四十英尺，而且它的马蹄拉得特别高，所以在马车上的感觉就好像是在暴风雨中上下摇摆的轮船上一样，而且上下摇摆的幅度更加剧烈。这趟旅程应该比伦敦到圣奥尔班的距离要远一点。我的主人在他熟悉的旅馆歇息，然后和旅馆主人商量了一番，做好了准备。他雇佣了一位喊话员，声称今天晚上在绿鹰旅店会有一只奇怪的动物做表演。这只动物还不及"斯普拉克奈克那么大"（这是当地的一种很美丽的动物，还不及六英尺长），而且看上去和人类没有什么区别，会说话，还能做出不下一百种把戏。

我被放到旅馆最大的房间里的一张桌子上，房间面积差不多有三百平方英尺。我的小保姆紧挨着桌子站在一张矮凳子上，一边照看我，一边指挥我表演。我主人为了避免人群拥挤，每次只让三十个人进来看我。我遵照小保姆的指令在桌子上走来走去。她用我所能听懂的几句话向我提问，我就高声地回答她。我一边向观众致敬一边在桌上绕行，说欢迎各位光临，还说了我学会的其他一些话。小保姆给了我一个针箍大小的容器作酒杯，我拿起这盛满酒的杯子，为大家的健康干杯。我抽出腰刀，学着英国击剑家的样子舞弄了一会。我又拿过小保姆给我的麦秆当作枪耍了一阵；我年轻时曾学过这把戏。那天我一共表演了十二场，常常被迫一遍又一遍地重复那些舞刀弄枪的把戏，累得我有气无力，苦不堪言。那些看过我表演的人大肆宣扬，以至于人们都想破门而入来观赏。我的主人为了维护他自身的利益，不让小保姆以外的任何人碰我；为了防止出危险，他在桌子四周设了一圈长凳，远远地将我与众人隔开，这样他们就没法接触到我了。但是，一个捣蛋鬼小学生拿起一颗榛子对准我的脑袋就扔了过来，差一点就击中了我。那榛子来势凶猛，真要是击中了，我肯定会被打得脑浆迸裂，因为它差不多有一只小南瓜那么大。不过我很开心看到这小流氓被痛打了一顿，然后被轰出了房间。

表演结束之后，我的主人宣布下一次集会他还会让我来表演，与此同时他也会准备一辆更加舒适的马车，这样的安排是有道理的，因为这一趟旅行让我精疲力尽。我整整表演了八个小时，几乎已经无法站立，一句话都说不出来了。我至少需要三天时间才能恢复过来，而在家里的我却是永无宁日。周围方圆百里的绅士们听闻了我的事情，纷纷慕名前来。至少有不下三十个人带着他们的妻子和孩子过来看我（因为这个国家人口众多）。每次我在家里表演的时候，哪怕屋子里没有坐满人，我的主人都要按照一屋子的人的价格来收费。所以很长一段时间以来，虽然我不需要进城，但是家里的频繁表演也让我累得不行（当然星期三除外，这是他们的安息日）。

主人很快就意识到我能够给他带来财富，于是他决心带我去这个国家的各个主要城市去碰碰运气。他做好了长途旅行的一切准备，并安排好家中事务，与妻子告别，随后就在 1703 年 8 月 17 日带着我出发了，大约是我来到这个国家的两个月以后了。我们朝着这个国家的京城出发，那个地方距离我们家大约三千英里。我的主人安排他的小女儿骑着马跟在他的身后，而我则被放在小姑娘腰间的一个盒子上面，然后固定在她的膝盖前方。整个盒子的四周都铺着最为柔软的棉被。同时她也带上了我的婴儿小床，上边铺设着厚厚的褥子。当然她还为我准备了一路上需要的各种必备品，确保我能够过得舒适惬意。和我们一起出发的还有家里的一个仆人，他拖着行李骑着马跟在我们身后。

我的主人的计划是在沿途的城镇一路表演，当然那些距离大路五十到一百英里的大村落也不会落下，因为那儿也可能会有生意。我们的旅途很轻松，一天也不过一百六十英里。我的小保姆为了让我得到充分的休息，好几次都故意抱怨说马儿太过于颠簸，借此要求休息。她经常把我从箱子里拿出来呼吸新鲜空气，同时还让我参观他们的国家，当然我的身上永远都被绑着一根带子。一路上我们跨过了五六条河，不管是宽度还是深度都要比尼罗河和恒河大多了，甚至都找不到一条比伦敦桥下的泰晤士河更小的小溪。这趟旅程一共花费了大约十个星期的时间，我们一共在十八个大城市里做过表演，这还没算上沿途的那些大村庄和大家庭。

我们10月26日抵达了这个国家的京城。用他们的语言来说，京城叫作"罗布鲁格路德"，意思是宇宙的荣耀。主人在京城的大街上找了个距离皇宫不算远的地方安顿下来，然后和往常一般张贴告示，宣传了一番我的模样和本领。他租了一间三四百英尺宽的房间，而供我表演的桌子也有六十英尺，而且在桌子边上还有三英尺高的围栏，防止我摔在地上。为了满足京城的观众的好奇心，每天我都要表演至少十次。现在我已经能够很好地掌握本地的语言了。我不仅能够很好地听懂他们的每句话，还学会了他们的字母表，甚至还能够解释几个句子。在家的时候，我的小保姆格兰姆达尔克里奇就开始教我本地语言，一路上都没有停下来。她的口袋里装着一本书，那是年轻姑娘的普通读物，专门讲解宗教教义的。平时她就用这本书来教授我字母，并且给我解释每个词语的意思。

第三章

作者被送进了皇宫。王后把他从农夫手里买了下来，然后献给了国王。他和这个国家的皇家学者辩论。之后他就有了属于自己的住所，受到王后的喜爱。他极力维护自己的祖国的荣誉，同时还和王后的侏儒辩论。

频繁的演出让我疲惫不堪，也让我的健康每况愈下。我的主人靠我赚得越多就越贪得无厌。我没了胃口，变得骨瘦如柴。农夫主人显然发现了这一点，他认为我很快就会死去了，所以他决定在我死之前再好好赚一笔。正当他在盘算这件事情的时候，皇宫里的一位特使找到了我的主人，命令他赶紧把我送进宫里，给王后和那些贵妇们解闷。有些夫人早已欣赏过我的表演，并且在王后面前大大夸赞了一番我的美貌绝伦、举止得体、见多识广。王后和她的侍从们听说了这事儿之后就迫不及待地想要欣赏一下我的风采。当我进宫觐见的时候，他们一个个简直喜出望外。我跪在地上，请求王后准许我亲吻她的脚表示恭敬；但是体贴的王后却安排我在桌子上，并且伸出了自己的小指头给我亲吻。我用自己的双臂抱住那根指头，然后把指尖凑到嘴唇边上，借此表达自己的敬意。她先是询问了我的祖国和我的这趟旅行的情况，我也简明扼要地向她做了解释。她询问我是否愿意留在皇宫里，我冲她鞠了一躬，然后诚恳地说："我是主人的奴隶，一切都要听从他的安排。但是，如果您询问我个人的意见的话，那么我非常愿意奉献自己，为您效劳是一种荣耀。"于是王后转过身去询问我的主人："你是否愿意卖一个好价格呢？"

我的主人认为我活不过一个月了，正巴不得把我脱手呢！于是他就开口要一千个金币；王后当场就把这笔钱支付清楚了。站在边上的我看得很清楚，这个国家的金币有大约八百个葡萄牙金币那么大；不过这个国家地大物博，而且金子的价格还比较高，所以我的价格大约是英国的一千个几尼。这笔交易完成之后，我说："现在我就是您的奴仆了，不过我请求您能够开恩把我的小保姆格兰姆达尔克里奇留下来，继续做我的保姆和老师，因为她是那么细心地照料我。"

格列佛亲吻了布罗丁格奈格的王后

王后陛下点头同意了，而我的农夫主人自然对此求之不得，他巴不得自己的女儿能够待在宫里呢！我的小保姆也十分开心。主人在离开的时候夸耀说给我找到了一个绝好的归宿，而我则是一言不发，只是轻轻鞠了一躬。

王后看出了我的冷淡，所以当他离开之后，王后便好奇地询问我其中的原因。我大胆地说道："我对我先前的这位主人并没有一丝亏欠，如果有什么是我亏欠他的，那就是他偶然在农田里发现我的时候并没有像捏死小动物一般把我给杀死。而这份恩情我已经报答了。他带着我在这个国家里不断地演出，赚了好大一笔钱，更别提这次把我卖出去的好价钱了。我在他手里所受的苦楚足够把比我强壮十倍的动物折磨致死。现在的我已经不再健康，还得被迫为那些客人表演节目。他之所以会以这样低廉的价格把我卖掉，是因为他觉得我命不久矣。而现在有仁慈的王后保护我，我自然就不会担心再受到虐待了。您是如此伟大而善良，是自然的结晶，是世界的瑰宝，是造物主钟爱的凤凰。我相信自己不会像前任主人所担忧的这般命不久矣，因为我现在在您的身边。在您的威仪之下，我感觉自己精神好极了。"

我就这样结束了我的发言，当然期间少不了一些结巴。后半段的恭维是这个国家特有的风格，其中有好几句还是我的小保姆格兰姆达尔克里奇在入宫的时候特意告诉我的。

虽然我在表达的时候错误百出，但是王后却对此不以为然，她被我的聪明程度给震惊了。她把我托在手里，把我带去给国王看。恰好这会儿国王已经处理完毕国家大事，正在休息。我第一眼看到国王的时候就觉得这是一位威严的国王。他扫了一眼王后手里的我，然后就漫不经心地询问王后："你从什么时候开始喜欢上'斯普拉克奈克'了？"他是把我当成他们国内的那种常见的小家伙了。当时的我趴在王后的掌心，没有爬起来，而王后也没有分辨什么，只是把我放在了国王的书桌上，让我简单自我介绍一下。我简单叙述了一下。这时候我的小保姆也来到了门外等候，她是那么关心我，一见不到我就会感到十分担忧。王后特意把她叫了进来，证实了我来到她家之后发生的这一切都是准确无误的。

国王虽然是这个国家里最为博学的人，也曾在哲学和数学领域有过刻苦的钻研，但是当他看到眼前这个挺直了身体来回踱步的小小的我的时候，就一眼断定我是一个机械产物，无非是制造者的手艺不错（这个国家的机械制造产业格外发达）。不过当他听到我流利的发音，终于忍不住流露出惊讶的表情。但是对于我来到这个国家的种种冒险经历，他却不以为意，认为这不过是格兰姆达尔克里奇和她的父亲为了哗众取宠，给我卖个好价钱才编织的一个骗人的故事而已。他还特意问了我好几个问题，我一一回答，一切都是那么顺理成章。唯一的缺陷可能就是我的发音了。这种夹杂着外国腔调和乡土音调的回答自然不符合宫廷礼仪，所以显得有些粗鲁。

国王派人请来了本周当值的三位宫廷学者。按照这个国家的习俗，这些人随时等候国王的传唤。当他们进来之后，先是对我的外貌做了一番仔细的研究，然后形成了不同意见。不过有一点是他们的共识，那就是按照自然规律，我是不可能存在的。因为他们认为我根本就没有在这个世界上保全自己的能力。我的身手不算敏捷，不可能通过爬树或者挖坑等手段生存下来。他们仔细检查了我的牙齿，认为我是肉食动物。但是实际上大部分动物都比我强壮得多，我不可能成功捕猎，就连田鼠都比我灵活太多。他们都很纳闷，我是如何活到今天的，除非我是以蜗牛之类的昆虫为食。但是很快他们就证实了我并不是以此为食的。其中有位学者认为我不过是个胚胎或者是早产儿，但是另外两位学者坚决反对，因为他们发现我是四肢健全的，而且他们也仔细检查了我的下巴，从我的胡子可以判断出，我已经活了不少年了。他们并不承认我是侏儒，因为我实在是太小了，这个国家的最小的侏儒也有接近三十英尺的身高。在讨论了许久之后，他们一致认为我是一个"瑞尔普拉姆·斯盖尔卡斯"，意思就是天生的奇物。这种判断方法和我们欧洲的哲学思维完全一致。出于对古老的神秘主义的逃避式的办法的摈弃，他们创造出了这种得以解决所有困难的定式，使得人类的知识积累获得了一种突破性的进步。亚里士多德的学生们曾经试图用这种逃避式的办法来掩饰他们的无知，但这一切都是徒劳。而眼下他们发明的这种办法却是屡试不爽。

当他们得出这样的结论之后，我自然要求发言。我郑重其事地对国王说："国王陛下，我来自一个有着千百万个和我一样身材的男女老少的国家，那儿的树木、房屋、动物的比例都和我很相称，所以在那儿生活的我完全可以像您的子民一般自卫和谋生。这就是我对这几位绅士的这一番辩论的回应。"听了我的这番话，他们不过是轻轻一笑，说："那个农民把你教得还不错！"幸好国王陛下深谋远虑，遣退了这几位学者，然后派人把还没来得及离开的农夫找了回来。他先是私下里盘问了有关我的情况，然后就和我以及我的小保姆的证词相互印证，确信我们的回答都是相同的。这时候国王才真正相信我的话。他吩咐王后一定要好好照顾我。他也看出我和格兰姆达尔克里奇的感情很好，所以他也安排她继续负责我的日常生活。国王吩咐为她准备一间舒适的房间，并且还为她指派了一位女教师来负责她的教育，一位女仆为她梳妆打扮，还有两位女仆负责各种粗重的杂活，她只需要照顾我就可以了。王后吩咐她的御用木匠专门为我打造一个箱子作为卧房，样式必须充分尊重我和格兰姆达尔克里奇的意见。御用工匠果然名不虚传，他按照我的吩咐，只用了三周时间就把这一切都完成了。卧房有十六平方英尺，高度是十二英尺，安装有好几扇窗户，一扇门和两个衣橱，和普通的伦敦式的衣橱没有什么区别。房间的天花板也是用木板做的，两边设置有开关，可以方便地打开。我的床就是这样从天花板上面放进去的。格兰姆达尔克里奇每天都会把我的床拿出去通风，然后每天晚上再放回去。当我安心躺在床上之后，她就把天花板给锁了。还有一位心灵手巧的木匠，特意为我打造了两把靠背椅子。椅子还有扶手，是一种类似象牙的材料做成的。为了让我有地方容纳一些小物件，他还专门为我打造了两张桌子和一个柜子。整个房间的墙壁、天花板和地板都很厚实，最大限度地保证我不会出意外。我要求他们在大门上放一把锁，这样就不会有老鼠闯入了。皇宫的铁匠几经周折，才打好了这把锁，他们说这是他们做过的最小的锁头了。但是在我看来，这比英国富豪家里大门的门锁还要大好多。门锁的钥匙我亲自保管，因为我很担心格兰姆达尔克里奇会把那么小的钥匙给弄丢。王后还吩咐下人用最轻薄的丝绸来为我做几身衣服，但是这些丝绸就和英国的毛毯差不多厚实，穿在身上显得分外笨重。这些衣服都是按照当地的风格来设计的，更偏向于波斯和中国的风格，却很合身。

王后是那么喜欢我，每天吃饭都要我陪在身旁。她吩咐下人在她就餐的座位的左边为我准备了桌椅。我在吃饭的时候，格兰姆达尔克里奇就站在边上的凳子上帮忙照顾我。我有一整套银子打造的碗、盘子和其他必备餐具一应俱全。不过和王后用的餐具比起来，我的餐具就好像是玩具店里的摆设一般。我的小保姆把我的餐具放在她口袋里的一个银子打造的小箱子里，在我需要的时候拿出来给我，这些餐具都是由她自己刷洗干净的。平时和王后一起进餐的还有两位公主，大一点的那一位十六岁，年轻一点的只有十三岁零一个月大。王后陛下每次都在我的碟子上放一小块肉，让我自己切着吃，她很喜欢看着我一口一口把这块肉给吃掉。王后的胃口算是当地人里很小的了，但是她一口就能吃掉十二个英国人一顿的饭量。对我来说，这样的场景一开始真的有些恶心。她一口就可以把一只云雀的翅膀连皮带肉全部吃掉，而他们国家的云雀有我们九只火鸡那么大。她吃的每一片面包都有我们国家的两个十二便士的面包那么大。她的金杯里容纳的酒都足以填满我们的一个人酒桶。她的餐刀有我们两把拉直的镰刀那么长，至于其他汤勺等餐具也都比例相当。当初好奇的我曾经央求格兰姆达尔克里奇带我去看宫廷里的人吃饭，看到十几把巨大的刀子和叉子一起挥舞，这样的场面真的是太过于恐怖了。

在每个星期三（也就是他们的安息日），国王和王后都会邀请他们的儿女们一起到内殿就餐。而现在我已经成了国王最为钟爱的小人，所以每次他们都把我的小桌椅放在他左手边的盐瓶跟前。国王陛下很喜欢和我聊天，听我描述欧洲的风俗、宗教、法律、政府和学术等方面的情况，每次我都能够解释得很清楚，而且对欧洲的现状有着独到的看法。不过当我谈论到贸易和海上战争的时候，讲到我们的宗教和政党之争的时候，我就忍不住多了很多的评论。而这位国王的固有的教育背景也让他忍不住对我的看法哈哈大笑。他用右手把我拿起来，然后用左手轻轻抚摸着我，说："你到底是托利党还是辉格党啊？"随后他就转身对边上手持白色手杖的首相说："你看我们的尊严是多么微不足道，就连那么大点的昆虫都能模仿。"随后他又说："我敢说这些小家伙的王国里还有爵位和官衔呢！他们造了一些小小的草窝，然后挖了一些小洞，就算是房屋和城镇了。他们不仅装饰打扮，而且还谈情说爱，甚至也有战争、争辩、欺骗和背叛。"他这么喋喋不休，语气中充满了对我的祖国的轻蔑。而我的伟大祖国曾经打败过法兰西，统治整个欧洲，有过永垂不朽的功绩，并且赢得了整个世界的敬仰，但是却被他们说得一文不值。

不过考虑到我当时的处境，我只能对这种公然的侮辱隐忍不发，不敢表示丝毫愤慨之情。好好思索了一番之后，我却开始怀疑自己是否真的受到了侮辱，因为在这个国家居住的几个月时间里，我已经习惯了这个国家的人的伟岸身躯，听惯了他们的语言，刚来时的那种对他们的身躯和面孔的恐惧感已经慢慢消失了。但是如果现在我看到一群英国的老爷和太太们身着盛装，在那儿装腔作势，一副高傲自大的模样，嘴里念叨着一些空洞无聊的大话，那么我非常有可能嘲笑他们，就像这儿的国王和贵族嘲笑我一样。当王后把我托在手心里照镜子，显现出两个相差如此之大的身躯时，我就会忍不住嘲笑自己。再没有比这更可笑的事情了，我甚至怀疑自己的身躯是不是真的缩小了好多倍。

这个国家里最让我感到气愤难平的屈辱，莫过于王后的侏儒对我的不敬了。他是这个国家有史以来个子最小的人（我相信他的身高不足三十英尺），但是当他看到比他个子还小的家伙的时候，却还是忍不住表现出傲慢的态度。每次我站在王后的会客室的桌子上和那些贵族们聊天的时候，他总是大摇大摆地从我身旁走过，然后说几句高傲的话。如果有哪次他不说几句嘲笑我身材的话，那简直是太意外了。作为报复，我总是叫他"我的兄弟"，还时常挑衅他，问他要不要一起摔跤比试什么的。不过这些也都是宫里的侍人常说的俏皮话而已。某一天晚上，我的一句话把他给惹恼了，这个坏家伙跳上了王后的座位，一把把我抓了起来，扔进了装满奶酪的银碗里，然后撒腿逃跑了。当时我正准备吃饭，根本没有想到有人会害我，所以没有一点防备就被扔到了碗里。幸亏我还是会游泳的，不然就真的不堪设想。王后被眼前的情景吓得惊慌失措，站在边上不知所措。幸好我的小保姆就在房间的另外一边，她马上跑过来把我从碗里捞出来。不过那时候的我已经吃下了整整一夸脱的奶酪。随后他们把我放到床上休息。幸好除了身上的衣服坏掉了，我没有受到其他什么伤害。之后这个侏儒被结实地暴打了一顿，然后作为惩罚，他被逼吃掉了那碗我泡过澡的奶酪。过了一段时间之后，王后就把他赏赐给了一个贵妇人，他的宠幸也就一去不返了，而我也不曾再见过他。这样的结局让我感到很满意，毕竟如果他还在宫里的话，指不定会想出什么坏点子来捉弄我呢！

之前他就曾经捉弄过我，虽然当时引得王后哈哈大笑，但是王后很快就变得出离愤怒，并且打算马上把他送出宫去，当时还是我好心地为他求情才幸免于难。那一天王后的盘子里有一根骨头，王后把骨髓敲出来之后，就把骨头放回到盘子里去。目睹了这一切的侏儒恰好看到格兰姆达尔克里奇去了餐具架，于是就趁机爬到了属于我的小保姆的位置，双手把我抓了起来，然后把我的双脚并拢，朝着骨头里面用力塞，一直塞到了我的腰部。我卡在那儿半天也不能动弹，样子十分可笑。直到大约一分钟之后，我的这副凄惨模样才被人发现，当时的我觉得因为这样的事情大吼大叫有失体面，所以我选择忍受。幸好王后的食物不是很烫，我的腿才得以保住，只是损失了我的袜子和裤子而已。我想如果不是我给他求情的话，当时他要受到的惩罚就不止一顿鞭子了。

王后经常嘲笑我胆子小，她还问我是否我的同胞们也和我一般胆小懦弱。当时的情形是这样的，到了夏天的时候，这儿的苍蝇就会四处飞窜。这些可恶的家伙在我看来，就和邓斯特堡的夜莺一般大小。每次我吃晚饭的时候，它们就会在我耳边嗡嗡嗡地飞来飞去，吵得我不得安宁。有的时候苍蝇们还会在我的食物上产卵，这样的景象当地人是看不到的，因为他们无法察觉到如此微小的细节，但是相比起来我却感官敏锐，所以我的眼睛能够看到这一切。有的时候这些苍蝇甚至会落在我的鼻子和额头上，狠狠叮咬一口，简直太恶心了。最让我印象深刻的就是它们身上的那种黏稠的物质，正是依靠这种物质的黏性，它们才得以倒立在天花板上。为了避开这些恼人的恶心家伙，我伤透了脑筋，因为我完全不想和它们在一起。每当苍蝇扑到我的脸上的时候，我都会被吓一跳。那个可恶的侏儒就经常抓苍蝇来戏弄我。他就像个淘气的小学生一样，手里抓着一把苍蝇，凑到我的鼻子边上然后一下子松开手，这样苍蝇就全部朝着我的脸飞过来。他总是试图以这样的办法来吓唬我，希望能够赢得王后的欢心。而我反抗的办法就是抽出腰刀，趁着那些苍蝇在四处乱飞的时候乱砍一顿。我敏捷的身手时常赢得大伙的赞叹。

我还记得有一天早晨，格兰姆达尔克里奇和往常一样把我容身的箱子拿到窗户边上去通风（我不敢冒险让她像英国人挂鸟笼一样把我挂在窗户外面）。当时我正拉起窗户，坐在窗边享用我的早餐——一块甜饼，没想到这时候有二十多只黄蜂闻到了甜饼的香味，一下子飞到了我的屋子里。它们的翅膀震动的声音比二十多支风笛齐声作响的声音还要响亮。其中好几只黄蜂甚至飞到了我的甜饼上，还叼走了好多块甜饼，而其余的黄蜂就在我的脑袋边上环绕飞翔着，把我弄得头昏脑涨。与此同时我也十分担心它们会伤害我。

幸好当时的我鼓起勇气，拔出了腰刀冲着它们挥舞。很快就有四只黄蜂的尸体落在了地上，其余的黄蜂也就飞走了。我赶紧把窗户关了起来。这些黄蜂差不多有我们的鹧鸪那么大，尾针有一英寸半那么长。我小心翼翼地把蜂刺收集起来，后来我曾在欧洲几个地方把这些尾针和其他稀奇古怪的东西展示给别人看。回到英国之后，我把其中三根捐赠给了格雷萨姆学院，另外一根留给了自己。

第四章

作者描述了这个国家的情形，并且提出修改现代地图的建议。作者随后又描述了国王的宫殿和这个国家首都的情况。除此之外还有对旅行和神庙的描述。

我曾经在首都罗布鲁格路德方圆两千英里的地方旅行过，所以我觉得有必要对我这一路的旅行见闻做一个简要的解说。我虽然常伴王后身边，但是王后在陪着国王出行的时候是绝对不会离开两千英里这个范围的。如果国王去了边境，那么王后就会在原地等待，这无疑影响了我的行动范围。这位国王的领土大约有六千英里长，三千到五千英里宽。所以我认为，欧洲的地理学家所认为的在加利福尼亚和日本之间只是一片汪洋的说法是荒谬的。我认为一定有一块和鞑靼大陆相对应的巨大陆地的存在，这样地球才能保持平衡。他们应该纠正他们的地图和海图的错误，在美洲的西北部画上一片广袤的大陆。如果他们需要的话，我愿意提供帮助。

这个王国确切地说是一个半岛，其东北边境有一条三十英里高的山脉，由于山顶有火山，所以难以跨越。这儿的居民也不清楚这座山的对面到底住着些什么人，或者有没有人居住。王国的其他三面都临海，但是没有一个海港，所有的河流入海的区域都布满锋利的礁石，而且海浪汹涌，没有人敢驾驶船只出海冒险，因此这里的人与外界没有任何往来。但是这个王国里有好几条宽阔的河流，盛产各种美味的鲜鱼。当地居民很少食用海鱼，因为这儿的海鱼的大小和欧洲常见的海鱼没有什么区别，所以在他们眼里也就根本不值得捕捞了。最令人感到惊讶的是，只有这一片土地上才能出产如此庞大的动物和植物，而到底为什么会这样，只能留给哲学家来解释了。当然偶尔也会有鲸鱼搁浅，这时候当地人就会把鲸鱼捉回来饱餐一顿。我也见过这种鲸鱼，的确算是庞然大物，一个人根本就没法扛起来。有的时候他们会把鲸鱼当成稀罕物，然后装箱送到这个国家的首都。有一次国王的宴会上就出现了这样一条鲸鱼，不得不说这是十分罕见的菜肴。但是国王仿佛并不是很喜欢，我想可能是因为鲸鱼的个头太大了吧，虽然我曾在格陵兰岛见过更大的鲸鱼。

这个国家人口稠密，一共有五十一座大城市和接近一百座有城墙的小镇，还有许许多多的村庄。为了满足读者的好奇心，我还是描述一下罗布鲁格路德。整座城市倚河而建，有一条巨大的河流从城市中穿过，将城市分成大致相同的两半。整座城市里大约有八万户人家，约有六十万人口。整座都城长约三个"格隆姆格伦"（大约有五十四英里），宽度则有两个半"格隆姆格伦"，这是我按照御制的地图来测量的，当时他们还特意把地图平铺在地上。整张地图有大约一百英尺那么长，我赤脚在地图上测量了好多次直径和周长，而且严格按照比例尺计算，所以我想这样的结果应该是可信的。

国王的皇宫占地大约七平方英里，外观不规则，但是满满的都是房屋。皇宫的主宫殿有两百四十英尺那么高，宽度和长度也都与之相称。国王曾经赐予我和我的小保姆格兰姆达尔克里奇一辆马车，她的女教师时常带她出去游玩或者去商店。每次我都在自己的箱子里，由我的小保姆紧紧抱在怀里。在我的请求之下，她也曾把我拿出来放在手心，这样我就能更好地观察沿街的建筑和居民了。我估计这儿的马车差不多和我们的威斯敏斯特大厅一般大，虽然看上去并没有那么高，不过这一点我也不是很确定。有一次，女教师吩咐车夫在几家店铺门口停了下来，因为她想要进去逛逛。周围的乞丐瞅准机会围了过来，这让我看到一幕在欧洲从没见过的可怕场景。有个女人的乳房上长了肿瘤，肿得很大，上面全是溃烂发炎的窟窿，其中有好几处能够轻松容纳我整个人。还有个家伙的脖子上长了一个巨大的瘤，差不多有五个装羊毛的包裹那么大。还有一个人装着一副木头做的假腿，每一条差不多有二十英尺长。但是最让人感到恶心的还是他们衣服上横行的虱子。我可以清清楚楚地看到它们的腿，这比我在欧洲时用显微镜看得还要清晰。这些吸血的家伙的嘴就像野猪一般，看上去十分丑陋。这是我第一次清楚地看到虱子，如果当时我身边有合适的工具的话，我一定会仔细解剖一只，以满足我的好奇心。但是我自己的解剖器械全都留在了船上，而且眼前的一幕也让我感到十分恶心。

除了我平时居住的大木箱子，王后还特别下令为我打造了一个稍稍小一些的木箱，大约有十二英尺见方，十英尺那么高，作为我出行时的移动住所，毕竟之前的那个大木箱子太大了，格兰姆达尔克里奇携带的时候很不方便，而且放在马车里也显得十分拥挤。这个箱子也是同一个木匠打造出来的，当然我全程在边上指导。这个箱子是正方形的，其中三面墙上各有一扇窗户。为了防止旅途中出现什么意外，窗户外面还特意加装了铁制的栅栏。第四面墙上没有窗户，只有两个粗壮的铁环。当我想要骑马的时候，人们就会在两个铁环中间穿进一根皮带，然后把皮带捆在腰上，这样箱子就能够牢牢固定了。当我打算陪着国王或者王后出巡，或者是游览花园，或者是去拜访那些达官贵人的时候，如果格兰姆达尔克里奇恰好有事没法陪伴，他们就会把我交给一位我可以信赖的老仆人。很快我就得到了那些贵人的赏识，当然我很清楚这是因为我赢得了国王和王后的钟爱，并非我个人的才干。在旅途中如果我在马车里感觉到疲累了，那位仆人就会把我所在的箱子在他身上扣好，然后放在他面前的垫子上。这样一来透过箱子里的三扇窗户，我就可以自由地欣赏沿途的风景。我的这个小房间里有一张行军床和一张吊床，以及两把椅子和一张桌子，所有的家具都是用螺丝固定在地板上，这样一来哪怕马车颠簸得再厉害，床和桌子都可以保持原位了。因为我早已习惯了海上的生活，所以哪怕有的时候马车摇晃得十分厉害，我都可以在箱子里坦然自若。

无论何时，只要我想去看看城里的风光，我就一定会坐在这个旅行用的小箱子里面。格兰姆达尔克里奇会把这个箱子抱在怀里，而她本人则坐在类似我们国家的敞篷轿子里面，由四个人抬着，后边还要跟着王后的两位侍女。镇子上的人经常听说我的事情，所以当他们看到格兰姆达尔克里奇的轿子的时候，就会跑上来围观。而彬彬有礼的小姑娘就会请轿夫停下，然后把我从箱子里拿出来捧在手心，让大伙看个清楚。

我一直对这个国家的神庙十分感兴趣，因为这座神庙有国内最高的钟楼，所以我一直很向往。我的小保姆后来终于带我去了，不过说实话看完之后的我感到十分失望，因为这号称是最高的钟楼不过才距离地面三千英尺。考虑到当地人和欧洲人的身高差异，按照比例计算还不如索尔兹伯里教堂的尖顶高（如果我没有记错的话）。不过出于对这个国家的尊敬，我并不想破坏它的声誉。虽然它可能并不算是高耸入云，但是建造得美丽而坚固，足以为整座钟楼增色不少。钟楼的墙壁差不多有一百英尺厚，由每块约四十英尺见方的石头砌成，墙壁的四周供奉着许多神像和帝王像。所有的雕像都是用大理石打造的，而且要比真人高出不少。我还发现有一个雕像的手指掉了下来，跌落在垃圾堆里面。我捡起来看了看，发现这手指差不多有四英尺一英寸长。格兰姆达尔克里奇发现了之后就赶紧用手帕包好放在口袋里，然后带回去和她收藏的那些小玩意放在一起，这也是这个年龄段的小姑娘常玩的游戏。

国王的厨房也十分雄奇。整个厨房呈拱形，高达六百英尺。厨房里的那个巨大的炉灶和圣保罗教堂的圆顶差不多大，可能只小了十几步。之所以那么精确，是因为我回国之后曾经亲自去丈量过圣保罗大教堂的宽度。如果我详细描述厨房里的炉子、铁锅和水壶、烤肉架上的烤肉和其他东西的话，也许会让人感到匪夷所思，甚至会招致某些吹毛求疵的批评家的质疑，认为我夸大其词。虽然这是许多旅行者的惯有经历，但是为了避免陷入另外一个极端，比如这本书被翻译成布罗丁格奈格的语言（这是当地人的说法）然后流传回这个国家的话，国王和这儿的百姓肯定会抗议我的描写太过于枯燥，进而抱怨我的描述是对他们的一种侮辱。

国王陛下在马厩里养的骏马很少超过六百匹。他的骏马一般都有五十四到六十英尺那么高。但是每当他在节日出巡的时候，就会带上五百名骑士组成的卫队以彰显他的威仪。当时的我认为那就是我见过的最为宏伟壮观的场面了。但是之后我又见过他的陆军演习，那场面就显得更加宏伟了。关于陆军演习的场面，以后有机会我再告诉你们。

第五章

作者描述了好几次冒险经历。他观看了处死罪犯的场景，并且表演了自己的航海技术。

我原本应该在这个国家过着快乐的生活，但是我的身形渺小，这也惹出了好几件滑稽而又麻烦的事情，现在就给读者们讲几件。我的小保姆格兰姆达尔克里奇经常把我放在小箱子里面，然后带着我去花园里玩耍。有的时候她还会把我捧在手心里，或者是把我放在地上让我随便溜达。我记得其中一次，当那个侏儒还没有被流放出宫的时候，他就悄悄地尾随我来到了花园。当时我们俩就站在一棵苹果树下边，调皮的我开了好几个玩笑，暗示这几棵低矮的苹果树和侏儒有某种相似之处。恰好在当地的语言里就有些相似之处，所以我的俏皮话自然引得侏儒愤怒。当我走到苹果树下边的时候，这个坏家伙趁机摇晃起我头顶的苹果树来，结果就有那么十几个苹果砸了下来。对我来说，这苹果就像布里斯托尔的酒桶一样大。当我弯腰躲避的时候，恰好有一颗苹果砸在我的腰上，一下子把我砸倒在地，摔了一个狗啃泥。幸好我只是受了一点轻伤，再加上是我挑起的事端，所以我请求王后能够宽恕他。幸好仁慈的王后并没有追究他的责任。

还有一天，格兰姆达尔克里奇把我一个人留在一块光滑的草地上，而她则和她的家庭女教师一起去稍远一些的地方散步去了。但是就在这时候突然下起了一阵凶猛的冰雹，一下子就把我打倒在地。趴在地上的我被一个个冰雹狠狠地砸中，那感觉就好像被许多的网球给击中一样。不过我还是用尽全力朝前方爬去，

苹果就这么砸了下来

脸朝下躲在了柠檬百里香花坛的背风一侧，躲过了这一劫。但是我全身上下都是伤，趴在床上整整十天都没有下床。这一切也没有什么值得大惊小怪的，毕竟这个国家发生的每一件事情都遵从同样的自然规律。这儿的冰雹的大小差不多是欧洲的冰雹的一千八百倍。之所以如此肯定，是因为好奇的我曾经测量过冰雹的尺寸。

在这个花园里我也碰上过更加危险的事情。有一次我的小保姆嫌那个箱子太麻烦，就没有带上箱子。她把我放在了一个她自以为安全的地方（我经常请求她这么做，因为这样一来我就可以沉浸在漫长的思考之中），然后就和她的家庭女教师以及其他几位女伴一起去了别的地方。当她离开之后，花园总管养的一条长毛小白狗不知道怎么回事闯进了这片花园，并且恰好跑到了我边上觅食。当它嗅到了我的味道之后，就径直冲着我的位置跑来，然后一口把我叼在嘴里，跑回它的主人身前，然后轻轻把我放在地上。幸运的是这条狗受过很好的训练，所以在它的嘴里的我安然无恙，连衣服都没有一点损坏。但是可怜的园丁却被吓坏了，因为我俩很熟悉，而且关系也不错。他温和地用双手捧着我，询问我有没有事情。不过当时的我被吓坏了，一句话都说不出。几分钟之后我回过神来，就被他送回到我的小保姆的身边。这时候我的小保姆已经回到了原先把我扔下的地方，看到我不见踪影的她已经急得团团转了。她狠狠训斥了一顿园丁，但是整件事情并没有声张，那些贵族们也都不知道，因为小保姆也很担心王后会因此迁怒于她。而且在我看来，这样不光彩的经历也没有必要大肆宣扬。

这一次的意外坚定了格兰姆达尔克里奇不让我离开她的视线的决心。而我很早以前就开始担心她会这样，所以先前几次独处时候的不幸的冒险我都没有告诉她。有一次一只鸢突然冲着我俯冲而来，要不是我当机立断地拔出腰刀跑到一个繁茂的树丛下边，没准就已经被它抓走了。还有一次我不小心走在一个刚挖出来的鼹鼠洞上面，结果一下子栽了进去，直接没过了我的脖子，我只好找了个借口解释我弄脏的衣服。还有一次则是我一边散步一边怀念可怜的英国的时候，不小心被一个蜗牛壳绊倒在地，把我的右小腿给摔伤了。

有一件事情我不知道到底应该感到欣慰还是恼怒，当我独自散步的时候，那些小鸟看上去一点都不害怕我，它们总是会在距离我不到一码的地方寻找毛虫或者是别的什么食物吃，就好像我根本不存在一样。我记得很清楚，有一次一只画眉竟敢把我手里的一块饼干抢走，那是格兰姆达尔克里奇为我准备的早饭。当我试图抓住它们的时候，总是会遭受它们的反抗，有的时候它们会啄我的手，几次三番之后，我就不敢伸手了，而它们也可以继续寻找食物。有一次我用一根粗重的棍子狠狠打中了一只红雀，然后提着它的脖子跑去见我的小保姆。但是这只小鸟不过是被打晕了，当它恢复知觉之后就扑扇着翅膀击打我的脑袋和身体。虽然当时的我伸直了手臂，防止它用爪子来挠我，但是我已经动了放它走的念头。幸好这时候一个仆人上前拧断了鸟脖子。第二天这只鸟就成了我的晚饭。这只红雀似乎要比英国的天鹅还要大一些。

侍女们时常邀请格兰姆达尔克里奇到她们的住所去玩，同时也要求小保姆能够带上我，这样就有机会见见我，摸摸我。她们经常把我脱个精光，让我躺在她们的胸脯上。说实在的我真的不想多谈这些事儿，因为她们的皮肤总是散发着一种难闻的臭味。当然我并不是想要诋毁这些姑娘，毕竟我总是对她们怀着一种尊敬之情。但是有一点是很明白的，那就是我的感官要比她们敏锐很多，所以其实这些姑娘就像英国的姑娘一样，在她们的情人的眼里同样是完美无缺的。不管怎么说，她们本身的体味我还是能够忍受的，可一闻到她们的香水我马上就要晕过去了。我记得很清楚，有一次我在利立浦特的一个暖和的天气里运动完毕之后，就有一位朋友直言我身上的味道十分刺鼻，虽然我和英国的大部分男同胞们一样都不曾有过这样的问题。现在回想起来，利立浦特的居民对我的味道的敏感程度就像我对于这儿的居民的体味的敏感程度一样。所以我必须要为深受我敬爱的王后以及我的小保姆格兰姆达尔克里奇说一句公道话，她们和英国的姑娘们一样甜美可人。

最让我感到坐立不安的是当她们带我去屋里玩耍的时候，完全不把我放在眼里，根本就不在意什么礼节问题。她们经常把我放在梳妆台上，当着我的面脱下所有的衣服，然后再换上衬衫。说实话，看到她们的裸体，我没有一点别的情绪，除了恐惧和恶心。在我的眼里，她们的皮肤粗糙不堪、凹凸不平，而且颜色还不均匀。如果我凑近一些，就会发现她们的皮肤上还有许多黑痣，大小就和我们切面包时用的垫板差不多大，而且那些黑痣上长出的毛发也有我们的绳索那么粗。至于她们身体的其他部位，我在这儿就不一一赘述了。她们也从来不忌讳在我面前小便，每次她们都会排出大约我们两个葡萄酒的酒桶的量。在这些女仆中最漂亮的一位只有十六岁，她经常会想出一些新花样，比如让我在她的乳头上劈叉之类的。希望读者能够原谅我讲得那么直白。这些把戏让我十分不开心，所以之后我就让格兰姆达尔克里奇找了个借口，再也不去拜访这位姑娘了。

有一天，一位年轻的绅士，也是小保姆的女教师的外甥来到了这儿，邀请她们去参观行刑的场面。罪犯谋杀的就是这位绅士的一位好朋友。格兰姆达尔克里奇是一个性格温和的姑娘，原本不想去看这样的场面，但是架不住盛情邀请，就同意和女教师一起去了。至于我，虽然打心眼里讨厌这样的场景，但是在好奇心的驱动下我还是和他们一起去看了。我一直觉得这样的场景会是非同一般的。在行刑场上，罪犯被绑在一张凳子上。用来行刑的大刀长达四十英尺，一刀下去就是人头落地，鲜血一下子喷涌了出来，哪怕是凡尔赛宫前边的喷泉也没有这般威势。人头落地的时候伴随着一声巨响，哪怕是在半英里之外，都能够吓我一跳。

王后很喜欢听我讲航海的事情，每当我感觉到郁郁寡欢的时候，她就会询问我一些有关航海的问题，比如我会不会扬帆，会不会划桨，这份行当会不会对我的身体有好处。我告诉她这两份工作我都很擅长，虽然我只是船上的外科医生，但是有必要的话我也能够充当船上的水手。不过我并没觉得我能够在这个国家展现我的技艺，因为这儿的一切东西都太大了，哪怕是最小的舢板也有我们国家的军舰那么大。能够让我驾驭的小船是不可能在他们的河流里出现的。王后陛下说，如果我能够提出设计方案，那么她手下的木匠就一定能够做出这么一艘船，让我可以好好享受一下划船的乐趣。这位木匠的确是一位技艺精湛的家伙，在我的指导之下，他只花费了十天时间就造出了一艘功能齐备的游艇，足以容纳整整八个欧洲人。这艘船完成之后，王后十分开心，并用自己的衣服兜着这艘船，跑去给国王看。国王下令把蓄水池蓄满水，然后让我进去展现一下身手。但实际上这个蓄水池太小了，根本没法让我划动手里的那两把短桨。幸好王后早已想到了这一点，她命令木匠打造一个长达三百英尺、宽约五十英尺、深度八英尺的水槽，再在上面涂上一层防水的沥青，然后把水槽放在皇宫外殿。在水槽底部有一个开关，专门负责更换水槽里的水，只需要两个仆人在边上忙活半个小时就可以把水槽灌满水。我经常在这个水槽上划船解闷，顺便也能给那些贵妇人一点乐子。我的技术不错，所以他们总能看得兴致勃勃。有的时候我还会把小船的船帆挂起来，一群妇人在边上用扇子扇风，帮助我的小船前进，而我只需要操控一下船舵就可以了。当那些贵妇人玩累了之后，就换内侍们用嘴吹气，而我就可以在船上大展身手。每次表演结束之后，格兰姆达尔克里奇都会把我的小船拿到她的房间里，挂在钉子上晾干。

但是我也曾经发生过意外，那一次差点就要了我的命。当时内侍正忙着把我的船放进水槽里，这时候格兰姆达尔克里奇的女教师多管闲事，她要把我举起来放在船上，可是我竟然从她的手指中间滑落了。幸好当时的我被她胸前的别针挡住了，不然的话等待我的就是从四十英尺高的空中跌落到空地。那枚胸针从我的衬衣和裤腰中间穿过，然后我就悬挂在了空中，幸好格兰姆达尔克里奇冲过来救下了我。

还有一次，负责每三天为我的木头水槽补水的内侍一不小心把一只硕大的青蛙倒进了水槽，结果那只青蛙就一直蛰伏在水槽下边。当我过几天去划船的时候，它觉得我的船是一个适合休息的地方，于是一下子就蹦了上来。结果我的船被它弄得晃动不休，我也不得不跑到小船的另外一头，拼命保持船体的平衡。这只青蛙一蹦就有大约半条船的距离，它时不时在我的脑袋上蹦跳，把我弄得浑身上下都沾满了恶心的黏液。这肥硕的动物简直就是世界上最为丑陋的存在了。不过我让格兰姆达尔克里奇不要插手，由我一个人来对付它。我挥舞木桨朝着青蛙一阵劈头盖脸地猛打，这才把它赶下了船。

但是我在这个国家面临的最大的危险却是来自于一只猴子，它是厨房的一位管理员的宠物。格兰姆达尔克里奇那天恰好有事外出，就把我锁在屋子里。那一天天气不错，所以我把所有的窗户都打开了。正当我坐在桌子旁边陷入沉思的时候，突然听到了有什么东西从宫殿的窗户闯入的声音，然后就听到这东西从房间这边跳到另外一边。惊恐万分的我鼓起勇气把脑袋探出窗外，发现了这只顽皮的猴子正在房间里上蹿下跳。最后它走到了我所在的木头箱子的边上，流露出一丝惊喜。它从箱子的各个角度朝里面张望，但是当时的我被这突如其来的猴子给吓呆了，并没有选择钻到床底下，而是退缩到屋子里最偏远的角落，所以很轻易就被发现了。这猴子龇牙咧嘴地叫了半天，然后伸进来一只爪子，就像猫抓老鼠一般逗弄了我一会儿。虽然我尽力躲闪，但最后还是被他抓住了衣服下摆，把我拽了出去。它用右前爪把我抓起来抱在怀里，就像护士照顾新生的婴儿一样，这和我在欧洲看到的大猴子怀抱小猴子的方式一模一样。我每每挣扎，它就把我抱得越紧，所以我觉得我还是顺从它比较好。

我有理由相信，它把我当成了一只小猴子，因为它很温柔地用另外一只爪子抚摸着我的脸。但是这样的举动很快就被门口传来的响动给打断了，应该是有人推门进来的声音。听到响声的猴子飞快地沿着来时的窗户跳了上去，然后沿着水管爬到了旁边的屋顶上。只见它用三只脚前进，剩下来的一只就紧紧抓着我。猴子把我抱出去的那瞬间，我听到了格兰姆达尔克里奇发出的一声尖叫。可怜的姑娘被吓坏了，很快整个皇宫都知道我被猴子给俘虏了，那些仆人们匆忙去找梯子，整整几百个人看到那只猴子坐在屋顶上，一只前爪像抱孩子一样搂着我，另外一只爪子忙着给我喂东西吃。它从自己的嗉囊里面挤出食物喂给我，而我闭着嘴坚决不吃，所以它只好用前爪轻轻拍打我，惹得下面的一帮人哈哈大笑。关于这一点我丝毫没有责怪他们的意思，因为这样的场景除了我本人，谁看到了都会觉得滑稽可笑。有好几个人想要往上扔石头，希望能把猴子给赶下来，但是很

格列佛和青蛙进行了激烈的搏斗

快就被禁止了，要不然我的脑袋都可能被砸烂。

梯子终于被安置好了，好几个人爬上了屋顶。猴子发现自己被包围了，它意识到三条腿是不可能逃脱的，于是它就把我扔在了屋顶的一块瓦片上面，然后自己逃跑了。而我就一个人坐在距离地面五百码的地方，冒着随时被风吹下屋檐的危险，也冒着因为头晕目眩而滚落房檐的危险。这时候我的小保姆的一个诚实的跟班爬了上来，把我塞进裤袋里，然后安全地把我带回了地面。

我几乎要被猴子强塞给我的那些食物噎死了，幸好我亲爱的小保姆小心翼翼地用一根缝衣针帮我掏了出来。我吐了几个小时之后，这才感觉缓过了一口气。猴子把我抓得生疼，再加上受到了惊吓，所以我一直在床上休养了半个月时间。国王、王后和其他人纷纷前来探望。那只猴子自然也被杀掉了，而且国王还颁布了新的命令，禁止皇宫里饲养猴子这种动物。

身体恢复后，我马上去朝见国王，感谢他对我的宠爱。这件事使他很开心，他好好地开了我一顿玩笑。他问我，躺在猴子怀里时有何感想？愿不愿意吃猴子给我的食物？它喂我吃东西的方式我觉得怎么样？屋顶的新鲜空气是不是很开胃？他还想知道，要是在我的祖国碰到这样的事，我会怎样？我告诉国王，我们欧洲没有猴子，有的都是从别的地方当稀罕东西运到那儿去的，而且都很小，如果它们敢向我进攻，我可以同时对付十二只。至于我最近碰到的那只可怕的畜生（它实际有一头象那么大），如果不是我当时吓坏了，没有想到在它把爪子伸进我房里来时，用我的腰刀狠狠地给它一下将其砍伤（说这话时我手按刀柄，样子十分凶狠），也许它那爪子都没时间缩回去，更不要说伸进来了。我说这番话时口气十分坚定，就像一个人唯恐别人对他的勇气有怀疑似的。可是我的话只引来哄堂大笑，就连陛下周围那些理应毕恭毕敬的人，也都忍不住大笑起来。这就使我想到，一个人身处根本无法与之相提并论也无法与之比较的人中间竟还企图死要面子，真是白费力气。可自从我回到英国后，像我这种行为的人还真不少见。就有那么一个卑鄙的小人，没有高贵的出身，没有丰采，缺少才智，连常识也不具备，却居然敢自高自大，想跟王国内最了不起的人物相提并论。

我每天都要给宫里的人提供几个笑话，格兰姆达尔克里奇虽然很喜欢我，但是如果我做了什么傻事，她也会马上报告给王后，以便讨王后的欢心。有一次小姑娘不太舒服，她的女教师就带着我们去三十英里以外的地方去散步，大概需要一个小时的路程。到了地儿之后她们就跳下了马车，漫步在乡间小路上。格兰姆达尔克里奇把我的小木箱给拿了下来，然后让我也出来透透气。路旁恰好有一堆牛粪，我想试试能不能跳过去。但不幸的是我过早起跳了，于是我就跳进了牛粪，膝盖以下的部分全部被淹没了。当我浑身脏兮兮的从牛粪里爬出来之后，其中有一个跟班赶紧上前用手帕把我擦干净，随后我的小保姆就把我锁在了箱子里，直到回去之后才把我放出来。当然王后很快就知道了我的丢人的事情，那些仆人也在皇宫里大肆宣扬，接下来的几天他们都拿这件事情来取笑我。

第六章

作者讲述了讨好国王和王后的几种办法，表现了自己在音乐上的才能。国王询问了他有关英国的情况，作者一一做了解答。国王也提出了自己的看法。

每个星期我都有一两次机会参加国王的朝会，经常看到理发师在给他剃胡子，我敢说第一次看到这般场景的人一定会被吓坏的，因为那剃刀差不多有我们的镰刀的两倍长。

这个国家的风俗习惯是，每个星期只刮两次胡子。有一次我说服理发师，请他把刮胡子用的肥皂泡沫送我一些，而我从泡沫中挑选了四五十根最粗壮的胡子茬。随后我找了一块好木头，削成了梳子背的模样，然后向格兰姆达尔克里奇要了一根最小的缝衣针。我在梳子背上钻出了许多小孔，然后把那些胡茬装了进去，再用小刀修理了一下，这样就完成了一把很不错的梳子，因为我原本的梳子的梳齿都断得差不多了。我很清楚，这个地方是不会有手艺如此精巧的工匠，能够做出像我原来那把一般大小的梳子的。

这让我想起了另外一件好玩的事情，那是我打发闲暇时光的一件好事情。我让王后的侍女帮我收集了不少王后梳头时掉下来的头发，并且收集在一起。随后我和我的木匠朋友商量了一下。在我的指导之下，他做成了两把和我的箱子里的几把椅子差不多大小的框架。我让他在原本是椅背和椅面的地方钻了许多的小孔，然后挑选了王后最粗壮的头发，像英国人编织藤椅一般做成了这把椅子。随后我就把这个玩意当作礼物送给了王后。她收下了这份礼物，并且时常拿出来给别人观赏，所有见到这把椅子的人都叹为观止。王后曾经要求我坐在椅子上，但是我拒绝了，因为我说，我宁可死也不想把自己的身体放到那些珍贵的头发上去，因为它们曾经为王后增添光彩。由于我在机械设计等方面的才能，我还用这些头发做了一只差不多有五英尺那么长的精美的小钱包，并且用金线绣上了王后的名字。在征得王后的同意之后，我把这个钱包送给了格兰姆达尔克里奇。说实话，这个钱包只是个好看的玩意，因为它根本无法容纳哪怕一枚大硬币，所以除了小姑娘的一些小玩具，其他就什么都不能装了。

国王十分喜欢音乐，也时常在宫里举办音乐会。他们有的时候也会带上我，把我安排在箱子里面，聆听演奏。但是音乐会的声音太响亮了，我简直没法分辨出其中的旋律。我敢说，就算英国的皇家乐队的乐器一齐在你耳边奏响，声音也不会比这儿的大。通常我都会让人把我的箱子搬到很远的地方，然后关上门窗放下窗帘，这才能欣赏他们的音乐。

年轻时代的我也曾学过一点钢琴。在格兰姆达尔克里奇的房间里就有一架钢琴，每周都会有一位教师教授她两次。我之所以这么称呼，是因为这件乐器和我们的钢琴的样子差不多，而且弹奏方法也是一样的。有一次我异想天开地想要给国王和王后表演一曲，但是这很难，因为这架钢琴有接近六十英尺那么长，每一个琴键都有大约一英尺那么长。就算我双臂平伸，也只能够得着五个琴键，而且弹奏的时候还得用尽力气砸下去。这样就很费力，而且效果也不好。后来我想到了一个办法，准备了两根圆棍，其中一头用老鼠皮包裹起来，这样我在敲击的时候就不会敲坏钢琴，也不影响演奏了。我在钢琴前边放了一条长凳，只比键盘低大约四英尺。他们把我放在凳子上，这样我就可以在凳子上跑来跑去，然后用手里的两根棍子演奏了。我努力表演了一首圆舞曲，赢得了国王和王后的赞赏，不过我发誓这是我这辈子干过的最累的活计了。但是就算这样我也只能敲击其中十六个琴键，而且还不能区分低音和高音，这无疑给我的表演带来了瑕疵。

之前我已经提到，这位国王拥有极好的理解能力。他时常命人把我连同箱子搬到他的房间去，放在桌子上，然后命令我从箱子里搬出一把椅子，在顶端放好，这样我和他的脸就几乎在一个水平线上了。我们就用这样的方式交谈了好几次。有一次我很大胆地对他说，我认为他对欧洲和这个世界的其他地方的那种鄙夷的态度与他的智力不太相符。人的智力并不完全取决于身高，恰恰相反，在我们国家，身材最高大的才是最缺乏才智的。而蜜蜂和蚂蚁相比其他体型更大的动物，更加具备勤劳和聪明的名气。所以，虽然他把我看得微不足道，我倒还希望有生之年能为他做几件了不起的事情，让他看看。国王仔细地听我说着，渐渐开始比以前对我更有好感。他要我尽可能详细地给他说说关于英国政府的情况，因为虽然君王们一般都喜欢他们自己的制度（他从我以前的谈话中推想，别的君主也都是这样的），要是有什么值得效法的，却也乐意听听。

可以想象一下，亲爱的读者，当时的我是多么希望自己有德摩西尼或者西塞罗的口才啊，这样一来我就可以用最恰如其分的描述来形容我那亲爱的祖国。

我先告诉这位国王，我们的国家由两座小岛组成，上边有三个王国，共同隶属于一位君主，这位君主同时也掌管着美洲的殖民地。我描述了好些有关我国那肥沃的土壤和温和的气候的信息，然后我又介绍了英国的议会。议会中最为著名的团体就是上议院，其中的成员都是血统最为高贵，掌握最古老也是最富足产业的家伙。我还介绍说，他们从出生开始就接受特殊的教育，因为他们生来就是担任国王或者参议的，能够帮助这个国家，能够成为合理处理每一次上诉的法官，能够充当捍卫君主和国家的最强大的战士。他们是帝国的荣耀，是他们的好祖先的好后代。他们的祖先由于种种美德而享有盛名，而他们的后代也会永远兴旺。除了这些人，上议院中还有一些神职人员，他们专门负责管理宗教事务，向人民宣传教义。这些人是由国王和参议从全国范围内挑选出来的品德最高尚、学识最渊博的教士，作为教士和人民的精神领袖。

议会的另一部分叫下议院，议员都是些重要的绅士，由人民民主选举产生。这些人才能卓越，爱国心强，能够代表全民的智慧。这两院人士组成了欧洲最严正的议会，整个立法机关就交由他们和君主一起掌管。

我把话题又转向了法庭，法官们都是些可敬的德高望重而又通晓法律的人，他们主持审判，对人们的权利及财产纠纷做出判决，同时惩恶扬善，保护弱小。我还提到了我国节俭的财政管理制度，提到了我国海陆军队的勇武与战绩。我先估算一下我们每个教会或政党拥有几百万人，然后再统算出我国的总人口是多少。我甚至提到了我们的体育和娱乐以及每一件我认为能为我国增光的琐碎的事。最后我对英国近百年来的主要事件作了一番简要的历史的叙述。

这一番描述足足花费了我五次觐见机会才讲完，每次我都要讲上好几个小时。国王饶有兴趣地聆听着，时不时还会把我说的内容给记下来，同时他也把准备好的问题一并写下来。

当我结束对英国的长篇大论的描述之后，国王陛下在他第六次召见我的时候翻看着自己的笔记本，然后提出了许多的疑问和反对意见。他问："你们是用什么办法来教育那些年轻贵族的呢？在他们最容易接受教育的时期，他们都在忙些什么？如果一位贵族没有后代的话，那要如何填补议会的空缺呢？议员需要满足什么资格和条件才能够胜任呢？如果是国王的心血来潮，或者是哪位贵族的贿赂，或者是出于党派利益的考虑而提拔一位新贵，这样的现象是否存在呢？那些负责裁决财务纠纷的贵族，他们对于法律法规又知道多少呢？他们是如何学习这个国家的法律法规的？难道他们从不贪婪、偏心、奢靡，从不接受贿赂，从来不搞阴谋诡计吗？还有那些神职人员，他们都是因为自己博学的见闻和高贵的生活品质而受到提拔的吗？当他们还是普通的教士的时候，难道就不曾趋炎附势？难道就不曾依附于贵族的门下？在当选入议会之后，他们难道就不会顺从于贵族的意志吗？"

随后他又想了解下议会的选举过程中有什么伎俩呢？如果一个腰缠万贯的外乡人鼓动选民投他的票，排挤当地的乡绅的话，有什么处理的办法呢？参选议员明显是一件劳民伤财的事情，而且也没有半点俸禄，为什么有那么多人不惜倾家荡产地去争取呢？听你的描述，大伙都很热情地为公共服务奉献自己，但那真的是出于热诚吗？他们会不会牺牲公共利益，屈从于那腐朽的君主和腐败的内阁的意志呢？他们会不会有什么办法来弥补自己在竞选过程中花费的金钱和精力呢？他提出了很多问题，并且表达了自己的质疑，而我在此就不再赘述了。

他还想了解一些有关法庭的情况，而我恰好对这一块比较熟悉，因为我曾经涉足一场几乎让我倾家荡产的审判。他问我："一般需要多少时间才能够做出判决，一般需要多少花费呢？如果案件审判存在明显的不公，那么辩护律师和原告有没有机会申诉呢？那些教派和政党会不会插手宣判呢？那些辩护律师是否受过教育呢？是否具备最基本的常识呢？他们是否了解国内所有地区的习俗呢？既然律师和法官可以解释司法条文，他们是否有机会参与法律起草呢？他们对某个案件的立场是否从一而终呢？是否会有援引完全矛盾的案例的尴尬时刻呢？他们到底是代表哪个阶层的呢？他们辩护的时候是否需要收取报酬？最重要的一点是，他们是否有参选下议院议员的资格呢？"

随后国王又质疑了我国的财政管理制度。他认为我的记忆力很差，因为据我的说法，英国的税收每年是五六百万，但是把提到的这个国家的各项开支统计一下，他就发现有时超支一倍还不止。这一点上他记的笔记非常具体详细，因为他说他本来倒是希望了解一下我们的做法或许对他是有用的，计算时不会被人欺蒙。但是，如果我对他说的是真的，他怎么也想不通，一个王国怎么也会像私人那样超支呢？他问我谁是我们的债权人，我们又上哪里去弄钱来还债。听我说到那些耗资巨大的大规模战争时，他非常吃惊，说我们一定是一个好争吵的民族，要不就是我们的四邻全是些坏人，而我们的将军肯定比我们的国王还有钱。他问，除了进行贸易、订立条约，或者出动舰队保卫海岸线，在我们自己岛国以外的地方还有我们什么事？最令他感到疑惑不解的是，他听我说起一个正处于和平时期的自由民族居然还要到国外去招募一支常备军。他说，既然领导、统治我们的是我们自己认可的代表，他真的难以想象我们还要怕谁，又要同谁去战斗。他说他愿意听听我的意见：一个人的家由他自己或者子女家人来保护，难道不比花费少许钱到街上胡乱找六七个流氓来保护要强得多吗？这些流氓要是把全家人都杀了，不就可以多赚一百倍的钱吗？

他嘲笑了我的计算方法，他觉得这样的说法很离奇，因为他很纳闷，为什么我们要强迫那些怀有不同意见的人改变主张，为什么不能让他们继续持有这样的主张？凡是强迫民众改变自己的观点的政府就都是专制。但是如果每个人都有权利表达对公众不利的消息，那么这样的政府就是软弱无能的。就好像每个人有权利私藏毒药，但是决不允许拿毒药当兴奋剂来四处兜售。

他还注意到，我们的贵族生活中很重要的娱乐方式是赌博。他很想知道，这种游戏大概是从什么年纪开始的，玩到什么时候才会住手。他们一般会在赌博上花费多少时间？会不会有人因为赌博而倾家荡产？会不会有人因为赌术高超而成为巨富？这样的人会不会控制那些贵族？而那些贵族会不会也去学习这种低劣、下流的伎俩？

当我简要叙述了这百年来我国发生的大事之后，国王显得十分惊讶。因为在他看来，这不过是充满了阴谋、叛乱、暗杀、屠杀、革命和流放，都是贪婪、党派斗争、虚荣、违背良心、残忍、愤怒、仇恨、淫乱、阴险和野心的最丑陋的结果罢了。

国王在他另一次召见我的时候又不厌其烦地将我所说的一切扼要地总结了一下。他把自己所提的问题与我的回答做了一番比较，接着把我拿到他手里，轻轻地摩挲着我，发表了这样一席话，这席话和他说话时的态度我永远也忘不了："我的小朋友格里尔特里格，你对你的祖国发表了一篇最为堂皇的颂词。你已十分清楚地证明：无知、懒散和腐化有时也许正是做一个立者所必备的唯一条件；那些有兴趣、有能力曲解、混淆和逃避法律的人，才能最好地解释、说明和应用法律。我想你们有几条规章制度原本还是可行的，可是那一半已被废除了，剩下的全被腐败所玷污。从你所说的一切来看，在你们那儿，获取任何职位似乎都不需要有一点道德，更不用说要有什么美德才能封爵了。教士地位升迁不是因为其虔诚或博学；军人晋级不是因为其品行或勇武；法官高升不是因为其廉洁公正；议会议员也不是因为其爱国，国家参政大臣也不是因为其智慧而分别得到升迁。至于你呢，"国王接着说，"你生命的大半时间一直在旅行，我很希望你到现在为止还未沾染上你那个国家的许多罪恶。但是，根据你自己的叙述以及我费了好大的劲才从你口里挤出的回答来看，我只能得出这样的结论：你的同胞中，大部分人是大自然从古到今容忍在地面上爬行的小小害虫中最有毒害的一类。"

第七章

作者表达了对祖国的爱。他向国王提了一项极为有利的建议，但是却遭到了拒绝。国王对政治几乎是一无所知。这个国家的学术范围十分小，作者随后又介绍了法律、军队和政党的相关情况。

出于对真理的追求和热爱，我把这段经历毫无保留地写了下来。当国王在讽刺英国的时候，哪怕我表现出愤慨或者不满，也是于事无补，因为这样的行为只会遭受他们的嘲笑。我不得不耐下性子，任凭他人嘲弄、侮辱和取笑我高贵的祖国，这样的场面真的让我十分难过。再加上这位国王的好奇心十分旺盛，事无巨细都要问个清清楚楚，如果我不交代清楚的话，那么就算是我忘恩负义了。所以在这儿我必须要坦白，在回答这些问题的时候我已经很注意避开一些问题了，而且我可以很负责任地讲，我回答的每一句话都比实际情况要美好很多。毕竟我生来就偏爱我的国家，而且这应该也算是一种美德。迪奥尼修斯就曾经告诫历史学家不要忘记这一点。所以我才不顾一切地掩盖我亲爱的祖国的各种制度缺陷和卑鄙肮脏的勾当，而选择宣扬她的美德。但是很不幸，在我和这位国王对话的过程中，这样的努力并没有成功。

但是我们有理由原谅这位国王，因为他与世隔绝，对于其他地方的风俗习惯也是一窍不通。他的观念都是由于无知而产生的偏见，而这样的偏见在欧洲的土壤是不可能出现的。如果我们坚定地把这样一位国王的观念当成全人类的是非标准，那么这也是不恰当的。

为了证明我的观点，证明在这样狭隘的观念下的教育成果，我可以再为大家讲述一小段插曲。当时为了获得国王的宠爱，我拿出了文明世界里的一项发明。当时我是这么描述这种威力极大的粉末的：哪怕只有一点点火星，也会瞬间把这种粉末引燃，哪怕这种粉末堆得如山一般高也是一样。这种点燃的粉末会爆发出如雷声一般的响声和冲击。如果把粉末装进铜管和铁管里面，那么粉末燃烧的时候就可以把铁管里的弹丸给打出去，其速度之快、威力之强，这世上没有任何东西能够阻挡。如果把这种发明应用到军事上，制造出最大的弹丸，可以很轻松地毁灭军队、夷平城池、击沉舰艇。哪怕轮船之间用铁链锁起，这种武器同样能够打断桅杆，毁灭舰队。我们时常把这种粉末装进空心大铁球，然后用机器把这种铁球发射到城池里边，摧毁城里的道路、房屋和军队。我对国王说，我对这种粉末的配方十分熟悉，可以指导他的手下制作这种粉末。按照两国之间的物件的尺寸比例，最大的武器不过一百英尺那么长。如果建造二三十根炮管，装入填着粉末的铁球，在几个小时之内就能够毁灭这个国家最为坚固的城池。如果城里有胆敢违背国王旨意的叛乱的话，那么只需要齐射几次，就足以毁灭整座城池。我就这样献出了我的计策，作为国王对我的恩典的回报。

国王对我描述的那些可怕的机器以及我提出的建议大为震惊。他很惊异，像我这么一只无能而卑贱的昆虫（这是他的说法），竟怀有如此非人道的念头，说起来还这么随随便便，似乎我对自己所描绘的那些毁灭性的机器所造成的流血和破坏丝毫无动于衷。他说，发明这种机器的人一定是一个恶魔，人类公敌。关于他本人，他坚决表示，虽然很少有什么东西能比艺术或自然界的新发现更使他感到愉快，但他还是宁可失去半壁河山，也不愿听到这样一件秘密。他严厉地告诫我，如果我还想保住一命，就不要再提这事了。

死板的教条和短浅的目光就产生了这么奇怪的结果！一位君王，具有种种令人崇敬、爱戴和敬仰的品质，他有卓越的才能，伟大的智慧，高深的学问，统治国家的雄才，臣民们对他都很爱戴；就是这么一位君王，出于一种完全没有必要的顾虑，竟将到手的机会轻轻放过了，这真是我们欧洲人意想不到的，要不然，他很可能成为他领导下的人民的生命、自由和财产的绝对主宰。我这么说倒也不是要减损这位杰出国王的许多美德。我清楚地知道，在这件事上，英国的读者会很看不起国王的这种性格。不过我认为他们有这种缺点是出于无知，他们至今还没能像欧洲一些比较精明的才子那样把政治变成一门科学。因为我记得很清楚，在有一天我和国王的谈话中，我曾偶然提到，关于统治这门学问，我们写过几千本书。使我没有想到的是，这反而使他非常鄙视我们的智慧。他表示，不论是君王还是大臣，心里每一点神秘、精巧和阴谋都令他厌恶、瞧不起。因为他那里既没有敌人也没有敌国，所以他不懂我说的国家机密到底是什么意思。他把治理国家的知识的范围划得很小，那不外乎是些常识和理智，正义和仁慈，从速判决民事、刑事案件，以及其他不值一提的一些简单事项。他还提出了这样的看法：谁能使原来只生产一串谷穗、一片草叶的土地长出两串谷穗、两片草叶来，谁就比所有的政客更有功于人类，对国家的贡献就更重大。

这个国家的学术体系不算很完整，只有伦理、历史、诗歌和数学等少数几门，但是这几门学科的成就不可小视。他们的数学完全应用于生活，比如改良农业，发展机械，但是在我们看来这样的用处完全是微不足道的。至于观念、本体、抽象、先验等概念，他们根本就一无所知。

他们的字母表只有二十二个字母，所有法律文件里没有一条超过这个长度。所有法律条文都简单明了，所有人都很淳朴，根本不会想着对法律条文做出什么曲解，而且凡是胆敢这么做的人都被处以死刑了。至于民事诉讼，由于他们平时的判例就很少，所以在这方面就没有什么值得吹嘘的了。

他们和中国人一样，很早就有了印刷术，但是他们的图书馆并不大，哪怕是皇家图书馆也就只有一千册藏书。所有的图书都被陈列在一条长达一千两百英尺的走廊里面，我可以随意翻阅。为了方便我阅读，王后的木匠在格兰姆达尔克里奇的房间里巧妙地制造了一架二十五英尺高的梯子，每层都有五十英尺宽，而且梯子可以随意移动。当我想看书的时候，我就把这本书靠在墙上，爬上最高层的梯子，从头开始读，一边读一边来回走动，走上八十到一百步就可以读完一行。周而复始，等到看不清下面一行字了，就来到梯子的下边一层，直到走到梯子的最底下一层。读完这一页之后自然就可以翻页了，这个动作我可以自己完成，因为他们的书页像硬纸板一样又厚又硬，最大也不过是十八到二十英尺长。

他们的文章清晰、雄辩、流畅，但又不华丽。他们竭力避免堆砌辞藻，最讨厌那些冗长的表达。我仔细研究过他们的书籍，特别是有关历史和道德方面的著作。至于其他类型的书，我最喜欢的是一本摆在格兰姆达尔克里奇的床头柜的一本小书，这本书是她的女教师，一位爱好道德和宗教信仰的老成持重的太太的。这本书阐述了人类的弱点，但是却只在女人和那些平民中广为流传。不过我还是很好奇，想知道这个国家的作者会对这个高深的话题发表怎样的看法。这本书的作者和欧洲的道德学家一样，论述了那些稀松平常的话题。他指出人类天性就是卑鄙渺小的，既不能抵抗恶劣的天气，也无法抵抗凶猛的野兽。力气、速度、视力、勤劳，全都不足以与其他动物相媲美。作者还认为，这个世界总体上都在衰弱，就连大自然本身都是一样。和古代的人类相比，现代出生的不过是一些矮小的早产儿。他认为古代人的体型不仅更为高大，而且时常还会有巨人出现。这一点不仅在典籍和传说中被证实，还有好多偶然被挖掘出来的头骨和骨骼都证明了这一点。大自然的法则要求我们长得和过去一般高大强壮，而不是如现在这般弱小。哪怕是屋顶掉落的瓦片、孩童手里的石头、偶然跌落的小溪都可能要我们的命。出于这几条原因，作者总结了几条道德准则，借此指导人类的生存，在这儿我就不多解释了。而我自己却是思绪万千，人类总是喜欢在与自然对抗的过程中吸取教训，普天之下莫不如是，但是实际上这不过是他们在发发牢骚而已。这个国家的人们与自然的抗争，和我们一样都是站不住脚的。

至于他们的军队，这个国家号称有十七万六千名步兵，三万两千名骑兵。其实这根本就不能算是步兵，因为这支军队不过是由几个城市的商人和乡下的农民组成的，他们的领袖是当地的贵族和乡绅，也没有任何的俸禄。虽然他们纪律严明，操练勤奋，但是我并没有看出什么优点，因为每一个农夫都在他的地主的统治之下，每一位市民都由本城的领袖统率，这些领袖又都是像威尼斯的做法那样用投票来选举，做到这样的事情又有什么大不了的呢？

我时常看到罗布鲁格路德的民兵操练。他们会被拉到距离京城不远的一块二十平方英里的空地上进行操练，总人数大约是两万五千步兵和六千骑兵，但是具体的数字我也说不清楚，毕竟他们占据的地盘太大了。这儿的战马有足足九十英尺那么高。我曾经见过骑兵队伍在他们指挥的命令之下，齐齐抽出马刀，在空中挥舞。难以想象当时的场景，简直是雄伟而又惊心动魄！就好像有千万道闪电在空中炸开一样。

一开始我很奇怪，这个国家和其他国家都没有接触，到底为什么要设立军队，要训练民兵呢？后来我通过和国王交谈，以及翻阅王国的历史等方式，了解了原因。原来多年以来，他们也犯了人类的通病：贵族争权夺势，人民向往自由，君主要求专制。这三方力量明争暗斗，哪怕是在法律的约束之下，也时常引发内战。最近一次内战就是被当今国王的祖父率领大军平定的。所以从那之后，三方势力都同意设立民兵团，并且严格履行职责。

第八章

国王和王后一起巡视边境，作者也得以一同前往。作者描述了自己离开这个国家的情形，他成功回到了英国。

我一直盼望着能够获得自由，虽然我一直没想清楚应该用什么样的方式去争取，但是这种念头却一直萦绕在我的心头。听说我当时乘坐的那艘小船是第一艘漂流到这一带海岸附近的船，所以国王已经下了严令，一旦发现了类似的小船，就一定要把小船和船上的人一起带上岸，并且送到罗布鲁格路德来。他很希望能够得到一位和我一般大小的女性，这样就可以在这儿延续子嗣了。但是我却宁死也不能忍受这样的安排，哪怕是在这儿传宗接代，我都免不了身陷囹圄，和金丝雀一般供人取笑。也许某一天我的后代会被当成玩物，在达官贵人当中转手出售。不过平心而论，在这个国家我还是受到礼遇的，国王和王后十分宠幸我，那些朝臣也十分喜欢我，但我的尊严却还是受到了侮辱。故乡和妻儿时常浮现在我的心头，我希望能够在人群中平等地生活，或者无拘无束地在大街小巷行走，而不用担心自己像小狗或者青蛙一般被人一脚踩死。但是我一点都没有想到，我逃离这种境遇的日子会来得如此迅速，而且逃离的办法会是那么出人意料。接下来我就好好叙述一番整件事情的经过。

　　我来到这个国家已经差不多有两年时间了，在第三年开头的时候，格兰姆达尔克里奇和我陪同国王和王后前往这个国家的南海岸线巡游。和往常一般，我坐在自己专用的小木箱子里。关于这个小木箱子我已经详细描述过了，有十二英尺宽，十分舒适。按照我的要求，这个箱子里面安装有吊床，吊床的四个角就固定在箱子的顶部。当仆人骑着马带着我的时候，他会把箱子抱在胸口，这样箱子就不会太过颠簸，而我也可以在吊床上休息。在木箱顶部稍稍偏离吊床的位置开着大约一英尺见方的天窗，这样就可以有效地让空气流通。在天窗上安装有木板，可以随时把天窗给关起来。

　　巡游结束之后，国王打算去弗兰弗兰斯尼克附近的行宫小住几天，这座行宫距离海岸只有大约十八英里。一路旅行的格兰姆达尔克里奇和我感觉到十分疲惫。我是有点感冒，而可怜的姑娘也病得不行，根本就不能出门。不过我很想去看看大海，因为那是我唯一逃生的路径。所以我就假装自己病得不轻，想要去海边呼吸一下新鲜空气。小保姆由于生病无法陪着我一起去，所以我希望由经常照看我的一位仆人带我去，他也深受国王的信任。格兰姆达尔克里奇虽然十分不情愿，但最终她还是同意了，不过分别时刻她流露出的关心的神情让我这辈子都忘不了。她一再叮嘱那位仆人要照顾好我，分别时还哭得相当厉害，就好像已经预料到即将发生的事情一样。那个仆人提着我的箱子离开了行宫，走了大约半个小时，就来到了满是岩石的海岸边上。我让这个仆人把我放了下来，然后拉开一扇窗户，一脸忧郁地凝望着大海。我感觉到有点不舒服，于是我就和仆人说我想在吊床上睡一会儿，希望这能够对我的身体有好处。我爬上了吊床，躺了一会儿，而仆人担心我着凉就把我的窗户给关上了。我很快就进入了梦乡，之后发生的事情就只是我事后的推测了。我猜测那个仆人看到我睡着了之后，就跑到岩石上去找鸟蛋，因为我在入睡之前就看到他在岩石间翻找。但是接下来我就感觉到箱子上的那个铁环被狠狠扯了一下，整个箱子就飞上了半空，然后飞快地前进。这突如其来的震动差点就把我甩下了吊床，不过很快箱子就稳当了起来。我大喊着救命，但是根本没有人理睬。窗外只有蓝天和白云，头上倒是传来一阵仿佛是拍打翅膀的声音，直到这时候我才意识到自己到底经历着什么。这是一只老鹰，用自己的鸟喙叼着木箱的铁环，想要找个机会把箱子扔到岩石上摔碎，就像它们经常对付乌龟那样。这种鸟非常机灵，嗅觉也十分敏锐，从很远的地方就能发现猎物，就是猎物躲在比我这两英寸厚的木板更安全的地方也起不到任何作用。

　　不一会儿工夫，我感觉到翅膀扇动的声音越来越快，我那箱子就像刮风天气的路标牌一样上下摇晃。我听到了几声撞击的声音，我想那是鹰遭到了袭击（我现在已完全肯定用嘴衔住我那箱子上的铁环的一定是只鹰）。接着，我猛然感觉到自己在垂直下落，一直下落了有一分多钟的样子，速度之快令人难以置信，我差点儿喘不上气来。忽然啪的一声巨响，我不再往下掉了，那声音我听起来比尼亚加拉大瀑布还要响。随后的一分钟时间里，我眼前一片漆黑。接着箱子高高地漂浮起来，我从最上面的窗子里看到了光亮。这时我才意识到我是掉进海里了。我那箱子，由于我身体的重量和里边的东西，再加上为了加固而在箱子顶部及底部四角钉上去的宽铁板，浸在水中大约有五英尺。我那时就猜想，现在还是这么认为，那只叼着我箱子往前飞的鹰大概正被另外两三只鹰追赶着，它们想分享我这一份活点心；那只鹰为了自卫，不得不扔下我去同它们搏斗。钉在箱子底部的铁板最坚固，所以箱子往下掉时得以保持平衡，也避免了在水面上碰得粉碎。所有的接缝处都被打造得十分严实，门也不是靠铰链来开关的，而是像窗户那样的上下拉动式，所以我这小屋关得严严实实，几乎没有一点水渗进来。但是因为缺乏空气，我都感到自己快要被闷死了，所以就先冒险拉开前面已提到的屋顶上那块透空气用的活板，这才好不容易从吊床上爬了下来。

我是多么希望我亲爱的格兰姆达尔克里奇能够和我在一起啊，毕竟我们分离的时间还没有一个小时！而且说实话，当时的我虽然身处困境，但是却忍不住为我可怜的小保姆担心起来，她会如何接受失去我的事实呢？王后知道了这件事情之后会如何生气，会不会迁怒于她呢？她在皇宫里的富足生活会不会因此而断送，会不会永远没有希望呢？我敢说许多旅行家都不曾有过比我当时还要艰难和痛苦的心境。毕竟当时我正处于千钧一发的关键时刻，我的木箱子随时都可能会散架，或者被一阵狂风给掀翻。哪怕是窗玻璃上的一个缝隙都可能置我于死地，如果不是窗户外面的铁丝网提供保护，我想这个窗户也早已毁坏。而当下从窗户外面已经慢慢渗进米一些水了，我必须要竭尽全力才能堵住那个裂缝。我想要打开天花板，但是我的力气根本不够，不然的话我还可以在海面上苟延残喘几个小时，总比被闷在这个封闭的箱子里要好很多。但是哪怕是这样，我也只能多存活那么一两天，严寒和饥饿会威胁我的生命，我要如何才能逃出生天呢？就这样，我熬过了四个小时，每一分每一秒都可能是我这辈子的终结。

我之前曾经说过，在木箱的没有窗户的那一面墙壁上安装着两个铁环，仆人们把我抱在怀里骑马的时候就会用皮带穿过铁环，借此来固定这个箱子。正当我陷入绝望的时候，我突然听到，或者是我觉得我听到了铁环那一面传来了巨大的响声。我开始想象有什么东西在海水里拖着箱子前进，因为我很快就感觉到了这种力量。不过这样一来波浪几乎漫过了我的窗户，所以在箱子里的我是一片黑暗。虽然我不知道这到底是怎么一回事，但是这至少给了我一点希望。我费尽力气把固定在地板上的一把凳子给卸了下来，然后搬到刚打开的天窗下边，又重新把螺丝拧了上去。随后我爬上椅子，把嘴巴贴近窗户，大声呼救。我用了平生所知晓的每一种语言，随后又找到了一块手帕，固定在我随身的一根手杖上面，然后把手杖伸出天窗，在空中挥舞。如果那会儿碰巧有轮船经过，也许会有水手发现我这个可怜的被关在箱子里的家伙。

我觉得自己的举动没有一点用处，但是我的确感觉到这个箱子一直在前进。差不多一个小时或者更长一点时间之后，铁环的那一边狠狠撞在了一个坚硬的物体上，据我猜测那可能是一块礁石。这时候我感觉到整个箱子颠簸得更加厉害了，我都能听到箱子发出了嘎嘎作响的声音，像是有缆绳穿过铁环一般。我再一次把绑着手帕的手杖伸出去，然后用自己最大的声音喊着救命，差点把我的喉咙都给喊破了。幸好我的呼喊终于有了回应，我听到外面传来三声回答，这种感觉真的是难以言表。头顶上传来一阵脚步声，有人通过那个小洞向我喊话，用的竟然是英语！"里面有人吗，请回答！"我赶忙说："我是一个英国人，时运不济，我敢说整个英国都找不到和我一般的可怜人了！我请求你们能够把我救出去。"那个声音回答说，我已经安全了，这个箱子已经固定在船上，木匠就在过来的路上，只需要在箱子顶上弄一个洞，就可以把我救出来。我说没有必要那么麻烦，那样太浪费时间了。只需要有个水手用手指勾着铁环把箱子拉出水面，放在船上就可以了。听到我这番胡话的一行人还以为我是个疯子，他们纷纷大笑起来。当时的我的确激动得忘记了，这些人和我一般大小。木匠来了之后很快就锯出了一个四平方英尺的通道，然后用一架小梯子把我弄到了大船上，当时的我几近虚脱。

水手们十分震惊，问了我许许多多的问题，而当时的我根本没有心情理会。最让我震惊的是看到那么多矮子，毕竟我的眼睛已经习惯了那些庞然大物了。不过船长托马斯·威尔科克斯是一个来自什罗普郡的老实人，他看出我当时的虚弱，就把我带进他的船舱里，给了我一些镇定药，让我缓了一口气。随后他又让我在他的床上睡一会儿，这正是我最需要的。休息之前我告诉船长，在那个木箱子里有一些珍贵的家具，丢了很可惜，有一张精致的吊床和一张好看的行军床、两把椅子、一张桌子和一个柜子。整个箱子的四周都挂着精美的丝绸。船长听我说这些稀奇古怪的东西，断定我是在说胡话了；不过（我猜想他当时是想我让安顿下来）他还是答应按照我的要求吩咐人去办这件事。他来到甲板上，派几个人到我的小屋里把我所有的东西都搬了出来，垫衬在墙壁上的东西也都扯了下来（这些都是我后来才知道的）；不过椅子、柜子还有床架都是用螺丝钉在地板上的，水手们不知道，硬使劲往上扯，结果大多毁坏了。他们又敲下了几块木板拿到船上来用，想要的东西全拿光后，就把空箱子扔进了海里；因为箱底和四壁有不少裂缝，箱子当即就沉了下去。说真的，我很高兴没有亲眼看着他们将东西毁坏，因为我相信，让一件件往事重新在脑海中浮现，我一定会感触万端的，而这些事我宁愿忘掉。

我睡了几个小时，但是睡得不安稳，我梦见了自己离开的那个地方，梦见了我刚刚躲过的种种危险。不过一觉醒来，我觉得自己精力已大为恢复。这时大约已是晚上八点钟了，船长考虑到我好长时间没有吃东西了，就立即吩咐开饭。他见我已不再是疯样，说话也前后连贯，就十分友好地招待我。当房间里只剩下我们两人的时候，他要我把旅行的情况告诉他，我是怎么乘坐那只大得吓人的木头箱子在海上漂流的。他说，中午十二点钟的样子，他正拿着望远镜在瞭望，忽然在远处发现了那东西，还以为是一艘帆船，心想离他的航线不太远，自己船上的饼干又快吃完了，就想赶上去从那船上买一些过来。当轮船靠近了才发现他错了，就派人坐着长舢板去探探这箱子到底是什么东西。他的水手们回来之后都显得十分害怕，发誓说他们看到了一座漂流着的房屋。他笑他们说傻话，就亲自坐小船去看，同时吩咐水手们随身带一根结实的缆绳。当时风平浪静，他绕着箱子划了几圈，发现了箱子上的窗户和保护窗户的铁框架，又发现一面全是木板，没有一点透光的地方，却安着两个锁环。他于是命令水手把船划到那一面去，将缆绳拴上其中的一只铁环后，就叫他们把我那柜子（这是他的话）向大船拖去。箱子到船边后，他又下令再挂一根缆绳到箱顶的铁环上，然后用滑车把箱子吊起来。可是全体水手一齐动手，也只不过吊起两三英尺。他说他们看到了我从洞里伸出来的手杖和手帕，断定一定有什么不幸的人被关在里面了。我问他起初发现我的时候，他和水手们可曾看见天空中有没有什么大鸟。他回答说，我睡觉的时候，他同水手们谈过这事，其中有一个水手说他看到有三只鹰朝北方飞去，不过他并没有说它们比普通的鹰大。我想那一定是因为它们飞得太高的缘故。他当时猜不透我为什么要问这个问题。我接着问船长，他估计我们离陆地有多远了。他说，据他最精确的计算，至少有一百里路。我告诉他，他肯定多算了差不多一半的路程，因为我掉进海里时，离开我来的那个国家还不到两个小时。听我这么一说，他又开始认为我的脑子有毛病了。他暗示我，我是神经错乱，劝我到他给我预备的一间舱房里去睡觉。我告诉他让他放心，他这么友好地招待我、陪我，我早已恢复过来了，神志也跟平时一样完全清醒。他这时却严肃起来，说想坦率地问我一句，是不是我犯了什么大罪，按照某个君王的命令受到惩罚，把我丢到那个柜子里面，就像别的一些国家对待重罪犯那样，不给食物，强迫他上一只破船到海上漂流。他说虽然很懊恼把这么一个坏人搭救上船，可他还是说话算话，一到第一个港口就送我平安上岸。他又补充说，我一开始对水手们尽说胡话，后来又对他去讲，什么小屋，柜子，加上我吃晚饭时神情举止都很古怪，他就越来越怀疑了。

　　我请求他能够耐心听我讲完我的故事，随后我就把自己从离开英国到最终被他们发现的这段时间的经历原原本本地讲了一遍。真相总是能够说服理性的人，这位诚实的绅士有几分学识，也有很好的判断力，他立刻就相信了我很坦诚，说的都是实话。为了进一步证明我的话，我让他安排手下把我的那个柜子拿来，因为钥匙还在我的口袋里，而他也已经把水手如何处理我的柜子的事情原原本本讲了一遍。我当着他的面打开了柜子，把我在那个奇怪国家收集的那些东西全部拿了出来。里面有我用国王的胡子做的一把梳子，还有一把也是用同样的材料做的，只不过是被安装在王后的手指甲做成的梳子的脊背上。当然还有好几根长度在一英尺到半码长的缝衣针和别针，四根硕大的黄蜂针，属于王后的几根头发，还有一枚金戒指。这枚戒指是王后某一天的赏赐，它原本是套在王后的尾指上的，但是在我身上几乎可以充当皇冠。为了报答船长的救命之恩，我请求他收下这枚戒指，但是被他拒绝了。我又拿出了亲自从一位侍女的脚上割下的鸡眼，那几乎有肯特郡出产的苹果那么大，回国之后我就把这个鸡眼雕刻成了一只杯子，并且镶嵌上了银子。随后我又给他们看了我身上的裤子，那是用一只老鼠的皮做成的。

　　不管我怎么说，船长就是什么都不接受。他只对一位仆人的牙齿产生了浓厚的好奇心，于是我就劝他收下。他千恩万谢地接受了这份礼物，虽然这在我看来根本微不足道。这枚牙齿是一位技术不熟练的牙医从格兰姆达尔克里奇的一位患牙病的仆人的嘴里错拔下来的，实际上这是一颗好牙。我把这枚牙齿洗干净然后放进了柜子里，这枚牙齿有差不多一英尺那么长，四英寸的直径。

　　船长对我的这一番解释十分满意，他希望我回到英国之后能够把这一切都写下来公之于众。我当时回答说，有关旅行的书实在是太多了，现在为了出彩，所以游记写得越来越离奇。而我是很怀疑他们的经历是否真实的，有些可能是出于对虚荣和利益的盲动，有些则是出于赢得读者的欢心的目的。而我的故事却只有一些普通的事情，而没有像大多数作者一样竭力描写那些奇怪的草木鸟兽，或者是对那些野蛮民族的风俗描写。但是不管怎么说，我还是感谢了船长的好意，并且答应会好好考虑这件事情。

　　船长说有一件事让我觉得很奇怪，为什么我平时说话的声音那么大，他询问我是不是因为那个国家的国王和王后的耳朵都有毛病。我说这两年来我早已熟悉这样的讲话方式了，所以听到他和他的水手的交谈，我差点以为他们是在窃窃私语，虽然我本人还是能够听得很清楚。在那个国家里，我说话的模样就好像是站在大街上冲着教堂的圆顶上的另外一个人说话。除非他们把我放在桌子上或者托在手上，我才没有必要用那么响亮的声音。我告诉他，我还注意到了另一件事，就是我刚上船那会儿，水手们全都围着我站着，我还以为他们是我平生见过的最不起眼的小人儿呢。真的，我在那个君王的国土上的时候，两眼已经看惯了庞然大物，一照镜子就受不了，因为相形之下，实在自惭形秽。船长说我们一道吃晚饭时，他就发觉我看什么东西都带一种惊奇的目光，好像总忍不住要笑似的，他也不清楚是怎么回事，只好认为我有点精神失常。我回答说他讲得很对。我看到那菜盘子只有三便士银币那么大，一条猪腿几乎不够一口吃的，酒杯还没有胡桃壳大，我怎么能忍住不笑。我接着又以同样的方式把他的其余家用器具和食物形容了一番。我在为王后效命时，虽然她吩咐人给我预备了一整套小型日用品，我却一门心思只在我周围看到的那些大东西上，就像人们对待自己的错误一样，我对自身的渺小故意视而不见。船长很能领会我这善意的嘲笑话，就引用了一句古老的英国谚语来回敬我，说他怀疑我的眼睛比肚子还大，因为我虽然饿了一天了，他却发现我的胃口并不怎么好。他还继续往下开玩笑，坚决说他乐意出一百英镑看鹰叼着我那小屋，再从极高的空中把它丢进海里。他觉得那样的场景一定十分惊心动魄，值得记录下来流传后世。这样的故事能够和法厄同的经历相提并论，虽然我并不是很欣赏这样的比喻。

当时船长正在从越南返回英国的途中，方位是北纬四十四度，东经一百四十三度。不过在我上船两天之后就遇到了信风，所以我们朝着南方走了很长一段路，绕过了新荷兰，然后一直朝着西南西方向前进，直到绕过了好望角。回程相当顺利，所以我也就不多赘述了。期间船长也曾在港口停船，并派人上岸补给。但是我一直等到达了唐兹才下船。我们在 1706 年 6 月 3 日抵达了唐兹，距离我脱险已经有九个月了。我建议留下我的收藏作为船票费用，但是船长并没有接受。离开的时候，船长答应以后一定会到雷德里夫看望我。我向船长借了五先令，雇佣了一匹马和一个向导，踏上了回家的旅程。

一路上看到小小的房屋、树木、牲口和行人，我都以为自己回到了利立浦特。我十分担心踩到遇到的每一个行人，时常大声提醒他们给我让路。这般无礼的做法害我差点被路人打破脑袋。

我向别人打听后才找到了自己的家。一位佣人开了门，因为我怕碰着头，所以就像鹅进窝那样弯腰走了进去。我妻子跑出来拥抱我，可我把腰一直弯到她的膝盖以下，认为如果不这样她就怎么也够不到我的嘴。我女儿跪下来要我给她祝福，可是我这么长时间以来已习惯于站着仰头看六十英尺以上的高处，所以直到她站起身来，我才看见她，这时才走上前一手将她拦腰抱起。我居高临下看了看佣人和家里来的一两个朋友，好像他们都是矮子，我才是巨人。我对妻子说，她太节省了，因为我发现她把自己和女儿都快饿得不像样了。总之，我的举动非常不可思议，大家就同那船长初见我时一样，断定我是神经失常了。我提这一点，是为了证明，习惯和偏见的力量是巨大的。

没过多久，我和家人、朋友就能互相理解了，只是我的妻子坚持不让我再次出海了。但是我的命运早已注定，她也没有办法阻拦。有关这一点读者们随后就会知晓，而我不幸的航行的第二部分游记就写到这儿吧！

第三卷

拉普塔、巴尔尼巴比、鲁格奈格、格鲁布杜德利卜、日本游记

第一章

作者开始了他第三次出海旅程。他被海盗给抓住了，随后遇到了狠毒的荷兰人。他登上了小岛，被接入了拉普塔。

我在家里才待了不到十天，威廉·罗宾逊船长就前来拜访了。他是康沃尔人，是"好望角"号轮船的船长。这艘船载重三百吨。之前他在另外一艘船上当船长的时候，我恰好是他手下的外科医生。他拥有那艘船四分之一的股份，我们曾经一起去过黎凡特。他待我很好，与其说他是我的上司，不如说我们就是亲生的兄弟。听说我孤身一人，就特意上来登门拜访。我原本以为这不过是因为我们深厚的友谊的关系，毕竟我们很久不曾见面，这般的看望和寒暄也实属平常。但是他却来访了很多次，特别是看到我身体健康他感到很高兴，问我是否决定就此安定下来。随后他自称要去一趟东印度，大概需要两个月时间，所以虽然他满怀歉意，仍然询问我是否愿意担任船上的外科医生。他说，除了两位助手，还会有另外一位外科医生安排在我的手下。我的工资将会是平时的两倍，毕竟我是一个航海经验丰富的老海员。随后，他又保证自己一定会采纳我的建议，甚至提出由我和他一起指挥这艘船。

他对我很客气，也说了不少好话。我知道他是一个诚实的人，所以在他的盛情邀请之下，我实在不知道该如何拒绝。虽然我过去遇上了那么多不幸，但是渴望去世界各地看看的念头却一点都不曾消退。现在唯一的困难就是如何说服我的妻子。最后出于对子女的前途的考虑，她还是答应了我的请求。

我们在 1706 年 8 月 5 日出发，于 1707 年 4 月 11 日抵达了圣乔治要塞。我们在那儿停留了三个星期，因为有许多船员都生病了。随后我们就朝着越南的东京进发。船长打算在那儿停留一段时间，因为需要置办的货物并没有买齐，大概还需要几个月的时间。为了应付必要的开支，他购买了一艘小帆船，和当地人做起了生意。这在这个地方是很普遍的现象。船上装满货物，还有十四名船员跟随，其中三个是当地人。他安排我当这艘小帆船的船长，授权我可以拍板任何交易，而他本人则在东京坐镇。

我们出发还不到三天，就遇上了可怕的暴风雨。我们被迫朝着东北偏北方向漂浮了整整五天，然后又转向东方。随后的天气虽然变好了，但是仍然有猛烈的西风。在第十天的时候我们被两艘海盗船追上了。由于我们的帆船载重太多，所以前进的速度很慢，我们也毫无抵抗能力，被追上之后只能束手就擒。

两艘海盗船的首领几乎是同时上船的，带着手下的人马，一副气势汹汹的模样。我命令所有人脸朝下趴在甲板上，他们顺手就用结实的绳索把我们捆绑了起来，只留下一个人看守，然后就去搜刮帆船的货物了。

我发现在海盗里有一个荷兰人，虽然不是一个头目，却似乎有些权势。他发现我们是英国人，就恶狠狠地用荷兰语诅咒了我们，并且发誓要把我们背靠背捆着扔进海里。我的荷兰语讲得不错，便把自己的遭遇坦白了，随后请求他看在我们都是基督徒和新教徒，并且我们两个国家相毗邻的份上，帮我们说说好话。没想到我的这一番央求却如同火上浇油一般，一下子把他给惹怒了。他重复念叨着刚才的话，并且和他的同伙说了好久，强调了好几次"基督徒"这个词。我猜他们说的应该是日语。较大的那艘海盗船的船长是个日本人，会讲一些荷兰语，但是并不熟练。他走到我的面前，问了我好几个问题，我毕恭毕敬地回答了之后，船长表示不会杀死我们。我深深鞠了一躬，然后转身对那个荷兰人说，看到外乡人能够给予我们怜悯，而同为基督徒的兄弟却没有一点同情之心，这让我感到很难过。不过我很快就后悔说了这些话，因为他之后好几次怂恿船长把我扔进海里（不过由于海盗们已经许下了承诺，所以并没有答应）；但是他却成功说服海盗们用一种比处死还要狠毒的办法来惩罚我。我手下的水手被分成了两队，被押上了两艘海盗船，而我们的帆船则被他们派人接管了。至于我本人，他们决定把我放上一条小船，只留给我船帆、船桨和四天的食物，然后就把我放逐了。最后好心的日本船长倒是给我多加了一倍的补给，并且不允许手下前来搜查。我登上了那条小船，而那个荷兰人就站在甲板上，用他们语言中所有恶毒的词语把我狠狠责骂了一顿。

在遇上海盗之前的一个小时我还观测过方位，当时我正处于北纬四十六度，东经一百八十三度的位置。当我驾驶着小船离开海盗船一段距离之后，我就掏出自己口袋里的袖珍望远镜，发现在东南方向有几座小岛。当时的风向也十分合适，所以我就扬帆起航，朝着最近的一座小岛前进。这段旅途十分顺利，不到三个小时我就顺利抵达了那座小岛。小岛上都是岩石，不过我捡到了不少鸟蛋。生火之后我用石南草和海藻把鸟蛋烤熟了。这顿晚饭我就用鸟蛋对付了过去，省下了不少粮食。我在岩石之中寻找到了一个避风的地方，然后在身子底下铺了一些干燥的石楠草，就这么睡了一个晚上。

第二天我抵达了第二个海岛，然后是第三个和第四个。有的时候我借助船帆前进，有些时候就借助船桨航行。但是在此我也不打算用我那困苦的旅程来烦扰读者了。总之在第五天的时候我抵达了最后一座小岛，位于前几座海岛的东南偏南方向。

这座海岛比我预估的要远一些，我几乎花了五个小时才抵达这座小岛。我绕着小岛转了一圈才发现一处可以登陆的地方。这是个很小的港湾，大约只有我的独木舟的三倍宽。登陆之后我才发现，这个小岛上也全是岩石，只有那么一点点地方生长着青草，还有一些闻着很香的药草。我拿出口粮吃了一会儿，恢复了一点体力，然后就把剩下的全部藏到一个山洞里面，这个小岛上有许许多多的山洞。我准备了许多的鸟蛋，然后又收集了一些干海草，这是我为第二天准备的食物。当晚我就睡在准备拿来当柴火的干海草上面。我睡得很浅，因为整个晚上我都心烦意乱。我获救的希望是如此渺茫，这种无形的威胁让我夜不能寐，我仿佛预料到了自己的结局。受到如此悲观的情绪影响，我几乎都不想起床了。当我强打起精神爬出山洞的时候，时间已经不早了。我在岩石间漫步了一会儿，晴空万里，阳光是如此猛烈，我不得不背对着太阳。但是突然间，眼前变得昏暗起来，而且这种变换和天空中飘来一片乌云截然不同。我发现太阳下面有一个完全透明的家伙，径直朝着小岛飞来。这个不明物体有整整两英里那么高，足足遮蔽了阳光有六七分钟的样子；但是我并没有感觉到空气变得凉爽，或者感觉到天空越发阴沉。实际上这种感觉还不如站在背阴处来得强烈。随着那不明物体朝着我所在的地方靠近，我才看清楚它是一个固体，底部平坦光滑，而且闪闪发光。当时我站在距离海面大约两百码的高处，看着这庞然大物降落到和我差不多的高度，就在距离我一英里不到的地方。我取出望远镜，清晰地看到上面有许许多多的人在边上忙碌着。整个边缘似乎是倾斜的，所以我看不到他们在做什么。

求生的本能让我的内心生起喜悦之情，原本绝望的我突然盼望着眼前的奇迹能够把我从这荒无人烟的绝境中拯救出来。但是与此同时我也感觉到无比惊讶，当时的情感波动想必很难引起读者的共鸣。看到满载着居民的空中孤岛竟然可以升降自如（看上去似乎如此）；如果他们愿意的话甚至还能够飞驰吧。但是就我当时的情况，我根本无暇考虑这些问题，而是关注着巨大的浮岛究竟要朝哪个方向去，毕竟它看上去已经静止了一会儿。很快，它越发靠近了，我看到这庞然大物的边缘有一层层走廊，都是以楼梯相连接的。而在最底层的走廊上还有垂钓和围观的人。我朝那个巨岛一边挥舞着自己的帽子

（已经破损不堪）和手帕，一边高声呼喊。随着岛屿越发靠近，我发现在底层已经聚集了好多人，朝着我的方向指指点点，显然是发现了我。但是他们并没有回应我，只是有四五个人急匆匆地跑上了楼梯。如果我猜得不错，他们这是去请示他们的领导了。

格列佛发现了浮岛

聚集的人群越来越庞大。不到半个小时，海岛继续移动了起来，慢慢地上升直到底层平台和我所站的地方相平行，距离也不过一百码。我在边上苦苦哀求，但是并没有得到任何回应。从他们的衣着来看，离我最近，站得最高的那些人应该是贵族。他们一边看着我，一边在那儿激烈讨论。最后其中一个人高声呼喊了起来，他的口齿清晰，声调悦耳，听起来像是意大利语。所以我也用意大利语回话，希望他们能觉得我的回应是顺耳的。虽然我们俩根本听不懂对方的语言，但是我想他们应该很清楚我的情况。

他们冲我做手势，让我从岩石上下来，然后走到岸边。我一一照做了。那个巨岛飞到了合适的位置，边缘恰好调整到我的头顶，然后从最底层的走廊里放下来一条链子，链子的末端拴着一把椅子。我坐上了椅子，固定好自己，然后就被他们拉了上去。

第二章

作者描述了拉普塔人的脾气和秉性，以及他们的学术情况。作者介绍了这儿的国王和朝臣，以及自己受到款待的过程。作者描述了当地居民的惶恐不安的生活现状，当然还有对当地女性的描述。

我上岛之后，很快就有一群人把我团团围住，距离我最近的似乎是一些有地位的人。看到我之后，都忍不住显露出惊叹的表情，当然我也是一样。这群人的外形、服装和模样都十分奇怪，以前我从来不曾见过。他们的脑袋不是向左歪就是向右歪，一只眼睛深深内凹，还有一只是笔直向天的。他们的衣服上画着太阳、月亮和星星的图案，当然还有小提琴、竖笛、军号、六弦琴和其他我在欧洲没有见过的乐器的图形。我发现边上有不少穿着仆人衣服的人，手里拿着一根手杖，手杖的其中一端挂着一个气囊，吹得很鼓。后来我才知道，气囊里面装的是干豆或者石子。那些仆人时不时地用气囊拍打站在他们附近的贵族的嘴和耳朵。当时的我对于这样的举动感到十分莫名其妙，后来我才明白了，原来当地的贵族很容易就陷入沉思，如果他们的嘴巴和耳朵没有得到来自外界的刺激的话，他们就没法说话，也听不到别人说话。所以那些贵族就会在仆人当中专门培育一个拍手（原文是克里门脑儿），出门的时候都会带上。这位拍手的职责就是，当两三个贵族凑在一起的时候，拍手要先用气囊拍一下发言人的嘴巴，然后再拍拍那位聆听的贵族的右耳。当他们的主人在走路的时候，他们还要负责拍打主人的双眼，以免深陷沉思的主人从悬崖上掉落，或者撞在柱子上面。走在街上，也很有可能会撞倒别人，或者被别人撞翻到路旁的水沟里面。

拉普塔贵族行走的模样

之所以要交代这些信息是很有必要的，不然的话读者就会对他们的行为万分茫然，当初他们领着我上楼梯，前往小岛顶端的王宫的时候，就曾几次三番地忘记他们的目的，把我扔在一边。如果不是有拍手在旁边提醒的话，我想我很难顺利抵达。哪怕是在见到我之后，他们也对我的外貌和服装无动于衷，甚至对于底层百姓的呼喊置若罔闻。倒是底层的百姓不像他们那样眉头紧锁，思虑重重。

我走进了皇宫，看到国王端坐在王座上，旁边侍立着许多贵族。在王座前面摆着一张桌子，放满了天球仪、地球仪和各种数学仪器。虽然我入宫的时候，所有的人都围了过来，引起了不小的骚动，但是国王仿佛一点都没有注意到我们的到来。当时他正在思考一个问题，所以我们足足等了一个小时，他才把这个问题给想清楚。国王的两旁各站着一位手里拿着拍子的侍从，看到国王思考完毕之后才拍打他的耳朵和嘴巴。国王苏醒过来，看到眼前的人群，才想起自己曾经召见过我。国王开口说了几句话之后，就有一个年轻人拿着拍子凑到我的旁边，拍打我的右耳。我做手势表示我并不需要这个工具。之后我才明白，这个举动让国王和贵族们十分鄙视我的智力水平。我猜测国王在问我问题，于是我就用我所掌握的各种语言来回答，但是他们仿佛并不能理会。之后国王命令手下把我带到另外一个房间，让两个仆人伺候我。这个国王显然十分热情。晚饭准备好之后，有整整四位贵人陪我吃饭。我记得这四位贵人都是陪伴在国王左右的人。晚饭一共有两道菜，每道菜有三盘。第一道菜是羊肩肉、牛肉和布丁。羊肉被切成了等边三角形，牛肉被切成了菱形，而布丁则是圆形的。第二道菜有鸭子、香肠、布丁和牛胸肉。鸭子被摆放成小提琴的模样，香肠和布丁则被摆成长笛形状，牛胸肉则是竖琴模样。就连面包都被切成了圆锥形、圆柱形、平行四边形和其他几何形状。

吃饭的时候，我询问了这几种食物在当地语言中应该如何表达。靠着拍手的帮助，这几位贵族做了回答。他们希望我能够和他们学习当地语言，这样我就能理解他们的伟大，进而敬佩他们。很快我就学会了如何让仆人送上面包、酒或者是我想要的别的东西。

晚饭之后，这些贵族们纷纷告辞。国王又派来了一个贵族和拍手，携带着笔墨纸砚和三四本书，做手势告诉我，他是来教授我语言的。这天晚上我学了大约四个小时。我把单词写在一旁，另外一侧则是解释。用这样的办法我又记住了好几个句子。我的语言老师让我的仆人做出了一系列动作，比如拿东西、转身、鞠躬、坐下、起立、走路等。他拿出了一本书，把月亮、星星、黄道、热带、南北极圈的图形指给我看，并且告诉我许多平面和立体几何形状的名称。随后他又告诉我各种乐器的名称和功能，以及演奏时使用的术语。之后我就把所有的单词和解释都按顺序排列了起来。就这样，几天之后我就凭借自己的记忆力，对他们的语言有了初步了解。之前我称之为浮岛的这个词，在当地被称为"Laputa"（拉普塔），但是直到现在我也没有考究清楚这个词的来源。"Lap"（拉普）这个词在古老的语言中代表高的意思，而"untuh"（恩图）这个词则代表统治者。所以他们就认为"Laputa"这个词是从"Lapuntuh"（飞翔的统治者）中派生而出的。但是我并不赞同，甚至觉得这有些牵强。我曾经向他们的学者提出异议，认为拉普塔的意思应该是"quasi lap outed"（海面上飞舞的翅膀）。不过我并不坚持这一点，而是把这个异议交给读者来判断。

照顾我的人发现我衣衫褴褛，就吩咐裁缝第二天帮我做衣服。这儿的手艺和欧洲的很不一样，裁缝先用四分仪测量我的身高，然后又用尺子和圆规把我的宽度和厚度，以及整个身体的数据记录下来。六天以后我的衣服就做好了，但是和我的身材完全不相符。后来我才知道，原来是裁缝不小心弄错了一个数字。这样的失误在这个国家简直司空见惯，都没有人在意。

由于没有合适的衣服，而且我身体也不是很舒服，于是我就在房间里面多待了几天，这让我的词汇量突飞猛进。等我再次进宫面见国王的时候我已经能够听懂他说的很多话，甚至还能简单回答几句。国王下令让浮岛朝东北偏东的方向前进，朝着拉格多的上空飞去。拉格多是这个王国的首都，距离这儿大约九十里格，而我们整整飞了四天半。浮岛在航行过程中就像陆地上一样平稳，我根本就感觉不出浮岛在前进。第二天早上十一点左右，国王和所有的贵族一起举办了一场三个小时的音乐会，但是我却被这嘈杂的音乐弄得十分昏沉。如果不是我的老师在边上讲解，我完全就是不知所谓。他介绍说岛上的居民都喜欢音乐，每隔一段时间都要演奏一次。所有人都必须使用自己最擅长的乐器。

在前往拉格多的途中，国王会命令浮岛在特定的镇子和村庄停留，以接受当地居民的请愿书。他会命令人垂下几根绳索，让底下的居民把请愿书拴在绳子上，他们再把绳子给拉上来，就好像欧洲的小学生喜欢把纸片固定在风筝线上。有的时候底下的居民也会送上酒水和饮食，他们也一样拉上来。

我的数学知识为我提供了很大帮助，因为他们的很多词汇都是和科学、音乐有关。关于音乐，我也不算陌生。他们的思想总是和线或者图形有关，比如在赞美妇女或者其他动物的美貌的时候，他们就会用菱形、圆形、平行四边形、椭圆形和其他几何术语来形容，或者就是一些起源于音乐的名词。在厨房里放着各种数学仪器和乐器，厨师们忙着按照这些东西的模样处理食物，然后送给国王享用。

他们的房子一点都不坚固，而且也不漂亮。所有的墙壁都是歪的，没有一个直角。这都是因为他们十分鄙视实用几何学，他们觉得这门科学呆板、机械。他们的指令往往十分准确，可惜匠人们没法领会他们的意图，所以总是出错。虽然他们可以在纸上用圆规和直尺熟练地作图，但是在日常行为中他们的表现只能用笨拙来形容。除了数学和音乐，他们对其他知识没有任何建树。他们不擅长辩论，只会直接表示反对。除非有人和他们的意见完全一致，但是这样的情况少之又少。他们对于幻想、发明一窍不通，甚至在他们的语言中根本没有类似的词汇。他们的心思完全局限于上述两门学科之中。

大多数岛民，特别是研究天文的那些人都对神判占星学十分热衷，虽然他们极为信奉，但却根本不敢公开承认。最让人感到惊讶的是他们对于政治的热衷。他们总是热衷于对公共事务发表评论，或者对某个党派的观点大加点评，这一点倒是和欧洲的很多数学家一样。但是我根本就没有发现在数学和政治这两门学科之间存在任何共同点。除非那群人假设说，因为所有的圆的度数都一样，所以治理国家也不需要多少本领，只要会转动地球仪就行了。但是我却认为，这种特质源于人性中普遍存在的一个弱点，人们总是喜欢介入那些和我们毫无关系，也没进行过一点研究的事情，还偏偏要怀着自以为是的态度。

这些人总是惶惶不安，心里一刻也得不到宁静，而搅得他们不安的原因，对其他的人类而言简直不可能发生任何影响。令他们担忧的是，天体会发生若干变化。比方说，随着太阳不断向地球靠近，地球最终会被太阳吸掉或者吞灭。太阳表面逐渐被它自身所散发出的臭气笼罩，形成一层外壳，阳光就再也照不到地球上来了。地球十分侥幸地逃过了上一次彗星尾巴的扫刷，要不然肯定早已化为灰烬；据他们推算，再过三十一年，彗星将再次出现，那时我们很有可能被毁灭。依据他们的计算，他们有理由害怕，当彗星运行到近日点时，在离太阳一定距离的位置上，彗星所吸收的热量，相当于赤热发光的铁的热量的一万倍。彗星离开太阳后，拖在后面的一条炽热的尾巴约有一百万零十四英里长。如果地球从距离彗核或者彗星主体十万英里的地方经过，那么运行过程中地球必然会被烧成灰烬，太阳光每天都在消耗，却得不到任何补充，到最后全部耗尽时，太阳也就完了，而地球以及一切受太阳光照的行星，也都将因此而毁灭。

正是由于这种杞人忧天式的恐惧，他们每天晚上都没法安稳入睡，白天也不能享受快乐。每天遇到熟人的第一句话就是关心太阳的运行是否正常，日出日落是否和往常一样，希望能够避免彗星的突然袭击。他们的举止就像孩童一般，一边对妖魔鬼怪的故事趋之若鹜，一边又被吓得不敢入睡。

岛上的女人们相当活泼。她们对丈夫总是十分鄙夷，但是对陌生人却十分热情。浮岛上时常有来自下方大陆的访客，有的是为了公事，有些则是个人私事。他们总是会被浮岛上的男人轻视，因为他们缺乏海岛上的居民的才能。但是岛上的女人们却总是在这些陌生人当中挑选情人。最让人气恼的是，她们可以十分轻松和安全地偷情，因为她们的丈夫总是在冥想。只要为他们准备纸笔和仪器，然后支开那些拍手，女人们就可以和她们的情夫光明正大地寻欢作乐了。

尽管我认为这岛是世界上最美好的地方，可那些人的妻女却都哀叹自己被困在岛上了。她们住在这里，生活富裕，应有尽有，想做什么就做什么，可她们一点都不满足，还是渴望到下面的世界去看看，去享受一下各地的娱乐。不过如果皇帝不答应的话，她们是不准下去的。获得国王的特许很不容易，因为贵族们已有不少经验，知道劝说自己的夫人从下面归来是多么困难。有人跟我说，一位朝廷重臣的夫人，已经都有几个孩子了，丈夫就是王国里最有钱的首相；首相人极优雅体面，对她宠爱有加。她住在岛上最漂亮的宫里，却借口调养身体，到下面的拉格多去了。她在那里躲了好几个月，后来国王签发了搜查令，才找到衣衫褴褛的她。原来她住在一家偏僻的饭馆里。为了养活一个年老而又丑陋的跟班，她将自己的衣服都当了。跟班天天都打她，即使这样，她被人抓回时，竟还舍不得离开他。她丈夫仁至义尽地接她回家，丝毫没有责备她，但过了没多长时间，她竟带着她所有的珠宝又设法偷偷地跑到下面去了，还是去会她那老情人，从此一直没有下落。

读者们也许会觉得，这与其说是发生在遥远国度的某个故事，不如说这就发生在欧洲或者英国。只要细细一想，就会发现女人的反复无常是通病，这不受气候或者国家的限制。这一点倒是出乎我们意料的。

差不多一个月之后我已经熟悉掌握了这个国家的语言，也能够回答国王提出的大部分问题了。国王对我所到过的国家的律法、政治、历史、宗教和习俗没有任何兴趣，只顾着询问数学问题。哪怕有拍手在边上提醒，他仍然对我的阐述漠不关心。

第三章

作者阐述了一种被现代哲学和天文学解释的现象。拉普塔人在天文学上有着十分伟大的成就，最后作者阐述了国王惩罚叛乱的方法。

我请求国王准许我参观一下这神奇的浮岛，而国王也欣然同意，同时安排我的翻译跟随着我。我最想弄清楚的是，这座海岛到底是在人力的驱使之下才能飘浮在空中，还是完全是出于自然的恩赐。所以我会作一个详细的解释。

这座飞岛，也被称为浮岛，直径 7837 码，或者说四英里半，总面积超过十万亩。浮岛的厚度是三百码。浮岛的底部是一块光滑而平坦的金刚石，厚度大约是两百码。从金刚石开始往上，按照通常的顺序，依次排列着各种矿物，最上面一层是肥沃的土壤，有十到十二英尺那么厚。浮岛的最上层从边缘到中心形成了凹坡，这样所有的雨水都可以汇集到浮岛中间，然后汇入四个巨大的池塘，每一个池塘都有大约半英里那么大，距离浮岛的中心两百码。白天在阳光的照射之下，池塘里的水分不断蒸发，所以不会溢出。而且国王随时都可以让浮岛上升到云层以上，这样一来雨水就没法落到浮岛上了。当地的科学家认为，云层是不会上升到两英里的高度的，至少他们从来不曾听说过有这样的云层。

浮岛的中心有一个直径大约五十码的洞穴，通往一个被称为"佛兰多纳·葛格诺尔"的圆顶洞穴。这个洞穴位于金刚石上表面以下一百码的深处。洞穴里有二十盏长明灯，灯光通过金刚石的反射投射到山洞的各个位置，所以整个山洞永远都亮如白昼。在洞穴里有许许多多的数学仪器，而最为珍贵的则是整个浮岛存在的关键，一块巨大的磁石。这块磁石呈梭子形状，长六码，厚度约三码。在磁石的中央固定着一根金刚石做成的转轴，这样磁石就可以自由转动了。整块磁石处于平衡状态，所以很轻易就可以转动。整块磁石被镶嵌在金刚石做成的圆筒里面，直径大约四码，就这么安装在地面上。整个圆筒由八根长达六码的金刚石柱子支撑，圆筒内壁有一道十二英寸深的凹槽，可以随时转动这个圆筒。

任何力量都无法将这块磁石移开，因为圆筒和底下的支柱已经完全和浮岛底部的金刚石连接在一起，再也不可分割了。

在这块磁石的帮助之下，整座浮岛可以自由地升降。这块磁石的一端有吸引力，而另外一端则有推动力，所以只要把磁石具有吸引力的那一端指向地球，浮岛就会下降；而如果把具有推动力的那一端指向地球，浮岛就会上升。如果磁石是倾斜的，那么浮岛也会倾斜移动，这是因为磁石的作用力方向完全在同一条直线上。

在这种复杂的作用力的作用之下，浮岛可以在这个国家自由地行动。为了解释岛的运行方式，我们假设 AB 代表横贯巴尔尼巴比领土的一条线，CD 代表着磁石的方向，其中 D 代表推动力的那一头，C 代表吸引力的那一头，此时浮岛恰好就位于 C 的上空。假如将磁石调整到 CD 方向，而且将有推力的那一头向下倾斜，那么整个浮岛就会朝着 D 的方向上升。抵达 D 点之后只需要调整磁石，使得具有吸引力的那一端指向 E，那么浮岛就会倾斜向 E 运行。如果继续调整磁石到 EF 的方向，并且将有推力的那一头向下，那么浮岛就会上升到 F 的位置。抵达 F 之后将具有吸引力的那一端指向 G，磁石就会向 G 运行。如果再转动磁石，那么浮岛就会从 G 处转移到 H 处。就这样，只需要随时调整磁石的位置，浮岛就可以朝着各个方向移动。通过这种移动，浮岛就可以自由地在领土上空移动了。

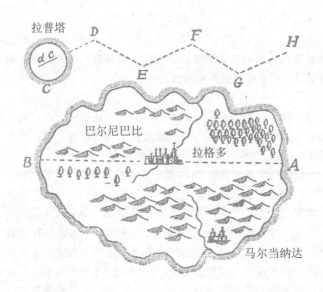

　　但必须注意，浮岛的运行不能超出下方的领土范围，也不能上升到四英里以上的高度。关于这一点，天文学家给出的解释是，这块磁石的磁力必须要在四英里的范围内才能够发挥作用。和磁石发生作用的物质就位于地球的深处以及距离海岸六英里的海中。所以在浮岛的帮助之下，国王能够轻易地统治处于磁场引力范围内的任何一个国家。

　　如果将磁石调整到水平位置的话，浮岛就可以静止在空中不动了。因为这时候磁石的两端和地球的距离相等，吸引力和推力是一样大的，所以就不会产生运动了。

　　这块磁石由专门的天文学家负责管理，他们会根据国王的命令随时移动磁石的位置。这些人一生中绝大部分时间都在观察天体，他们是用望远镜来完成这项工作的。他们的望远镜要比我们的精密太多。虽然他们最大的望远镜不过三英尺那么长，但是却比我们长达数百英尺的望远镜的效果好很多。先进的望远镜帮助他们在天文学上取得了巨大的成就，远远超过了我们欧洲的天文学家。他们已经观测到大约一万颗恒星，而在欧洲，我们的观测数目只有他们的三分之一。他们甚至已经发现在火星的周围还有两颗卫星。靠近火星的那一颗距离火星的距离恰好是火星直径的三倍，而外围的那一颗距火星的距离则是火星直径的五倍。前者运转一周大概需要十个小时，而后者则需要二十一个半小时。因此，它们运转周期的平方，和它们距离火星的距离的立方是相同的。所以这两颗卫星肯定也受到影响其他天体的万有引力的支配。

　　他们已经观察到九十三颗彗星，每一颗都有属于自己的运行周期。如果这一切属实的话，我倒希望他们能够把这份观察结果公布出来。这样我们国家才刚刚起步的彗星学说就一定会和天文学的其他分支一样进入成熟发展的阶段。

　　如果说国王和他的重臣能够齐心合力的话，他一定会成为最强大的国王。但是他的大臣们都在底下的大陆拥有产业，并且考虑到宠臣的地位是非常不稳定的，所以他们绝对不会同意和国王一起奴役自己的国家。

　　如果有哪座城市发生了叛乱，或者拒绝朝贡的话，一般有两种手段来平息。第一种就是把浮岛开到那座城市的上空，让这座城市失去阳光和雨水，这座城市很快就会暴发瘟疫，死去许多的市民。浮岛还可以朝下方投掷巨大的石块，把当地居民的房屋全部砸烂，让他们只能躲进地窖。如果叛乱的居民仍然执迷不悟的话，国王就会命令浮岛直接降落，把所有的房屋和居民都压成碎片。不过国王很少会采取这种极端的办法，一方面，国王不愿意这样做，另一方面，大臣们也不敢向他建议采取这样的行动，因为如果浮岛落下去了，下面的人民就会憎恨他们，大臣们在下方的产业也会受到极大的损害。而浮岛是属于国王的，不会受到影响。

不过不到万不得已的时候，国王是不会采取这种极端的手段的。其中更为重要的原因是，如果在他想毁灭的城市里有高耸的岩石的话，那么浮岛很有可能会被毁坏。虽然整座浮岛的底部是由一块大约两百码厚的金刚石组成的，但巨大的震动也可能毁坏金刚石板，或者被底下的炉火烤裂，就像我们的烟囱一样，尽管是用铁和石头制成的，有时也会爆裂。这些情况底下的居民也十分清楚，所以他们也很懂得适可而止。如果国王已经忍无可忍的话，他也会命令浮岛缓缓下降，这样一来金刚石岛底就不会被毁坏了。有一点是确定的，那就是浮岛的底部如果坏掉了，那么浮岛就会掉落到地面上。

而且根据这个王国的一项基本法律规定，国王和他的两个儿子是不准离开浮岛的。王后在没有超过生育年龄的时候也是无法离开的。

第四章

作者离开拉普塔，前往巴尔尼巴比。他到达了这个国家的首都，并对首都以及郊区的景象进行了描写。作者受到一位贵族的热情款待，并与其相谈甚欢。

尽管不能说我在浮岛上受到了虐待，但我必须要承认，我受到了冷落，甚至有几分蔑视。因为无论是国王还是浮岛上的居民都对数学和音乐这两门学科以外的其他学科嗤之以鼻，所以我在上面并不受人待见。

从另一方面来说，在领略了浮岛的所有的奇妙之后，我也迫切希望能够早日离开，因为我对这座浮岛上的人已经开始有点厌倦了。他们在上述两门学科的研究中的确取得了令人仰视的成就，我也十分崇拜他们。但他们却总是陷入无尽的沉思之中，这样一来就显得十分乏味了。我只能和浮岛上的女人、商人、拍手还有仆从们一起交谈，很快两个月时间就过去了，而我的举动也招致了他们的蔑视，但是我只有从这些人的口中才能得到合乎情理的回答。

通过刻苦学习，我已经熟练掌握了他们的语言。我不甘心一辈子待在这个浮岛上受人轻视，所以我决定只要有机会就赶紧离开。

宫廷里有一位贵族，是国王的近亲，就因为这个，大家才尊重他。他被公认为浮岛上最无知也是最愚蠢的人，虽然他曾经立下赫赫战功，而且在天分上也无可挑剔，在品性上也是无懈可击。但他唯一的缺点就是对音乐和数学这两门学科一窍不通。他时常会打错拍子，更不用说他在最浅显的数学定理的学习上所遇到的困难了。但是他却对我另眼相待，时常来拜访我，而且对于欧洲发生的各类事情，包括法律、风俗、习惯和礼节都十分有兴趣。他总是认真聆听我的讲话，对于我的描述总能提出许多真知灼见。虽然他时常安排两个拍手陪在身旁，但是他从来不需要他们，除非是在上朝等隆重场合。如果只有我们两个人的时候，他就会让拍手们退下。

我请求这位贵族帮助我求得国王的允许，让我离开这座浮岛。后来他果然这么做了，他说自己感到十分遗憾，因为他已经为我安排好了好几份好工作。我虽然十分感激，但最终还是婉言谢绝了。

在2月16日这一天，我告别了国王陛下和他的朝臣。国王赐予我一份价值大约两百英镑的礼物，庇佑我的这位贵族也送了一份同样贵重的礼物，同时还准备了一封介绍信，让我带给住在首都拉格多的一位老友。这座浮岛当时恰好位于距离拉格多大约两英里的地方，于是我去了浮岛的最底层，然后用先前上岛的办法下到了地面。

这块隶属于浮岛的大陆被称为巴尔尼巴比，首都是我先前提到过的拉格多。当我踏上坚实的土地的时候，我还是很满意的，随后我就一路朝着首都前进。一切都很正常，因为我的衣着和当地人完全相同，我也能够和他们熟练交谈。我很快就找到了介绍信上写的地址，我送上了介绍信，见到了我的老友在首都的朋友，并受到了热情款待。这位贵人的名字叫蒙诺帝，他安排我住在他家里，并且热情地招待了我。我在首都的这段时间就一直住在他家里。

我抵达拉格多的第二天早晨，蒙诺帝就带着我坐马车参观首都，这座城市差不多有半个伦敦那么大，但是城里的房屋看上去很奇怪，而且大部分都是年久失修的。街道上的人们行色匆匆，他们的面相粗野，目光呆滞，大多数人还衣衫褴褛。我们从一道城门走出，来到了大约三英里以外的郊区，在那儿有许多农夫拿着各种工具在劳动，但是我却没有看清楚他们到底在伺候什么庄稼。一路上这些奇怪的景象都让我分外迷惑，于是我鼓起勇气询问带领我参观的蒙诺帝，为什么街上和田里的人看上去十分忙碌，但是我却看不到任何效果？这儿的土地早已荒芜，这儿的房屋也摇摇欲坠，每个人看上去都那么辛苦，每个人的衣服也都破烂不堪，这到底是怎么一回事呢？

这位蒙诺帝老爷地位很高，曾多年担任拉格多政府首脑。但是由于底下官员们的阳奉阴违，他就因能力不足被罢官了。幸好国王认为他虽然治国不利，但还是个品性纯良的人，于是就网开一面了。

我如此这般直白地指责这个国家和它的人民，但是蒙诺帝却没有任何回应。他只是说我来这儿的时间还比较短，尚不足以做出公平的论断。而且每一个国家都有属于自己的习俗。随后他又说了好多话，但都是一个意思。当我们回到他的府上之后，他就询问我对他的府上有什么看法，有没有发现任何荒唐的地方，以及对他门下的仆从的面貌和着装有什么意见。我觉得他能够问出这样的问题也是合情合理，因为他衣着端正，看上去十分有教养。我回答说这是由于阁下的人品和出身都是无懈可击的缘故，并认为之前见到的那些缺点都是由于乡民的愚蠢和穷困所造成的。他问我是否愿意去参观距此二十英里不到的庄园，在那儿我们就可以畅所欲言了。我点头答应了，于是第二天一早我们就出发了。

旅途中，他要我注意农民经营管理土地的各种方法，我看了却完全摸不着思路，因为除了极少的几个地方，我看不到一穗谷子，一片草叶。但走了三小时后，景色却完全变了。我们走进了一片美丽无比的田野；农舍彼此相隔不远，修建得十分整齐；田地被围在中间，里边有葡萄园、麦田和草地。我记不得自己在哪还见过比这更赏心悦目的景象。那位贵族见我脸上开始晴朗起来，就叹了口气对我说，这些是他的产业，一直到他的住宅都是这样子。但他说，他的同胞们都讥讽他、瞧不起他，说他自己的事料理得都不行，哪还能给王国树立好榜样。虽然也有极少一些人学他的样子，可那都是些老弱而又任性的人。

我们终于到了他的家。那的确是一座高贵的建筑，合乎最优秀的古代建筑的典范。喷泉、花园、小径、大路、树丛都安排布置得极有见识、极有趣味。我每见一样东西都适当地赞赏一番，可他却毫不理会，直到没有其他人在场的晚餐之后，他才带着一副忧郁的神情告诉我：他正在考虑拆掉他现在城里和乡下的房子，因为他得按照目前的式样重新建造，所有的种植园也得毁掉，把它们改建成现在流行的样子，还得指示他所有的佃户都这么去做，不然他就会遭人责难，被人说成是傲慢、标新立异、做作、无知、古怪，说不定还会更加不讨国王的喜欢。他还对我说，等他把具体的一些事告诉我之后，我也许就不会那么惊奇了；这些事我在朝廷时可能闻所未闻，因为那里的人一心埋头沉思，注意不到下方发生的事情。

他谈话的内容总结起来大致是这样的：约在四十年前，有人或是因为有事，或是为了消遣，到拉普塔上面去了。一住就是五个月，虽然数学只学了一点皮毛，却带回了浮岛上的好冲动的风气。这些人一回来，就对地上的任何东西都感到厌烦，无论是艺术、科学、语言、技术，统统要求重新设计。为了达到这个目的，他们努力取得了皇家特许，在拉格多建立了一所皇家科学院。这一古怪的想法在百姓中倒是十分流行，结果就是王国内所有重要的城市都建有这么一所科学院。在这些科学院里，教授们设计出新的农业与建筑的规范和方法，为一切工商业设计了新型的工具和仪器。应用这些方法和工具，他们保证一个人可以干十个人的活；七日内就可以建成一座宫殿，并且建筑材料经久耐用，永远也不用维修；地上所有的果实，我们让它什么时间成熟它就什么时间成熟，产量比现在还要多一百倍。他们还提出了无数巧妙的建议。唯一让人觉得烦恼的是，所有这些计划到现在一项都没有完成，全国上下一片废墟，房屋倒塌，百姓缺衣少食，景象十分悲惨。所有这一切，他们见了不仅不灰心，反而在希望与绝望的同时驱使下，变本加厉地要去实施他们的那些计划。至于他自己，因为没有什么进取心，也就满足于老式的生活方式，住在先辈们建造的房子里，生活中的事情都完全模仿祖辈，没有什么革新。还有少数一些贵族和绅士也都像他这么做，但他们却遭人冷眼和讽刺，被认为是艺术的敌人，是国人中无知的败类，全国普遍都在改革发展，他们却一味懒散，自顾逍遥。

这位贵族非要我去参观一下科学院，他坚持说我肯定会感兴趣的，而他自己则不想多谈以前的事情了。他指了指大约三英里远的山坡上的一幢破烂房子，举了一个例子。原本在距离他的房子不到半英里的地方有一座水磨，是依靠河水来带动的，不仅满足他的庄园的需要，同时也能帮助那些佃户。但是在大约七年以前，这些设计师们建议他把水磨拆掉，然后在山坡上重建一个。他们计划开凿一条水渠，用水管和机器把水送上山，然后用这些水来推动水磨，毕竟高处的水的动力更强，所以只需要一半的水就可以推动水磨了。当时他和朝廷的关系不是很好，再加上一群朋友的劝告，他就同意了这个建议。他雇了一百人，花了两年工夫，结果失败了。设计家们走了，把责任全都推到他身上，并且一直都在怪他。他们又去拿别人做试验，同样说是保证成功，结果却一样令人失望。

几天后，我们回到了城里。他考虑到自己在科学院名声不好，没有亲自陪我去，只介绍了他的一个朋友陪我前往。我这位老爷喜欢说我是个设计的崇拜者，而且是个十分好奇和容易轻信于人的人。他这话并不是没有道理，我年轻时自己就做过设计家之类的人物。

格列佛参观科学院

第五章

作者得到许可前去参观拉格多皇家科学院，并且描述了这个地方。同时对于教授们的学术研究也做了简单描述。

　　这所科学院不是一整座独立的建筑物，而是一条街道两侧连在一起的几所房子，因为年久失修，才买下来给科学院使用。

　　科学院院长很客气地接待了我，我就在科学院里待了一段时间。每一个房间里都有一位或一位以上的设计家。我相信我参观了至少五百个房间。

　　我见到的第一个人样子枯瘦，双手和脸得就像刚刚被烟熏过一样，头发胡子一把长，衣衫褴褛，有几处都被火烤糊了，他的外衣、衬衫和皮肤全是一种颜色。八年来他一直在从事一项设计，想从黄瓜里提取阳光，装到密封的小玻璃瓶里，遇到阴雨湿冷的夏天，就可以放出来让空气温暖。他告诉我，他相信再有八年，他就可以以合理的价格向总督的花园提供阳光了；不过他又抱怨说原料不足，请求我给他点什么，也算是对他尖端设计的鼓励吧，特别是现在这个季节，黄瓜价格那么贵。我就送了他一份小小的礼物，因为我那位老爷特意给我准备了钱，他知道他们惯于向前来参观的人要钱。

　　我走进了另一间屋子，差点儿被一种臭气熏倒，急着就要退出来。我的向导却硬要我往前走，悄悄地求我不要得罪他们，要不他们会恨我入骨。我因此吓得连鼻子都不敢堵。这间屋里的设计家是科学院里年资最高的学者，他的脸和胡子呈淡黄色；手上、衣服上布满了污秽。我被介绍给他的时候，他紧紧拥抱了我，我当时本可以找个借口不受他这种礼遇的。自从他到科学院工作以来，就是研究怎样把人的粪便还原为食物。他的方法是把粪便分成几个部分，去除从胆汁里来的颜色，让臭气蒸发，再把浮着的唾液除去。每星期人们供应他一桶粪便，那桶大约有布里斯托尔酒桶那么大。

　　我还看到另外一个人在做将冰煅烧成火药的工作。他给我看了他撰写的一篇关于火的可锻性的论文，他打算发表这篇论文。

　　还有一位最巧妙的建筑师，他发明了一种建造房屋的新方法，即先从屋顶造起，自上而下一直盖到地基。他还为自己的这种方法辩护，对我说，蜜蜂和蜘蛛这两种最精明的昆虫就是这么做的。

　　有一个眼睛先天失明的人，他有几名徒弟也都如此。他们的工作是为画家调颜色，先生教他们靠触觉和嗅觉来区分不同的颜色。真是不幸，那一阵子我见他们的功课学得很不到家，就是教授自己也往往弄错。不过这位艺术家在全体研究人员中极受鼓励和推崇。

　　在另一个房间里，我饶有兴致地看到有位设计家发明了一种用猪来耕地的方法。那方法不用犁和牲口，也省劳力，是这样的：在一亩地里，每隔六英寸，在八英寸深的地方埋上一些橡子、枣子、栗子和这种动物最爱吃的其他山毛榉果及蔬菜；然后把六百头以上的猪赶到地里去；猪为了觅食，几天工夫就可以把所有的土翻遍，这样不仅适于下种，猪拉下的屎也正好给土上了肥。当然，尽管通过实验他们发现费用太大，也很麻烦，而且几乎没有获得什么收成，可大家都相信这一发明大有改进的可能。

　　我走进了另一个房间，这里边除了有一条狭小的通道供学者进出，其他的地方，像墙上和天花板上全都挂满了蜘蛛网。我刚一进门，他就大声叫喊让我不要碰坏他的蜘蛛网。他悲叹世人犯了个极大的错误，长久以来竟一直在用蚕丝，而他这里有许多家养昆虫，比蚕不知要好多少倍，因为它们既懂得织又懂得纺。他又进一步建议说，要是用蜘蛛，织网的费用就可以全部省下来。这一点，在他把一大堆颜色极其漂亮的飞虫给我看了过后，我就完全明白了。他用这些飞虫喂他的蜘蛛，他告诉我们，蛛网的颜色就是从这些飞虫而来，又因为他各种颜色的飞虫都有，就能满足每个人的不同喜好。只要他能给飞虫找到适当的食物如树脂、油或者其他什么黏性的物质，他就能够使蜘蛛纺出来的丝线牢固而坚韧。

还有一位天文学家，他承担了一项设计，要在市政厅房顶的大风标上安装一架日晷，通过调整地球与太阳在一年中和一天中的运转，使它们能和风向的意外转变正好一致。

我忽然感到一阵腹痛，于是我的向导就带我走进了一间屋子，那儿住着一位以治疗这种毛病而闻名的医生。他能用同一种器具施行作用相反的两种手术。他有一个很大的、装有一个细长象牙嘴的吹风器。他把象牙嘴插入肛门内八英寸，将肚子里的气吸出来；他肯定地说他这样能把肚子吸得又细又长，像一个干瘪的膀胱。不过要是病情来得又顽劣又凶，他就要把吹风器先鼓满气体再将象牙嘴插入肛门，把气打进病人的体内，然后抽出吹风器重新将气装满，同时用大拇指紧紧地堵住屁眼。这样重复打上三四次，打进去的气就会喷出来，毒气也被一同带出（就像抽水机一样），病人的病也就好了。我看到他在一只狗的身上同时做了这两种试验，第一种不见任何效果，第二种手术后，那畜生胀得都快要炸了，接着就猛屙了一阵，可把我和我的同伴熏坏了。狗当场就死了，可我们走的时候，那医生还在设法用同样的手术让它起死回生呢！

我还参观了其他房间，但是所见的那些奇怪的情景我就不再说出来劳读者的神了，所以接下来我会说得简单一些。

至此，我只参观了科学院的一侧房间，另一侧都是为那些思考者准备的。在介绍这些思考者之前，我想先介绍一位十分有名的人物，他被称为"全能学者"。他告诉我们，他花费了整整三十年的时间来研究改善人类生活的途径。他一个人就拥有两个巨大的房间，里面有许多奇怪的东西，还有五十个人在协助他干活。有些试图把空气凝结成固体，他们先从固体中提取出氮元素，然后再把液体部分给蒸发掉。还有一些人忙着软化大理石，用来制造枕头或者针垫；还有人在研究如何将马匹的马蹄硬化，这样它们就不会摔倒了。至于这位学者本身，当时正忙着两件大事：第一件就是用米糠来播种，关于这一点他宣称已经有好几个试验结果支持他的论断。还有一件则是用树脂、矿物质和蔬菜混合而成的东西抹在羊羔背上，防止羊羔长出羊毛。他希望通过一段时间的努力，培养出不长羊毛的绵羊，并且推广到全国。

我们穿过一条通道，就来到了科学院的另外一侧。正如先前我讲的，这一部分是专门留给思考者的。

我见到的第一位教授正和他的四十个学生在一个巨大的房间里工作。在房间里有一个巨大的架子，几乎占据了房间的所有空间。只听他介绍说这项工程能够用切实可行的、机械的办法来改变人类的思维。世人很快就能够感觉到它的用处了。而在他之前，从未有人想到过这般伟大的计划。众所周知，要想在艺术和科学这两门领域取得一点成就是多么困难啊！但是如果采用了他的办法，那么不管是多么愚蠢的人，只需要支付一笔相当的费用就足以创作出哲学、诗歌、政治、法律、数学和神学的专著。他领着我来到了架子前面，在这架子四周站着他的学生。整个架子差不多有二十英尺见方，就放在屋子中间。这个架子的表面是由许许多多像骰子一般大小的木块组成的，木块的每一面都贴着一张纸，上面写着他们的语言中的词汇，由各种不同的语态、时态和派生变化组成。教授接下来要我注意看，因为他现在要准备开动机器了。一声令下，学生们各抓住了一个铁把手。原来架子的四边装有四十个把手，每个学生转动一个把手，单词的布局就完全改变了。然后他又吩咐三十六个学生轻声念出架子上出现的文字，只要有三四个词连起来可以凑成一个句子，他们就念给剩下的四名做抄写员的学生听，由他们记录下来。这项工作要重复做三四次。由于机器构造巧妙，每转动一次，木方块就彻底翻个身，上面的文字也会换到其他位置。

这些年轻的学生每天花六个小时在这项劳动上。教授把几卷对开的书拿给我看，里边已经收集了不少支离破碎的句子，他打算把它们全都拼凑到一起，用这丰富的材料，编撰一部包括所有文化和科学门类的全书贡献给这个世界。不过，要是公众能筹一笔资金在拉格多制造五百个这样的架子来从事这项工作，同时要求负责这些架子的人把他们各自搜集到的材料都贡献出来，那么，这项工作将得以改进，并加速完成。

他还对我说，他从青年时代起就沉浸在这项发明之中，他已经把所有的词汇都记录上去了，而且还刻意调整了虚词、名词、动词和其他类型的词汇的比例。

我向这位滔滔不绝的思考者致以诚挚的感谢，感谢他的详尽说明。我保证说如果我有幸回到故土，我一定会告诉世人他是这架精妙的机器的发明者。我请求他能够允许我把这机器的模样画在纸上。我对他说，现在欧洲有一股歪风邪气，总是喜欢剽窃他人成果。如果让他们知道有这么伟大的发明，一定会趋之若鹜，前来抢夺这个宝贵的荣誉，尽管如此，我一定会多加小心，让他独享盛名。

随后我们就去了语言学校，有三位教授正坐在那儿，严肃地谈论如何改进本国的语言。

他们的第一项计划就是简练他们的语言，比如将多音节词改成单音节的，然后去掉所有的动词和分词，毕竟在现实生活中能想到的事物都是名词。

另一项计划则是，无论什么词汇，一概废除。他们坚决主张，不论从健康的角度考虑，还是从简练的角度考虑，这一计划都大有好处，因为大家都清楚，我们每说一个词，或多或少会对肺部有所侵蚀，这样也就缩短了我们的寿命。因此他们就想出了一个补救

两位大学问家就像小商贩一样

的办法：既然词只是事物的名称，那么，大家在谈到具体事情的时候，把表示具体事情所需的东西带在身边，不是来得更方便吗？本来这一发明早就应该实现了，百姓们会感到很轻松，对他们的健康也大有好处。可是妇女们联合了俗人和文盲，要求像他们的祖先那样能有用嘴说话的自由，否则他们就要起来造反。这样的俗人常常就是科学势不两立的敌人。不过，许多最有学问最有智慧的人还是坚持这种以物示意的新方法。这方法只有一点不便，就是如果一个人要办的事很大，种类又很多，那他就必须将一大捆东西背在身上，除非他有钱，能雇上一两个身强力壮的佣人随侍左右。我就常常看到有两位大学问家，背上的负荷压得他们腰都快断了，就像我们这里的小贩一样。如果他们在街上相遇，就会把背上的东西放下来，然后打开背包，在一起谈上个把钟头，再收起各自的东西，互相帮忙将负荷重新背上，然后分手道别。

但如果是简短的谈话，只需要把工具放在

口袋里，或者夹在胳膊中间就够了。如果是在家里也不会为难，毕竟房间里早已准备好了一切。

这种发明还有一个巨大的优势，那就是可以不受到国别的影响，因为每个国家的工具其实都是大同小异的，所以他们的用处也得到了共识。这样哪怕那些驻外使节们对外国语言一窍不通，都可以和所在国家的国王和大臣交谈。

我还到了数学学校，那里的先生用一种我们欧洲人很难想象的方法教他们的学生。命题和证明都用头皮一样颜色的墨水清清楚楚地写在一块薄而脆的饼干上。这饼干学生得空腹吞食下去，接下来的三天，除面包和水，什么都不准吃。饼干消化之后，那色彩就会带着命题涂进脑子里。不过到现在为止还不见有什么成效，一方面是因为墨水的成分有错误，另一方面也因为小孩子们顽劣不驯，这么大的药片吃下去总觉得太恶心，所以他们通常偷偷溜走，不等药性发作，就朝天把它吐了出来。他们也不听劝告，不愿像处方上要求的那样等待那么长时间不吃东西。

第六章

作者继续参观学院，并提出了许多建议，而且都被采纳了。

在政治工程学院，我受到了冷遇。在我看来，这儿的教授都失去了理性，这让我感到十分悲伤。这些不幸的家伙正在畅想着有关未来的美好规划和愿景。他们打算向国王提出建议，要根据一个人的智慧、才能和品德来选拔宠臣。他们还强调公共利益的重要性，提议要加大对那些具有卓越的功勋、出众的才能、不凡的贡献的人的奖励。同时他们也希望国王能够将自己的利益和人民的利益放在一起，要选择那些有才能的人担任要职。同时他们也提出了一些无法实现的空想，都是前人从来没有想过的可怕念头。不过他们的举动倒是让我想到了一句至理名言：凡是被认为是荒诞不经的，都被哲学家奉为真理。

哪怕是这样，我也得为这些人说一句公道话，因为并不是所有人都是幻想家。有一位才华横溢的医生，对于政府的体制架构和运营机制十分熟悉。他擅长将自己所学应用在各个行政机关，帮助治疗各种堕落腐化的行为。在他看来，这些弊端之所以会产生，是由于统治者本身的陋习和缺点所造成的，另一方面则是来源于被统治者的自由散漫。所有作家和理论家都同意，在人体和政治体制之间是存在关联性的。既然这两个系统都必须要保持健康，那么它们的病症是否可以通过同样的办法来解决呢？这是一个很浅显的道理。众所周知，那些参议员和顾问最大的毛病就是说话啰啰唆唆，而且还很容易生气。当然还有其他问题，比如说他们在思想上的巨大问题。有的时候他们会剧烈痉挛，两手的神经和肌肉会痛苦地收缩，右手更是如此；有时还会肝火旺，肚子胀，头晕，说胡话；也会长满是恶臭和脓疮的淋巴性结核瘤；会口沫直飞地吐出酸气扑鼻的胃气；吃起东西来胃口像狗却又消化不良；还有许许多多其他的病症，就不一一列举了。因此，这位医生建议：每次参议员开会，头三天请几位大夫列席；每天辩论完毕，由他们替每位参议员诊脉；之后，经过深思熟虑，讨论出各种毛病的性质和治疗方法；然后，在第四天带着药剂师，准备好相应的药品赶回参议院，在议员们入席之前，根据各人病情的需要，分别让他们服用镇静剂、轻泻剂、去垢剂、腐蚀剂、健脑剂、治标剂、通便剂、头痛剂、黄疸剂、去痰剂、清耳剂，再根据药性及作用决定再服、换服，或者停服。

这项计划并不会对公众造成多么严重的负担，在我看来，在那些由参议员来参与立法的国家，这一项计划将对提高办事效率有着很大的帮助。这种做法不仅能够缓和现场的氛围，减少辩论的时间，还可以让那些总是沉默的人开口，让说个没完的人能够歇口气。同时还能够缓解年轻人的急躁脾气，纠正老家伙们的那种倚老卖老的态度，能够让糊涂鬼变得清醒，让冒失鬼变得谨慎。

同时，由于重臣的记性太差，所以这位医生建议，当人们面见大臣，汇报完毕之后应该狠狠拧一下大臣的鼻子，或者踢他的肚子，踩他脚上的鸡眼，或者捏着他的耳朵狠狠扯三下，或者在他的屁股上戳一针，要么就把他的胳膊拧出淤青。之所以要这么做，是为了杜绝大臣们的健忘症。要坚持每天都这么做，直到交代给他的事情顺利完成或者被拒绝办理为止。

他还提出，每一位参加议会的议员在发表意见和参与答辩之后，都应该投票反对自己的提议，因为只有这样做，才能做出真正对公众有利的判决。

针对不同党派之间的激烈纷争，医生同样提出了一个绝妙的建议。具体的操作办法是这样的：每个党派可以选出一百个重要人物，然后把脑袋差不多大的两个人凑成一组。随后由两名手艺精湛的外科医生同时取下脑袋的一部分，要保证取下来的部分恰好是大脑的一半。随后把两个人取下来的部分互换一下，然后安在另外一个人的脑袋上。这项手术对于外科医生的精准度有着很高的要求，不过这位医生向我们保证，只要手术进展顺利，疗效是绝对可以保证的。这样一来，在两个思维完全相反的半脑的共同作用下，他们就很容易达成和解，随后就可以平和地进行思考了。我们也同样希望那些自以为生下来就是为了观察和统治这个世界的家伙能够怀着一种平和的心态去思考啊。如果遇到两个人的大脑的大小和质量相差甚大，那其实也没有什么大不了。因为在这位医生看来，这样的差异根本就无足轻重。

我还听到两个教授正在进行一场激烈的讨论，他们正在争辩如何才能在不让百姓受苦的前提下最方便也最有效地完成筹款工作。其中一位教授认为应该对那些丑陋而愚蠢的行为征税。每个人应缴纳的税额都应该由他的邻居组成的审判团体进行公平裁决。而第二位教授的意见恰好相反。他认为有些人就爱炫耀自己的过人的才能，对于这样的人来说，他们应缴纳的税额应该由他们自认为的出众程度来决定。最受异性欢迎的男人应该缴纳最高的税额，而具体的评判标准则应该由他接受的爱情的性质和次数来决定。至于这两项指标，则应该在实事求是的基础上允许他们自由裁定。他还建议对聪明、勇敢和礼貌征收同样的税额，具体的方法和上述一样。至于荣誉、正义、智慧和学问这类更加稀有的品德，那就不需要征税了。因为没有人会承认别人拥有这样的品德，而真正拥有这些品德的人也不会觉得自己高人一等。

那些妇女应该按照她们的美貌和打扮手段来征税。她们可以和男人一样自己决定税额。但是像忠贞、节操、辨别是非和温柔善良等品性也是不需要征税的，因为如果要征收的话，这部分税额将会是很大的负担。

为了保证议员们始终对皇室忠诚，他建议他们用抽签的办法来分配职位。所有人在抽签之前都必须宣誓，无论自己抽到了什么什么岗位，都会保持对皇室的忠诚，而那些没有抽中的人也可以安排在下次继续抽签，这样他们就会对朝廷怀有希望，不会抱怨朝廷的失信。这样一来，他们的落选就只是命运的安排，和其他内阁大臣就没有一点关系了。而命运的肩膀可要比那些内阁大臣的肩膀宽厚太多了。

另一位教授拿了一大本关于如何侦破反政府阴谋诡计的文件给我看。他建议政治家们要对一切可疑人物进行检查，看他们什么时间吃饭，睡觉时脸朝哪边，擦屁股用的是哪一只手；要严格检查他们的粪便，从粪便的颜色、气味、味道、浓度以及消化的程度来判断他们的思想和计划，因为人没有比在排便时思考更严肃、周密和专心致志了，这是他经过无数次实验才发现的。这种时候他如果在考虑怎样暗杀国王，粪便就会呈绿色；但他盘算的如果只是搞一次叛乱或者焚烧京城，粪便的颜色就大不一样了。

这篇论文写得十分犀利，其中不少见解对政治家来说是既有趣又有用，不过我觉得有些地方还不够完善。这一点我冒昧地对作者说了，并且提出，要是他愿意，我可以再提供他一点补充意见。他很高兴地接受了我的建议，这在作家中，尤其在设计家之流的作家中，是十分罕见的。他表示很愿意听听我还有什么意见。

我对他说，我曾在特列布里亚的首都兰顿停留了一段时间，我发现那儿的居民都是由侦探、告密者、证人、控告者、检举人、证人、咒骂者和他们的手下组成的。他们全部受正、副官员的指使和资助。在那个国家，阴谋诡计往往都是那些身怀高位的政治家的所作所为。他们试图保住那个摇摇欲坠的王国，试图镇压或者转移群众的不满情绪，试图将财富收入自己囊中，试图影响舆论来满足自己的私欲。他们会私下里先达成协议，明确那些作为目标的可疑分子，控告他们图谋不轨。随后他们就有理由去搜查这些可疑分子的书信和文件，并且冠冕堂皇地把他们抓起来。至于那些搜出来的文件，则由一伙擅长从词语和音节中搜寻出神秘意义的能手们去处理。比如他们会强行把马桶翻译成枢密院，认为"一群鹅"指"参议院"，"瘸腿狗"指"侵略者"，"呆头"指"——"（"——"代表"国王"，当时作者不便明白写出，故以"——"代之），"瘟疫"指"常备军"，"秃鹰"指"大臣"，"痛风"指"祭司长"，"绞刑架"指"国务大臣"，"夜壶"指"贵族委员会"，"筛子"指"宫廷贵妇"，"扫帚"指"革命"，"捕鼠器"指"官职"，"无底洞"指"财政部"，"阴沟"指"朝廷"，"滑稽演员戴的系铃帽"指"宠臣"，"折断的芦苇"指"法庭"，"空酒桶"指"将军"，"流脓的疮"指"行政当局"。

如果这一招行不通的话，他们还有两种好办法。分别是拆分法和颠倒法。第一个办法就是用每个单词的第一个字母来解释其中的政治含义。比如 N 代表的就是阴谋，B 代表的是骑兵团，而 L 代表着舰队。第二种办法就是颠倒文件上的可疑的字母，用来拼凑出某种对当局不满的阴谋。比如我写了一封信给我的朋友，说我的兄弟汤姆最近得了痔疮。这时候那些本领高超的专家经过一通分析之后，就会得出以下这句话："反抗吧——条件已经成熟！"这就是所谓的颠倒法。

这位教授对我的建议大为重视，他十分感激，表示一定要在自己的论文中提及我的名字以表敬意。

我觉得这个国家已经没有什么吸引我的地方了，便开始思索着返回英国。

第七章

作者离开拉格多，来到马尔多纳达。由于没有船只，所以他就去格鲁布杜德利卜做了短暂的拜访，并且受到当地长官的热情招待。

巴尔尼巴比只是这块大陆的一部分。我有理由相信，这块一直向东延伸的大陆应该是通往美国加利福尼亚以西的无名地带。这块大陆的北边临近太平洋，距离拉格多不过才一百五十英里。那儿有一个不错的港口，这个港口与被称为鲁格奈格的巨大海岛有很多贸易往来。鲁格奈格就位于这座大陆西北方向大约北纬二十九度，东经一百四十度的位置。而在鲁格奈格的东南方向大约一百里格的地方就是日本了。日本天皇和鲁格奈格国王结成了亲密的同盟关系，两个岛国因此交易频繁。于是我决定沿着这条路线返回欧洲。我雇佣了两头驴子还有一个向导，带上了我为数不多的行李就出发了。我在拉格多和我亲爱的朋友告别，他一直以来都对我很好，临别时还赠予我一份丰厚的礼物。

我的旅程平淡无奇，所以我也就不赘述了。当我到达马尔多纳达海港时（这个海港的名字就是如此），却发现并没有马上出发去鲁格奈格的船只，而且在一段时间内都不会有。这座海港小镇和朴次茅斯差不多大小。我很快就在城里认识了几个好友，并且受到了热情的招待。其中一位有名望的先生建议我说，既然在一个月以后才会有通往鲁格奈格的船只，为什么不趁着这段时间去格鲁布杜德利卜岛参观一下呢，也许我会在那儿找到很好玩的事情。这座海岛就在西南方向距此大约五里格的地方。他主动要求陪我一起去，同行的还有另外一位朋友。他们专门为我准备了一艘轻便的小帆船。

按照我的理解，"格鲁布杜德利卜"这个词的含义和我们的"魔法岛"差不多。这座海岛的面积大概有英国南海岸的怀特岛的三分之一，而且物产十分丰富。住在海岛上的居民都是身怀魔法的人，由这个部落的首领统治。他们只允许内部通婚，由岛上年龄最大的人担任首领或长官。首领有一座雄伟的宫殿，还有一座大约三千亩大小的花园，花园的四周是大约二十英尺高的石头围墙。花园里还有几块田地，用来养牛、种庄稼，以及栽培花草。

首领和他的家人都是不同寻常的人。这位首领可以随时召唤出亡灵，并且让他们在二十四小时之内都听从他的命令。不过这时间一秒钟都不能延长，不然魔法就会失效。而且除非是特殊情况，否则在三个月之内他无法再次召唤同样的亡灵。

当我们来到海岛上的时候已经差不多是上午十一点了，陪同我的一位绅士前去拜见首领，并且告诉他有一位远道而来的陌生人希望能够拜见他。而这位首领也很爽快地答应了，于是我们三人就这样走进了宫殿的大门。在大门的两侧各有一排卫兵把守，他们的服饰以及武器都十分奇怪。这些卫兵的表情十分恐怖，简直无法用言语来形容。我们穿过了几座宫殿，一路上都有卫兵把守。我就这样怀着恐惧之心来到了大殿上，并向首领深深地鞠了三个躬。在回答了首领的问题之后，他安排我们坐在宝座下方的最后一级台阶旁的三个凳子上。虽然岛上有属于他们的语言，但是这位首领其实也掌握巴尔尼巴比的语言。他希望我能够讲讲一路上的见闻。为了表现他对我们的热情，只见他挥了挥手，侍立在两旁的卫兵就这么不见了。这样的景象真让我大吃一惊，就好像一个清醒的人突然发现身边的一切如同梦境一般失踪了一样。首领安慰我说不要激动，而我身旁的两个同伴也是一副习以为常的模样，想必他们已经见识过很多次了。我这才鼓起勇气谈了谈这一路上的见闻，但是我并没有完全放下心来，而是时不时回头望向之前侍卫们站立的地方。我很荣幸能够和首领共进午餐。用餐的时候又有一批新的亡灵在边上服侍着。这时候的我已经没有先前那般惊慌了。我们一直待到傍晚才离开。首领盛情邀请我留宿，但是我拒绝了他，然后和同伴一起在附近的镇子上找了一家小旅馆。第二天一早我们再次上门拜访，他一如既往地热情接待了我们。

就这样我们在岛上住了十天。白天我们大部分时间都在和首领聊天，晚上则回到我们的住处。很快我就对亡灵习以为常了，三四次之后，我就完全无动于衷了。可能还是有一点点害怕，但更多的还是好奇。首领说我可以随意召见我想要见到的灵魂，他都能够满足我的要求，无论是多么古老的亡灵都可以。而且只要我的问题合情合理，他们都会回答我，前提是我不能询问发生在他们所在的年代之后发生的事情。我不用担心他们会说谎，因为在冥界是不能撒谎的。所以他们绝对会诚实回答我的问题。

对于这样的恩典，我真是感恩不尽。我跟着他去了内殿，在那儿欣赏花园的美景。这让我联想到了雄伟壮观的场面，所以我希望能够见到亚历山大大帝在阿贝拉之战之后统帅军队的雄奇景象。首领的大手一挥，我们所在的窗户下面很快就出现了一个宏伟的战场。亚历山大大帝本人被召唤了进来，他的话很难懂，毕竟我不是很擅长希腊语，但是他很严肃地告诉我，他并不是被毒死的，而是因为饮酒过度而发热病死的。

随后我又见到了正在穿越阿尔卑斯山的汉尼拔，他说他的军营里面根本就没有醋。

我看到了凯撒和庞贝正准备开战，凯撒获得了胜利。我想看看古罗马的元老院开会时的场景，也想看看现代的议会议事的模样。相比之下，元老院的成员都是英雄和半神，而现代的议会则是一群乌合之众，充斥着商贩、小偷、土匪和暴徒。

在我的请求之下，首领示意凯撒和布鲁特斯上前。看到布鲁特斯的我不禁肃然起敬，他的面庞透露出他那崇高的品德和坚定的信念，对于国家的热情和对于人类的热爱。看到两位伟人能够达成和解，我感到十分开心。特别是凯撒承认说，自己这辈子虽然有许多的功绩，但是和布鲁特斯相比，这一切都相形见绌了，因为正是布鲁特斯为他的一生画上了句号。我和布鲁特斯谈了很久，他说自己和自己的祖先尤尼乌斯、苏格拉底、埃帕米农达、小加图和托马斯·摩尔爵士在一起。他们这个六人集团是那么伟大，人类的历史上根本就无法找出第七个人能够和他们的功绩相提并论。

我希望各个历史时期的风流人物都能够出现在眼前，这样我就可以好好欣赏了。为了满足我的愿望，首领召唤了许多的历史人物。如果我在此一一赘述的话，读者们一定会感到十分沉闷。许多推翻了暴君的英雄，为被奴役的民族争取到自由的名人都出现在我的面前，让我十分过瘾。我简直无法表达自己内心的喜悦之情，所以我的读者应该也无法体验这样的美妙感觉。

第八章

继续对格鲁布杜德利卜的情况进行描述，对古今历史的修正。

我很想见见古代那些最有名的圣贤和学者。于是我特意安排了一天时间，请求首领帮我把荷马和亚里士多德请过来，当然还有所有对他们的作品做过注释的人。这些评述家加起来差不多有上百位，很多人只能等在院子里和宫殿外面。但是我一眼就认出了那两位英雄，而且立即就分辨清楚了两人的身份。荷马长得比较高大俊美，在他这个年纪的人来说，他算是站得很直的了，而且眼神活泼而锐利。亚里士多德伛偻着身体，手里拿着一根拐杖。他长得很清瘦，头发稀少而又偏长，嗓音低沉。很快我就发现，这两人根本就不认识其余的人，他们从来没有见过也没有听说过这些人。其中有一位不愿意透露姓名的鬼魂说，在冥界这些评注家从来不敢靠近这两位贤者，因为他们很清楚自己的评注不过是胡说八道，所以感到十分羞愧。我把迪选莫斯和尤思台修斯介绍给了荷马，请求他能够对他们好一点，不过荷马很快就发现了这两人缺乏天分，根本无法了解一位诗人的内在精神。我还把司格特斯和拉莫斯介绍给亚里士多德，但是他一听两人的介绍就十分不耐烦了。他直截了当地问，这伙人是不是都像他们两个一样是十足的蠢蛋呢？

随后我请首领帮我把笛卡儿和伽桑狄召来，并且说服他们把自己的思想体系解释给亚里士多德听。这位伟大的哲学家坦然承认了自己在自然哲学方面犯下的错误，因为他和很多人一样，在一些事情上难免臆测。但是他也发现，宣扬伊壁鸠鲁学说的伽桑狄和笛卡儿的涡动学说同样存在很大的缺陷。因此他预测，当代学者热衷的万有引力学说也会遭遇同样的命运。他说大自然的体系不过是新的风尚，时时刻刻随着时间而改变，哪怕是那些能够用数学定理来证明的人，都只能在短短一段时间内风靡，很快就会被时光所湮没。

我花费了五天时间和许多古代的学者会面。我也看到了罗马第一帝国的大部分的皇帝。我还请首领为我召唤了伊里欧伽布鲁斯的厨师为我做了一顿丰盛的晚餐，但是由于缺乏材料，他们并不能最大限度地发挥自己的才能。阿格西劳斯的奴隶为我们准备了一盆典型的斯巴达式肉羹，但是我吃了一口就再也不想吃了。

陪同我造访的两位绅士因为急于去处理一些私事，三天之后就得回去，所以我就抓紧机会在这三天时间里见了一些近代的名人，都是三百年来我国和欧洲其他各国最为有名的人物。因为我一向对血统十分崇拜，所以我请求首领帮我把所有的国王和他们的祖先都召集过来。但是结果却让我大为失望。在他们的谱系当中并不全是国王，我就看到一个族谱里面有两位提琴师、三位朝臣和一位意大利教廷的主管。而在另外一个家族里竟然还有一名理发匠、一位修道院的主管和两名红衣主教。由于我对这些头顶皇冠的人过于尊崇，所以在此就不多阐述这个问题了。至于那些公爵、伯爵、侯爵、子爵之类的我就顾不上那么多了，毕竟还是能够从他们的祖先身上找出一些名门望族的特征，这一发现倒是让我十分欣慰。因为我看得很清楚，这一家人的长长的下巴到底是怎么出现的，而另外一家为什么两代都出恶棍，而接下来的都是傻子；第三家人为什么都发疯，第四家人都是骗子。这一切怎么会像坡里道尔·维吉尔在说到某家名门时所讲的那样："男子不勇敢，女子不贞洁。"残暴、欺诈、懦弱怎么会像盾牌纹章那样，渐渐成了某些家族出名的特征。是谁第一次给一个高贵的家族带来了梅毒，由此代代相传使子子孙孙都生上瘰疬毒瘤。我看到皇家世系中断原来是因为出了这么些仆人、佣人、走卒、车夫、赌棍、琴师、戏子、军人和扒手，对以上种种也就一点不觉得奇怪了。

最让我感到恶心的就是现代历史了。我仔细检查了一下近一百年来宫廷里的所有大人物，发现这个世界都被这群恶心的作家给欺骗了！他们吹嘘说懦夫立下了赫赫战功，傻瓜提出了最聪明的建议，阿谀奉承的人成了最真诚的，而那些出卖祖国的却具备古罗马人的品德。那些无神论者成了最虔诚的，而强奸犯成了最忠贞的代表，告密的奸细说的都是真话。而又有多少无辜的好人，由于腐败的法官和党派斗争等内幕遭到屠杀和流放。那些身处高位，享受荣华富贵的又有多少是恶棍。在枢密院和参议院里发生的事情，其肮脏程度简直可以和鸨母、妓女和皮条客相媲美。世界上的伟大节点的出现也不过如此，它们之所以能够成功，所依靠的无非就是一些微不足道的偶然事件。得知了这样的真相之后，我对人类的成就和品格产生了浓浓的鄙夷之情。

我在这里还发现，那些装模作样要写什么轶闻秘史的人原是多么的诡诈而无知。许多国王都被他们用一杯毒药送进了坟墓；君王和首相在无人在场时的谈话也会被他们记录下来；驻外使节和国务大臣的思想和密室他们都能打开；不幸的是他们永远也没有弄对过。我还发现了许多震惊世界的大事背后的秘密：一名妓女怎么把持着后门的楼梯，后门的楼梯怎么把持着枢密院，枢密院又怎么把持了上议院。一位将军当着我的面承认，他打的一次胜仗纯粹是由于他的怯懦和指挥无方；一位海军大将说，因为没有正确的情报，他本打算率舰队投敌，不知为何却打败了敌人。三位国王对我明言，他们在位期间从来就没有提拔过一个有功之人，除非是一时弄错，或者中了某个亲信大；他们就是再世，也不会这么做的。他们提出了充足的理由来证明：不贪污腐败就无法保住王位，因为道德灌输给人的那种积极、自信和刚强的性格，对办理公务将是一种永久的阻碍。

出于好奇，我还特意询问过他们，这么多人获取高官贵爵和巨大产业，到底用的是什么手段？我的提问只限于近代，不触及当代，因为我得保证做到，即使是外国人也不能得罪。当然，我这里所说的没有一点是针对我的祖国来的，这一点我想就不必向读者解释了吧。大量有关的人物都被召唤了来，我只稍稍一看，就发现景象真是一片狼藉，以致我每每想起，都免不了心情沉重。伪证、欺压、唆使、欺诈、拉皮条等错误还是他们提到的最可以原谅的手段，因为都还说得过去，我也就原谅了他们。可是，有人承认，他们伟大富贵都是因为自己鸡奸和乱伦，有的强迫自己的妻女去卖淫，有的是背叛祖国或者君王，有的给人下毒药，更有人为了消灭无辜滥用法律。地位高贵的人仪表堂皇，本该受到我们这些卑贱的人的尊敬，然而我看到的这种种现象不免要使我减少对他们的崇敬；我这么做，希望大家能够原谅。

我还经常读到一些忠君爱国的丰功伟绩，对于那些建立了卓越功勋的人物相当敬仰。但是我实际一打听才知道，他们的名字根本就没有被记录，仅有的几个却被历史写成了卑鄙无耻的恶棍和卖国贼，以及其他我从来没有听到过的名字。所有人都很沮丧，因为大多数人都穷困潦倒而死，剩下的则被送上了断头台。

在这些人当中，有一个人的经历十分不寻常。他身边有一个十八岁的青年。他告诉我，他在一艘战舰上当了多年的舰长，艾克丁姆海战当中，他幸运地冲破了敌军的防线，击沉了三艘主力舰并且俘虏了一艘，直接促成了安东尼的大败溃逃。站在他身边的青年就是他的独子，也在这一次战役中丧生了。战后他凭借着自己的功绩，前往罗马请求奥古斯都朝廷提升他的职位，恰好有一艘大战舰的舰长阵亡了。但是朝廷根本不理会他的要求，竟将舰长一职给了一名连大海都从未见过的青年，他是皇帝的一个情妇的仆人李柏丁那的儿子。回到自己原来的舰上，他就被加上了玩忽职守的罪名，战舰则移交给了海军副将帕勃利可拉的一位亲随。从此他退居到远离罗马的一个穷乡，并在那里结束了自己的一生。我极想知道这个故事的真相，就请求长官把那次战役中任海军大将的阿格瑞帕召来。阿格瑞帕来了，他证明舰长所说毫无虚假。他还说了舰长许多好话。舰长因为生性谦逊，自己的大部分功劳不是少说就是整个儿不提。

我感到很奇怪，这个帝国明才刚兴起奢侈之风，为什么一下子就腐化堕落了呢？至于那些早已恶贯满盈的国家，类似的情形倒让我见怪不怪了。在那些国家里，名利往往都被总指挥一个人霸占着，而实际上他可能根本就不配。

每个亡灵都和生前的模样完全一样，看到我们人类在这一百年时间里退化了那么多，我感到十分忧伤。各种病毒改变了英国人的面貌，使他们变得身材矮小，面目可憎，肌肉松弛，面色灰黄。

我还提出要见几个古代的英国农民，发现他们一个个淳朴而又老实，日常生活是那么简单，具备真正的自由、爱国、勇敢等珍贵品质。把现在的人和这些亡灵一比较，我不禁感慨万千。祖先那些珍贵的美德都被他们的子孙给败坏了。那些原本在宫廷里蔓延的罪恶和腐化，就这样肆意传播，沾染荼毒了他们的子孙后代。

第九章

作者返回了马尔多纳达。并且乘船前往鲁格奈格。作者被拘捕并送往朝廷。国王接见了他，这是一位对臣民十分宽大的国王。

分别的日子到了，我向格鲁布杜德利卜的首领告别之后，就和我的两位同伴一起返回了马尔多纳达。在那儿等待了半个月，等到了一艘前往鲁格奈格的船只。两位慷慨的先生还有其他好心人为我准备了食物，把我送上了船。这次航行足足有一个月的时间，我们遇上了风暴，所以只能在信风的作用下向西行驶了差不多六十里格。1708 年 4 月 21 日，我们顺利进入了柯兰木格聂格河。柯兰木格聂格是一个位于鲁格奈格的东南角的海港城市。我们在距离港口不到一里格的地方停了下来，发出信号请求对方派一个领航员过来。不到半个小时，就有两位领航员来到了船上，一路带着我们穿过了暗礁和岩石，来到了一个宽阔的内港，距离城墙不过才一点点距离。

我们船上的几名水手不知道是心怀恶意还是别的原因，告诉那两位领航员我是一个外地人，而且是一位"大旅行家"。领航员把这个消息告诉了海关，于是在上岸的时候我就经受了十分严苛的盘查。这位官员用巴尔尼巴比语和我交谈，因为两地之间来往密切。这个城市里的人，特别是海关人员和水手都对这种语言不陌生。我简要说明了我的情况，不过我觉得有必要隐瞒一下自己的国籍，因为整个欧洲就只有荷兰人能够进入日本。于是我就对巴尔尼巴比的海关官员说，我的船只在巴尔尼巴比触礁沉没，而我则侥幸找到了一块礁石，之后我就被接到了拉普塔，也被称为浮岛（这才是他们知道的名字），现在正想办法去日本，因为只有那儿才有机会回国。那位官员却坚持在拿到朝廷的命令之前必须先把我拘留起来。他立即就给当地的朝廷写了信，希望两个星期之内就能拿到回信。我被带到了一处住所，虽然门口有哨兵把守，但是里面却有一个巨大的花园，可以让我自由活动。必须承认的一点是我的日子过得不错，而拘禁时间内的费用全部都由皇家负担。当然也有人来拜访我，不过大部分人都是出于好奇，因为我来自遥远的他们从未听说过的一个国家。

我雇佣了同船的一个人充当翻译。他是鲁格奈格人，不过在马尔多纳达生活了很多年，所以对这两种语言都丝毫不陌生。在他的帮助之下我可以和前来看望我的那些人交谈，但是对话一般都是他们提问我回答。

朝廷的回文在预期的时间到了。其实就是一纸命令，要求十名骑兵把我和我的随从一起押送到特拉尔德拉格达布，或者叫特利尔德拉格达布（这两种叫法好像都有）。我的随从就是那位可怜的翻译，而他也是我好说歹说才答应陪同我的。在我的请求之下，我们每个人都有了一头驴子代步。那位信使比我们早去半天，向国王报告我快要到来的消息，请陛下安排出一个时间来接见我，这样我也许还能有幸亲吻他宝座前方的尘土。这是朝廷礼仪，不过我发现这不仅仅是一种仪式。因为当我两天后被允许接见的时候，他们竟然命令我趴在地上向前爬，一边爬一边还得亲吻地板。幸好他们看在我是个外国人的份上，事先把地板清理了一遍，使得这味道没有那么令人作呕。不过据说这还是一种十分高规格的礼仪，只有等级很高的官员入宫时才能享受这样的待遇。不仅这样，要是被召见的人碰巧有几个有权有势的仇敌在朝，有时地板上还故意撒上尘土。我就看到过一位大臣满嘴尘土，等他爬到御座前规定的地点时，已经一句话都说不出来了。这也没有别的办法，因为那些被召见的人如果当着国王陛下的面吐痰或抹嘴，就会被处以死刑。另外还有一种风俗，说实话我也不能完全赞同：如果国王想用一种温和宽大的方法来处死一位贵族，他就下令在地板上撒上一种褐色的毒粉，舔到嘴里，二十四小时后毒发身亡。但是说句公道话，这位君王还是非常仁慈的，对臣子的性命相当爱护（这一点上，我很希望欧洲的君王都能向他学习）。为了他的荣誉，我一定要说一下，每次以这种方法将人处死后，他都严令叫人将地板上有毒粉的地方洗刷干净，侍从们要是大意了，就会因惹恼了国王而受刑。我曾亲耳听他下令要把一个侍从鞭打一顿，因为有一次行刑之后，轮到他去叫人洗刷地板，他却玩忽职守，故意不通知。由于他的失职，一位前途无量的贵族青年就在一次被召入宫时不幸中毒身亡了，而国王当时并没有打算要他的命。这位好君王非常宽厚仁慈，饶了那个可怜的侍从一顿鞭子，只要他保证，以后没有特别的命令，不许再干这样的事。

回到我的仪式上来。当我爬到距离王座四码的距离的时候，我可以慢慢支起身子，但是仍然跪在地上，磕头七次。然后我就说出了前天晚上他们教导过我的那句话，每一个见到国王的人都要这么说，大意是"祝愿国王陛下的寿命比太阳还要长十一个半月"。国王回答了一句，我虽然不明白其中的意思，但我还是严格按照之前学会的那样回答说："我的舌头在别人的嘴里。"这句话的意思就是希望国王能够允许召见我的翻译。随后先前那位充当翻译的可怜人就被带了进来。在接下来的一个多小时的时间里，我回答了国王的很多问题。我用巴尔尼巴比语回答，而我的翻译负责把我的意思翻译成鲁格奈格语。

国王好像很喜欢和我聊天，命令他的侍卫队长在宫里给我和我的翻译安排一间住所，每天好吃好喝地伺候着，还送给我一大袋金币。

我遵从国王的旨意，在这个国家停留了三个月。他很欣赏我，几次都想封我一个大大的官职。但是我觉得还是回家和我的妻子、孩子在一起比较合适。

第十章

作者称赞了那些鲁格奈格人。作者详细描述了斯特鲁尔德布鲁格斯，并和许多著名人士多次谈论这个话题。

鲁格奈格人既有礼貌又大方，虽然他们身上也带有东方国家所特有的那种傲气，但对于陌生人还是十分客气的，特别是那些受到朝廷器重的陌生人。我就认识了不少达官贵人，而且由于我的翻译一直陪在我的身边，所以我们的谈话进行得十分愉快。

有一天，我们好些人坐在一起，一位贵族询问我有没有见过当地的"斯特鲁尔德布鲁格斯"，意思就是"长生不老的人"。我坦承自己并没有见过，并且询问他为什么要在凡人前边加上这样一个前缀。他对我说，虽然概率很小，但是有的时候一户人家恰好就能够生出这样一个孩子，这个孩子的额头上会有一个红色的斑点，就在左边眉毛的上方，这个标记的含义就是这个孩子将永生不死。

按照他的说法，这个标记差不多有一枚三便士的硬币那么大，随着孩子的长大会慢慢变大，而且还会转变颜色。在十二岁那年，这块标记会变成绿色，持续到二十五岁之后就会变成蓝色；到了四十五岁那年就会变成一枚和先令一般大小的黑色斑点，以后就不再变化了。他说，这样的孩子很稀少，整个国家估计都没有超过一千一百个，在首都可能只有大约五十个，其中一个小姑娘就是三年前刚刚出生的。这类孩子并不是哪一家血统特有的产物，哪怕是"斯特鲁尔德布鲁格斯"的孩子，也可能和别的孩子一样生为凡人。

不得不承认，在听了这一番言论之后，我真的是说不出的开心。我的巴尔尼巴比语讲得不错，恰好和我交谈的这位贵人也听得懂这门语言，所以我情不自禁地讲了几句可能有点过分的话。我大喊着："幸福的民族啊！每个孩子都可能会长生不老！幸福的民族啊！你们能够享受到来自上古的恩泽！有来自上古的大师传授你们超越时代的智慧！但是最幸福的莫过于这些

斯特鲁尔德布鲁格斯

伟大的'斯特鲁尔德布鲁格斯'，他们生来就不用担心生老病死，所以活得那么超脱！"但是同时我也感到十分奇怪，为什么这样杰出的人物我一个都没有见过呢？前额上有那么大一块斑点，这么明显的特征我是不可能看不到的。而这样一位贤明的君主，怎么会拒绝这样一群充满智慧的帮手的协助呢？不过也有可能是因为他们那高风亮节和宫廷里的污秽格格不入吧！毕竟从我自己的角度来看，年轻人总是太有主见，不肯接受老年人的指导。不过既然国王经常会见我，那么下一次我一定要把整件事情交代清楚。我已经下定了决心，只要那些神奇的"斯特鲁尔德布鲁格斯"愿意接纳我，那么我愿意一辈子和他们相处在一起。

在前边我已经叙述过，和我谈话的那位先生会讲巴尔尼巴比语。他面带着一种微笑——这种微笑一般都是因为对无知者的可怜——跟我说，他很高兴有机会留我下来和他们在一起，并希望我允许他把我刚才说的话向大家解释一下。他解释过后，他们又在一起用本国话交谈了一会儿，不过我什么都听不懂，从他们脸上我也看不出我的话到底给他们留下了什么印象。一阵短暂的沉默之后，还是这位先生对我说，他的朋友们和我的朋友（指他自己，他觉得这样比较恰当）在听了我关于长生不老的幸福和好处的一番高谈阔论后，都欣喜至极，很想具体知道，如果我命中注定生下来就是个"斯特鲁尔德布鲁格斯"，我会怎样安排自己的生活。

我回答说："这样一个精彩而又令人愉悦的话题是很容易发挥的，特别是对于我这样喜欢设想的人来说。因为平时我就经常设想我当了国王、将军或者大臣之后应该如何行事。有关于这件事情我也想了很多，假如我真的长生不老的话，我该做些什么事情来度过我的无尽的美好时光。

"如果我真的有幸成为一个'斯特鲁尔德布鲁格斯'，当我了解到生和死之间的区别之后，我就会意识到自己的幸福所在。首先我要用各种手段来发家致富，我想依靠着我的勤俭和用心经营，大约两百年之后我就能够成为整个国家最富有的人。而且我天生就喜欢艺术和科学，所以我终将成为这个世界上最为博学的人。最后我要记录下每一件具有历史意义的大事件，并且根据自己的观察描述出历代君王和大臣的性格。我还会记录下风俗习惯、语言、服装、饮食和娱乐活动的演变情况。有了这些知识，我就能够成为一座鲜活的知识和智慧的宝库，终将成为整个民族的先知。

"六十岁以后我就不会再结婚了。我会成为一个慷慨的人，但同时也很节约。我会发挥好自己的记忆、经历和观察，以及我记录下来的所有的例子的作用，用心教导那些有希望的青年，让他们意识到道德在公众生活和私人事务中的重要作用。我会挑选出和我一样长生不老的同伴作为我的朋友，如果这些人中有没有产业的，那么我就会在自己的产业附近为他准备一处住所，这样我就可以经常请他们来做客。至于普通的凡人，我可能只会让少数几个出类拔萃的和我交往，但是时间长了之后我就会处之淡然了。哪怕是你们死去了，我也不会惋惜，就好像一个人种在花园里的石竹和郁金香，每年枯萎的时候绝对不会让他感到悲伤。

"这些'斯特鲁尔德布鲁格斯'可以和我交流在这漫长的岁月中所观察到的一切。我们会谈论这个世界是如何被腐蚀。我们会不断警示人类提防这样的腐化。也许以我们自己为榜样，可以在人类世界产生更大的影响力，才能阻止人类陷入每个时代都会发生的这种堕落。

"同时我们也能看到很多大国和小邦发生的革命，在上层社会和下层社会中都可能发生的各种变化，看到古老的城市变成废墟，看到那些平凡的村庄最终变成国王的皇宫，看到著名的河流变成小溪，看到沧海桑田。我们会看到许多不为人知的国家，看到那些野蛮民族入侵文明国家，随后变得文明起来。这一切都让我那么兴奋。而在这漫长的时间中，我会发现黄道、永动机和万能灵药，以及其他伟大的发明。

"在天文学上我们会取得多么奇妙的发现！在我们活着的时候，我们就可以看到自己的预言得以实现。我们会观测到彗星的运行轨道，以及其他日月星辰的运动变化。"

对长生和无尽的幸福的憧憬让我说了许多。随后我的翻译就原原本本地把我的意见翻译给了其他人听。他们先是用当地话交谈了一会儿，然后就开始嘲笑我。最后还是由我的翻译对我说，大家一致认为我的想法中有许多错误，而这些错误之所以会出现，是因为人性中的愚蠢。他告诉我，"斯特鲁尔德布鲁格斯"是这个国家特有的产物，在巴尔尼巴比和日本是不存在这样的人的。而他曾经有幸担任过这两个国家的大使，发现当地人的看法和我很相似。他发现长寿是人类普遍的愿望，无论是谁，只要他一只脚踏进了坟墓，就会想着保全另外一只脚。古稀老人总希望能够再多活几天，死亡在他们看来是最为可怕的事情，他们的本能促使他们躲避死亡。只有在鲁格奈格岛上，人们才没有那么渴望生命的延续，因为眼前有活生生的"斯特鲁尔德布鲁格斯"的例子。

他认为我设想的那种生活方式是很不合理的，因为那必须在永葆青春，永远健康、永远精力充沛的基础上才可以继续推进。一个人可以幻想，但是问题在于，他是否愿意在衰老中度过他永恒的生命呢？虽然极少有人愿意在这样极为不利的条件下长生不老，但是在先前提到的巴尔尼巴比和日本这两个国家，每个人都希望自己的死亡会推迟一点，他也没有见过有谁愿意心甘情愿地接受死亡，除非他面临着痛苦和折磨。他询问我在我旅行过的国家和我的祖国，这是否是一种十分普遍存在的心理。

他详细地描述了"斯特鲁尔德布鲁格斯"的情况。他说这些人在三十岁之前和普通人没有什么区别，随后就开始变得忧郁，一直到八十岁。这是他亲自听那些长生不死的人说的。当他们活到八十岁的时候（这也被认为是这个国家的寿命的极限），他们身上不仅能够看到一般老人的所有毛病，由于自己还面临着永生不死的烦恼，所以他们往往还会变得顽固、暴躁、贪婪、忧伤，所有的友谊和爱情都顾不上了，最多也就对自己的后代有一点感情。只要想到那些年轻人，他们的欢乐就烟消云散了。而看到那些送葬的队伍，他们只会满心羡慕。除了他们在年轻时代所经历过的东西，其他的一切注定被遗忘，哪怕是这一点点东西也是不完整的。所以他们的记忆是靠不住的。这一类人中最不悲惨的应该就属那些老眼昏花的、完全失忆的人，因为他们身上没有那么多的恶劣品质，反而能够得到大家的怜悯。

如果一个"斯特鲁尔德布鲁格斯"恰好跟他的同类结婚，按照王国的恩典，等到夫妇二人中较年轻的一人活到八十岁时，婚姻就可以解除。法律认为这种优待是很合理的，因为那些无辜受惩罚要在世上永远活下去的人，不应再受妻子的连累而使自己加倍痛苦。

他们年满八十岁，法律上就认定为死亡了，后嗣马上就可以继承其产业，只留极可怜的一点钱供他们维持生活，贫穷的则由公众来负担。过了八十岁，大家认为他们不能再担任任何工作，因为人们相信他们已经无法再为公众谋福利了。他们不能购买和租赁土地，也不准他们为任何民事或刑事案件作证，甚至都不允许他们参加地界的勘定。

九十岁之后，牙齿和头发就全部脱落了。活到这把年纪已不能辨别气味，有什么吃什么，有什么喝什么，没有食欲，不谈胃口。患的老毛病既不加重也不减轻，一直就这么维持下去。谈话时连一般事物的名称、人们的姓名都忘掉了，即使是自己的至亲好友的姓名也记不起来。因此，读书自娱也是不可能了，因为记忆力太差，一个句子看了后面却把前边忘了，这一缺陷把本来还有可能享受的唯一的乐趣也给剥夺了。

这个国家的语言时刻都在变化，所以一个时代的"斯特鲁尔德布鲁格斯"很难听懂另外一个时代的同类的话。到了两百年以后，他们只能和身边的人交流几个最为简单的词汇，他们就和来自外国的陌生人一样感到生活不便。

这就是我记忆中他们对"斯特鲁尔德布鲁格斯"的描述。后来我还真看到了五六个来自不同时代的这样的人，其中最年轻的不过两百岁，都是由我的几个朋友带来的。他们虽然听说我是一个去过世界各地的旅行家，却一点都不觉得好奇，也提不出一个问题。他们只希望我能给他们一个"司兰木斯库达斯科"，也就是一种纪念品。实际上那是乞讨的一种委婉的方式，以躲避严苛的法律。虽然他们的津贴很少，但的确是由公众抚养的。

人人都轻视、痛恨他们生下一个这样的人来，大家都认为是不祥之兆。他们出生的情况记载得十分详细，所以查一查登记簿就可以知道他们的年龄。不过登记簿上记载的还不到一千年，要不就是因为年代久远或者社会动乱，一千年前的记载早都被毁掉了。通常计算他们年龄的方法，还是问一问他们脑子里记得哪些国王或者大人物，然后再去查历史，因为他们记得的最后一位君王，毫无疑问不会在他们八十岁之后登基。

他们是我生平所见到的最令人痛心的人，而女人比男人还要来得可怕。她们除了具有极度衰老的人普遍存在的缺陷，还有一些更可怕的地方；这种可怕的程度是和她们的年岁成正比的，实在令人难以形容。我在五六个人当中很快就能分辨出谁年龄最大，虽然她们彼此之间相差还不到一二百岁。

读者不难相信，自从我亲耳听到、亲眼看到这种人以后，我长生不老的欲望为之大减。我为自己先前那些美妙的幻想感到由衷的羞愧，心想，与其这样活着真还不如死掉，无论哪一位暴君发明什么可怕的死法，我都乐于接受。我和我的朋友们在这件事上所谈论的一切，国王都听说了，他于是得意扬扬地挖苦我，说希望我能带一对"斯特鲁尔德布鲁格斯"回自己的国家，使我国人民不至于再怕死。不过这似乎是这个王国的法律所不允许的，否则我还真乐意费些力气花些钱把他们运回来。

我不得不赞成，这个王国制定关于"斯特鲁尔德布鲁格斯"的法律，具有最强有力的理由，其他任何国家处在那种情况下，都有必要执行那些法律。否则，由于贪婪是年老的必然结果，那些长生不老的人最终就会成为整个国家的财产的业主，独霸全民的权力，却又因为缺乏经营管理的能力，最终必将导致整个社会的毁灭。

第十一章

作者离开鲁格奈格，前往日本。他在那里搭乘一艘荷兰船只前往阿姆斯特丹，随后从阿姆斯特丹返回英国。

我认为读者应该会对"斯特鲁尔德布鲁格斯"的情况有点兴趣，因为这多少有点不同寻常，至少我从来不曾在别的游记中读到过类似的描述。如果我记错了，那么恳求大家原谅，因为旅行家们在描述同一个国家时总免不了在同一个细节上发表长篇大论，而且还不用担心会受到有关抄袭的指责。

这个国家和日本经常有贸易往来，所以很可能日本的作家已经有过关于"斯特鲁尔德布鲁格斯"的描述，但是我在日本停留的时间不长，而且还不懂他们的语言，所以我也没法去调查。不过我倒是希望荷兰人在看到这一份介绍的时候能够在好奇心的驱使下完成我的调查。

国王陛下虽然多次要求我接受他的官职，但是看到我执意回国也就准许我离开了。他亲自给日本天皇写了一封介绍信，并且赐予我四百四十四块巨大的金币（这个国家喜欢偶数），还有一颗红色的钻石，回到英国之后我卖了一千一百英镑。

　　1709 年 5 月 6 日，我正式和国王以及我的朋友们告别。这位高尚的国王派了一支卫队送我到位于这座海岛西南部的皇家港口格兰古恩斯达尔德。六天之后我就乘坐一艘前往日本的船只出发了。这一次航行持续了十五天，最后在日本东南部一个叫滨关的地方上了岸。在港口的西边有个镇子，旁边有一条狭长的海峡，而江户就在这座海湾的西北岸。上岸之后我马上就把鲁格奈格写给日本天皇的介绍信给了海关官员，他们对上面的印章十分熟悉。那印章差不多有我的手掌那么大，图案是一个国王扶起一位乞丐。地方长官听闻了这事儿之后，就以大臣之礼来接待我，不仅为我准备好了马车，还免费护送我去江户。抵达江户之后天皇就召见了我。我递上介绍信，拆信的仪式十分隆重，一名翻译将信的内容解释给天皇听。随后，翻译转达天皇的命令，让我表明自己的请求，无论我提出什么要求都会照准（这当然是看他鲁格奈格王兄的面子）。这位翻译是专门同荷兰人打交道的，他从我的面相立即就猜出我是个欧洲人，于是又用纯熟的低地荷兰语把天皇陛下的命令重复一遍。我按照事先想好的主意回答说，我是一名荷兰的商人，在一个遥远的国家航海时翻了船，之后从那里先海路后陆路一直到了鲁格奈格，再后来就坐船来到了日本。我知道我的同胞常在这里经商，希望有机会能随他们中的一些人回欧洲去。说完我就极为低声下气地请求天皇开恩，希望他能下令把我安全地送到长崎。我还提出了另一个请求，能否看在鲁格奈格国王的面上，免我履行踩踏十字架这一仪式（踩踏十字架是日本人探明外人是否为基督徒的一种仪式）；我的同胞到这儿来都得履行这样的仪式，可我是因为遭遇了不幸才来到他的王国的，丝毫没有做生意的意思。当翻译把我的后一个请求说给天皇听之后，他显得有几分吃惊，说他相信在我的同胞中不愿履行这种仪式的人我是首例，因而开始怀疑我是不是真正的荷兰人；他都疑心我一定是个基督徒。尽管如此，根据我提的那些理由，而更主要是看在鲁格奈格国王的面上，他特别开恩迁就了我这与众不同的脾气。不过事情还得安排得巧妙，他吩咐他的官吏像是一时忘了那样把我放过去，因为要是我的同胞荷兰人发现了其中的秘密，他们一定会在途中将我的喉管割断。我通过翻译感谢天皇对我格外开恩。那时恰巧有一支军队要到长崎去，天皇就命令指挥官护送我前往那里，关于十字架的事还特别作了关照。

　　于是在 1709 年 6 月 9 日我终于抵达了长崎，并且认识了几个荷兰水手，他们都是一艘载重量为 450 吨的"阿姆波伊娜号"商船上的水手，即将前往阿姆斯特丹。我在荷兰住过很长一段时间，曾经在莱顿上学，所以我的荷兰话说得不错。水手们不知道我的来历，便好奇询问我的航海经历。我尽量编了个可信的故事，很小心地隐藏了真相。我在荷兰认识不少人，所以我撒谎说自己的父母是盖尔德兰的穷人。我原本应该支付船费，但是当船长听说我是个外科医生之后就高兴地免了我一半船费，前提是我得为船员提供服务。在开船之前有好几位水手询问我是否履行了那种仪式，而我则巧妙地避开了这个问题，只推脱说天皇的所有要求我都满足了。但是尽管如此还是有个歹毒的家伙跑到海关官员面前询问我有没有踩过十字架。而那位官员却用毛竹在他的肩膀上敲了二十下，之后就再也没有人询问我这个问题了。

　　一路上没有发生什么值得一提的事情，我们顺利抵达好望角，并在那儿停留了一会儿补充淡水。1710 年 4 月 10 日，我们成功抵达阿姆斯特丹，一路上只有三名水手病死，还有一个在几内亚失足落水了。随后我搭乘一艘前往英国的小船返程了。

　　我在 4 月 16 日抵达了唐兹。第二天我就上了岸，在离开了五年零六个月之后再次回到了自己的祖国。我马上启程前往雷德里夫，并于当天下午两点抵达了自己的家。我的妻子和孩子都很健康。

第四卷
慧骃国游记

纳 特 地 区

爱 德 尔 地 区   圣彼得岛

路 温 地 区   圣芳济岛

斯维尔士岛

马德苏卡岛

德维茨岛

慧骃国

公元 1711 年发现

第一章

作者以船长的身份再次出发。他的手下图谋不轨，将他长期囚禁在船舱里，又把他流放到了一片未知的土地上。他深入探索这个国家，记录下一种名叫"野猢"的奇怪动物。作者还遇到了两只"慧骃"。

　　我在家陪妻子、儿女度过了五个月的快乐时光，要是我当时知道什么才是真正的快乐就好了。我接受了一份待遇优厚的邀请，再次离开了我那可怜的妻子，当时她已经怀孕很久了。这次是去一艘载重量三百五十吨的"冒险号"商船上担任船长，因为我对航海十分精通，而且我也很熟悉医生这份活计。不过我对做外科医生这件事已经有些厌倦了，所以我就雇佣了一位技术熟练的年轻医生罗伯特·飘尔佛伊担任船上的外科医生。我们在1710年9月7日从朴次茅斯港出发，到了14日的时候我们在特内里费遇上了来自布里斯托尔的泊柯克船长，他正准备去坎披契湾采伐木材。但是16日的一场风暴把我们给吹散了。直到这次航海结束之后我才听闻他的船只沉没了，除了一位服务员，其他人无一幸免。他是一个正直的人，一位优秀的海员，虽然有些固执己见。我想应该是这种固执让他和他的水手一起遇难了。如果当时他能够听从我的建议，也许这会儿他就能和我一样平安地在家里过着好日子。

　　由于我手下好几个水手都患了热病死去了，所以我不得不在巴巴多斯和背风群岛招募新水手，雇佣我的那些商人曾经指示我可以在当地停留。但是很快我就后悔自己的举动了，因为这次新招募的水手很多都做过海盗。我的船上一共有五十个水手，我的雇主希望我可以去南洋和印度人做生意，有机会的话还可以开辟新商机。但是后来招募的那群恶棍把船上的水手们都拖下了水，还共同策划了夺船的阴谋，并把我囚禁起来。一天早晨他们冲进船舱，捆住我的手脚，并恐吓我说，要是乱动就把我扔进海里。我被迫发誓愿意听话，做他们的俘虏。然后他们给我松绑，只用一根铁链拴住我的脚，另一头固定在床头；同时他们还安排了一个哨兵随时监视我，一旦我有逃跑的迹象就把我打死。他们每天都会送吃的到船舱来，而船上的一切都在他们的掌握之中。他们的计划是去当海盗，抢劫那些西班牙人，不过首先他们得招募更多的人。他们打算先把船上的货物处理掉，然后再去马达加斯加招募新人，因为在我被囚禁以后，他们中又死了几个人。他们航行了几周并与印度人做了点生意，但是我不知道他们到底走了哪条航线。他们好多次威胁说要杀死我，我当时真的觉得自己只有死路一条了。

　　1711年5月9日，一个叫詹姆斯·韦尔奇的人走进我的船舱，说他奉船长的命令，把我送上岸。我哀求着他，但这一切都是徒劳，他甚至都不肯告诉我新船长是谁。他们押送我上了一条长舢板，让我带上自己最好的一套衣服和一小包内衣。但是除了我的腰刀，他们不让我带任何武器。不过他们并没有搜查我的口袋，所以里面的钱财和其他的物品都保留了下来。他们划行了差不多有一里格，然后就把我丢在了一片浅滩上面。我请问他们这是什么地方，而他们发誓说自己也不清楚，因为他们只奉行船长的命令，只要货物处理完毕之后，他们就把我扔在看到的第一片陆地上面。随后他们就划船离开了，并且建议我赶紧上岸，不然可能会被潮水冲走。

　　我在这荒凉的岛上朝前走着，没过多久便走到了一片硬地上。我在岸上休息了一会儿，并考虑接下去该怎么办。稍稍缓过劲来之后，我就进入了这个国家，决定一碰上什么野人就向他投降，用些手镯、玻璃戒指以及别的小玩意贿赂他们，用这些东西让他们能够饶我一命；当海员的在航海途中总要随身携带这些东西，而我也带了几件在身上。

这儿的土地被一长排一长排的树木分隔开；树并非人工种植，而是天然地长在那儿，毫无规则。到处是野草，还有几块燕麦田。我小心翼翼地走着，生怕受到突然袭击，或者突然有一支箭从身后或两边飞来将我射死。我走上了一条踩踏出来的路，看见上面有许多人的脚印，还有一些牛蹄印，不过多数是马蹄印。最后我在一块地里发现了几只动物，还有一两只同类的在树上坐着。它们的形状非常奇特、丑陋，这让我感觉到几分不安，所以我就在一处灌木丛后伏下来仔细观察它们。其中有几只往前一直走，来到了我躺着的地方，这使我有机会把它们的样子看得清清楚楚。它们的头部和胸脯都覆盖着一层厚厚的或卷曲或挺直的毛。下巴上长着山羊一样的胡子，脊背上和腿脚的前面都长着长长的一道毛，不过身上其他地方就光光的了，所以我能看到它们那浅褐色的皮肤。它们没有尾巴，除了肛门周围，臀部都没有毛，我猜想是自然进化保留下它们，以便直接坐在地上时起到保护作用。因此坐、卧以及用后腿站立都是它们常用的姿势。它们爬起树来像松鼠一样敏捷，因为它们的前后脚都长着尖利如钩的长爪。它们时常蹦蹦跳跳，窜来窜去，行动灵巧至极。母的没有公的那么高大，头上长着长而直的毛发，除了肛门和阴部的周围，身上其他地方就都只有一层茸毛。乳房吊在两条前腿的中间，走路时几乎常常要碰到地面。公兽和母兽的毛发都有褐、红、黑、黄等几种不同的颜色。总之，在我历次旅行中，还是第一次见到这么让人不舒服的动物，也从来没有一种动物天然地就叫我感到这般厌恶。我想我已经看够了，心中充满了轻蔑和厌恶，就站起身来走到了原先那条人行道上，希望沿路走最终能找到一间印第安人的小屋。我还没走多远，就碰上了一只动物严实地挡在路上，并且径直向我走来。那丑八怪见到我，就做出种种鬼脸，两眼紧紧地盯着我，就像看一件它从未见过的东西。接着它向我靠拢过来，不知是出于好奇还是想伤害我，一下抬起了前爪。我拔出腰刀，用刀背猛击了它一下；我不敢用锋刃的一面砍它，怕当地居民知道我砍死或砍伤了他们的牲口而被激怒。那畜生挨了这一击之后就一面往后退去，一面狂吼起来；这一下立刻就有至少四十头这样的怪兽从邻近的地里跑过来将我团团围住，它们又是嗥又是扮鬼脸。我跑到一棵树干底下，背靠着树，

格列佛遇上了"慧骃"

挥舞着腰刀不让它们接近。有几只该死的畜生抓住了我身后的树枝窜到了树上，并往我的头上拉屎。我把身子紧贴在树干上，总算躲了过去，但差点儿被从四周落下来的粪便的臭气熏死。

就在这紧要关头，我看到它们突然飞快地跑开了，于是我就离开了大树，继续赶路，心里也纳闷到底是什么东西让它们变得如此恐惧。这时我发现在我的左手边有一匹马在田野里慢慢走着，看来那些恶心的家伙是先看到了这匹马才会跑开的。那马儿看到我的时候明显吃了一惊，但是很快就安静下来了，并用一种好奇的眼神打量着我。他先是看了看我的手，又看了看我的脚，还围着我转了好几圈。我原本想要继续赶路，但是却被他牢牢挡住了。不过他的举止很温和，丝毫没有要伤害我的意思。我们就这样对视了一会儿，随后我大着胆子冲他吹了个口哨，模仿那些职业的驯马师打算去抚摸他的脖子，但是他却摇摇脑袋皱着眉头，用他的前蹄推开了我的

手。随后他就用高低不同的声调嘶叫了好几声，这不由得让我怀疑他是在用某种语言自言自语。

正当我和这匹马相持不下的时候，又有一匹马凑了过来。只见他很有礼貌地走到第一匹马的跟前，两匹马互相碰了碰对方的前蹄，然后就用不一样的声音嘶叫了几声，就好像是在说话一样。随后他们稍稍走开了几步，就像人类在思考和讨论问题一样，眼神还时不时落回我身上，仿佛是害怕我逃跑一般。看到这种动物竟然能够表现出如此文明的一幕，我真的惊讶万分。这个地方的动物都那么有灵性，那这儿的居民该是多么聪明啊！这个念头给了我莫大安慰，于是我打算继续前进，去找找房子、村庄或当地的居民，而这两匹马既然愿意在这儿交谈，那么就随便他们吧！但是第一匹马看到我要走，马上就在我身后长鸣了一声，那夸张的声音让我一下子就明白了他的意思。我转过头来走到他面前，看看他是否有别的吩咐。当时的我内心已经有一些恐慌了，因为我不知道这件事情该如何收场。我想读者们也不难发现当时我的处境有多么尴尬。

那两匹马凑到我的跟前，仔细看着我的脸和手。那匹灰色的马用他的前蹄摸了一圈我的帽子，把它弄得有点乱，所以我只好摘下来整理一下然后再重新戴回去。没想到他和他的同伴（那匹棕色的马）却更加惊讶了。那匹棕色的马碰了碰我的上衣，发现原来我的衣服是披挂在身上的，这让他们露出了更加惊讶的神色。他摸了摸我的右手，仿佛是在羡慕右手的光滑和肤色。但是他很快就用他的几瓣蹄子夹住我的手，把我疼得大叫起来，之后他们的举动就变得温和了起来。他们对我的鞋子和袜子也很好奇，时常去碰一碰，然后互相嘶叫几声，就好像两个试图解释新现象的哲学家一样。

总之这两只动物的举止十分得体，而且看上去很有理性，再综合他们的敏锐的观察力和判断力，我认为他们可能是两个魔法师，施了某种法术把自己变成了现在这个模样，然后用这样的办法来逗弄我这个陌生人。要么就是被我这样一个言行举止和他们完全不一样的人给弄得十分惊讶。这样的推断也是很有可能的，所以我就大着胆子对他们说："先生们，如果你们是魔法师，那么我想你们一定可以听懂任何语言。我要告诉你们，我是一个可怜的英国人，遭遇不幸流落到你们的领土。我请求你们两位能够让我骑在你们的背上，带我去某个有人烟的地方，这样我就有救了。作为报答，我可以把刀子和手镯送给你们。"说着我就把这两件东西掏出了口袋。说这话的时候两只动物就这么静静听着，仿佛很有耐心的样子；而当我说完了之后，他们又互相交流了一会儿，仿佛是在进行什么严肃的谈话。我发现他们的语言很简单，他们的字母拼写可能比中国话还要言简意赅。

我时不时可以分辨出"野猢"这个单词，他们讲了好几遍。虽然我不知道这到底是什么意思，但是这两匹马交谈的时候我就试着学习这个词。当他们讲完了之后我就大着胆子叫了一句"野猢"，还尽量模仿出他们的那种语调。他们仿佛很吃惊的样子，随后灰色的马又重复了两次，就好像是在校正我的口音一样。我跟着学了几次，虽然还算不上标准，但是讲得越来越好了。随后他们又教了我第二个词，这次可比第一个难发音多了，按照英文的拼写法，这个词念"慧骃"。这个词我发的不好，但是尝试了两三次以后我就讲得好多了，这两匹马显得十分惊讶。

他们又谈了一会儿，然后就分手了，离开之前他们同样碰了碰蹄子。灰色的马做了个手势，让我在他前面走，我想最好的办法就是遵从他的意见。每当我放慢脚步的时候他就会发出某种声响，我猜到了他的意思，竭力让他明白，我太累了，根本就走不快。于是他就站在那儿让我休息了一会儿。

第二章

作者跟着"慧骃"回到了家里。作者描述了"慧骃"的房屋以及他们的食物。作者因为吃不到肉而感到痛苦，但是很快就找到了解决的办法。作者描述了在这个国家吃饭的方式。

　　我们走了大约三英里路，来到了一座长长的房子前，它是用木桩打在地上，再用柳条编织起来的。屋顶上盖着草，看上去很低矮的样子。我感到些许心安，就拿出了几件玩具，这是旅行家们经常用来馈赠美洲的印第安人的礼物。我希望这些玩具能够帮助自己赢得一个好印象。那匹马做了个姿势，要我先走进房里。这是一个巨大的房间，泥土地面铺得很平整，边上有一排排马厩。房间里有三匹小马和两匹母马，但是都没有在吃草，好几匹马都是屁股着地坐在地上，这样的景象让我十分惊讶。其余几匹马在边上干活，看上去和那种普通的牲口差不多，这更加坚定了我当时的想法，一个能够把野兽驯化成这样文明的民族，其智力程度肯定远超过所有人。灰马跟了进来以避免我可能受到他人的伤害，不然的话我可能还要吃点苦头呢！只见灰马用一种威严的姿态冲着房间里的马儿们嘶叫几声，而他们也纷纷回应。

　　在这个房间后面还有三个房间，通过三扇门依次相连，就像街道一样。我们穿过了第二个房间，朝着第三个房间走去。灰马先走了进去，然后示意我在外面等着。我就在第二个房间里等着，顺便把我为男、女主人准备的礼物拿了出来，分别是两把小刀、三只假的珍珠手镯、一小面镜子和一串链子。那匹马嘶叫了好几声，我原本以为会有一个人的声音响起，但是除了马儿的声音，其他什么声音都没有。我心想着这一定是某种礼节，在召见之前需要走许多的程序。但是这样一位贵人竟然是由马匹来伺候的，这样的情形我可是从来没见过。我很担心自己被这样的遭遇和不幸弄得神志不清，于是就打起精神观察了一下自己所在的房间。这个房间的摆设和前一个房间是一样的，可能还更加雅致一点。我擦了好几次眼睛，但是眼前的一切都和第一个房间一模一样。我拧了拧自己的胳膊，想要确定自己并不是在梦里。随后我得出了一个结论，那就是这一切都是魔法。但是我已经没时间继续这么想了，因为那匹灰色的马已经来到了门口，示意我走进第三个房间。进门之后我就看到一匹很漂亮的母马，在一匹公马和一匹母马的陪伴下坐在一张整洁而又精致的草席上面。

　　我进入房间之后，母马就从草席上站了起来，走到我的面前仔细地打量了我一番，然后就露出了轻蔑的神色。随后她就转过身去对着那匹灰马，我听到她说出了"野猴"这个词。那是我学会的第一个词语，虽然当时我不清楚这个词的意思，但是很快我就弄清楚了，而且这让我感到十分耻辱。灰马冲着我点点头，然后又发出那熟悉的声音，我明白那是让我跟着他走的意思。他带我走出房间，来到了一个和院子差不多的地方。距离马儿的房子不远处还有一座房子，我们走进去之后就看到三只我上岸那会儿看到的那种恶心的畜生在那儿吃着树根和肉，后来我才发现那是驴肉和狗肉，有的时候还有病死或者偶然死去的母牛。他们的脖子上都拴着看上去很结实的枝条，另外一头就拴在横木上。他们的两只前爪抓着食物，然后用牙齿撕扯下肉来吃。

　　这匹马吩咐他的仆人，一匹棕色的小马，把最大的一头"野猴"解下来牵到了院子里。当我和那只"野猴"被放在一起之后，他们就开始仔细比较起我们的面貌，嘴里还一直重复着"野猴"这个词。当我看到边上那只恶心的畜生竟然真的像是个人的模样的时候，我的惊讶和恐惧简直难以形容。那张脸又扁又宽，鼻子塌陷，嘴唇很厚，嘴巴很大，这样的特征在那些野蛮民族身上都是很常见的。因为野蛮人总是把孩子们扔在地上，或者把孩子们背在背上，所以孩子的脸在摩擦之后就变形了。"野猢"的指甲很长，手掌粗糙，整只手掌是棕黄色而且带毛的，其余就和我们的手没有任何区别了。我们的脚的差异也是一样的，这一点我很清楚，但是那些马并不清楚，因为我穿着鞋子和袜子。除了毛发和肤色，身体的其他部分也没有什么区别了。

　　看上去最让这两匹马感到困惑的就是我身体的其他部分和"野猢"截然不同，这一点完全归功于我的衣服，而那些马对于衣服是没有一点概念的。那匹棕色的小马用蹄子拿了一根树枝（具体的手法我会在合适的时候详细介绍），我拿在手里闻了一下，然后礼貌地还给他了。他又从"野猢"的住所拿来一块驴肉，闻起来很臭，所以我根本就不想吃，小马见状就把驴肉扔给了"野猢"，结果那只野猢一下子就吃完了。随后小马又给了我一捆干草和一些燕麦，但是我摇摇头，表示这两样东西都不符合我的胃口。我很担心，要是找不到同类的话，自己可能就会饿死了。至于那些"野猢"，虽然我十分渴望见到自己的同类，但我无论如何都不承认它们就是我的同类，毕竟我从未见过那么恶心的生物。住在这个国家的这段时间里，我越看它们就越觉得恶心。那匹马也发现了这一点，于是他就吩咐把"野猢"牵走，然后把自己的前蹄凑到最边上，看上去十分从容，这样的举动让我大吃一惊。后来他又做了好几个手势，询问我到底想吃什么。但是我没法做出简明的回答。就算他明白了，我也很难理解他有什么办法为我弄到粮食。就在这时候我看到了一头母牛，于是我指了指那头牛，表明自己想要喝奶。这动作倒是有了效果。他把我领回了家，让一匹母马打开了一个房间，里面存放着许多用陶盆盛放的牛奶。母马递给我一大碗，我一下子就喝完了，顿时就感觉自己精神了不少。

　　大约中午时分，我看到四只"野猢"拉着一种像雪橇一样的车子朝房子这边走来。车上是一匹老马，看上去像是有些身份的；他下车时后蹄先着地，因为他的左前蹄不小心受了伤。老马是来我的马主人家里赴宴的，马主人十分客气地接待了他。他们在最好的一间屋里用餐，第二道菜是牛奶熬燕麦，老马吃热的，其余的马都吃冷的。他们的食槽在房间的中央摆成一个圆圈，分隔成若干格，他们就围着食槽在草堆上坐成一圈。食槽圈的中间是一个大草料架，上有许多尖角，分别对准食槽的每一个格子，这样每一匹公马和母马都能规规矩矩、秩序井然地吃自己那一份干草和牛奶燕麦糊。小马驹似乎行动很讲规矩，马主人夫妇对他们客人的态度则极为热情而殷勤。灰色马让我在它的身边站着，他就和他的朋友谈了许多关于我的话，因为我发现客人不时地朝我看，而且一再地说到"野猢"这个词儿。

　　我那时恰好戴着一副手套，灰色马主人看上去十分迷惑，难以理解我把自己的前蹄弄成这样。他用蹄子在我的手套上碰了三四次，仿佛是要我把蹄子恢复原样。我赶紧把手套摘了下来，放回到口袋里。这一举动越发吸引了他们的注意，我发现他们对我的做法十分满意，看来这一举动产生了很好的效果。在吃饭的时候他们又要求我说一遍我学会的几个单词，随后主人又教了我燕麦、牛奶、水、火等名词，幸好我从小就有很好的语言天赋，所以很快就学会发音了。

　　吃完饭以后，主人把我拉到一边，比画着告诉我，他很担心我没有吃东西。燕麦在他们的语言中被称作"赫伦"。我把这个词念了三四遍，虽然一开始我拒绝吃这种东西，但是我转念一想，觉得自己可以制作燕麦面包，再加上牛奶，我就可以活下去，直到想到办法逃往别的国家，寻找我的同类。马主人马上就吩咐一匹白色的母马拿来许多燕麦。我把燕麦拿到火上去烤了一会儿，然后把外皮搓了下来，全部吹走。随后我用两块石头模仿石磨把燕麦磨成粉，然后加水搅拌成面糊糊，再拿到火焰上去烤熟，做成了一种类似饼干的东西，这种东西在欧洲的很多地方都很普遍，虽然一开始我觉得毫无美味可言，但是很快我就习惯了。我这一生常常要落到吃粗饭的地步，可人的天性是很容易满足的，这不止一次从经验中得到证明。另外我还不得不说一下，我在这座岛上居留期间，连一个小时的病都没有生过。我有时设法用"野猢"的毛发编织罗网来捕兔子或鸟儿什么的；也常常去采集一些卫生的野菜，煮熟了就着面包一起吃，或者就当沙拉吃；间或我也做点奶油当稀罕物，而且把做奶油剩下来的乳清也都喝了。起初我吃不到盐简直不知该怎么办，可是习惯成自然，不久以后，没有它也无所谓了。我相信，我们老是要吃盐其实是奢侈的结果，因为把盐放到饮料中起初是用来刺激胃口的，所以除了在长途的航海中，或者在远离大市场的地方贮存肉食需要用盐，其他时候食盐是没有必要的。我们发现，除了人，没有一种动物喜欢吃盐。就我自己而言，离开这个国家之后，过了好长一段时间，我才吃得下有咸味的食物。

我想我已经讲了不少有关饮食的事情了，其他旅行家的书中也有许多这方面的内容，好像读者们很关心我们是否吃得好。不过我觉得还是有必要讲一讲这件事情，否则读者们如何相信我在这样一个国家，和这样的居民一起生活了三年。

到了晚上，主人吩咐为我准备住处，就在距离他们的房子六码远的地方，和"野猢"的窝是分开的。我在底下铺了一层干草，身上盖着自己的衣服，睡得很香甜。不过我的居住条件很快就得到了改善，之后我会更加详细地叙述一番。

第三章

作者开始学习当地语言。他的"慧骃"主人教导他。作者介绍了这种语言。有好几位"慧骃"贵族出于好奇前来探访。他简要描述了自己的旅途。

我那时候唯一的愿望就是学习当地的语言，而我的主人（之后我都这么称呼他）和他的孩子们以及家里的奴仆们都愿意教我。因为他们认为一头牲畜竟然能表现出理性，这简直就是一个奇迹。我指着身边的每一样东西，询问他们该如何发音，然后记在自己的日记本里面。发音不标准的地方我会请他们多念几次帮我纠正。这方面，家里的仆人，那匹棕色的小马很愿意帮助我。

说到发音，他们主要是依靠鼻音和喉音，这一点倒是和高地荷兰语或者德语相类似，不过他们的发音更加柔和，含义也更加丰富。查尔斯五世就有过类似的观点，如果他要和他的马对话，一定会选用高地荷兰语。

我的主人很好奇，也很有耐心，所以每天他都会花费好几个小时来教导我。他坚信（这是他后来告诉我的）我就是一只"野猢"，但是我愿意学习，文明而又干净，这样的特质和"野猢"是大不相同的。他感到最困惑的就是我的衣服，有时候他会思考那是不是我身体的一部分，因为我每次都要等他们都睡了才脱下衣服睡觉，而早上他们还没有起来的时候我就又穿上了。我的主人很想知道我到底是从哪儿来的，因为我的言行举止都很有理性。他非常想让我把自己的故事讲给他听。当我已经熟悉他们的语言、单词和句法之后，他就希望我能够亲自把自己的经历告诉他。为了熟悉他们的语言，我把所有的单词都用英文拼好，然后连着译文一起写下来。一段时间之后我就可以当着他们的面说话了，不过我花费了不少时间向他解释清楚这到底是怎么一回事，因为他们对书本和文献没有任何概念。

差不多十个星期之后我已经可以明白他提出的大部分问题了。三个月之后我就差不多能够完整地回答问题了。他很好奇我到底是从哪儿来的，怎么会和那些有理性的动物一样，因为那些"野猢"（他从我们的头、手和脸中分辨出我是一只"野猢"）虽然很机灵，但是却总爱调皮，是最难驯化的动物。我回答说我是从一个很远的地方来，而且是和许多同类一起坐在一个用树干做成的容器中一起漂洋过海来到这儿。我的同伴们把我抛弃在这儿的海岸，让我自生自灭。我费了许多口舌，又用了不少手势，这才让他明白了我的意思。他却说我肯定是弄错了，要么就是我说的事情和真实情况不一样，因为在他们的语言中并没有表达欺骗或谎言的词语。他认为海那边不会有别的国家，而一群野蛮的畜生也是不可能在水面上用这样的容器前进，因为没有一只"慧骃"能够做出这样的容器，他们也不可能允许"野猢"去这么做。

　　"慧骃"的意思是马，就它的词源而言，是指大自然中最好的存在。我对我的主人说我不知道该如何表达，不过我会改变这种情形，愿意把各种奇怪的事情都告诉他。他感到非常高兴，于是就让家里的母马、小马和奴仆用各种机会教导我，他也会花费两三个小时来教导我。住在附近的几位"慧骃"贵族听说家里有一只神奇的"野猢"，不仅能像"慧骃"一样说话，而且还是一只有理性的动物，所以就经常上门拜访。他们仿佛很喜欢和我谈话，并且提出了许多问题，而我也尽可能回答。这样一来我的语言能力也就突飞猛进，差不多五个月之后，我就能够听懂他们所说的所有的话，也能够表达我自己的所有意思了。

　　前来拜访的"慧骃"们都不相信我是一只"野猢"，因为我的身体和"野猢"并不一样。他们看到我除了头发、脸蛋和手脚，并没有那种毛发，不过两个星期之前发生的意外倒是让我不得不向主人坦白了自己的秘密。

　　之前我曾经对读者说，每天晚上等这家"慧骃"入睡了之后我才脱下衣服，但是一天早上，主人派他的棕色小马来喊我起床。但是那时候我正在熟睡，身上的衣服也滑落在一边。小马看到我的模样的时候，讲话都有些颠三倒四了。随后他就回到了自己的主人那边，报告了自己看到的情况。我马上就意识到了，因为当我穿好衣服去拜见主人的时候，他劈头就问刚才那是怎么回事，为什么我睡觉的模样和平时不一样。他的仆人告诉他，我身上有些地方是白色的，有些是黄色的，还有些地方是棕色的。

　　为了尽量显示我与那该死的"野猢"不是一个族类，我至此一直严守着我穿着衣服这一秘密，但现在再也没有办法保密了。另外，考虑到我的衣服和鞋子已越来越糟，很快就要穿破，我得想个法子用"野猢"或者别的兽类的皮另做一套换上，那样一来，整个秘密就要被他们知道了。因此我就对主人说，在我来的那个国家，我的那些同类总是用加工过的某种动物的毛皮来遮蔽身体，那一方面是为了体面，另一方面也是为了抵御炎热和寒冷的恶劣气候；要是他愿意看的话，我马上就可以证实这一点。不过要请他原谅，有些地方不能暴露，因为大自然教我们要把那些地方遮盖起来。他说我讲的话真是稀奇，特别是最后那一句，因为他不明白，大自然既已赐给我们的东西，为什么又要教我们藏起来？他说，不论他自己还是他家人，对自己身体的每一部分都不觉得有什么羞耻；不过，他允许我按自己的意愿去做。他这么一说，我就先脱了上衣，接着我又把背心脱掉，再把鞋、袜和裤子都扯了下来。我把衬衣放下来盖到腰部，再拉起下摆拦腰打一个结，遮住赤裸裸的肉体。

　　我的主人惊讶地看着我的表演，他用蹄子拿起我的衣服仔细观察，然后又轻轻抚摸着我的身体，还仔细检查了好几遍。最后他得出结论，认为我是一只"野猢"，只不过我和我的同类有一些不同而已。我的皮肤更加柔软洁白，身上还没有毛。我的前爪和后爪都短一些，形状也和"野猢"不一样，而且我是用两只后脚走路的。他不想再看了，就准许我把衣服重新穿上，因为当时我已经冷得瑟瑟发抖了。

对他时时把我称为"野猢"的做法，我表示十分不安；对于那种恶心的动物，我只有痛恨和鄙夷。我请求他不要这样称呼我了，也请求他在那些前来探访的朋友们面前别这么称呼我。我还请求他为我保密，因为我现在的这身衣服还是可以穿的，不要让他之外的其他人知道我身上有这么一层伪装了。至于那位仆人，他可以命令他不许说出这个事儿。

他答应了我的一切诚恳请求，这样秘密就一直守到我的衣服再也不能穿的时候。我不得不想些办法来添制衣服，这件事我以后还会有交代。与此同时，他还要我继续努力学习他们的语言，因为他最感到惊奇的还是我那说话和推理的能力，而对我身体的样子，则不论有没有穿着衣服，他都不像对前者那样感到惊奇。他又说，我曾答应过给他讲一些稀奇古怪的事，他都有点等不及了。

从这时候起，他就加倍努力来教我学习它们的语言。并带我会见了他所有的客人，同时要求他们以礼待我，因为他私下里对他们说，那样会使我高兴，我也就会变得更加有趣了。

每天我在侍候他的时候，他除了教导我，还要问几个与我有关的问题，我就尽我所能回答他。他用这种方法已经大致了解了一些情况，不过还很不全面。至于我怎么一步步提高到能同他做更加正式的交谈，说起来就未免冗长乏味了，不过我第一次比较详细而有次序地叙述我身世的谈话，大概内容是这样的：

我告诉他我来自一个遥远的国家，我和大约五十个同类坐在一艘比他们的房子还要大的木头容器在海面上航行。我简单描述了自己的船，然后又用手帕解释如何利用风力推动大船前进。在一次争执之后，我被遗弃到这里。当我探索这个小岛的时候，就被那些"野猢"给困住了，幸好主人把我救了出来。他询问我船是谁造的，我们国家的"慧骃"怎么会把船交给我们这样的"野猢"来管理呢？我对他说我已经不敢继续说了，除非他保证不会生气，我才敢继续说下去。他做了保证之后，我就告诉他船是我这样的人建造的。在我旅行过的所有的国家和我自己的国家里，我这样的人类是唯一的统治者，也是唯一拥有理性的动物。我坦白当我看到"慧骃"是一个有理性的动物的时候，也感到十分吃惊，就像他们在"野猢"身上发现理性一样吃惊。我承认我和"野猢"可能在外表上有一点相似，但是我难以理解他们为何本性残忍。我还说，如果我有幸回国，把这次旅行的见闻告诉我的族人的话，他们一定会说我的见闻是胡编乱造的。虽然我对他和他的家人十分尊敬，但是我还是要说，我的族人肯定难以接受"慧骃"会成为一个国家的主宰，而"野猢"竟然只是一群畜生。

第四章

作者描述了慧骃国的真理观和伪善观。主人对作者的看法提出了反对意见。作者详细描述了自己的身世和他的旅途经历。

听完我的这一番话，主人露出了不安的神色，因为怀疑和不相信这两个概念在这个国家是不存在的。遇到这样的情况，当地居民往往不知道如何是好。我记得很清楚，当我和主人描述其他地方的人人的性时，我也曾经提到过"说谎"或者"胡说八道"的概念。虽然他有着强大的判断力，但是对于这两个词语的意思他却还是茫然无知的。他是这么认为的：语言的功能是让我们能够彼此了解，也能够方便我们更好地明白事情的真相。

但是如果一个人胡说八道，那么语言的作用就被破坏了。既然不能了解对方，也不能掌握事情的真相，这种颠倒黑白的做法简直比无知还要可怕。这就是他对说谎这件事情的看法，而我们人类早已把这门技艺掌握得炉火纯青。

让我们回到原来的话题。当我说在我们国家，"野猢"是唯一的统治者的时候，我的主人说这是出乎意料的。他询问在我们国家是否有"慧骃"，他们又是担任什么角色的。我告诉他，在我们国家有许多"慧骃"，夏天的时候它们在田里吃草，冬天的时候就在家吃干草和燕麦。"野猢"仆人会帮它们擦洗身体，梳理鬃毛，清洁马蹄，投喂食料，还要负责整理他们的床铺。"我完全明白你的意思，"我的主人说，"无论你描述的'野猢'是多么有理性，'慧骃'还是你们的主人。当然我也很希望我们的'野猢'能像你那么温顺。"我恳求他不要让我再说下去，因为我知道接下来我要说的话肯定不是那么愉快。但是他坚持要我讲清楚，不管好坏他都要听听。我说，我承认我们国家的"慧骃"，在我们国家被称为"马"的那种生物，是所有动物中最奔放也是最英俊的，在力量和速度上超越了其他所有动物。那些被贵族驯养的马匹能够得到很好的照顾，专门负责旅行、比赛或者拉车，除非它们不小心生病或者是受伤了，才会被卖去当苦力，死后被剥皮，剩下来的尸体就丢给那些野狗吃掉。而普通的马匹就不会有这样的福气，它们属于农夫、搬运工和其他出卖力气的人，每天要干很多活，而且吃的饲料也不好。我还详细介绍了我们骑马的方式，包括缰绳、马鞍、马刺、马鞭以及马儿拉的那种车，包括我们专门设计的为了防止马蹄磨破的那种蹄铁。

主人听完了我的描述之后十分生气，他很纳闷，我们怎么敢骑到"慧骃"的背上，因为在家里，哪怕是最孱弱的仆人也能轻松地把"野猢"打翻在地，只需要在地上打个滚就可以把那畜生压死。我解释说我们那儿的马三四岁就开始接受训练，让它们听从我们的命令。如果有些马敢违抗命令，那么就要接受惩罚。那些用来骑或者用来拉车的马在两岁左右就会被阉割，这样它们就会变得十分温顺。当然最重要的是让它们明白什么是奖励，什么是惩罚。对于那些马来说，它们所拥有的理性并不比这儿的"野猢"多多少。

我费尽口舌才让主人明白了我的意思。他们的语言中词汇不是很丰富，因为他们的欲望和情感需求比我们要少。但是我仍然无法形容他在听闻我们如此对待"慧骃"时的那种咬牙切齿的痛恨，特别是当我说到把马儿阉割，让它们变得更加温顺的时候。他说，如果一个国家里只有"野猢"拥有理性，那么毫无疑问他们应该是这个国家的统治者，毕竟理性总是能够战胜野蛮。但是从我们这个物种的体格，特别是像我这样的体格来说，简直是所有动物中体型最为糟糕的了，所以他很难想象我们是如何在日常生活中运用理性的。他询问我们那个国家的"野猢"到底是更像我还是更像这个国家的"野猢"。我告诉他，我们那儿的同龄人大多数和我长得差不多，年纪小一些的人和女人们会矮小一点，而女人们的皮肤就像牛奶一样洁白。我的主人承认我和这儿的"野猢"不太一样，至少看上去干净很多，而且样子也比较顺眼。但是在身体优势上，我的这些特点可能还比不上这个国家的"野猢"。我的指甲几乎没有什么用处，至于我的前腿，根本就不能算是前腿，因为他从没见过我用前腿走路。我走路时前腿通常不戴套子，尽管偶尔也戴一下，但没有后脚的套子那么结实，导致我走起路来一点都不稳当，因为只要我的一条腿打了滑，我就肯定会摔在地上。随后他又开始对我身体的其他部分吹毛求疵，比如我的面庞太扁，鼻子太高，双眼太向前，如果不转动脑袋的话根本就看不到边上的东西。而且如果我不用前脚把食物送到嘴边的话是不可能吃到食物的，所以我才需要那么多关节。但是他想不明白为什么我的后脚还需要有那么多指节。我的后脚是那么柔嫩，不穿上兽皮做成的套子就不能在石子路上行走。我也缺乏御寒的能力，所以每天都得把这一身衣服穿上又脱下，这实在是太麻烦了。最后他总结说，这个国家的每一种动物都讨厌"野猢"，比"野猢"弱小的会想办法躲开，而比它们强壮的会驱逐它们。所以就算我们国家的"野猢"具备理性，又怎么才能驯服其它动物，让它们心甘情愿地为我们效劳呢？不过他说他不想再继续讨论这件事了，他对我的个人经历更感兴趣，包括我出生的那个国家和我到这儿之前的生活经历。

我向他保证说我是多么愿意把这一切都告诉他，但是我很怀疑能否解释清楚，因为在这个国家根本就不会发生类似的事情，所以我的主人可能一点概念都没有。不过我还是会尽力用各种办法来表达清楚。如果我一时间找不到最合适的词语，还希望主人能够理解。他欣然答应了。

我说我出生在距离这个国家很远的一个叫英格兰的岛上，哪怕是主人最强壮的仆人都需要跑上整整一年时间才能到达。我的父母都是很老实的人，他们培养我成为一位外科医生，专门负责治疗各种创伤，可能是由意外造成的，也有可能是各种暴力伤害。我们的国家由女王统治。我之所以出海是为了赚钱养家。在最近一次航行中我是船长，带领着五十名和"野猢"一样的水手出海。在路途中死了不少人，所以我不得不沿途招募新人。我们的船有两次险些沉没，第一次是遇到了风暴，第二次是触了礁。说到这里，我的主人插了一句，他问我，既然我蒙受了那么多损失，又遭遇了种种危险，我怎么还能说服不同国家的陌生人跟我一同出来冒险呢？我说他们都是一些亡命之徒，由于贫穷所迫或是犯了什么罪，才不得不离开故乡。有的人因为吃官司弄得倾家荡产；有的人则因为吃喝嫖赌把财产全部花光；有的人背叛了祖国；还有不少人是因为犯了凶杀、偷窃、放毒、抢劫、假证、伪证、私铸假币、强奸、鸡奸、变节、投敌等罪行才被迫出走的。这帮人大多是越狱而跑的，没有一个敢回到祖国去，他们害怕回去受绞刑或者关在牢里饿死，因此是外出逃生。

在这次谈话中我被主人打断了好多次，我不得不花费了好多力气来解释那几种罪行。我船上的水手大部分都是因为犯罪所以才不得不离开的。这次谈话花费了好几天时间，幸好他最终还是明白了我的意思。原本他根本就不理解为什么要做这些坏事。为了解释清楚，我就尽量把争夺权力、淫欲、放纵、怨恨和嫉妒解释了一遍，而且我只能用举例和假设的方法。听我说完之后，他不由得抬起头，表现出惊奇和愤慨，就像一个人看到或听到了从未见闻的事时受了震惊一样。权力、政府、战争、法律、刑罚以及无数其他的东西在他们的语言中根本就找不到可以表达的词汇。在这种情况下，要使我的主人弄明白我说话的意思，几乎是不可克服的困难。但是，他的理解力非常出色，又经他沉思细想，加上我们的交谈，他的理解力大有提高，因此终于对我们那个世界里人类能做出些什么事来，有了充分的了解。他希望我能把我们叫作欧洲的那块土地，特别是我自己国家的情形，也详细地说明一下。

第五章

作者奉命汇报了英国的情况，解释了欧洲君王之间的战争的原因，还解释了英国宪法。

读者们请注意，以下是我和我的主人的谈话的摘录，包括在这两年时间里几次会谈的重要内容。当我对"慧骃"的语言的掌握有了进一步提升之后，主人就好几次要求我更加详细地阐述一下欧洲的情况。我谈到了贸易和制造业，谈到了艺术和科学，对他的每一个问题都做了回答。这些问题涉及许多学科，在短时间内可能很难解释清楚，不过我现在只想把其中的要点记录下来。一方面我会按照逻辑思路进行整理，而忽略其中的时间先后顺序；另一方面我会严格遵守事实。唯一让我感到担忧的是我很难确切表达主人的观点，因为我还没有能力把他们的语言翻译成我们粗俗的英语。

在主人的要求之下，我先讲述了奥伦治亲王发动的对法国的战争。之后他的继承者，也就是我们的现任女王继续发动了战争，基督教世界的所有强国都参战了，哪怕到现在这场战争都没有结束。根据主人的要求我大致测算了一下，在这场战争中大概有一百万只"野猢"死去，超过一百座城市被摧毁，三百多艘战舰被击沉。

我的主人问我，两个国家之间的战争是否有原因或者是动机呢？我回答说这样的例子数不胜数，不过我可以举例说明几个特别有代表性的，有时候是因为雄心勃勃的君主认为自己的国土太小，治下的人民数量太少；有的时候是腐化堕落的大臣唆使君王发动战争，以转移人民对他们的无能的不满。有的时候观念不合都可能会让成千上万的人丧生。比如说，究竟面包是肉呢还是肉是面包？葡萄汁到底是血呢还是酒呢？吹口哨到底是好事还是坏事？十字架是亲吻一下比较好还是扔进火里比较好？什么颜色的上衣最好，是黑色、白色、红色还是灰色，应该长一点还是短一点，窄一点还是宽一点，脏一点还是干净一点，诸如此类。再没有什么能够比意见不合所引发的战争更加残忍、血腥以及持久，特别是那些在无关紧要的事情上所产生的意见不合所引发的战争。

有时两位君王为谁该夺取另一位君王的领土而发生争吵，但事实上他俩谁都无权统治那片领地。有时一位君王跟另一位君王争吵，是怕那位君王要来跟他争吵。有时发动战争是因为敌方太强大了，有时则是因为敌方太软弱。有时候是因为邻国没有的东西我们有，或者我们没有的东西他们有，结果双方打起来，直到两方中有任何一方被打败战争才结束。如果一个国家的人民为饥荒、瘟疫所害，或者国内党派纷争，局势紊乱，这时发动战争侵略这个国家就有了十分正当的理由。如果我们最紧密的盟国有一座我们唾手可得的城市，或者有一块领域我们夺过来就可以使我们的疆土圆满完整，那我们就很有理由同他们打一仗。如果一个国家的人民又贫穷又无知，那么君王的军队一进入这个国家，就可以合理合法地将一半的人都处死，剩下的为奴隶，这么做是为了让他们开化，放弃那野蛮的生活方式。一位君王请求另一位君王帮助他抵御敌国的侵略，那位援助者把侵略者赶走之后，竟自己占下这领土，而把他前来援助的那位君王或杀，或监禁，或流放；这样的事经常发生，对德高望重的君王来说是多么的无耻。血缘或者婚姻关系也常常是君王之间发生战争的原因，关系越亲，还越容易引起争吵。穷国挨饿，富国骄横，骄横与饥饿则永不能相容。由于这种种原因，士兵这一职业在所有职业中最受人尊敬，因为士兵也就是一只受人雇佣的"野猢"，尽管它的同类从来都没有冒犯过它，它却可以将它们无情屠杀，并且杀得越多越好。

在欧洲还有穷得像乞丐一样的国王，虽然无力发动战争，但是却可以把自己的军队出租给富有的国家，每天收取租金。国王可以获得这笔收入的四分之三，而他们也依靠这笔收入来维持国家的正常开支，欧洲北部国家基本都属于这一类。

我的主人说："你对战争这个问题的解释倒是揭示了所谓的理性的后果。幸好你们的羞耻心还是要比你们的危险性大一些，所以就决定了你们不会过分作恶。你们的嘴是那么平，所以很难互相撕咬。再加上你们的前后爪子是那么短小娇嫩，这儿的一只"野猢"就可以打败你们十二个。所以在重新计算了战争的伤亡人数之后，我觉得你所说的都是子虚乌有。"

我忍不住摇头微笑，嘲笑他没有见识。我对战争一点都不陌生，于是就把加农炮、重炮、滑膛枪、卡宾枪、手枪、子弹、火药、剑、刺刀、战役、围攻、撤退、进攻、挖地道、反地道、轰炸、海战等描述给他听。我还叙述到载有千名士兵的许多战舰被击沉，两军各有两万人丧生；还有那临死时的呻吟，飞在半空中的肢体，硝烟，嘈杂，混乱，马蹄下人被践踏致死；逃跑，追击，胜利；尸横遍野，等着狗、狼和其他猛兽来吞食；掠夺，抢劫、强奸，烧杀。还有，为了说明我亲爱的同胞的勇敢，我还告诉他我曾经亲眼看到在某次围城战役中他们一次就炸死一百个敌人，还看过他们在一艘船上炸死了一百名士兵；看到被炸得粉碎的尸体从云端往下掉，在一旁观看的人大为快意。

正当我准备继续描述的时候，我的主人却制止了我。他说，任何了解"野猢"的本性的"慧骃"都不难发现，如果这样邪恶的牲畜的体力和狡诈程度能够匹配它那凶残的性格，那么我所说的每一件事情都是可能发生的。但是我所说的这些情况只会加深主人对"野猢"的憎恶。这种情况是他从来不曾听说过的，他很担心自己听惯了这种恶心的词语，变得逐渐接受这样的事实，而不像先前那般厌烦"野猢"了。主人说他虽然憎恶这个国家的"野猢"，但是这种憎恶其实和对格纳耶（一种猛禽）或者对弄伤他的蹄子的石头一样，没有什么区别。但是自认为有理性的动物竟然能够做出这么罪孽深重的事情，他很担心理性堕落之后会比本能的残暴更加可怕。所以他很肯定地认为我们所拥有的并不是理性，而是某种能够助长我们的罪恶天性的品性。就好像一条被搅动的溪水，能够把原本丑陋的倒影弄得更大更丑陋。

他说对于战争这个话题他已经在几次对话中了解了一些，现在他还有另外一个问题没有弄明白。我曾经说过，我的水手中有些人是被法律害得倾家荡产，背井离乡的；而根据我先前解释的法律的定义，原本旨在保护公民的法律为什么会毁掉这些人呢？所以他很想知道，这所谓的法律到底是什么意思？为什么法律不能保护任何人的财产，而且还加剧了财产的丢失，这到底是怎么情况呢？他完全没有看出法律存在的必要性，因为理想和目标可以在自然规律中得到实现。既然我们自命为有理性的动物，那么天性和理性就能够指引我们的言行。

我告诉我的主人，关于法律我了解得不多，有限的法律知识都是自己的利益受到侵害之后聘请律师的经历。但这一切都是徒劳。还有就是和其他有着相同经历的人交谈所获得的法律知识。有好些人因此受到了伤害，所以就离开了。至于我，还是决定尽我所能告诉主人我所知道的一切。

我告诉他说，我们那里就有那么一帮人，从年轻时起就接受培养，学习怎样通过搬弄文字将白说成黑、黑说成白这么一种本领。他们怎么说全看你给他们多少钱而定。这帮人狂妄自大，厚颜无耻，却还赢得群众的信任，群众还都依附他们，这样他们也就以某种方式使群众变成了他们的奴隶。比方说，我的邻居看中了我的一头母牛，他就会聘请这么一位律师来证明，牛是他的，该由他把牛从我这儿牵走。由于任何人都不准为自己辩护，因为这样做违反法律规定，所以我就必须聘请另一位律师来替自己的权利辩护。就这桩案子来说，我作为母牛真正的主人，却有两大不利之处。第一，我的律师几乎从摇篮时代起就一直为虚假辩护，现在要他来为正义辩护，他就很不适应。由于违反他的常规，即使他对我没有恶意，辩护起来也一定是极不熟练的。第二个不利之处是，我的律师还得谨慎从事，因为那么多人都得靠干执法这一行活着，速判速决，律师的生意就要减损，这样即使他不招来法官们的斥责，也肯定会引起同行弟兄的敌意和仇恨。这种情况下，要保住我那头母牛，我只有两种办法。第一是出双倍的钱将我对手的律师买通，因为他所受的训练就是那样，我完全有理由指望他受金钱诱惑背叛他的当事人而倒向我这一边。第二种办法是让我的律师不要硬坚持说公理在我这边，要说得好像那母牛就属于我的对手似的。这种办法要是做得巧妙，我最终就会赢得有利于我的裁决，这是通过对种种事件的仔细观察而发现的。在这些律师的筹划安排下，过错一方更有机会获胜，特别是当那些派来裁决财产纠纷以及审判罪犯的人，都是经前面提到的那一宗派中的大宠臣或朝廷贵妇推荐，从这一职业中挑选出来的最有学问、最聪明的律师时（我和我朋友的案子就碰到了这种情况），错的一方就更有机会获胜了。这帮人因为一辈子都对公正和公道持有强烈的偏见，所以急需搞偏袒、两面派和压制的手段；另外，由于年老体弱脾气差，他们到头来变得又懒又随便，几乎完全无力胜任与他这一职业的责任要求相符合的任何工作。如此教养、如此素质的人所做出的裁决，我们完全可以想到裁决一定是有利于错误的一方；这也并不奇怪，那些能把高谈阔论、吵吵嚷嚷就当是论理说道的人（只要说得慷慨激昂，洋洋洒洒），一定会推断，谁在那儿使劲地辩护，谁就是论争的胜方。

还有一条准则就是，只要以前做过这样的事情，那么再做的话就是合理合法的。所以他们会特别留心把每一条裁决都记录下来，哪怕是那些明显和公理相违背的判决。他们称之为判例，可以作为依仗的权威。凭借这样的规则，他们的意见就能够变得那么公正，而且他们的裁决又都是符合他们的心意的。

在辩护时，他们避而不谈案件的本质，而是大着嗓门，言辞激烈，啰啰唆唆地大谈特谈与案件毫不相干的其他所有情况。就以上面提到的案子为例，他们根本不想知道我的对手有什么理由或权利要占有我那头母牛，却只是问那母牛是红色还是黑色，牛角是长还是短，我放牧的那块地是圆还是方，是在家挤奶还是在户外挤奶，那牛容易得什么病，等等。问完之后，他们就去查以前的判例，这案子则一拖再拖，十年、二十年、三十年之后也弄不出个结果来。

还有一点值得注意，这帮人有自己的行话，外人是无法理解的，他们所有的法律条文就都用这样的术语撰写，他们还特别注意对法律进行增订。依靠这些东西，他们把真和假、对和错的实质差不多全都搞混了。所以他们也许要花上三十年的时间来裁决，经六代祖传留到我手上的一块地，到底是属于我还是属于三百英里外的一个外乡人。

他们审判叛国罪犯的方法却简单得多，这倒是很值得称道的。法官先要了解一下有权人的意见，然后就能轻而易举地判处罪犯是绞死还是赦免，还说他是严格遵守了所有的法律法规。

说到这里，我的主人接过去说，照我描述的情形来看，像这些律师这样具有如此巨大才能的人，你们却不鼓励他们去教导别人，传授智慧和知识，实在是可惜了。听他这话，我回答说，律师们所有的心思和时间都用在处理和研究本职工作上了，其他任何事都漠不关心，所以除了他们自己的本行，其他各方面他们大多是又无知又愚蠢，从一般的交谈中，还真很难找得出别的行业中有什么人比他们更卑鄙。大家也都认为他们是一切知识和学问的公开的敌人，无论跟他们谈哪一门学问，他们都会像在本行业务中的表现那样，违反人类的理性。

第六章

作者继续描述在安妮女王统治下的英国。作者描述了欧洲宫廷中首相的性格。

我的主人仍然不明白为什么会有这么一帮律师，专门为了迫害自己的同类而组织了这么一个不公平的组织。他们到底是受到别人的雇佣还是怎么回事呢？所以我只好给他普及了一下有关钱财的作用。我先是解释了钱财是由什么材料制成的，以及各种金属的内在价值。我告诉他，如果一只"野猢"拥有大量的钱财，那么他就可以购买任何想要购买的东西，比如最好的衣服，最美的房子，大片的土地，最昂贵的肉类和饮料，还能够挑选最漂亮的女人。既然用金钱就能够换来那么多的东西，我们的"野猢"自然认为钱财是越多越好，而且永远都不会满足，因为挥霍浪费和贪得无厌是他们的天性。那些有钱人可以享用穷人的劳动成果，而穷人和富人的人数比例是一千比一，大多数穷人都只能过着悲惨的日子，为了一点点报酬就得付出艰辛的劳作，而结果则是让极少数人过上幸福的生活。

我在这些问题上讲了很多，但是我的主人仍然还在追问，因为在他看来，地球上出产的东西理应交给所有动物分享，而占据统治地位的动物显然享有更高的待遇，所以他不明白那些昂贵的肉到底是什么，为什么有那么多人想要吃呢？于是我就把脑海里能够想到的所有的种类都讲了一遍，还有琳琅满目的烹调方法。如果不派人前往世界各地搜寻美酒、调料和其他食物，这一切都是无米之炊。我告诉我的主人，在我们那个地方，一只地位很高的母"野猢"的一顿早餐或者一只餐具，至少得绕着地球跑三圈才能够准备齐全。我的主人说，一个国家连最基本的食物都无法提供，这一定是一个很悲惨的国家。但是我的描述中最让他感到惊奇的是，我们国家那么大的一片土地竟然没有淡水，还得千里迢迢跑到海外去弄饮料？我回答他说，我亲爱的英国生产的粮食大约是居民需求的三倍，而从谷物和某种果实中提取发酵的液体可以制作成最好的饮料，和其他日用品一样，产量也是需求的三倍，但是为了满足国人的虚荣和奢侈，我们都把这些东西送出国门，换回了疾病、愚蠢和罪恶，于是我们大多数人民就没有生存的依靠，只好靠讨饭、抢劫、偷窃、欺骗、拉皮条、作伪证、谄媚、教唆、伪造、赌博、说谎、奉承、威吓、搞选举、滥作文、星象占卜、放毒、卖淫、侈谈、诽谤、想入非非以及各种类似的事来糊口过日子。这其中的每一个名词我都费了不少劲来解释，最后他终于明白了。

我还告诉我的主人，从海外进口的酒类并不是用来补充我们饮料的缺乏，而是因为这种酒喝多了能够让人变得麻木而兴奋，可以缓解我们的忧愁，同时激发我们的灵感，让理智失去效用，让四肢无法运动，最后把我们送进梦乡。但是有一点必须承认，每次喝完睡醒之后我们总是精神萎靡，而这种液体还会给我们带来很多种疾病，让我们的生命变得痛苦而短暂。

除了这一切，我们的大多数人还得向富人提供必需品才能够维持生存。比如我在家的时候，身上穿的衣服就需要一百位工匠的手艺，我的房子和家具也需要那么多人来制造；而我的妻子打扮整齐就需要整整五百个人的辛劳。

随后我又谈到了另外一种人，依靠服侍病人来维持生活。之前我曾经和我的主人交代过，我船上有不少水手是生病去世的。但是这的确花费了我不少力气来解释这种现象，因为"慧骃"只会在临死前的几天变得衰弱，或者在遇到意外的时候弄伤自己的腿，这一切都能够被我的主人所理解。但是自然界既然创造出了那么多的完美，为什么会让我们的身体遭受那么多的痛苦呢？所以他就很难理解，也想知道这些不可理解的灾难到底是如何产生的。

我告诉他，我们平时吃的东西就有上千种，还有许多是互相冲突的。我们的肚子不饿的时候还得继续吃，一点不渴却还要拼命喝。我们经常整夜地空腹喝烈酒，一直把人喝到昏昏欲睡，浑身乏力。那些卖淫的母"野猢"身上有一种病，谁要是投入她们的怀抱就得烂骨头，而这种病和其他许多病一样都是遗传的，所以很多人一生下来就有这种病。如果我把人类身上的所有病症都讲一遍，一时间还真讲不完，因为至少有五六百种，分布在人体的四肢和所有的关节。所以为了治疗这些毛病，我们就专门有人负责治病，当然其中还有不少是假冒的。我也是这一行的人，所以为了感谢主人的恩德，我愿意把治疗疾病的秘密和方法都交代清楚。

治病的基本原理就是所有的疾病都是由无规律、不合理的饮食所导致的，所以他们得出结论，要想治病就得把人体内部清理一次，既可以通过排泄口，也可以通过嘴将内部的污秽排出。第一步就是用药草、矿物质、树脂、油、贝壳、盐、果汁、海藻、粪便、树皮、蛇、癞蛤蟆、青蛙、蜘蛛、死人的肉和骨头、鸟、兽、鱼等，想尽办法做成一种气味和味道都最令人难受、恶心和反感的混合物，一吃进胃里就叫你恶心得往外吐；他们管这种混合物叫催吐剂。他们还用同样的这些药再加进别的几样有毒的东西制成一种同样叫人反胃的药，让我们从上面的孔（嘴）或者下面的孔（肛门）灌入（从哪个孔灌要看医生当时的意向如何）。这种药可把肚子里的东西全清理出来；他们管这种药叫泻药或者灌肠剂。从自然规律上来说，我们的嘴是用来吃喝，而肛门则是用来排泄的；既然生病的人的这一切都被打乱了，那么为了让身体恢复正常，就必须用截然相反的办法来治疗疾病，也就是把固体和液体从肛门处灌进去，然后从嘴里排出来。

除了这些切实存在的病症，还有不少属于臆想症，所以医生们也发明了各种对付的药品。由于这些病症各有名称，所以也有相应的药品。我们国家的母"野猢"就经常会犯这样的病症。

这些人的本领都很强，能够预测疾病的后果，这一点倒是很少会弄错。因为一般来说疾病恶化之后就会导致死亡，而且无药可医，所以他们的预言也是很有把握的。如果有被宣判死刑的病例却出人意料地痊愈了，病人们也不会去咒骂他们，因为他们知道如何用一剂恰到好处的药来向世人证明自己是有先见之明的。

对于那些对自己的配偶感到厌倦的丈夫或者妻子，对那些长子和权臣，特别是对君主来说，这些医生都有着特殊的存在意义。

之前我已经和主人说过政府的性质，特别是我们那优越的宪法，这真是令全世界赞叹羡慕的制度啊！在这里我偶然提到了大臣这个词语，过了一段时间之后他就要求我讲讲大臣到底是怎样的一种"野猢"。

我告诉他，国家的首相必须得是一个喜怒不形于色的人，除了对财富、权利和爵位有欲望，其余的一切都不能引起他的注意。他说的话都是万金油，但就是不表明自己的态度。他的每一句实话都会被你当成是谎言，而他的谎言你却信以为真。那些被他在背后数落的人可能是他最喜欢的，而要是他在你面前夸奖你，那么你就要倒霉了。最为严重是你得到了他的许诺，特别是这个许诺还伴随着誓言的时候，那就最糟糕了。聪明人遇到这样的事情都会识趣地离开，放弃自己所有的希望。

一般来说有三种办法能够获得首相的宝座。首先就是要知道如何妥善地利用自己的妻子、女儿或者姐妹；第二种是依靠背叛和暗杀前任首相；第三种就是在公开场合抨击朝廷的腐败。不过聪明的君王一般都会选择第三种，因为这种人往往最能遵从君王的爱好。他们一旦手握大权，就会选择去贿赂元老院或者枢密院的重臣，以保全自己的势力。当然他们还得推行免于处罚的条令（我向我的主人介绍了这样的法令）来保证自己没有后顾之忧，可以放心地带着自己的巨额财产功成身退。

首相的官邸则是他们的大本营。他手下的随从、仆人和看门狗都能够一人得道鸡犬升天。他们的蛮横、撒谎和贿赂的本领简直就是青出于蓝，很快他们就有了自己的势力范围，得到贵族的奉承。他们当中的有些人还会依靠自己的投机取巧，最终成为他们主子的继承人。

所谓的首相往往会受到荡妇或者亲信的影响，而这些趋炎附势之徒往往会通过这样的渠道平步青云，所以说到底，他们的确是这个国家的统治者。

有一次，当我的主人在听我描述国内的贵族的时候，他倒是夸赞了我一句，虽然这样的夸赞我却是受不起。他竟然认为我是出自贵族家庭，因为我长得很干净，皮肤又白，这几个方面都比他们那儿的"野猢"要好很多。虽然我可能没有"野猢"那般强壮敏捷，不过这可能是因为两者在生活方式上的巨大差异。除此之外，我不仅有说话的能力，而且还有理性，他的所有朋友都觉得我是个难得的存在。

他告诉我，"慧骃"中的白马、栗色马和青色马的地位和红马、深灰色马以及黑马的地位截然不同，由于这是天生的，绝对无法改变，所以他们永远都是仆人。如果他们试图改变这一情况，这在慧骃国会被认为是可怕和反常的事情。

我的主人十分看重我，我对此十分感激。我承认说我其实并没有高贵血统，我的父母只是普通的百姓，勉强能够承担我的教育。我告诉他，我们那儿的贵族和他想象的截然不同，那些年轻贵族从小就游手好闲、骄奢淫逸。成年之后他们也忙着在女人中穿梭，时常会因此染病。等到自己把家财挥霍一空的时候，他就会娶一个自己都瞧不上的出身卑贱、脾气古怪的、身体还不好的女人做妻子，因为那女人可能有点钱。这种婚姻下的孩子往往先天不足。要是女主人不留心在邻居和佣人当中找一个强壮的父亲来改善后代的基因的话，这样的家族肯定传承不过三代。身体虚弱、脸色苍白是贵族的标志，强壮的身体在他们看来反而是一种侮辱，因为别人会觉得他的父亲是个马夫或者车夫。他的头脑同样有缺陷，那是古怪、迟钝、无知、任性、荒淫和傲慢的综合体。

不得到这帮贵族的同意，任何法令都不能颁布，既不能废除，也不能修改。这些贵族还对我们所有的财产拥有决定权，而不用征求我们的意见。

第七章

作者对于祖国的热爱。他的主人根据作者的描述对英国的宪法和行政手段发表了自己的看法，并且提出了佐证。主人表达了自己对于人性的看法。

我的读者们也许会感到很奇怪，我为什么会在这样一种平凡的动物面前坦率地揭露自己的同类的缺点呢？他们不仅认为我和"野猢"一模一样，而且还做出了那么糟糕的评价。但是有一点我必须承认，这些四足动物的美德和人类的堕落形成了鲜明的对比。在他们的帮助下，我开阔了自己的视野，我意识到了另外一种观察人类的行为和感情的角度。同时我也意识到了，保全人类所谓的尊严的念头是十分可笑的，而且在思维敏捷，判断能力极强的"慧骃"面前（尤其是我的主人面前），这样的掩饰也是没有一点用处的。每一次和我的主人交谈，我都能够意识到人类的许多错误，其中有好些是我从来不曾意识到，或者一点不觉得那是人类的错误一般。同时，我的主人教会了我痛恨一切虚伪和假装，我从不曾那般坚定地认为，我愿为真理牺牲一切。

让我更加坦率地承认吧，我之所以那么愿意揭露这些事，其中还有一个很强烈的驱动因素就是，在这不到一年的时间里，我已经对这个国家的居民产生了强烈的热爱和尊敬的情感，我甚至都打定主意不再回去人类的世界，而在这些值得尊敬的"慧骃"当中安定下来，并且在我的后半生去琢磨并且实践这些美德。在这个国度不会有任何原因诱导我去作恶。但是命运毕竟是我的敌人，不肯赐予我这样的福分。不过现在回想起来，我仍然感到欣慰。因为我的主人在谈论我的同胞的时候，我仍然愿意为他们的错误辩护，每一件事情我都尽自己的努力做出徒劳的解释。毕竟这个世界上的每个人都对自己的出生地怀有私心。

在我侍奉我的主人的时间里，我们谈论了许多次，具体的内容之前就已经交代清楚了。不过限于篇幅，我省略掉了其中大部分的内容。

当我回答完他的所有问题之后，他的好奇心似乎得到了满足。一个清晨，他早早把我叫了过去，命令我坐在距离他不远的地方（这种恩典还是第一次）。他说自己认真考虑了一番有关我和我的国家的一切，他认为我们不过是碰巧得到了一点理性的动物，至于这点理性到底是如何得来的他也想不明白。但是重要的是我们并没有好好利用我们的理性，并借此来克服我们的天性，反而获得了自然从未赐予我们的新欲望。更为严重的是，我们这一生似乎都在用自己的发明来满足这些欲望。至于我本人，在体力和敏捷上还不如一只普通的"野猢"，而且用两只后脚站立的方式是那么不稳当，两只前爪毫无用处，连基本的防卫功能都没有，就连下巴上用来阻挡阳光和恶劣天气的毛发都不见了。我既不能快跑，也不能爬树，和这个国家的"野猢"真是一点都不一样。

我们的国家之所以有政府和司法机构，那是因为我们的道德和理性存在严重的缺陷。理性足够对一切拥有理性的动物产生约束效应，所以哪怕我为自己的同类辩护，我们仍然无法自认为有理性的动物。我的主人认为我偏袒我的同胞，隐瞒了许多的真相，而且还说了许多子虚乌有的事情。

他坚信自己的看法是正确的，因为他注意到我的身体和"野猢"的构造一模一样。除了我的力气更小，速度更慢，动作更笨拙，爪子更短。当我详细叙述了我们的生活、习惯和日常行为之后，他发现我们的性情也和"野猢"的很相似。他告诉我，在这个国家，"野猢"对于同类的痛恨要超过对其它所有动物的痛恨，他们归咎于"野猢"那丑陋而可怕的面貌。它们只能看清自己的同类的丑陋，却没有意识到自己的丑陋，所以像我们这样发明遮蔽身体的衣服倒是一种不错的办法，因为这样一来我们就看不见彼此身上的诸多缺陷了。他还意识到自己先前的想法是错误的，因为这儿的"野猢"之间发生争执的原因和我们国内的冲突是完全一样的。如果把足够五十人吃的食物发给五只"野猢"，他们就不会守本分，而是想要独占所有食物，这样一来他们就会大打出手。所以在这个国家，在给"野猢"喂食的时候必须要有一位奴仆在旁边监视，那些关在房间里的"野猢"也必须用绳子捆缚住，免得出现什么意外。如果有一头母牛身故了，而"慧骃"还没有来得及拿走作为自己家里的"野猢"的食物，周围的"野猢"就会闻风前来，并且打得不可开交。不过由于这儿的"野猢"并不像我们国家那样发明许多杀人的武器，所以结局倒是没有那么凄惨。有的时候"野猢"还会趁着另一个地方的"野猢"没有备战准备而发动偷袭。如果计划失败就会提前撤退。如果没有外部敌人，他们也许还会在内部发动战争。

在这个国家的一些土地里面埋藏着各种不同颜色的闪光的石头。"野猢"们十分喜欢这种石头，它们整天都忙着用爪子挖掘这样的石头，然后运回去藏在家里，一边藏一边还得小心防备被自己的伙伴给发现。他一直都弄不清楚那些"野猢"为什么会有这样违反天性的欲望，因为这些石头对"野猢"来说没有一点用处。不过他现在倒是认为，这可能就是我说过的那种贪婪的习性。他曾经做过一个实验，那就是悄悄把"野猢"埋着的石头给搬走。那只可怜的"野猢"发现自己宝贝失踪了，就大声哭号，吸引所有的"野猢"在边上围观，还会不依不饶地撕咬那些同伴。从那之后，这只"野猢"就日渐消瘦，变得无精打采了起来。这时候主人就吩咐一个仆人悄悄把石头放回原来的那个坑里。"野猢"发现自己的石头失而复得之后，就变得十分正常了。

我的主人还发现，在埋有许多石头的地段时常会出现大规模的战争，因为生活在附近的"野猢"团体经常会入侵。

我的主人告诉我，当两只"野猢"在争夺地里发现的一块石头的时候，时常会有第三只"野猢"捡了便宜。我的主人认为这样的情形和我描述的法庭上的纷争有着异曲同工之妙。我倒是觉得，他所说的这种方法比我们的法律还要公平，因为那两只"野猢"不过就是丢失了争夺的石头，并不会有别的损失。而在我们的法庭里，不把原告和被告一起整得倾家荡产，是不会结案的。

我的主人继续往下讲，他说，"野猢"最叫人厌恶的是它们那好坏都不分的食欲，无论碰到什么，草也好，根也好，浆果也好，腐烂的兽肉也好，或者乱七八糟全都混在一起的东西也好，它们统统吞吃下去。它们还有一种怪脾气，家里给它们准备的好好的食物放着不吃，却喜欢从老远的地方去偷或者抢。弄来的东西哪怕一时吃不完，它们还是会直吃到肚子要炸。这之后大自然会指引它们去吃一种草根，吃下去肚子就会拉得干干净净。

还有另外一种根茎，肥厚多汁，但是比较稀少。"野猢"们对这种根茎也十分感兴趣。找到了之后就会开心地吮吸一会儿。这种根茎的作用和我们的酒类十分相似。吮吸完之后的"野猢"一会儿搂抱着，一会儿厮打着，在那儿闹个没完，最后就会在烂泥地里昏睡过去。

我的确观察到，这个国家里只有"野猢"会生病，不过得的病还是要比我们国家的马少很多，而且大多不是因为受虐待，而是由于它们贪吃并且不注重卫生。这些病症在当地的语言中有一个统一的名字，就被称为"野猢病"。而且这种病症的治疗方法就是用"野猢"的屎尿灌进喉咙。据我所知，这种办法是很有效的。为了我们的公共利益，我愿意向我的同类宣传这种办法，对于因为过度饮食而引起的疾病，这种疗法是切实有效的。

在学术、政治、艺术等方面，我的主人承认，他看不出他们国家的"野猢"和我们之间有不同之处，因为他只想看看我们在本性上有什么共同点。他也确曾听一些好奇的"慧骃"说过，在大多数"野猢"群落当中总有一头是首领。这种"野猢"总是长得比别的"野猢"更难看，性情也更刁钻。这领头的一般总要找一只尽可能像它自身一样的"野猢"做宠儿，给领头的舔脚和屁股，并带母"野猢"到领头的窝里去。为此领头的常常会赏它一块驴肉吃。大家都恨这个宠儿，因此为了保护自己它只好一步不离地跟着主人。在找到比它还要恶劣的"野猢"之前，它一般是不会被解职的；可它一被蹬开，继任它的"野猢"就会率领这一地区的男女老幼"野猢"们一齐赶来，对它从头到脚撒尿拉屎。不过这种现象与我们这里的朝廷、宠臣和大臣到底有几分相像，我的主人说只有我最能说得准了。

对于这种嘲讽，我也没有吱声，因为这一番话已经把人类贬损得不如一头普通的猎犬了，至少猎犬还有准确的判断力，能够分辨出同伴中最厉害的那一头，并且追随强者。

我的主人告诉我，"野猢"还有好几种十分明显的特性，之前在听我谈论人类的特点的时候并没有听到类似的阐述。他说，"野猢"和别的牲畜并没有什么区别，同样有供所有"野猢"共用的母"野猢"，唯一的区别是，那些母"野猢"就算怀孕了还是要和公"野猢"交配。此外，公"野猢"和母"野猢"之间同样会爆发争执，这两个特点是任何有感情的动物都没有的。

另外一点让他感到不解的是，"野猢"为什么格外喜欢肮脏呢？而别的动物都很喜欢干净。对于前面那两项责难，我并不想辩白什么，因为我没有什么有力的辩护，虽然我打心里想要做这样的辩护。但是关于最后一条，他指责我们有喜脏的怪毛病，如果这个国家有猪（可惜他们没有），我原本可以为我们人类辩解一下的。猪这种四足动物虽然可能比"野猢"要来得温顺，可是说句公道话，在下以为它没有资格说自己比"野猢"更干净。要是主人亲眼看到猪那脏兮兮的吃相，看到猪在烂泥中打滚、睡觉的习惯，他一定会承认我说的话是对的。

我的主人还提到了另外一个特性，那是他的仆人在几只"野猢"身上发现的，在他看来却完全不能理解。他说，"野猢"有时不知怎么会想到要躲进一个角落里去，在那里躺下来，又是嚎叫又是呻吟，谁走近它都把人家一脚踢开，虽然年轻体胖，却可以不吃不喝，仆人们也看不出它哪里不舒服。后来他们发现，唯一可以治疗它的办法是让它去干重活，重活一干，肯定恢复正常。由于我偏向自己的同类，所以听了这话我只好默不作声。这倒也使我找到了忧郁症的病源，也只有懒惰、奢侈的人以及有钱人才得这样的病，如果强迫他们接受同样方法的治疗，我可以保证他们的病马上就会好。

我的主人还说，有些母"野猢"经常会站在土堆或者是灌木后面，盯着路过的年轻公"野猢"。她们扭扭捏捏地做出许多丑态，而且还会发出很难闻的气味。要是有一只公"野猢"走上前来，她们就会慢慢后退，做出一副欲拒还迎的模样，然后跑到了一个方便的地方，她很清楚，公"野猢"一定会跟来的。

有的时候，如果从哪儿来了一只陌生的母"野猢"，三四只本地的母"野猢"就会围上去打量、议论。她们一边冷笑一边把新来的母"野猢"闻了个遍，然后就装模作样地离开了，借此表达自己的不屑。

这些都是我主人自己的观察所得，或者也可能是别人告诉他的，当然话也许可以再说得文雅一点。不过我想起来倒不免有几分惊讶，同时也很悲哀，在女性的本能中竟可以找到淫荡、风骚、苛刻和造谣的萌芽。

我时刻都等待着我的主人来指责男女"野猢"身上那些违反自然的欲望，那在我们中间很常见。造物主似乎还不是一位手段非常高明的教师；这些较为文雅的享乐，在我们这一边，却完全是艺术和理性的产物。

第八章

作者描述了"野猢"的情况，随后又描述了"慧骃"的美德，他们对年轻"慧骃"的教育。最后作者交代了他们的代表大会。

我对人性的理解显然要比我的主人清楚许多，所以我觉得他所描述的有关"野猢"的性格和我的同胞是截然不同的。同时我坚信如果我亲自去观察的话，一定会有进一步的发现。于是我就时常请求他允许我到附近的"野猢"群体中去观察。他一向都很清楚我对这些畜生只有痛恨之情，是绝对不会被它们所引诱的，所以每一次他都会答应，而且还命令一位仆人充当我的警卫。这是一匹健壮的栗色小马，诚实而敦厚。如果不是有他的保护的话，我还真不敢冒险。毕竟先前我已经讲过了，在我刚来到这个地方的时候曾经吃过这群畜生的苦头，之后还有好几次身临险境，因为我有几次是没有带腰刀出门的。不过我有理由相信它们是我的同类，因为当我和我的同类在一起的时候，时常会卷起袖子，露出胳膊和胸脯。而这时候那些"野猢"们就会靠拢过来，和猴子一样模仿我的动作，只不过眼睛里满是仇视。我就像一只被人驯化的寒鸦，戴着帽子穿着衣服跑到陌生的野鸟群中，只能落得被迫害的下场。

它们从小就十分敏捷。有一次我抓到过一只大约三岁大的公"野猢"，我用尽了一切手段，想要哄它安静下来，但是这家伙总是哭闹，还拼命用嘴咬我，无奈之下我只能把它给放掉。当时有一群成年"野猢"闻风而来；不过看到那只小"野猢"安然无恙，又看到我的边上站着那匹栗色小马，就没有敢靠近。我察觉到那小家伙的肉带着一股子臭味，有点像黄鼠狼，又有点像狐狸，不过要难闻很多。我还忘了另外一件事情（如果我不说的话，我想读者们也是会原谅我的），那就是当我把这只小"野猢"抓在手里的时候，它拉了一泡黄色的屎，把我的衣服都弄脏了。幸好边上有一条小河，我就跑到河里去洗了个干净，这才敢回去见我的主人。

在我看来，"野猢"应该是所有动物里最难以调教的。它们除了会拉东西和扛东西，就没有别的本领了。不过我倒是觉得，之所以会这样完全是因为"野猢"那种乖张的性格。它们十分狡诈恶毒，而且有很强的报复心。虽然它们身体强壮，但是性格懦弱，所以就变得蛮横而下贱，卑鄙而残忍。听说红毛的"野猢"要比一般的"野猢"更加残忍淫荡，当然在身体的灵活程度上也比它们的同类要好很多。

"慧骃"把自己要使唤的"野猢"养在距离他们的屋子不远的茅草屋里，其余的就被赶到外面的田里去，由得它们在那儿刨树根野草吃，或者以动物的死尸或者是黄鼠狼之类的为生。它们的吃相分外地贪婪。造物主教会它们在土坡旁边挖洞，平时它们就在里面休息。那些母"野猢"的窝会大一些，可以容纳两三个幼崽。

"野猢"和青蛙一样会游泳，而且能够在水底下待很长时间。它们也时常在水里捉鱼，那些母"野猢"会把鱼带回家给它们的幼崽。说到这里，我还要讲一件奇怪的事情。

有一次我和我的护卫小马一起外出，那天十分炎热，所以我请求他同意我去边上的一条小河里洗个澡。他同意之后我马上就把衣服给脱光了，然后朝着小河走去。这时候一只站在土堆后面的年轻母"野猢"看到了我，一下子就有了兴致，然后在距离我不到五码的地方跳进了水里。我这辈子还从来没有那么惊恐过。那时候的小马还在远处吃草，他根本就没想到会出这样的事情。当母"野猢"用一种恶心的动作把我搂在怀里的时候，我拼了命地大喊着。一直等到小马闻声赶来，那只母"野猢"才松开了手，但是她的眼里却仍然是那般依依不舍。只见她跳到了对岸，冲着正在穿衣服的我嗷嗷大叫。

我的主人和他的家人一直把这件事情当作笑谈，而我则感觉到十分羞耻。母"野猢"竟然把我当成是它的同类，并且还表达了自己的爱慕之情，这无疑让我无法否认自己和"野猢"不是同一物种了。那只"野猢"的毛发也不是红色的（这就不能说她的欲望不正常），而是和李子一般黑，看上去也不像一般的"野猢"那么丑陋。我想它应该还不到十一岁。

我在这个国家生活了三年，我想读者们一定希望我能够像其他旅行家一样把这个国家的风俗习惯给讲一讲。实际上，这也是我迫切想要学习的东西。

这些高贵的"慧骃"天生就具备各种美德，根本就不知道理性动物的罪恶是怎么一回事。他们的最高准则就是培育理性，因为所有的一切都受到理性的支配。在这个国家，理性不存在值得争论的问题，这一点和我们的国家不一样。在我们国家，你可以正面回答一个问题，也可以换一个角度来反证。而在这儿，理性是不会受到感情或者利益的蒙蔽，所以理性是唯一值得信服的存在。我记得我花了好长时间才让我的主人明白了"观点"这个词的含义，也花费了好多工夫才能让他明白为什么一个问题会引发各种争论。因为理性告诉他，只有确凿的事情才值得肯定或者否定，如果是不确定的事情，不管如何争辩都无法改变事实。所以那些争议、吵闹之类的把戏在"慧骃"看来都是从未接触过的罪恶。至于我们的自然哲学的几套体系，他更是嗤之以鼻，因为他觉得一群冒充理性的动物竟然会重视别人的猜想。而这样的事情过于虚无缥缈，就算彻底了解了也没有什么用处。关于这方面他倒是赞同柏拉图对于苏格拉底的思想的阐述。而我之所以提出这些，完全是出于对这位哲学之王的敬意。从那时候我就时常回想，这样一种学说不知道要摧毁多少图书馆的藏书，又要堵塞多少条成名之路。

友谊和仁慈是"慧骃"的两种主要美德，这两种美德不局限于个别"慧骃"，而是这个种族普遍存在的美德。不管是从最遥远的地方来的陌生客人，还是住在附近的邻居，他们一视同仁。所以不管他们去哪儿，都有种在家的感觉。他们很讲究礼貌，但是不拘小节。他们从来不溺爱子女，凡事都以理性为准。我就曾经见过他们对待邻居的孩子和对待自己的孩子没有什么区别。"慧骃"遵从大自然的教导，热爱自己的同类。只有理性才能够给他们划分等级。

当"慧骃"生下一对孩子之后，他们就不再同居了；除非有意外情况出现，其中的一个孩子不幸夭折，只有在这样的情况下他们才会再次同居。或者是当别的"慧骃"遭遇了这样的不幸，而他们的配偶又无法生育的话，另外一对"慧骃"夫妇就会把其中一个孩子过继给他，然后再同居准备迎接一个新生命。这样的做法可以有效防止人口过剩。至于那些做仆人的"慧骃"，就没有这样的严格限制了。他们一生可以生产三对子女，而他们的子女也可以去贵族家里当仆人。

在婚姻这件事上，他们非常注意对毛色的选择，这样做是为了避免造成血统混乱。男方主要看是否强壮，女方则看是不是美丽，这倒并不是为了爱情，而是为了防止种族退化。如果偶有女方力气过人，就找一个漂亮的伴侣配给她。

他们对求婚、谈情说爱、送礼、寡妇得丈夫遗产、财产赠送等一无所知，他们的语言中也没有可用来表达这些概念的专门术语。年轻夫妇的结识和结合全由他们的父母和朋友来定夺，他们每天都看到这样的事，并认为那是理性动物必要的一种行为。婚姻受到破坏或者不忠不贞的事却从来都没有听说过，夫妇俩像对待他们碰到的所有同类一样，相互友爱、相互关心着度过一辈子，没有嫉妒，没有溺爱，不吵架，舒心满意。

在教育年轻人方面，他们的办法值得敬佩，十分值得我们学习。除了某几天特殊的日子，他们吃不到一粒燕麦，喝不到几次牛奶，就这样一直长到十八岁。夏天的清晨他们都要出去吃两个小时的青草，晚上也是一样，这样的训练都要求有父母在边上监督。那些仆人只能吃一个小时，大部分的草都被他们带回家，在不干活的时候拿出来吃。

节俭、勤劳、运动和卫生是他们必须掌握的习惯。我的主人认为，除了家务管理，女子的教育和男子的教育不该有任何差别。我十分赞同这样的观点，这样一来我们国家就不会有一半人除了生孩子，其他什么都不会做了。把我们的子女交给这样一无是处的动物来照看，本身就是一件残忍的事情。

"慧骃"们总是训练他们的孩子在陡峭的山坡上快速奔跑，或者是在坚硬的土地上奔跑，借此锻炼孩子们的体力、速度和毅力。浑身大汗之后就命令他们跳进池塘里游泳。每年会有四次大型集会，所有的年轻人都可以展现他们的体力和运动技巧，所有人都会赞颂比赛的优胜者。那些仆人会押着一群负责搬运燕麦、牛奶和干草的"野猢"来到比赛场地。东西送到之后这些畜生就会被马上赶走，免得它们影响到大会。

每隔四年的春分都会举行全国代表大会，地点就在距离主人家不到二十英里的平原上，每次会议都要持续五六天。他们在会上讨论各个地区的情况，有关干草、燕麦、母牛、"野猢"等数量是否富足，如果有哪里缺什么（这种情况很少见）就会由大家捐助来补齐。有关孩子的问题同样是在这样的场合解决。比如一个"慧骃"生下了两个男孩子，就可以和生下两个女孩的"慧骃"交换。如果有孩子意外死亡，而母亲又失去了生育能力，那么大家也会决定由哪一对夫妇再生育一个来补充损失。

第九章

"慧骃"们举行了一场大辩论，并且做出了决定。"慧骃"的学术成就，他们的建筑，他们的葬礼，他们的语言缺陷。

在我离开这个国家三个月之前，慧骃国召开了一次全国代表大会，我的主人作为我们这个地区的代表出席了会议；在这次会议上，他们辩论了一个老话题，这也是这个国家自古以来唯一一个辩题。主人回来之后就把有关辩论的情况全部告诉我了。

辩论的问题是：是否有必要把"野猢"消灭干净。其中一位主张消灭"野猢"的代表提出了几个很有力的观点。他认为"野猢"是世界上最肮脏、最丑陋，也是害处最大的动物，它们性格执拗，脾气暴躁，而且内心恶毒。如果不好好监管的话，它们就会偷喝属于"慧骃"的牛奶，把猫给弄死吃掉，破坏燕麦和干草，还会干出许多放肆的事情来。这位代表注意到一个很盛行的传说，"野猢"并不是这个国家的本土动物，而是在许多年前突然出现在一座山上的。至于它们到底是从阳光下的污泥中出现的还是从海水里冒出来的就没人知晓了。在此之后这一对"野猢"就开始拼命繁殖，它们的后代一下子遍布全国，成了巨大的灾害。"慧骃"曾经举行过一次规模庞大的狩猎活动，把"野猢"们团团包围，然后杀死其中的大部分，剩下来的"野猢"，每一只"慧骃"分走了两只，驯养它们出卖苦力。能把如此野蛮的动物驯养到这个程度也算是难能可贵了。这个传说倒是有几分道理，这种动物不可能是土生土长的。因为所有的动物都对它们恨之入骨。就算是它们生性恶毒，但是如果它们是本地动物，那么大家绝对不会想要消灭它们。而且由于驯养"野猢"，他们还忽略了对驴的培养。这种动物文雅而温顺，更加适合饲养，还没有那种令人作呕的臭味。虽然它们可能没有"野猢"那么灵活，但是足够对付繁重的劳作。虽然它们的声音也很刺耳，但是总比"野猢"那种可怕的嚎叫声要好很多。

另外几个代表也持有相同的看法，这时候我的主人向大会提出了一个权宜之计，这个想法显然是从我身上想到的启示。他先是对前一位代表的传说表示赞同，并且进一步证实了那两只最先出现的"野猢"是从海上来的。由于被同伴抛弃，它们就被留在了这片陆地上，流落在山野之间，慢慢退化，最后变得比它们在祖国的同类还要野蛮。之所以这么说，是因为他现在就拥有这么一只神奇的"野猢"（指的就是我），并且有许多代表都曾来参观过。随后我的主人就详细讲述了自己最初是如何发现的我，当时的我浑身上下都用别的动物的皮毛覆盖着，还有属于我们自己的语言，还有本领学会"慧骃"的语言。我也曾经告诉过他我先前的奇遇。他认为我不穿覆盖物的时候和"野猢"没有什么两样，只是显得皮肤较白，毛发较少，爪子也短一些而已。我的主人还转述了我曾经描述过的关于我的祖国和别的一些国家的截然相反的情况。那儿的"野猢"是处于统治地位的，而"慧骃"却受到奴役。我的主人觉得我拥有"野猢"的全部特征，只不过相比之下我更有理性。但是总的来说我身上的理性远远不如"慧骃"，就如同这儿的"野猢"比不上我一样。我的主人又提出了一种办法，那是我们国家用来让"慧骃"变得温顺的一种办法，那就是在年幼的时候就把"慧骃"给阉割了，这样的手术简单而安全。我的主人说，向地位比我们低下的动物学习也不算是什么丢人的事情，毕竟蚂蚁教会了我们勤劳，而燕子也教会了我们筑巢（其实这是一种大很多的鸟类，但是我只能翻译成燕子了）。这项发明完全可以应用于年轻的"野猢"身上，这样它们就会变得温顺而善良，同时避免了"野猢"的无序繁殖，温和地断绝了这个种族的传承。同时我的主人也十分赞成培养驴这个种族。一方面是驴比别的兽类更有价值；此外，驴长到五岁就可以干活了，而其他种类的野兽则需要长到十二岁。

这就是我的主人觉得可以告诉我的全部内容，不过他却隐瞒了有关我个人的一件事情。由此引发的不幸后果很快就被我预料到了，而我生命中的不幸也就由此开始。这件事情我之后会详细解释的。

"慧骃"没有文字，他们的知识都是口口相传的。这个民族十分团结，天赋和美德都受到理性的支配，和周围的国家丝毫没有往来，所以国内几乎没有什么重大事件，这样有利于历史的传承。前边我已经交代过，他们几乎不会生病，所以也不需要找大夫。但是他们却有用草药配成的用来治疗蹄子划伤的良药，这种药同时也可以用来治疗身体其他部位的损伤。

他们根据太阳和月亮的运转来计算一年的时间，但是不会区分星期的概念。他们对于两个发光天体很了解，也明白日食和月食的原理，这一切就是他们在天文学方面的最高成就。

在诗歌方面，他们的成就超过其他所有动物。他们的比喻贴切，描写细致，我们简直望尘莫及。他们的韵律丰富，题材大多不是歌功颂德，而是赞颂在赛跑和其他运动中的优胜者。他们的建筑虽然粗糙简陋，但是设计巧妙，足以抵御寒暑的侵蚀。在这个国家有一种树木，差不多四十年之后树根就开始松动，被狂风一刮就会倒伏。这种树的树干笔直，"慧骃"用锋利的石头把它们削成木桩（他们对铁器一窍不通），然后按照间隔十英寸的距离打在地面上，然后在两根木桩之间用燕麦秸秆或者柳条编织起来。屋顶和门也用同样的办法建成。

"慧骃"用前蹄中间的中空部分来拿东西，就像我们的手一样。一开始我还真没想到他们的蹄子会有那么灵巧。我还见过有母"慧骃"用蹄子来穿针线（针线是我借给她的）。他们可以完成挤牛奶、收割燕麦等工作。他们会使用一种十分坚硬的石头，通过摩擦就可以打造类似我们的斧头和锤子等工具。他们也用这样的工具来收割干草和燕麦。这些燕麦都是自然生长的，"野猢"把燕麦运到家里，然后由仆人们用脚踩碎，把麦粒归到粮仓里面。他们也会制造简陋的陶器和木器，是放在太阳底下烘干的。

如果他们的一生不发生什么意外的话，他们就只会自然衰老而死，然后被埋葬到最为偏远的地方，他们的朋友和亲人们也从不表示高兴或者悲伤。那些"慧骃"在临死之前也不会因为要离开这个世界而感到遗憾，就好像是拜访了一位邻居之后自然而然地要回家一样。我记得有一次，我的主人邀请他的朋友带着家人一起来商量要事，但是那一天，客人的妻子带着两个孩子姗姗来迟。她先是忙着道歉，说她的丈夫"回到了第一个母亲那里"去了。随后她又为自己的迟到表示道歉，因为她丈夫在上午晚些时候才去世的，她和仆人们商量了好久该挑选哪一块合适的地方来安葬。我发现她的神情并没有一点悲伤，大约三个月以后，她也死去了。

一般来说他们都能够活到七十或者七十五岁，很少会超过八十岁。在死前的几个星期，他们会感觉到自己的身体衰弱了下去，但是一点都不痛苦。这时候他的朋友们会时常来看望他，因为他已经不能像往常一般欢快地外出了。但是在死前十天左右，这个时间很少会推算错，他们就会坐上"野猢"拉着的车前去回访那些亲近的朋友。这种车不仅仅是在这种情形下才会使用，他们在上了年纪，出远门或者摔断了腿的时候也会用这样的车。临死前的"慧骃"去拜访自己的好友的时候往往会语气郑重，就好像要去某个遥远的地方度过余年一般。

有一点我不知道是否值得提出，那就是"慧骃"的语言中是没有罪恶这个词的，和他意思相近的几个词都是从形容"野猢"的丑陋的外表和品性之中借来的。所以当他们在表达仆人懒惰、孩子调皮、不小心弄伤了脚、天气不好等坏意思的时候，都会加上"野猢"一词。包括那些造得很差劲的房子，都会被冠以"野猢"的名号。

我十分乐意叙述这个优秀民族的美德，我也打算专门出版一本书来谈这个问题。读者们如果有兴趣的话可以去参考那本书，而接下来我要继续讲述我的悲惨遭遇了。

第十章

作者描述了自己的日常生活，在和"慧骃"一起生活时的幸福。他在道德方面有了十足的进步。但是他的主人却通知他必须要离开这个国家。他伤心欲绝，但是只能遵从。在仆人的帮助下他制作了一艘小船，冒险出发了。

我的日常生活十分顺心。我的主人吩咐在距离他家大约六码的地方按照他们的建筑风格给我盖一间房子。我在房间的四壁和地面上涂了一层黏土，然后铺上我自己编织的草席。我自己采麻然后做成了被套，里面填上各种鸟类的羽毛，那都是我用"野猢"毛做成的捕鸟网抓到的，那些鸟肉也是绝佳的食物。我用小刀做了两把椅子，其中大部分粗活都是栗色小马帮我完成的。我的衣服都已经破烂不堪，所以我就用兔子和另外一种和兔子差不多大小的动物的皮缝制了几件新衣服。随后我又用相同的材料做了几双长筒袜。至于鞋子，我用木片来当鞋底，鞋帮就用晒干的"野猢"皮。我在树洞里时常能够找到蜂蜜，不管是掺水还是抹在面包上都很美味。有两句名言我深以为然，"需求是很容易满足的"，"需求是发明的动力"。我觉得自己亲身验证了这两句话。在这儿我过得很健康，不会有人来算计我、背叛我，也不会有明里暗里的危险。我不用贿赂别人，也不需要卑躬屈膝地讨好那些大人物和他们手下的走狗。我不用担心受到欺骗和伤害。这儿没有医生来残害我的身体，没有律师来败毁我的财产，没有告密者在旁监视我的一言一行，没有人会受人雇佣捏造罪名对我妄加控告。这儿没有人冷嘲热讽、批驳非难、背地里说人坏话，也没有扒手、盗匪、入室窃贼、讼棍、鸨母、小丑、赌徒、政客、才子、性情乖戾的人、说话冗长乏味的人、辩驳家、强奸犯、杀人犯、强盗、古董贩子；没有政党和小集团的头头脑脑以及他们的扈从；没有人用坏榜样来引诱、唆使人犯罪；没有地牢、斧钺、绞架、笞刑柱或颈手枷；没有骗人的店家和工匠；没有骄傲、虚荣、装腔作势；没有花花公子、恶霸、醉汉、游荡的娼妓、梅毒病人；没有喜欢吹牛、淫荡而奢侈的阔太太；没有愚蠢却又自傲的学究；没有盛气凌人、吵吵嚷嚷、大喊大叫、脑袋空空、自以为是、赌咒发誓的同伴；没有为非作歹却平步青云的流氓，也没有因为有德行而被贬为庶民的贵族；没有大人老爷、琴师、法官和舞蹈教师。

我非常有幸能和几位"慧骃"见面，并一起进餐，这种时候我的主人总是十分仁慈地准许我在房里侍候，听他们谈话。他和他的客人常常会屈尊问我一些问题，并且听我回答。我有时也很荣幸能陪主人去拜访朋友。除了要回答问题，我从来都不敢多说一句话，就是回答问题的时候，我内心也感到惭愧，因为这使我丧失了不少进步和自我提升的时间。我非常喜欢做一个谦卑的听众，听他们在那儿交谈。他们的交谈总是言简意赅；最讲礼貌，却丝毫不拘于形式；每一句对话都能让双方感到快乐；没有人会打断别人的话头，会冗长乏味地说个不停，会争得面红耳赤，会话不投机。他们认为大家碰在一起的时候，短暂地沉默一会儿确实对谈话有很大好处。这一点倒是真的，因为在那不说话的短时间的沉默里，新的见解会在他们的脑子里油然而生，谈话也就变得越发生动。他们谈论的题目通常是友谊和仁慈，秩序和经济；有时也谈到自然界的各种现象和活动，或者谈古代的传统；他们谈道德的范围、界限；谈理性的正确规律，或者下届全国代表大会要做出的一些决定；还常常谈论诗歌的各种妙处。我还可以补充一点，但这并不是我虚荣，我在场还往往给他们提供了很多谈话资料，因为我的主人可以借此机会向他的朋友介绍我和我的祖国的历史。他们都非常喜欢谈这个话题，不过对于人类不是很有利，因此我也就不想在此复述他们的话了。不过有一点我想请大家允许我说一下，我的主人似乎对"野猢"的本性了解得比我要清楚，这是非常令我钦佩的。他把我们的罪恶和蠢事一一抖了出来，其中有许多是我从来都没有向他提起过的，他只是从他们国家的"野猢"来推想，这种品性的"野猢"要是再有几分理性，可能会干出什么样的事来呢？他的结论颇为肯定：这样的动物该是多么的卑鄙而可怜啊！

我必须要承认，我所掌握的一点点有价值的知识都是在我主人的教诲以及他和他的朋友的谈话之中学到的。听他们交谈要比听欧洲最伟大、最聪明的人物谈话还要让人感到自豪。我钦佩他们那充沛的体力，那俊美的体态和迅捷的行动力。他们拥有那么高尚的品德，足以让我产生最为崇高的敬意。起初我的确不明白为什么"野猢"和别的动物会对他们产生敬畏之情，现在我也有了这种感觉，而且要比我预料得更加快。除了敬畏，我还充满了对他们的敬爱和感激，因为他们对我另眼相待，一点都不认为我和"野猢"是同类。

当我想到我的家人、朋友、同胞和全人类的时候，我认为他们从形体和性情上都和"野猢"没有什么分别，只是具备说话的能力，稍稍进步一些而已。但是理性只会被他们用来犯罪，而不像这个国家的"野猢"，只有本能的原罪。有的时候我看到自己的影子会忍不住产生恐惧和讨厌的情绪，觉得自己还不如一只"野猢"好看。因为我时常和"慧骃"一起交谈，所以慢慢就开始模仿他们的步法和姿势，并逐渐养成了习惯。我的朋友们经常指出我走起路来就像一匹马。我倒觉得这是对我的赞美。就连我的发音和习惯都和"慧骃"差不多了。虽然这样一来我经常遭受嘲笑，但是我一点都不生气。

正当我沉浸在快乐之中，畅想着就这样度过余生的时候，一天早晨，主人比平时更早地把我叫了过去。看着他的脸色我就知道一定出事了。一阵短暂的沉默之后，他开口道，上一次在代表大会上谈起"野猢"的时候，许多代表都为他家里养着一只"野猢"（指的就是我）而感到反感，因为我并没有受到普通"野猢"的待遇，反而像招待一只"慧骃"一般。这些代表都很清楚我的主人时常和我谈话，难道和我谈话会得到什么好处或者乐趣吗？他们坚持认为这样的做法是违背理性的，所以劝告他，要么把我和普通的"野猢"放在一起，要么就命令我回到原来的地方。凡是在主人家里见过我的"慧骃"都反对第一种做法，因为我除了"野猢"的劣性，还是有一点理性的。他们十分担心我引诱"野猢"到偏远地带，然后趁着夜色带他们来破坏"慧骃"的劳动成果，因为我生来就是懒惰而贪婪的。

我的主人补充道，住在附近的"慧骃"时常来催促他履行代表大会的决议，所以他再也拖延不下去了。他觉得我是没法靠游泳去到另外一个国家的，所以他希望我能够做出先前向他描述过的那种可以在海面上行走的车子，他可以让仆人和邻居家的仆人一起帮助我。他坦白说自己还是愿意把我留下来的。虽然我天性卑劣，但是却在努力学习"慧骃"的品格，并且也改掉了身上的一些缺点。

在这里我需要强调的是，代表大会形成的决议类似我们国家的"郑重劝告"，因为他们不会强迫动物去做什么事情，只能劝说他们这么做。这一切都无法违反理性的原则，否则他们就称不上是理性动物了。

听了我主人的话之后我可真是伤心欲绝，我当时一下子就昏倒在了他的面前。等我苏醒之后他才告诉我，他还以为我就这么死去了，因为"慧骃"从来不会有这样的情况。我虚弱地回答说，死亡也许是真正的幸福。我虽然不能埋怨他们做出这样的决定，也不能责怪他的邻居们，但是从我的表现来看，对我宽容一点也是符合理性的吧！我最多只能游一里格的距离，而距离这儿最近的陆地大约在一百里格以外。制作一艘尺寸合适的小船的材料在这个国家也是很难找到的，所以我当时十分失望。不过既然是我的主人的意见，我也愿意试一试。当时我还说，我肯定是要死在路上了，但这并不算是什么巨大的不幸。一想到回去之后又要和"野猢"生活在一起，我就不寒而栗。以后没有主人的榜样和指引，我又如何沿着道德之路前进呢？想到这些我又悲伤起来。但是我很清楚，"慧骃"做出的决定是经过深思熟虑的，是不可能因为我的悲惨境遇而动摇的。于是我先是表达了自己的感谢，感谢他主动提出让仆人来帮助我，同时请求他给我充分的时间来完成这项艰巨的工作。随后我又对他说，我一定会努力保护自己的这条性命，这样万一能够回到英国的话，至少还能赞颂"慧骃"的美德，号召人类向他们学习。

我的主人简单回答了我几句，并且答应给我两个月的时间来造船，同时安排那匹栗色小马来和我搭伙（现在我们已经相距那么远，我可以这样称呼他了），听我的指挥。因为我对主人说，有他帮忙就够了，因为他对我很和善。

我要做的第一件事就是让他陪我去当初那些叛变的水手逼我登陆的那一带海岸。我爬上了附近最高的地方，然后朝四周眺望。我发现东北方向好像有一座小岛。于是我拿出了自己的望远镜，发现在大约五里格之外还真有一座小岛。但是身旁的栗色小马却只能看到一片白色的云彩，因为他从没想过除了自己的国家，还有别的国家存在，所以也不能像我们那样辨别出大海远处的东西。

当我发现了那座小岛之后我就不再多考虑什么了。如果有可能的话那就是我第一个流放地，至于接下来会怎样，那就听天由命吧！

回到家之后我和栗色小马商量了一番，然后就来到了附近的灌木丛里。我用我的小刀，而他用一块锋利的石头，一起砍下了好几根差不多有手杖粗细的橡树枝。不过我不想在这些细节上过多描述，总之六个星期之后，在栗色小马的帮助下（他分担了最吃力的那份活计），我制成了一艘印第安式的小船，不过尺寸要大很多。我用自制的麻线把"野猢"皮缝制在一起，包在船外面还用小"野猢"皮做了一面船帆。不过我找的都是最小的"野猢"，老一些的"野猢"皮太粗糙了。同时我还准备了四把船桨，在船上准备了一些煮熟的兔子肉和其他干粮，还带了两个瓦罐，一个装着牛奶，一个装着水。

我先是在主人家旁边的大池塘里试验了一番，然后再进行调整，最后用"野猢"的油脂把裂缝堵好。一切都准备就绪之后，我就让"野猢"把小船搬到一辆车上，在栗色小马和另外一名仆人的带领下把小船拖到了海边。

一切都准备好了，离开的日子也就到了。我和我的主人，以及家里的所有人告别。我的眼里满是泪水，心情十分沉重。我的主人也许是出于好奇，也许是出于对我的好感（这么说并不算自负），决定送我到海边看我上船，还叫来了好几个朋友一起前去。为了等潮水上涨，我在岸上多等了一个小时。当风吹向我要去的那座小岛时，我就和我的主人告别。正当我打算趴下去亲吻他的蹄子的时候，他还特意把蹄子抬了起来，凑到我的嘴边。我不是不知道自己由于提到刚才这个细节而受到了多少责难，那些诽谤者可能认为我的主人是不会赐予我这等恩惠的。我也没有忘记有些旅行家吹嘘的所谓的恩典。但是如果他们对于"慧骃"的高贵品格有一点点了解的话，他们马上就会改变自己的想法。

我又向陪着我的主人一起来的其他"慧骃"一一致敬，然后就推着船离开了岸边。

第十一章

作者那危险的旅程。他抵达了新荷兰，打算在那儿定居。他被当地人射伤了，然后又被葡萄牙人抓住，并且带上了船。船长热情款待了他。作者回到了英国。

　　这趟令人绝望的旅程开始于1714年或者是1715年的2月15日的上午9点。当时是顺风，不过我仍然在划桨。考虑到这样下去我很快就会疲累，而风向也可能会发生变化，所以我就扯起了船帆。在海浪的帮助下，我以每小时一里格半的速度前进（这是我尽可能精确地估算的结果）。我的主人和他的朋友一直站在海滩上，直到我消失在他们的视野里。我还时不时能听到那匹栗色小马（他一直很喜欢我）在那儿喊着："保重了，温柔的'野猢'！"

　　我原本打算找一座无人岛，依靠自己的劳动就这样生活下去，因为我觉得这样比在欧洲的宫廷里当首相还要幸福。一想到回去接受那些"野猢"的统治，我就感到十分害怕。如果我能够过上这种隐居的生活，至少还能自由自在地思考，回想那些"慧骃"的美德，而避免堕入我的同类的罪恶当中去。

　　读者们可能还记得，我之前曾叙述过我手下的水手是如何谋反并把我囚禁在船舱里，让我一连几个星期都不知道航行的方向；随后他们就把我押上了这个海岛。我记得他们曾赌咒发誓说不知道这是什么地方，不知道是真是假。不过当时我推测他们是朝着东南方向前进，打算去马达加斯加的。所以我相信当时我是在好望角以南大约十度，也就是南纬四十五度左右的地方。虽然这只是一种推测，但我还是决定朝着东方前进，希望能够抵达新荷兰的西南边，在那儿找到一座无人小岛。这时的风向偏西，所以到了晚上六点的时候我至少已经向东前进了十八里格。这时候我看到半里格之外好像有一座小岛，我很快就抵达了那里。这座小岛是由一整块岩石组成的，只有一个被风暴侵蚀形成的港湾。我把小船停靠过去，然后爬上了一块岩石，发现由南向北延伸出一片陆地。我在小船里躺了一晚上，然后第二天一早继续前进。差不多七个小时之后我就来到了新荷兰的西南角。这就验证了我长期以来的观点，地图和海图把这个国家的位置给弄错了，实际位置至少应该西偏三度。我记得好多年前我就和好友赫尔曼·摩尔先生讲过这件事情，并且提出了自己的理由，但是他仍然选择相信别人的意见。

　　我登陆的地方没看到任何居民，不过因为我手无寸铁，所以我并不敢过分深入，只是在岸边寻找了一些贝壳充饥。由于害怕被当地人发现，我也没有生火，只能生吃下去。为了节约自己的食物，我连吃了三天这样的东西。幸运的是我找到了一条水质很好的小溪，这不得不说是一大宽慰。

　　第四天我朝着内陆深入了一点，发现在距离我大概五百码的高地上有二三十个土著。他们浑身上下都没有穿衣服，围成一团。其中一个人发现了我，马上告诉了其他人，然后就有五个人朝着我的方向前进，其余的女人和孩子留在篝火边上。我拼命朝着岸边跑去，卖力地划桨准备逃开。他们追得很快，还冲我射了一箭，正好射中了我的左膝盖，这个伤疤我得带去坟墓了。我担心那是一支毒箭，就在离开他们的射程之后用嘴吮吸伤口，然后仔细包扎了一下。

　　当时的我有些不知所措，也不敢回到原先登陆的那个地方，只能继续向北前进。当时的风虽然不大，但却是迎面来的西北风。正当我忙着寻找一个安全的停靠地点的时候，发现北边来了一艘帆船。我有些犹豫，要不要和他们汇合，但是对于"野猢"的憎恨还是占了上风，于是我调转船头回到了早上出发时的那个港湾。因为我已经下定决心，哪怕是在这些野蛮人手里送命，也好过和欧洲的"野猢"们一起生活。我把小船停靠在岸边，自己则躲在小溪旁边的一块石头后面。正如我先前所说，这条小溪的水很好。

这艘小船距离小溪已经不到半里格了，只见它放下了一条长长的舢板，看来是来取水的。不过当我发现舢板的时候，已经距离我很近了，所以我也来不及躲避了。水手们先是发现了我的小船，在仔细端详了一番之后就推测出船主就在附近。四个全副武装的水手把周围搜了个遍，终于发现了我。他们还打量了好一会儿我身上那怪异的衣服，因为当时的我穿着皮外衣、木头鞋子和毛皮袜子。不过从我的衣着当中他们判断出我并不是土著，因为他们是不穿衣服的。其中一个水手用葡萄牙语询问我的来历。而葡萄牙语是我很熟悉的一门语言，于是我站起来，承认自己是一只可怜的"野猢"，被"慧骃"放逐了。我请求他们能够放我一马。当他们听到我的回答的时候，显得分外惊奇，因为从我的外貌看，我显然是一个欧洲人，但是这所谓的"野猢"和"慧骃"却让他们有些茫然。而且我讲话的腔调也很奇怪，就好像是一匹马一样，他们就这样被逗笑了。我的心里充斥着害怕和厌恶，一直在边上瑟瑟发抖。我再次请求他们放走我，并朝着我的小船靠拢。但他们还是把我给控制住了，并且追问我从哪里来。我坦白说我是个英国人，只不过五年前就离开祖国了。当时我们和葡萄牙的关系还是不错的，所以他们也并没有把我视作敌人。我再三强调自己不过是一只可怜的"野猢"，想要找一个安静的地方度过余生。

当他们在交谈的时候，我突然感觉自己从来没有见过那么不自然的事情，这就像英国的一条狗或者一头母牛，或者是"慧骃国"的"野猢"会说话一样。而那些葡萄牙人也对我的奇装异服和我怪异的口音感到吃惊，不过还是能听懂的。他们的态度十分友好，并且告诉我他们的船长可以免费把我送回里斯本，这样我就可以返回祖国了。他们决定先派遣两位水手回到大船上去把情况告诉船长，同时决定把我控制起来，免得我逃跑。权衡利弊之下我只好顺从他们的要求。他们都十分好奇，想听听我的故事，可我几乎没有满足他们的愿望，于是他们就猜测是我的不幸遭遇使我丧失了理智。两小时之后，装载淡水回去的小船带着船长的命令又回来了，命令说要把我带到大船上去。我双膝跪地，哀求他们给我自由，可一切全是白搭。水手们用绳索将我绑好，扔进了舢板，我被带到了大船上，接着就被押进了船长室。

船长的名字叫彼得罗·德·孟德斯，是一个豪爽的人。他先是请我讲讲自己的情况，然后又询问我想吃点什么。他告诉我，我在这船上能够享受到和他一样的待遇，不说了很多的客气话。这不禁让我感到怀疑，一只"野猢"怎么会那么有礼貌呢？我依旧沉默不言，闻到他和边上的水手身上那股子味道就足以把我熏晕过去了。最后我提出要求，从我自己的小船上拿点东西来吃，但是他却吩咐人给我拿来了一只鸡和一些酒，然后又把我安排在一间很干净的房间里。我不愿意脱下衣服睡，就穿着衣服躺下了。大约半个小时之后，我趁着水手们吃饭的工夫想要偷偷溜到船边，跳海逃生。但是这一举动被一个水手给发现了，他拦下我，并且告诉了船长。这样一来我就被锁在了船舱里面。

晚饭过后，彼得罗先生来到我的房间，询问我为什么要冒那么大风险逃跑。他向我保证他是没有恶意的，他只想要帮助我。他的一番话很真挚，所以我最终还是把他当作一个有几分理性的动物来看待了。我简要叙述了自己的航海经历，坦白我的手下是如何背叛我，然后把我流放到一个陌生的小岛，以及之后在那儿生活了五年的情形。但他却说我的经历不过是一场大梦，这样的话语让我十分反感，因为我已经忘记如何撒谎了。撒谎这种本领在"野猢"统治的国家是司空见惯的，所以他们对真话也有颇多质疑。于是我询问他，他们国家是否有撒谎的习惯。我告诉他我已经基本不明白他所说的虚假是什么意思了。就算在"慧骃国"住上一千年，都不会从最低劣的仆人口中听到一句谎言。

不管他信不信，我已经和他们截然不同了。当然为了报答他的恩情，我可以原谅他堕落的天性。如果他有什么质疑的地方的话，我可以一一讲述，这样他就能够发现事情的真相了。

船长是一个十分聪明的人，他花费了好多心思来寻找我谈话中的漏洞，但是慢慢地，他开始相信我所说的都是事实了。而且他自己也说过，他先前碰到过一位荷兰船长，那位船长宣称自己在和手下五名水手在新荷兰以南的某个岛屿或大陆取水的时候，看到过一匹马赶着好几只和我描述的"野猢"很像的动物的情景，还有一些别的情况。船长承认当时他还以为这一切不过是一个谎言。不过他接着对我说，既然我宣称忠于真理，那么必须说话算话，再也不能有什么舍命逃跑的念头。他要求我老老实实地和他一起完成这趟旅行，否则在抵达里斯本之前他只能把我锁在船舱里。我虽然答应了他的要求，但是我同时申明，我宁愿遭受最痛苦的折磨也不想回去和"野猢"生活在一起。

一路上风平浪静，为了报答船长，我有时也会陪他一起坐坐。在交谈的时候我已经竭力掩饰对"野猢"的憎恶，但是有的时候难免会有所显露。不过船长是一个大度的人，并没有追着不放。不过一天中的大部分时间我都是躲在自己的房间里不和水手见面。船长好几次要求我把身上的衣服换下来，他愿意拿出自己最好的衣服借给我。但是我并不愿意接受，因为我讨厌把"野猢"的东西穿在身上。我只需要他借给我两件衬衫，因为我想他穿了之后总是要洗的，这样好歹会干净一点。这两件衬衫我每两天就洗一次，而且每次都是我亲自动手洗的。

1715 年 11 月 5 日，我们抵达了里斯本。上岸的时候船长硬是把自己的外套披在我的身上，免得我被人围观。他先是把我带回了家。在我的不断恳求之下，他终于同意把我安排在房子后面最高的房间，并且同意不透露有关"慧骃"的任何事情。因为只要有一点风声，不仅会有许多人来围观我，我还可能会被当成异教徒审判，落得个监禁或者被烧死的结局。船长劝说我做一套新衣服，但是我不能接受裁缝来给我量尺寸。幸好彼得罗先生和我的体型差不多，所以他的衣服穿着也十分合身。他还给我准备了许多崭新的必需品，我足足把他们晾晒了一天才能使用。

船长没有妻子，家里只有三个仆人，我要求在吃饭的时候不用他们伺候。船长是一个很有礼貌，而且还善解人意的人，所以我倒是能够容忍和他在一起。慢慢地我也敢从后窗张望外面的风景了。过了一段时间之后我就搬到了另外一间屋子。虽然我大着胆子伸头出去看了看大街上的情景，但我还是飞快地把头缩了回来。大约一个星期之后他带着我走到门口，我发现我已经不那么恐惧了，只是对"野猢"的仇恨和鄙夷又多了几分。最后我已经可以在他的陪同下在街上走走了，但是我的鼻子总得用香料或者烟草堵起来。

格列佛回家了

我大致和彼得罗先生讲过自己家里的情况，所以差不多十天之后他就劝我多考虑一下所谓的荣誉和面子，让我回家去和老婆孩子生活在一起。他告诉我在海港里有一艘英国船只即将启航，他也可以提供路上所需的一切。我提出了不少反对意见，但是过于冗长，在这儿就不多赘述了。他告诉我，找一座无人的荒岛去隐居是不大可能实现的。但是如果住在家里，至少可以想怎么安排都可以。

意识到也没有什么更好的办法，我最终还是同意了。我在 11 月 24 日离开了里斯本，搭乘一艘商船出发了，不过我从来没有去打听过船长是谁。彼得罗先生亲自送我上了船，并且借给我二十英镑。在分别的时候他大力拥抱了我，而我只能尽力忍受。在这趟旅程中我和船长以及所有的船员都没有什么往来，我推说自己生病了，在自己的船舱里一步都没有离开。1715 年 12 月 5 日上午九点钟，我们抵达了唐兹。下午三点的时候我就回到了自己在雷德里夫的家。

我的妻子和孩子惊喜万分地迎接我的归来，因为他们认为我早已死在了旅途中。但是我必须承认，见到他们之后我的心里只有痛恨、厌恶和鄙夷，特别是联想到我和他们之间的亲密关系。虽然我不幸被驱逐出"慧骃"国，不得不忍受着和"野猢"们打交道，同彼得罗先生交谈，但是我的内心依然被"慧骃"的美德和崇高思想所包围着。联想到我曾经和一只"野猢"生下过好几只"野猢"，这不由得让我感到万分羞耻和惶恐。

我一到家我的妻子就拥抱、亲吻了我。但是我已经多少年不曾触碰这种讨厌的生物了，所以我当场就昏了过去，整整一个小时之后我才苏醒过来。在写这本书的时候我已经回国五年了。在第一年中我都不允许我的妻子和孩子来到我的面前，更不用说在一个房间里吃饭了，因为我根本忍受不了他们的气味。哪怕是到今天，我都不能接受让他们触碰我的面包，或者用我的杯子喝水，而我也从来不和他们牵手。我花的第一笔钱就是买了两匹小马，然后养在一个很好的马厩里面。除此之外，马夫就是我最能接受的人了，因为他身上带着那种马厩里的独有的味道。我的马很能理解我，每天我都要和它们说上四个小时的话。我从来不给它们戴什么马缰绳，而我们之间相处得也很愉快。

第十二章

作者强调自己叙述的真实性。他试图出版这部作品的计划。作者对于那些歪曲事实的游记作者的谴责。他强调自己写作没有任何险恶目的。作者回应了一些质疑。描述了殖民扩张的方法。对英国的赞美。占领作者所描述的那几个国家的权利基础。征服那些国家会遇到的困难。作者和读者告别，谈到了自己未来的生活方式，并且做出了总结。

亲爱的读者们，我已经原原本本地把我十六年零七个月的旅行经历讲给你们听了。我保证我所叙述的都是事实。虽然我原本可以和别人一样用那种荒诞不经的故事来吸引眼球，但最终我还是决定用最简朴的方式来叙述这些平凡的事实，因为我的初衷是告知而非娱乐。

英国人和欧洲其他国家的人是很难得去一些遥远的国家旅行的。像我这种去过这些地方的人，想要描述一点海上和陆上的奇异见闻是很容易的一件事情。但是旅行家之所以推出游记，最主要的目的还是让人变得更加聪明，要通过不同国家的见闻来改善人们的思想，使人增长见识。

我发自内心地希望能够制定一项法律，每一位旅行家必须在大法官面前宣誓，保证自己发表的内容是真实的，这样世人就会少一些被欺骗的可能了。有些作家为了能够博得大众的注意力，就想尽办法撒谎来欺骗读者。年轻时候的我也曾看过类似的几本游记，但是自从走遍地球的大部分角落，观察的心得让我可以轻易驳斥其中明显不符合事实的叙述，我对于这类游记的印象也就急转直下了，对于自己年轻时如此轻信于人也感到懊悔。所以既然我熟悉的人对于我辛苦写出的这本书还是持接受态度，那么我就要坚决恪守实事求是的原则。实际上我是不可能受到欺骗或者诱惑的，因为我的内心一直牢记我的"慧骃"主人的谆谆教诲，并对自己有幸能够聆听主人的教诲而感到无比自豪。

虽然厄运让西农落难，
但是却不曾让他撒谎骗人。

我很清楚，这类作品不需要天分，也不需要学问，只需要记忆力好，精准记录下自己的见闻就可以了。我也很清楚，这类作家和那些编纂词典的人一样，总是没什么名声，而且会被后来者居上，因为后继者不管是在内容还是在细节上都会超过他们。那些读了我的作品的旅行家如果去了我说过的那些国家旅游，很容易就能够发现其中的谬误（如果有的话），然后增补上自己的新发现。这样一来他们就会取代我的位置，让我消失在世人的视野当中。如果我写作是为了名气的话，那么我不得不说这是一种侮辱，然而我出书的唯一目的是为了大众的利益，所以我完全不会感到失望。那些自认为是理性的统治者在读到有关"慧骃"的美德的时候，会不会为自己的罪恶感到羞愧呢？那些同样由"野狷"统治的国家我就不想多说了；其中布罗丁格奈格的腐败程度最轻，所以他们在道德和统治上的准则应该是我们最乐于遵从的。但是这个问题我就不多谈了，我相信那些贤明的读者会有自己的想法。

我非常高兴我的这部作品大概不会受到什么责难。一个作家，他只叙述发生在那么遥远的国度里的一些平凡的事实，我们既没有半点兴趣同这些国家做生意，又不想同它们谈判，对于这样的一个作家，还有什么能反对的呢？我曾十分谨慎地避免了一般游记作家所出现的毛病，他们因为这些毛病常常受到指责也是罪有应得，另外，我不插手干涉任何政党的事。我的作品没有情绪，不带偏见，对任何人或者任何团体的人都没有敌意。我写作的目的是最高尚的：只想给人类传递见闻，教育人类。我也不是谦虚，我认为自己的想法要高过一般人，因为我曾那么长时间同最有德行的"慧骃"在一起交谈，我自有优势。我写作既不为名也不图利。我从来都不肯用任何一个看起来像是影射或者哪怕有一点冒犯别人的词，即使对那些最爱认为自己是受了指责的人，我也尽可能不去得罪他们。因此，我希望我能够公正合理地表明自己是个绝对无可指摘的作家，任何抗辩家、思想家、观察家、沉思家、挑毛病专家、评论家对我都无计可施。

我承认，有人曾悄悄地对我说，作为一个英国的臣民，我有义务回来后就向国务大臣递交一份报告，因为一个英国臣民发现的任何土地都是属于国王的。但是，我怀疑如果我们要去征服我说到的那些国家，是不是会像弗迪南多·柯太兹征服赤身裸体的美洲人那么轻松。征服利立浦特所得的好处几乎都抵不上派遣一支海陆军队的消耗；对布罗丁格奈格人有所企图，我又怀疑是否慎重或安全；而如果英国军队的头顶上浮着那么一座浮岛，他们会不会感到很不自在。"慧骃"看来倒真的对战争没有什么准备，他们对战争这门科学而尤其是对大规模的武器完全是不在行。尽管如此，假如我是国务大臣，是决不会主张去侵犯他们的。他们审慎、团结、无畏、爱国，足可弥补他们在军事方面所有的缺陷。想想看，两万"慧骃"冲进一支欧洲的军队，冲乱队伍，掀翻车辆，用后蹄将士兵的脸踢得稀烂，因为他们和奥古斯都的性格没有什么两样。但是我不会建议去征服那样一个高尚的民族，我倒希望他们能够或者愿意派遣足够数量的"慧骃"居民来欧洲教化我们，教我们学习关于荣誉、正义、真理、节制、公德、刚毅、贞洁、友谊、仁慈和忠诚等基本原则。在我们的大部分语言中还保留着这全部美德的名词，在古今作家的作品中也经常见到这些名词；我自己虽然读书不多，这些名词倒还能说得出来。

不过我还有一个理由支持我不赞同国王陛下去我发现的几个国家扩张领土。说实话，对于君王们统治这些地区的合法性我是有怀疑的。举个例子，假如有一群海岛被风暴刮到了一个不知名的地方，一位水手在桅杆上发现了陆地，于是他们就打算当一回强盗。当他们上岸之后发现的是一个手无寸铁的民族，还在那儿热情招待他们，但是他们却给这个地方起了个名字，以国王的名义侵占了这块土地，同时用一块烂木板或者石头来留作纪念。他们杀死二三十个土著，再抓走几个当地人，回到祖国就能够得到赦免。一块崭新的领土就这样开辟了。国王会马上派遣舰队去攻占这块新大陆，杀死所有的土著，搜刮所有的黄金，让他们的君主受尽磨难。到那时候所有的罪行都会被合法化，这片新大陆上染遍了当地居民的鲜血。这群被指派的远征军，本质上就是伪君子，打着改造未开化民族的旗号，实行侵略的本质。

不过必须承认的一点是，这一切和英国没有关系。英国人在开辟殖民地方面所表现出的智慧、关心和正义可以做全世界的楷模。他们在宗教和学术方面具有很大的促进作用；他们选派虔诚、能干的教士传布基督教义；他们谨慎小心从本王国挑选出生活正派、谈吐清楚的人移居各地；他们派出最能干、最廉洁的官员到各殖民地管理行政，严守正义；更使人高兴的是，他们派出去的总督都是些最警醒、最有德行的人，全心全意只考虑到人民的幸福和他们国王主子的荣誉。

但是，我谈到的那几个国家一定都不愿意被殖民者征服、奴役或者赶尽杀绝，他们那里也不盛产黄金、白银、食糖和烟草。所以我认为，他们并不是我们表现热情、发挥勇武或者捞点实惠的合适的对象。然而，如果那些和这事更有利害关系的人觉得应该持与我相反的意见，那么我在依法被召见的时候就准备宣誓作证：在我之前还从未有任何一个欧洲人到过那几个国家。我的意思是说，如果我们相信当地居民的话，事情是不会引起纷争的，除非是关于那两只据说是许多年前出现在"慧骃"国一座山上的"野猢"可能会引起争议。根据那种意见，"野猢"种就是它俩的后裔，而据我所了解，那两只"野猢"可能就是英国人。这一点，说实话，从它们后代面容的特征来看，我是有点怀疑的，但这是否就构成我们占据那地方的理由，只有留给精通殖民法的人去考虑了。

但是以国王的名义去占领这些地方，这样的想法我从未有过；而且就我当时面临的情形来看，出于自我保护，我也不可能会有这样的想法。

这可能是我作为旅行家所受到的唯一的责难了，而我也已经做了回答。所以我想是时候向我的每一位读者告别，因为我要回到我位于雷德里夫的小花园去享受思考的快乐，我要去实践从"慧骃"那儿学来的道德品质，去教导家里的几只"野猢"，让他们能够成为善良的动物。我要坚持对着镜子看，希望这样能够让我改变无法忍受人类的面孔的习惯。我对国内的"慧骃"的野蛮表现也很失望，但是看在我那高贵的主人以及其他"慧骃"的面子上，我仍然对他们崇敬有加。他们的外表虽然和"慧骃"没有任何区别，但是智力却有所退化了。

上个星期我已经允许我的妻子和我一起吃饭了，当然她得坐在长餐桌的另一头，还询问了她几个问题（只需要最简单的回答）。但是"野猢"的气味仍然让我难以忍受，所以我就用香料或者烟草堵住鼻子。虽然老人很难改掉自己的习惯，但是我仍然在努力。一段时间之后我就能够忍受邻居家的"野猢"和我见面，而不用担心他用爪子或者牙齿来伤害我。

如果"野猢"只有天生的愚蠢和罪恶的话，那么和他们一起打交道倒也不是那么难以忍受；哪怕是看到律师、扒手、上校、傻子、绅士、赌棍、政客、嫖客、医生、证人、罪犯和卖国贼的时候我也不会有任何生气的感觉。但是当我看到一个丑陋的笨蛋，身心都有病，却还骄傲不堪，我马上就会失去全部的耐心。我怎么也弄不明白这样一种动物怎么会和这么一种罪恶搅和到一起。聪明而有德行的"慧骃"富于理性动物所能有的一切美德，而在他们的语言中却没有表达这种罪恶概念的名词。他们的语言中，除了那些用来描述"野猢"的可恶品性的名词，没有任何可以表达罪恶的术语。因为他们对人性缺乏透彻的理解，所以在"野猢"身上还辨认不出这种骄傲的罪恶，可在"野猢"这种动物统治的国家中，"骄傲"这种特性是显而易见的。而我比较有经验，所以能够清清楚楚地在"野猢"的身上看到几分骄傲的本性。

但是在理性支配下的"慧骃"却不会因为自己的优点感到骄傲，就好像我不会因为自己没有少一条腿或者少一只胳膊而感到骄傲一样。四肢不健全的人当然会很痛苦，但是正常人也不会因此而感到骄傲。在这个问题上我讲得比较多，为的是努力让英国的"野猢"们变得让人可以接受。所以在这儿我请求那些犯下这种荒唐的罪恶的家伙不要出现在我的视野里。